Program Authors

Peter Afflerbach
Camille Blachowicz
Candy Dawson Boyd
Elena Izquierdo
Connie Juel
Edward Kame'enui
Donald Leu
Jeanne R. Paratore
P. David Pearson
Sam Sebesta
Deborah Simmons
Alfred Tatum
Sharon Vaughn
Susan Watts Taffe
Karen Kring Wixson

Glenview, Illinois • Boston, Massachusetts
Chandler, Arizona • Upper Saddle River, New Jersey

We dedicate Reading Street to
Peter Jovanovich.

His wisdom, courage,
and passion for education
are an inspiration to us all.

ISBN-13: 978-0-328-47032-7
ISBN-10: 0-328-47032-5
2 3 4 5 6 7 8 9 10 V003 14 13 12 11 10
CC1

Any Path, Any Pace

CALLE de la Lectura

"Welcome to Reading Street! Bienvenidos too."

PEARSON SCOTT FORESMAN

PEARSON

Find Your Place on Reading Street!

Who said so?

The Leading Researchers,

Program Authors

Peter Afflerbach, Ph.D.
Professor
Department of Curriculum and Instruction
University of Maryland at College Park

Camille L. Z. Blachowicz, Ph.D.
Professor of Education
National-Louis University

Candy Dawson Boyd, Ph.D.
Professor
School of Education
Saint Mary's College of California

Elena Izquierdo, Ph.D.
Associate Professor
University of Texas at El Paso

Connie Juel, Ph.D.
Professor of Education
School of Education
Stanford University

Edward J. Kame'enui, Ph.D.
Dean-Knight Professor of Education and Director
Institute for the Development of Educational Achievement and the Center on Teaching and Learning
College of Education
University of Oregon

Donald J. Leu, Ph.D.
John and Maria Neag Endowed Chair in Literacy and Technology
Director, The New Literacies Research Lab
University of Connecticut

Jeanne R. Paratore, Ed.D.
Associate Professor of Education
Department of Literacy and Language Development
Boston University

P. David Pearson, Ph.D.
Professor and Dean
Graduate School of Education
University of California, Berkeley

Sam L. Sebesta, Ed.D.
Professor Emeritus
College of Education
University of Washington, Seattle

Deborah Simmons, Ph.D
Professor
College of Education and Human Development
Texas A&M University

Alfred W. Tatum, Ph.D.
Associate Professor and Director of the UIC Reading Clinic
University of Illinois at Chicago

Sharon Vaughn, Ph.D.
H. E. Hartfelder/Southland Corporation Regents Professor
Director, Meadows Center for Preventing Educational Risk
University of Texas

Susan Watts Taffe, Ph.D.
Associate Professor in Literacy
Division of Teacher Education
University of Cincinnati

Karen Kring Wixson, Ph.D.
Professor of Education
University of Michigan

Consulting Authors

Jeff Anderson, M.Ed.
Author and Consultant
San Antonio, TX

Jim Cummins, Ph.D.
Professor
Department of Curriculum, Teaching and Learning
University of Toronto

Lily Wong Fillmore, Ph.D.
Professor Emerita
Graduate School of Education
University of California, Berkeley

Georgia Earnest García, Ph.D.
Professor
Language and Literacy Division
Department of Curriculum and Instruction
University of Illinois at Urbana-Champaign

George A. González, Ph.D.
Professor (Retired)
School of Education
University of Texas-Pan American, Edinburg

Valerie Ooka Pang, Ph.D.
Professor
School of Teacher Education
San Diego State University

Sally M. Reis, Ph.D.
Board of Trustees Distinguished Professor
Department of Educational Psychology
University of Connecticut

Jon Scieszka, M.F.A.
Children's Book Author
Founder of GUYS READ
Named First National Ambassador for Young People's Literature 2008

Grant Wiggins, Ed.D.
Educational Consultant
Authentic Education
Concept Development

Lee Wright, M.Ed.
Pearland, TX

Practitioners, and Authors

Consultant

Sharroky Hollie, Ph.D.
Assistant Professor
California State University
Dominguez Hills, CA

Teacher Reviewers

Dr. Bettyann Brugger
Educational Support Coordinator–Reading Office
Milwaukee Public Schools
Milwaukee, WI

Kathleen Burke
K–12 Reading Coordinator
Peoria Public Schools, Peoria, IL

Darci Burns, M.S.Ed.
University of Oregon

Bridget Cantrell
District Intervention Specialist
Blackburn Elementary School
Independence, MO

Tahira DuPree Chase, M.A., M.S.Ed.
Administrator of Elementary English Language Arts
Mount Vernon City School District
Mount Vernon, NY

Michele Connor
Director, Elementary Education
Aiken County School District
Aiken, SC

Georgia Coulombe
K–6 Regional Trainer/ Literacy Specialist
Regional Center for Training and Learning (RCTL), Reno, NV

Kelly Dalmas
Third Grade Teacher
Avery's Creek Elementary, Arden, NC

Seely Dillard
First Grade Teacher
Laurel Hill Primary School
Mt. Pleasant, SC

Jodi Dodds-Kinner
Director of Elementary Reading
Chicago Public Schools, Chicago, IL

Dr. Ann Wild Evenson
District Instructional Coach
Osseo Area Schools, Maple Grove, MN

Stephanie Fascitelli
Principal
Apache Elementary, Albuquerque Public Schools, Albuquerque, NM

Alice Franklin
Elementary Coordinator, Language Arts & Reading
Spokane Public Schools, Spokane, WA

Laureen Fromberg
Assistant Principal
PS 100 Queens, NY

Kimberly Gibson
First Grade Teacher
Edgar B. Davis Community School
Brockton, MA

Kristen Gray
Lead Teacher
A.T. Allen Elementary School
Concord, NC

Mary Ellen Hazen
State Pre-K Teacher
Rockford Public Schools #205
Rockford, IL

Patrick M. Johnson
Elementary Instructional Director
Seattle Public Schools, Seattle, WA

Theresa Jaramillo Jones
Principal
Highland Elementary School
Las Cruces, NM

Sophie Kowzun
Program Supervisor, Reading/ Language Arts, PreK–5
Montgomery County Public Schools
Rockville, MD

David W. Matthews
Sixth Grade Teacher
Easton Area Middle School
Easton, PA

Ana Nuncio
Editor and Independent Publisher
Salem, MA

Joseph Peila
Principal
Chappell Elementary School
Chicago, IL

Ivana Reimer
Literacy Coordinator
PS 100 Queens, NY

Sally Riley
Curriculum Coordinator
Rochester Public Schools
Rochester, NH

Dyan M. Smiley
Independent Educational Consultant

Michael J. Swiatowiec
Lead Literacy Teacher
Graham Elementary School
Chicago, IL

Dr. Helen Taylor
Director of English Education
Portsmouth City Public Schools
Portsmouth, VA

Carol Thompson
Teaching and Learning Coach
Independence School District
Independence, MO

Erinn Zeitlin
Kindergarten Teacher
Carderock Springs Elementary School
Bethesda, MD

Any Path, Any Pace

Turning Points

Key

- SI Strategic Intervention
- OL On-Level
- A Advanced
- ELL ELL

In this Teacher's Edition Unit 1, Volume 1

In the First Stop on Reading Street

GO Digital!

See It!

- Big Question Video
- Concept Talk Video
- Envision It! Animations

Hear It!

- eSelections
- eReaders
- Grammar Jammer
- Leveled Reader Database

Do It!

- Vocabulary Activities
- Story Sort
- 21st Century Skills Activities
- Online Assessment
- Letter Tile Drag and Drop

Turning Points

Key
- SI Strategic Intervention
- OL On-Level
- A Advanced
- ELL ELL

Teamwork

Key
- SI Strategic Intervention
- OL On-Level
- A Advanced
- ELL ELL

Patterns in Nature

Key
- SI Strategic Intervention
- OL On-Level
- A Advanced
- ELL ELL

Puzzles and Mysteries

Key
SI Strategic Intervention
OL On-Level
A Advanced
ELL ELL

Adventures by Land, Air, and Water

Key
- SI Strategic Intervention
- OL On-Level
- A Advanced
- ELL ELL

UNIT 6

Reaching for Goals

Key
SI Strategic Intervention
OL On-Level
A Advanced
ELL ELL

UNIT 1

Skills Overview

Key
T Tested Skill
Target Skill

		WEEK 1	WEEK 2
		 **Because of Winn-Dixie** Realistic Fiction pp. 26–37 **A Film with a Message of Hope** Movie Review pp. 42–43	 **Lewis and Clark and Me** Historical Fiction pp. 52–67 **Ellen Ochoa: Space Pioneer** Biography pp. 72–75
Get Ready to Read	**Question of the Week**	What experiences bring diverse people together?	What opportunities can be found in new places?
	Amazing Words	*attention, kindness, variety, similar, distinct, courteous, teach, understanding, social, introduce*	*pioneer, traveled, experiences, foreign, improve, settlers, territories, seek, prepared, fortune*
	Word Analysis	Word endings *-ed*	Suffixes *-or, -er*
	Literary Terms	Point of View	Sensory Words
	Story Structure/ Text Features	Sequence	Setting
Read and Comprehend	**Comprehension**	T **Skill** Sequence **Strategy** Summarize Review **Skill** Cause and Effect	T **Skill** Author's Purpose **Strategy** Questioning Review **Skill** Sequence
	Vocabulary	T **Skill** Affixes: Suffixes	T **Skill** Word Endings
	Fluency	Expression	Appropriate Phrasing/Punctuation Cues
Language Arts	**Writing**	Realistic Story/Word Choice	Expository Composition/Organization
	Conventions	Declarative and Interrogative Sentences	Imperative and Exclamatory Sentences
	Spelling	Short Vowel VCCV	Long *a* and *i*
	Speaking/Listening	Dramatic Retelling	Introduction
	Research Skills	Map/Globe/Atlas	Skim and Scan

The Big Question

What can we discover from new places and people?

WEEK 3	WEEK 4	WEEK 5	WEEK 6
On the Banks of Plum Creek Historical Fiction pp. 84–99 **Laura Ingalls Wilder** Online Reference Sources pp. 104–107	**The Horned Toad Prince** Trickster Tale pp. 116–129 **The Fox and the Tiger** Fable pp. 134–135	**Letters Home from Yosemite** Expository Text pp. 144–155 **The Bison of Caprock Canyons** Magazine Article pp. 160–163	**Interactive Review**
Why do we want to explore new places?	What can we discover in the landscape of the Southwest?	How does Yosemite reflect the unique qualities of the West?	Connect the Question of the Week to the Big Question
coast, route, landscape, sights, landmarks, desert, valleys, enormous, magnificent, navigate	*frontier, rodeo, cacti, plains, mesa, corral, creeks, range, grassland, sagebrush*	*earthquake, eruptions, volcano, geyser, elk, magma, lava, wildlife, sequoia, wildflowers*	Review Amazing Words for Unit 1
Word ending *-ing*	Compound Words	Related Words	
Foreshadowing	Dialect	Imagery	
Conflict/Resolution	Rising Action	Description/Definition	
T **Skill** Literary Elements: Character, Setting, Plot **Strategy** Background Knowledge Review **Skill** Sequence	T **Skill** Author's Purpose **Strategy** Story Structure Review **Skill** Literary Elements: Character, Setting, Plot	T **Skill** Main Idea and Details **Strategy** Text Structure Review **Skill** Author's Purpose	Review Unit 1 Target Comprehension Skills
T **Skill** Multiple-Meaning Words	T **Skill** Synonyms and Antonyms	T **Skill** Affixes: Suffixes	Review Unit 1 Target Vocabulary Skills
Rate and Accuracy	Expression	Appropriate Phrasing	Review Unit 1 Fluency Skills
Parody/Voice	Friendly Letter/Conventions	Personal Narrative/Voice	Quick Write for Fluency
Complete Subjects and Predicates	Compound Sentences	Clauses and Complex Sentences	Review Unit 1 Conventions
Long *e* and *o*	Long *e*	Long *u*	Review Unit 1 Spelling Patterns
Advertisement	Report	Travel Show	
Alphabetical Order	Illustrations, Captions, Label	Print Sources	

Monitor Progress

Don't Wait Until Friday SUCCESS PREDICTOR	WEEK 1	WEEK 2	WEEK 3	WEEK 4
WCPM **Fluency**	Expression 95–105 WCPM	Appropriate Phrasing/ Punctuation Cues 95–105 WCPM	Rate and Accuracy 95–105 WCPM	Expression 95–105 WCPM
Vocabulary **Oral Vocabulary/ Concept Development** (assessed informally)	attention kindness variety similar distinct courteous teach understanding social introduce	pioneer traveled experiences foreign improve settlers territories seek prepared fortune	coast route landscape sights landmarks desert valleys enormous magnificent navigate	frontier rodeo cacti plains mesa corral creeks range grassland sagebrush
Lesson Vocabulary	T memorial T prideful T recalls T peculiar T grand T positive T selecting	T yearned T wharf T docks T scan T migrating T scent	T badger T bank T bristled T jointed T patched T ruffled T rushes	T prairie T lassoed T riverbed T bargain T favor T offended T shrieked
Retelling **Text Comprehension**	T **Skill** Sequence **Strategy** Summarize	T **Skill** Author's Purpose **Strategy** Questioning	T **Skill** Literary Elements: Character, Setting, Plot **Strategy** Background Knowledge	T **Skill** Author's Purpose **Strategy** Story Structure

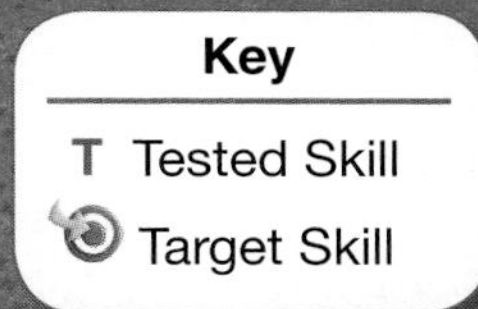

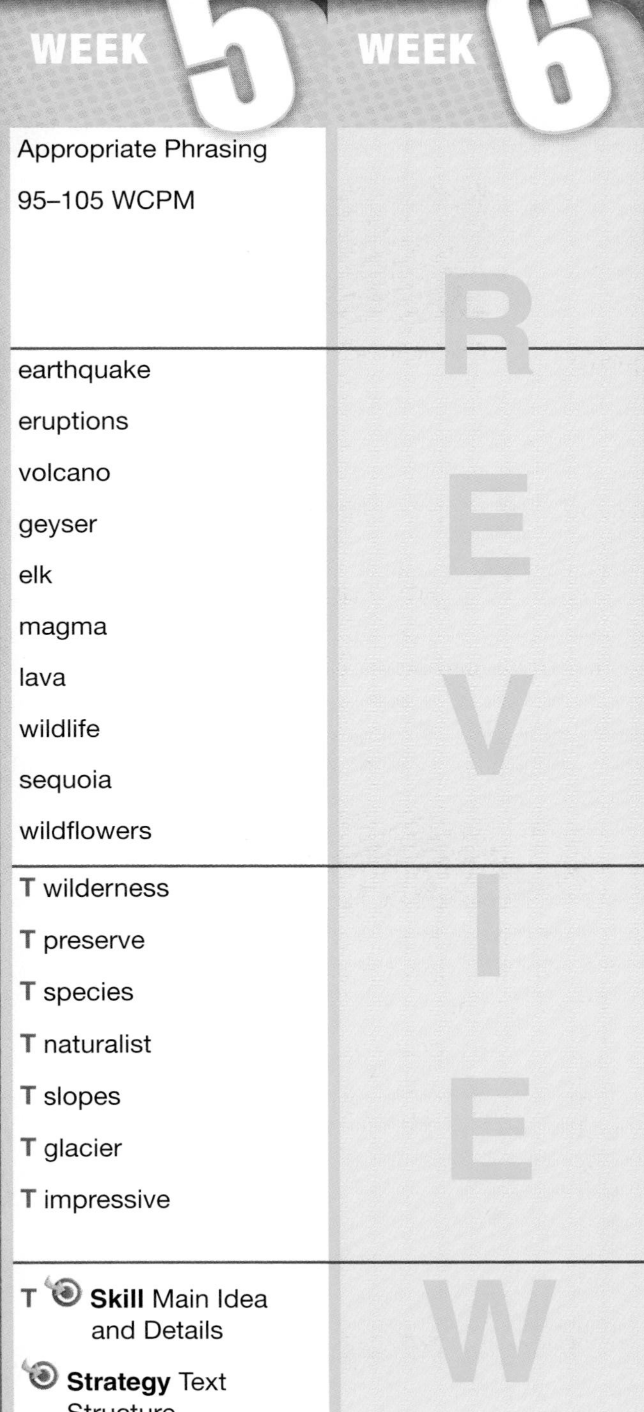

WEEK 5	WEEK 6
Appropriate Phrasing 95–105 WCPM	REVIEW
earthquake eruptions volcano geyser elk magma lava wildlife sequoia wildflowers	
T wilderness T preserve T species T naturalist T slopes T glacier T impressive	
T **Skill** Main Idea and Details **Strategy** Text Structure	

Online Classroom

Manage Data

- Assign the Unit 1 Benchmark Test for students to take online.
- Online Assessment records results and generates reports by school, grade, classroom, or student.
- Use reports to disaggregate and aggregate Unit 1 skills and standards data to monitor progress.
- Based on class lists created to support the categories important for AYP (gender, ethnicity, migrant education, English proficiency, disabilities, economic status), reports let you track adequate yearly progress every six weeks.

Select a Class: Reading 101

Make Assignments	View Reports and Logs
Assign Tests Search by: Unit GO!	Class Reports View by: Standard GO! Assignment Log View by: Entire Class GO!

Other Resources and Information

Certificates Motivate your students with printable certificates.

The User's Guide and Quick Start Guide get you the help you need fast. Learn how to make the most of the Reading Success Tracker System with our simple to use guides.

Group

- Use results from Unit 1 Benchmark Tests taken online through Online Assessment to measure whether students have mastered the English-Language Arts Content Standards taught in this unit.
- Reports in Online Assessment suggest whether students need Extra Support or Intervention.

Individualized Instruction

- Tests are correlated to Unit 1 tested skills and standards so that prescriptions for individual teaching and learning plans can be created.
- Individualized prescriptions target instruction and accelerate student progress toward learning outcome goals.
- Prescriptions include remediation activities and resources to reteach Unit 1 skills and standards.

Assessment and Grouping

for Data-Driven Instruction

4-Step Plan for Assessment
1 Diagnose and Differentiate
2 Monitor Progress
3 Assess and Regroup
4 Summative Assessment

STEP 1 Diagnose and Differentiate

Baseline Group Tests

Diagnose

To make initial grouping decisions, use the Baseline Group Test, the *Texas Primary Reading Inventory (TPRI),* or another initial placement test. Depending on student's ability levels, you may have more than one of each group.

Differentiate

If... student performance is  **then...** use the regular instruction and the daily **Strategic Intervention** small group lessons.

If... student performance is  **then...** use the regular instruction and the daily **On-Level** small group lessons.

If... student performance is  **then...** use the regular instruction and the daily **Advanced** small group lessons.

Small Group Time

SI Strategic Intervention
- Daily small group lessons provide more intensive instruction, more scaffolding, more practice, and more opportunities to respond.
- Reteach lessons in the *First Stop on Reading Street* provide more instruction with target skills.
- Leveled readers build background and provide practice for target skills and vocabulary.

OL On-Level
- Explicit instructional routines teach core skills and strategies.
- Daily On-Level lessons provide more practice and more opportunities to respond.
- Independent activities provide practice for core skills and extension and enrichment options.
- Leveled readers provide additional reading and practice for core skills and vocabulary.

A Advanced
- Daily Advanced lessons provide instruction for accelerated learning.
- Advanced Leveled readers provide additional reading tied to lesson concepts and skills.

Additional Differentiated Learning Options

Reading Street Response to Intervention Kit
- Focused intervention lessons on the five critical areas of reading: phonemic awareness, phonics, vocabulary, comprehension, and fluency

My Sidewalks on Reading Street
- Intensive intervention for struggling readers

STEP 2 Monitor Progress

Use these tools during lesson teaching to **monitor student progress.**

- **Skill and Strategy** instruction during reading
- **Don't Wait Until Friday** boxes to check retelling, fluency, and oral vocabulary
- **Weekly Assessment** on Day 5 to check comprehension and fluency
- **Reader's and Writer's Notebook** pages at point of use
- **Weekly Tests** assess target skills for the week
- **Fresh Reads** for Fluency and Comprehension

Weekly Tests

Fresh Reads for Fluency and Comprehension

STEP 3 Assess and Regroup

Use these tools during lesson teaching to **assess and regroup.**

- **Weekly Assessments** Record results of weekly assessments in retelling, comprehension, and fluency to track student progress.
- **Unit Benchmark Tests** Administer this assessment to check mastery of unit skills.
- **Regroup** We recommend the first regrouping to be at the end of Unit 2. Use weekly assessment information and Unit Benchmark Test performance to inform regrouping decisions. Then regroup at the end of each subsequent unit.

Unit Assessment Chart in First Stop

Group Baseline Group Test → Regroup Units 1 and 2 → Regroup Unit 3 → Regroup Unit 4 → Regroup Unit 5 → End of Year

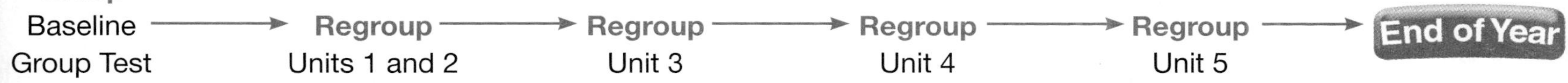

Outside assessments, such as *TPRI, DRA,* and *DIBELS,* may recommend regrouping at other times during the year.

STEP 4 Summative Assessment

Use these tools after lesson teaching to **assess students.**

- **Unit Benchmark Tests** Use to measure a student's mastery of each unit's skills.
- **End-of-Year Benchmark Test** Use to measure a student's mastery of program skills covered in all six units.

Unit and End-of-Year Benchmark Tests

Concept Launch

Understanding By Design

Grant Wiggins, Ed. D.
Reading Street Author

"A big idea is a concept, theme, or issue that gives meaning and connection to discrete facts and skills…In an education for understanding, a vital challenge is to highlight the big ideas, show how they prioritize the learning, and help students understand their value for making sense of all the 'stuff' of content."

Turning Points

Reading Street Online

www.ReadingStreet.com

- Big Question Video
- eSelections
- Envision It! Animations
- Story Sort

What can we learn from exploring new places and things?

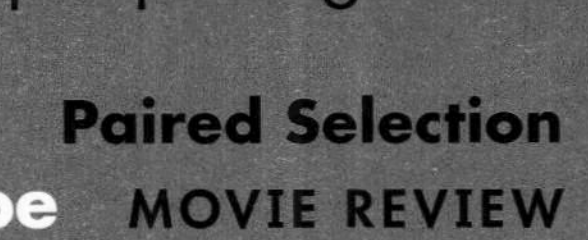

Let's Think About Reading!

connect to SOCIAL STUDIES

Because of Winn-Dixie REALISTIC FICTION

What experiences bring diverse people together?

Paired Selection
A Film with a Message of Hope MOVIE REVIEW

Lewis and Clark and Me HISTORICAL FICTION

connect to SOCIAL STUDIES

What opportunities can be found in new places?

Paired Selection
Ellen Ochoa: Space Pioneer BIOGRAPHY

connect to SOCIAL STUDIES

On the Banks of Plum Creek HISTORICAL FICTION

Why do we want to explore new places?

Paired Selection
Laura Ingalls Wilder ONLINE REFERENCE SOURCES

connect to SOCIAL STUDIES

The Horned Toad Prince TRICKSTER TALE

What can we discover in the landscape of the Southwest?

Paired Selection
The Fox and the Tiger FABLE

connect to SCIENCE

Letters Home from Yosemite EXPOSITORY TEXT

How does Yosemite reflect the unique qualities of the West?

Paired Selection
The Bison of Caprock Canyons MAGAZINE ARTICLE

Small Group Time

Flexible Pacing Plans

Key

- SI Strategic Intervention
- OL On-Level
- A Advanced
- ELL ELL

SI OL A

5 Day Plan

DAY 1	• Reinforce the Concept • Read Leveled Readers Concept Literacy Below Level
DAY 2	• Comprehension Skill • Comprehension Strategy • Revisit Main Selection
DAY 3	• Vocabulary Skill • Revisit Main Selection
DAY 4	• Practice Retelling • Read/Revisit Paired Selection
DAY 5	• Reread for Fluency • Reread Leveled Readers

4 Day Plan

DAY 1	• Reinforce the Concept • Read Leveled Readers Concept Literacy Below Level
DAY 2	• Comprehension Skill • Comprehension Strategy • Revisit Main Selection
DAY 3	• Vocabulary Skill • Revisit Paired Selection
DAY 4	• Practice Retelling • Read/Revisit Paired Selection • Reread for Fluency • Reread Leveled Readers

3 Day Plan

DAY 1	• Reinforce the Concept • Read Leveled Readers Concept Literacy Below Level
DAY 2	• Comprehension Skill • Comprehension Strategy • Revisit Main Selection
DAY 3	• Practice Retelling • Read/Revisit Paired Selection • Reread for Fluency • Reread Leveled Readers

ELL

5 Day Plan

DAY 1	• Frontload Concept • Preteach Skills • Conventions/Writing
DAY 2	• Review Concept/Skills • Frontload and Read Main Selection • Conventions/Writing
DAY 3	• Review Concept/Skills • Reread Main Selection • Conventions/Writing
DAY 4	• Review Concept/Skills • Read ELL or ELD Reader • Conventions/Writing
DAY 5	• Review Concept/Skills • Read ELL or ELD Reader • Conventions/Writing

4 Day Plan

DAY 1	• Frontload Concept • Preteach Skills • Conventions/Writing
DAY 2	• Review Concept/Skills • Frontload and Read Main Selection • Conventions/Writing
DAY 3	• Review Concept/Skills • Reread Main Selection • Conventions/Writing
DAY 4	• Review Concept/Skills • Read ELL or ELD Reader • Conventions/Writing

3 Day Plan

DAY 1	• Frontload Concept • Preteach Skills • Conventions/Writing
DAY 2	• Review Concept/Skills • Frontload and Read Main Selection • Conventions/Writing
DAY 3	• Review Concept/Skills • Read ELL or ELD Readers • Conventions/Writing

This Week's ELL Overview

Grade 4 • Unit 1 • Week 1
Because of Winn-Dixie
20a–45r
and DI•16–DI•25

ELL Handbook

- Maximize Literacy and Cognitive Engagement
- Research Into Practice
- Full Weekly Support for Every Selection

Because of Winn-Dixie
- Multi-Lingual Summaries in Five Languages
- Selection-Specific Vocabulary Word Cards
- Frontloading/Reteaching for Comprehension Skill Lessons
- ELD and ELL Reader Study Guides

- Transfer Activities
- Professional Development

Daily Leveled ELL Notes

ELL notes appear throughout this week's instruction and ELL Support is on the DI pages of your Teacher's Edition. The following is a sample of an ELL note from this week.

English Language Learners

Beginning Ask students yes/no questions about characters, settings, and events in realistic fiction. Ask whether the following characters could be in a realistic fiction story: a 12-year-old girl (yes); a Martian (no); a talking dog (no); an old man (yes).

Intermediate Ask students multiple-choice questions following the same procedure.

Advanced Have students describe realistic characters, events, and settings.

Advanced High Have students use a T-chart to list examples of characters, events, and settings that are realistic and those that could not happen in real life.

ELL by Strand

The ELL lessons on this week's Support for English Language Learners pages are organized by strand. They offer additional scaffolding for the core curriculum. Leveled support notes on these pages address the different proficiency levels in your class. See pages DI•16–DI•25.

ELL Strands	The Three Pillars of ELL Instruction		
	Activate Prior Knowledge	**Access Content**	**Extend Language**
Vocabulary pp. DI•17–DI•18	Preteach	Reteach	Leveled Writing Activities
Reading Comprehension p. DI•22	Frontloading	Sheltered Reading	After Reading
Phonics, Spelling, and Word Analysis p. DI•20	Preteach	Model	Leveled Practice Activities
Listening Comprehension p. DI•19	Prepare for the Read Aloud	First Listening	Second Listening
Conventions and Writing pp. DI•24–DI•25	Preteach	Leveled Practice Activities	Leveled Writing Activities
Concept Development p. DI•16	Activate Prior Knowledge	Discuss Concept	Daily Concept and Vocabulary Development

This Week's Practice Stations Overview

Grade 4 • Unit 1 • Week 1
Because of Winn-Dixie
20a–45r

Six Weekly Practice Stations with Leveled Activities can be found at the beginning of each week of instruction. For this week's Practice Stations, see pp. 20h–20i.

Classroom Management Handbook for Differentiated Instruction Practice Stations

Practice Stations

Daily Leveled Center Activities

- Below
- On-Level
- Advanced
- ELL

Practice Stations Flip Charts

	 Word Wise	 Word Work	 Words to Know	 Let's Write	 Read for Meaning	 Get Fluent
Objectives	• Spell words with the VCCV pattern.	• Identify and write words that have the VCCV pattern.	• Identify words with suffixes.	• Write realistic fiction.	• Identify a sequence of events.	• Read aloud with expression.
Materials	• *Word Wise* Flip Chart Activity 1 • Teacher-made word cards • Letter Tiles • paper • pencil	• *Word Work* Flip Chart Activity 1 • Teacher-made word cards • paper • pencil	• *Words to Know* Flip Chart Activity 1 • Teacher-made word cards • dictionary • paper • pencil	• *Let's Write* Flip Chart Activity 1 • paper • pencil	• *Read for Meaning* Flip Chart Activity 1 • Leveled Readers • paper • pencil	• *Get Fluent* Flip Chart Activity 1 • Leveled Readers

This Week on Reading Street!

Question of the Week

What experiences bring diverse people together?

Daily Plan

Whole Group

- Sequence
- Affixes: Suffixes
- Fluency/Expression
- Research and Inquiry

Don't Wait Until Friday

MONITOR PROGRESS **Success Predictor**

Day 1	Days 2–3	Day 4	Day 5
Check Oral Vocabulary	Check Retelling	Check Fluency	Check Oral Vocabulary

Small Group

- Reading Support
- Skill Support
- Fluency Practice

Practice Stations

Independent Activities

Customize Literacy More support for a Balanced Literacy approach, see pp. CL•1–CL•47

Customize Writing More support for a customized writing approach, see pp. CW•1–CW•10

Whole Group

- Writing: Realistic Fiction
- Conventions: Declarative and Interrogative Sentences
- Spelling: Short Vowels VCCV

Assessment

- Weekly Tests
- Day 5 Assessment
- Fresh Reads

This Week's Reading Selections

Main Selection
Genre: **Realistic Fiction**

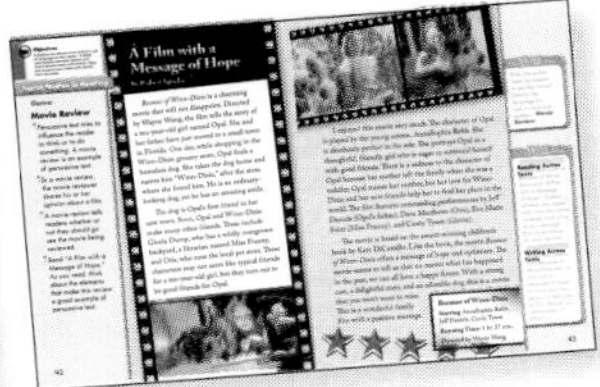

Paired Selection
Genre: **Movie Review**

Leveled Readers

ELL and ELD Readers

Resources on Reading Street!

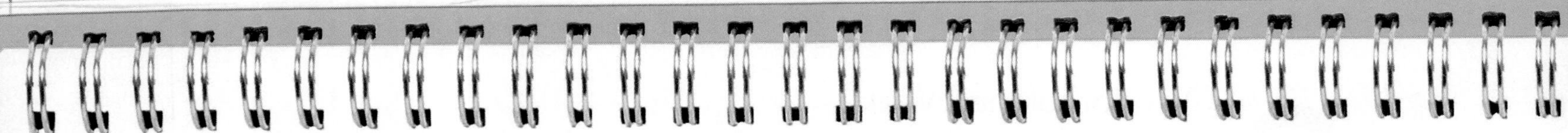

	Build Concepts	Comprehension 
Whole Group	 Let's Talk About pp. 20–21	 Envision It! Skills/ Strategies 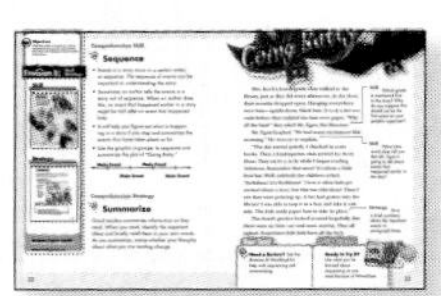 Comprehension Skills Lesson pp. 22–23
 *Go Digital*	• Concept Talk Video	• Envision It! Animations • eSelections
Small Group and Independent Practice	 Because of Winn-Dixie pp. 26–27  ELL and ELD Readers  Leveled Readers	 Because of Winn-Dixie pp. 26–27  ELL and ELD Readers  Leveled Readers  Envision It! Skills/ Strategies  Reader's and Writer's Notebook 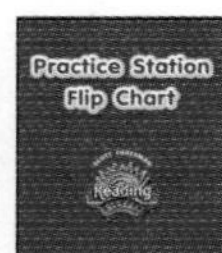 Practice Station Flip Chart
 *Go Digital*	• eReaders • eSelections	• Envision It! Animations • eSelections • eReaders
Customize Literacy	• Leveled Readers	• Envision It! Skills and Strategies Handbook • Leveled Readers
 *Go Digital*	• Concept Talk Video • Big Question Video • eReaders	• Envision It! Animations • eReaders

Question of the Week

What experiences bring diverse people together?

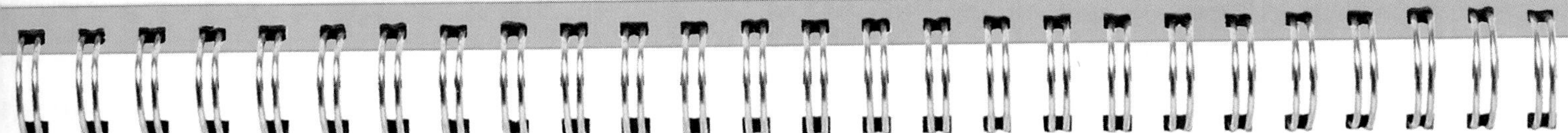

Vocabulary

Envision It! Vocabulary Cards

Vocabulary Skill Lesson pp. 24–25

- Envision It! Vocabulary Cards
- Vocabulary Activities

Envision It! Vocabulary Cards

Because of Winn-Dixie pp. 26–27

Practice Station Flip Chart

Words! W•6

Reader's and Writer's Notebook

- Envision It! Vocabulary Cards
- Vocabulary Activities
- eSelections

- Envision It! Vocabulary Cards

- Vocabulary Activities

Fluency

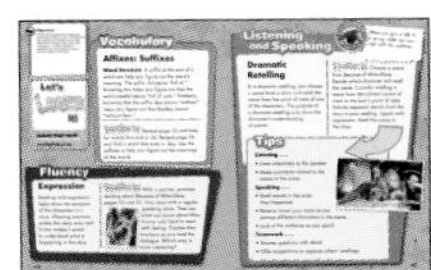
Let's Learn It! pp. 44–45

- eSelections
- eReaders

Because of Winn-Dixie pp. 26–27

Practice Station Flip Chart

Leveled Readers

ELL and ELD Readers

- eSelections
- eReaders

- Leveled Readers

- eReaders

Conventions and Writing

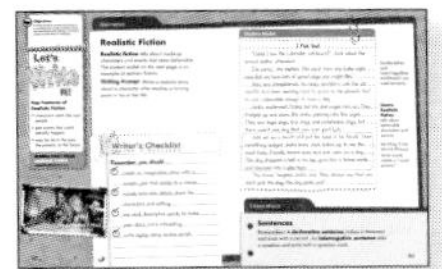
Let's Write It! pp. 40–41

- Grammar Jammer

Reader's and Writer's Notebook

Because of Winn-Dixie pp. 26–27

Practice Station Flip Chart

- Grammar Jammer

- Reader's and Writer's Notebook

- Grammar Jammer

Week 1

My 5-Day Planner for Reading Street!

Don't Wait Until Friday MONITOR PROGRESS	Check Oral Vocabulary **Day 1** pages 20j–23f	Check Retelling **Day 2** pages 24a–31e
Get Ready to Read	**Concept Talk,** 20j **Oral Vocabulary,** 21a kindness, attention, teach, understanding **Listening Comprehension,** "Child of the Silent Night," 21b	**Concept Talk,** 24a **Oral Vocabulary,** 24b variety, introduce **Word Analysis,** 24c Word Ending *-ed* **Literary Terms,** 24d Point of View **Story Structure,** 24d Sequence
Read and Comprehend	**Comprehension Skill,** ◎ Sequence, 21c **Comprehension Strategy,** ◎ Summarize, 21c READ **Comprehension,** 22–23 **Model Fluency,** Expression, 22–23 **Introduce Lesson Vocabulary,** 23a memorial, prideful, recalls, peculiar, grand, positive, selecting	**Vocabulary Skill,** ◎ Affixes: Suffixes, 24e **Vocabulary Strategy,** Word Structure, 24e **Lesson Vocabulary,** 24–25 memorial, prideful, recalls, peculiar, grand, positive, selecting READ **Vocabulary,** 24–25 **Model Fluency,** Expression, 24–25 READ **Main Selection,** *Because of Winn-Dixie*, 26–31a
Language Arts	**Research and Inquiry,** Identify Questions, 23b **Spelling,** Short Vowels VCCV, 23c **Conventions,** Declarative and Interrogative Sentences, 23d **Handwriting,** Letter Size and Proportion, 23d **Writing,** Realistic Fiction, 23e–23f	**Research and Inquiry,** Navigate/Search, 31b **Conventions,** Declarative and Interrogative Sentences, 31c **Spelling,** Short Vowels VCCV, 31c **Writing,** Realistic Fiction, Organization, 31d–31e

Question of the Week

What experiences bring diverse people together?

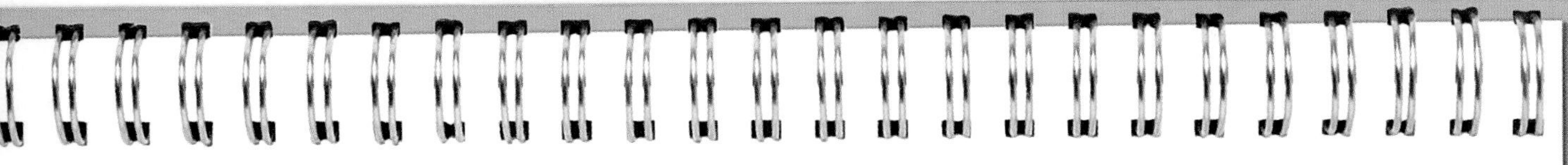

Check Retelling **Day 3** pages 32a–41c	Check Fluency **Day 4** pages 42a–45e	Check Oral Vocabulary **Day 5** pages 45f–45q
Concept Talk, 32a **Oral Vocabulary,** 32b similar, distinct **Comprehension Check,** 32c **Check Retelling,** 32d	**Concept Talk,** 42a **Oral Vocabulary,** 42b social, courteous **Genre,** Persuasive Text, 42c	**Concept Wrap Up,** 45f **Check Oral Vocabulary,** 45g kindness, attention, teach, understanding, variety, introduce, similar, distinct, social, courteous **Amazing Ideas,** 45g Review ◎ Sequence, 45h Review ◎ Affixes: Suffixes, 45h Review **Word Analysis,** 45i Review **Literary Terms,** 45i
READ **Main Selection,** *Because of Winn-Dixie*, 32–37a **Retelling,** 38–39 **Think Critically,** 39a **Model Fluency,** Expression, 39b **Research and Study Skills,** Map, Globe, Atlas, 39c	READ **Paired Selection,** “A Film with a Message of Hope,” 42–43a **Let's Learn It!** 44–45a Fluency: Expression Vocabulary: Affixes: Suffixes Listening and Speaking: Dramatic Retelling	**Fluency Assessment,** WCPM, 45j–45k **Comprehension Assessment,** ◎ Sequence, 45l–45m
Research and Inquiry, Analyze, 39d **Conventions,** Declarative and Interrogative Sentences, 39e **Spelling,** Short Vowels VCCV, 39e **Let's Write It!** Realistic Fiction, 40–41a **Writing,** Realistic Fiction, Vivid Words, 41a–41c	**Research and Inquiry,** Synthesize, 45b **Conventions,** Declarative and Interrogative Sentences, 45c **Spelling,** Short Vowels VCCV, 45c **Writing,** Realistic Fiction, Revising, 45d–45e	**Research and Inquiry,** Communicate, 45n **Conventions,** Declarative and Interrogative Sentences, 45o **Spelling Test,** Short Vowels VCCV, 45o **Writing,** Realistic Fiction, Declarative and Interrogative Sentences, 45p–45q **Quick Write for Fluency,** 45q

Week 1

Grouping Options for Differentiated Instruction
Turn the page for the small group time lesson plan.

Planning Small Group Time on Reading Street!

Look for this Small Group Time box each day to help meet the individual needs of all your students. Differentiated instruction lessons appear on the DI pages at the end of each week.

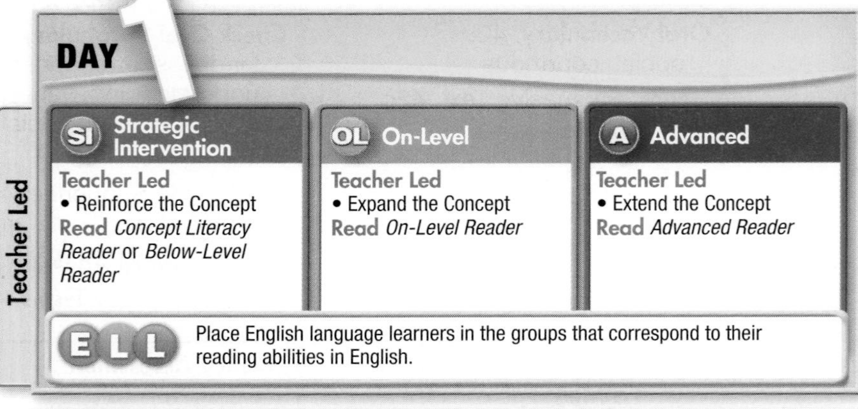

DAY 1
Teacher Led
SI Strategic Intervention
Teacher Led
• Reinforce the Concept
Read Concept Literacy Reader or Below-Level Reader
OL On-Level
Teacher Led
• Expand the Concept
Read On-Level Reader
A Advanced
Teacher Led
• Extend the Concept
Read Advanced Reader
ELL
Place English language learners in the groups that correspond to their reading abilities in English.
Practice Stations
• Read for Meaning
• Get Fluent
• Word Work
Independent Activities
• Concept Talk Video
• Reader's and Writer's Notebook
• Research and Inquiry

ELL Reader
Advanced
Advanced High

ELD Reader
Beginning
Intermediate

ELL Poster

Day 1	
SI Strategic Intervention	**Reinforce the Concept,** DI•1–DI•2 Read **Concept Literacy Reader** or **Below-Level Reader**
OL On-Level	**Expand the Concept,** DI•7 Read **On-Level Reader**
A Advanced	**Extend the Concept,** DI•12 Read **Advanced Reader**
ELL English Language Learners	DI•16–DI•25 **Frontload Concept** **Preteach Skills** **Writing**

You Are Here! Unit 1 Week 1

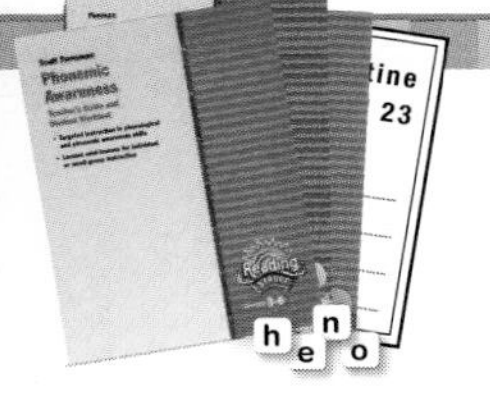

Reading Street Response to Intervention Kit

Reading Street Practice Stations Kit

Question of the Week

What experiences bring diverse people together?

SI Strategic Intervention

Below-Level Reader

Concept Literacy Reader

Because of Winn-Dixie pp. 26–27

On-Level Reader

OL On-Level

A Advanced

Advanced Reader

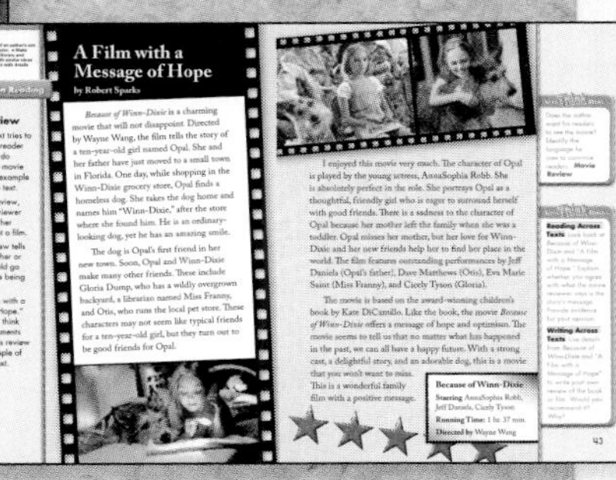

A Film with a Message of Hope pp. 42–43

Small Group Weekly Plan

Day 2	Day 3	Day 4	Day 5
Reinforce Comprehension, DI•3 Revisit **Main Selection**	**Reinforce Vocabulary,** DI•4 Read/Revisit **Main Selection**	**Reinforce Comprehension,** Practice Retelling, DI•5 Genre Focus Read/Revisit **Paired Selection**	**Practice Fluency,** DI•6 Reread **Concept Literacy Reader** or **Below-Level Reader**
Expand Comprehension, DI•8 Revisit **Main Selection**	**Expand Vocabulary,** DI•9 Read/Revisit **Main Selection**	**Expand Comprehension,** Practice Retelling, DI•10 Genre Focus Read/Revisit **Paired Selection**	**Practice Fluency,** DI•11 Reread **On-Level Reader**
Extend Comprehension, DI•13 Revisit **Main Selection**	**Extend Vocabulary,** DI•14 Read/Revisit **Main Selection**	**Extend Comprehension,** Genre Focus, DI•15 Read/Revisit **Paired Selection**	**Practice Fluency,** DI•15 Reread **Advanced Reader**
DI•16–DI•25 **Review Concept/Skills** **Frontload Main Selection** **Practice**	DI•16–DI•25 **Review Concept/Skills** Reread **Main Selection** **Practice**	DI•16–DI•25 **Review Concept** Read **ELL/ELD Readers** **Practice**	DI•16–DI•25 **Review Concept/Skills** Reread **ELL/ELD Readers** **Writing**

Week 1

Practice Stations for Everyone on Reading Street!

Word Wise
Short-vowel pattern VCCV

Objectives
- Spell words with the VCCV pattern.

Materials
- *Word Wise* Flip Chart Activity 1
- Teacher-made word cards
- Letter tiles • paper • pencil

Differentiated Activities
● Choose four word cards. Use the letter tiles to spell the words. Write a sentence for each of the words.

▲ Choose six word cards. Use the Letter Tiles to spell the words. Write a sentence for each word.

■ Choose eight word cards. Use the Letter Tiles to spell each word. Write sentences using the words.

Technology
- Online dictionary

Word Work
Short vowel-sounds in VCCV pattern

Objectives
- Identify and write words that have the VCCV pattern.

Materials
- *Word Work* Flip Chart Activity 1
- Teacher-made word cards
- paper • pencil

Differentiated Activities
● Choose five word cards. Write the words in a list. Quietly say each word aloud.

▲ Choose seven word cards, and write the words. Say each word aloud. Think of other words with these sounds. Add them to the list.

■ Choose nine word cards, and write the words. Make a five-column chart with the vowels *a, e, i, o, u* as headings. Write your words in the correct column.

Technology
- Online dictionary

Words to Know
Words with suffixes

Objectives
- Identify words with suffixes.

Materials
- *Words to Know* Flip Chart Activity 1
- Teacher-made word cards
- dictionary • paper • pencil

Differentiated Activities
● Choose four word cards. Write the words. Circle the base word in each word. Use the dictionary to find the meanings. Write a sentence for each word.

▲ Choose six word cards, and write the words. Circle the base word in each word. Use the dictionary to find the meanings. Write a sentence for each word.

■ Choose eight word cards, and write the words. Circle the base word in each word. Use the dictionary to find the meanings. Write a sentence for each word.

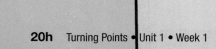

Technology
- Online dictionary

Use this week's materials from the Reading Street Leveled Practice Stations Kit to organize this week's stations.

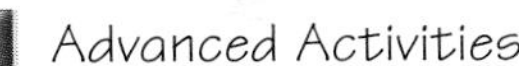

Key

- ● Below-Level Activities
- ▲ On-Level Activities
- ■ Advanced Activities

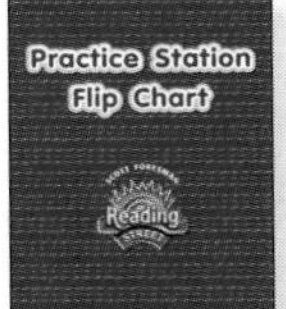

Practice Station Flip Chart

Let's Write!

Realistic fiction

Objectives

- Write realistic fiction.

Materials

- *Let's Write!* Flip Chart Activity 1
- paper
- pencil

Differentiated Activities

● Write a realistic story about an unexpected event. Give details about the characters and setting and tell what happens. Use vivid words.

▲ Write a realistic story about an unexpected event. Use vivid words to describe the characters and setting. Tell what happens to the characters.

■ Write a realistic story about an unexpected event. Use vivid words to describe the characters and setting and tell what happens. Proofread for word choice.

Technology

- Online Graphic Organizers

Read for Meaning

Sequence of events

Objectives

- Identify a sequence of events.

Materials

- *Read for Meaning* Flip Chart Activity 1
- Leveled Readers
- paper
- pencil

Differentiated Activities

● Choose a book from those your teacher provided. Think about the order of events in the story. List three important events from the book in the correct order. Use signal words to show the sequence.

▲ Read one of the books your teacher provided. Think about the order of events. Write three sentences that tell the sequence. Use signal words.

■ Choose and read a leveled reader. Think about the sequence of events. Write a short paragraph that uses signal words to tell the sequence of events.

Technology

- Leveled Reader Database

Get Fluent

Practice fluent reading.

Objectives

- Read aloud with expression.

Materials

- *Get Fluent* Flip Chart Activity 1
- Leveled Readers

Differentiated Activities

● Work with a partner. Choose a Concept Literacy Reader or Below-Level Reader. Take turns reading a page from the book. Use the reader to practice correct expression. Provide feedback as needed.

▲ Work with a partner. Choose an On-Level Reader. Take turns reading a page from the book. Use the reader to practice correct expression. Provide feedback as needed.

■ Work with a partner. Choose an Advanced Reader. Take turns reading a page from the book. Use the reader to practice correct expression. Provide feedback as needed.

Technology

- Reading Street Readers CD-ROM
- Leveled Reader Database

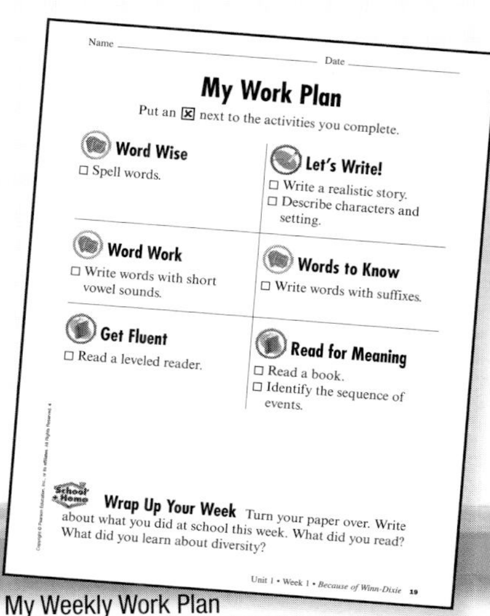

Name ____________ Date ______

My Work Plan

Put an ☒ next to the activities you complete.

Word Wise
☐ Spell words.

Let's Write!
☐ Write a realistic story.
☐ Describe characters and setting.

Word Work
☐ Write words with short vowel sounds.

Words to Know
☐ Write words with suffixes.

Get Fluent
☐ Read a leveled reader.

Read for Meaning
☐ Read a book.
☐ Identify the sequence of events.

Wrap Up Your Week Turn your paper over. Write about what you did at school this week. What did you read? What did you learn about diversity?

Unit 1 • Week 1 • *Because of Winn-Dixie*

My Weekly Work Plan

Week 1

Objectives

- Introduce the weekly concept.
- Develop oral vocabulary.

Today at a Glance

Oral Vocabulary
kindness, attention, teach, understanding

Comprehension
◉ Sequence
◉ Summarize

Reading
"Going Batty"

Fluency
Expression

Lesson Vocabulary
Tested vocabulary

Research and Inquiry
Identify questions

Spelling
Short vowels VCCV

Conventions
Declarative and interrogative sentences

Handwriting
Letter size and proportion

Writing
Realistic fiction

Concept Talk

Question of the Week

What experiences bring diverse people together?

Introduce the concept

To explore the unit concept of Turning Points, this week students will read, write, and talk about how common experiences can bring people of diverse backgrounds together. Write the Question of the Week on the board.

ROUTINE Activate Prior Knowledge **Team Talk**

1. **Think** Have students think about common experiences that bring diverse people together.
2. **Pair** Have pairs of students discuss the Question of the Week
3. **Share** Call on a few students to share their ideas and comments with the group. Guide the discussion and encourage elaboration with prompts such as:
   - What kinds of places do many communities have where people spend time or do activities?
   - What kinds of events have you been to where you notice people of all backgrounds and ages?

Routines Flip Chart

Anchored Talk

Develop oral vocabulary

Have students turn to pp. 20–21 in their Student Editions. Look at the photos. Then, use the prompts to guide discussion and create the *Experiences that bring diverse people together* concept map. Remind students to ask and answer questions with appropriate detail.

- What are the people in the photos doing? (They are all working to accomplish something.) Work helps bring different people together. Let's add *work* to the concept map.
- What else do you notice about the people? (There are boys, girls, and adults of different backgrounds.)

Concept Talk Video

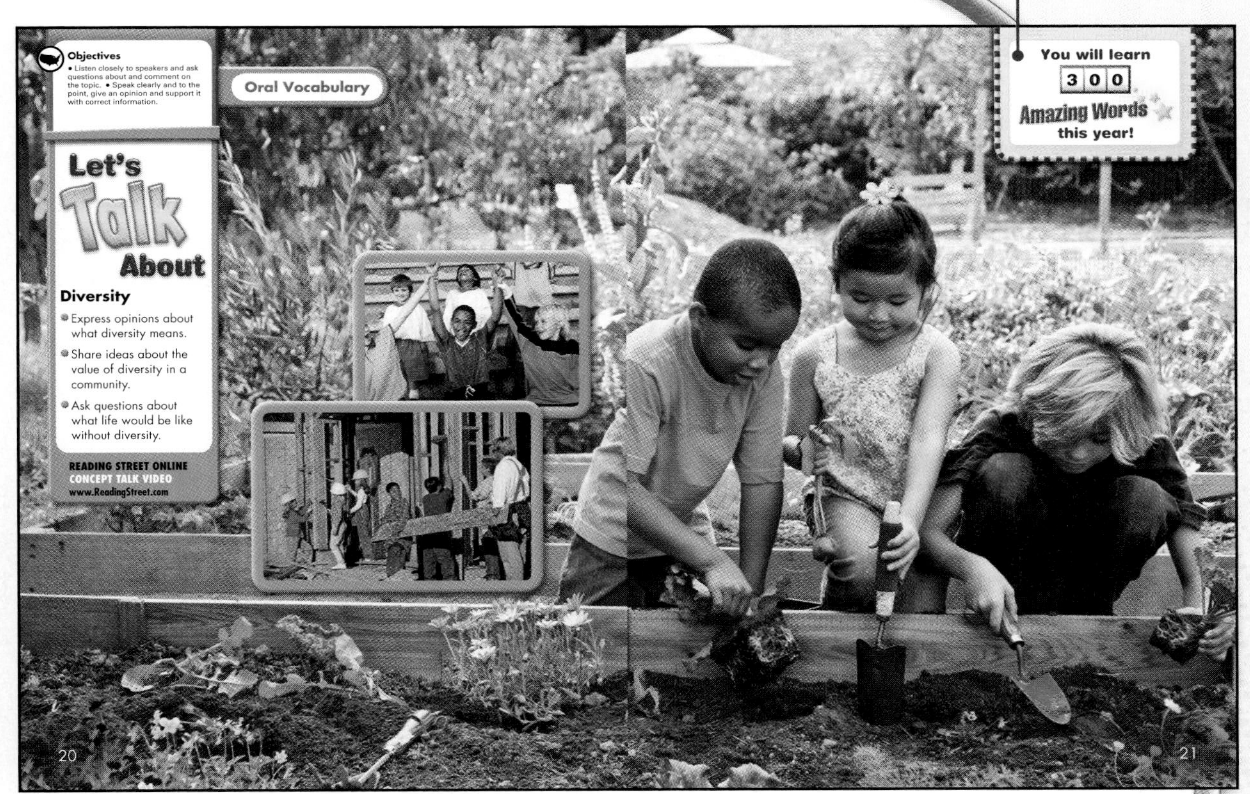

Objectives
• Listen closely to speakers and ask questions about and comment on the topic. • Speak clearly and to the point, give an opinion and support it with correct information.
Oral Vocabulary
Let's Talk About
Diversity
• Express opinions about what diversity means.
• Share ideas about the value of diversity in a community.
• Ask questions about what life would be like without diversity.
READING STREET ONLINE
CONCEPT TALK VIDEO
www.ReadingStreet.com
You will learn
300
Amazing Words
this year!
20
21

Student Edition pp. 20–21

Amazing Words

You've learned 0 0 0 words so far

You'll learn 0 1 0 words this week!

kindness	introduce
attention	similar
teach	distinct
understanding	social
variety	courteous

• How might this group of people have gotten together? (Maybe they attend the same school or are taking part in a community event.) Let's add *school* and *community events* to our concept map.

• After discussing the photos, ask: What experiences bring diverse people together?

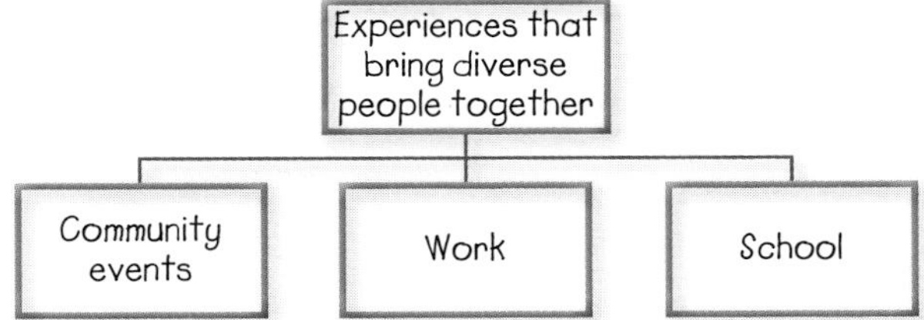

Connect to reading Tell students that this week they will be reading about experiences that bring diverse people together. Encourage students to add concept-related words to the map.

ELL Preteach Concepts Use the Day 1 instructions on ELL Poster 1 to assess and build background knowledge, develop concepts, and build oral vocabulary.

ELL Poster 1

Writing on Demand

Writing Fluency
Ask students to respond to the photo on pp. 20–21 by writing as well as they can and as much as they can about what experiences bring diverse people together.

ELL

English Language Learners

ELL support Additional ELL support and modified instruction is provided in the *ELL Handbook* and in the ELL Support lessons on pp. DI•16–DI•25.

Listening comprehension English learners will benefit from additional visual support to understand the key terms in the concept map. Use the photo on pp. 20–21 to scaffold understanding.

Frontload for Read Aloud Use the modified Read Aloud on p. DI•19 of the ELL Support lessons to prepare students to listen to "Child of the Silent Night" (p. 21b).

Objectives

- Develop listening comprehension.
- Develop oral vocabulary.

Check Oral Vocabulary
SUCCESS PREDICTOR

Oral Vocabulary
Amazing Words

Introduce Amazing Words "Child of the Silent Night" on p. 21b is about a child who loses her abilities to see, hear, or speak because of an illness. Tell students to listen for this week's Amazing Words—*kindness, attention, teach,* and *understanding*—as you read.

Model fluency As you read "Child of the Silent Night," model appropriate expression by adjusting your voice to demonstrate a lively, fluent reader.

Teach Amazing Words

Amazing Words Oral Vocabulary Routine

kindness
attention
teach
understanding

1. **Introduce** Write the word *kindness* on the board. Have students say the word aloud with you. In "Child of the Silent Night," we find out that Laura wanted someone to show her kindness. What is *kindness*? Supply a student-friendly definition.
2. **Demonstrate** Have students answer questions to demonstrate understanding. Would you be showing kindness if you got someone a drink of water on a hot day? Why or why not?
3. **Apply** Ask students to give a personal example of *kindness.*

See p. OV•1 to teach *attention, teach,* and *understanding.*

Routines Flip Chart

Apply Amazing Words To build oral language, lead the class in a discussion about the meanings of the Amazing Words. Remind students to listen attentively to speakers and to build on the ideas of others in a discussion.

Don't Wait Until Friday **MONITOR PROGRESS** **Check Oral Vocabulary**

During discussion, listen for students' use of Amazing Words.

If... students are unable to use the Amazing Words to discuss the concept,

then... use Oral Vocabulary Routine in the Routines Flip Chart to demonstrate words in different contexts.

Day 1	**Days 2–3**	**Day 4**	**Day 5**
Check Oral Vocabulary	Check Retelling	Check Fluency	Check Oral Vocabulary

Child of the Silent Night

by Edith Fisher Hunter

For several months after the fever Laura had lain in a large old cradle in a darkened room. Gradually her father and mother discovered that the sickness had made her blind and deaf. For weeks she could only drink liquids and could not even sit up. It was a whole year before she could walk by herself again and it was not until she was about five years old that she was nearly as strong as most children her age.

Perhaps she would never have become very healthy if it had not been for her friend Mr. Asa Tenney. The Bridgman family called him Uncle Asa, but he was not a real uncle to them. Most people thought that Asa Tenney was a little odd. Although he seemed very old, he wasn't, really. But his clothes were. He didn't care about things like clothes. All he cared about were out-of-door things—like birds and flowers and brooks, and the little dumb animals that he found on his walks.

And now he had come to care about Laura Bridgman too. In a way she seemed almost like one of the little helpless creatures of the woods. Like them, she could not tell people what she was thinking and what she wanted. But he knew that she wanted kindness and attention and love.

Mr. Tenney had no family of his own. When he discovered this little girl at neighbor Bridgman's house he felt that at last he had found someone who needed him.

Daniel and Harmony Bridgman, Laura's father and mother, were kindly people and wanted to do what they could for this poor child of theirs. But they had little time to give her. Mr. Bridgman was a busy farmer and a selectman of the town of Hanover. Mrs. Bridgman had two little boys younger than Laura to care for. In addition, she had to do all the things that any farm wife did in those days.

No, Mrs. Bridgman did not have much time to teach her little deaf, blind, mute daughter. Even if there had been time, how could she have taught Laura anything? Can a person who cannot see or hear or talk learn anything?

Asa Tenney was sure Laura could learn. He believed that she was learning every minute and that she wanted to learn a great deal more. He knew that he had plenty of time in which to teach her too.

He explained it to himself this way: "It is as though Laura is living in a room without windows or doors. I must make windows and doors into that room. Somehow, I must get behind the cloth band that she wears over her eyes and bring the light of understanding to her."

DAY 1 Read and Comprehend

Objectives

- ◎ Sequence events to aid comprehension.
- ◎ Use the summarize strategy to aid comprehension.

Skills Trace

◎ **Sequence**

Introduce U1W1D1; U4W3D1; U6W3D1

Practice U1W1D2; U1W1D3; U4W3D2; U4W3D3; U6W3D2; U6W3D3

Reteach/Review U1W1D5; U1W2D2; U1W3D2; U1W3D3; U4W3D5; U6W3D5; U6W4D2; U6W4D3

Assess/Test Weekly Tests U1W1; U4W3; U6W3 Benchmark Tests U1

KEY:
U=Unit W=Week D=Day

Skill ↔ Strategy

◎ Sequence

◎ Summarize

Student Edition p. El•13

Introduce sequence **Envision It!**

Sequence is the order that events happen in a story. How can noticing the sequence of events help me as a reader? (When I read I will need to know when things happen to fully understand the story.) Authors sometimes tell events out of order. For example, an author might tell about something that happened one afternoon before telling what happened that morning. How can I keep track of sequence if an author tells events out of order? (I can ask myself which events happened first, next, and so on. As I read, I may have to adjust the sequence.) Have students turn to p. El•13 in the Student Edition to review sequence. Then read "Going Batty" with students.

Model the skill

Today we're going to read about a class visit to the school library. Have students follow along as you read the first two paragraphs of "Going Batty." The first thing the author mentions is a fourth grade class visiting the library and seeing bats hanging everywhere. I know that happens in the afternoon. Then Mr. Egan starts to tell what happened that morning. The words *afternoon* and *morning* help me keep track of the sequence.

Guide practice

Have students finish reading "Going Batty" on their own. Then have them use a graphic organizer like the one on p. 22 to sequence the main events.

Strategy check

Summarize Remind students that good readers summarize the plot's main events as they read. Encourage them to think about the important ideas in "Going Batty" as they read and to retell the ideas in their own words.

Model the strategy **Envision It!**

I'm going to summarize the first two paragraphs to help me keep track of what's happening. A fourth-grade class goes to the library in the afternoon and sees bats hanging everywhere. They ask the librarian what this is all about and he says there was some excitement earlier in the day. Have students review the strategy of summarize on p. El•23 of the Student Edition.

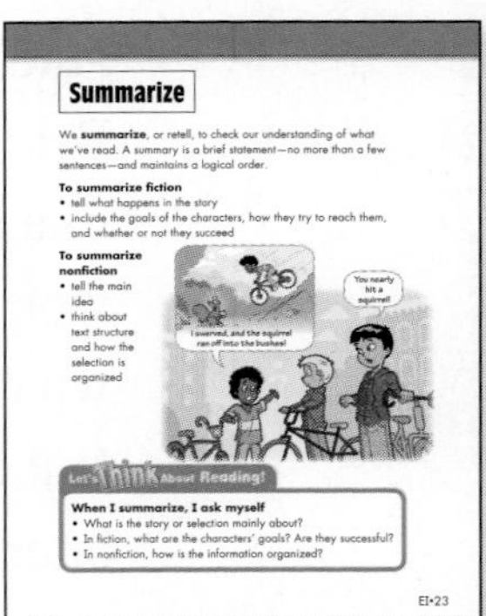

Student Edition p. El•23

On their own

Use p. 40 in the *Reader's and Writer's Notebook* for additional practice with sequence.

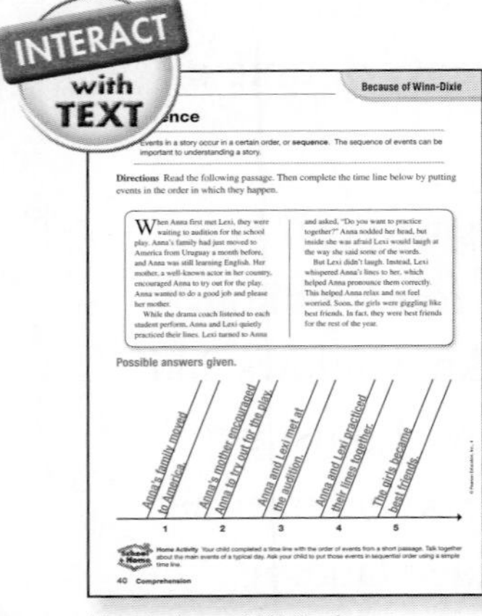

Reader's and Writer's Notebook p. 40

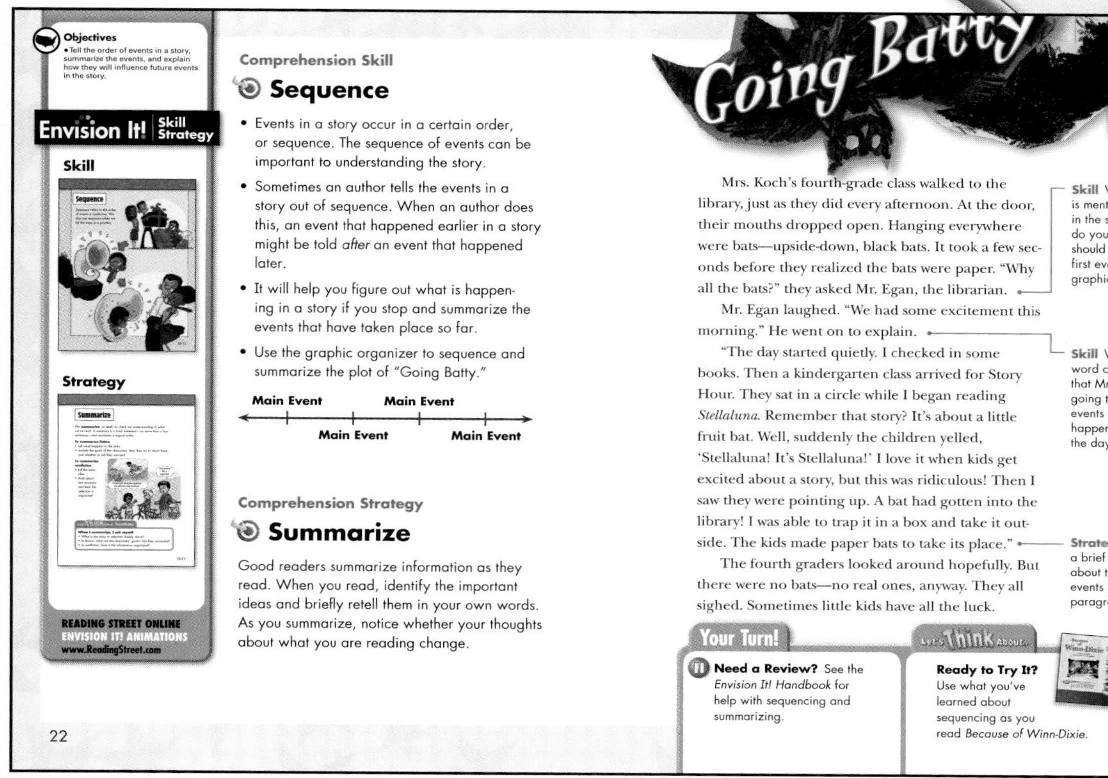

Objectives
- Tell the order of events in a story, summarize the events, and explain how they will influence future events in the story.

Envision It! Skill Strategy

Skill

Strategy

READING STREET ONLINE
ENVISION IT! ANIMATIONS
www.ReadingStreet.com

Comprehension Skill

Sequence

- Events in a story occur in a certain order, or sequence. The sequence of events can be important to understanding the story.
- Sometimes an author tells the events in a story out of sequence. When an author does this, an event that happened earlier in a story might be told *after* an event that happened later.
- It will help you figure out what is happening in a story if you stop and summarize the events that have taken place so far.
- Use the graphic organizer to sequence and summarize the plot of "Going Batty."

Main Event — Main Event — Main Event — Main Event

Comprehension Strategy

Summarize

Good readers summarize information as they read. When you read, identify the important ideas and briefly retell them in your own words. As you summarize, notice whether your thoughts about what you are reading change.

22

Going Batty

Mrs. Koch's fourth-grade class walked to the library, just as they did every afternoon. At the door, their mouths dropped open. Hanging everywhere were bats—upside-down, black bats. It took a few seconds before they realized the bats were paper. "Why all the bats?" they asked Mr. Egan, the librarian.

Mr. Egan laughed. "We had some excitement this morning." He went on to explain.

"The day started quietly. I checked in some books. Then a kindergarten class arrived for Story Hour. They sat in a circle while I began reading *Stellaluna.* Remember that story? It's about a little fruit bat. Well, suddenly the children yelled, 'Stellaluna! It's Stellaluna!' I love it when kids get excited about a story, but this was ridiculous! Then I saw they were pointing up. A bat had gotten into the library! I was able to trap it in a box and take it outside. The kids made paper bats to take its place."

The fourth graders looked around hopefully. But there were no bats—no real ones, anyway. They all sighed. Sometimes little kids have all the luck.

Skill Which grade is mentioned first in the story? Why do you suppose this should not be the first event on your graphic organizer?

Skill What time-word clues tell you that Mr. Egan is going to tell about events that happened earlier in the day?

Strategy Give a brief summary about the important events in paragraph three.

Your Turn!

Need a Review? See the *Envision It! Handbook* for help with sequencing and summarizing.

Let's Think About...

Ready to Try It? Use what you've learned about sequencing as you read *Because of Winn-Dixie.*

23

Student Edition pp. 22–23

Skill Fourth grade is mentioned first. It is not the first event on the graphic organizer because the author is telling the story out of sequence.

Skill The clues are *morning* and *the day started.*

Strategy The librarian was reading *Stellaluna* to a kindergarten class and the children got very excited. They were shouting that *Stellaluna* was in the library. Actually, a real bat had gotten in. The librarian carefully set it free.

Academic Vocabulary

sequence the order in which events happen in a story

summarize to retell in your own words

Model Fluency
Expression

Model fluent reading

Have students listen as you read paragraph 1 of "Going Batty" with appropriate expression. Explain that your voice will rise and fall as you read, just as it does when you are talking.

ROUTINE Oral Rereading

1. **Read** Have students reread paragraph 3 of "Going Batty" orally.
2. **Reread** To achieve optimal fluency, students should reread the text three to four times with appropriate expression.
3. **Corrective Feedback** Have students read aloud without you. Provide corrective feedback about their expression and encourage them to vary their tone of voice to make their reading sound natural. Listen for appropriate expression.

Routines Flip Chart

ELL

English Language Learners

Sequence Provide oral practice by having students sequence events about the school day. Have students state several activities that happen during the school day. Write these on sentence strips and read them aloud. Then have students arrange them in order. Add time order words to the beginning of the sentences after students have sequenced them.

Objectives

- Activate prior knowledge of words.
- Identify questions for research.

Vocabulary
Tested Vocabulary

Lesson vocabulary Use the following Question and Answer activity to help students acquire word knowledge that improves reading, speaking, listening, and writing vocabularies.

Activate prior knowledge Display the lesson words. Give students the opportunity to tell whatever they already know about these words. Then ask oral questions like those below. Students should respond *yes* or *no* and give reasons for their choice.

- Would you expect to have a *grand* time at a carnival?
- Do you know of a *memorial* building or statue in your community?
- Do you think a hedgehog is a *peculiar* pet?
- Are you *positive* that the school cafeteria will serve lunch tomorrow?
- Is a person who shouts, "I'm the best player ever!" during a game *prideful?*
- Are you someone who *recalls* jokes easily?
- Is *selecting* a good library book a difficult task?

Old English suffixes Use the word *memorial* to point out that the suffix *-al* comes from Old English and can be added to words to mean "of or like." Have students identify the base word and suffix in *memorial*. (*memory* and *-al*) Ask students if thinking about the base word and suffix helped them understand the meaning of the word. By the end of the week, students should know the lesson words. Students can use lesson words to write yes or no questions for classmates to answer.

Preteach Academic Vocabulary  **Academic Vocabulary** Write the following words on the board:

point of view	**summarize**
sequence	**expression**
complex sentences	**clauses**

Have students share what they know about this week's Academic Vocabulary. Use the students' responses to assess their prior knowledge. Preteach the Academic Vocabulary by providing a student-friendly description, explanation, or example that clarifies the meaning of each term. Then ask students to restate the meaning of the Academic Vocabulary term in their own words.

Research and Inquiry
Identify Questions

Teach Discuss the Question of the Week: *What experiences bring diverse people together?* Tell students they will research how common experiences can bring diverse people together. Students will present their findings in a report to the class on Day 5.

Model Think Aloud: I can use my own personal interests to generate some research topics. I'll start by asking how people are diverse. I play on the soccer team and I know there are diverse people on our team. *Do other youth sports teams in our area show diversity? What kinds of other events draw big crowds that are diverse?*

Guide practice After students have formulated open-ended inquiry questions from their personal interests, explain that tomorrow they will research their questions and conduct a survey. To generate a research plan, help students identify whom they will ask to participate in their survey and where they will gather relevant information about their research question.

On their own Have students work individually, in pairs, or in small groups to write an inquiry question.

Small Group Time

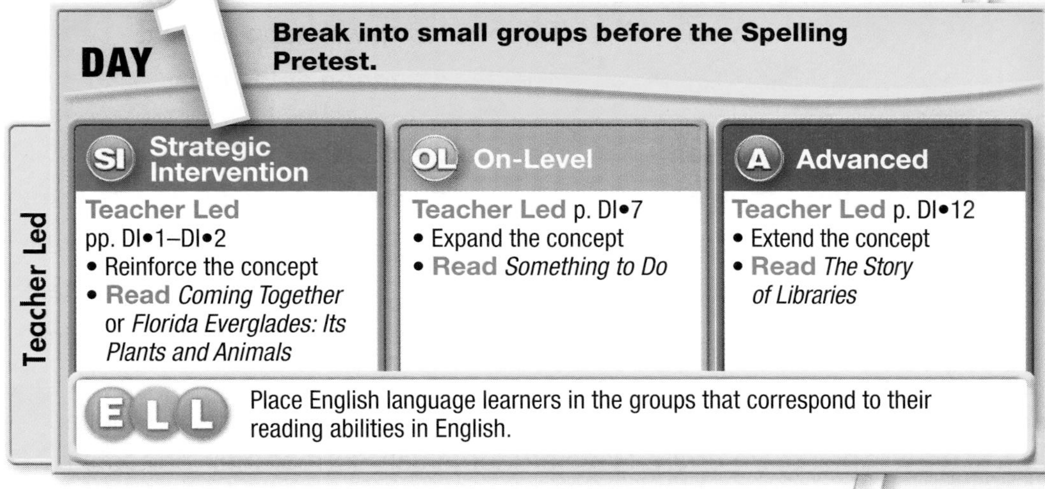

DAY 1 Break into small groups before the Spelling Pretest.

Teacher Led

SI Strategic Intervention	OL On-Level	A Advanced
Teacher Led pp. DI•1–DI•2 • Reinforce the concept • Read *Coming Together* or *Florida Everglades: Its Plants and Animals*	Teacher Led p. DI•7 • Expand the concept • Read *Something to Do*	Teacher Led p. DI•12 • Extend the concept • Read *The Story of Libraries*

ELL: Place English language learners in the groups that correspond to their reading abilities in English.

Practice Stations
- Read for Meaning
- Get Fluent
- Word Work

Independent Activities
- Concept Talk Video
- *Reader's and Writer's Notebook*
- Vocabulary Activities

INTERNET GUY
Don Leu

21st Century Skills

Weekly Inquiry Project

Day 1 Identify Questions
Day 2 Navigate/Search
Day 3 Analyze
Day 4 Synthesize
Day 5 Communicate

Academic Vocabulary

Expression is used to make reading sound natural, as if the reader were having a conversation with someone. Expression makes use of the rise and fall of the reader's voice. Expression can be used to communicate feelings or the mood of a story.

English Language Learners

Multilingual Vocabulary
Students can apply knowledge of their home languages to acquire new English vocabulary by using Multilingual Vocabulary Lists (*ELL Handbook*, pp. 431–442).

Objectives

- Spell words with the VCCV pattern.
- Identify and use declarative and interrogative sentences.
- Practice letter formation, focusing on size and proportion.

Spelling Pretest
Short Vowels VCCV

Introduce This week we will spell words with a vowel, consonant, consonant, vowel pattern.

Pretest Use these sentences to administer the spelling pretest. Say each word, read the sentence, and repeat the word.

1. admire	I **admire** people who are kind.
2. magnet	A **magnet** picks up nails.
3. contest	The girls won the **contest.**
4. method	Do you have a good **method** for doing homework?
5. custom	It is our **custom** to stand during the parade.
6. rally	We had a pep **rally** before the game.
7. soccer	Terry loves to play **soccer.**
8. engine	The car's **engine** wouldn't start.
9. sudden	The car made a **sudden** turn.
10. finger	I cut my **finger.**
11. accident	No one was hurt in the **accident.**
12. mitten	I always seem to lose one **mitten.**
13. intend	How do you **intend** to solve the puzzle?
14. fabric	The wool **fabric** made me itch.
15. flatten	I used my hand to **flatten** the clay.
16. rascal	That playful puppy is a **rascal**.
17. gutter	The leaves clogged the **gutter.**
18. mammal	A camel is a **mammal.**
19. happen	I wonder what will **happen** next.
20. cannon	There is a **cannon** at the park.

Challenge words

21. dungeon	The **dungeon** is dark and dank.
22. magnify	My reading glasses **magnify** the letters.
23. festival	The town has its annual **festival** each July.
24. thunderstorm	Windows blew open during the **thunderstorm.**
25. injury	His **injury** from the accident was healing nicely.

Self-correct After the pretest, you can either display the correctly spelled words or spell them orally. Have students self-correct their pretests by rewriting misspelled words correctly.

On their own For additional practice, use *Let's Practice It!* p. 1 on the *Teacher Resources DVD-ROM*.

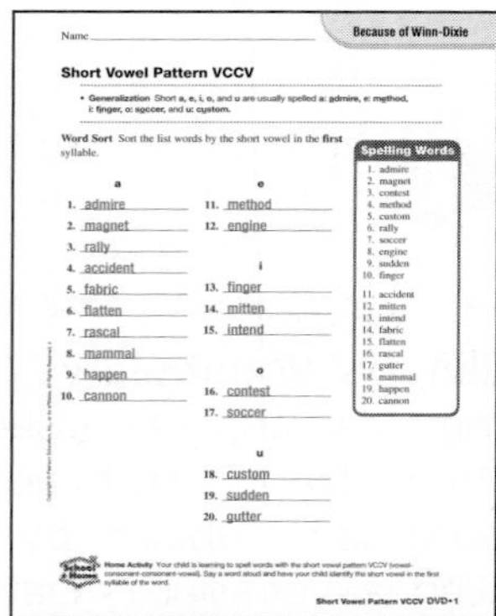
Name ______ Because of Winn-Dixie

Short Vowel Pattern VCCV

- **Generalization** Short **a, e, i, o,** and **u** are usually spelled **a: admire, e: method, i: finger, o: soccer,** and **u: custom.**

Word Sort Sort the list words by the short vowel in the **first** syllable.

a
1. admire
2. magnet
3. rally
4. accident
5. fabric
6. flatten
7. rascal
8. mammal
9. happen
10. cannon

e
11. method
12. engine

i
13. finger
14. mitten
15. intend

o
16. contest
17. soccer

u
18. custom
19. sudden
20. gutter

Spelling Words
1. admire
2. magnet
3. contest
4. method
5. custom
6. rally
7. soccer
8. engine
9. sudden
10. finger
11. accident
12. mitten
13. intend
14. fabric
15. flatten
16. rascal
17. gutter
18. mammal
19. happen
20. cannon

Home Activity Your child is learning to spell words with the short vowel pattern VCCV (vowel-consonant-consonant-vowel). Say a word aloud and have your child identify the short vowel in the first syllable of the word.

Short Vowel Pattern VCCV DVD•1

Let's Practice It!
TR DVD•1

Conventions
Declarative and Interrogative Sentences

Teach Display Grammar Transparency 1, and read aloud the explanation and examples. Point out the declarative and interrogative sentences. Remind students that they will be using complete simple sentences with subjects and verbs that agree in number.

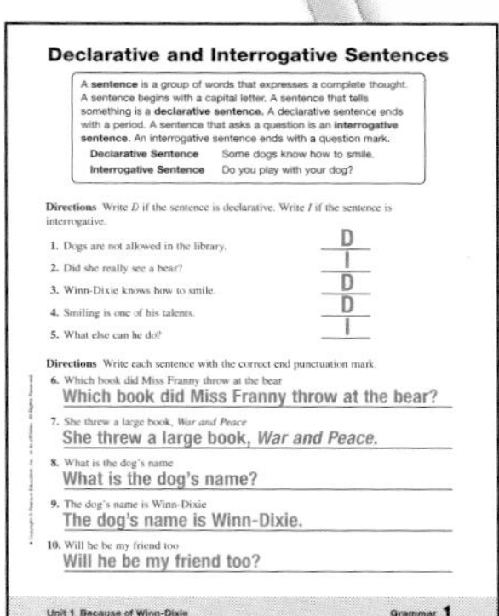

Declarative and Interrogative Sentences

A **sentence** is a group of words that expresses a complete thought. A sentence begins with a capital letter. A sentence that tells something is a **declarative sentence.** A declarative sentence ends with a period. A sentence that asks a question is an **interrogative sentence.** An interrogative sentence ends with a question mark.

Declarative Sentence	Some dogs know how to smile.
Interrogative Sentence	Do you play with your dog?

Directions Write *D* if the sentence is declarative. Write *I* if the sentence is interrogative.

1. Dogs are not allowed in the library. D
2. Did she really see a bear? I
3. Winn-Dixie knows how to smile. D
4. Smiling is one of his talents. D
5. What else can he do? I

Directions Write each sentence with the correct end punctuation mark.

6. Which book did Miss Franny throw at the bear
   Which book did Miss Franny throw at the bear?
7. She threw a large book, *War and Peace*
   She threw a large book, *War and Peace.*
8. What is the dog's name
   What is the dog's name?
9. The dog's name is Winn-Dixie
   The dog's name is Winn-Dixie.
10. Will he be my friend too
    Will he be my friend too?

Unit 1 Because of Winn-Dixie — Grammar 1

Grammar Transparency 1, TR DVD

Model Write the answers to numbers 1 and 2. Explain how you applied the rules for identifying declarative and interrogative sentences.

Guide practice Guide students to complete items 3–5. Remind them to determine if the sentence is a statement or a question. Record the correct responses on the transparency. Have students try to come up with one of each on their own, making sure to use complete sentences.

Connect to oral language Have students read sentences 6 to 10 on the transparency and write the correct punctuation mark for each sentence.

Daily Fix-It Use Daily Fix-It numbers 1 and 2 in the right margin.

Handwriting
Letter Size and Proportion

Model proportion Display the triangles, circles, and squares. You can tell the proportion of an object is correct when the object keeps the same form or shape no matter what the size.

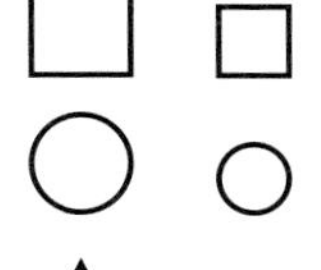

Model letter size Explain that when writing in cursive, the size of the letters should fit properly in the writing space. Draw two boxes, one smaller than the other. Each should have three lines to write on, with the lines more closely spaced in the smaller box. In each box write *I am thinking about the size of my letters.*

Guide practice Have students draw the same boxes. In each box have them write *I am thinking about the size of my letters.* Circulate around the room, guiding students to focus on letter size and proportion.

Daily Fix-It

1. My dog Bella is a real rascul? *(rascal.)*
2. Does stray dogs make good pets. *(Do; pets?)*

English Language Learners

Language production: Declarative and interrogative sentences Model an interrogative sentence: *What is your name?* and the answer in a complete declarative sentence: *My name is Ann.* Have partners practice asking and answering questions about each other. Call on volunteers to share their interrogative and declarative sentences with the group.

Handwriting To support students in learning the concept of proportion, choose three objects in the room that differ in size but are similar in proportion (e.g., square, circular, or spherical objects of varying sizes). Discuss the fact that these objects differ in size but are similar in proportion.

Objectives

- Understand and identify the features of realistic fiction.

Writing—Realistic Fiction
Introduce

MINI-LESSON

Read Like a Writer

INTERACT with TEXT

Reader's and Writer's Notebook p. 41

- **Introduce** This week you will write a **realistic fiction** story. Realistic fiction is fiction writing that tells a made-up story about something that could really happen.

Prompt	Write a realistic story about a character who reaches a turning point in his or her life.
Trait	Organization
Mode	Narrative

- **Examine Model Text** Let's read an example of a realistic fiction story about a character who reaches a turning point. Have students read "The Most Important Moment," on p. 41 of the *Reader's and Writer's Notebook.*

- **Key Features** Realistic fiction stories have **made-up people and events.** Have students circle the name of the main character in the story and one event.

  A realistic fiction story has **events that could happen in real life.** Have students read aloud the event they circled and discuss why it could or could not happen in real life.

  A realistic fiction story happens in **a setting that seems real.** Have students underline one setting in the story that seems real.

  A realistic fiction story discusses **problems that people in real life could have.** Have students draw a box around a problem the main character has in this story and then discuss why it could or could not be a problem that people in real life have.

MINI-LESSON

5-Day Planner
Guide to Mini-Lessons

DAY 1	Read Like a Writer
DAY 2	Story Sequence Chart
DAY 3	Using Vivid Words
DAY 4	Revising Strategy: Deleting
DAY 5	Proofread Declarative and Interrogative Sentences

Review key features

Review the key features of a realistic fiction story with students. You may want to post the key features in the classroom for students to reference as they work on their stories.

Key Features of Realistic Fiction

- has made-up people and events
- has events that could happen in real life
- happens in a setting that seems real
- discusses problems that people in real life could have

Write Guy *Jeff Anderson*

What Do You Notice?

When students are examining the model text, ask, "What do you notice?" By being given the responsibility of sharing what they find effective in the text, students build self-confidence and notice features of the writing they might have missed. They might try them in their writing.

ROUTINE Quick Write for Fluency Team Talk

1. **Talk** Have partners share what they learned about the features of a realistic fiction story.
2. **Write** Each student writes a sentence using his or her own words to define a realistic fiction story.
3. **Share** Have partners exchange and read each other's definitions.

Routines Flip Chart

English Language Learners

Leveled support: Activate prior knowledge

Beginning Ask students yes/no questions about characters, settings, and events in realistic fiction. Ask: Could this character be in a realistic fiction story? A 12-year-old girl (yes); a Martian (no); a talking dog (no); an old man (yes).

Intermediate Ask students multiple-choice questions following the same procedure.

Advanced/Advanced High Have students describe realistic characters, events, and settings.

Wrap Up Your Day

✔ **Build Concepts** What did you learn about the types of experiences that bring different people together?

✔ **Oral Vocabulary** Have students use the Amazing Words they learned in context sentences.

✔ **Homework** Send home this week's Family Times Newsletter on *Let's Practice It!* pp. 2–3 on the *Teacher Resources DVD-ROM.*

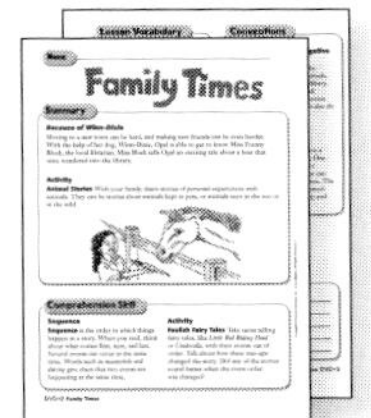

Let's Practice It! TR DVD•2–3

Tell students that tomorrow they will read about a 10-year-old girl who moves to a new town where she doesn't know anyone.

Objectives

- Expand the weekly concept.
- Develop oral vocabulary.

Today at a Glance

Oral Vocabulary
variety, introduce

Word Analysis
Word ending *-ed*

Literary Terms
Point of view

Story Structure
Sequence

Lesson Vocabulary
◎ Affixes: suffixes

Reading
"The Storyteller"
Because of Winn-Dixie

Fluency
Expression

Research and Inquiry
Navigate/Search

Spelling
Short vowels VCCV

Conventions
Declarative and interrogative sentences

Writing
Realistic fiction

Concept Talk

Question of the Week

What experiences bring diverse people together?

Expand the concept

Remind students of the Question of the Week. Tell students that today they will begin reading *Because of Winn-Dixie*. As they read, encourage students to think about how diverse people live, play, and work together in a community.

Anchored Talk

Develop oral vocabulary

Use the photos on pp. 20–21 and the Read Aloud "Child of the Silent Night," to talk about the Amazing Words: *kindness, attention, teach,* and *understanding.* Add these and other concept-related words to the concept map to develop students' knowledge of the topic. Discuss the following questions. Remind students to listen attentively to other students and to answer the questions with appropriate detail. Encourage students to build on the ideas of others.

- Why is it important for each person to receive *attention*?
- Discuss times when you showed *kindness* or *understanding*.
- How does someone's willingness to *teach* help others?

Oral Vocabulary
Amazing Words

Teach Amazing Words

Amazing Words Oral Vocabulary Routine

1. **Introduce** Write the Amazing Word *variety* on the board. Have students say it with you. Relate *variety* to the photograph on pp. 20–21. Think about the different jobs the people in the photo are doing. A variety of jobs are shown. Have students determine the definition of the word. (A variety is a number of different kinds of things within the same group or category.)
2. **Demonstrate** Have students answer questions to demonstrate understanding. Say that you found a recipe for Fruit *Variety* Salad. What would you expect the ingredients to be? Is it true that the school library offers a *variety* of books?
3. **Apply** Have students apply their understanding. Describe a day when you did a *variety* of activities.

See p. OV•1 to teach *introduce.*

Routines Flip Chart

Apply Amazing Words As students read "The Storyteller" on p. 25, have them think about the *variety* of people Ms. Ada tells about in her stories and whether or not they would like for Ms. Ada to *introduce* them to these people.

Connect to reading Explain that today students will read about a girl, her dog, and a librarian in *Because of Winn-Dixie.* As they read, they should think about how the Question of the Week and the Amazing Words *variety* and *introduce* apply to the characters and events.

Amazing Words

kindness	introduce
attention	similar
teach	distinct
understanding	social
variety	courteous

ELL Reinforce Vocabulary Use the Day 2 instruction on ELL Poster 1 to teach lesson vocabulary and discuss the lesson concept.

ELL Poster 1

Objectives

- Use word endings to understand word meaning.
- Identify whether the narrator of a story is first person or third person.
- Sequence the plot's events to aid comprehension.

Word Analysis
Word Ending *-ed*

Teach word ending *-ed* Tell students that many verbs have an ending that helps readers figure out when the action happened. On the board, write the ending *-ed.* Explain that this ending indicates that the action has already happened. Tell students that sometimes the spelling of a word changes with this ending.

Model

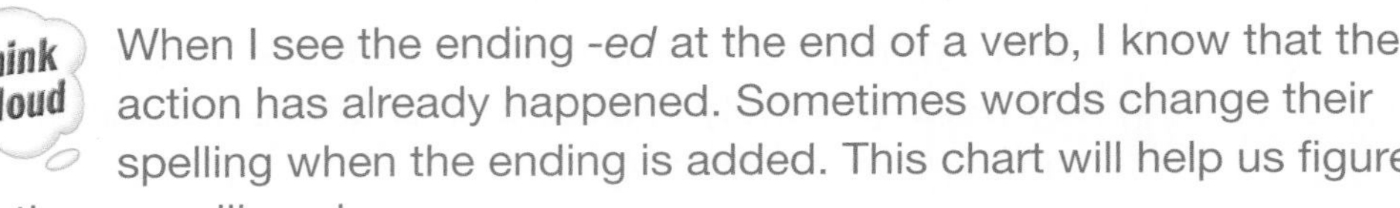

When I see the ending *-ed* at the end of a verb, I know that the action has already happened. Sometimes words change their spelling when the ending is added. This chart will help us figure out those spelling changes.

Base Word	Word with Ending *-ed*
jump	jumped
pack	packed
plan	planned
bake	baked
cry	cried

Guide practice Lead students to notice that words that end with two consonants don't require a spelling change. Words that have a short vowel often double the consonant before adding *-ed.* Words with long vowels and final silent *e* drop the *e* before adding *-ed.* And, words that have only *y* as a vowel and end in that letter change the *y* to *i* before adding *-ed.*

On their own Have students brainstorm more examples of words that follow each pattern of adding *-ed.* Follow the Strategy for Meaningful Word Parts to teach *jumped.*

ROUTINE Strategy for Meaningful Word Parts

1. **Introduce word parts** Circle the ending. I will circle *-ed.*
2. **Connect to meaning** Define the base word and ending. To *jump* is to hop. The ending *-ed* shows this already happened.
3. **Read the word** Blend the parts together to read *jumped.* Then blend the meanings. *Jumped* means that someone or something hopped, and it has already happened.

Continue the routine with the words *planned, baked,* and *cried.*

Routines Flip Chart

Literary Terms
Point of View

Teach point of view

Explain to students that the point of view of the story is how the author presents the actions and characters. The author may tell the story through a narrator or speaker who is a character in the story. When a narrator tells a story using *I* and *we,* this is called first-person point of view. When the narrator or speaker is not a character and uses pronouns such as *he, she, it,* and *they,* this is called third-person point of view. Make sure students understand that the author and narrator are not always the same.

Model point of view

Let's look back at "Going Batty" on p. 23 and think about the point of view. Who is telling the story? Is a character telling what happened? I don't think so. Someone who is not a part of the story is telling it, so the point of view is third-person.

Guide practice

Have students look ahead to *Because of Winn-Dixie,* beginning on p. 26. Help them determine whether the narrator of the story is first-person or third-person.

On their own

Have students browse other selections in their Student Edition to identify the point of view of the narrator or speaker as first-person or third-person.

Story Structure
Sequence

Teach sequence

Events in stories happen in a certain order, or sequence. The author doesn't always tell about the events in order.

Model the strategy

"Going Batty" began with a visit to the library. But something had happened *before* then that was important to the story. Good readers keep track of events as they read.

Guide practice

Brainstorm with students ways to keep track of events, such as making a time line.

On their own

Have students identify the sequence of events in a story they have read recently.

Differentiated Instruction

Strategic Intervention

Point of view Work with a small group of students and have them brainstorm a list of things they did in class yesterday. Use those events to write several sentences. First, write the sentences from first-person point of view. Then write them from third-person. Read the mini-stories with students. Help them compare and contrast the way the stories are written and determine the point of view of each.

Academic Vocabulary

Point of view is the way an author presents the characters and events of a story. The story is told from first-person point of view when one of the characters in the story narrates. The story is told from third-person point of view when it is told from a perspective outside the story.

Objectives

- ◎ Determine meanings of words with affixes.
- Read grade-level text with expression.

Vocabulary Strategy for ◎ Affixes: Suffixes

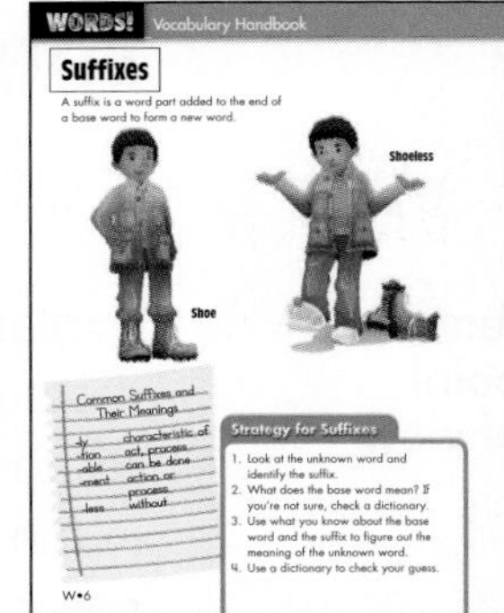
WORDS! Vocabulary Handbook

Suffixes

Student Edition p. W•6

Teach affixes: suffixes

Envision It!

Tell students that when they encounter an unknown word, they should check to see if the word has a suffix they recognize. Explain that they can use the word structure strategy to help them figure out the meaning of the word. Refer students to *Words!* on p. W•6 in the Student Edition for additional practice with suffixes. Then read "The Storyteller" on p. 25 with students.

Model the strategy

Think Aloud Write on the board: *We read a memorial plaque outside the old building.* I'm not sure about the meaning of *memorial*. When I scan the word, I notice a suffix *-al*. I know that this Old English suffix means "of, or having to do with." I look at the rest of the word and I notice the base word *memory*. I'll put the parts together. *Memorial* must mean "having to do with a memory." I'll try that meaning in the sentence. Yes, that makes sense.

Guide practice

Write this sentence on the board: *The man sounded prideful when he spoke about his son's good report card.* Have students determine the meaning of *prideful* by using the meanings of the suffix and the base word. For additional support, use *Envision It! Pictured Vocabulary Cards* or *Tested Vocabulary Cards.*

On their own

Read "The Storyteller" on p. 25. Have students write a definition for the lesson vocabulary words with the Old English suffixes *-ful* and *-al*. Challenge students to find an additional word for each of those suffixes and write definitions for them as well. (*Magical* means "full of magic." *Boastful* means "full of boasting," or "boasting too much.") For additional practice, use the *Reader's and Writer's Notebook* p. 42.

INTERACT with TEXT

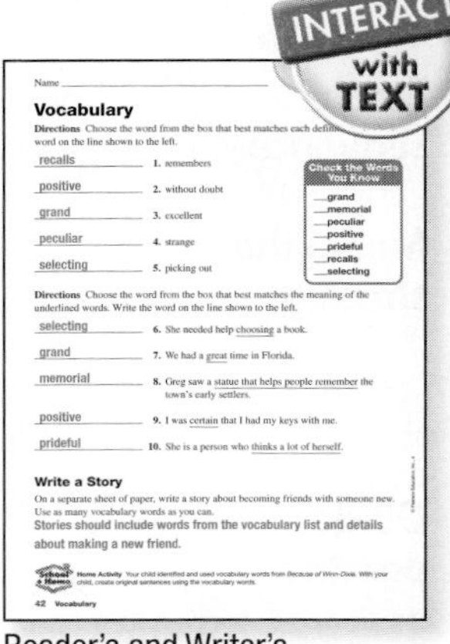
Vocabulary

Reader's and Writer's Notebook p. 42

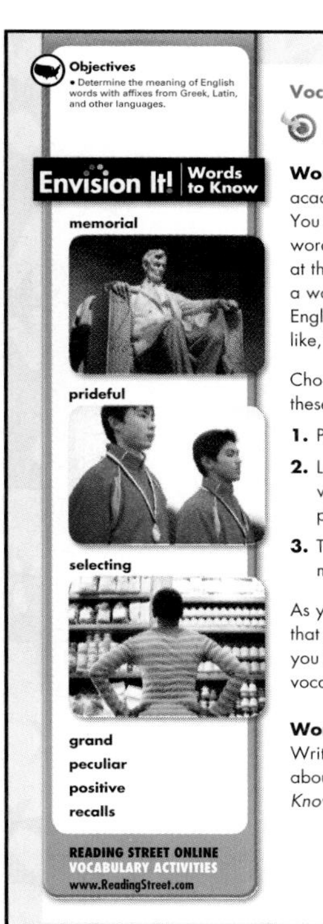

Objectives
• Determine the meaning of English words with affixes from Greek, Latin, and other languages.
Envision It! Words to Know
memorial
prideful
selecting
grand
peculiar
positive
recalls
READING STREET ONLINE
VOCABULARY ACTIVITIES
www.ReadingStreet.com

Vocabulary Strategy for

Affixes: Suffixes

Word Structure Suppose you read an academic vocabulary word you don't know. You can use the suffix to help you figure out the word's meaning. Does the word have *-ful* or *-al* at the end? The Old English suffix *-ful* can make a word mean "full of," as in *tasteful*. The Old English suffix *-al* can make a word mean "of or like," as in *magical*.

Choose one of the *Words to Know* and follow these steps.

1. Put your finger over the *-ful* or *-al* suffix.
2. Look at the base word, the part of the word without the suffix. Put the base word in the phrase "full of ______" or "of or like ______."
3. Try that meaning in the sentence. Does it make sense?

As you read "The Storyteller," look for words that end in *-ful* or *-al*. Use the suffixes to help you figure out the meanings of academic vocabulary words.

Words to Write Reread "The Storyteller." Write a short essay about what you like best about the library. Use words from the *Words to Know* list in your essay.

24

The Storyteller

Thursday mornings at the James P. Guthrie Memorial Library are magical. That's because every Thursday morning Ms. Ada Landry tells historical fiction stories to anyone who wants to listen. But she does not just tell the stories. She acts them out. She makes them come alive.

When Ms. Ada describes what she calls "a prideful person," she puffs out her chest and looks down her nose. She talks in a loud, boastful, powerful voice. When she tells about a sly person, she narrows her eyes and pulls up her shoulders. She talks in a shady kind of voice. When she recalls things that happened long ago, she gets a faraway look in her eyes, and she talks in a quiet, dreamy, hopeful voice.

Ms. Ada's stories are entertaining, but they nearly always have a lesson in them too. A person who everyone thinks is a bit peculiar turns out to be kind or brave. A person who everyone thinks is grand proves to be cowardly or mean. A mistake or disaster ends up having a positive effect.

When it comes to selecting and telling stories, Ms. Ada is the best.

Need a Review? For help with word structure and working with suffixes, see *Words!*

Ready to Try It? Read *Because of Winn-Dixie* on pp. 26–37.

25

Student Edition pp. 24–25

Lesson Vocabulary

grand great; wonderful
memorial serving to remember a person or event
peculiar strange; odd
positive in a good way
prideful in a way that shows a person thinks he or she is better than others
recalls remembers
selecting choosing; picking

Differentiated Instruction

Strategic Intervention

Word structure Remind students of the strategy to use to help them figure out the meanings of words with suffixes.

Reread for Fluency
Expression

Model fluent reading Read paragraph 1 of "The Storyteller" aloud, communicating excitement through your tone of voice. Tell students that you are reading the passage with expression, paying special attention to new vocabulary. Point out that by making your voice rise and fall, your reading sounds the same as when you are talking.

ROUTINE Oral Rereading

 **Read** Have students reread paragraph 2 of "The Storyteller" orally.

 **Reread** To achieve optimal fluency, students should reread the text three to four times with appropriate expression.

 **Corrective Feedback** Have students read aloud without you. Provide corrective feedback about their expression and encourage them to make their reading sound like talking. Listen for use of appropriate expression.

Routines Flip Chart

English Language Learners

Build Academic Vocabulary Use the lesson vocabulary pictured on p. 24 to teach the meanings of *memorial, prideful,* and *selecting.* Call on pairs to write the words on sticky notes and use them to label images of the words on the ELL Poster.

Read and Comprehend

Objectives

- Understand the elements of realistic fiction.
- Use text features to preview and predict.
- Set a purpose for reading.

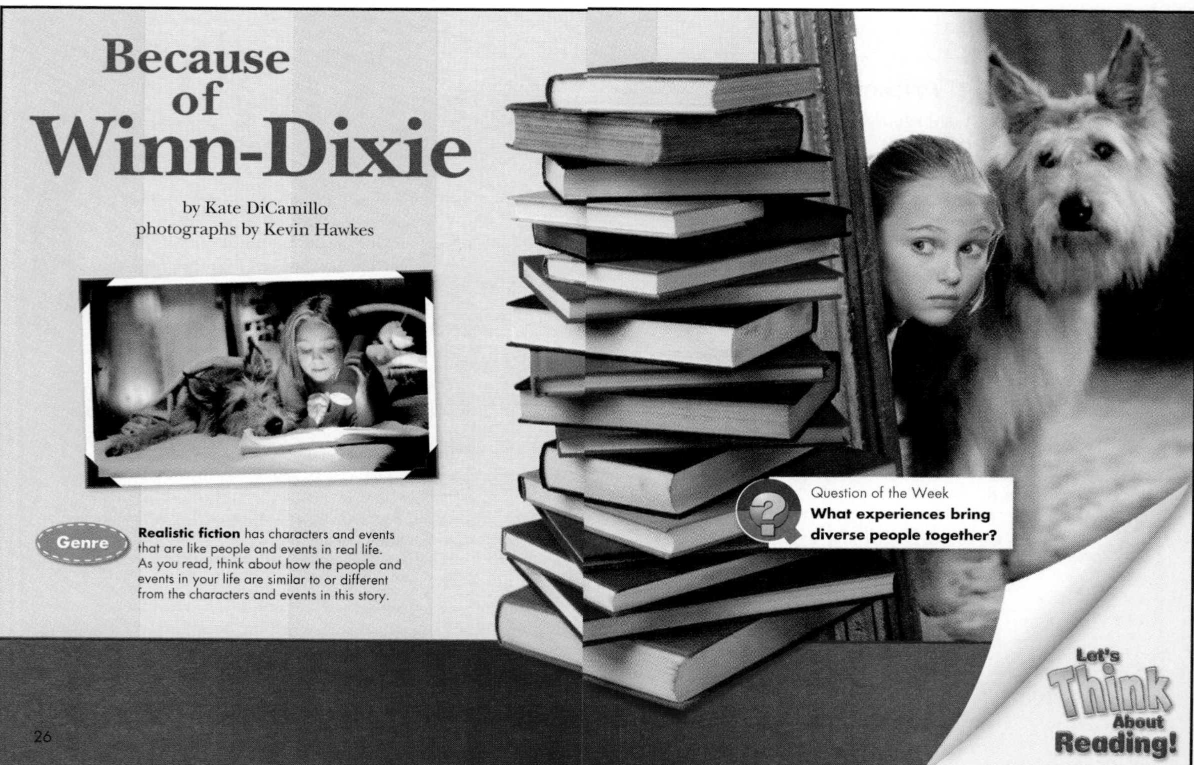

Because of Winn-Dixie
by Kate DiCamillo
photographs by Kevin Hawkes
Genre
Realistic fiction has characters and events that are like people and events in real life. As you read, think about how the people and events in your life are similar to or different from the characters and events in this story.
Question of the Week
What experiences bring diverse people together?
Let's Think About Reading!
26

Student Edition pp. 26–27

Build Background

Discuss communities

Team Talk Have students turn to a partner and discuss the Question of the Week and these questions about communities. Remind students to ask and answer questions with appropriate detail and to give suggestions that build on the ideas of others.

- How do people in a community get to know each other?
- What are some places in a community where people might gather?
- What can you learn about people by listening to their stories?

Connect to selection

Have students discuss their answers with the class. Remind students to listen attentively to speakers and to make relevant, pertinent comments. Possible responses: People get to know each other as they go about their lives in the community. They talk to people they see as they work, go to school, or do errands. People in a community might gather in parks, schools, or libraries. You can learn about a person's personality and beliefs by listening to his or her experiences and stories. For additional opportunities to build background, use the Background Building Audio.

Prereading Strategies

Genre Remind student that fiction tells stories of imaginary people and events. Point out that *Because of Winn-Dixie* is a type of fiction called **realistic fiction** because the characters are believable and the events that happen could happen in real life.

Preview and predict Have students preview the story title and illustrations and then discuss who the characters might be and predict what might happen.

Set purpose Prior to reading, have students set their own purposes for reading this selection. To help students set a purpose, ask them to think what might have happened because of Winn-Dixie.

Strategy Response Log

INTERACT with TEXT

Have students use the Strategy Response Log on p. 7 in the *Reader's and Writer's Notebook* to identify the characteristics of realistic fiction.

Small Group Time

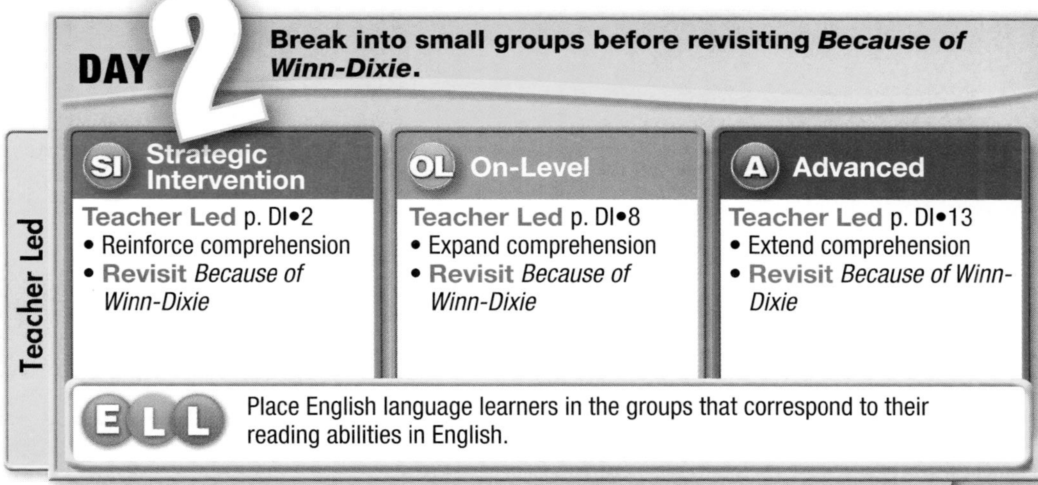

DAY 2 Break into small groups before revisiting *Because of Winn-Dixie*.

Teacher Led

SI Strategic Intervention	OL On-Level	A Advanced
Teacher Led p. DI•2 • Reinforce comprehension • Revisit *Because of Winn-Dixie*	Teacher Led p. DI•8 • Expand comprehension • Revisit *Because of Winn-Dixie*	Teacher Led p. DI•13 • Extend comprehension • Revisit *Because of Winn-Dixie*

ELL Place English language learners in the groups that correspond to their reading abilities in English.

Practice Stations
- Words to Know
- Get Fluent
- Word Wise

Independent Activities
- Background Building Audio
- *Reader's and Writer's Notebook*
- Research and Inquiry

Differentiated Instruction

 Advanced

Have students write a paragraph about the benefits of friendship between a younger person and an elderly person.

Multidraft Reading

For **Whole Group** instruction, choose one of the reading options below. For each reading, have students set the purpose indicated.

Option 1

Day 2 Read the selection. Use Guide Comprehension to monitor and clarify understanding.

Day 3 Reread the selection. Use Extend Thinking to develop higher-order thinking skills.

Option 2

Day 2 Read the first half of the selection, using both Guide Comprehension and Extend Thinking instruction.

Day 3 Read the second half of the selection, using both Guide Comprehension and Extend Thinking instruction.

English Language Learners

Build background To build background, review the selection summary in English (*ELL Handbook*, p. 31). Use the Retelling Cards to provide visual support for the summary.

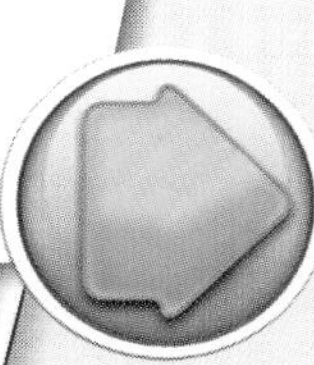

DAY 2 Read and Comprehend

Objectives

◎ Sequence the plot's main events to improve comprehension.

OPTION 1 Guide Comprehension Skills and Strategies

Teach Sequence

◎ **Sequence** Write *first*, *next,* and *last* on the board. Then read p. 28 aloud as students follow along. Have students list the main events in sequence.

Corrective Feedback

If... students are unable to determine the sequence,
then... use the model to guide students in identifying the order of events.

Let's Practice It!
TR DVD•4

Model the Skill

Think Aloud How can I figure out the order of events? (Ask what happened first, next, then last.) I read in the first sentence that Opal moved to Florida. That must be what happened first.

India Opal Buloni, known best as Opal, has recently moved to Naomi, Florida, with her preacher father. Shortly after her arrival, Opal rescues a scrappy dog that she names Winn-Dixie, after the store in which she finds him.

She convinces her father, who often preaches about caring for the needy, that this dog is certainly in need. Thus a summer of adventures begins.

28

Student Edition pp. 28–29

Let's Think About...

1 Opal is telling the story. The author might want to tell the story from a character's point of view to make it more realistic.

OPTION 2 Extend Thinking Think Critically

Higher-Order Thinking Skills

◎ **Sequence • Analysis** Opal is telling this story in her own words. How is the way she uses sequence on page 29 different from the way she uses it on page 28? Opal tells the beginning of her story in sequence first, next, last, but she doesn't use the same order on p. 29. She tells about Miss Franny Block and how they are friends first, which didn't happen until after Opal taught Winn-Dixie to look in the window and scared Miss Franny.

When I read the words *shortly after her arrival,* that must mean it happened after she moved, so that must be what happened next. Then Opal couldn't adopt Winn-Dixie until after she rescued him, so that must be what happened last. By sequencing the main events, I can monitor and adjust my understanding of the text.

I spent a lot of time that summer at the Herman W. Block Memorial Library. The Herman W. Block Memorial Library sounds like it would be a big fancy place, but it's not. It's just a little old house full of books, and Miss Franny Block is in charge of them all. She is a very small, very old woman with short gray hair, and she was the first friend I made in Naomi.

It all started with Winn-Dixie not liking it when I went into the library, because he couldn't go inside, too. But I showed him how he could stand up on his hind legs and look in the window and see me in there, selecting my books; and he was okay, as long as he could see me. But the thing was, the first time Miss Franny Block saw Winn-Dixie standing up on his hind legs like that, looking in the window, she didn't think he was a dog. She thought he was a bear.

Let's Think About...

Who is telling the story? Why would the author tell the story through a first-person narrator? **Story Structure**

1

29

Visualize • Evaluation How can visualizing the events help you keep track of the sequence? As you create sensory images of what the words are saying, it can help make sense of the order in which they would most likely happen.

Draw Conclusions • Analysis How does Opal feel about Miss Franny Block? What in the text makes you think so? Opal likes Miss Franny Block. The text says that Miss Franny Block is the first friend Opal made in Naomi.

On Their Own

Have students reread pp. 28–29 to understand sequence. For additional practice use *Let's Practice It!* p. 4 on the *Teacher Resources DVD-ROM*.

Differentiated Instruction

Strategic Intervention

Point of view Explain that the story is told from Opal's point of view. Have students read the first paragraph on p. 29 and explain how a story told in the first person uses words such as *I, me,* and *we*. This means that the story events are told as seen by one of the characters.

Connect to Social Studies

When people recount events from the past, they are passing along oral history.

ELL

English Language Learners

Activate prior knowledge Create a word web on a chart or on the board with the word *Bears* in the center circle. Guide students to complete the web with words that describe bears. Then have them list the words in order starting with the biggest reason why people are afraid of bears.

DAY 2 Read and Comprehend

Objectives

- Summarize plot events to improve comprehension.

OPTION 1 Skills and Strategies, continued

Teach Summarize

Summarize Have students reread p. 30. Ask a volunteer to tell what happened in his or her own words. Point out that this is summarizing. Remind students that summarizing the plot's main events will help them understand what they have read.

Corrective Feedback

If... students are unable to summarize using important events and a few details,
then... use the model to help them focus on summarizing.

Model the Strategy

Now that I have read the page, I can summarize the main ideas to make sure I understand what is happening in the story. In this part of the story, Miss Franny Block thinks she has seen a bear.

Let's Think About...

Can you hear Miss Franny and Opal talking to each other? How does the author use the dialogue to create these characters? **Story Structure**

This is what happened: I was picking out my books and kind of humming to myself, and all of a sudden, there was this loud and scary scream. I went running up to the front of the library, and there was Miss Franny Block, sitting on the floor behind her desk.

"Miss Franny?" I said. "Are you all right?"

"A bear," she said.

"A bear?" I asked.

"He has come back," she said.

"He has?" I asked. "Where is he?"

"Out there," she said and raised a finger and pointed at Winn-Dixie standing up on his hind legs, looking in the window for me.

"Miss Franny Block," I said, "that's not a bear. That's a dog. That's my dog. Winn-Dixie."

"Are you positive?" she asked.

"Yes ma'am," I told her. "I'm positive. He's my dog. I would know him anywhere."

Miss Franny sat there trembling and shaking.

30

Student Edition pp. 30–31

Let's Think About...

2. Yes. The author uses the dialogue to make the reader feel like they are part of the conversation. The dialogue can give clues about the character's personality by the words being said.

3. Miss Franny tells Opal the story to explain why she screamed and was embarrassed.

OPTION 2 Think Critically, continued

Higher-Order Thinking Skills

Summarize • Evaluation Opal has just moved to a new town. How are things working out for her there so far? (Opal is enjoying her dog and spending time at the library. She is starting to meet new people.)

Character • Analysis Describe the interaction between Opal and Miss Franny. What does this tell you about Opal? Use details from the text to support your answer. (Opal acts in a kind way. She helps Miss Franny up. She tells her it's okay. She asks about the bear.)

She is telling Opal that a bear is outside. Opal assures Miss Block that it isn't a bear at all, only her dog Winn-Dixie.

"Come on," I said. "Let me help you up. It's okay." I stuck out my hand and Miss Franny took hold of it, and I pulled her up off the floor. She didn't weigh hardly anything at all. Once she was standing on her feet, she started acting all embarrassed, saying how I must think she was a silly old lady, mistaking a dog for a bear, but that she had a bad experience with a bear coming into the Herman W. Block Memorial Library a long time ago, and she never had quite gotten over it.

"When did that happen?" I asked her.

"Well," said Miss Franny, "it is a very long story."

"That's okay," I told her. "I am like my mama in that I like to be told stories. But before you start telling it, can Winn-Dixie come in and listen, too? He gets lonely without me."

"Well, I don't know," said Miss Franny. "Dogs are not allowed in the Herman W. Block Memorial Library."

"He'll be good," I told her. "He's a dog who goes to church." And before she could say yes or no, I went outside and got Winn-Dixie, and he came in and lay down with a *"buummmppff"* and a sigh, right at Miss Franny's feet.

She looked down at him and said, "He most certainly is a large dog."

"Yes ma'am," I told her. "He has a large heart, too."

Let's Think About...

Why does Miss Franny tell Opal the story?
Questioning

3

31

Background Knowledge • Synthesis • Text to Self Look at the illustration on page 30. How would you feel if you were Miss Block and thought you saw a bear? Why would some people be afraid of bears and some not? If you had a bad experience with an animal and thought it was going to happen again, what would you do? (Answers will vary.)

Check Predictions Have students look back at the predictions they made earlier and discuss whether they were accurate. Then have students preview the rest of the selection and either adjust their predictions accordingly or make new predictions.

On Their Own

Have students reread the first paragraph on p. 31. Have students work with a partner to write a short summary. Remind them to use their own words and summarize the main ideas in the correct sequence.

Differentiated Instruction

Strategic Intervention
Organize students into pairs to create a summary of the story so far. Have students begin by making several quick sketches to show important events. Help them use their drawings to sum up the story to this point.

Advanced
Pose the question, *Might a bear really go into a library?* Have students search the Internet to find out more about how bears behave. Have them use a student-friendly search engine and use the keywords *bear behavior*. Be sure to follow classroom rules for Internet use.

ELL

English Language Learners
Build Academic Vocabulary Point to the word *hind* (paragraph 7, p. 30). Explain to students that when Winn-Dixie stood on his hind legs, he stood on his back legs. Have students find Winn-Dixie in the illustration on page 31 and ask how it supports the meaning of the word.

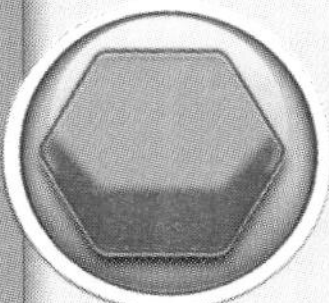

If you want to teach this selection in two sessions, stop here.

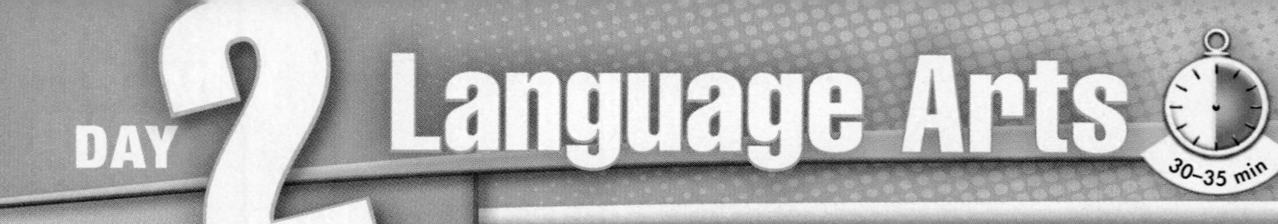

Objectives

- Collect information from student-initiated surveys to answer the research question.
- Recognize and correctly use declarative and interrogative sentences.
- Practice correctly spelling words with the short vowel VCCV pattern.

Research and Inquiry
Navigate/Search

Teach

Explain to students that they will be initiating a survey to gather relevant information about their research questions. They can give the survey to their classmates or to teachers in other classes. Before students begin working on their survey, have them search the Internet for background information. Students can use this information to focus their survey questions.

Model

Think Aloud When I did my search on the Internet, I found many examples of school sports programs that promote diversity by helping students from different backgrounds learn how to work together on the same team. This information helped me think of these questions for our survey: *Does our school sports program encourage diversity? Does our school have any sports teams with a diverse group of students? Do students think such a program would help them understand others who are different from themselves?*

Guide practice

Have students continue their research. Discuss the types of questions that are best suited to a survey. Explain that questions that require a yes or no answer, as well as multiple-choice questions, are good choices, because the results are easier to tally at the end of the survey. Encourage students to think of additional survey questions.

On their own

Have students work together to list possible survey questions. To create the survey, have them narrow the choices down to the most important questions. Then, have students administer the survey to the class. If possible, have students ask students and teachers in other classes to take the survey.

Grammar Jammer

Conventions
Declarative and Interrogative Sentences

Teach Write these sentences on the board: *The girl took the dog to her house. Why did she take the dog?* Point out that the first sentence makes a statement and ends in a period. The second asks a question and ends with a question mark.

Guide practice Students can vary their sentence style using interrogative sentences along with declarative sentences. Have students add an interrogative sentence to each of the following:

Animals are interesting. **School can be fun.**

Daily Fix-It Use Daily Fix-It numbers 3 and 4 in the right margin.

Connect to oral language Have students look for, read, and identify declarative and interrogative sentences in *Because of Winn-Dixie. (You asked for a whole library?* p. 32; *I raised my eyes slowly.* p. 34.)

On their own For additional practice, use the *Reader's and Writer's Notebook* p. 43.

Spelling
Short Vowels VCCV

Teach Remind students that VCCV words usually have a short vowel followed by two consonants. Write *admire* and *mitten*. Explain that in some words the two consonants are the same, as in *mitten.* In others they are different, as in *admire.*

Guide practice Have one partner write same-consonant spelling words from the list and the other write different-consonant spelling words. Then have students read aloud each word and say the vowel sound in the first syllable.

On their own For additional practice, use the *Reader's and Writer's Notebook* p. 44.

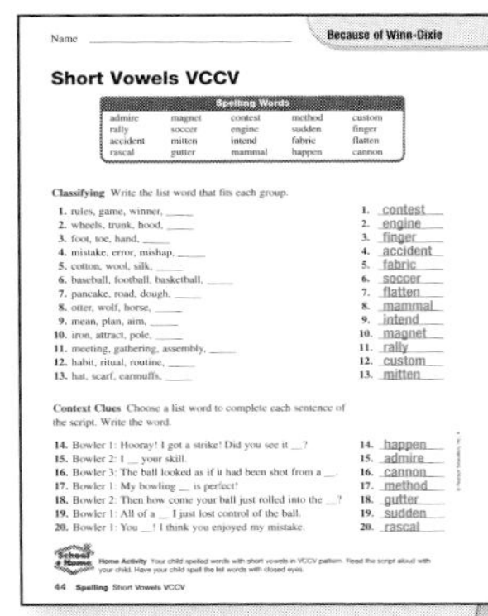

Name ______ Because of Winn-Dixie

Short Vowels VCCV

Spelling Words				
admire	magnet	contest	method	custom
rally	soccer	engine	sudden	finger
accident	mitten	intend	fabric	flatten
rascal	gutter	mammal	happen	cannon

Classifying Write the list word that fits each group.

1. rules, game, winner, ____ — 1. contest
2. wheels, trunk, hood, ____ — 2. engine
3. foot, toe, hand, ____ — 3. finger
4. mistake, error, mishap, ____ — 4. accident
5. cotton, wool, silk, ____ — 5. fabric
6. baseball, football, basketball, ____ — 6. soccer
7. pancake, road, dough, ____ — 7. flatten
8. otter, wolf, horse, ____ — 8. mammal
9. mean, plan, aim, ____ — 9. intend
10. iron, attract, pole, ____ — 10. magnet
11. meeting, gathering, assembly, ____ — 11. rally
12. habit, ritual, routine, ____ — 12. custom
13. hat, scarf, earmuffs, ____ — 13. mitten

Context Clues Choose a list word to complete each sentence of the script. Write the word.

14. Bowler 1: Hooray! I got a strike! Did you see it __? — 14. happen
15. Bowler 2: I __ your skill. — 15. admire
16. Bowler 3: The ball looked as if it had been shot from a __. — 16. cannon
17. Bowler 1: My bowling __ is perfect! — 17. method
18. Bowler 2: Then how come your ball just rolled into the __? — 18. gutter
19. Bowler 1: All of a __ I just lost control of the ball. — 19. sudden
20. Bowler 1: You __! I think you enjoyed my mistake. — 20. rascal

Home Activity Your child spelled words with short vowels in VCCV pattern. Read the script aloud with your child. Have your child spell the list words with closed eyes.

44 **Spelling** Short Vowels VCCV

Reader's and Writer's Notebook p. 44

Daily Fix-It

3. I teaching my dog to rol over. *(I am teaching; roll)*
4. Dogs can learn to help blind people. Or works with the police. *(people or work)*

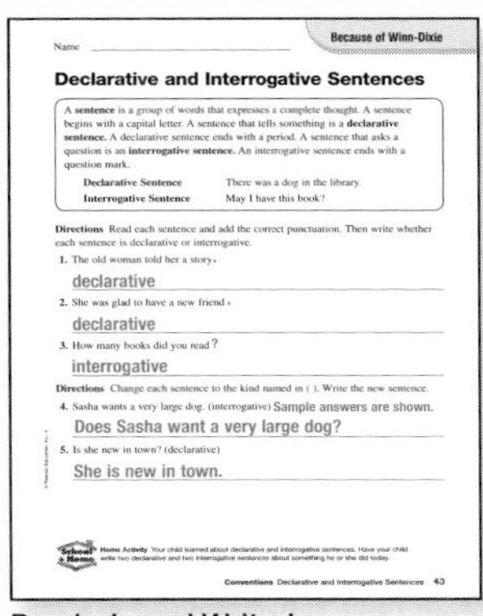

Name ______ Because of Winn-Dixie

Declarative and Interrogative Sentences

A **sentence** is a group of words that expresses a complete thought. A sentence begins with a capital letter. A sentence that tells something is a **declarative sentence.** A declarative sentence ends with a period. A sentence that asks a question is an **interrogative sentence.** An interrogative sentence ends with a question mark.

Declarative Sentence	There was a dog in the library.
Interrogative Sentence	May I have this book?

Directions Read each sentence and add the correct punctuation. Then write whether each sentence is declarative or interrogative.

1. The old woman told her a story.
declarative
2. She was glad to have a new friend.
declarative
3. How many books did you read?
interrogative

Directions Change each sentence to the kind named in ( ). Write the new sentence.

4. Sasha wants a very large dog. (interrogative) Sample answers are shown.
Does Sasha want a very large dog?
5. Is she new in town? (declarative)
She is new in town.

Home Activity Your child learned about declarative and interrogative sentences. Have your child write two declarative and two interrogative sentences about something he or she did today.

Conventions Declarative and Interrogative Sentences 43

Reader's and Writer's Notebook p. 43

English Language Learners

Conventions To provide students with practice using declarative and interrogative sentences, use the modified grammar lessons in the *ELL Handbook* and Grammar Jammer online at: www.ReadingStreet.com

Language transfer: Interrogative and declarative sentences In English, questions often have a different word order than in statements, which is not always the case in other languages. Provide students with additional practice in making statements and questions with the correct word order.

Objectives

- Organize ideas to prepare to writing about characters.

Writing—Realistic Fiction
Writing Trait: Organization

Introduce the prompt

Remind students that the selection they'll be reading this week, *Because of Winn-Dixie,* is an example of realistic fiction. Review the key features of realistic fiction. Remind students to think about these features as they plan their own writing. Then explain that they will begin the writing process for a realistic fiction story today. Read aloud the writing prompt.

Writing Prompt

Write a realistic story about a character who reaches a turning point in his or her life.

Select a topic

To help choose a topic, let's make a chart with a list of realistic characters and the problems a character might have. Display a T-chart. In *Because of Winn-Dixie* you read about a young, friendly girl, Opal, who had no friends in a new town. I'll put that character and problem in my chart. Ask students to brainstorm other realistic characters and the problems they might have. Fill in the chart as they give their suggestions.

Gather information

Remind students that they can use people and events they have read about in books or have seen in movies or in real life to give them ideas about characters and problems. Remember to keep this chart as the students will refer back to it tomorrow as they draft.

Possible Characters	Possible Problems
Young, friendly girl named Opal	Has no friends in a new town
Young, determined boy	Doesn't make basketball team
Marco, a boy from Mexico	Has no confidence in sports or in English

Corrective feedback

Circulate around the room as students use their charts to help them plan what they will write about. Talk individually with students who seem to be having difficulty completing their charts or choosing a topic. Ask struggling students to think about which problem they think they can solve.

MINI-LESSON

Story Sequence Chart

- A story sequence chart helps you plan and organize your story. I'm going to write about a boy named Marco who moved to the U.S. from Mexico and has no confidence in English or in sports. I'll use my story sequence chart to organize the events in my story. Display a story sequence chart. In the "Beginning" box on the chart, write the name of the character and his problem.
- In the middle box I'll write about Sam asking Marco to join the basketball team. I'll write details about how he teaches Marco to play. In the ending box I'll write how Marco does well in the game and now has confidence.

  Have students begin their own story sequence chart using the form on p. 45 of their *Reader's and Writer's Notebook.* Explain that they will fill in their chart with the character and events.

Teacher Tip

Check students' graphic organizers to be sure they have included the events in a sensible sequence and the characters and events are realistic.

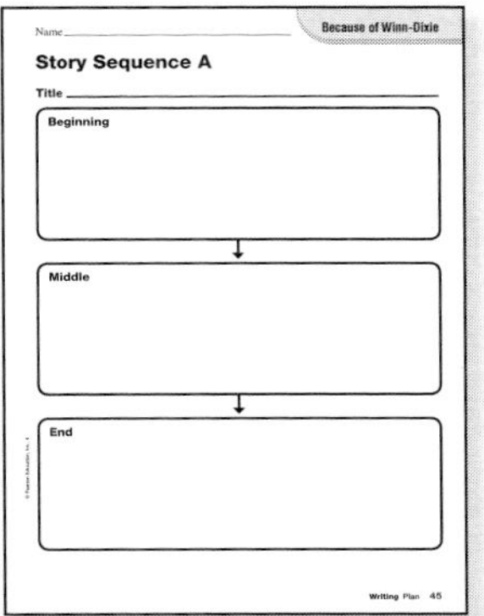
Name
Because of Winn-Dixie
Story Sequence A
Title
Beginning
Middle
End
Writing Plan 45

Reader's and Writer's Notebook p. 45

ROUTINE **Quick Write for Fluency** Team Talk

1. **Talk** Have pairs discuss the main problem the character in their story has.
2. **Write** Each student writes a sentence about the problems discussed.
3. **Share** Partners read their writing to each other and then each asks a question about what the other has written.

Routines Flip Chart

Wrap Up Your Day

- ✔ **Build Concepts** What did you learn about what it might be like to move to a new community?
- ✔ **Sequence** What happens in the beginning of the story? What happens next?
- ✔ **Summarize** How does identifying the order of events in a story help you understand the text?

Tell students that tomorrow they will continue reading about Opal and her life in a new town.

Objectives

- Expand the weekly concept.
- Develop oral vocabulary.

Today at a Glance

Oral Vocabulary
similar, distinct

Comprehension Check/Retelling
Discuss questions

Reading
Because of Winn-Dixie

Think Critically
Retelling

Fluency
Expression

Research and Study Skills
Map, globe, atlas

Research and Inquiry
Analyze

Spelling
Short vowels VCCV

Conventions
Declarative and interrogative sentences

Writing
Realistic fiction

Concept Talk

Question of the Week

What experiences bring diverse people together?

Expand the concept

Remind students of the Question of the Week. Discuss how the question relates to *Because of Winn-Dixie.* Remind students to make pertinent comments in a discussion. Tell students that today they will read more about Opal, Winn-Dixie, and Miss Franny Block. Encourage students to think about how Opal and Miss Franny represent diversity, and what experience brought them together.

Anchored Talk

Develop oral vocabulary

Use the illustrations to review pp. 26–31 of *Because of Winn-Dixie.* Discuss the Amazing Words *similar* and *distinct.* Add these and other concept-related words to the concept map. Use the following questions to develop students' understanding of the concept. Remind students to ask and answer questions with appropriate detail and to give suggestions based on the ideas of others.

- Opal and Miss Franny are alike because they both seem a little lonely. What are some other ways that people of different ages can be *similar?*
- Winn-Dixie is an average-looking dog, but he has something quite *distinct* about him. Which of Winn-Dixie's features is *distinct?*

Oral Vocabulary
Amazing Words

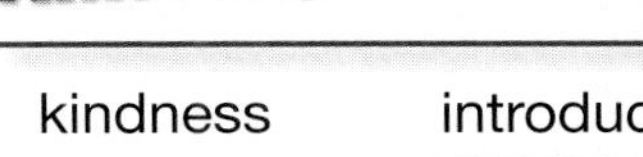

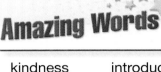

kindness	introduce
attention	similar
teach	distinct
understanding	social
variety	courteous

Amazing Words Oral Vocabulary Routine

Teach Amazing Words

1. **Introduce** Write the word *similar* on the board. Have students say it with you. Yesterday we learned that a bear once went into the Herman W. Block Memorial Library, and Miss Franny thought that something *similar* was happening when she saw Winn-Dixie. Have students determine a definition of *similar.* (When things are *similar*, they are alike.)
2. **Demonstrate** Have students answer questions to demonstrate understanding. In what way does Opal say that she is *similar* to her mama? (They both like to be told stories.) After Miss Franny saw Winn-Dixie, she was trembling and shaking. Are trembling and shaking *similar* actions? Why or why not? (Trembling and shaking are similar because they mean almost the same thing.)
3. **Apply** Have students apply their understanding. How is your favorite thing to do *similar* to your friend's favorite thing to do?

See p. OV•1 to teach *distinct*.

Routine Flip Chart

Apply Amazing Words As students read pp. 32–37 of *Because of Winn-Dixie,* have them consider how the Amazing Words *similar* and *distinct* apply to the details of Miss Franny's stories.

Connect to reading Explain that today students will read about more events from Miss Franny's past, as well as things that are happening now in Naomi. As they read, students should think about how the Question of the Week and the Amazing Words *similar* and *distinct* apply to the details of the story.

ELL **Expand Vocabulary** Use the Day 3 instruction on ELL Poster 1 to help students expand vocabulary.

ELL Poster 1

ELL

English Language Learners

Cognates Point out that both of today's Amazing Words have Spanish cognates: *similar* and *distinto.*

Objectives

- ◎ Identify sequence to aid comprehension
- ◎ Use the summarize strategy to aid comprehension.
- ◎ Identify suffixes to aid with unfamiliar words.

Comprehension Check

Have students discuss each question with a partner. Ask several pairs to share their responses.

☑ **Genre • Analysis**
How is *Because of Winn-Dixie* a good example of a realistic fiction story? Use specific examples from the text. Possible response: *Because of Winn-Dixie* is a good example of realistic fiction because the places and people could be real and the things that happen could really happen in life. There really are small towns in Florida. A little girl and her dog could really visit a library and meet a librarian.

☑ **Sequence • Analysis**
Restate the main events in sequence and explain how the sequence of events helped you understand why Opal was at the library with Winn-Dixie looking in the window. Possible response: The sequence of events told me how Opal liked to go to the library and how she showed Winn-Dixie to stand on his hind legs and look in the window to know Opal didn't leave him behind.

☑ **Summarize • Synthesis**
What are some questions you can ask yourself to help you summarize the first part of *Because of Winn-Dixie?* Possible response: Who is the story about? What is important about Winn-Dixie? What are the main things that have happened so far?

☑ **Affixes: Suffixes • Synthesis**
Read the following sentence aloud: *Opal was helpful to Miss Franny when Miss Franny was scared*. Use what you know about suffixes to figure out the meaning of *helpful*. Possible response: *-ful* means "full of, or having the qualities of," so *helpful* must mean "someone or something that is full of help."

☑ **Connect text to self**
How would you feel if, like Opal, you moved to a new town and didn't know many people? What do you think about Opal going to the library to pass the time? What might you do in this situation? Possible response: I would want to make new friends. It is a good idea to go places where you might meet people, such as the library or swimming pools or parks.

Strategy Response Log

INTERACT with TEXT

Have students revisit p. 7 in the *Reader's and Writer's Notebook* to add additional information about realistic fiction.

Check Retelling

Have students retell Miss Franny Block's story of the bear in the library section of *Because of Winn-Dixie,* summarizing information in the text in a logical order. Encourage students to use the text features in their retellings.

Corrective feedback

If... students leave out important details,
then... have students look back through the illustrations and photographs in the selection.

Small Group Time

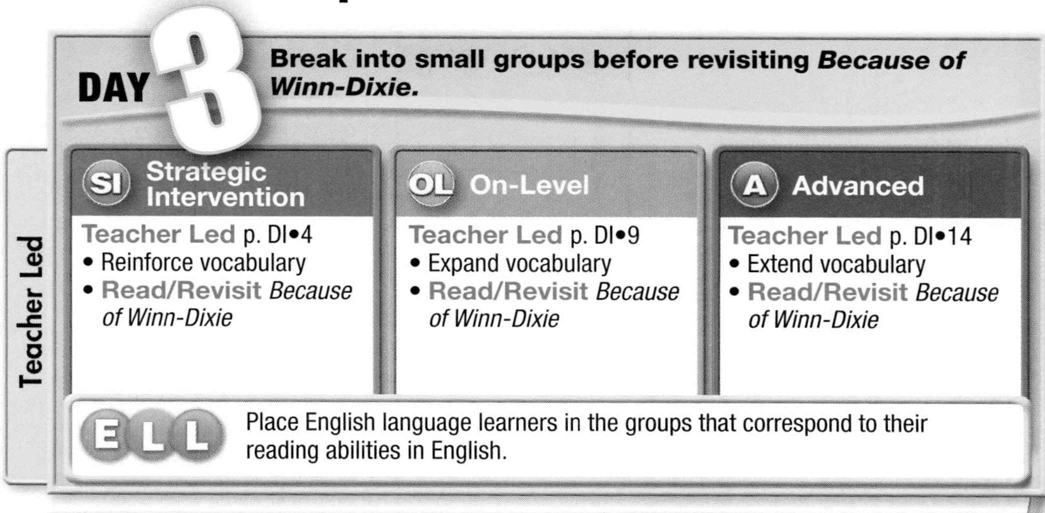

DAY 3
Break into small groups before revisiting *Because of Winn-Dixie.*
Teacher Led
SI Strategic Intervention
Teacher Led p. DI•4
• Reinforce vocabulary
• Read/Revisit *Because of Winn-Dixie*
OL On-Level
Teacher Led p. DI•9
• Expand vocabulary
• Read/Revisit *Because of Winn-Dixie*
A Advanced
Teacher Led p. DI•14
• Extend vocabulary
• Read/Revisit *Because of Winn-Dixie*
ELL
Place English language learners in the groups that correspond to their reading abilities in English.

Practice Stations
- Let's Write
- Get Fluent
- Word Work

Independent Activities
- AudioText: *Because of Winn-Dixie*
- *Reader's and Writer's Notebook*
- Research and Inquiry

English Language Learners

Check retelling To support retelling, review the multilingual summary for *Because of Winn-Dixie,* with the appropriate Retelling Cards to scaffold understanding.

Read and Comprehend

Objectives

◎ Determine the meanings of words with affixes.

OPTION 1 Skills and Strategies, continued

Teach Affixes: Suffixes

◎ **Affixes: Suffixes** Remind students that some words have parts added to the end of the word. Have students use their knowledge of the Old English suffix *-ful* to determine the meaning of *prideful* on p. 32.

Corrective Feedback

If… students are unable to determine the meaning of *prideful*,
then… model using word structure to figure out the meaning.

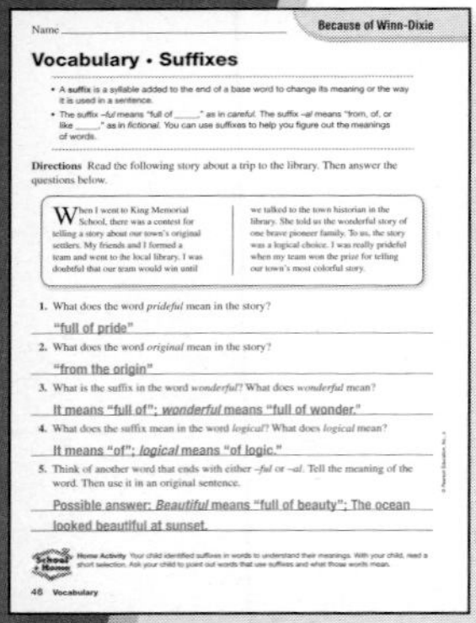

Name ______________ Because of Winn-Dixie

Vocabulary • Suffixes

- A **suffix** is a syllable added to the end of a base word to change its meaning or the way it is used in a sentence.
- The suffix *-ful* means "full of _____," as in *careful*. The suffix *-al* means "from, of, or like _____," as in *fictional*. You can use suffixes to help you figure out the meanings of words.

Directions Read the following story about a trip to the library. Then answer the questions below.

When I went to King Memorial School, there was a contest for telling a story about our town's original settlers. My friends and I formed a team and went to the local library. I was doubtful that our team would win until we talked to the town historian in the library. She told us the wonderful story of one brave pioneer family. To us, the story was a logical choice. I was really prideful when my team won the prize for telling our town's most colorful story.

1. What does the word *prideful* mean in the story?
"full of pride"
2. What does the word *original* mean in the story?
"from the origin"
3. What is the suffix in the word *wonderful*? What does *wonderful* mean?
It means "full of"; *wonderful* means "full of wonder."
4. What does the suffix mean in the word *logical*? What does *logical* mean?
It means "of"; *logical* means "of logic."
5. Think of another word that ends with either *-ful* or *-al*. Tell the meaning of the word. Then use it in an original sentence.
Possible answer: *Beautiful* means "full of beauty"; The ocean looked beautiful at sunset.

School + Home **Home Activity** Your child identified suffixes in words to understand their meanings. With your child, read a short selection. Ask your child to point out words that use suffixes and what those words mean.

46 Vocabulary

Reader's and Writer's Notebook p. 46

Model the Skill

Think Aloud When I read the word *prideful*, right away I notice the word *pride*. I see the suffix *-ful*. I remember that the suffix can mean "full of." That would mean the whole word means "full of pride."

"Well," Miss Franny said. She bent over and gave Winn-Dixie a pat on the head, and Winn-Dixie wagged his tail back and forth and snuffled his nose on her little old-lady feet. "Let me get a chair and sit down so I can tell this story properly."

"Back when Florida was wild, when it consisted of nothing but palmetto trees and mosquitoes so big they could fly away with you," Miss Franny Block started in, "and I was just a little girl no bigger than you, my father, Herman W. Block, told me that I could have anything I wanted for my birthday. Anything at all."

Miss Franny looked around the library. She leaned in close to me. "I don't want to appear prideful," she said, "but my daddy was a very rich man. A very rich man." She nodded and then leaned back and said, "And I was a little girl who loved to read. So I told him, I said, 'Daddy, I would most certainly love to have a library for my birthday, a small little library would be wonderful.'"

"You asked for a whole library?"

Let's Think About… How does Miss Franny feel about Winn-Dixie now? What details tell you? **Inferring**

32

Student Edition pp. 32–33

Double Day Read! Multidraft Reading

If you chose…

Option 1 Return to Extend Thinking instruction starting on p. 28–29.
Option 2 Read pp. 32–37.
Use the Guide Comprehension and Extend Thinking instruction.

OPTION 2 Think Critically, continued

Higher-Order Thinking Skills

◎ **Affixes • Analysis** How can you use what you know about base words and affixes to figure out the meaning of the word *librarian* on page 33? Think about the base word and whether a prefix or suffix has been added. The base word is *library*. The suffix is *-an*. I know that this suffix can have to do with jobs. I think that a *librarian* is a person who works in a library.

Let's Think About…

4. You can tell she likes him because she bends over and gives him a pat on the head, and lets him snuffle his nose on her feet.

5. She is a bit of a know-it-all, and she loves to read. She is brave and sometimes likes to exaggerate. I can picture the setting because of these details: it was hot, the doors and windows were open, Miss Franny was bent over her book.

I'll try that meaning in the sentence. Yes, that makes sense with what Miss Franny says.

On Their Own

Have students think about base words and suffixes to figure out the meanings of *certainly, properly,* and *wonderful* on p. 32. For additional practice, use *Reader's and Writer's Notebook* p. 46.

Connect to Social Studies

Florida, along with other southeastern states, forms part of the Atlantic Coastal Plain. The region's warm, sunny climate makes it a popular destination for tourists and retirees who enjoy swimming, fishing, and boating along miles of sandy coastline. The climate also makes it a good place for agriculture. Cotton, vegetables, citrus fruits, peanuts and tobacco all grow well in the Southeast, and farming has long been a way of life in the area.

"A small one," Miss Franny nodded. "I wanted a little house full of nothing but books and I wanted to share them, too. And I got my wish. My father built me this house, the very one we are sitting in now. And at a very young age, I became a librarian. Yes ma'am."

"What about the bear?" I said.

"Did I mention that Florida was wild in those days?" Miss Franny Block said.

"Uh-huh, you did."

"It was wild. There were wild men and wild women and wild animals."

"Like bears!"

"Yes ma'am. That's right. Now, I have to tell you, I was a little-miss-know-it-all. I was a miss-smarty-pants with my library full of books. Oh, yes ma'am, I thought I knew the answers to everything. Well, one hot Thursday, I was sitting in my library with all the doors and windows open and my nose stuck in a book, when a shadow crossed the desk. And without looking up, yes ma'am, without even looking up, I said, 'Is there a book I can help you find?'

What kind of person is Miss Franny? What details help you picture this setting? **Story Structure**

5

33

Draw Conclusions • Synthesis How does the author use dialogue, or the conversation, to enable the reader to get to know the characters? Give examples from the text. Possible response: Miss Franny uses interesting language, such as *mosquitoes so big they could fly away with you*. This shows she exaggerates.

Genre • Evaluation A bear going into a library is not something the reader would expect to happen. How does this detail fit with the definition of realistic fiction? Possible response: The bear going into the library is very unusual, but it could really happen. So this detail still fits with the definition of realistic fiction.

ELL

English Language Learners

Idioms Point out the last paragraph on p. 33 and explain to students that *my nose stuck in a book* means that Miss Franny was concentrating hard on reading her book and was not distracted by anything.

Read and Comprehend

Objectives

- Identify cause-effect relationships.

OPTION 1 Skills and Strategies, continued

Teach Cause and Effect

Review **Cause and Effect** Review the terms *effect* ("what happened") and *cause* ("why it happened"). Remind students that readers have to ask themselves questions as they read, such as *What happened?* and *Why did it happen?* Ask students why Miss Franny looked up from her book that day. (She smelled something peculiar.)

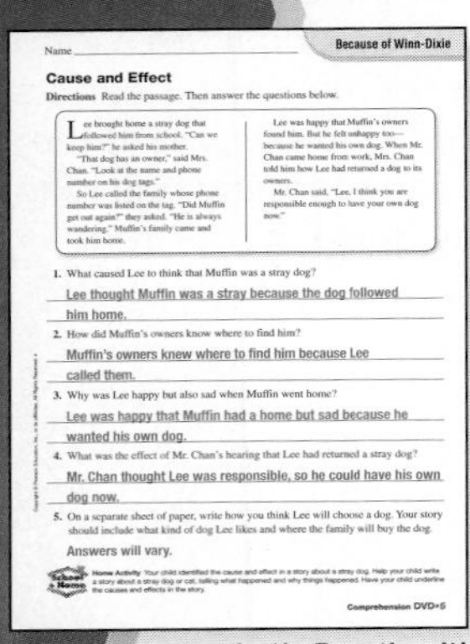

Let's Practice It!
TR DVD•5

Corrective Feedback

If... students have difficulty recognizing cause-effect relationships, **then...** model how to identify what happened and why it happened.

Model the Skill

Think Aloud Miss Franny was talking without looking up because she was interested in what she was reading. So I ask myself, *Then what happened?* She looked up. I ask myself *Why?*

"Well, there was no answer. And I thought it might have been a wild man or a wild woman, scared of all these books and afraid to speak up. But then I became aware of a very peculiar smell, a very strong smell. I raised my eyes slowly. And standing right in front of me was a bear. Yes ma'am. A very large bear."

"How big?" I asked.

"Oh, well," said Miss Franny, "perhaps three times the size of your dog."

"Then what happened?" I asked her.

"Well," said Miss Franny, "I looked at him and he looked at me. He put his big nose up in the air and sniffed and sniffed as if he was trying to decide if a little-miss-know-it-all librarian was what he was in the mood to eat. And I sat there. And then I thought, 'Well, if this bear intends to eat me, I am not going to let it happen without a fight. No ma'am.' So very slowly and very carefully, I raised up the book I was reading."

"What book was that?" I asked.

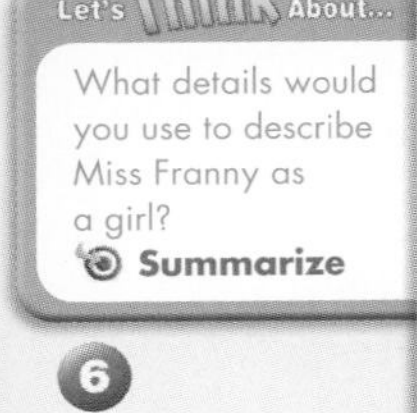

Let's Think About...
What details would you use to describe Miss Franny as a girl?
Summarize
6

34

Student Edition pp. 34–35

Let's Think About...

6 As a girl, Miss Franny loved to read and she was someone who was happy to share her books with others.

OPTION 2 Think Critically, continued

Higher-Order Thinking Skills

Review **Cause and Effect • Analysis** Why did the bear leave the library? Miss Franny threw a book at it.

I reread and find out that she smelled something peculiar. Now I know what happened, and why it happened.

"Why, it was *War and Peace,* a very large book. I raised it up slowly and then I aimed it carefully and I threw it right at that bear and screamed, 'Be gone!' And do you know what?"

"No ma'am," I said.

"He went. But this is what I will never forget. He took the book with him."

"Nuh-uh," I said.

"Yes ma'am," said Miss Franny. "He snatched it up and ran."

"Did he come back?" I asked.

"No, I never saw him again. Well, the men in town used to tease me about it. They used to

35

Literary Elements: Character • Analysis What more does the reader learn about Miss Franny's personality on pages 34–35? Possible response: Miss Franny is a quick thinker. She is brave when faced with danger.

Point of View • Evaluation Is the story told in first or third person? (first person) How effective do you think it was it for the story to be told in the first person? Possible response: It was very effective because the story events were told in the informal language of a young girl, which helped me relate to the character better than if the story had been told by a third-person narrator.

On Their Own

Have students work in small groups and use a T-chart with the headings *What happened* and *Why it happened* to list other cause-effect relationships on pp. 34–35. For additional practice use *Let's Practice It!* p. 5 on the *Teacher Resources DVD-ROM*.

Differentiated Instruction

SI Strategic Intervention

Summarize Help students use cause and effect to summarize this part of the story. Encourage them to use words such as *so* and *because* to help them link events.

English Language Learners

Monitor comprehension Model using the strategy of monitor comprehension. Reread the last two paragraphs on p. 34. Say, When I'm reading, I'm asking myself, does this make sense? Do I understand? If not, I'll go back and reread. I'm not sure what is going on here. Why is the bear sniffing the air? Let me reread. Oh, Miss Franny thought the bear was sniffing to see if it wanted to eat her.

Objectives

- Summarize plot events to improve comprehension.

OPTION 1 Skills and Strategies, continued

Teach Summarize

 **Summarize** Have students reread p. 36 beginning with the second paragraph. Ask: What are the big ideas about what happens in this part of the story? Point out that a good summary tells what a character is trying to do and how it is working out for the character. Have students summarize the events on p. 36.

Corrective Feedback

If... students are unable to summarize the important events,
then... use the model to help them focus on summarizing.

Model the Strategy

Think Aloud: Let's summarize what is happening. Opal notices that Miss Franny seems sad and lonely, which is the way Opal feels.

They used to say, 'Miss Franny, we saw that bear of yours out in the woods today. He was reading that book and he said it sure was good and would it be all right if he kept it for just another week.' Yes ma'am. They did tease me about it." She sighed. "I imagine I'm the only one left from those days. I imagine I'm the only one that even recalls that bear. All my friends, everyone I knew when I was young, they are all dead and gone."

She sighed again. She looked sad and old and wrinkled. It was the same way I felt sometimes, being friendless in a new town and not having a mama to comfort me. I sighed, too.

Winn-Dixie raised his head off his paws and looked back and forth between me and Miss Franny. He sat up then and showed Miss Franny his teeth.

"Well now, look at that," she said. "That dog is smiling at me."

"It's a talent of his," I told her.

"It is a fine talent," Miss Franny said. "A very fine talent." And she smiled back at Winn-Dixie.

"We could be friends," I said to Miss Franny. "I mean you and me and Winn-Dixie, we could all be friends."

Miss Franny smiled even bigger. "Why, that would be grand," she said, "just grand."

Let's Think About...
How will friendship with Miss Franny help Opal? How will it help Miss Franny? **Questioning**

7

36

Student Edition pp. 36–37

Let's Think About...

7. Opal won't be lonely because she now has a friend in her new town. Miss Franny will have a friend who likes to visit her in the library and who shares her interest in stories.

8. Amanda's personality is not like Opal's or Miss Franny's. She is not friendly, like Opal and Miss Franny. The author helps us visualize this character by describing her as *old pinch-faced Amanda*. The author also describes how Amanda boasts that she is an advanced reader, ignores Opal, and then tries to get Opal in trouble by asking if dogs are allowed in the library.

OPTION 2 Think Critically, continued

Higher-Order Thinking Skills

Summarize • Evaluation What questions can you ask yourself to make sure your summary of the end of the story is a good one? Possible response: What are the main things that happened to Opal at the end of the story? What does that mean for her?

Author's Purpose • Synthesis Why do you think the author chose to have Amanda Wilkinson come into the library at the exact moment Opal and Winn-Dixie and Miss Franny decide to be friends? Possible response: Amanda isn't being nice to Opal. She ignored Opal and acted snobby. Miss Franny notices and winks at Opal. The author probably put this part here to show that Miss Franny and Opal really are friends.

Winn-Dixie smiles at Miss Franny, and Opal says they should all be friends. Miss Franny happily agrees. Things are working out well for Opal.

On Their Own

Have students reread p. 37. Ask them to work with a partner to write a summary of the end of the story. Remind students to focus on the main points and to summarize what happened in their own words.

And right at that minute, right when the three of us had decided to be friends, who should come marching into the Herman W. Block Memorial Library but old pinch-faced Amanda Wilkinson. She walked right up to Miss Franny's desk and said, "I finished *Johnny Tremain* and I enjoyed it very much. I would like something even more difficult to read now, because I am an advanced reader."

"Yes dear, I know," said Miss Franny. She got up out of her chair.

Amanda pretended like I wasn't there. She stared right past me. "Are dogs allowed in the library?" she asked Miss Franny as they walked away.

"Certain ones," said Miss Franny, "a select few." And then she turned around and winked at me. I smiled back. I had just made my first friend in Naomi, and nobody was going to mess that up for me, not even old pinch-faced Amanda Wilkinson.

Let's Think About...

Is Amanda's personality like Opal's or Miss Franny's? How does the author create a different kind of character? **Story Structure**

8

37

Differentiated Instruction

Strategic Intervention

Questioning Help students make notes about their thinking as they read. Have them make a T-chart with the headings *What's happening? What am I thinking?* Have students share their thoughts. Point out when students are making personal connections or wonderings about the story.

Advanced

Critical thinking Have students discuss the topic of friendship. Pose the questions *What makes a good friend?* and *How do friendships help people?* Have them brainstorm other stories they have read about friendships and explain how they connect.

Six Pillars of Character

Caring To be caring is to show compassion and help others in need. Have students discuss how Opal shows Miss Franny that she cares about her.

Comprehension Check

Spiral Review

Literary Elements: Theme • Synthesis How does this story remind you of something you know about friendships? Possible response: Everyone needs to have friends. Friends can help you when you feel lonely.

Literary Elements: Character • Analysis How does Opal go about making friends with Miss Franny? Possible response: She goes to the library and listens to Miss Franny's story. Opal shows she is interested in Miss Franny and notices her feelings. She says they could be friends.

Check Predictions Have students return to the predictions they made earlier and confirm whether they were accurate.

ELL

English Language Learners

Idioms Explain that the expression *old pinch-faced Amanda Wilkinson* on p. 37 does not refer to the girl's age. The word *old* can refer to something we don't like. Demonstrate a pinch-faced expression. Have students do the same. Ask: How does this feel?

DAY 3 Read and Comprehend

Objectives

- ◎ Sequence events to aid comprehension.
- ◎ Use the strategy of summarize to aid comprehension.

Check Retelling

SUCCESS PREDICTOR

Objectives
• Read independently for long periods of time and paraphrase the reading, including the order in which events occur. • Write responses to texts using details to show understanding.
Envision It! Retell
READING STREET ONLINE
STORY SORT
www.ReadingStreet.com

Think Critically

1. Do you or does someone you know own a pet? What is the relationship between a person and a pet like? Why do you think people bond so strongly with their pets? Text to Self
2. This author has won prizes for her books. Why? Find a part of this story you think could win a prize. Think Like an Author
3. Think about the events in the story. How does Miss Franny feel about Winn-Dixie at the beginning of the story? How does she feel at the end? ◎ Sequence
4. When summarizing a story, you only include important details. Which two of the following statements would you leave out of a summary of the story? Why?
   A. The Herman W. Block Memorial Library is a little old house full of books.
   B. Miss Franny Block is afraid of Winn-Dixie because she thinks he is a bear.
   C. Amanda Wilkinson returns a book to the library. ◎ Summarize
5. **Look Back and Write** Look back at pages 32–36. Do you think the story Miss Franny tells Opal about her encounter with a bear is factual or fanciful? Provide evidence from the text to support your answer.

38

Meet the Author

Kate DiCamillo

As a child, Kate DiCamillo was often sick. When Kate was five, a doctor said warm weather would be better for her health. She and her mother moved to a town in Florida. The people were friendly, and Kate loved the way they talked. "I also had a dog I loved. I spent a lot of time dressing Nanette up—in a green ballet tutu and then later as a disco dancer."

After college, Ms. DiCamillo moved to Minneapolis and got a job at a bookstore. She lived in a tiny apartment and never had enough money. "I wrote *Because of Winn-Dixie* because I was homesick for Florida. Also, my apartment building didn't allow dogs. So I made up one to keep me company." She got up at 4:00 every morning to write before going to work.

Since then, Ms. DiCamillo's life has really changed. She has now written three award-winning books. She bought a new home and a new car. And she no longer has to work at the bookstore. "I couldn't have imagined in my wildest dreams what's happened to me!"

Here are other books by Kate DiCamillo.

The Tiger Rising *The Tale of Despereaux*

Reading Log: Choose a book from your library and read independently for 30 minutes. Record your reading by paraphrasing, or telling in your own words, in a logical order and meaningful way what you have read.

Student Edition pp. 38–39

Retelling

Envision It! Have students work in pairs to retell the selection, using the Envision It! Retelling Cards as prompts. Remind students that they should accurately describe the characters and plot and use key vocabulary in their retellings. Monitor students' retellings.

Scoring rubric

Top-Score Response A top-score response makes connections beyond the text, describes the characters and plot, and draws conclusions from the text.

Plan to Assess Retelling

- ☑ **This week assess Strategic Intervention students.**
- ☐ **Week 2** Assess Advanced students.
- ☐ **Week 3** Assess Strategic Intervention students.
- ☐ **Week 4** Assess On-Level students.
- ☐ **Week 5** Assess any students you have not yet checked during this unit.

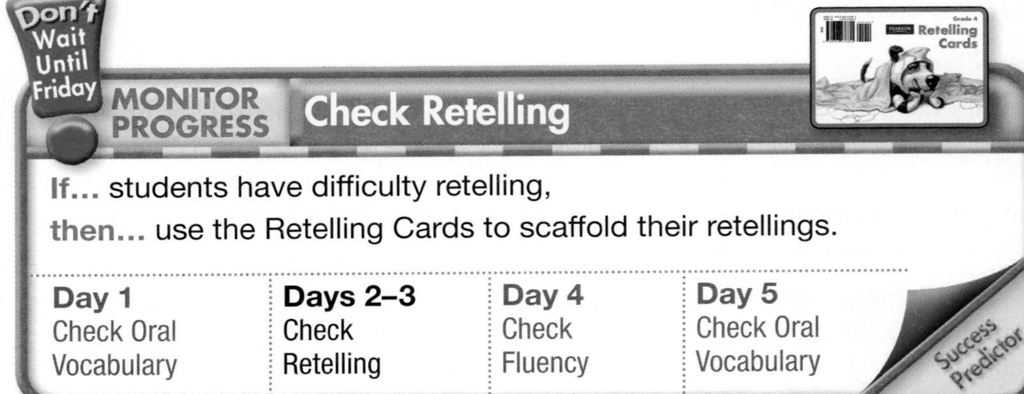

Don't Wait Until Friday
MONITOR PROGRESS
Check Retelling
Retelling Cards
If... students have difficulty retelling,
then... use the Retelling Cards to scaffold their retellings.
Day 1 Check Oral Vocabulary
Days 2–3 Check Retelling
Day 4 Check Fluency
Day 5 Check Oral Vocabulary
Success Predictor

Think Critically

Text to self

1. Responses will vary. Possible response: I have a cat and she is one of my best friends. I help take care of her and I play with her every day. She jumps in my lap and takes naps. Pets are important to people because we love them and they love us.

Think like an author

2. The author wins prizes because people enjoy reading her books. The part of this story I think could win a prize is when Opal says that she, Winn-Dixie, and Miss Franny could all be friends. It shows how much she wants a friend and that is something everyone wants.

Sequence

3. At first, Miss Franny is really afraid of Winn-Dixie, but at the end she begins to like him and they become friends. Her feelings change because Opal helps Miss Franny understand Winn-Dixie. Also, Winn-Dixie is a very nice dog and is well-behaved.

Summarize

4. Statements *A* and *C* are not important details in the story. They are not essential to understanding the main points of the story.

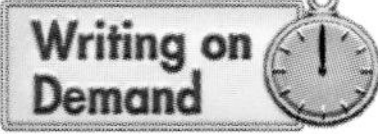

5. **Look Back and Write** To build writing fluency, assign a 10–15 minute time limit.

Suggest that students use a prewriting strategy, such as brainstorming or using a graphic organizer, to organize their ideas. Remind them to establish a topic sentence and support it with facts, details, or explanations. As students finish, encourage them to reread their responses, revise for organization and support, and proofread for errors in grammar and conventions.

Scoring rubric

Top-Score Response A top-score response uses evidence from the text to support students' position on Miss Franny's bear story.

A top-score response should include:

- A statement about student's position on factual or fanciful.
- Details about the bear's behavior.
- Details about Miss Franny's actions.

Differentiated Instruction

Strategic Intervention

Have pairs of students decide whether or not they think Miss Franny's bear encounter really happened. Have them ask questions as they look for supporting details, such as *Could a bear really do that? Is that how a person would most likely react?*

Meet the Author

Have students read about author Kate DiCamillo on p. 39. As they read, ask them what connections they can make between Ms. DiCamillo's life and the story *Because of Winn-Dixie*.

Independent Reading

After students enter their independent reading information into their Reading Logs, have them paraphrase a portion of the text they have just read. Remind students that when we paraphrase, we express the meaning of a passage using other words and maintaining logical order.

ELL

English Language Learners

Retelling Randomly place the Retelling Cards in an incorrect order. Then have students explain where each card should go as they describe the sequence of the selection.

Retelling
Success Predictor

Read and Comprehend

Objectives

- Read grade-level text with expression.
- Reread for fluency.
- Use visual sources of information to collect information.

Model Fluency
Expression

Model fluent reading Have students turn to p. 29 of *Because of Winn-Dixie*. Have students follow along as you read this page. Tell them to listen to the expression of your voice as you read Opal's words. Point out that the tone of your voice will rise and fall, just as it does when you are talking to a friend.

Guide practice Have students follow along as you read the page again. Then have them reread the page as a group without you until they read with the right expression and make no mistakes. Ask questions to be sure students comprehend the text. Continue in the same way on p. 30.

Reread for Fluency

Corrective feedback **If...** students are having difficulty reading with the right expression, **then...** prompt:

- Which word is a problem? Let's read it together.
- Read the sentence again to be sure you understand it.
- Tell me the sentence. Now read it as if you are speaking to me.

ROUTINE **Oral Rereading**

1. **Read** Have students reread p. 37 of *Because of Winn-Dixie*.
2. **Reread** To achieve optimal fluency, students should reread the text three to four times with appropriate expression.
3. **Corrective Feedback** Have students read aloud without you. Provide corrective feedback about their expression and encourage them to vary their tone of voice to make their reading sound natural. Listen for appropriate expression.

Routines Flip Chart

Research and Study Skills
Map, Globe, Atlas

Teach

Ask students where they have seen maps. Students may mention road maps, classroom displays, textbooks, newspapers, magazines, websites, and GPS (global positioning system) devices. Show a map from a content-area text and use it to review these points:

- A **map** is a drawing of a place. It shows where something is or where something happened.
- There are many different kinds of maps.
- A map's **legend** is the most important part of a map and is key to understanding the information on the map. Legends usually show directions, a scale to show distances, and symbols to show landmarks.

Also explain these terms:

- An **atlas** is a book of maps.
- A **globe** is a sphere with a map of the world on it.

Guide practice

Provide groups with a map. Have each group interpret the legend and generate a question that could be answered by using this map. Have each group share their map and question-and-answer with the class.

On their own

Have students complete pp. 47–48 of the *Reader's and Writer's Notebook*.

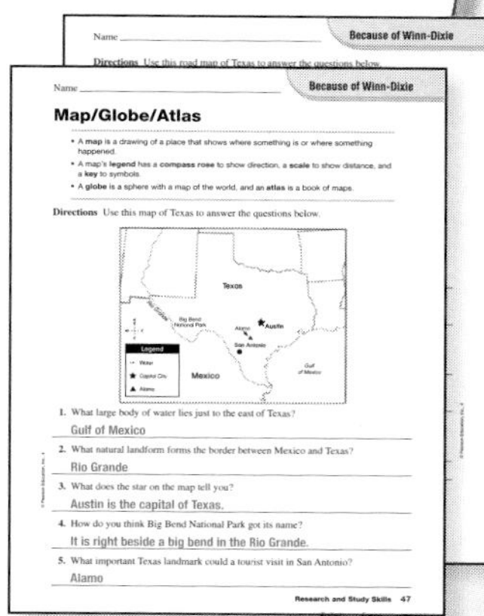

Name ______ Because of Winn-Dixie

Directions Use this road map of Texas to answer the questions below.

Name ______ Because of Winn-Dixie

Map/Globe/Atlas

- A **map** is a drawing of a place that shows where something is or where something happened.
- A map's **legend** has a **compass rose** to show direction, a **scale** to show distance, and a **key** to symbols.
- A **globe** is a sphere with a map of the world, and an **atlas** is a book of maps.

Directions Use this map of Texas to answer the questions below.

1. What large body of water lies just to the east of Texas?
Gulf of Mexico
2. What natural landform forms the border between Mexico and Texas?
Rio Grande
3. What does the star on the map tell you?
Austin is the capital of Texas.
4. How do you think Big Bend National Park got its name?
It is right beside a big bend in the Rio Grande.
5. What important Texas landmark could a tourist visit in San Antonio?
Alamo

Research and Study Skills 47

Reader's and Writer's Notebook pp. 47–48

ELL

English Language Learners

Maps Explain that maps can help readers better understand a selection. Help students create a map of their own. Some options: a map of the school, their backyard, or their neighborhood. Help them to include a title, labels, and a legend showing symbols and what they represent. Encourage them to use the direction words *north*, *south*, *east*, *west* on their maps.

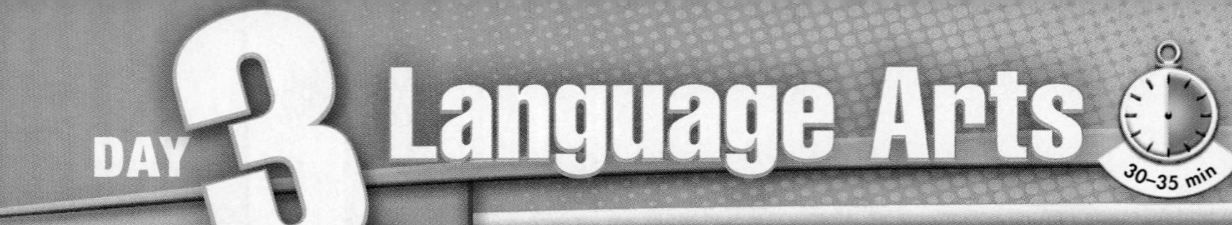

Objectives

- Analyze data for usefulness.
- Identify and correctly use interrogative sentences.
- Spell frequently misspelled words correctly.

Research and Inquiry
Analyze

Teach

Tell students that today they will analyze their findings and may need to change the focus of their original inquiry question.

Model

Think Aloud We gave our survey to the students in our class. Once we tallied the results, we found that it might be useful to give the same survey to teachers in this school, to see how their opinions are the same as or different from the students' opinion. First, we can look through the questions to see if they are all appropriate for teachers.

Guide practice

Have students analyze their findings. They may need to refocus their inquiry question to better fit the information they found. Students may wish to rewrite some of the survey questions to obtain more specific results from the survey.

Remind students that if they have difficulty improving their focus, they can ask a local expert, such as the PE teacher or organizer of student sports, for guidance.

On their own

Have students give additional surveys, if necessary. Students should then compare the information they gathered from the student survey(s) with the information they found in their online research.

Grammar Jammer

Conventions
Declarative and Interrogative Sentences

Review Remind students that this week they learned about declarative and interrogative sentences.

- A *declarative* sentence is a statement that tells about something. It ends with a period.
- An *interrogative* sentence asks a question. It ends with a question mark.

Daily Fix-It Use Daily Fix-It numbers 5 and 6 in the right margin.

Connect to oral language Practice subject and verb order with declarative and interrogative sentences. Begin a statement and let students finish it. Then reverse the order of the subject and verb and turn it into a question. Remind them to use a complete subject and a complete predicate and make sure they agree.

The classroom is ________.

Is the classroom ________?

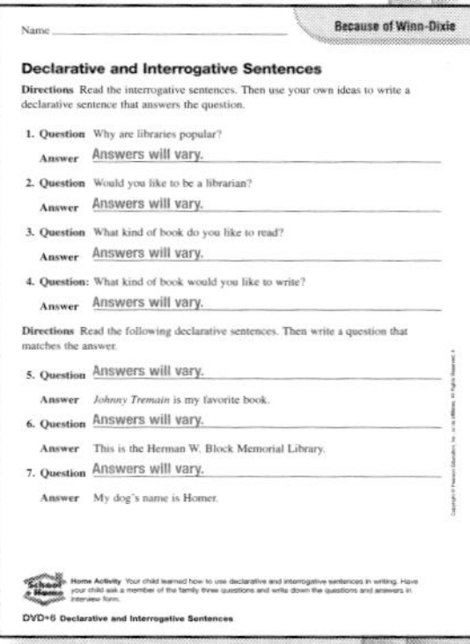

Name ________ Because of Winn-Dixie

Declarative and Interrogative Sentences

Directions Read the interrogative sentences. Then use your own ideas to write a declarative sentence that answers the question.

1. **Question** Why are libraries popular?
   Answer Answers will vary.
2. **Question** Would you like to be a librarian?
   Answer Answers will vary.
3. **Question** What kind of book do you like to read?
   Answer Answers will vary.
4. **Question:** What kind of book would you like to write?
   Answer Answers will vary.

Directions Read the following declarative sentences. Then write a question that matches the answer.

5. **Question** Answers will vary.
   Answer *Johnny Tremain* is my favorite book.
6. **Question** Answers will vary.
   Answer This is the Herman W. Block Memorial Library.
7. **Question** Answers will vary.
   Answer My dog's name is Homer.

Home Activity Your child learned how to use declarative and interrogative sentences in writing. Have your child ask a member of the family three questions and write down the questions and answers in interview form.

DVD•6 Declarative and Interrogative Sentences

Let's Practice It!
TR DVD•6

On their own For additional support, use *Let's Practice It!* p.6 on the *Teacher Resources DVD-ROM.*

Spelling
Short Vowel VCCV

Frequently misspelled words Students often misspell the words *with* and *cousin. Accident* and *custom* are also difficult to spell. I'm going to read a sentence. Choose the correct word to complete the sentence and then write it correctly.

1. **Darian was hurt in a car ________.** (accident)
2. **I enjoy playing with my ________, Lynda.** (cousin)
3. **Did Lynda play ________ you today?** (with)
4. **What is the ________ here for thanking your hosts?** (custom)

On their own For additional support, use *Reader's and Writer's Notebook* p. 49.

Differentiated Instruction

Advanced
Have students create declarative and interrogative sentences using spelling words that are difficult to spell.

Daily Fix-It

5. Our class study in the library every tuesday. *(studies; Tuesday)*
6. We read quietly for an our, we can read any book we like. *(hour. We)*

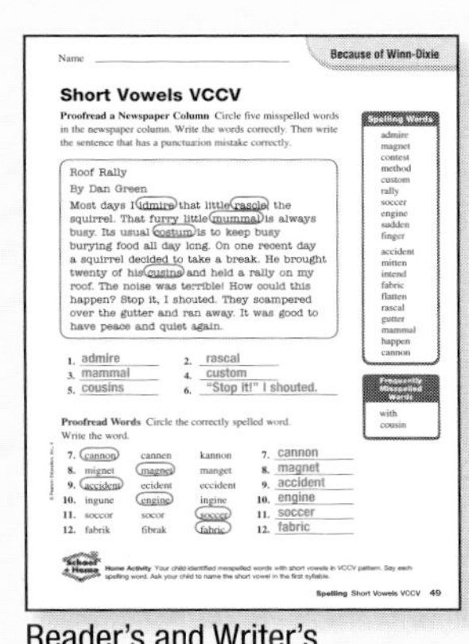

Name ________ Because of Winn-Dixie

Short Vowels VCCV

Proofread a Newspaper Column Circle five misspelled words in the newspaper column. Write the words correctly. Then write the sentence that has a punctuation mistake correctly.

Roof Rally
By Dan Green
Most days I idmire that little rascle, the squirrel. That furry little mummal is always busy. Its usual costum is to keep busy burying food all day long. On one recent day a squirrel decided to take a break. He brought twenty of his cusins and held a rally on my roof. The noise was terrible! How could this happen? Stop it, I shouted. They scampered over the gutter and ran away. It was good to have peace and quiet again.

1. admire 2. rascal
3. mammal 4. custom
5. cousins 6. "Stop it!" I shouted.

Spelling Words: admire, magnet, contest, method, custom, rally, soccer, engine, sudden, finger, accident, mitten, intend, fabric, flatten, rascal, gutter, mammal, happen, cannon

Frequently Misspelled Words: with, cousin

Proofread Words Circle the correctly spelled word. Write the word.

7.	cannon	cannen	kannon	7. cannon
8.	mignet	magnet	manget	8. magnet
9.	accident	ecident	eccident	9. accident
10.	ingune	engine	ingine	10. engine
11.	soccor	socor	soccer	11. soccer
12.	fabrik	fibrak	fabric	12. fabric

Home Activity Your child identified misspelled words with short vowels in VCCV pattern. Say each spelling word. Ask your child to name the short vowel in the first syllable.

Spelling Short Vowels VCCV 49

Reader's and Writer's Notebook p. 49

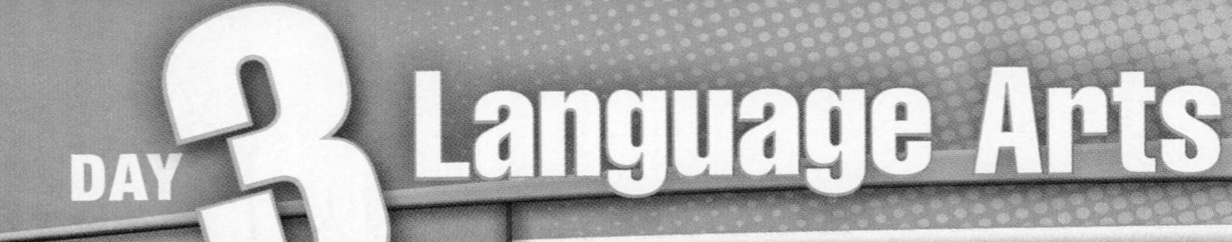

Objectives

- Understand the criteria for writing an effective realistic fiction story.
- Understand the characteristics of declarative and interrogative sentences.

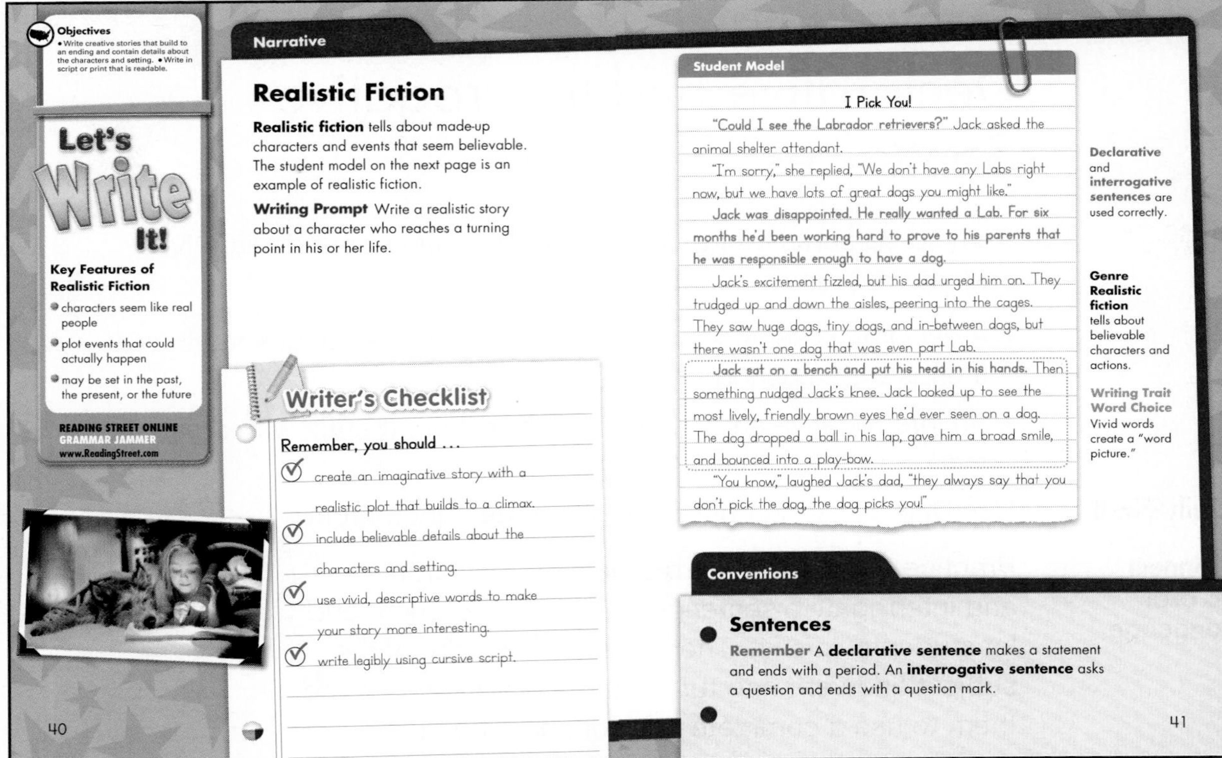

Objectives
• Write creative stories that build to an ending and contain details about the characters and setting. • Write in script or print that is readable.

Let's Write It!

Key Features of Realistic Fiction
- characters seem like real people
- plot events that could actually happen
- may be set in the past, the present, or the future

READING STREET ONLINE
GRAMMAR JAMMER
www.ReadingStreet.com

Narrative

Realistic Fiction

Realistic fiction tells about made-up characters and events that seem believable. The student model on the next page is an example of realistic fiction.

Writing Prompt Write a realistic story about a character who reaches a turning point in his or her life.

Writer's Checklist

Remember, you should ...
- create an imaginative story with a realistic plot that builds to a climax.
- include believable details about the characters and setting.
- use vivid, descriptive words to make your story more interesting.
- write legibly using cursive script.

40

Student Model

I Pick You!

"Could I see the Labrador retrievers?" Jack asked the animal shelter attendant.

"I'm sorry," she replied, "We don't have any Labs right now, but we have lots of great dogs you might like."

Jack was disappointed. He really wanted a Lab. For six months he'd been working hard to prove to his parents that he was responsible enough to have a dog.

Jack's excitement fizzled, but his dad urged him on. They trudged up and down the aisles, peering into the cages. They saw huge dogs, tiny dogs, and in-between dogs, but there wasn't one dog that was even part Lab.

Jack sat on a bench and put his head in his hands. Then something nudged Jack's knee. Jack looked up to see the most lively, friendly brown eyes he'd ever seen on a dog. The dog dropped a ball in his lap, gave him a broad smile, and bounced into a play-bow.

"You know," laughed Jack's dad, "they always say that you don't pick the dog, the dog picks you!"

Declarative and **interrogative sentences** are used correctly.

Genre Realistic fiction tells about believable characters and actions.

Writing Trait Word Choice Vivid words create a "word picture."

Conventions

Sentences

Remember A **declarative sentence** makes a statement and ends with a period. An **interrogative sentence** asks a question and ends with a question mark.

41

Student Edition pp. 40–41

Let's Write It!
Realistic Fiction

Teach Use pp. 40–41 in the Student Edition. Direct students to read the key features of realistic fiction which appear on p. 40. Remind students that they can refer to the information in the Writer's Checklist as they write their own realistic fiction story.

Read the student model on p. 41. Point out the characterization, setting, and realistic events in the model.

Connect to conventions Remind students that a declarative sentence makes a statement and an interrogative sentence asks a question. Point out the correct use of a period and question mark at the end of these sentences in the model.

Writing—Realistic Fiction
Writer's Craft: Vivid Words

Display rubric Display Scoring Rubric 1 from the *Teacher Resources DVD* and review the criteria for each trait under each score. Then, using the model in the Student Edition, have volunteers explain why the model should score a 4 for one of the traits. If a student offers that the model should score below 4 for a particular trait, the student should offer support for that response. Remind students that this is the rubric that will be used to evaluate the realistic fiction story they write.

Scoring Rubric: Realistic Fiction

	4	3	2	1
Focus/Ideas	Story clearly focused on one event	Story generally focused on one event	Story lacks focus; event unclear	Story without focus; no event
Organization	Organized with clear beginning, middle, and end	Organized, with beginning, middle, and end	Lacks clear beginning, middle, and end	Lacks organization
Voice	Voice of character/narrator believable and engaging	Voice of character/narrator mostly believable	Character or narrator lacking distinct voice	Voice of character or narrator not believable
Word Choice	Word choice vivid, strong, and precise	Word choice adequate	Word choice weak, few examples of strong and precise choices	Dull and/or inaccurate word choices throughout
Sentences	Clear, varied sentences; excellent flow	Mostly clear sentences with good variety	Some sentences unclear; little or no variety	Incoherent sentences; dull, choppy style
Conventions	Few, if any errors. Correct end punctuation for declarative and interrogative sentences	Several minor errors	Many errors, some serious. Incorrect end punctuation in declarative and/or interrogative sentences	Numerous errors; hard to understand

Story Sequence Chart Have students take out the sequence charts they created yesterday. If they have more information to add to their charts give them time to add it.

Write You will use your story sequence chart to help you write the draft of your realistic fiction story. As you write your draft, try to get all of your ideas down on paper, using vivid words wherever possible. You will have time to revise your draft tomorrow.

Differentiated Instruction

Advanced

Author's purpose Have students discuss what emotions the author wanted the reader to feel when reading this story. Encourage them to support their answers with evidence from the story.

English Language Learners

Leveled support: Word choice Help students use vivid adjectives and strong verbs.

- **Beginning**: Ask yes/no questions to elicit vivid adjectives, such as Is your character shy? sloppy? embarrassed?
- **Intermediate** Help students choose strong verbs by having them circle the verbs they used and providing some alternatives such as *walk* vs. *dash*; *enter* vs. *intrude*.
- **Advanced/Advanced High** Have students use an online or hard copy of a thesaurus to include vivid and precise adjectives and verbs in their drafts.

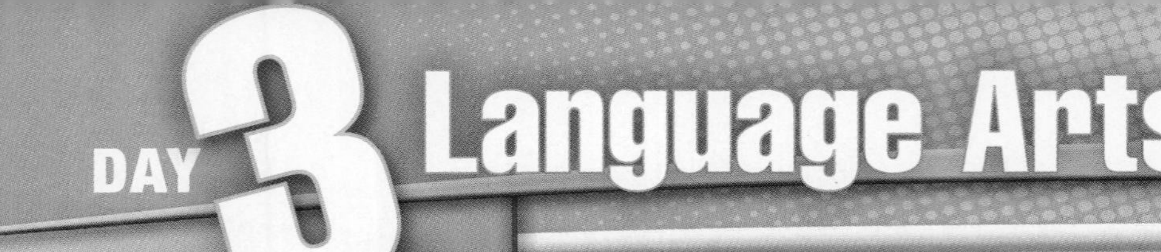

Objectives

- Write a first draft of a realistic fiction story
- Use strong, precise, and vivid words in writing.

Writing, continued
Writer's Craft: Vivid Words

MINI-LESSON

Using Vivid Words

Introduce Explain to students that when writing their stories, they should choose their words carefully to describe both the characters and actions precisely. Explain that they should use descriptive adjectives to let the reader clearly visualize the characters and setting. Point out that strong verbs will help the reader more clearly understand the actions in the story. Remind them to use their story sequence charts to work on their drafts. Display the Drafting Tips for students. Then display Writing Transparency 1A.

Joining the Team

Marco Juarez had just moved to Illinois from Mexico. It was his first day at school. Marco did not know English too well, so he did not feel confident at making new friends. At lunch Matt and Sam started up a conversation with Marco.

"Hi, my name is Matt. This is my friend Sam," said Matt.

Marco smiled. He was shy and nervous. "I'm Marco," he whispered.

Then Matt had a great idea.

"Hey Marco, we need a center for our 5th grade basketball team. Do you want to play on the team? " he asked.

Marco did not feel very confident about sports. He told the boys that he did not know how to play very well. Sam and Matt convinced him to come to practice after school.

In the gym Marco stood quietly watching the boys play.

"Come on, "Sam said encouragingly. "Give it a try." Sam and Matt demonstrated to Marco how to stand under the basket and bank the ball off the backboard into the hoop. They showed him and then they asked him to try it. Shooting the ball felt really very awkward to Marco at first, but Sam and Matt were encouraging.

"Try it again," they said.

Soon, with their instruction, Marco began to get the hang of it. He reached up and aimed at the very, exact same spot each time and the ball bounced neatly into the hoop.

When it was time for the team to play their first game, Marco made five bakets as the team's center. It was different playing with the other team guarding him, but Marco enjoyed it. His Dad enjoyed it too he cheered from the crowd.

"Do you like playing basketball," Sam asked Marco after the game.

"I do, " Marco said.

"See," Sam said with a smile. "I told you, you'd be good?"

" Thanks," Marco said, smiling back. "Could it be because I had a good teacher."

Unit 1 Because of Winn-Dixie — Writing: Model 1A

Writing Transparency 1A, TR DVD

Drafting Tips

- ✔ To get started, review your story sequence chart.
- ✔ As you draft, think about vivid adjectives and strong verbs that you can use to make your story come to life.
- ✔ Don't worry about grammar and mechanics when drafting. Focus on getting a complete story down on paper.

I'm going to write the first draft of my story called *Joining the Team.* When I draft, I develop my ideas. I do not worry about revising or editing because I will do these tasks after I finish my draft. I will refer to my story sequence chart to make sure I write my story in the correct sequence. I'll carefully choose my words to clearly and vividly describe how shy Marco felt when he first met Sam. I'll use strong verbs to show how he looks as he talks with Sam and Matt.

Direct students to use the drafting tips for help with writing their drafts. Remind them to make sure that their characters, setting, and events are realistic.

ROUTINE **Quick Write for Fluency** Team Talk

1. **Talk** Pairs talk about some vivid words they used to describe characters in their stories.
2. **Write** Each partner writes a few sentences about his or her character. Have students include declarative and interrogative sentences.
3. **Share** Have partners read each other's writing and check that they wrote both the declarative and interrogative sentences correctly.

Routines Flip Chart

Differentiated Instruction

SI Strategic Intervention
Discuss why using a strong verb in a phrase such as "*crashed* to the floor" is a better writing tool than saying "*fell* to the floor." Have students brainstorm other strong verbs that can replace ordinary verbs such as *go, come, look,* or *say.*

Wrap Up Your Day

- ✔ **Build Concepts** What did you learn about how people become friends?
- ✔ **Sequence** What time-word clues helped you place the events of the story in the right order?
- ✔ **Summarize** How did summarizing or retelling the story's events help you understand the text?

Tell students that tomorrow they will read a review of the movie *Because of Winn-Dixie.*

Objectives

- Expand the weekly concept.
- Develop oral vocabulary.

Today at a Glance

Oral Vocabulary
social, courteous

Genre
Persuasive text

Reading
"A Film with a Message of Hope"

Let's Learn It!
Fluency: Expression
Vocabulary: Affixes: Suffixes
Listening and speaking: Dramatic retelling

Research and Inquiry
Synthesize

Spelling
Short vowels VCCV

Conventions
Declarative and interrogative sentences

Writing
Realistic fiction

Concept Talk

Question of the Week

What experiences bring diverse people together?

Expand the concept Remind students that this week they have read about diverse people coming together through common experiences. Tell students that today they will read a movie review of *Because of Winn-Dixie* that explores the relationship between diverse characters.

Anchored Talk

Develop oral vocabulary Use the text features, including illustrations, to review pp. 32–37 of *Because of Winn-Dixie.* Discuss the Amazing Words *social* and *courteous.* Add these and other concept-related words to the concept map. Use the following questions to develop students' understanding of the concept. Remind students to ask and answer questions with appropriate detail and to build on other students' answers.

- A trip to the library turns into a social occasion for Opal because she visits with Miss Franny Block about Miss Franny's past experiences. When do you have a chance to be social with other people?
- Winn-Dixie is such a courteous dog that he is even allowed to attend church. What are some places that you go where courteous behavior is especially important?

Strategy Response Log

INTERACT with TEXT

Have students review the characteristics of realistic fiction on p. 7 of the *Reader's and Writer's Notebook*. Then have them compare *Because of Winn-Dixie* to another example of realistic fiction that they have read or know about.

Oral Vocabulary
Amazing Words

Amazing Words

kindness	introduce
attention	similar
teach	distinct
understanding	social
variety	courteous

Teach Amazing Words

Amazing Words Oral Vocabulary Routine

1. **Introduce** Write the word *social* on the board. Have students say it with you. We read about Opal visiting Miss Franny at the library. Opal does check out books, but the visit seems more like a social event. When an activity is *social,* it allows people to meet and interact in a friendly way. In other words, *social* activities are more about spending time with people than about conducting business.
2. **Demonstrate** Have students answer questions to demonstrate understanding. Which of these is more of a social activity—a party at a friend's house or a trip to the post office to mail a letter? What makes it more *social?* Which of these is *social*—studying in your room by yourself or meeting new people at a neighborhood gathering? Why?
3. **Apply** Have students apply their understanding. Describe a social event you've attended recently. Explain what made it a social activity.

See p. OV•1 to teach *courteous.*

Routines Flip Chart

Apply Amazing Words

As students read "A Film with a Message of Hope" on pp. 42–43, have them think about how Opal shows that she is a *courteous* 10-year-old and how she can turn everyday errands into *social* interactions.

Connect to reading

As students read today's selection about the movie *Winn-Dixie,* have them think about how this week's concept question and the Amazing Words *social* and *courteous* apply to the film.

ELL Produce Oral Language Use the Day 4 instruction on ELL Poster 1 to extend and enrich language.

ELL Poster 1

Get Ready to Read

Objectives

- Introduce movie review as a form of persuasive text.

Let's Think About Genre

Persuasive Text

Introduce persuasive text

Explain to students that one reason authors write is to persuade, or convince, a reader to do something or think a certain way. Authors may try to convince readers that an idea, activity, or product is a good one. Authors may try to convince readers to change their opinion about a topic.

Discuss the genre

Persuasive writing tries to convince readers in two ways. Authors may try to make readers think. They may present facts, statistics, or specific information in order to get the reader to come around to their way of thinking. Another technique authors may use to persuade is to appeal to a reader's feelings. To help readers relate to an idea, authors may tell a story or describe something in a way that is meant to bring out strong feelings in the reader.

Ask the following questions:

- What forms of writing are you familiar with that are designed to persuade the reader to think a certain way about a topic or take an action? Possible response: advertisements, TV commercials, some newspaper articles, movie reviews, and donation request letters
- What should a reader keep in mind when reading a persuasive text? Possible response: The reader should keep in mind that the author is trying to persuade the reader to come around to his or her way of thinking. The reader should evaluate what the author has to say and make his or her own decision about it.
- How could you apply what you know about persuasive text when you want to convince someone about something? Possible response: I can write to persuade by using facts or appealing to a reader's feelings.

Guide practice

Have students work in pairs to summarize their learning about persuasive texts and record their thoughts in a chart such as the following:

What persuasive text is	How it persuades
text written for the purpose of changing readers' minds or getting them to take an action	by presenting facts, statistics, information by telling stories or giving descriptions

Connect to reading

Tell students they will now read a movie review for the film version of *Because of Winn-Dixie.* Have students think about what they learned about persuasive texts as they read.

Small Group Time

DAY 4 **Break into small groups before reading or revisiting "A Film with a Message of Hope."**

Teacher Led

SI Strategic Intervention	OL On-Level	A Advanced
Teacher Led p. DI•5 • Practice retelling • Genre focus • **Read/Revisit** "A Film with a Message of Hope"	**Teacher Led** p. DI•10 • Practice retelling • Genre focus • **Read/Revisit** "A Film with a Message of Hope"	**Teacher Led** p. DI•15 • Genre focus • **Read/Revisit** "A Film with a Message of Hope"

Place English language learners in the groups that correspond to their reading abilities in English.

Practice Stations
- Read for Meaning
- Get Fluent
- Words to Know

Independent Activities
- AudioText: "A Film with a Message of Hope"
- *Reader's and Writer's Notebook*
- Research and Inquiry

English Language Learners

Cognates The Spanish word *persuasivo* may be familiar to Spanish speakers as the cognate for *persuasive*.

Objectives

- Analyze a persuasive text.
- Compare and contrast across texts.

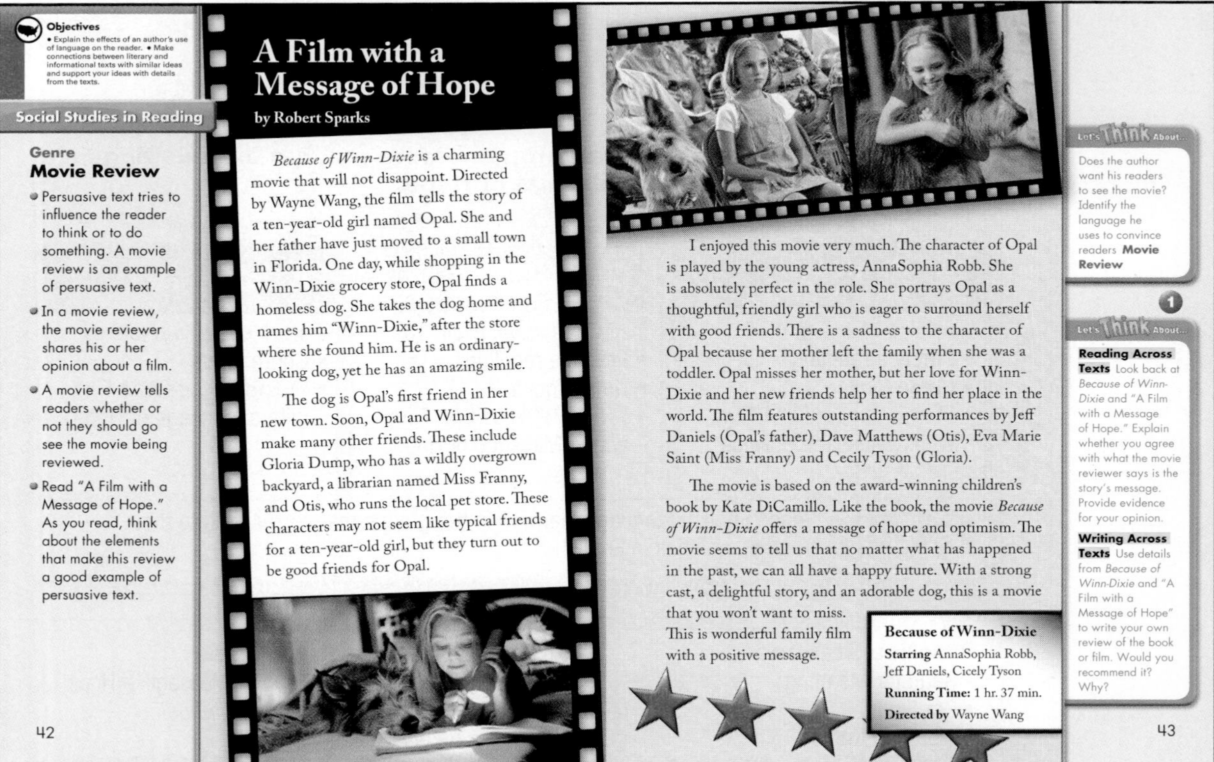

Objectives
• Explain the effects of an author's use of language on the reader. • Make connections between literary and informational texts with similar ideas and support your ideas with details from the texts.

Social Studies in Reading

Genre
Movie Review

- Persuasive text tries to influence the reader to think or to do something. A movie review is an example of persuasive text.
- In a movie review, the movie reviewer shares his or her opinion about a film.
- A movie review tells readers whether or not they should go see the movie being reviewed.
- Read "A Film with a Message of Hope." As you read, think about the elements that make this review a good example of persuasive text.

42

A Film with a Message of Hope

by Robert Sparks

Because of Winn-Dixie is a charming movie that will not disappoint. Directed by Wayne Wang, the film tells the story of a ten-year-old girl named Opal. She and her father have just moved to a small town in Florida. One day, while shopping in the Winn-Dixie grocery store, Opal finds a homeless dog. She takes the dog home and names him "Winn-Dixie," after the store where she found him. He is an ordinary-looking dog, yet he has an amazing smile.

The dog is Opal's first friend in her new town. Soon, Opal and Winn-Dixie make many other friends. These include Gloria Dump, who has a wildly overgrown backyard, a librarian named Miss Franny, and Otis, who runs the local pet store. These characters may not seem like typical friends for a ten-year-old girl, but they turn out to be good friends for Opal.

I enjoyed this movie very much. The character of Opal is played by the young actress, AnnaSophia Robb. She is absolutely perfect in the role. She portrays Opal as a thoughtful, friendly girl who is eager to surround herself with good friends. There is a sadness to the character of Opal because her mother left the family when she was a toddler. Opal misses her mother, but her love for Winn-Dixie and her new friends help her to find her place in the world. The film features outstanding performances by Jeff Daniels (Opal's father), Dave Matthews (Otis), Eva Marie Saint (Miss Franny) and Cecily Tyson (Gloria).

The movie is based on the award-winning children's book by Kate DiCamillo. Like the book, the movie *Because of Winn-Dixie* offers a message of hope and optimism. The movie seems to tell us that no matter what has happened in the past, we can all have a happy future. With a strong cast, a delightful story, and an adorable dog, this is a movie that you won't want to miss. This is wonderful family film with a positive message.

Because of Winn-Dixie
Starring AnnaSophia Robb, Jeff Daniels, Cicely Tyson
Running Time: 1 hr. 37 min.
Directed by Wayne Wang

Let's Think About...

Does the author want his readers to see the movie? Identify the language he uses to convince readers **Movie Review**

1

Let's Think About...

Reading Across Texts Look back at *Because of Winn-Dixie* and "A Film with a Message of Hope." Explain whether you agree with what the movie reviewer says is the story's message. Provide evidence for your opinion.

Writing Across Texts Use details from *Because of Winn-Dixie* and "A Film with a Message of Hope" to write your own review of the book or film. Would you recommend it? Why?

43

Student Edition pp. 42–43

Guide Comprehension

Teach the genre

Genre: Persuasive Text Have students preview "A Film with a Message of Hope" on pp. 42–43. Have them skim the review and discuss what they notice. Then ask: How can you tell this is a persuasive text?

Corrective feedback

If... students are unable to explain the elements of a persuasive text, **then...** use the model to guide students in recognizing persuasive text.

Model the skill

The first thing I notice about the review is the title, "A Film with a Message of Hope." That sounds like someone's opinion. Then I notice that the writer starts the review right away with another opinion. It seems that the writer is trying to influence people about this movie by sharing his opinion.

On their own

Have students discuss with a partner how an author uses language to present information to influence what the reader thinks or does. Then have them discuss what the reader's job should be when reading a movie review or other persuasive text.

Extend Thinking
Think Critically

Higher-order thinking skills

Summarize • Evaluation How effective was the author at using a summary of the movie in the movie review? Possible response: The summary tells the main points of the story. The author was effective in making the story sound lively and interesting.

Draw Conclusions • Analysis Which specific word choices by the author in the last paragraph of the review support the idea that this is a film that you won't want to miss? Possible response: award-winning, hope and optimism, happy future, strong cast, delightful story, adorable dog, family film, positive message

1 Possible response: The author wants people to see the movie. He says it is a movie you won't want to miss.

Reading Across Texts

Have students look back at *Because of Winn-Dixie* and "A Film with a Message of Hope." Have them ask themselves whether or not they agree with what the movie reviewer says is the message of the story. Have them write the following sentence, beginning with *I agree because* _______ or *I disagree because* _______.

Writing Across Texts

Have students reread *Because of Winn-Dixie* and "A Film with a Message of Hope" and jot down details as they read. Tell students to use those details to support what they write for their review of the book or the film. Have them tell whether or not they would recommend it to other people and why. Remind them use the techniques of persuasive writing.

Differentiated Instruction

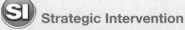

 **Strategic Intervention**

Persuasive text Work with students to brainstorm a list of questions they can ask themselves as they read a persuasive text, such as *What is the author trying to say here? Why is this important? What does the author want us to think or do? How is the author trying to convince us—through facts or through feelings?*

 **Advanced**

Persuasive writing Have partners work together to write a guide for how to write a persuasive text. Encourage them to include what they know about persuasive text and techniques the author of the movie review used.

Read and Comprehend

Objectives

- Read with fluency and expression.
- ◎ Use affixes to figure out the meanings of words.
- Provide a dramatic retelling.

Check Fluency WCPM
SUCCESS PREDICTOR

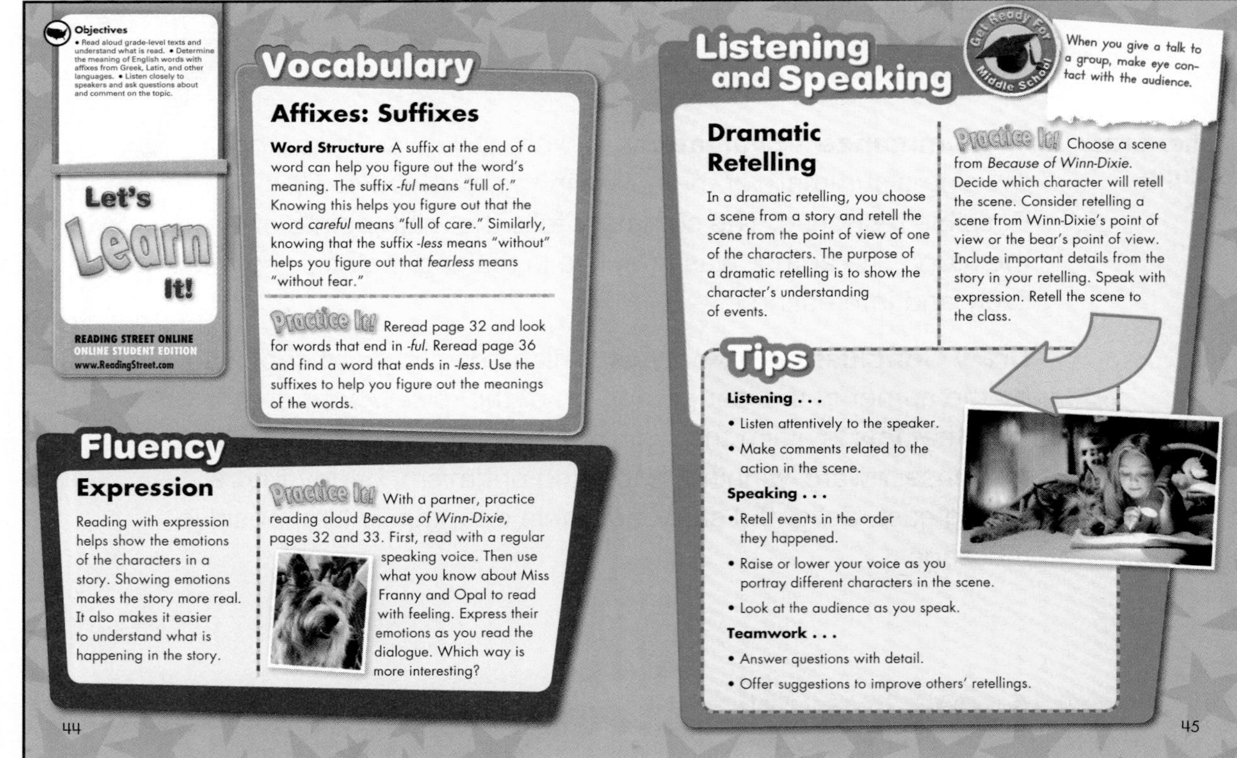

Objectives
• Read aloud grade-level texts and understand what is read. • Determine the meaning of English words with affixes from Greek, Latin, and other languages. • Listen closely to speakers and ask questions about and comment on the topic.

Let's Learn It!

READING STREET ONLINE
ONLINE STUDENT EDITION
www.ReadingStreet.com

Vocabulary

Affixes: Suffixes

Word Structure A suffix at the end of a word can help you figure out the word's meaning. The suffix *-ful* means "full of." Knowing this helps you figure out that the word *careful* means "full of care." Similarly, knowing that the suffix *-less* means "without" helps you figure out that *fearless* means "without fear."

Practice It! Reread page 32 and look for words that end in *-ful*. Reread page 36 and find a word that ends in *-less*. Use the suffixes to help you figure out the meanings of the words.

Fluency

Expression

Reading with expression helps show the emotions of the characters in a story. Showing emotions makes the story more real. It also makes it easier to understand what is happening in the story.

Practice It! With a partner, practice reading aloud *Because of Winn-Dixie*, pages 32 and 33. First, read with a regular speaking voice. Then use what you know about Miss Franny and Opal to read with feeling. Express their emotions as you read the dialogue. Which way is more interesting?

Listening and Speaking

Get Ready For Middle School

When you give a talk to a group, make eye contact with the audience.

Dramatic Retelling

In a dramatic retelling, you choose a scene from a story and retell the scene from the point of view of one of the characters. The purpose of a dramatic retelling is to show the character's understanding of events.

Practice It! Choose a scene from *Because of Winn-Dixie*. Decide which character will retell the scene. Consider retelling a scene from Winn-Dixie's point of view or the bear's point of view. Include important details from the story in your retelling. Speak with expression. Retell the scene to the class.

Tips

Listening . . .
- Listen attentively to the speaker.
- Make comments related to the action in the scene.

Speaking . . .
- Retell events in the order they happened.
- Raise or lower your voice as you portray different characters in the scene.
- Look at the audience as you speak.

Teamwork . . .
- Answer questions with detail.
- Offer suggestions to improve others' retellings.

44 45

Student Edition pp. 44–45

Fluency
Expression

Guide practice Use the Student Edition activity as an assessment tool. Make sure the reading passage is at least 200 words in length. As students read aloud with partners, walk around to make sure their expression is appropriate and that it changes to enhance the meaning of what they are reading.

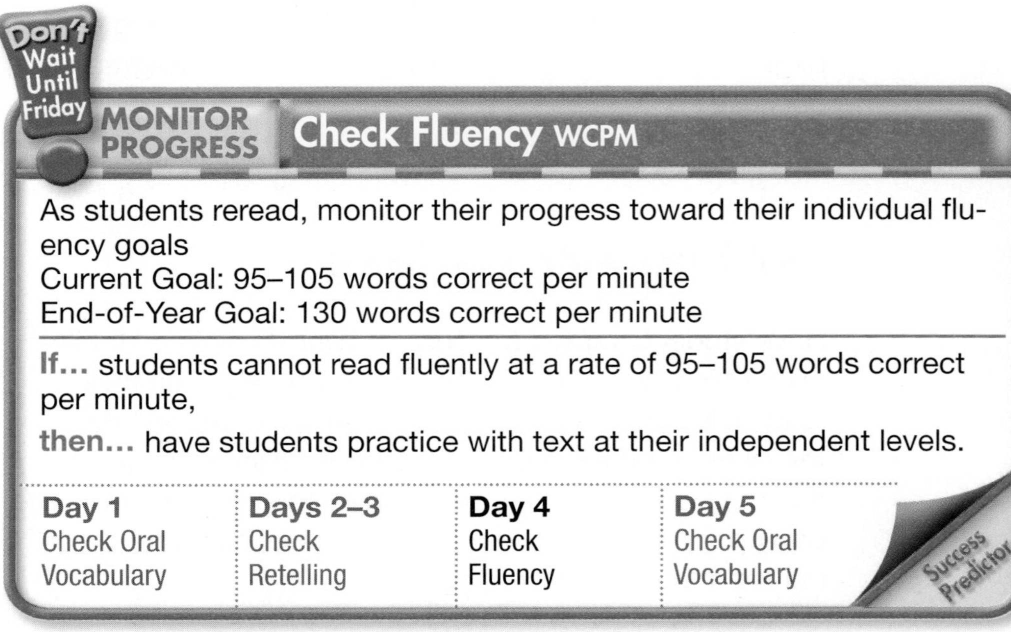

Don't Wait Until Friday

MONITOR PROGRESS **Check Fluency** WCPM

As students reread, monitor their progress toward their individual fluency goals
Current Goal: 95–105 words correct per minute
End-of-Year Goal: 130 words correct per minute

If... students cannot read fluently at a rate of 95–105 words correct per minute,
then... have students practice with text at their independent levels.

Day 1	Days 2–3	Day 4	Day 5
Check Oral Vocabulary	Check Retelling	Check Fluency	Check Oral Vocabulary

Success Predictor

Vocabulary
Affixes: Suffixes

Teach suffixes

Word Structure On the board, write this sentence: *We were fearful about the storm.* Read it aloud and discuss the meaning of *fearful* and how the suffix helps you understand the meaning. Erase *fearful* and replace it with *fearless.* Compare the meanings of the two sentences and discuss how the suffix affects the meanings.

Guide practice

On the board, write the words *pain, thought,* and *harm.* Have partners work together to add the suffixes *-ful* and *-less* to each word. Have them use each word in a sentence. Circulate to monitor students' discussions.

On their own

Have students write a sentence or two to summarize what they have learned about using suffixes to figure out word meaning.

Listening and Speaking
Dramatic Retelling

Teach

Point out that two characters might have differing opinions on the same event. Explain that a dramatic retelling allows the speaker to present a character's point of view. Encourage students to apply what they know about reading with expression to a dramatic retelling—they will want to use their voice to convey feelings and add emphasis and interest.

Guide practice

Point out to students that a dramatic retelling does not have to reflect the point of view of the story. Specifically, Opal does not have to be telling about events. Students can present a character who does not actually speak in the story, such as Winn-Dixie or the bear. Encourage students to speak expressively and make eye contact with the audience. Remind the audience to listen attentively to speakers and make pertinent comments.

On their own

Have students practice their scenes with their small groups and then present them to the class.

Dramatic Retelling

Remind students that key elements of a dramatic retelling are presenting a character's understanding of events, retelling events in the order they happened, and using expression when speaking. Have students take a minute to summarize the main features of a dramatic retelling with a partner. Give them prompts, such as *What are we trying to do with a dramatic retelling?* or *What are the main things to remember about a dramatic retelling?*

ELL

English Language Learners

Practice pronunciation Assist pairs of students by modeling the correct pronunciation for words that give students difficulty. Have students repeat after you. Pair students with mixed language proficiencies together to practice pronunciation and employ self-corrective techniques.

Grammar support Since students will be posing and answering questions with their groups, provide support for English sentence structure for questions and answers.

DAY 4 Language Arts

30–35 min

Objectives

- Draw conclusions from research.
- Synthesize research into a written report.
- Review declarative and interrogative sentences.
- Spell words with the short vowel VCCV pattern.

Research and Inquiry
Synthesize

Teach Have students synthesize their research findings and results. Encourage students to use a visual representation, such as a bar graph, to show the results of their surveys. Suggest that students use their graphs, as well as the other relevant information they have gathered, to draw conclusions about diversity in school sports programs. Review how to choose relevant information from a number of sources and organize it logically.

Guide practice Have students use a word processing program to prepare for their presentations on Day 5. If students are using graphs, they may prepare their graphs on a piece of poster board. Remind students to label their graphs accurately.

On their own Have students create their reports by drawing conclusions through a brief written explanation of the information they gathered in their research. Students should incorporate the results of the student survey into their reports. Then have students organize and combine information and plan their presentations.

Conventions

Declarative and Interrogative Sentences

Test practice Remind students that grammar skills, such as identifying declarative and interrogative sentences, are often assessed on important tests. Remind students of the definitions:

- *Declarative* sentences make a statement and end with a period.
- *Interrogative* sentences ask a question and end with a question mark.

Daily Fix-It Remind students that all sentences should have a complete subject and complete predicate. Use Daily Fix-It numbers 7 and 8 in the right margin.

On their own For additional practice, use *Reader's and Writer's Notebook* p. 50.

Reader's and Writer's Notebook p. 50

Spelling

Short Vowels VCCV

Practice spelling strategy Have pairs of students take turns giving each other clues about the spelling words. Tell them to give one clue about the word's meaning. For the other clue, students should say the vowel sound in the word's first syllable. Students should keep track of how many words they are able to guess correctly based on the clues.

On their own For additional practice, use *Let's Practice It!* p. 7 on the *Teacher Resources DVD-ROM.*

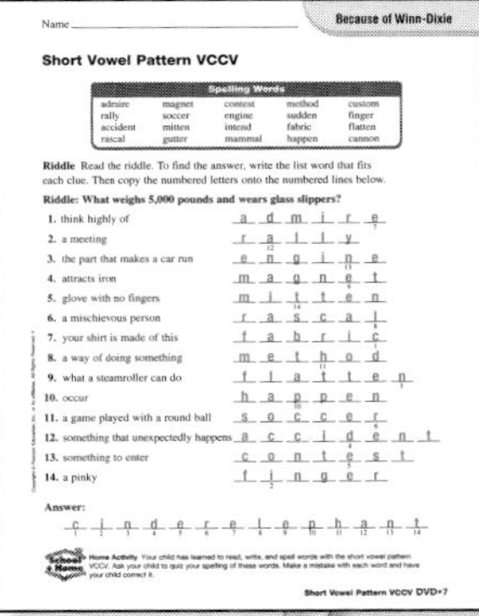
Because of Winn-Dixie

Short Vowel Pattern VCCV

Let's Practice It! TR DVD•7

Daily Fix-It

7. A bear is a large mammal? *(mammal.)*

8. Grizzly bears is bigger then black bears. *(are; than)*

Objectives

- Use revising strategy of deleting to improve draft.

Writing—Realistic Fiction
Revising Strategy

MINI-LESSON

Revising Strategy: Deleting

- Yesterday, we wrote a realistic story about a character who reaches a turning point in his or her life. Today we will revise our drafts. The goal is to make our writing clearer, more coherent, and more interesting.

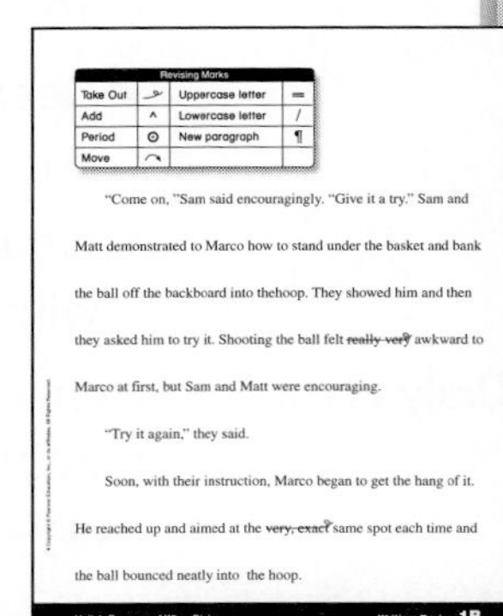

Revising Marks			
Take Out	⌐	Uppercase letter	≡
Add	^	Lowercase letter	/
Period	⊙	New paragraph	¶
Move	⌒		

"Come on, "Sam said encouragingly. "Give it a try." Sam and Matt demonstrated to Marco how to stand under the basket and bank the ball off the backboard into thehoop. They showed him and then they asked him to try it. Shooting the ball felt ~~really very~~ awkward to Marco at first, but Sam and Matt were encouraging.

"Try it again," they said.

Soon, with their instruction, Marco began to get the hang of it. He reached up and aimed at the ~~very, exact~~ same spot each time and the ball bounced neatly into the hoop.

Unit 1 Because of Winn-Dixie Writing: Revise 1B

Writing Transparency 1B, TR DVD

- Display Writing Transparency 1B. Remind students that revising does not include corrections of grammar and mechanics. Tell them that this will be done as they proofread their work. Introduce the revising strategy of deleting.

- When you revise, ask yourself, *What information remains in this story that does not fit with my topic?* The revising strategy of deleting is the process by which unnecessary words are deleted to make writing clearer and more to the point. Notice that I can delete the words *really* and *very* and make my story clearer without losing any meaning.

Tell students that as they revise, not only should they look for places where they can delete unnecessary words to help make their writing clearer and more interesting, but they should also look at their word choice to make sure they used vivid adjectives and verbs.

Revising Tips

- ✔ Review the story to delete any unnecessary words, or even whole sentences, that aren't needed to make the point.
- ✔ Review story to make sure that adjectives are vivid and precise and verbs are strong.
- ✔ Be sure your story is well organized and engaging.

Peer conferencing

Peer Revision Have pairs of students exchange papers for peer revision. Provide partners with sticky notes. Have them use the notes to write questions, suggestions, or compliments and place them in the appropriate places in their partner's stories.

Have students revise their compositions. They should use the information their partner gave during the Peer Revision as well as the key features of realistic fiction to guide their revision. Be sure that students are using the revising strategy of deleting.

Corrective feedback

Circulate around the room to monitor students and confer with them as they revise. Remind students correcting errors that they will have time to proofread tomorrow. They should be working on content and organization today, as well as deleting unnecessary words.

ROUTINE Quick Write for Fluency

Team Talk

1. **Talk** Have pairs discuss how Opal made a new friend.

2. **Write** Each student should write a few sentences describing the event that happened in the story where Opal made a friend.
3. **Share** Have partners read each other's writing to check that the event described could happen in real life.

Routines Flip Chart

Wrap Up Your Day

- ✔ **Build Concepts** Have students discuss why the story has a positive message.
- ✔ **Oral Vocabulary** Monitor students' use of oral vocabulary as they respond to this question: What can you learn about friendship by reading about Opal and her adventures in the town of Naomi?
- ✔ **Text Features** Discuss how the photos from the movie helped students understand the movie review.

Write Guy
Jeff Anderson

Life in a Fishbowl

When a teacher can't confer with every student, a "fishbowl conference" with one willing student can allow other students to observe, listen, and explore how to appropriately respond to others' writing. It's important to reflect what the student is doing well and how a draft might be revised and improved.

ELL

English Language Learners
Have students work in pairs to write a descriptive paragraph (e.g., describing their favorite food), making their writing purposefully wordy. Ask students to switch papers and revise their partner's work, deleting unnecessary words. Ask partners to read the revised paragraphs aloud to each other.

Remind students to think about what they can discover from new places and new people.

Objectives

- Review the weekly concept.
- Review oral vocabulary.

Today at a Glance

Oral Vocabulary

Comprehension
◎ Sequence

Lesson Vocabulary
◎ Affixes: Suffixes

Word Analysis
Word ending *-ed*

Literary Terms
Point of view

Assessment
Fluency
Comprehension

Research and Inquiry
Communicate

Spelling
Short vowels VCCV

Conventions
Declarative and interrogative sentences

Writing
Realistic fiction

Check Oral Vocabulary SUCCESS PREDICTOR

Concept Wrap Up

Question of the Week

What experiences bring diverse people together?

Review the concept Have students look back at the reading selections to find examples that demonstrate diverse people interacting with each other.

Review Amazing Words Display and review this week's concept map. Remind students that this week they have learned ten Amazing Words related to people interacting with each other. Have students use the Amazing Words and the concept map to answer the question of the week, *What experiences bring diverse people together?*

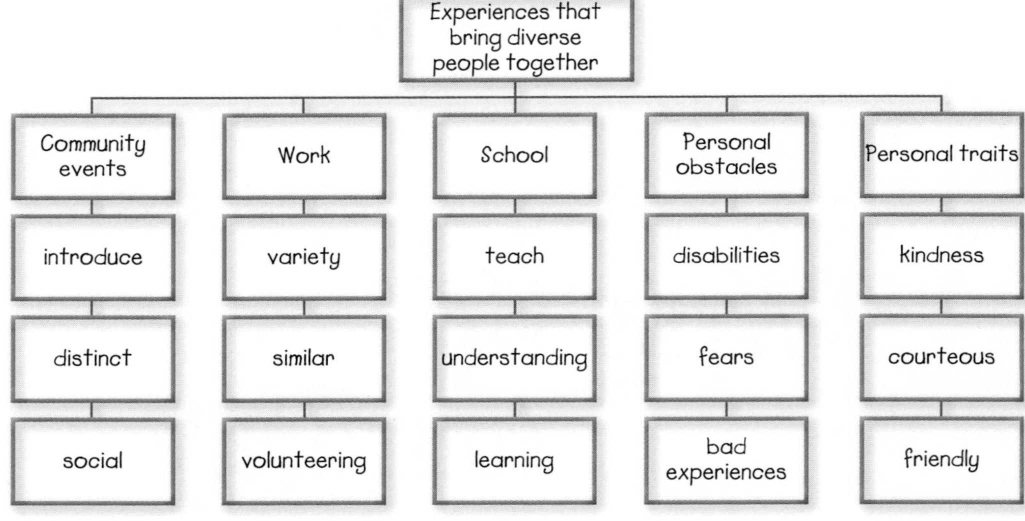

ELL Check Concepts and Language Use the Day 5 instructions on ELL Poster 1 to monitor students' understanding of the lesson concept.

ELL Poster 1

Amazing Ideas

Connect to the Big Question

Have pairs of students discuss how the Question of the Week connects to the Big Question: *What can we discover from new places and people?* Tell students to use the concept map and what they have learned from this week's Anchored Talks and reading selections to form an Amazing Idea—a realization or "big idea" about Turning Points. Remind partners to pose and answer questions with appropriate details and to give suggestions that build on each other's ideas. Then ask pairs to share their Amazing Ideas with the class.

Amazing Ideas might include these key concepts:

- You never know where you might find an interesting friend who might be quite different from you in some ways.
- Everyday experiences can bring diverse people of all ages, backgrounds, and abilities together to help one another.

Write about it

Have students write a few sentences about their Amazing Idea, beginning with "This week I learned . . ."

It's Friday

MONITOR PROGRESS **Check Oral Vocabulary**

Have individuals use this week's Amazing Words to describe common experiences that can bring diverse people together. Monitor students' abilities to use the Amazing Words and note which words you need to reteach.

If... students have difficulty using the Amazing Words,
then... reteach using the Oral Vocabulary Routine, pp. 21a, 24b, 32b, 42b, OV•1.

Day 1	Days 2–3	Day 4	Day 5
Check Oral Vocabulary	Check Retelling	Check Fluency	**Check Oral Vocabulary**

Success Predictor

Amazing Words

kindness	introduce
attention	similar
teach	distinct
understanding	social
variety	courteous

ELL

English Language Learners
Concept map Work with students to add new words to the concept map.

Objectives
- ◎ Review sequence.
- ◎ Review suffixes.
- Review word ending *-ed*.
- Review point of view.

Comprehension Review
Sequence

Teach sequence

Envision It!

Review the definition of sequence on p. 22. Remind students that understanding the sequence of the plot's main events can be important to understanding a story, and that sometimes authors tell the events out of order. For additional support, have students review p. EI•13 on sequence.

Student Edition EI•13

Guide practice

Have partners discuss the order of events in *Because of Winn-Dixie.* Have them make a time line. Remind them that authors sometimes include events that happened long ago, such as Miss Franny's bear experience.

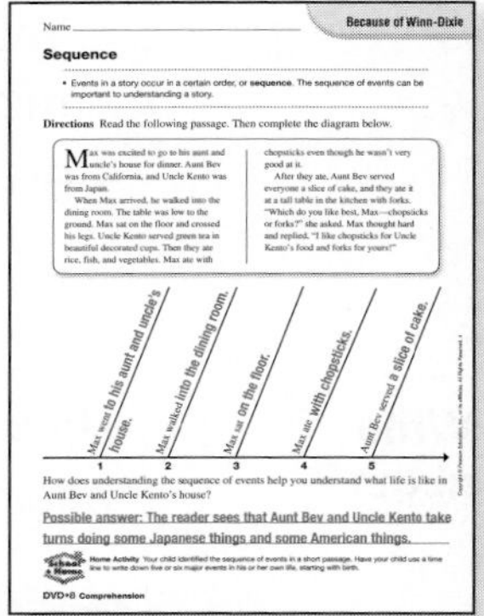
Let's Practice It!
TR DVD•8

On their own

For additional practice, use *Let's Practice It!* p. 8 on the *Teacher Resources DVD-ROM.*

Vocabulary Review
Affixes: Suffixes

Teach suffixes

Remind students that knowing the meanings of suffixes can help them figure out the meanings of unknown words.

Guide practice

On the board, write the words *functional* and *truthful.* Review with students how to use the suffixes to help figure out the meanings of the words.

On their own

Tell students to notice words with *-ful* and *-al* suffixes as they do their independent reading. Have them add examples to a class list.

Word Analysis Review
Word Ending *-ed*

Teach word ending *-ed* Review with students that the *-ed* ending added to verbs shows that an action has already happened. Use the words *walk* and *walked* in separate sentences and have students explain what the ending *-ed* indicates.

Guide practice Display the following words: *checked, listened, wondered, asked.* Use the Strategy for Meaningful Word Parts routine to teach the word *checked.*

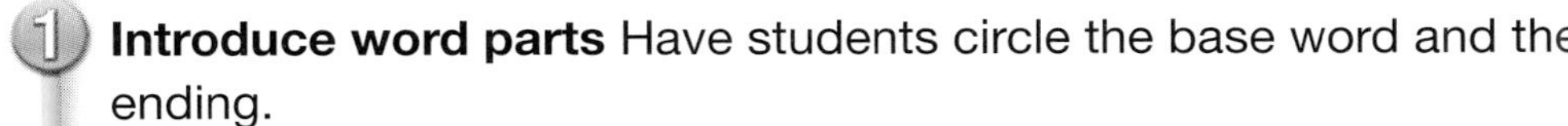

ROUTINE **Strategy for Meaningful Word Parts**

1. **Introduce word parts** Have students circle the base word and the ending.
2. **Connect to meaning** Define the word and the ending. *Check* can mean "to look over." The ending *-ed* shows that the action already happened.
3. **Read the word** Blend the meaningful word parts together to read *checked*. Then use the meanings of the base word and the ending to determine the meaning of the word. *Checked* means that someone has looked over something.

Routines Flip Chart

On their own Have students work in pairs to circle the base word and ending in each word.

Literary Terms Review
Point of View

Teach point of view Have students reread p. 34 of *Because of Winn-Dixie.* Have them identify the point of view and support their answer with examples from the text.

Guide practice Help students create a T-chart to compare first and third person points of view. (First person talks about the characters as *I, we, me, us.* Third person talks about the characters as *he, she, they, them.*)

On their own Have partners work together to identify the point of view in books they are reading independently.

Lesson Vocabulary

grand great; wonderful
memorial serving to remember a person or event
peculiar strange; odd
positive in a good way
prideful in a way that shows a person thinks he or she is better than others
recalls remembers
selecting choosing; picking

ELL

English Language Learners

Word ending *-ed* Supply students with a list of verbs that do not undergo a spelling change when *-ed* is added, such as *walk, jump, brush, clean.* Remind students that to show that an action has already happened, we often add *-ed* to the end of a verb. Pair more fluent students with less fluent ones. Have partners work together to say sentences using a word from the list in the present tense and then another sentence with the word with *-ed* added.

DAY 5 Wrap Up your Week

10–15 min

Objectives

- Read grade-level text with fluency.

Assessment

Check words correct per minute

Fluency Make two copies of the fluency passage on p. 45k. As the student reads the text aloud, mark mistakes on your copy. Also mark where the student is at the end of one minute. To check the student's comprehension of the passage, have him or her retell you what was read. To figure words correct per minute (WCPM), subtract the number of mistakes from the total number of words read in one minute.

WCPM

Corrective feedback

If... students cannot read fluently at a rate of 95–105 WCPM,
then... make sure they practice with text at their independent reading level. Provide additional fluency practice by pairing nonfluent readers with fluent readers.

If... students already read at 130 WCPM,
then... have them read a book of their choice independently.

Plan to Assess Fluency

- ☑ **This week assess Advanced students.**
- ☐ **Week 2** Assess Strategic Intervention students.
- ☐ **Week 3** Assess On-Level students.
- ☐ **Week 4** Assess Strategic Intervention students.
- ☐ **Week 5** Assess any students you have not yet checked during this unit.

Set individual goals for students to enable them to reach the year-end goal.

- Current Goal: 95–105 WCPM
- Year-End Goal: 130 WCPM

Small Group Time

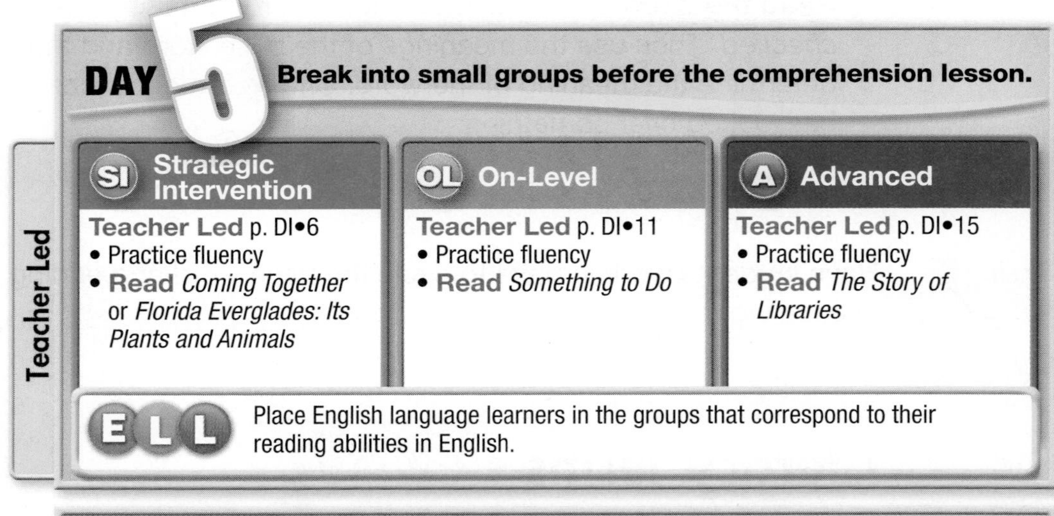

DAY 5 Break into small groups before the comprehension lesson.

Teacher Led

SI Strategic Intervention	OL On-Level	A Advanced
Teacher Led p. DI•6 • Practice fluency • **Read** *Coming Together* or *Florida Everglades: Its Plants and Animals*	**Teacher Led** p. DI•11 • Practice fluency • **Read** *Something to Do*	**Teacher Led** p. DI•15 • Practice fluency • **Read** *The Story of Libraries*

ELL Place English language learners in the groups that correspond to their reading abilities in English.

Practice Stations
- Words to Know
- Get Fluent
- Read for Meaning

Independent Activities
- Grammar Jammer
- Concept Talk Video
- Vocabulary Activities

Name ______________________________

A Lasting Friendship

For as long as she could remember, Kim had felt more comfortable 12
with animals than people. She was shy and quiet at school and she was 26
quiet at home now, too, with her mother, who'd been sick. When Kim 39
found five abandoned kittens, she didn't feel shy at all. She talked to 52
them, petted them, and fed them milk. 59

Kim knew that she wouldn't be able to keep the kittens, though. 71
Instead, she brought them to a new animal shelter. As soon as she 84
arrived there, she felt comfortable with the sounds of the animals, 95
barking and meowing. They feel lonely, like me, she thought. 105

"May I come back," Kim asked a worker, "to help?" The next 117
Saturday, Kim went to the shelter to work. That's when she met Mira. 130
Mira was bent over talking to a sad-looking puppy. Kim watched as 142
Mira stroked the puppy and told it that she felt sad also. When Mira 156
saw Kim, she turned away, blushing. 162

"It's okay," said Kim. "I feel sad a lot too. Looks like we have a lot in 179
common—you and me and the animals." From then on, Kim and Mira 192
met at the shelter each Saturday. They talked to the animals and to each 206
other too. It was the beginning of a lasting friendship. 216

MONITOR PROGRESS

• Check Fluency

Objectives

- Read grade-level text with comprehension.

Assessment

Check sequence

Sequence Use "Camp Grove" on p. 45m to check students' understanding of sequence.

1. How does the author use sequence in "Camp Grove"? (Possible response: The author tells about events in the order they happen.)
2. What are some words in the story that give you clues about when the plot's main events are happening? (July, After, During, ended)
3. Compare Bruce's feelings about Camp Grove at the beginning of his stay to his feelings at the end. Why did Bruce's feelings change? (Possible response: At the beginning, Bruce did not like outdoors, adventure, or meeting new people, but at the end he seemed to like it. He tried new things and made friends, so his feelings changed.)

Corrective feedback

If... students are unable to answer the comprehension questions,
then... use the Reteach lesson in the *First Stop* book.

Name ______________________________

Camp Grove

Bruce went to Camp Grove because his parents made him go. Camp Grove was an outdoor adventure camp. Bruce did not like the outdoors or adventures.

Still, July found Bruce in the mountains of South Carolina unpacking his bags at Camp Grove. He peeked around at the other boys in his cramped cabin. They all seemed so different from him. One drummed on his cot, singing a rap tune. Another grunted as he lifted hand weights. Two more argued about who had the best cell phone. Bruce was quiet, and he just liked to read and play cards. Why was he here?

Their counselor, a lanky guy named Tim, came into the cabin. "Cabin four is the best!" he said. "Let's gather round and get to know each other."

They played a get-to-know-you game. Bruce thought the game would be dumb, but he learned that the weight-lifting boy, Justin, had a grandfather who lived in Bruce's town. He also learned that another boy, Sam, liked to play cards too.

After they all went to the lake to canoe, Bruce and Sam came back to the cabin and played cards.

During his two weeks at camp, Bruce made many discoveries. He discovered that he did like the outdoors after all. He even discovered that meeting new people was not so bad. Justin taught him about lifting weights.

When camp ended, Justin said he'd call Bruce the next time he visited his Grandpa. Sam and Bruce agreed they'd be back to play card games next year.

MONITOR PROGRESS

• Sequence

Objectives

- Communicate inquiry results.
- Review declarative and interrogative sentences.
- Administer spelling test.

Research and Inquiry
Communicate

Present ideas Have students share their inquiry results by presenting their information and giving a brief talk on their research. Have students display any visual representations they created on Day 4.

Listening and speaking Remind students how to be good speakers and how to communicate effectively with their audience.

- Respond to relevant questions with appropriate details.
- Speak clearly and loudly.
- Keep eye contact with audience members.

Remind students of these tips for being a good listener.

- Listen attentively to speakers.
- Wait until the speaker has finished before raising your hand to ask a relevant question or make a pertinent comment.
- Be polite, even if you disagree.

Spelling Test
Short Vowels VCCV

Spelling test To administer the spelling test, refer to the directions, words, and sentences on p. 23c.

Conventions
Extra Practice

Teach Remind students that a declarative sentence makes a statement and ends in a period. An interrogative sentences asks a question and ends in a question mark. Sentences must have correct subject-verb agreement.

Guide practice Have partners write an interrogative sentence asking each other about a favorite realistic fiction character and then write a declarative sentence answering the question.

Who is your favorite character in *Because of Winn-Dixie*?

My favorite character is Miss Fanny.

Daily Fix-It Use Daily Fix-It numbers 9 and 10 in the right margin.

On their own Write these sentences. Have students look back in *Because of Winn-Dixie* to find the missing first two words and end punctuation to fill in the blanks. Remember a declarative sentence ends in a period and an interrogative sentence ends in a question mark.

1. ________ **he was a bear**________ (She thought; .)
2. ________ **all right** ________ (Are you; ?)
3. ________ **sat there trembling and shaking**________ (Miss Fanny; .)
4. ________ **weigh hardly anything at all** ________ (She didn't; .)
5. ________ **for a whole library**________ (You asked; ?)

For additional practice, use *Let's Practice It!* p. 9 on the *Teacher Resources DVD-ROM.*

Daily Fix-It

9. I love to here Miss Block tell his stories. *(hear; her)*

10. Some off her stories are hard to believe *(of; believe.)*

Let's Practice It!
TR DVD•9

Objectives

- Proofread revised drafts of realistic fiction stories, including watching for correct punctuation for declarative and interrogative sentences.
- Create and present final draft.

Writing—Realistic Fiction
Declarative and Interrogative Sentences

Review Revising

Remind students that yesterday they revised their realistic fiction stories, focusing on deleting words and information to make the writing clearer and less wordy. Today they will proofread their stories.

MINI-LESSON

Proofread Declarative and Interrogative Sentences

- **Teach** When we proofread, we search for errors in spelling, capitalization, punctuation, and grammar. Today we will focus on proofreading declarative and interrogative sentences.

- **Model** Let's look at the final paragraph from the story we revised yesterday. Display Writing Transparency 1C. Explain that you will look for errors in the use of declarative and interrogative sentences. I see a problem in the sentence, *"Do you like playing basketball," Sam asked Marco after the game.* This is an interrogative sentence, so it needs a question mark at the end. Point out that the sentence *"I told you, you'd be good?"* is a declarative sentence that needs a period at the end. Explain to students that they should reread their story a number of times, each time looking for different types of errors: spelling, punctuation, capitalization, and grammar.

Writing Transparency 1C, TR DVD

Proofread

Display the Proofreading Tips. Ask students to proofread their stories, using the Proofreading Tips and paying particular attention to declarative and interrogative sentences. Circulate around the room answering students' questions. When students have finished editing their own work, have pairs proofread one another's stories.

Proofreading Tips

- ✓ Be sure all declarative and interrogative sentences are used correctly.
- ✓ Use correct indentation when beginning new paragraphs and using dialogue.
- ✓ Begin proofreading only after you have completed drafting, revising, and editing.

Present

Have students incorporate revisions and proofreading edits into their stories to create a final draft.

Give students two options for presenting: an oral presentation to the class or a class book. For oral presentations, have students create art to go along with the main events in their story, which they can display as they read their story to the class. For a class book, have groups work together to create a table of contents, design a cover, and bind the stories into a book. When students have finished, have each complete a Writing Self-Evaluation Guide.

ROUTINE Quick Write for Fluency — Team Talk

1. **Talk** Have students discuss what they learned about turning points in people's lives.
2. **Write** Each student writes a paragraph summarizing what he or she has learned.
3. **Share** Partners read their own writing to one another.

Routines Flip Chart

Teacher Note

Writing self-evaluation Make copies of the Writing Self-Evaluation Guide on p. 39 of the *Reader's and Writer's Notebook* and hand out to students.

ELL

English Language Learners

Support editing Provide practice with declarative and interrogative sentences. Ask partners to write two interrogative sentences. Then have them switch papers and write two declarative sentences in response to their partner's questions.

Poster preview Prepare students for next week by using Week 2, ELL Poster 2. Read the Poster Talk-Through to introduce the concepts and vocabulary. Ask students to identify and describe objects and actions in the art.

Selection summary Send home the summary of *Lewis and Clark and Me,* in English and the students' home languages, if available. Students can read the summary with family members.

Preview NEXT WEEK

What opportunities can be found in new places? Tell students that next week they will read about the explorers Lewis and Clark.

Assessment Checkpoints for the Week

Weekly Assessment

Use pp. 1–6 of *Weekly Tests* to check:

- ✔ **Word Analysis** Word ending in *-ed*
- ✔ **Comprehension Skill** Sequence
- ✔ Review **Comprehension Skill** Cause and Effect
- ✔ **Lesson Vocabulary**

memorial	grand
prideful	positive
recalls	selecting
peculiar	

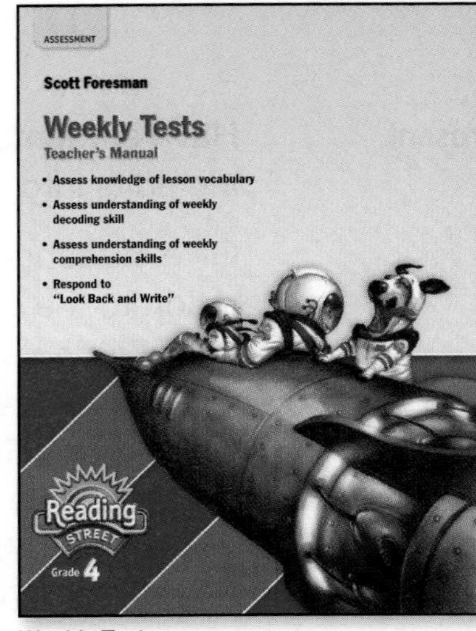

Weekly Tests

Advanced

Differentiated Assessment

On-Level

Strategic Intervention

Use pp. 1–6 of *Fresh Reads for Fluency and Comprehension* to check:

- ✔ **Comprehension Skill** Sequence
- ✔ Review **Comprehension Skill** Cause and Effect
- ✔ **Fluency** Words Correct Per Minute

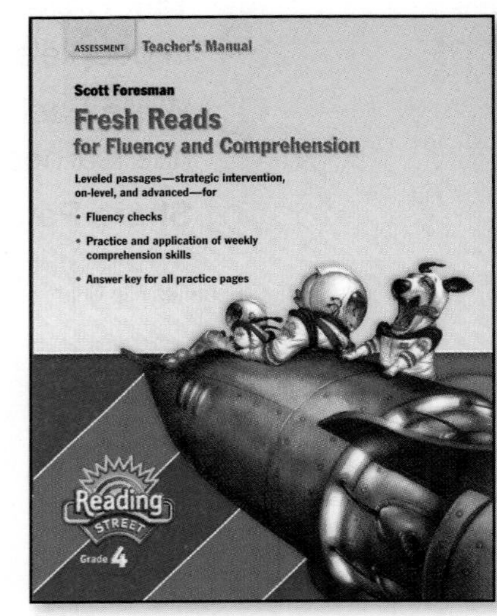

Fresh Reads for Fluency and Comprehension

Managing Assessment

Use *Assessment Handbook* for:

- ✔ **Weekly Assessment Blackline Masters for Monitoring Progress**
- ✔ **Observation Checklists**
- ✔ **Record-Keeping Forms**
- ✔ **Portfolio Assessment**

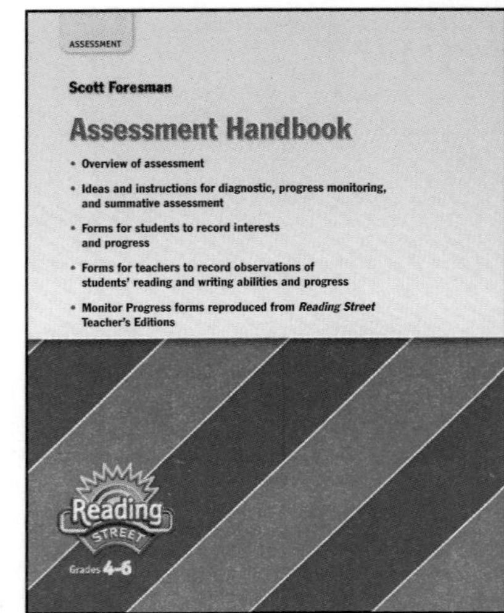

Assessment Handbook

Teacher Notes

Pacing Small Group Instruction

5-Day Plan

DAY 1	• Reinforce the concept • Read Leveled Readers Concept Literacy Below Level
DAY 2	• Sequence • Summarize • Revisit Student Edition pp. 26–31
DAY 3	• Suffixes • Revisit Student Edition pp. 32–37
DAY 4	• Practice Retelling • Read/Revisit Student Edition pp. 42–43
DAY 5	• Reread for fluency • Reread Leveled Readers

3- or 4-Day Plan

DAY 1	• Reinforce the concept • Read Leveled Readers Concept Literacy Below Level
DAY 2	• Sequence • Summarize • Revisit Student Edition pp. 26–31
DAY 3	• Suffixes • Revisit Student Edition pp. 32–37
DAY 4	• Practice Retelling • Read/Revisit Student Edition pp. 42–43 • Reread for fluency • Reread Leveled Readers

3-Day Plan: Eliminate the shaded box.

DAY 1

Build Background

- **Reinforce the Concept** Discuss the weekly question *What experiences bring diverse people together?* We often visit new places together with people we have never met before. We take tours through museums or parks. When we visit new outdoor places, we can share what we learn about the plants and animals there. For example, if you visit the desert, you might learn how cactuses can store water. You can talk about this new fact with other visitors. Sharing this kind of experience brings different kinds of people together. Discuss the words on the concept map.
- **Connect to Reading** This week you will read about the friendship that develops between a young person and an older person. Which young person and older person become friends in "Child of the Silent Night"? Why? (*Laura Bridgman and Asa Tenney become friends. Laura is deaf and Asa wants to help her learn.*)

Objectives

- Participate in teacher-led discussions by answering questions with appropriate detail.

DAY 1

For a complete literacy instructional plan and additional practice with this week's target skills and strategies, see the **Leveled Reader Teaching Guide.**

Concept Literacy Reader

- **Read** *Coming Together*
- **Before Reading** Preview the book with students, focusing on key concepts and vocabulary. Then have them set a purpose for reading.
- **During Reading** Read the first two pages of the book aloud while students track the print. If students are able, have them read and discuss the remainder of the book with a partner.
- **After Reading** After students finish reading the book, have them use what they learned to answer the weekly question *What experiences bring diverse people together?*

Below-Level Reader

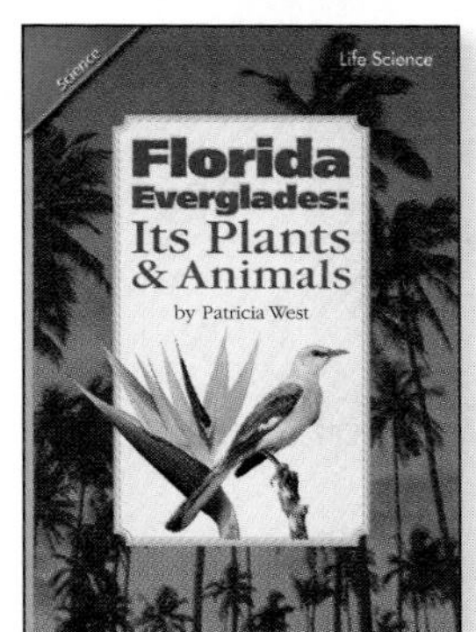

- **Read** *Florida Everglades: Its Plants & Animals*
- **Before Reading** Have students preview the story using the illustrations. *What kinds of plants and animals do you see?* Then have students set a purpose for reading.
- **During Reading** Do a choral reading of the first two pages. As students finish reading the book with a partner, have them discuss these questions:
  - How did the mockingbird get its name? (*It can mock the sounds of other birds.*)
  - What happened after people killed many egrets to get their beautiful feathers? (*The egret became a protected species.*)
- **After Reading** Have students review the Concept Map. Connect the reader to the weekly question *What experiences bring diverse people together?* How could you share what you learned about black bears in *Florida Everglades: Its Plants & Animals* with another person?

MONITOR PROGRESS

If... students have difficulty reading the selection with a partner,
then... have them follow along as they listen to the Leveled Readers DVD-ROM.

If... students have trouble understanding the facts about birds,
then... reread pp. 10–11 and discuss the various plants and animals that are described.

Objectives

- Participate in teacher-led discussions by answering questions with appropriate detail.

Reinforce Comprehension

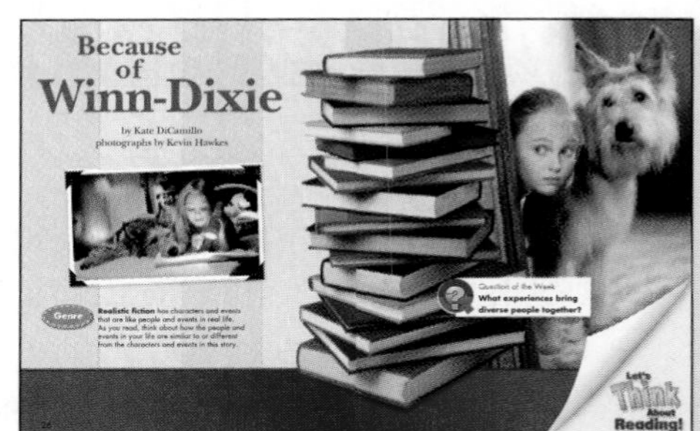

Skill Sequence Review with students *Envision It!* p. EI•13 on sequence. Then use p. 22 to review the definition of sequence. Clue words such as *first, second,* and *last* can tell you the order of events. Sometimes clues are in groups of words, such as *In the beginning* or *It was not until later.*

Strategy Summarize Review the definition of summarize. Remind students that, as they read, they should sum up the important ideas or events. This will help them follow the story. For additional support, refer students to *Envision It!* p. EI•23.

Read *Because of Winn-Dixie* on pp. 26–31. As students read, have them apply the comprehension skill and strategy.

- What is the sequence of events in paragraph 2 on p. 29? (First, Opal shows Winn-Dixie how to look in the window. Then Opal goes inside the library. Then Miss Franny Block sees the dog at the window and thinks he's a bear.)
- What clue word or phrase in the text helped you figure out the sequence? (*"It all started"*)

Use the During Reading Differentiated Instruction for additional support for struggling readers.

MONITOR PROGRESS

If... students have difficulty reading along with the group,
then... have them follow along as they listen to the AudioText.

Student Edition, p. EI•13

More Reading

Use additional Leveled Readers or other texts at students' instructional levels to reinforce this week's skills and strategies. For text suggestions, see the Leveled Reader Database or the Leveled Readers Skills Chart on pp. CL 24–CL 29.

Objectives

- Sequence the plot's main events.
- Summarize the plot's main events.

DAY 3

Reinforce Vocabulary

Suffixes/Word Structure Say the word *prideful* as you write it on the board. Circle the suffix *-ful.* When I circle the suffix, I see that the base word is *pride*. I know the suffix *-ful* means "full of." When I combine this meaning with the meaning of *pride,* I find that the word *prideful* means "full of pride.

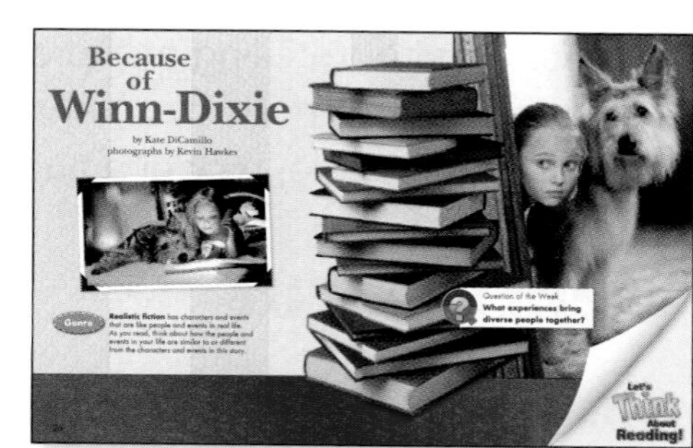

Revisit *Because of Winn-Dixie* on pp. 32–37. Then review *Words!* on p. W•6. Encourage students to use suffixes to figure out the meanings of any unfamiliar words.

- Point out the word *fancy* on the first page of the story. If I add the suffix *-ful* to *fancy,* how would it change the word? (Fanciful *would mean "full of fancy." It turns the word into an adjective.*)
- Write these suffixes and definitions on the board: *-less* = "without"; *-ly* = "in the manner of"; *-ness* = "quality of." Look at the words *friend, sudden,* and *loud* on this page. Try to make new words using the suffixes *-less, -ly,* and *-ness.* What do the new words mean? (Friendless *means "without friends."* Suddenly *means "in a sudden manner."* Loudness *means "the quality of being loud."*)
- What did the bear do after Miss Franny threw the book at him? (*He left, taking the book with him.*)
- What did Winn-Dixie do that helped bring Opal and Miss Franny together? (*Winn-Dixie smiled at Miss Franny.*)

Use the During Reading Differentiated Instruction for additional support for struggling readers.

MONITOR PROGRESS

If... students need more practice with the lesson vocabulary,
then... use *Envision It! Pictured Vocabulary Cards*.

Objectives

- Determine meaning of grade-level academic English words derived from other linguistic affixes.
- Use word structure to analyze and decode new words.

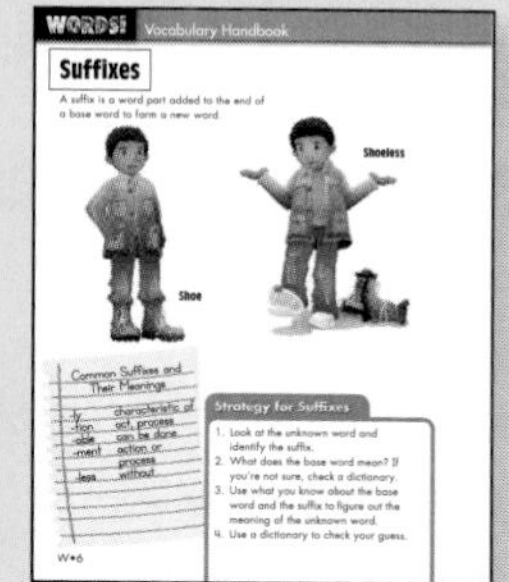

Student Edition, p. W•6

More Reading

Use additional Leveled Readers or other texts at students' instructional levels to reinforce this week's skills and strategies. For text suggestions, see the Leveled Reader Database or the Leveled Readers Skills Chart on pp. CL 24–CL 29.

Practice Retelling

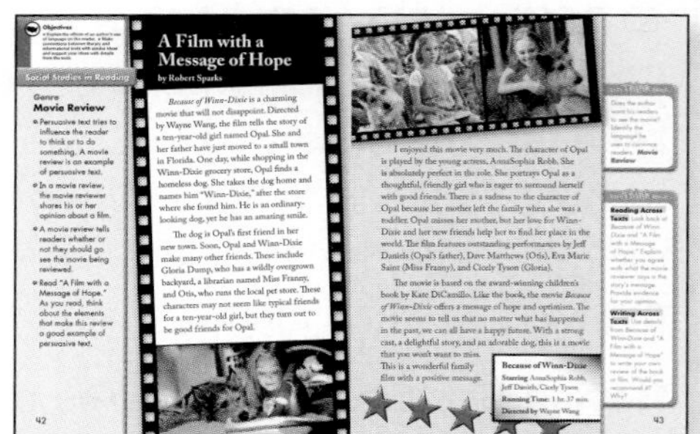

- **Retell** Students work in pairs and use the Retelling Cards to retell *Because of Winn-Dixie.* Monitor retelling and prompt as needed. Who are the main characters? If students struggle, model a fluent retelling.

Genre Focus

- **Before Reading or Revisiting** "A Film with a Message of Hope" on pp. 42–43, read aloud the information about movie reviews on p. 42. Explain that a movie reviewer tries to persuade readers to see or avoid a movie. A movie reviewer forms an opinion based on the plot, the message, or the actors' performances. Some movie reviewers use a star system to tell how good or bad a movie is, with five stars being the best.

  Help students preview "A Film with a Message of Hope."

  - What features do you see? (*scenes from the movie, boxed information, five stars*) What does the boxed information tell you? (*names of the stars, running time, and name of the director*)

  Then have students set a purpose for reading based on their preview.

- **During Reading or Revisiting** Have students read along with you while tracking the print. Stop to discuss any unfamiliar words, such as *typical* and *optimism.*

- **After Reading or Revisiting** Have students share their reactions to the review. What was the reviewer's idea about the message of the story? (*The relationship between Opal and her dog offers a positive message about the value of friendship.*) Then guide them through the Reading Across Texts and Writing Across Texts activities.

MONITOR PROGRESS

If... students have difficulty retelling the main selection,
then... have them review the story using the photos.

Objectives

- Explain how an author uses language to present information to influence what the reader thinks or does.

Strategic Intervention

DAY 5

For a complete literacy instructional plan and additional practice with this week's target skills and strategies, see the **Leveled Reader Teaching Guide.**

Concept Literacy Reader

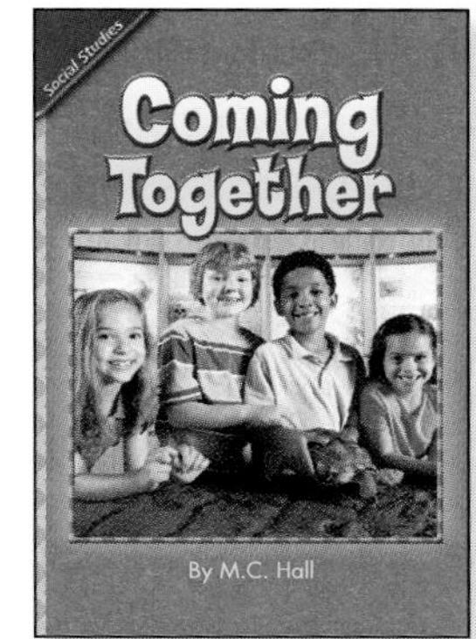
Coming Together

- **Model** Model the fluency skill, appropriate phrasing, for students. Ask students to listen carefully as you read aloud the first two pages of *Coming Together.* Have students note the grouping of your words and the rise and fall of your voice.
- **Fluency Routine**
  1. Have students reread passages from *Coming Together* with a partner.
  2. For optimal fluency, students should reread three to four times.
  3. As students read, monitor fluency and provide corrective feedback. Have students note the grouping of your words and the rise and fall of your voice.

  See *Routines Flip Chart* for more help with fluency.
- **Retell** Have students retell *Coming Together* and prompt as necessary.

Below-Level Reader

Florida Everglades: Its Plants & Animals

- **Model** Ask students to listen carefully as you read aloud the first two pages of *Florida Everglades: Its Plants & Animals,* emphasizing appropriate phrasing.
- **Fluency Routine**
  1. Have students reread passages from *Florida Everglades: Its Plants & Animals* with a partner or individually.
  2. For optimal fluency, they should reread three to four times.
  3. As students read, monitor fluency and provide corrective feedback. Discuss how stressing important words creates a more natural rhythm.

  See *Routines Flip Chart* for more help with fluency.
- **Retell** For additional practice, have students retell *Florida Everglades: Its Plants & Animals* page by page, using the illustrations. Prompt as necessary.
  - What happens in this part?
  - What dangers do the bears face?

MONITOR PROGRESS

If... students have difficulty reading fluently,
then... provide additional fluency practice by pairing nonfluent readers with fluent ones.

Objectives
- Read aloud grade-level stories with fluency.

Pacing Small Group Instruction

5-Day Plan

DAY 1	• Expand the concept • Read On-Level Reader
DAY 2	• Sequence • Summarize • Revisit Student Edition pp. 26–31
DAY 3	• Suffixes • Revisit Student Edition pp. 32–37
DAY 4	• Practice Retelling • Read/Revisit Student Edition pp. 42–43
DAY 5	• Reread for fluency • Reread On-Level Reader

3- or 4-Day Plan

DAY 1	• Expand the concept • Read On-Level Reader
DAY 2	• Sequence • Summarize • Revisit Student Edition pp. 26–31
DAY 3	• Suffixes • Revisit Student Edition pp. 32–37
DAY 4	• Practice Retelling • Read/Revisit Student Edition pp. 42–43 • Reread for fluency • Reread On-Level Reader

3-Day Plan: Eliminate the shaded box.

Build Background

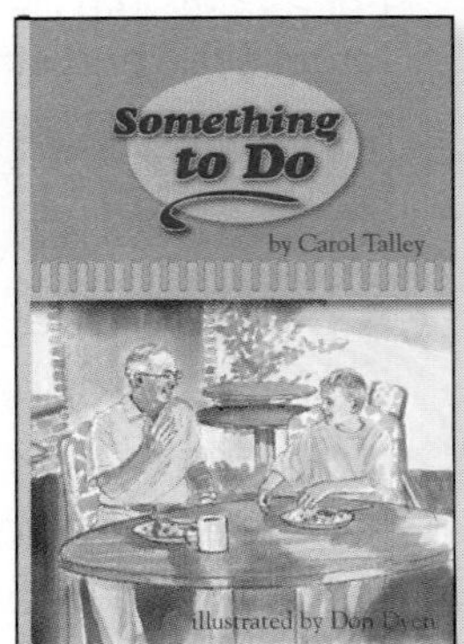

Something to Do

■ **Expand the Concept** Connect to the weekly question (*What experiences bring diverse people together?*) and expand the concept. When we spend time with older people, such as grandparents, we can learn from them and they can learn from us. Discuss the meanings of the words on the concept map.

On-Level Reader

For a complete literacy instructional plan and additional practice with this week's target skills and strategies, see the **Leveled Reader Teaching Guide.**

■ **Before Reading** *Something to Do*, have students preview the reader by looking at the title, cover, and all the pictures in the book. Notice that the grandfather appears more often in the pictures than any other character.

- Who is this story mostly about?
- What is the topic of this book?

■ **During Reading** Read aloud the first three pages of the book as students follow along. Then have them finish reading the book on their own. Remind students that keeping track of the sequence, or order, of events in a story can help them understand what happens. Tell them that sometimes a sequence describes steps in a process. Suggest that they look for clue words as they read, such as *while, then, now, next,* and *after.*

■ **After Reading** Remind students that remembering information in a book can help them keep track of the main idea in a story.

- What activities were suggested to the grandfather? (*walking, pyrography, making fried pies*) How did the grandfather respond to these suggestions?
- How does this story relate to the weekly question *What experiences bring diverse people together?* (*It shows how the grandfather learns to do something new as he adjusts to his new environment.*)

Objectives
- Participate in teacher-led discussions by answering questions with appropriate detail.

On-Level

DAY 2

Expand Comprehension

Skill Sequence Use p. 22 to review the definition of sequence. For additional review, see p. EI•13 in *Envision It!* Sometimes the sequence in a story is interrupted by a flashback that tells about something that happened in the past. Flashbacks might begin with clue words such as "a long time ago" or "back then."

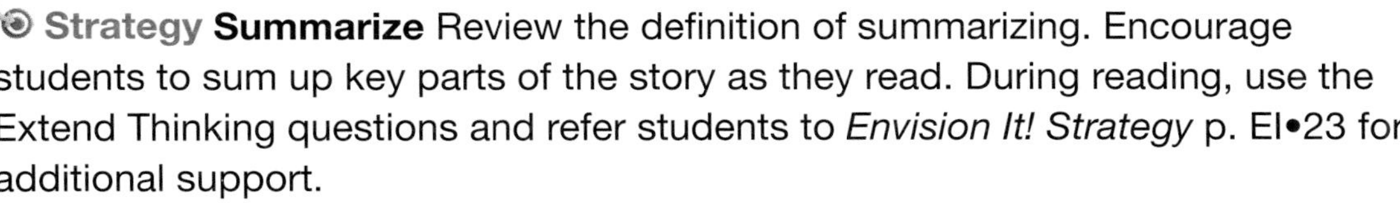

Strategy Summarize Review the definition of summarizing. Encourage students to sum up key parts of the story as they read. During reading, use the Extend Thinking questions and refer students to *Envision It! Strategy* p. EI•23 for additional support.

Revisit *Because of Winn-Dixie* on pp. 26–31. As students read, help them apply the comprehension skill and strategy to the story.

- Summarize the reason Winn-Dixie looks in the window of the library. (*The dog does not like being separated from Opal, so she teaches him to watch her through the window.*)
- When did a bear come into the Herman W. Block Memorial Library? How do you know? (*It came into the library long ago. The words "a long time ago" tell when it happened.*)

Objectives

- Sequence the plot's main events.
- Summarize the plot's main events.

Student Edition, p. EI•13

More Reading

Use additional Leveled Readers or other texts at students' instructional levels to reinforce this week's skills and strategies. For text suggestions, see the Leveled Reader Database or the Leveled Readers Skills Chart on pp. CL 24–CL 29.

Expand Vocabulary

Suffixes/Word Structure Write the word *memorial* as you say it aloud. Ask students to identify the suffix (*-al*). Then ask:

- What word is the base word? (*memory*)
- What does the suffix *-al* mean? Look it up in *Words!* on p. W•6 or in a dictionary. (*"of" or "like"*)
- What meaning do you get when you combine the meaning of *memory* with the suffix? (*"a memory of"*)

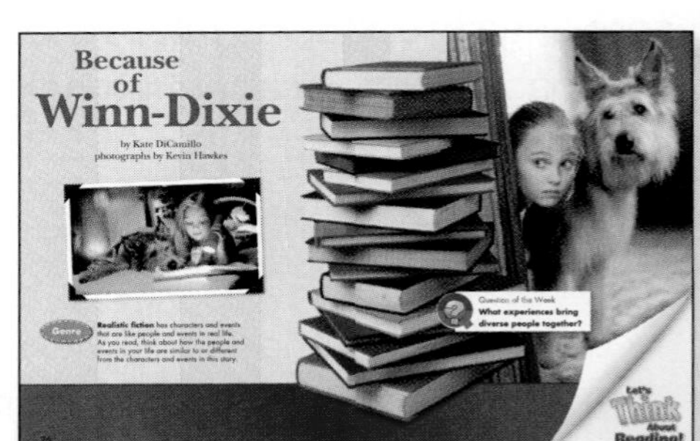

Revisit *Because of Winn-Dixie* on pp. 32–37. Then review *Words!* on p. W•6. Encourage students to apply the skill and strategy as they read to figure out any unfamiliar words.

- Notice the word *wonderful* on p. 32. What does the suffix *-ful* mean? (*"full of"*)
- How did Miss Franny get the bear to leave? (*She threw a book at him.*)

Critical Thinking Prompt students to think critically as they read. How do you know the story about the bear is a flashback? (*Miss Franny was a young girl in the story.*)

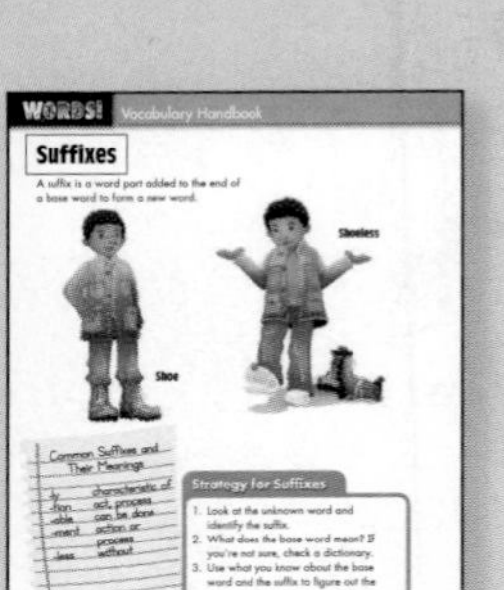

Student Edition, p. W•6

More Reading

Use additional Leveled Readers or other texts at students' instructional levels to reinforce this week's skills and strategies. For text suggestions, see the Leveled Reader Database or the Leveled Readers Skills Chart on pp. CL 24–CL 29.

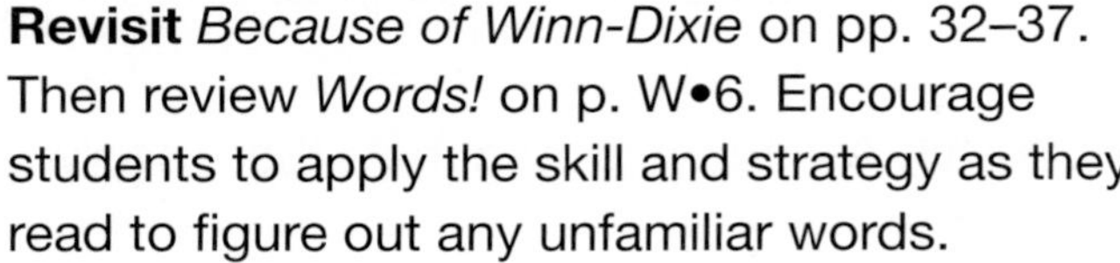

Objectives

- Determine meaning of grade-level academic English words derived from other linguistic affixes.
- Use word structure to analyze and decode new words.

On-Level

DAY 4

Practice Retelling

- **Retell** To assess students' comprehension, use the Retelling Cards. Monitor retelling and prompt students as needed.

Genre Focus

- **Before Reading or Revisiting** "A Film with a Message of Hope" pp. 42–43, read aloud the genre information about movie reviews on p. 42. Have students preview "A Film with a Message of Hope." Then have students set a purpose for reading based on their preview.
- **During Reading or Revisiting** Have students read along with you while tracking the print, or do a choral reading. Stop to discuss any unfamiliar words, such as *typical* and *optimism.* What does the author think about the actors' performances in the movie?
- **After Reading or Revisiting** Have students share their reactions to the movie review. Then guide them through the Reading Across Texts and Writing Across Texts activities.
    - Do you agree with the reviewer's ideas about the message of the story?
    - How is this movie review different from *Because of Winn-Dixie*?

  Have students write a brief review of a movie they have seen.

Objectives

- Explain how an author uses language to present information to influence what the reader thinks or does.

On-Level Reader

Something to Do

- **Model** Have students listen closely as you read aloud pp. 3–4 of *Something to Do,* emphasizing appropriate phrasing. Read the pages again as students track the print. Ask them to notice how you use punctuation to help phrase your reading.
- **Fluency Routine**

1. Have students reread passages from *Something to Do* with a partner.
2. For optimal fluency, students should reread passages three to four times.
3. As students read, monitor fluency and provide corrective feedback. Have students note the grouping of their words into phrases and the rise and fall of their voices. Discuss how reading with a natural rhythm is much more pleasing than reading word by word.

See *Routines Flip Chart* for more help with fluency.

- **Retell** For additional practice, have students use illustrations as a guide to retell *Something to Do.* Prompt as necessary.
  - What did you learn from reading this page?
  - Why do you think the artist chose to draw this illustration? How does it relate to the story?
  - Do you think it was easy or difficult for the grandfather to move in with his son and grandson? Why?

Objectives

- Read aloud grade-level stories with fluency.

DAY 1

Build Background

The Story of Libraries

- **Extend the Concept** Discuss the weekly question *What experiences bring diverse people together?* When you meet new people, you can learn about their customs, attitudes, and backgrounds. Think about a time you went somewhere new. What did you learn about people there? Discuss the meaning of each word in the concept map.

Advanced Reader

For a complete literacy instructional plan and additional practice with this week's target skills and strategies, see the **Leveled Reader Teaching Guide.**

- **Before Reading** *The Story of Libraries*, have students skim the text and predict what they will learn about libraries from the selection. Have students set a purpose for reading.
- **During Reading** Have students read *The Story of Libraries* independently.
  - What happened to libraries after the fall of the Roman Empire? (*Muslims preserved libraries, which continued to thrive in the East.*)
  - How did the codex influence how books look today? (*The codex gave books the shape we know today.*)
  - What prompted the Junto to form a lending library? (*Members needed books to write their essays, but not all members could afford to buy books.*)
- **After Reading** Have students review the concept map and explain how *The Story of Libraries* helps students answer the weekly question.
  - What information about faraway places can you find in libraries?
  - How do libraries provide information about diverse people in the world?
- **Now Try This** Assign "Now Try This" at the end of the Advanced Reader.

Objectives

- Participate in teacher-led discussions by answering questions with appropriate detail.

Pacing Small Group Instruction

15–20 min

5-Day Plan

DAY 1	• Extend the concept • Read Advanced Reader
DAY 2	• Sequence • Summarize • Revisit Student Edition pp. 26–31
DAY 3	• Suffixes • Revisit Student Edition pp. 32–37
DAY 4	• Genre Focus • Read/Revisit Student Edition pp. 42–43
DAY 5	• Reread for fluency • Reread Advanced Reader

3- or 4-Day Plan

DAY 1	• Extend the concept • Read Advanced Reader
DAY 2	• Sequence • Summarize • Revisit Student Edition pp. 26–31
DAY 3	• Suffixes • Revisit Student Edition pp. 32–37
DAY 4	• Genre Focus • Read/Revisit Student Edition pp. 42–43 • Reread for fluency • Reread Advanced Reader

3-Day Plan: Eliminate the shaded box.

Use additional Leveled Readers or other texts at students' instructional levels to reinforce this week's skills and strategies. For text suggestions, see the Leveled Reader Database or the Leveled Readers Skills Chart on pp. CL 24–CL 29.

Extend Comprehension

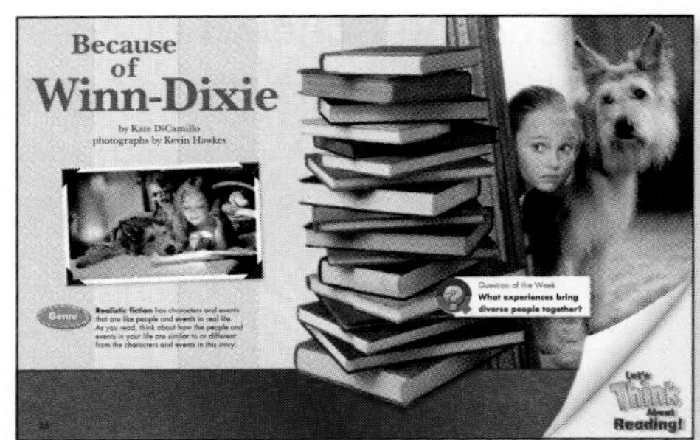

Skill Sequence Use p. 22 to review the definition of *sequence.* Explain that some clue words indicate events happening at the same time (*meanwhile, during,* etc.). Also explain that a flashback takes the reader to an event in the past. Think of *The Story of Libraries,* which you just read. Name two events that happened at about the same time. Name two events that happened at very different times. Then explain how libraries changed over time.

Strategy Summarize Review the definition of summarizing. Remind students to sum up parts as they read the rest of *Because of Winn-Dixie.* During reading, use the Extend Thinking questions and the During Reading Differentiated Instruction for additional support.

- **Revisit** *Because of Winn-Dixie* on pp. 26–31, reminding students to track the sequence and summarize key events.
- **Critical Thinking** As students read, encourage them to think critically.
  - What happened in Opal's life before the story opens?
  - How does Miss Franny react to seeing Winn-Dixie in the window?
  - Why did she react this way?
  - What part of the story do you think will be a flashback?
- **Problem Solving** Encourage students to problem solve. How could Miss Franny Block make her library safe from unwanted visitors, such as wild animals?

Objectives

- Sequence the plot's main events.
- Summarize the plot's main events.

Extend Vocabulary

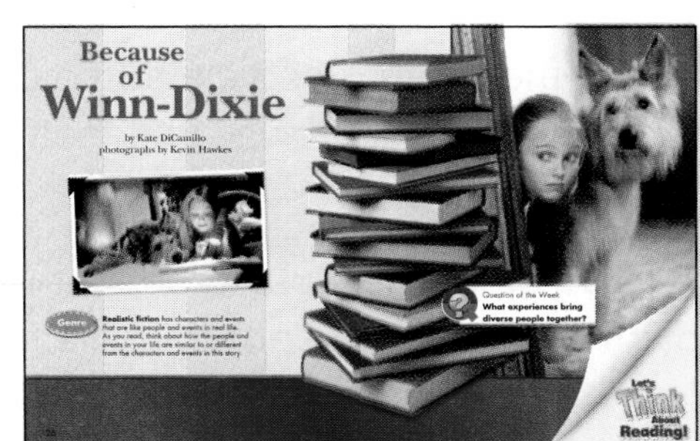

Suffixes/Word Structure Read this sentence: "I spent a lot of time that summer at the Herman W. Block Memorial Library." Model interpreting suffixes. I recognize the suffix *-al* in the word *memorial.* I know that *-al* can mean "of" or "like." I think *memorial* relates to being "a memory of" someone or something. Perhaps the library was named in memory of Herman W. Block.

Read these sentences from the story: "He most certainly is a large dog." "Let me get a chair and sit down so I can tell this story properly." What suffix do you hear in both sentences? (*-ly*) The suffix *-ly* means "in the manner of." Therefore, the words you heard mean "in a certain manner" and "in a proper manner." Challenge students to find other words in the story that end with *-ly* (*hardly, silly, lonely, slowly*) and to use a dictionary to find out if the letters make up a suffix in each case.

- **Revisit** *Because of Winn-Dixie* on pp. 32–37.
- **Critical Thinking** Encourage students to think critically about the vivid language. For example, ask:
  - Why do you think Miss Franny says "mosquitoes so big they could fly away with you" instead of just "big mosquitoes"?
  - Why do you think the author describes how the bear smelled and how big he was?
- **Creative Thinking** Encourage students to think creatively.
  - What might happen next in the story?
  - What might Opal's next adventure be?

Objectives

- Determine meaning of grade-level academic English words derived from other linguistic affixes.
- Use word structure to analyze and decode new words.

More Reading

Use additional Leveled Readers or other texts at students' instructional levels to reinforce this week's skills and strategies. For text suggestions, see the Leveled Reader Database or the Leveled Readers Skills Chart on pp. CL 24–CL 29.

Genre Focus

- **Before Reading or Revisiting** “A Film with a Message of Hope” pp. 42–43, have students preview the article on their own. Read aloud the panel information on movie reviews. Then have students use text features to set a purpose.
- **During Reading or Revisiting** Have students find words that reveal the author’s purpose. Then prompt students to remember details. The author says several positive things about the film. Name at least three. (*It is a “charming movie that will not disappoint.” The actress playing Opal is “absolutely perfect in the role.” The other actors give “outstanding performances.” It is a “wonderful family film with a positive message.”*) Point out that movie reviews are not always positive. Often, they criticize a movie and advise readers not to see it.
- **After Reading or Revisiting** Have students discuss Reading Across Texts and do Writing Across Texts independently.

“A Film with a Message of Hope”

Objectives

- Explain how an author uses language to present information to influence what the reader thinks or does.

DAY 5

- **Reread for Fluency** Have students silently reread passages from *The Story of Libraries.* Then have them reread aloud with a partner or individually. As students read, monitor fluency and provide corrective feedback. If students read fluently on the first reading, they do not need to reread three to four times. Assess the fluency of students in this group using p. 45j.
- **Retell** Have students summarize the main idea and key details from *The Story of Libraries.*
- **Now Try This** Have students complete their projects. You may wish to review their initial floor plans to see if they need additional ideas.

The Story of Libraries

Objectives

- Read aloud grade-level stories with fluency.

The ELL lessons are organized by strands. Use them to scaffold the weekly curriculum of lessons or during small group time instruction.

Academic Language

Students will read the following academic language in this week's core instruction. As students encounter the vocabulary, provide a simple definition or concrete example. Have students speak giving an example or synonym of the word and identify available cognates. This allows students to internalize new English words.

Skill Words	sequence summarize cause *(causa)*	expression *(expressión)* vivid words effect *(efecto)*
Concept Words	diversity *(diversidad)* concert *(concierto)*	orchestra *(orquesta)*

** Spanish cognates in parentheses*

Concept Development

What experiences bring diverse people together?

■ **Preteach Concept**

- **Prior Knowledge** Have students turn to pp. 20–21 in the Student Edition. Call attention to the pictures of the children working in the garden and on the house and tap into students' knowledge of working together. What are these children doing together? Have you ever worked with other kids on a project? What was it? Do you like working with other kids? Why or why not?
- **Discuss Concept** Elicit students' knowledge and experience of diverse people being brought together. Did you notice that the people in the pictures come from different backgrounds and yet they are all working together? Why do you think this is so? What are some reasons people like to work together?
- **Poster Talk-Through** Read aloud the Poster Talk-Through on ELL Poster 1 and work through the Day 1 activities.

■ **Daily Concept and Vocabulary Development** Use the daily activities on ELL Poster 1 to build concept and vocabulary knowledge

Objectives

- Use prior knowledge to understand meanings in English.
- Speak using grade-level content area vocabulary in context to internalize new English words and build academic language proficiency.

Daily Planner

DAY 1	• **Frontload Concept** • **Preteach** Comprehension Skill, Vocabulary, Phonics/Spelling, Conventions • **Writing**
DAY 2	• **Review** Concept, Vocabulary, Comprehension Skill • **Frontload Main Selection** • **Practice** Phonics/Spelling, Conventions/Writing
DAY 3	• **Review** Concept, Comprehension Skill, Vocabulary, Conventions/Writing • **Reread Main Selection** • **Practice** Phonics/Spelling
DAY 4	• **Review Concept** • **Read ELL/ELD Readers** • **Practice** Phonics/Spelling, Conventions/Writing
DAY 5	• **Review** Concept, Vocabulary, Comprehension Skill, Phonics/Spelling, Conventions • **Reread ELL/ELD Readers** • **Writing**

See the ELL Handbook for ELL Workshops with targeted instruction.

Concept Talk Video

Use the Concept Talk Video Routine (*ELL Handbook*, p. 477) to build background knowledge about bringing diverse people together. Have students respond orally to information presented in the video to build and reinforce concept attainment.

Language Objectives

- Understand and use basic vocabulary.
- Learn meanings of grade-level vocabulary.

Cognates

For Spanish learners, point out that the word for *grand* is spelled *grandioso* in Spanish. Reinforce the concept that these languages share many words that are the same or similar.

ELL Workshop

Provide opportunities for students to practice new basic and academic vocabulary by working with *Learn New Words* (*ELL Handbook,* pp. 402–403).

ELL English Language Learners

Basic Vocabulary

- **High-Frequency Words** Use the ELL Vocabulary Routine on p. 471 of the *ELL Handbook* to systematically teach newcomers the first 300 sight words in English necessary for identifying and describing people, places, and objects. Students will learn words 1–10 this week *(ELL Handbook,* p. 447). Page 446 of the handbook contains a bank of strategies to use to ensure students' mastery of high-frequency words needed to internalize new basic language and to build academic language.

Lesson Vocabulary

- **Preteach** Introduce the Lesson Vocabulary using this routine:

1. Distribute copies of this week's Word Cards (*ELL Handbook*, p. 29).
2. Display ELL Poster 1 and reread the Poster Talk-Through.
3. Using the poster illustrations, model how a word's meaning can be expressed with other similar words: The *prideful* band thought they did a good job of playing the song.
4. Use these sentences to reveal the meanings of the other words.
   - After Coach Brown's retirement, our school renamed the football field "Mark Brown *Memorial* Field." (preserving the memory of someone)
   - My grandmother *recalls* the days when there was no television. (remembers)
   - The fruit had a *peculiar* taste to it. (unusual)
   - We had a *grand* time at the lake. (great)
   - I'm *positive* I locked the back door. (certain)
   - Juan spent a lot of time *selecting* his clothes for today. (choosing)

Objectives

- Expand and internalize initial English vocabulary by learning and using high-frequency English words necessary for identifying and describing people, places, and objects, by retelling simple stories and basic information represented or supported by pictures, and by learning and using routine language needed for classroom communication.
- Use visual and contextual support and support from peers and teachers to read grade-appropriate content area text, enhance and confirm understanding, and develop vocabulary, grasp of language structures, and background knowledge needed to comprehend increasingly challenging language.

- **Reteach** Ask questions to check students' understanding of the vocabulary.
  - Can you think of an example of a *memorial* in our area? (answers will vary)
  - What is one characteristic of a *prideful* person? (overly proud)
  - What is the earliest memory you can *recall*? (answers will vary)
  - What is another word that means *peculiar*? (possible answer: unusual)
  - Is a *grand* time good or bad? (very good)
  - If you are *positive* you know the answer, you are ________. (absolutely certain)
  - What is the root word in *selecting*? (select)
  - What is a synonym of *select*? (choose)
- **Writing** Distribute the Word Cards facedown. Working in pairs, have one student look at the word and complete the Word Grid, leaving the box for "Word" blank. Have the other student read the clues aloud, and then write the correct word in the box. Shuffle and redistribute the Word Cards so that each student has the opportunity to write a sentence and to guess a word.

Beginning Have students draw pictures or use gestures to show their understanding. Then write the word for them and have them copy it.

Intermediate students give an example or use phrases.

Advanced/Advanced High Have students use complete sentences. Assist if necessary.

Directionality

The directionality of some languages is different from English. For example, Arabic and Hebrew read from right to left, and some Asian languages read from top to bottom. Students who speak these languages need more exposure to print concepts through oral reading activities of books and classroom materials. When students write, have them think about the left-to-right direction in which they are writing. Point out that when writing in English they should write from left to right.

Objectives

- Speak using learning strategies such as requesting assistance, employing non-verbal cues, and using synonyms and circumlocution (conveying ideas by defining or describing when exact English words are not known).
- Recognize directionality of English reading such as left to right and top to bottom.
- Write using newly acquired basic vocabulary and content-based grade-level vocabulary.

Language Objectives

- Produce drawings, phrases, and short sentences to show understanding of Lesson Vocabulary.

ELL Teacher Tip

Have students learn new words, while speaking, using this learning strategy. When asking the vocabulary questions at the top of the page, tell students they should convey ideas by defining or describing when exact English words are not known. Tell students to ask for assistance when they do not understand the questions. Employ non-verbal clues for students when necessary.

Graphic Organizer

Word	Definition
Picture	Example

ELL Workshop

Provide opportunities for students to give information using new abstract and content-based vocabulary. *Give a Speech* (*ELL Handbook*, pp. 412–413) supports students with their speaking.

Content Objectives

- Monitor and adjust oral comprehension.

Language Objectives

- Use and discuss oral passages to learn new and essential language.
- Use a graphic organizer to take notes.

Graphic Organizer

Beginning
↓
Middle
↓
End

ELL Teacher Tip

Have students contribute to the reading of the text by chorusing repetitive words or phrases or reading sight words that you point to.

ELL English Language Learners

Listening Comprehension

Read Aloud

A Perfect Match

Laura had a fever for several months. The sickness made her blind and deaf. It took a whole year before she could walk again. It took a couple of years until she was nearly as strong as most children her age.

Laura's neighbor was a man named Asa Tenney. Most people thought that Asa was a little odd. He didn't have many friends. Since he didn't have many friends, he cared about other living things. He made friends with many animals. All the neighborhood dogs loved him because he always had a treat for them.

When Asa found out Laura was sick, he felt bad. He wanted to help her. He asked Laura's parents if he could help Laura in any way. They thought visiting her to keep her company would help. He began to visit her every day. He helped teach her things. He also helped her get strong again.

Asa helped Laura get healthy. And she helped him have someone to care about. They were a perfect match.

Prepare for the Read Aloud The modified Read Aloud and the graphic organizer prepares students for listening to the oral reading "Child of the Silent Night" on p. 21b. These pre-reading supports enhance comprehension.

- **First Listening: Listen to Understand** Use the Read Aloud to help students learn new and essential language. Write the title of the Read Aloud on the board. This is a story about an older man and a little girl. Listen to find out how they become friends. What experience brings them together? Afterward, ask the questions again and have students share their answers using essential language in the process.
- **Second Listening: Listen to Check Understanding** Using Story Map B (*ELL Handbook,* p. 484) work with students to describe the characters and relate the events of the story. How would you describe Laura? How would you describe Asa? How do Asa and Laura come together? Fill in the Story Map together as students answer the questions.

Objectives

- Use accessible language and learn new and essential language in the process.
- Use prereading supports such as graphic organizers, illustrations, and pretaught topic-related vocabulary and other prereading activities to enhance comprehension of written materials.

Phonics and Spelling

- **Short vowel VCCV** Use Sound-Spelling Card 147 to teach the sounds, pronunciations, and spellings of short vowel VCCV pattern.
  - Display card 147 to teach short vowel spelling VCCV pattern. This is *basket*. /b/ /a/ /s/ /k/ /i/ /t/. Point out that there are two vowel sounds in *basket* and therefore two syllables. How many consonants do you see between the vowels *a* and *e* in the word *basket*? That's right, there are two consonants between the vowels. Now, let's break the word into syllables: *bas/ket*. *Basket*. How many syllables does the word *basket* have?
  - Write *finger* on the board. *Finger*. /f/ /i/ /n/ /g/ /ə/ /r/. Underline the two consonants between the vowels *i* and *e*. There are two consonants between two vowels in this word. Each vowel means that there is a syllable, so we know that there are two syllables in this pattern. Remind students that a word has as many syllables as it has vowel sounds. Let's break the word into syllables: *fin/ger*. *Finger*. How many syllables does the word *finger* have?
  - Have students write out the spelling patterns to reinforce this lesson by repeating this routine using the words *admire, soccer,* and *happen.*

Word Analysis: Word Ending *-ed*

- **Preteach/Model** Write these verbs on the board. Then read them, asking students to pay close attention to the sound at the end of each word: *walked*, *enjoyed*, *liked*, *talked*, *played*, *measured*. Ask students if they noticed a difference in the way the final *-ed* was pronounced. Confirm that *enjoyed*, *played*, and *measured* are pronounced with the /d/ sound and *walked*, *liked*, and *talked* are pronounced with the sound of /t/.
- **Practice** Write these verbs on the board: *call*, *fix, rub*, *help*, *open*, *wash*. Provide practice for students at their language proficiency level.

Beginning/Intermediate Read the words aloud with students. Have Beginners come to the board and form *-ed* words. Call on Intermediates to read the words aloud and say whether the words end with the /d/ or /t/ sound.

Advanced/Advanced High Have students say and write the past tense form of these verbs, and then write a sentence using each word.

Objectives

- Spell familiar English words with increasing accuracy, and employ English spelling patterns and rules with increasing accuracy as more English is acquired.
- Write using newly acquired basic vocabulary and content-based grade-level vocabulary.

Content Objectives

- Identify and define words ending in *-ed.*
- Identify words with short vowel VCCV pattern.
- Review multisyllabic words.

Language Objectives

- Write using phonics patterns and decoding skills with newly acquired vocabulary.
- Write and discuss the meanings and sounds of words ending in *-ed.*

Transfer Skills

Multisyllabic Words

Speakers of monosyllabic languages such as Cantonese, Hmong, Khmer, Korean, and Vietnamese may pronounce a two-syllable word as two separate words. Have students practice saying multisyllabic words.

ELL Teaching Routine

For more practice with short vowel words, use the Sound-by-Sound Blending Routine (*ELL Handbook,* p. 472).

Content Objectives

- Order the sequence of events in a text.

Language Objectives

- Discuss following directions in a text.
- Retell sequence from a reading.
- Write sequence from personal experience.

ELL Workshop

Encourage students to ask questions to monitor their understanding of instruction of comprehension skills. Use *Ask Clarifying Questions* (*ELL Handbook,* pp. 404–405) for practice.

ELL English Language Learners

Comprehension
Sequence

■ **Preteach** Events in a text take place in a certain time-order called sequence. We use sequence when we list the steps in a process. Have students turn to p. 22 in the Student Edition. Read aloud the text together on Sequence. Tell students that it is important for them to develop basic sight vocabulary written in classroom materials. Have students identify the correct sequence. Point out that students can use the arrows as clues.

■ **Reteach** Distribute copies of the Picture It! *(ELL Handbook,* p. 30). Have students read the captions next to the pictures in order. What happens first? What happens next? Read the directions aloud and help students complete the organizer. Remind students to seek clarification if they have difficulty following directions. (First: Ayako and Julie decide to share lunches. Next: Ayako gives Julie a rice ball. Then: Julie gives Ayako a cheese sandwich. Last: The girls praise each other's lunches.)

Beginning/Intermediate Display a copy of the graphic organizer. Write students' responses as you ask, "What happened first?" and so on. Have students copy the organizer and retell the story to a partner.

Advanced/Advanced High Have pairs of students cut out the pictures without the text. Have them arrange the pictures in chronological order and retell the story in their own words.

MINI-LESSON

Social Language

Have students look at the Envision It! on p. EI•13. Remind students that when they describe events in sequence, they tell specific details about what happens first, next, then, and last. Have students practice these expressions by asking them questions such as: What do we do first when we start our school day? What do we do next? After that what do we do? What is the last thing we do before we start our school day? Be sure students describe the events with increasing specificity and detail as more English is acquired.

Objectives

- Describe with increasing specificity and detail as more English is acquired.
- Develop basic sight vocabulary, derive meaning of environmental print, and comprehend English vocabulary and language structures used routinely in written classroom materials.

Reading Comprehension
Because of Winn-Dixie

Student Edition pp. 26–27

- **Frontloading** Read the title aloud. Tell students that "Winn-Dixie" is a chain of grocery stores in the southeast United States. I wonder what important experience takes place in Winn-Dixie? Let's look through the selection to find out. Guide students on a picture walk. Have advanced students read captions and subheads aloud for visual and contextual support to develop background knowledge for comprehension. Ask students to predict what important event takes place in Winn-Dixie and record their predictions. During reading, have students adjust their predictions by filling out Story Map B.

  Sheltered Reading Ask questions to guide students' comprehension:

  - p. 28: Which character in the selection is named Winn-Dixie? (Opal's dog) Why did she give him that name? (because she found him in a Winn-Dixie)
  - pp. 29–30: Why was Miss Franny frightened by Winn-Dixie at first? (She thought he was a bear.)
  - pp. 30–36: Describe the characters of Opal and Miss Franny. How are they the same? How are they different? (Both characters are friendly and sympathetic. They are different because they are different ages and have had different experiences.)
  - p. 37: Is Amanda Wilkerson a nice character? What clues help you? (She is described as "pinch-faced" and she is not friendly at all to Opal.)

- **Fluency: Read with Expression** Remind students that reading with expression means to read with emotion. Read the first paragraph on p. 31 and model how to read expressively using intonation by raising or lowering their tone of voice. Point out the quotation marks at the beginning of the paragraph, and tell students that quotation marks show that a character is speaking. Have pairs choose a paragraph on p. 32 to read with intonation as their partners listen and offer feedback.

  After Reading Help students summarize the text with the Retelling Cards. Ask questions that prompt students to summarize important parts of the text.

Objectives
- Distinguish sounds and intonation patterns of English with increasing ease.
- Use visual, contextual, and linguistic support to enhance and confirm understanding of increasingly complex and elaborated spoken language.

Content Objectives
- Monitor and adjust comprehension.
- Make and adjust predictions.

Language Objectives
- Read grade-level text with expression and intonation.
- Summarize text using visual and contextual support to aid comprehension.

Graphic Organizer

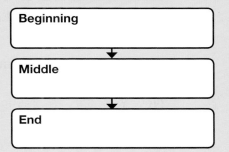

Beginning
↓
Middle
↓
End

Audio Support
Students can prepare for reading *Because of Winn-Dixie* by using the eSelection or the AudioText CD (*ELL Handbook,* page 477).

ELL English Language Learners

For additional leveled instruction, see the **ELL/ELD Reader Teaching Guide.**

Comprehension
World Concert

- **Before Reading** Distribute copies of the ELL and ELD Readers, *World Concert*, to students at their reading level.
  - **Preview** Read the title aloud with students. This is realistic fiction about a group of children from all over the world who go to New York City to play in a concert together. Invite students to look through the pictures and name what they see. Have them predict what kinds of experiences the children will have based on the picture clues and their prior knowledge.
  - **Set a Purpose for Reading** Let's read to learn more about the children's experience of going to New York City to play in a concert together.

ELD Reader ELL Reader

- **During Reading** Follow the Reading Routine for both reading groups.

1. Read the entire Reader aloud slowly.
2. Reread pp. 1–4, pausing to build background or model comprehension. Use the questions in the chart to check students' comprehension.
3. Have students reread pp. 1–4 in pairs, taking turns reading alternate pages.
4. Repeat steps 2–3 above for pp. 5–8 of the Reader.

- **After Reading** Use the exercises in each Reader and invite students to share their writing. Ask students, Which character did you find most interesting? Why? Record their answers on the board and invite them to point to pictures in the book to support their answers.

ELD Reader Beginning/Intermediate

- **p. 2** Where did children from all over the world go to play a concert? (New York)
- **p. 8** Pedro was nervous at the beginning of the concert. How did he feel at the end of the concert? (He wasn't nervous anymore.)

Writing Which character in the story is most interesting to you? Find the sentence in the book that describes this character. Copy the sentence. Then read it aloud to your partner.

ELL Reader Advanced/Advanced High

- **p. 2** Describe what happens first in the story. (Children from all over the world come to New York to play in a concert.)
- **pp. 4–8** How do Pedro's feelings change from the beginning of the concert to the end of the concert? (At first he was nervous, but afterward he wasn't.)

Study Guide Distribute copies of the ELL Reader Study Guide (*ELL Handbook*, p. 34). Scaffold comprehension of event sequence by helping students look back through the Reader in order to answer the questions in the graphic organizer. (See *ELL Handbook*, pp. 209–212.)

Objectives

- Understand the general meaning, main points, and important details of spoken language ranging from situations in which topics, language, and contexts are familiar to unfamiliar.

Conventions
Declarative and Interrogative Sentences

- **Preteach** Display these sentences: *What is your favorite food? My favorite food is oatmeal.* Read the sentences aloud. Look at these two sentences. The first sentence asks something and ends with a question mark. A sentence that asks something is called an interrogative sentence. The second sentence starts with a capital letter and ends with a period. It tells something. A sentence that tells something is called a declarative sentence. Model the difference in intonation between these two sentences and emphasize the difference between the sentence lengths.

- **Practice** Have pairs of students ask each other questions about what they did yesterday using varying sentence lengths and intonation in their tone.

Beginning Students can draw pictures or use gestures.

Intermediate Have students use the following sentence frames: *What did we do in school yesterday? Yesterday we ________. What is your favorite subject? My favorite subject is ________.* Challenge students to use these sentence frames as models for their own questions.

Advanced/Advanced High Have students speak using complete sentences.

- **Reteach** Have students reread the story on the Picture It! page *(ELL Handbook*, p.1). Then display the following question: Who is sitting with Ayako? What kind of sentence did I write? (interrogative) How do you know? (It asks a question and ends with a question mark.) Who can write a sentence that answers the question? Invite a volunteer to write the answer. (Julie is sitting with Ayako.) What kind of sentence did you write? (declarative) How do you know? (It tells something and ends with a period.)

- **Practice** Have pairs of students ask more questions about the events in the story. Then have them exchange papers and write declarative sentences to answer their partner's questions in varying lengths.

Beginning Have students can point to the pictures and use gestures or draw pictures.

Intermediate Have students can write using single words or phrases.

Advanced/Advanced High Have students write using complete sentences.

Objectives
- Distinguish sounds and intonation patterns of English with increasing ease.
- Speak using a variety of grammatical structures, sentence lengths, sentence types, and connecting words with increasing accuracy and ease as more English is acquired.

Content Objectives
- Distinguish and use declarative and interrogative sentences.

Language Objectives
- Speak using varying patterns of declarative and interrogative sentences with intonation.
- Write declarative and interrogative sentences.

Transfer Skills
Speakers of Chinese, Vietnamese, and other Asian languages often form questions by adding words to statements, comparable to *The food is hot, no?* or *You see or not see the bird?* Provide model English questions for students to understand and to follow the patterns.

Content Objectives

- Identify vivid words in a text.

Language Objectives

- Write a narrative paragraph using vivid words.
- Edit for appropriate verb tense.

ELL Teaching Routine

For practice spelling words related to bringing diverse people together, use the Spelling Routine (*ELL Handbook,* p. 476).

ELL Workshop

Students can collaborate with peers to discuss their writing. *Discuss with Classmates* (*ELL Handbook,* pp. 418–419) provides assistance with discussion.

ELL English Language Learners

Writing with Vivid Words

- **Introduce** Display the narrative paragraph model and read it aloud. Review that vivid words make our writing more interesting and provide details. Vivid words help us say exactly what we want to say. The writer of this paragraph did not use vivid words. Instead of writing "There are trees in my backyard," you can write "There are tall trees with full green leaves towering over my backyard." Write the new sentence and underline the vivid words. Tell students to close their eyes and listen as you read the two sentences again. Which sentence helped you create more vivid images in your mind? Vivid words make our writing come alive.

Writing Model

My new backyard is not very interesting. There is some grass. There are trees in my backyard. Every once in a while, Winn-Dixie might go out there and bark. Even he doesn't think it's very interesting.

- **Practice** Work together to say and rewrite the narrative paragraph model using vivid words.
- **Write** Have students write a narrative paragraph using vivid words and details about someone they know who is from a different country. Ask students to narrate the experience of meeting this person for the first time. Have students use the Writer's Checklist found on p. 158 for contextual support. Remind students to edit using appropriate verb tense.

Beginning Have students write the name of their subject at the top of their paper. Then have them provide details about this person using gestures or drawings and dictate to you one sentence for each detail. Write out their sentences and have students copy them.

Intermediate Supply students with this sentence frame. *I met ________ when ________.* Have partners work together to write three interesting details about this person in the form of a paragraph.

Advanced/Advanced High Have students write their paragraph independently. Then have pairs exchange papers and provide feedback for revising verb tenses and editing. Encourage partners to star the details that they find most interesting and underline any places that they find hard to understand.

Objectives

- Narrate, describe, and explain with increasing specificity and detail as more English is acquired.
- Narrate, describe, and explain with increasing specificity and detail to fulfill content area writing needs as more English is acquired.

This Week's ELL Overview

Grade 4 • Unit 1 • Week 2
Lewis and Clark and Me
46a–77s
and DI•41–DI•50

ELL Handbook

- Maximize Literacy and Cognitive Engagement
- Research Into Practice
- Full Weekly Support for Every Selection

Lewis and Clark and Me
- Multi-Lingual Summaries in Five Languages
- Selection-Specific Vocabulary Word Cards
- Frontloading/Reteaching for Comprehension Skill Lessons
- ELD and ELL Reader Study Guides

- Transfer Activities
- Professional Development

Daily Leveled ELL Notes

ELL notes appear throughout this week's instruction and ELL Support is on the DI pages of your Teacher's Edition. The following is a sample of an ELL note from this week.

English Language Learners

Beginning Read a sentence from the model. Ask students if it is the main idea or not.

Intermediate Read a main idea from a paragraph of the model. Have students identify a detail to support it.

Advanced Have students identify the main idea and one supporting detail of two paragraphs of the model.

Advanced High Have students write, in their own words, the main idea of several paragraphs from the model. After each main idea have them write one supporting detail.

ELL by Strand

The ELL lessons on this week's Support for English Language Learners pages are organized by strand. They offer additional scaffolding for the core curriculum. Leveled support notes on these pages address the different proficiency levels in your class. See pages DI•41–DI•50.

ELL Guy
Dr. Jim Cummins

The Three Pillars of ELL Instruction

ELL Strands	Activate Prior Knowledge	Access Content	Extend Language
Vocabulary pp. DI•42–DI•43	Preteach	Reteach	Leveled Writing Activities
Reading Comprehension p. DI•47	Frontloading	Sheltered Reading	After Reading
Phonics, Spelling, and Word Analysis p. DI•45	Preteach	Teach/Model	Leveled Practice Activities
Listening Comprehension p. DI•44	Prepare for the Read Aloud	First Listening	Second Listening
Conventions and Writing pp. DI•49–DI•50	Preteach	Leveled Practice Activities	Leveled Writing Activities
Concept Development p. DI•41	Activate Prior Knowledge	Discuss Concept	Daily Concept and Vocabulary Development

This Week's Practice Stations Overview

Six Weekly Practice Stations with Leveled Activities can be found at the beginning of each week of instruction. For this week's Practice Stations, see pp. 46h–46i.

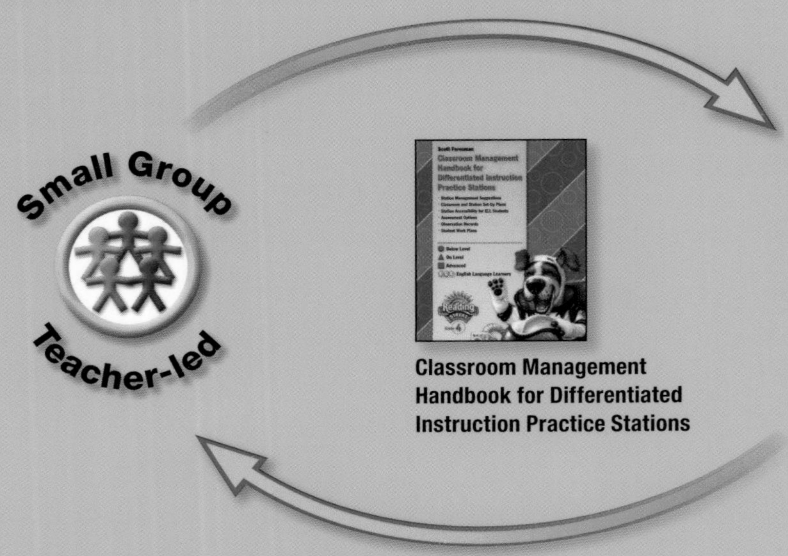

Classroom Management Handbook for Differentiated Instruction Practice Stations

Practice Stations

Daily Leveled Center Activities

Below
Advanced
On-Level

Practice Stations Flip Charts

	 **Word Wise**	 **Word Work**	 **Words to Know**	 **Let's Write**	 **Read for Meaning**	 **Get Fluent**
Objectives	• Spell words with short-vowel pattern VCCV.	• Identify and write words that have short-vowel sounds with the VCCV pattern.	• Determine the meanings of words with suffixes.	• Understand the main features of realistic fiction.	• Identify a sequence of events.	• Read aloud with expression.
Materials	• *Word Wise* Flip Chart Activity 2 • Teacher-made word cards • paper • pencil	• *Word Work* Flip Chart Activity 2 • Teacher-made word cards • paper • pencil	• *Words to Know* Flip Chart Activity 2 • Teacher-made word cards • paper • pencil	• *Let's Write* Flip Chart Activity 2 • paper • pencil	• *Read for Meaning* Flip Chart Activity 2 • Leveled Readers • paper • pencil	• *Get Fluent* Flip Chart Activity 2 • Leveled Readers

This Week on Reading Street!

Question of the Week

What opportunities can be found in new places?

Daily Plan

Whole Group

- Author's Purpose
- Word Endings
- Fluency/Appropriate Phrasing
- Research and Inquiry

Success Predictor

Day 1	Days 2–3	Day 4	Day 5
Check Oral Vocabulary	Check Retelling	Check Fluency	Check Oral Vocabulary

Small Group

Teacher Led

- Reading Support
- Skill Support
- Fluency Practice

Practice Stations

Independent Activities

Customize Literacy More support for a Balanced Literacy approach, see pp. CL•1–CL•47

Customize Writing More support for a customized writing approach, see pp. CW•1–CW•10

Whole Group

- Writing: Expository Composition
- Conventions: Imperative and Exclamatory Sentences
- Spelling: Long *a* and *i*

Assessment

- Weekly Tests
- Day 5 Assessment
- Fresh Reads

This Week's Reading Selections

Main Selection
Genre: **Historical Fiction**

Paired Selection
Genre: **Biography**

Leveled Readers

ELL and ELD Readers

Resources on Reading Street!

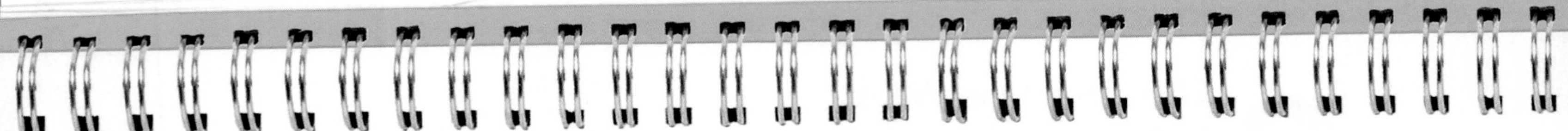

	Build Concepts	 Comprehension
Whole Group	 Let's Talk About pp. 46–47	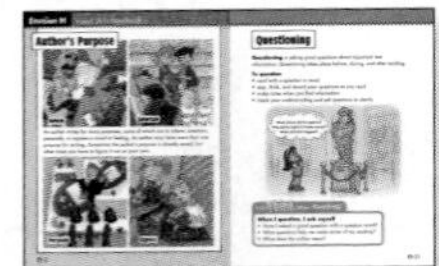 Envision It! Skills/ Strategies 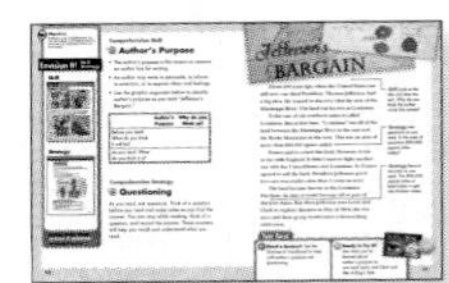 Comprehension Skills Lesson pp. 48–49
 Go Digital	• Concept Talk Video	• Envision It! Animations • eSelections
Small Group and Independent Practice	 Lewis and Clark and Me pp. 52–53  ELL and ELD Readers  Leveled Readers	 Lewis and Clark and Me pp. 52–53  ELL and ELD Readers  Leveled Readers 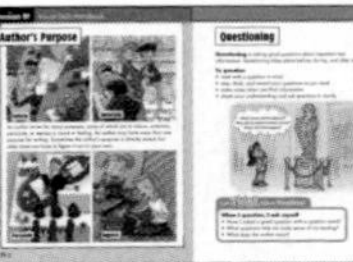 Envision It! Skills/ Strategies  Reader's and Writer's Notebook  Practice Station Flip Chart
 Go Digital	• eReaders • eSelections	• Envision It! Animations • eSelections • eReaders
 **Customize Literacy**	• Leveled Readers	• Envision It! Skills and Strategies Handbook • Leveled Readers
Go Digital	• Concept Talk Video • Big Question Video • eReaders	• Envision It! Animations • eReaders

Question of the Week

What opportunities can be found in new places?

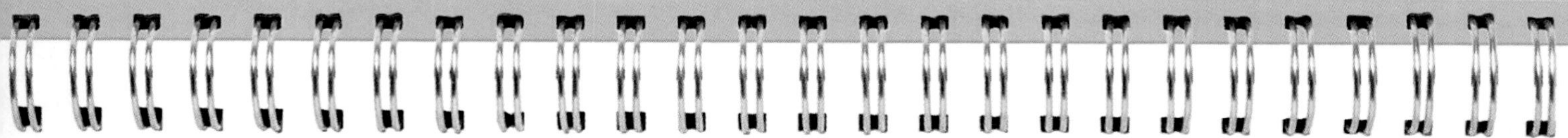

Vocabulary

Envision It! Vocabulary Cards

Vocabulary Skill Lesson pp. 50–51

- Envision It! Vocabulary Cards
- Vocabulary Activities

Envision It! Vocabulary Cards

Lewis and Clark and Me pp. 52–53

Practice Station Flip Chart

Words! W•6

Reader's and Writer's Notebook

- Envision It! Vocabulary Cards
- Vocabulary Activities
- eSelections

- Envision It! Vocabulary Cards

- Vocabulary Activities

Fluency

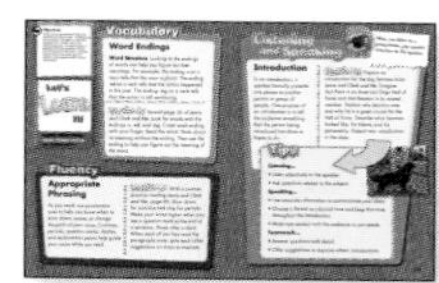
Let's Learn It! pp. 76–77

- eSelections
- eReaders

Lewis and Clark and Me pp. 52–53

Practice Station Flip Chart

Leveled Readers

ELL and ELD Readers

- eSelections
- eReaders

- Leveled Readers

- eReaders

Conventions and Writing

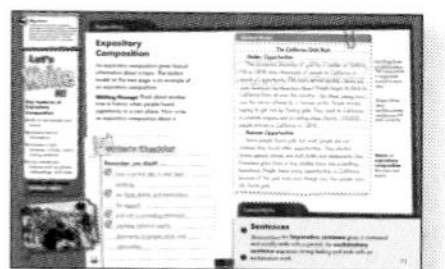
Let's Write It! pp. 70–71

- Grammar Jammer

Reader's and Writer's Notebook

Lewis and Clark and Me pp. 52–53

Practice Station Flip Chart

- Grammar Jammer

- Reader's and Writer's Notebook

- Grammar Jammer

Week 2

My 5-Day Planner for Reading Street!

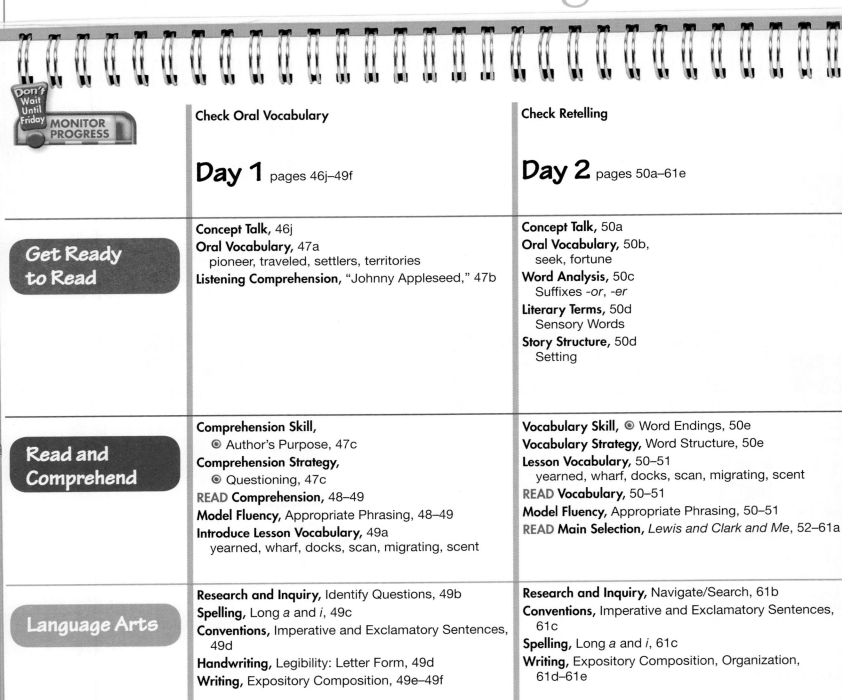

Don't Wait Until Friday MONITOR PROGRESS	Check Oral Vocabulary **Day 1** pages 46j–49f	Check Retelling **Day 2** pages 50a–61e
Get Ready to Read	**Concept Talk,** 46j **Oral Vocabulary,** 47a pioneer, traveled, settlers, territories **Listening Comprehension,** "Johnny Appleseed," 47b	**Concept Talk,** 50a **Oral Vocabulary,** 50b, seek, fortune **Word Analysis,** 50c Suffixes *-or*, *-er* **Literary Terms,** 50d Sensory Words **Story Structure,** 50d Setting
Read and Comprehend	**Comprehension Skill,** ◎ Author's Purpose, 47c **Comprehension Strategy,** ◎ Questioning, 47c READ **Comprehension,** 48–49 **Model Fluency,** Appropriate Phrasing, 48–49 **Introduce Lesson Vocabulary,** 49a yearned, wharf, docks, scan, migrating, scent	**Vocabulary Skill,** ◎ Word Endings, 50e **Vocabulary Strategy,** Word Structure, 50e **Lesson Vocabulary,** 50–51 yearned, wharf, docks, scan, migrating, scent READ **Vocabulary,** 50–51 **Model Fluency,** Appropriate Phrasing, 50–51 READ **Main Selection,** *Lewis and Clark and Me*, 52–61a
Language Arts	**Research and Inquiry,** Identify Questions, 49b **Spelling,** Long *a* and *i*, 49c **Conventions,** Imperative and Exclamatory Sentences, 49d **Handwriting,** Legibility: Letter Form, 49d **Writing,** Expository Composition, 49e–49f	**Research and Inquiry,** Navigate/Search, 61b **Conventions,** Imperative and Exclamatory Sentences, 61c **Spelling,** Long *a* and *i*, 61c **Writing,** Expository Composition, Organization, 61d–61e

Question of the Week

What opportunities can be found in new places?

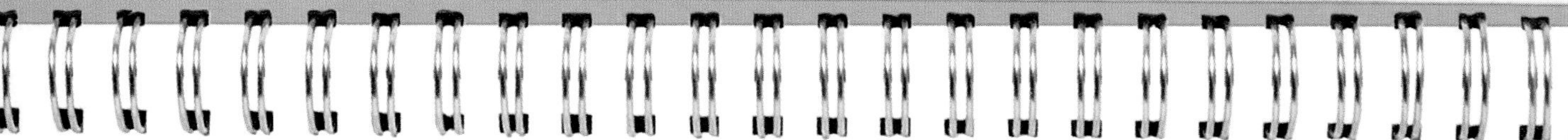

Check Retelling **Day 3** pages 62a–71c	Check Fluency **Day 4** pages 72a–77e	Check Oral Vocabulary **Day 5** pages 77f–77q
Concept Talk, 62a **Oral Vocabulary,** 62b experiences, prepared **Comprehension Check,** 62c **Check Retelling,** 62d	**Concept Talk,** 72a **Oral Vocabulary,** 72b foreign, improve **Genre,** Biography, 72c	**Concept Wrap Up,** 77f **Check Oral Vocabulary,** 77g pioneer, traveled, settlers, territories, seek, fortune, experiences, prepared, foreign, improve **Amazing Ideas,** 77g Review ◎ Author's Purpose, 77h Review ◎ Word Endings, 77h Review **Word Analysis,** 77i Review **Literary Terms,** 77i
READ **Main Selection,** *Lewis and Clark and Me,* 62–67a **Retelling,** 68–69 **Think Critically,** 69a **Model Fluency,** Appropriate Phrasing, 69b **Research and Study Skills,** Skim and Scan, 69c	READ **Paired Selection,** "Ellen Ochoa: Space Pioneer," 72–75a **Let's Learn It!** 76–77a Fluency: Appropriate Phrasing Vocabulary: Word Endings Listening and Speaking: Introduction	**Fluency Assessment,** WCPM, 77j–77k **Comprehension Assessment,** ◎ Author's Purpose, 77l–77m
Research and Inquiry, Analyze, 69d **Conventions,** Imperative and Exclamatory Sentences, 69e **Spelling,** Long *a* and *i*, 69e **Let's Write It!** Expository Composition, 70–71a **Writing,** Expository Composition, Chronological Order, 71a–71c	**Research and Inquiry,** Synthesize, 77b **Conventions,** Imperative and Exclamatory Sentences, 77c **Spelling,** Long *a* and *i*, 77c **Writing,** Expository Composition, Revising, 77d–77e	**Research and Inquiry,** Communicate, 77n **Conventions,** Imperative and Exclamatory Sentences, 77o **Spelling Test,** Long *a* and *i*, 77o **Writing,** Expository Composition, Imperative and Exclamatory Sentences, 77p–77q **Quick Write for Fluency,** 77q

Week 2

Grouping Options for Differentiated Instruction
Turn the page for the small group time lesson plan.

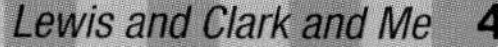

Planning Small Group Time on Reading Street!

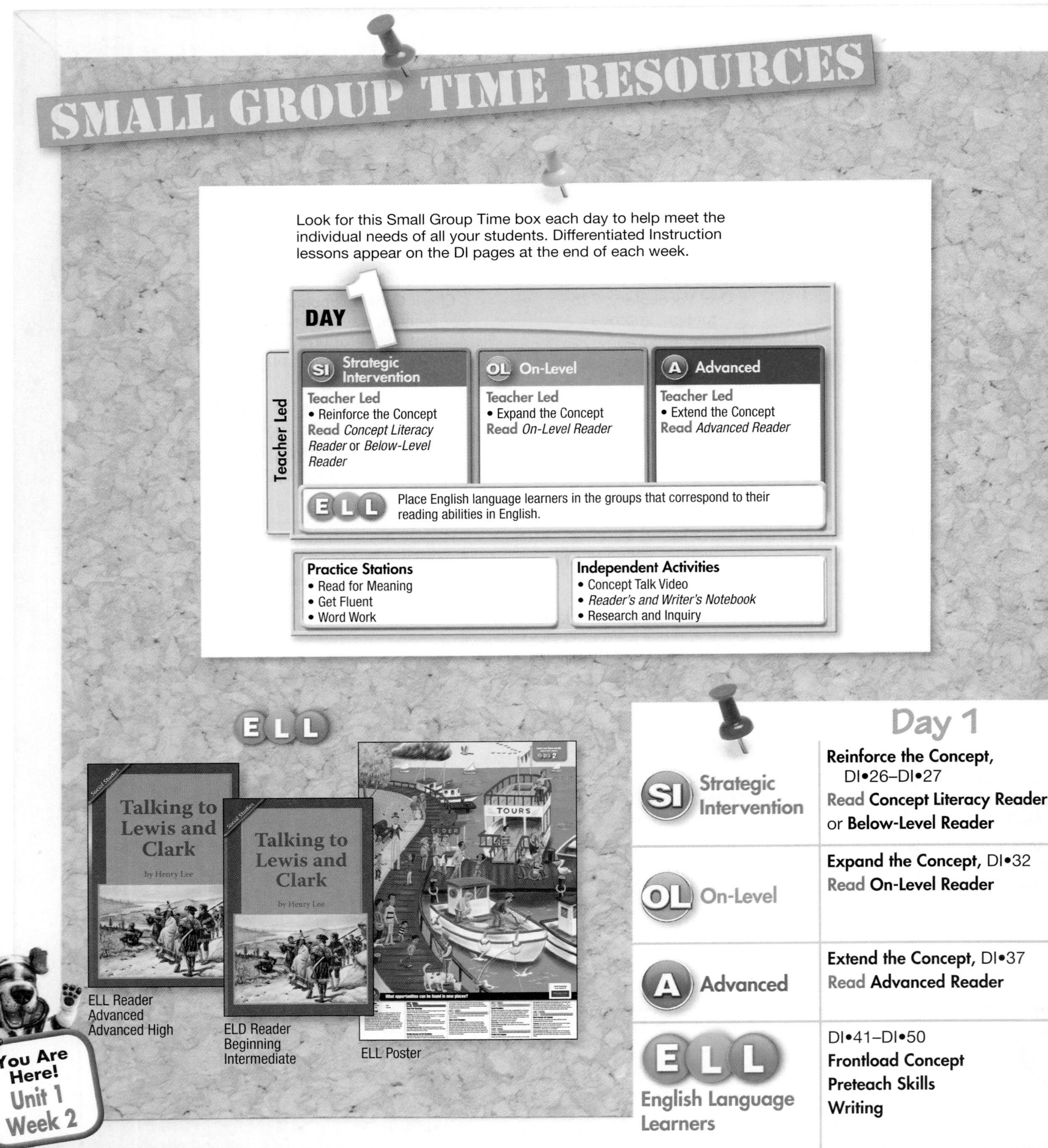
SMALL GROUP TIME RESOURCES
Look for this Small Group Time box each day to help meet the individual needs of all your students. Differentiated Instruction lessons appear on the DI pages at the end of each week.
DAY 1
Teacher Led
SI Strategic Intervention
Teacher Led
• Reinforce the Concept
Read Concept Literacy Reader or Below-Level Reader
OL On-Level
Teacher Led
• Expand the Concept
Read On-Level Reader
A Advanced
Teacher Led
• Extend the Concept
Read Advanced Reader
ELL
Place English language learners in the groups that correspond to their reading abilities in English.
Practice Stations
• Read for Meaning
• Get Fluent
• Word Work
Independent Activities
• Concept Talk Video
• Reader's and Writer's Notebook
• Research and Inquiry
ELL
Talking to Lewis and Clark
by Henry Lee
Talking to Lewis and Clark
by Henry Lee
TOURS
You Are Here!
Unit 1
Week 2

ELL Reader
Advanced
Advanced High

ELD Reader
Beginning
Intermediate

ELL Poster

	Day 1
SI Strategic Intervention	**Reinforce the Concept,** DI•26–DI•27 Read **Concept Literacy Reader** or **Below-Level Reader**
OL On-Level	**Expand the Concept,** DI•32 Read **On-Level Reader**
A Advanced	**Extend the Concept,** DI•37 Read **Advanced Reader**
ELL English Language Learners	DI•41–DI•50 **Frontload Concept** **Preteach Skills** **Writing**

Reading Street Response to Intervention Kit

Reading Street Practice Stations Kit

Question of the Week

What opportunities can be found in new places?

Below-Level Reader

Concept Literacy Reader

Lewis and Clark and Me pp. 52–53

On-Level Reader

Advanced Reader

Ellen Ochoa: Space Pioneer pp. 72–73

Small Group Weekly Plan

Day 2	Day 3	Day 4	Day 5
Reinforce Comprehension, DI•28 Revisit **Main Selection**	**Reinforce Vocabulary,** DI•29 Read/Revisit **Main Selection**	**Reinforce Comprehension,** Practice Retelling, DI•30 Genre Focus Read/Revisit **Paired Selection**	**Practice Fluency,** DI•31 Reread **Concept Literacy Reader** or **Below-Level Reader**
Expand Comprehension, DI•33 Revisit **Main Selection**	**Expand Vocabulary,** DI•34 Read/Revisit **Main Selection**	**Expand Comprehension,** Practice Retelling, DI•35 Genre Focus Read/Revisit **Paired Selection**	**Practice Fluency,** DI•36 Reread **On-Level Reader**
Extend Comprehension, DI•38 Revisit **Main Selection**	**Extend Vocabulary,** DI•39 Read/Revisit **Main Selection**	**Extend Comprehension,** Genre Focus, DI•40 Read/Revisit **Paired Selection**	**Practice Fluency,** DI•40 Reread **Advanced Reader**
DI•41–DI•50 **Review Concept/Skills** **Frontload Main Selection** **Practice**	DI•41–DI•50 **Review Concept/Skills** Reread **Main Selection** **Practice**	DI•41–DI•50 **Review Concept** Read **ELL/ELD Readers** **Practice**	DI•41–DI•50 **Review Concept/Skills** Reread **ELL/ELD Readers** **Writing**

Week 2

Practice Stations for Everyone on Reading Street!

Word Wise
Short-vowel pattern VCCV

Objectives
- Spell words with short-vowel pattern VCCV.

Materials
- *Word Wise* Flip Chart Activity 2
- Teacher-made word cards
- paper • pencil

Differentiated Activities
● Choose four word cards. Write the words. Circle the short-vowels in each word. Write sentences using the words.

▲ Choose six word cards, and write the words. Circle the short-vowels in each word. Write sentences using the words.

■ Choose eight word cards, and write the words. Circle the short-vowels in each word. Write sentences using the words. Add other words with two-syllables and short vowels to your list.

Technology
- Online Dictionary

Word Work
Short vowel sounds VCCV

Objectives
- Identify and write words that have short-vowel sounds with the VCCV pattern.

Materials
- *Word Work* Flip Chart Activity 2
- Teacher-made word cards
- paper • pencil

Differentiated Activities
● Choose six word cards. Write the words. Say each word. Think of other words you know with these short-vowel sounds. Add the words to your list.

▲ Choose eight word cards, and write the words. Say each word. Think of other words you know with these short-vowel sounds. Add them to your list.

■ Choose ten word cards, and write the words. Say each word. Make a five-column chart with short-vowel sounds as headings. Write the words in the correct column.

Technology
- Modeled Pronunciation Audio CD

Words to Know
Words with suffixes

Objectives
- Determine the meanings of words with suffixes.

Materials
- *Words to Know* Flip Chart Activity 2
- Teacher-made word cards
- paper • pencil

Differentiated Activities
● Choose six word cards. Write the words. Circle the suffix in each word. Use the dictionary to check definitions. Write a sentence for each of your words.

▲ Choose eight word cards, and write the words. Circle the suffix in each word. Use the dictionary to check definitions. Write a sentence for each word.

■ Choose six word cards, and write the words. Circle each word's base word. Write a sentence for each word and its base word to show how suffixes can change word meaning.

Technology
- Online Dictionary

Use this week's materials from the Reading Street Leveled Practice Stations Kit to organize this week's stations.

Key

- Below-Level Activities (circle)
- On-Level Activities (triangle)
- Advanced Activities (square)

Practice Station Flip Chart

Let's Write!

Explore realistic fiction.

Objectives

- Understand the main features of realistic fiction.

Materials

- *Let's Write!* Flip Chart Activity 2
- paper • pencil

Differentiated Activities

● Write a realistic story about two characters who travel somewhere. Tell where the characters go and how they travel. Tell what happens when they arrive.

▲ Write a realistic story with two characters who travel to a place they want to visit. Explain where they are going and what happens when they arrive.

■ Write a realistic story about two characters traveling to a place they want to visit. Include details explaining where they are going, how they get there, and what happens when they arrive.

Technology

- Online graphic organizers

Read for Meaning

Identify a sequence.

Objectives

- Identify a sequence of events.

Materials

- *Read for Meaning* Flip Chart Activity 2
- Leveled Readers
- paper • pencil

Differentiated Activities

● Choose a book from those your teacher provided. Think about the sequence of events in the story. Write sentences telling three events in the story. Use signal words such as *first, next,* and *finally* to show the sequence.

▲ Read one of the books your teacher provided, and think about the sequence of events in the story. Write three sentences that tell the sequence. Use signal words such as *first, next, then,* and *finally* to show sequence.

■ Choose and read a leveled reader, and think about the story's sequence of events. Write a short paragraph telling the sequence of at least four important story events. Use signal words.

Technology

- Leveled Reader Database

Get Fluent

Practice fluent reading.

Objectives

- Read aloud with expression.

Materials

- *Get Fluent* Flip Chart Activity 2
- Leveled Readers

Differentiated Activities

● Work with a partner. Choose a Concept Literacy Reader or Below-Level Reader. Take turns reading a page from the book. Use the readers to practice correct expression. Provide feedback as needed.

▲ Work with a partner. Choose an On-Level Reader. Take turns reading a page from the book. Use the reader to practice correct expression. Provide feedback as needed.

■ Work with a partner. Choose an Advanced Reader. Take turns reading a page from the book. Use the reader to practice correct expression. Provide feedback as needed.

Technology

- Reading Street Readers CD-ROM
- Leveled Reader Database

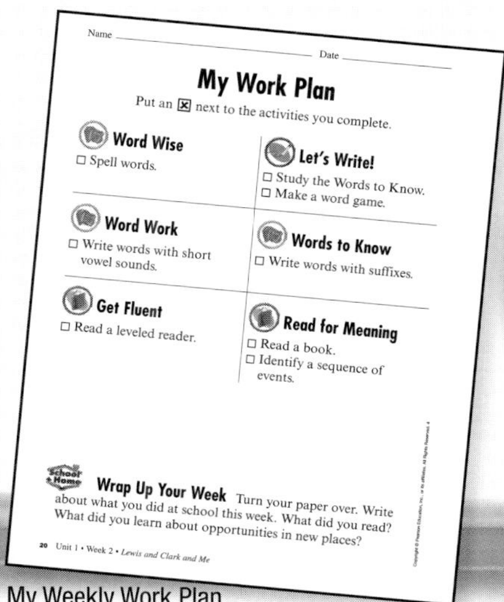

Name ______ Date ______

My Work Plan

Put an ☒ next to the activities you complete.

Word Wise
☐ Spell words.

Let's Write!
☐ Study the Words to Know.
☐ Make a word game.

Word Work
☐ Write words with short vowel sounds.

Words to Know
☐ Write words with suffixes.

Get Fluent
☐ Read a leveled reader.

Read for Meaning
☐ Read a book.
☐ Identify a sequence of events.

Wrap Up Your Week Turn your paper over. Write about what you did at school this week. What did you read? What did you learn about opportunities in new places?

20 Unit 1 • Week 2 • *Lewis and Clark and Me*

My Weekly Work Plan

Week 2

30–35 min

Objectives

- Introduce the weekly concept.
- Develop oral vocabulary.

Today at a Glance

Oral Vocabulary
pioneer, traveled, settlers, territories

Comprehension
◎ Author's purpose
◎ Questioning

Reading
"Jefferson's Bargain"

Fluency
Appropriate phrasing

Lesson Vocabulary
Tested vocabulary

Research and Inquiry
Identify questions

Spelling
Long *a* and *i*

Conventions
Imperative and exclamatory sentences

Handwriting
Legibility: Letter form

Writing
Expository composition

Concept Talk

Question of the Week

What opportunities can be found in new places?

Introduce the concept

To further explore the unit concept of Turning Points, this week students will read, write, and talk about what opportunities can be found in new places. Write the Question of the Week on the board.

ROUTINE **Activate Prior Knowledge** Team Talk

1. **Think** Have students think about the different opportunities that can be found in new places.

2. **Pair** Have pairs of students discuss the Question of the Week.

3. **Share** Call on a few students to share their ideas and comments with the group. Guide the discussion and encourage elaboration with prompts such as:
   - How does it feel to start a new school year in a new school or new classroom? What opportunities does each new school year bring?
   - Why do people move or travel to a new place? What opportunities do they hope to find?

Routines Flip Chart

Anchored Talk

Develop oral vocabulary

Have students turn to pp. 46–47 in their Student Editions. Look at each of the photos. Then, use the prompts to guide discussion and create the *What opportunities can be found in new places* concept map. Remind students to answer questions with appropriate details and provide suggestions that build upon the ideas of others.

- What is the man claiming in the picture with the covered wagons? (He is a pioneer claiming new land.) *Pioneers traveled* west in our country in the 1800s to start a new life. Let's add *Why people go* and *Where people go* to our concept map.

Objectives
• Speak clearly and to the point, give an opinion and support it with correct information. Make eye contact, change how fast, loud, and clearly you speak, and get your ideas across clearly.
Oral Vocabulary
Let's Talk About
Opportunity
• Share opinions about why people want to explore new lands.
• Speak clearly when explaining what opportunities await those who explore new places.
• Describe what opportunities you would pursue in a new place.
READING STREET ONLINE
CONCEPT TALK VIDEO
www.ReadingStreet.com
You've learned
0 1 0
Amazing Words
so far this year!
46
47

Student Edition pp. 46–47

Amazing Words

You've learned 0 1 0 words so far

You'll learn 0 1 0 words this week!

pioneer	fortune
traveled	experiences
settlers	prepared
territories	foreign
seek	improve

Writing on Demand

Writing Fluency
Ask students to respond to the photos on pp. 46–47 by writing as well as they can and as much as they can about what opportunities people find in new places.

- Why do you think the people are exploring the mountain area? Why have they *traveled* there? (They want to see new places.)
- Look at the photo of the ships. Many explorers left their country and sailed to new places. What do you think they hoped to find? (new opportunities, new homes, new people) Let's add *People* to our concept map.

Connect to reading Tell students that this week they will be reading about different people who have explored new places in our country. Encourage students to add concept-related words to this week's concept map.

ELL **Preteach Concepts** Use the Day 1 instruction on ELL Poster 2 to assess and build background knowledge, develop concepts, and build oral vocabulary.

ELL Poster 2

ELL

English Language Learners

ELL support Additional ELL support and modified instruction is provided in the *ELL Handbook* and in the ELL Support lessons on pp. DI•41–DI•50.

Listening comprehension English learners will benefit from additional visual support to understand the key terms in the concept map. Use pictures on pp. 46–47 to scaffold understanding.

Frontload for Read Aloud Use the modified Read Aloud on p. DI•44 of the ELL Support lessons to prepare students to listen to "Johnny Appleseed" (p. 47b).

Objectives
- Develop listening comprehension.
- Develop oral vocabulary.

Check Oral Vocabulary
SUCCESS PREDICTOR

Oral Vocabulary
Amazing Words

Introduce Amazing Words "Johnny Appleseed" on p. 47b is about a man who planted apple trees as he traveled the United States. Tell students to listen for the Amazing Words—*pioneer, traveled, settlers,* and *territories*—as you read.

Model fluency As you read "Johnny Appleseed," model appropriate phrasing by using punctuation cues.

Teach Amazing Words

Amazing Words Oral Vocabulary Routine

pioneer
traveled
settlers
territories

1. **Introduce** Write the word *pioneer* on the board. Have students say the word aloud with you. Johnny Appleseed was an American *pioneer*. What context clues does the author include to help you determine the meaning of *pioneer?* Supply a student-friendly definition.
2. **Demonstrate** Have students answer questions to demonstrate understanding. How was Johnny Appleseed a *pioneer* in the Midwest? What do *pioneers* do?
3. **Apply** Ask students what characteristics a *pioneer* would have to possess.

See p. OV•2 to teach *traveled, settlers,* and *territories.*

Routines Flip Chart

Apply Amazing Words To build oral language, lead the class in a discussion about the meanings of the Amazing Words. Remind students to listen attentively to speakers and to build on the ideas of others in discussion.

MONITOR PROGRESS Check Oral Vocabulary

During discussion, listen for students' use of Amazing Words.

If... students are unable to use the Amazing Words to discuss the concept,

then... use Amazing Word Routine in the Routines Flip Chart to demonstrate words in different contexts.

Day 1	Days 2–3	Day 4	Day 5
Check Oral Vocabulary	Check Retelling	Check Fluency	Check Oral Vocabulary

Johnny Appleseed

John Chapman was born in Massachusetts shortly before the beginning of the American Revolution. As the new nation began taking root, John Chapman became an American pioneer, and before long he would become a legend, earning the nickname Johnny Appleseed.

As a young man, Chapman set out alone traveling west from his birthplace. As he traveled, Appleseed claimed land, cleared it, and planted seeds. Johnny began by collecting apple seeds from cider presses. Until about the age of seventy, he traveled alone throughout the Midwest, planting apple trees on the land he cleared. Johnny looked for good land that could support trees. Wherever he went, Johnny pulled weeds, took care of the soil, and planted apple seeds. He eventually owned over 1,000 acres of orchards throughout Ohio and Indiana. Johnny's dream was to enrich the land with blossoming apple trees for everyone to enjoy.

Johnny Appleseed worked hard caring for his orchards. He did not simply plant the seeds and abandon the orchards. He returned to care for the young trees as they grew. It is said that he traveled hundreds of miles simply to take care of one of his orchards. He was truly dedicated to his apple trees.

Johnny was a good-natured man, so he made friends with people wherever he went. He became friends with Native Americans and settlers in the territories he visited. Because he spent his time outdoors, he naturally respected the animals. He may even have shared his apples with them.

Johnny may have become well known because of his character. People noticed this friendly, kind-hearted man who planted and cared for apple orchards. To people he met along the way, he sold his apple seeds and saplings for a few pennies each. Sometimes he even gave away his apple trees. Some stories say that he accepted almost anything for payment, even old clothes. According to stories, settlers didn't need money to buy Appleseed's trees.

Of course, those who told about Johnny Appleseed remembered to mention his unusual appearance. They said that he traveled barefoot in ragged pants. According to the stories, he carried a pot that he sometimes wore as a hat! He cut holes in a coffee sack and wore it as a shirt. Johnny was also said to have very long hair that had seldom been cut. Can you imagine how he must have looked? But Johnny wasn't

Continued on p. 77s

DAY 1 Read and Comprehend

Objectives

- ◎ Identify author's purpose to aid comprehension.
- ◎ Use the questioning strategy to aid comprehension.
- Read grade-level text with appropriate phrasing.

Skills Trace

◎ **Author's Purpose**

Introduce U1W2D1; U1W4D1; U5W1D1

Practice U1W2D2; U1W2D3; U1W2D4; U1W4D2; U1W4D3; U1W4D4; U5W1D2; U5W1D3; U5W1D4

Reteach/Review U1W2D5; U1W4D5; U1W5D2; U1W5D3; U2W2D2; U2W2D3; U5W1D5; U5W3D3

Assess/Test Weekly Tests U1W2; U1W4; U5W1

Benchmark Tests U1; U5

KEY:
U=Unit W=Week D=Day

Skill ↔ Strategy

◎ Author's Purpose

◎ Questioning

Student Edition p. EI•2

Introduce author's purpose

Envision It!

The author's purpose is the reason an author has for writing. Authors write to persuade, to inform, to express an idea or feeling, or to entertain. Can an author have more than one purpose for writing a text? (Yes.) Have students turn to p. EI•2 in the Student Edition to review author's purpose. Then read "Jefferson's Bargain" with students.

Model the skill

Have students follow along as you read the title and the first paragraph. The first paragraph talks about the new land west of the Mississippi that Jefferson wanted to explore. The language the author uses in this paragraph makes me think that the author's purpose is to inform, or present information. I also think about the clever title the author chose. How does the way the title is written suggest another purpose the author might have for writing this selection? (I think the author wants to express the idea that this new land was acquired in an interesting way.) Sometimes writers can have more than one purpose for writing.

Guide practice

Have students finish reading "Jefferson's Bargain" on their own. After they read, have them use a graphic organizer like the one on p. 48 and identify the author's purpose for writing the passage.

Strategy check

Questioning Remind students that if they have difficulty understanding "Jefferson's Bargain," they can use the questioning strategy. Guide students in asking literal, interpretive, and evaluative questions to monitor and adjust understanding.

Model the strategy

Envision It!

Before I began to read I looked at the title and wondered about the word *bargain.* I asked myself, *Why does the author use the word* bargain *in the title?* I read on and found the answer to my question in the third paragraph. The author used the word *bargain* because Jefferson bought the land for less than 3 cents an acre, and that is a bargain. Have students review the strategy of questioning on p. EI•21 of the Student Edition.

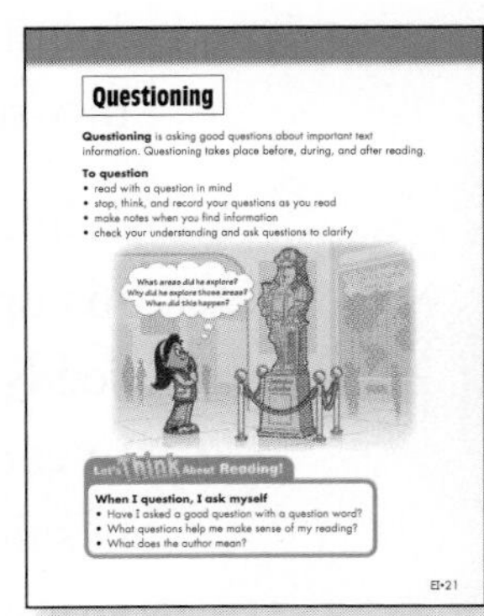

Questioning

Questioning is asking good questions about important text information. Questioning takes place before, during, and after reading.

To question
- read with a question in mind
- stop, think, and record your questions as you read
- make notes when you find information
- check your understanding and ask questions to clarify

Let's Think About Reading!

When I question, I ask myself
- Have I asked a good question with a question word?
- What questions help me make sense of my reading?
- What does the author mean?

EI•21

Student Edition p. EI•21

On their own

Use p. 51 in the *Reader's and Writer's Notebook* for additional practice with author's purpose.

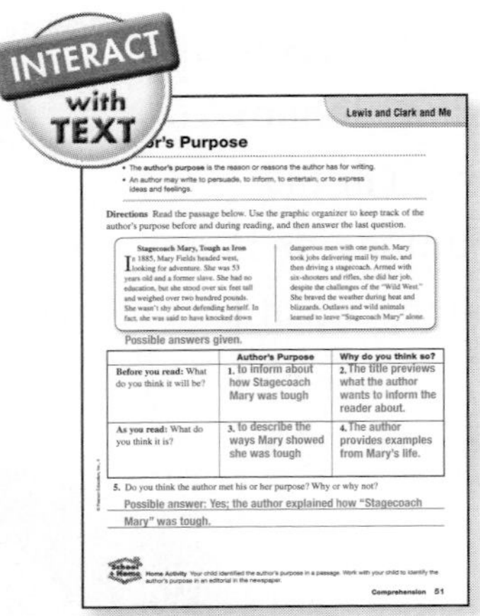

Lewis and Clark and Me

...or's Purpose

- The **author's purpose** is the reason or reasons the author has for writing.
- An author may write to persuade, to inform, to entertain, or to express ideas and feelings.

Directions Read the passage below. Use the graphic organizer to keep track of the author's purpose before and during reading, and then answer the last question.

Stagecoach Mary, Tough as Iron

In 1885, Mary Fields headed west, looking for adventure. She was 53 years old and a former slave. She had no education, but she stood over six feet tall and weighed over two hundred pounds. She wasn't shy about defending herself. In fact, she was said to have knocked down dangerous men with one punch. Mary took jobs delivering mail by mule, and then driving a stagecoach. Armed with six-shooters and rifles, she did her job, despite the challenges of the "Wild West." She braved the weather during heat and blizzards. Outlaws and wild animals learned to leave "Stagecoach Mary" alone.

Possible answers given.

	Author's Purpose	Why do you think so?
Before you read: What do you think it will be?	1. to inform about how Stagecoach Mary was tough	2. The title previews what the author wants to inform the reader about.
As you read: What do you think it is?	3. to describe the ways Mary showed she was tough	4. The author provides examples from Mary's life.

5. Do you think the author met his or her purpose? Why or why not?
Possible answer: Yes; the author explained how "Stagecoach Mary" was tough.

Home Activity Your child identified the author's purpose in a passage. Work with your child to identify the author's purpose in an editorial in the newspaper.

Comprehension 51

Reader's and Writer's Notebook p. 51

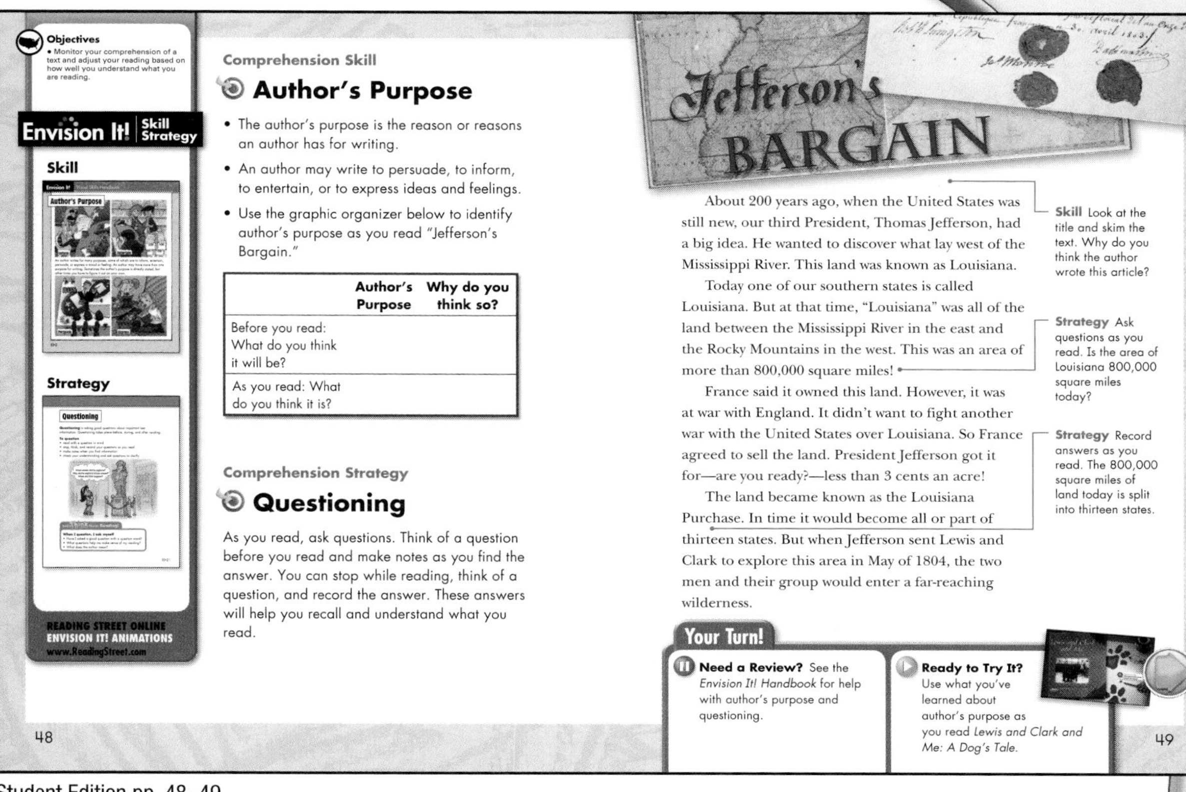

Student Edition pp. 48–49

Skill The author wrote this article to inform readers about how President Jefferson added the land known as the Louisiana Purchase to our country.

Strategy Questions will vary. Students should ask literal, interpretive, and evaluative questions to monitor and adjust comprehension of the text.

Strategy Students' responses should demonstrate a clear understanding of the text.

Model Fluency
Appropriate Phrasing

Model fluent reading

Have students listen as you read the first paragraph of "Jefferson's Bargain" with appropriate phrasing. Explain that you will use punctuation to emphasize pauses and set off phrases. Explain that commas and periods are cues to read text with appropriate phrasing.

ROUTINE Choral Reading

1. **Select a passage** For "Jefferson's Bargain," use the first paragraph.
2. **Model** Have students listen as you read with appropriate phrasing.
3. **Guide practice** Have students read along with you.
4. **On their own** For optimal fluency, students should reread three or four times with appropriate phrasing.

Routines Flip Chart

English Language Learners

Author's purpose On the board, list the different reasons why authors write. Then give the following examples. Have students identify the author's purpose for writing and provide support for their answers.

- a report about Thomas Jefferson (to inform)
- an article about why everyone should recycle (to persuade)
- a silly story (to entertain)
- a journal entry about a happy memory (to express feelings)

DAY 1 **Read and Comprehend**

Objectives

- Activate prior knowledge of words.
- Identify questions for research.

Vocabulary
Tested Vocabulary

Lesson vocabulary

Use the following Question and Answer activity to help students acquire word knowledge that improves reading, speaking, listening, and writing vocabularies.

Activate prior knowledge

Give oral clues that help students think about the categories in which the lesson words belong. Display the lesson words. Have students check their glossary for the meanings of any unknown words. Read aloud each three-item list below. Ask students to name the word that fits in the same category. Discuss reasons.

- search, peek, glance (scan—All are ways of looking.)
- desired, wished, hoped (yearned—All are ways to want something.)
- traveling, moving, wandering (migrating—All are ways of moving from one place to another.)
- odor, perfume, smell (scent—All are synonyms for a type of smell.)
- pier, shore, dock (wharf—All have to do with where boats are kept.)

Tell students that analogies are comparisons between pairs of related words. Incorporate lesson words into oral analogies, as shown below. Have students explain the relationships.

Migrating is to resting as waking is to sleeping. (antonyms)

Wharf is to ***dock*** as car is to automobile. (synonyms)

By the end of the week, have students demonstrate their understanding by using each word in a sentence.

Preteach Academic Vocabulary

ELL **Academic Vocabulary** Write the following words on the board:

sensory images	**historical fiction**
skim & scan	**biography**
eye contact	**organization**

Have students share what they know about this week's Academic Vocabulary. Use the students' responses to assess their prior knowledge. Preteach the Academic Vocabulary by providing a student-friendly description, explanation, or example that clarifies the meaning of each term. Then ask students to restate the meaning of the Academic Vocabulary term in their own words.

Research and Inquiry
Identify Questions

Teach Discuss the Question of the Week: *What opportunities can be found in new places?* Tell students they will research the discoveries of Lewis and Clark. They will create a report and present their findings to the class on Day 5.

Model **Think Aloud** I'll start by brainstorming a list of questions about things Lewis and Clark discovered on their journey. I know that Lewis and Clark encountered many Native American tribes along their route west. Some possible questions could be: *What did Lewis and Clark learn from the different Native American tribes they encountered?, How did Lewis and Clark communicate and trade with Native American tribes they met?,* and *How were Lewis and Clark able to survive in the wilderness?*

Guide practice After students have formulated open-ended inquiry questions about the research topic, explain that tomorrow they will conduct online and library research of their questions. Help students identify key-words that will guide their search.

On their own Have students work individually, in pairs, or in small groups to write an inquiry question.

INTERNET GUY
Don Leu

21st Century Skills

Weekly Inquiry Project

Day 1	Identify Questions
Day 2	Navigate/Search
Day 3	Analyze
Day 4	Synthesize
Day 5	Communicate

Small Group Time

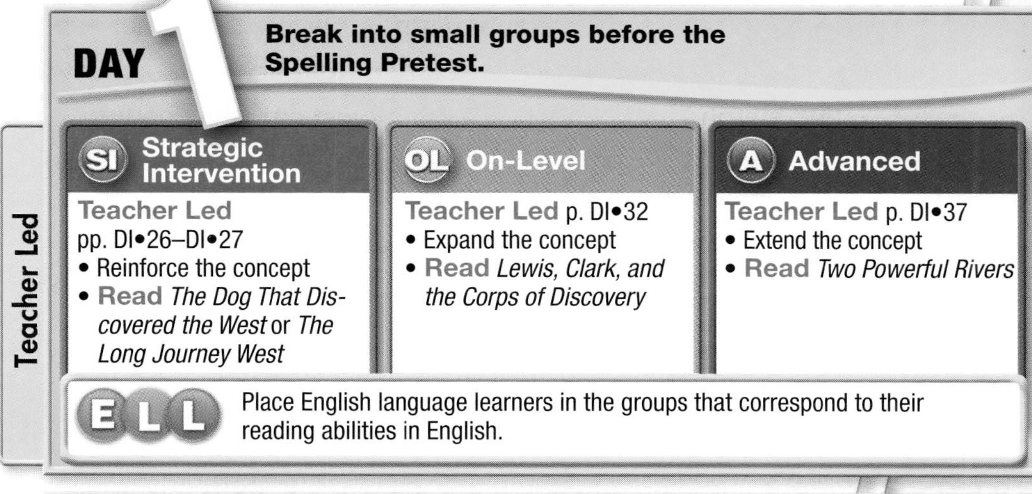

DAY 1 **Break into small groups before the Spelling Pretest.**

Teacher Led

SI Strategic Intervention	OL On-Level	A Advanced
Teacher Led pp. DI•26–DI•27 • Reinforce the concept • **Read** *The Dog That Discovered the West* or *The Long Journey West*	**Teacher Led** p. DI•32 • Expand the concept • **Read** *Lewis, Clark, and the Corps of Discovery*	**Teacher Led** p. DI•37 • Extend the concept • **Read** *Two Powerful Rivers*

ELL Place English language learners in the groups that correspond to their reading abilities in English.

Practice Stations
- Read for Meaning
- Get Fluent
- Word Work

Independent Activities
- Concept Talk Video
- *Reader's and Writer's Notebook*
- Vocabulary Activities

English Language Learners

Multilingual Vocabulary
Students can apply knowledge of their home languages to acquire new English vocabulary by using Multilingual Vocabulary Lists (*ELL Handbook* pp. 431–442).

Objectives

- Practice spelling words with long *a* and long *i* sounds.
- Use and understand imperative and exclamatory sentences.
- Practice handwriting, focusing on proper letter form.

Spelling Pretest
Long *a* and *i*

Introduce Tell students to think of words with long *a (rain)* and long *i (light).* This week we will spell words with long *a* and long *i* sounds.

Pretest Use these sentences to administer the spelling pretest. Say each word, read the sentence, and repeat the word.

1. sigh	People **sigh** when they are sad.
2. right	Chad got all the answers **right.**
3. weigh	The scale shows how much you **weigh.**
4. eight	One week is less than **eight** days.
5. detail	Tell every **detail** of the story.
6. height	The wall's **height** is five feet.
7. spray	Will you **spray** some water on the plants?
8. braid	Ann wears her hair in a **braid.**
9. bait	Bring your fishing pole and some **bait.**
10. grain	The cow ate the **grain.**
11. slight	There is a **slight** change of plans.
12. thigh	The **thigh** is part of the leg.
13. tight	My shoes are too **tight.**
14. raisin	A dried grape is a **raisin.**
15. trait	Kindness is a good **trait.**
16. highway	Take the **highway** to the last exit.
17. frighten	Did the big dog **frighten** you?
18. dismay	To our **dismay,** we lost the game.
19. freight	Trucks carry **freight** across the country.
20. sleigh	The **sleigh** moved over the snow.

Challenge words

21. eighteen	We went away for **eighteen** days.
22. mayonnaise	I do not like **mayonnaise.**
23. campaign	Come join the **campaign** for a clean city.
24. daylight	It is better to travel in **daylight.**
25. twilight	**Twilight** comes just before the sun sets.

Self-correct After the pretest, you can either display the correctly spelled words or spell them orally. Have students self-correct their pretests by writing misspelled words.

On their own For additional practice, use *Let's Practice It!* p. 10 on the *Teacher Resources DVD-ROM*.

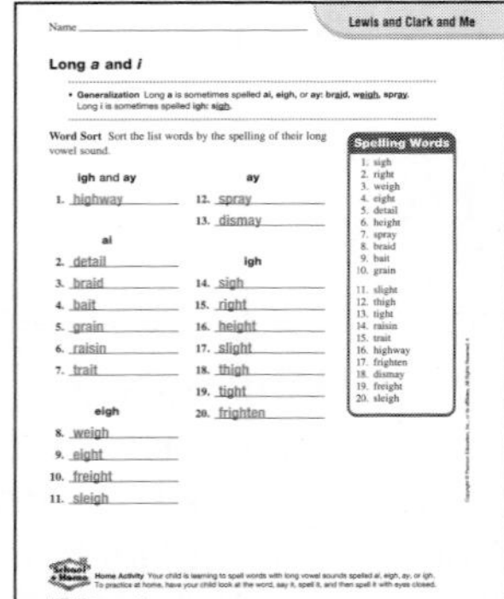

Name ____________ Lewis and Clark and Me

Long *a* and *i*

- **Generalization** Long **a** is sometimes spelled **ai, eigh,** or **ay: braid, weigh, spray.** Long **i** is sometimes spelled **igh: sigh.**

Word Sort Sort the list words by the spelling of their long vowel sound.

igh and ay
1. highway

ai
2. detail
3. braid
4. bait
5. grain
6. raisin
7. trait

eigh
8. weigh
9. eight
10. freight
11. sleigh

ay
12. spray
13. dismay

igh
14. sigh
15. right
16. height
17. slight
18. thigh
19. tight
20. frighten

Spelling Words
1. sigh
2. right
3. weigh
4. eight
5. detail
6. height
7. spray
8. braid
9. bait
10. grain
11. slight
12. thigh
13. tight
14. raisin
15. trait
16. highway
17. frighten
18. dismay
19. freight
20. sleigh

Home Activity Your child is learning to spell words with long vowel sounds spelled *ai, eigh, ay,* or *igh.* To practice at home, have your child look at the word, say it, spell it, and then spell it with eyes closed.

DVD•10 Long *a* and *i*

Let's Practice It!
TR DVD•10

Conventions
Imperative and Exclamatory Sentences

Teach Display Grammar Transparency 2, and read aloud the explanation and examples in the box. Point out the imperative and exclamatory sentences.

Model Write the correct answers to numbers 1 and 2. Explain how you applied the rules to identify imperative and exclamatory sentences.

Guide practice Guide students to complete items 3–5. Remind them to determine if the sentence gives a command or if it shows strong feeling or surprise. Record the correct responses on the transparency.

Daily Fix-It Use Daily Fix-It numbers 1 and 2 in the right margin.

Connect to oral language Have students read sentences 6–10 on the transparency and write the correct punctuation mark to correctly complete each sentence.

Handwriting
Legibility: Letter Form

Model letter formation Display the letters *l, h, t, i,* and *j.* Follow the stroke instruction pictures to model letter formation.

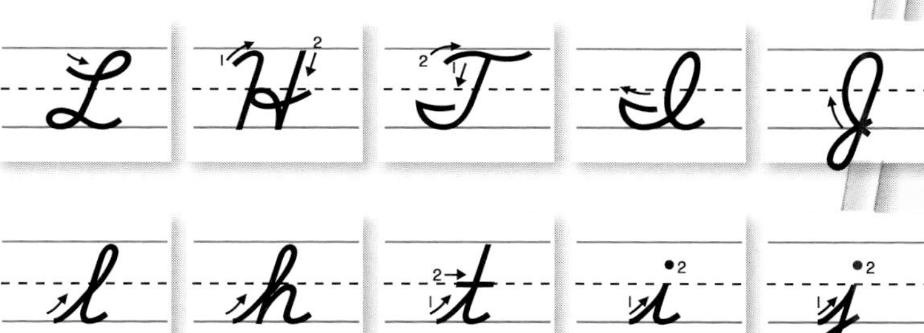

Model form Explain that writing legibly means that letters are correctly formed. The letters are written in cursive and look like they are supposed to. The height and width of the letter is correct. Model writing this sentence, paying attention to letter form. *This is not my lost jacket.*

Guide practice Have student write these humorous book titles, paying attention to letter formation. *How to Speak Clearly by Whujuh Sey; 101 Excuses by I.M. Lion.* Circulate around the room, guiding students to focus on proper form as they write.

Daily Fix-It

1. A move to a big city like San francisco might frightin some people. *(Francisco; frighten)*
2. Do you think, we will stay at a hotel. *(think we; hotel?)*

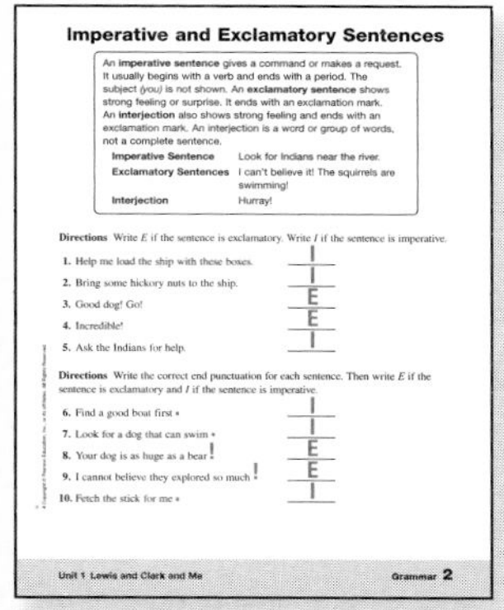

Imperative and Exclamatory Sentences

An **imperative sentence** gives a command or makes a request. It usually begins with a verb and ends with a period. The subject (*you*) is not shown. An **exclamatory sentence** shows strong feeling or surprise. It ends with an exclamation mark. An **interjection** also shows strong feeling and ends with an exclamation mark. An interjection is a word or group of words, not a complete sentence.

Imperative Sentence	Look for Indians near the river.
Exclamatory Sentences	I can't believe it! The squirrels are swimming!
Interjection	Hurray!

Directions Write *E* if the sentence is exclamatory. Write *I* if the sentence is imperative.

1. Help me load the ship with these boxes. I
2. Bring some hickory nuts to the ship. I
3. Good dog! Go! E
4. Incredible! E
5. Ask the Indians for help. I

Directions Write the correct end punctuation for each sentence. Then write *E* if the sentence is exclamatory and *I* if the sentence is imperative.

6. Find a good boat first . I
7. Look for a dog that can swim . I
8. Your dog is as huge as a bear ! E
9. I cannot believe they explored so much ! E
10. Fetch the stick for me . I

Unit 1 Lewis and Clark and Me Grammar 2

Grammar Transparency 2, TR DVD

English Language Learners

Language production: Imperative and exclamatory sentences Model an imperative sentence: *Come to my house.* Have students take turns changing one word in the sentence to make a new sentence. Repeat the same activity using an exclamatory sentence: *I just won first prize!*

Handwriting For students who are not accustomed to writing the letters *l, h, t, i* and *j,* provide extra practice with words such as *hilly, tattle,* and *jungle.*

DAY 1 Language Arts

Objectives

- Understand and identify the features of an expository composition.

MINI-LESSON

5-Day Planner

Guide to Mini-Lessons

DAY 1	Read Like a Writer
DAY 2	Main Idea and Details
DAY 3	Chronological Order
DAY 4	Revising Strategy: Adding
DAY 5	Proofread Imperative and Exclamatory Sentences

Writing—Expository Composition
Introduce

MINI-LESSON

Read Like a Writer

INTERACT with TEXT

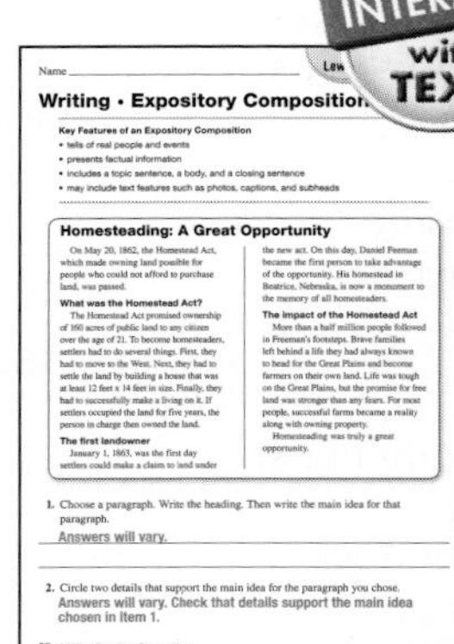
Reader's and Writer's Notebook p. 52

- **Introduce** This week you will write an expository composition. An expository composition gives factual information about a topic.

Prompt	Think about another time in history when people found opportunity in a new place. Now write an expository composition about it.
Trait	Organization
Mode	Expository

- **Examine Model Text** Let's read an example of an expository composition about a time in history when people found opportunity in a new place. Have students read "Homesteading: A Great Opportunity," on p. 52 of the *Reader's and Writer's Notebook.*

- **Key Features** An expository composition tells of **real people and events.** Have students circle the name of a real person and one real event.

An expository composition presents **factual information.** Have students read aloud the event they circled and discuss what makes it fact.

An expository composition includes **a topic sentence, a body, and a closing sentence.** Have students draw a box around the topic sentence, another box around the body, and another box around the closing sentence.

An expository composition may include text features such as **photos, captions,** or **subheads.** Have students tell what text features they see in this expository composition and read them aloud. Guide students to use the subheads to help them predict the topic of each paragraph.

Review
Key features

Review the key features of an expository composition with students. You may want to post the key features in the classroom for students to refer to as they work on their stories.

Key Features of an Expository Composition

- tells of real people and events
- presents factual information
- includes a topic sentence, a body, and a concluding sentence
- may include text features such as photos, captions, and subheads

Write Guy
Jeff Anderson

Conferencing Is Listening

Conferring about student's writing is about teachers listening. What is the student trying to say? What help does he need? We can ask questions to keep students speaking. *What do you want your reader to know?*

ROUTINE **Quick Write for Fluency** **Team Talk**

1. **Talk** Have partners tell each other what they know about the features of an expository composition.
2. **Write** Each student writes a few sentences using his or her own words to describe the features of an expository composition.
3. **Share** Have partners read their sentences to each other.

Routines Flip Chart

English Language Learners

Leveled support: Main idea Prepare students to write main ideas and details by having them identify them in the model.

Beginning Read a sentence from the model. Ask students if it is the main idea or not.

Intermediate Read a main idea from a paragraph of the model. Have students identify a detail to support it.

Advanced/Advanced High Have students write, in their own words, the main idea of several paragraphs from the model. After each main idea have them write one supporting detail.

Wrap Up Your Day

- ✔ **Build Concepts** What did you learn about why people want to explore new lands?
- ✔ **Oral Vocabulary** Have students use the Amazing Words they learned in context sentences.
- ✔ **Homework** Send home this week's Family Times newsletter on *Let's Practice It!* pp. 11–12 on the *Teacher Resources DVD-ROM.*

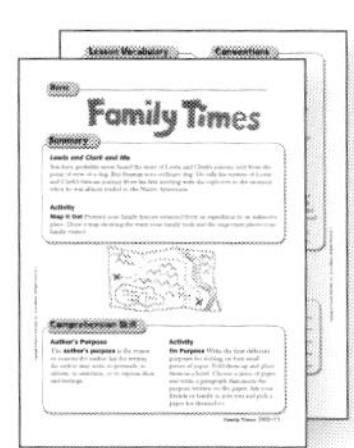

Let's Practice It!
TR DVD•11–12

Preview DAY 2

Tell students that tomorrow they will read about the adventures of Lewis's dog on the Lewis and Clark Expedition.

Objectives

- Expand the weekly concept.
- Develop oral vocabulary.

Today at a Glance

Oral Vocabulary
seek, fortune

Word Analysis
Suffixes *-or, -er*

Literary Terms
Sensory words

Story Structure
Setting

Lesson Vocabulary
◉ Word endings

Reading
"Westward Ho!"
Lewis and Clark and Me

Fluency
Appropriate phrasing

Research and Inquiry
Navigate/Search

Spelling
Long *a* and *i*

Conventions
Imperative and exclamatory sentences

Writing
Expository composition

Concept Talk

Question of the Week

What opportunities can be found in new places?

Expand the concept

Remind students of the weekly concept question. Tell students that today they will begin reading *Lewis and Clark and Me*. As they read, encourage students to think about how exploring new territories provides for new opportunities.

Anchored Talk

Develop oral language

Use the photos on pp. 46–47 and the read aloud "Johnny Appleseed" to talk about the Amazing Words: *pioneer, traveled, settlers, territories*. Add these and other concept-related words to the concept map to develop students' knowledge of the topic. Discuss the following questions. Remind students to listen attentively to other students and to answer with appropriate detail. Encourage students to build upon the ideas of others when they answer.

- How does a *pioneer* help create opportunities for others?
- What kinds of things do you think *settlers* looked for before deciding to settle in **new** *territories?*
- What are some places you have *traveled?* What kinds of opportunities do travelers look for in new places?

Oral Vocabulary
Amazing Words

Amazing Words Oral Vocabulary Routine

Teach Amazing Words

1. **Introduce** Write the Amazing Word *seek* on the board. Have students say it aloud with you. Relate *seek* to the photographs on pp. 46–47 and "Johnny Appleseed." What did Johnny Appleseed *seek* as he traveled the Midwest? What do pioneers *seek*? Have students determine the definition of the word. (*Seek* means "to try and find or get.")
2. **Demonstrate** Have students answer questions to demonstrate understanding. What did settlers *seek* back in the 1800s? Do you think people who come to live in our country today *seek* similar things?
3. **Apply** Have students apply their understanding. What would you *seek* if you had the opportunity?

See p. OV•2 to teach *fortune*.

Routines Flip Chart

Apply Amazing Words

As students read "Westward Ho!" on p. 51, have them think about how the settlers went West to *seek* their *fortune*.

Connect to reading

Explain that today students will read about the experiences of a dog that accompanied the explorers Lewis and Clark. As they read, they should think about how this week's concept question and the Amazing Words *seek* and *fortune* apply to the story of the dog that accompanied Lewis and Clark.

Amazing Words

pioneer	fortune
traveled	experiences
settlers	prepared
territories	foreign
seek	improve

ELL **Reinforce Vocabulary** Use the Day 2 instruction on ELL Poster 2 to teach lesson vocabulary and the lesson concept.

ELL Poster 2

Objectives

- Use the suffixes *-or* and *-er* to determine the meaning of an unknown word.
- Understand how authors use sensory words.
- Identify setting as an element of story structure.

Word Analysis
Suffixes *-or, -er*

Teach suffixes *-or, -er*

Tell students that the suffixes *-or* and *-er* are affixes added to the end of verbs to create nouns. These suffixes come from Middle English and German and can mean "someone who." Have students choose a word from the chart and use the meanings of the base word and the suffix to generate a definition of the word.

Model

Think Aloud I will choose the word *contractor* from the chart. Write *contractor* on the board and circle the suffix *-or*. I see the suffix *-or* and the base word *contract.* I know the verb *contract* can mean "to hire someone." The suffix *-or* means "someone who." *Contractor* means "someone who hires people."

-or	*-er*
contractor	seeker
director	employer
counselor	settler
navigator	explorer

Guide practice

Have students choose two words from each column. Have them identify the base words and use the suffix to generate a definition of the word.

On their own

Have students check their definitions in a dictionary. Then have students identify the base words and define the rest of the words in the chart. Follow the Strategy for Meaningful Word Parts to teach the word *seeker*.

ROUTINE Strategy for Meaningful Word Parts

1. **Introduce word parts** Display the word *seeker.* I will circle the suffix *-er* and underline the base word *seek.*
2. **Connect to meaning** Define each smaller word part. *Seek* means "to try and find or get." The suffix *-er* means "one who."
3. **Read the word** Blend the meaningful word parts together to read the word *seeker.* Then blend meanings to find the meaning of *seeker.* A *seeker* is "someone who is trying to find or get something."

Continue the routine with the words *employer* and *counselor*.

Routines Flip Chart

Literary Terms
Sensory Words

Teach sensory words Sensory words are words or phrases that help the reader experience the way things look, smell, taste, sound, or feel. Authors use sensory words to make the characters and setting seem real by appealing to the reader's senses.

Model Think Aloud Let's look back at "Jefferson's Bargain" on page 49. The sensory language the author uses in the last sentence gives me an image of what it might be like for pioneers to see the country for the first time. When the author talks about a far-reaching wilderness, it appeals to my sense of how the land might look.

Guide practice Look back at "The Storyteller," from the previous week. Direct students to paragraph 2 on p. 25. Point out how sensory words help the reader better understand how Ms. Ada tells stories.

On their own Have students look for examples of sensory words in other selections of their Student Edition.

Story Structure
Setting

Teach setting Setting is the time and place in which the events in a story occur. It is important for readers to understand how the setting influences the plot and characters in a story.

Model Think Aloud I see that *Lewis and Clark and Me* is historical fiction. I know that setting is very important in historical fiction because the events in the story are based on real events in history. The events in the plot could not occur the same way at any other time or place.

Guide practice Look back at "Jefferson's Bargain" to come up with details for a setting for a possible pioneer historical fiction story. Have students tell how the setting would influence the story's events and characters.

On their own Have students think of a story they have read in which the setting was very important to the characters and plot. Have them explain how the story would have been different in another time or place.

Academic Vocabulary

sensory images A sensory image is any detail that stimulates any of the senses or imagination.

historical fiction Historical fiction takes place in a factually historical setting. Sometimes real historical people may be characters in the story.

Objectives

- ◎ Use word endings to determine the meanings of words.
- Read grade-level text with appropriate phrasing.

Vocabulary Strategy for ◎ Word Endings

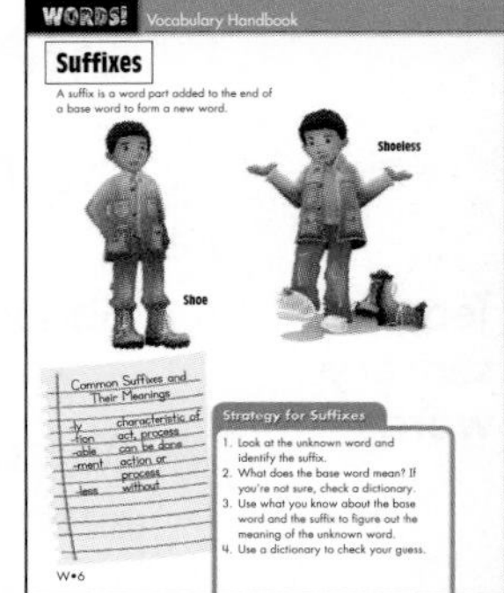

Student Edition p. W•6

Teach word endings

Envision It!

Tell students that when they encounter an unknown word, they may be able to use the strategy of word structure to figure it out. Explain how separating word endings and base words can help students figure out the meanings of unknown words. Refer students to *Words!* on p. W•6 in the Student Edition for additional practice. Then read "Westward Ho!" on p. 51 with students.

Model the strategy

Think Aloud Write the word *migrating* on the board. I know that the ending *-ing* is a common ending added to verbs. When I cover the *-ing* ending, I see *migrat*. If I put back the final *e*, I recognize the word *migrate*. I know that birds migrate south in winter. *Migrating* must have something to do with moving from place to place.

Guide practice

Write this sentence on the board: *The students yearned for a longer recess.* Have students determine the base word and ending in the vocabulary word *yearned*. Discuss the meaning of *yearn* and how adding *-ed* affects its meaning. Point out that if students do not know the meaning of a base word, they should use context clues or look up the word in a dictionary. For additional support, use *Envision It! Pictured Vocabulary Cards* or *Tested Vocabulary Cards*.

On their own

Read "Westward Ho!" on p. 51. Have students use word structure to determine the meanings for the lesson vocabulary and other words that they may not know in the selection. For additional practice, use *Reader's and Writer's Notebook* p. 53.

INTERACT with TEXT

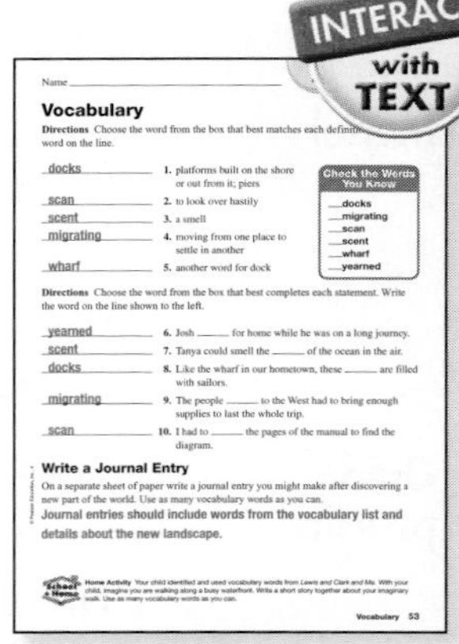

Reader's and Writer's Notebook p. 53

Objectives
• Determine the meaning of English words with affixes from Greek, Latin, and other languages.
Envision It! Words to Know
docks
migrating
scent
scan
wharf
yearned
READING STREET ONLINE
VOCABULARY ACTIVITIES
www.ReadingStreet.com

Vocabulary Strategy for

Affixes: Word Endings

Word Structure When you read an academic vocabulary word you don't know, you may be able to use the ending to figure out its meaning. Is *-ed* or *-ing* at the end of the word? The ending *-ed* is Old English and is added to a verb to make it past tense, or tell about past actions. The ending *-ing* is added to a verb to make it tell about present or ongoing actions.

1. Find a word that ends in *-ed* or *-ing*. Put your finger over the *-ed* or *-ing*.
2. Look at the base word. Do you know what the base word means?
3. Try your meaning in the sentence.
4. If it makes sense, add the ending and read the sentence again.

Read "Westward Ho!" Use what you know about endings to help you figure out this week's *Words to Know.*

Words to Write Reread "Westward Ho!" Imagine you are exploring an unknown river. Describe your first day on the water. Include details on what you see, hear, smell, and feel to help the reader experience your trip. Use words from the *Words to Know* list.

50

WESTWARD HO!

In the 1800s, America grew ever larger as land in the West was bought. As it grew, men and women of a certain kind yearned to travel west into the unknown. They had pioneer spirit.

There were no roads, of course. However, rivers made good highways for boats. In my mind I can see the pioneers with all their goods, waiting on the wharf in St. Louis. Sailors are busy loading and unloading ships. The pioneers load their belongings onto flatboats tied to the docks.

As they traveled, pioneers would scan the country for food and Indians. There were no grocery stores. And they never knew how the Indians would receive them. If the Indians were friendly, they might talk and trade. If a trapper was present, they were lucky. Trappers knew the country and the Indians well.

It must have been exciting to see this country for the first time. Pioneers saw endless herds and flocks of animals migrating. They breathed pure air full of the scent of tall grasses and wildflowers.

Your Turn!

Need a Review? For help with using word structure to determine the meanings of words, see *Words!*

Ready to Try It? Read *Lewis and Clark and Me* on pp. 52–67.

51

Student Edition pp. 50–51

Reread for Fluency
Appropriate Phrasing

Model fluent reading Read paragraph 2 of "Westward Ho!" aloud, pausing at commas to meaningfully set off phrases and pausing appropriately at the end of each sentence. Tell students that you are reading the passage with appropriate phrasing, paying special attention to how punctuation divides words and sentences into meaningful phrases and provides clues for pausing.

ROUTINE Choral Reading

1. **Select a passage** Read paragraph 2 of "Westward Ho!" aloud.
2. **Model** Have students track the print as you read with the appropriate phrasing.
3. **Guide practice** Have students read along with you.
4. **On their own** For optimal fluency, students should reread three or four times with appropriate phrasing.

Routines Flip Chart

Lesson Vocabulary

docks platforms built on the shore or out from the shore; wharves; piers

migrating going from one region to another with the change in seasons

scan to glance at; look over hastily

scent smell

wharf platform built on the shore or out from the shore beside which ships can load or unload

yearned felt a longing or desire

Differentiated Instruction

SI Strategic Intervention

Word endings Have students identify the word endings in this week's lesson vocabulary. Have students separate the base word and the ending and explain how the word ending changes the meaning of the base word.

ELL

English Language Learners

Build Academic Vocabulary Use the lesson vocabulary pictured on p. 50 to teach the meanings of *docks*, *migrating*, and *scent*. Call on pairs to write the words on sticky notes and use them to label images of the words on the ELL Poster.

Objectives

- Understand the elements of historical fiction.
- Use text features to preview and predict.
- Set a purpose for reading.

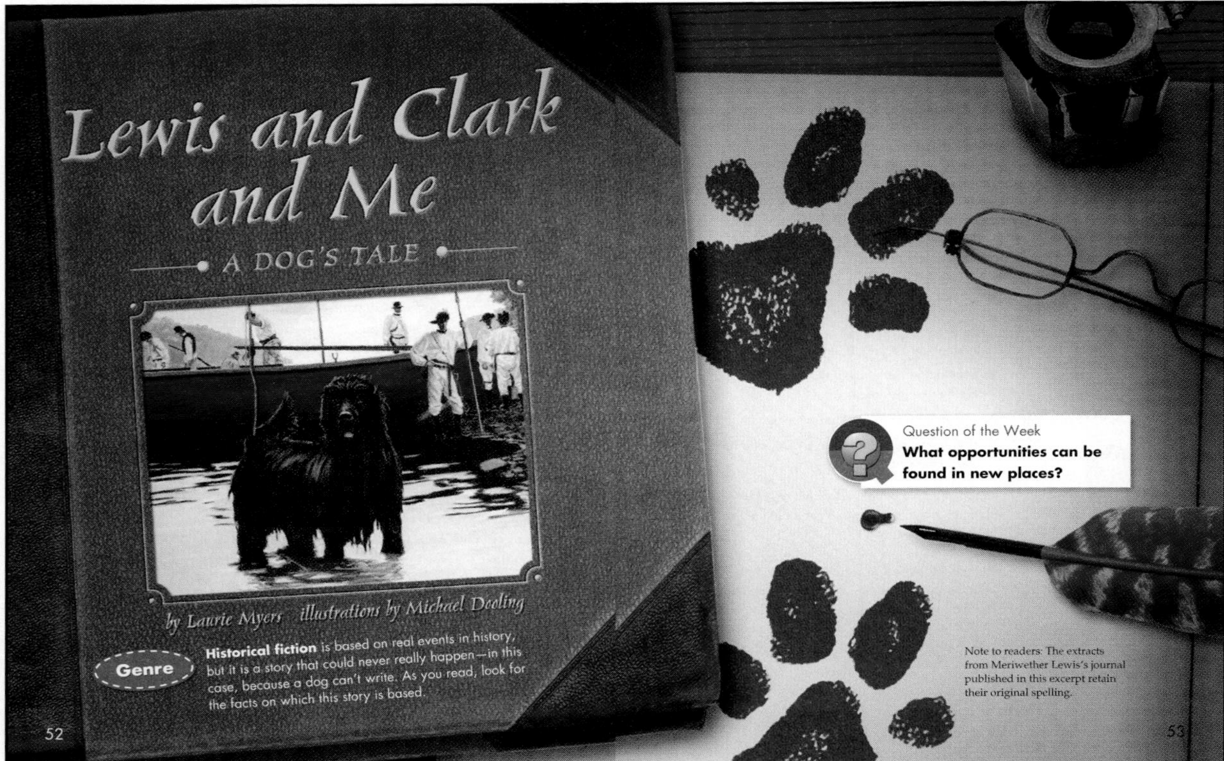

Student Edition pp. 52–53

Build Background

Discuss expedition of Lewis & Clark

Team Talk Have students turn to a partner and discuss the Question of the Week and these questions about the expedition of Lewis and Clark. Remind students to ask and answer questions with appropriate detail and to give suggestions that build on the ideas of others.

- What do you know about the explorations of Lewis and Clark?
- What kinds of experiences do you think Lewis and Clark might have had as they explored these new lands?
- Who or what do you think Lewis and Clark would have brought with them on their journey? Why might a dog be useful on an expedition?

Connect to selection

Have students discuss their answers with the class. Possible responses: Lewis and Clark explored the lands from the Mississippi all of the way to the Pacific Ocean. I think Lewis and Clark saw a lot of animals and landscapes that they had never seen before. I think that Lewis and Clark must have brought lots of supplies. Bringing a dog along would be useful because dogs are loyal, they protect, and they can smell other animals. For additional opportunities to build background, use the Background Building Audio.

Prereading Strategies

Genre Explain that **historical fiction** is realistic fiction that takes place in the past. It is a combination of imagination and fact because fictional characters are placed in a factually historical setting. Real historical people sometimes appear as characters. Their speeches and actions may be fictional or could be based on factual experiences.

Preview and predict Have students preview the title, illustrations, and insets in *Lewis and Clark and Me*. Have them gain an overview of the text and predict what they will find out as they read.

Set purpose Prior to reading, have students set their own purposes for reading this selection. To help students set a purpose, ask them to think about what opportunities could be found by joining Lewis and Clark on their exploration.

Strategy Response Log

INTERACT with TEXT

Have students use p. 8 in the *Reader's and Writer's Notebook* to review and use the strategy of questioning.

Small Group Time

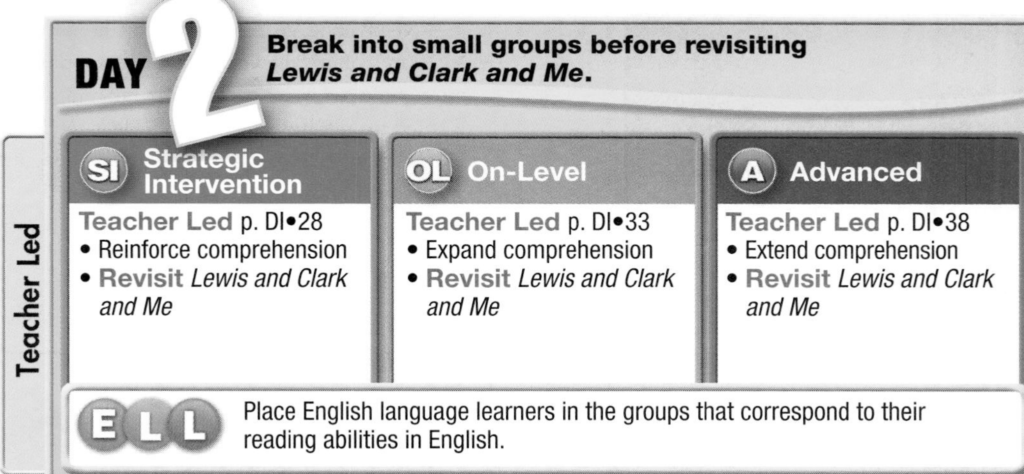

DAY 2 **Break into small groups before revisiting *Lewis and Clark and Me*.**

Teacher Led

SI Strategic Intervention	OL On-Level	A Advanced
Teacher Led p. DI•28 • Reinforce comprehension • Revisit *Lewis and Clark and Me*	Teacher Led p. DI•33 • Expand comprehension • Revisit *Lewis and Clark and Me*	Teacher Led p. DI•38 • Extend comprehension • Revisit *Lewis and Clark and Me*

ELL Place English language learners in the groups that correspond to their reading abilities in English.

Practice Stations	Independent Activities
• Words to Know • Get Fluent • Word Wise	• Background Building Audio • *Reader's and Writer's Notebook* • Research and Inquiry

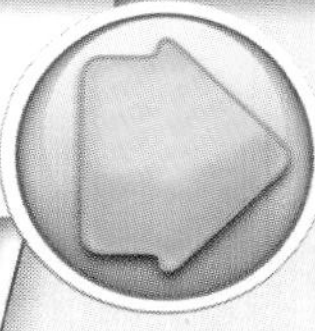

Differentiated Instruction

Advanced
Have students create a T-Chart with one column labeled *Dog's Point of View* and the other *Human Point of View*. Have students list how humans and dogs would explore and experience a new place differently.

Multidraft Reading

For **Whole Group** instruction, choose one of the reading options below. For each reading, have students set the purpose indicated.

Option 1
Day 2 Read the selection. Use Guide Comprehension to monitor and clarify understanding.
Day 3 Reread the selection. Use Extend Thinking to develop higher-order thinking skills.

Option 2
Day 2 Read the first half of the selection, using both Guide Comprehension and Extend Thinking instruction.
Day 3 Read the second half of the selection, using both Guide Comprehension and Extend Thinking instruction.

English Language Learners
Build background To build background, review the selection summary in English *(ELL Handbook* p. 37). Use the Retelling Cards to provide visual support for the summary.

Objectives

◎ Identify author's purpose to improve comprehension.

OPTION 1 Guide Comprehension Skills and Strategies

Teach Author's Purpose

Author's Purpose Remind students that authors often have more than one purpose, or reason for writing, such as to entertain, to persuade, to inform, or to express ideas and feelings. Have students read p. 54 to identify the author's purpose for writing.

Corrective Feedback

If... students are unable to identify the author's purpose,
then... use the model to guide students in identifying author's purpose.

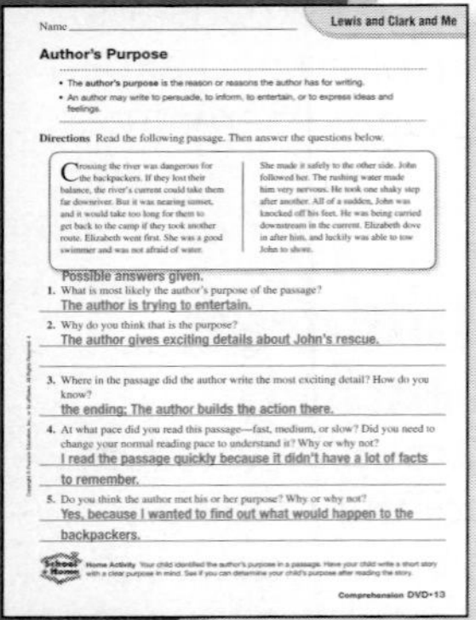

Lewis and Clark and Me

Author's Purpose

Possible answers given.

1. What is most likely the author's purpose of the passage? The author is trying to entertain.
2. Why do you think that is the purpose? The author gives exciting details about John's rescue.
3. Where in the passage did the author write the most exciting detail? How do you know? the ending; The author builds the action there.
4. At what pace did you read this passage—fast, medium, or slow? Did you need to change your normal reading pace to understand it? Why or why not? I read the passage quickly because it didn't have a lot of facts to remember.
5. Do you think the author met his or her purpose? Why or why not? Yes, because I wanted to find out what would happen to the backpackers.

Let's Practice It
TR DVD•13

Model the Skill

Think Aloud I read the entry at the beginning of the story at the top of page 54. What is this entry about? **(It tells what is going to happen in the story.)** After reading the entry, what do you think is the author's purpose? **(to inform)**

The year is 1803. Lewis and Clark are planning their expedition to explore the territory west of the Mississippi River. Lewis is looking for a dog to accompany the expedition, and as the story opens, he meets a 150-pound Newfoundland dog named Seaman, who goes on to tell of their adventures.

"Seaman!"

I glance at the man beside me.

"Look alive. Here's buyers."

Something caught my attention beyond him, down the wharf—a group of men, but I saw only one. It was Lewis. He was a full head taller than the other men I had known on the docks. And he was dressed in a different way—white breeches and a short blue coat with buttons that shone in the sun. A tall pointed hat with a feather made him look even taller.

Lewis walked along the dock with a large stride. There was a purpose about him. My life on the wharves was good, but I was a young dog and yearned for more. At the time I didn't know exactly what. I sensed that this man was part of what I wanted. I sat straighter as he approached. The man who owned me stood straighter, too. Lewis slowed.

"Need a dog, sir?" my man asked.

"I'm lookin'," Lewis replied. He stooped down and looked me right in the eye. I wagged my tail and stepped forward. I wanted to sniff this strange man. He extended his hand for me. He didn't smell like any I had ever smelled, and it made me want to sniff him all over.

Lewis scratched the back of my neck, where I liked to be scratched.

54

Student Edition pp. 54–55

Inferring • Analysis Reread page 54. Why does Seaman sit up straighter as Lewis approaches? Describe the interaction between the characters. What inference can you make about what Seaman thinks of Lewis? Use evidence from the text to support your understanding. Possible response: Seaman sits straighter because he wants to look good for Lewis. Seaman thinks that Lewis is different from other men. He wants Lewis to buy him so he can be with Lewis.

OPTION 2 Extend Thinking Think Critically

Higher-Order Thinking Skills

Author's Purpose • Evaluation The author tells this story from Seaman's point of view. Do you think this was a good choice? Use details from pages 54–55 to explain your evaluation. Possible response: I think it was a good choice because it is very interesting and fun to hear about this historical event through the eyes of a dog. I like the detailed way that the author has Seaman describe meeting Lewis.

But, Seaman, the dog, is telling the story. Using a dog as a storyteller is a fun and unusual way to tell about this historic trip. What other purpose do you think the author had? (to entertain)

"I'm headed out west, up the Missouri River," Lewis said.

My man's face brightened.

"This dog be perfect, sir. These dogs can swim. Newfoundlands, they call them. Rescue a drowning man in rough water or in a storm. Look at these paws. You won't find another dog with paws like that. They's webbed." He spread my toes to show the webbing.

"So they are," Lewis replied. Lewis began feeling my chest and hindquarters. His hands were large and muscular.

"Water rolls off this coat," my man added. He pulled up a handful of my thick, dense double coat.

Lewis examined my coat and nodded.

"I know the Mississippi, sir, but I don't know the Meesori," my man said.

"It's off the Mississippi, headin' northwest."

55

Literary Elements: Character • Evaluation
If you were Captain Lewis, would you choose Seaman to go with you on this trip? Provide details to support your answer. Possible response: Yes, I'd take Seaman because Lewis's trip is on a river. Seaman can swim and rescue drowning men. He can catch fish too.

On Their Own

Have students reread p. 54 and list one or more of the author's purposes for writing this story. Have them include an explanation for each purpose. For additional practice, use *Let's Practice It!* p. 13 on the *Teacher Resources DVD-ROM.*

Differentiated Instruction

SI **Strategic Intervention**
Have students point out details from the text that show this story is told from a dog's point of view.

 **Advanced**
Have students rewrite the meeting of Seaman and Captain Lewis from Lewis's point of view.

Connect to Social Studies

President Thomas Jefferson asked Meriwether Lewis and William Clark to explore the territory acquired by the Louisiana Purchase of 1803. Jefferson hoped they would discover a waterway leading to the Pacific Ocean. The two explorers led their Corps of Discovery westward along the Missouri and Columbia Rivers to the Pacific and back. Although a direct waterway to the Pacific does not exist, the explorers brought back a great deal of information about the lands they explored.

ELL

English Language Learners
Activate prior knowledge Create a web to record students' prior knowledge of dogs. We're going to read about how a dog gets to go on Lewis's expedition. What kind of dog is Seaman? What other kinds of dogs do you know? What are some things that dogs can do? Use students' answers to create a web.

DAY 2 Read and Comprehend

Objectives

◎ Ask questions to monitor and adjust comprehension.

OPTION 1 Skills and Strategies, continued

Teach Questioning

Questioning Have students read p. 56 and then, in order to monitor their comprehension, have them generate a question about the characters or about why something happened.

Corrective Feedback

If... students cannot generate a question,
then... use the model to help them use questioning to monitor and adjust comprehension.

Model the Strategy

Think Aloud After reading the first two paragraphs on page 56, I ask myself, *Why did Lewis get a piece of wood and throw it?* How can I find the answer to this question? (read on) I read on and find the answer to my question: he threw it to test Seaman. This answer

"North, you say. Ah. It'll be cold up that river. Won't bother this one, though." He patted me firmly on the back.

Lewis stood and looked around. He found a piece of wood that had broken off a crate. He showed it to me, then threw it.

"Go," he said.

I wanted to go. I wanted to do whatever this man asked. But I belonged to another. I looked at my man.

"Go on," he said.

I ran for the stick and returned it to Lewis.

"How much?" Lewis asked.

"Twenty dollars. And a bargain at that."

Lewis looked down at me. I lifted my head proudly.

"Won't find a better dog than this. Perfect for your trip," my man said, trying to convince Lewis.

It wasn't necessary. Lewis wanted me. I could tell. He had liked me the minute he saw me. The feeling was mutual. Lewis paid my man twenty dollars.

"Does he have a name?" Lewis asked.

"I been callin' him Seaman, but you can name him anything you like."

"Come, Seaman," Lewis called.

As we walked away, my rope in his hand, he put his other hand on my head. After that, he didn't need a rope. I would follow this man to the ends of the Earth.

...the dog was of the newfoundland breed one that I prised much for his docility and qualifications generally for my journey....

Meriwether Lewis November 16, 1803

56

Student Edition pp. 56–57

Text Structure • Evaluation Why do you think the author shows an excerpt from one of Captain Lewis's journals at the bottom of page 56? Possible response: The journal shows the story was based on an actual event. The contrast between Seaman's and Lewis's viewpoints makes the story more interesting to read.

OPTION 2 Think Critically, continued

Higher-Order Thinking Skills

Questioning • Synthesis What kinds of interpretive and evaluative questions can you ask yourself to be sure you have understood what you have read? Possible response: What is the author trying to tell me by including the detail that Seaman says he would follow Lewis to the ends of the earth? Why did the author write the meeting of Lewis and Seaman in this particular way? How would I say it instead?

leads me to another question: *Why does Lewis want to test Seaman?* How can I find the answer to this kind of question? (combine what I know with what I have read) I think he tests Seaman because he wants to know if Seaman was loyal to his owner and if he follows directions.

Squirrels

I caught fish off the docks. I chased animals in the woods. But hunting came alive for me on the river—the Ohio, Lewis called it.

I have always loved the water, so the day we boarded the boat and pushed out onto the Ohio River was just about the happiest day of my life. Lewis was excited, too. I could tell by the way he walked. And his voice was louder than usual.

The men were also excited. I could hear it in their voices. They didn't complain when they loaded the boat. Lewis was telling them what to load and how to load it. Anyway, that afternoon, Lewis and I and some men started down the river.

I rode in the back of the boat. It was the highest place and gave me the best view. From there I could scan both banks and the water with just a glance. The first two weeks I couldn't get enough of it. There were animals I had not seen before. Smells I had not smelled. My skin tingled with excitement.

57

Draw Conclusions • Analysis How does Seaman infer and conclude that both Lewis and the crew are excited the day the boat is boarded and they push off onto the river? Possible response: Seaman notices their voices, and he notices that Lewis was walking faster.

Cause and Effect • Analysis What are the effects for Seaman of boarding the boat and pushing out onto the Ohio River for Seaman? Seaman is excited and happy because he sees animals he had not seen before and notices smells he had not smelled before.

On Their Own

Have students check their understanding and record another literal question they have as they reread pp. 56–57.

Connect to Social Studies

For three years Meriwether Lewis and William Clark kept journals about their expedition. They sketched and collected samples of the unusual plants and animals they saw. They also met and traded with Native American peoples such as the Mandan (in what is now North Dakota) and the Shoshone (in what is now Montana). The maps they drew of the areas they explored led a great number of explorers, traders, and settlers to make their way across the West.

ELL

English Language Learners

Activate prior knowledge Ask students to share what they know about journal writing. Ask: Who is the author of the journal entry on page 56? (Lewis)

Questioning Read aloud the last line on p. 57. Model using the questioning strategy to monitor comprehension. The last sentence says: *My skin tingled with excitement.* I wonder why Seaman says this. I ask myself, "Why is Seaman so excited?" I look back at the sentences before the last sentence to find an answer to my question. What is the answer to the question? (He sees animals he had not seen before. He smells things he has not smelled before.) Are there any questions you can ask about why something happened?

DAY 2 Read and Comprehend

Objectives

- Use word endings to determine meanings of unknown words.

OPTION 1 Skills and Strategies, continued

Teach Word Endings

Word Endings Have students name the base words and meanings for *hiring, hunting,* and *scanned* on p. 58. (Base words: *hire, hunt, scan.* Meanings: *hiring*—paying someone to do something for you; *hunting*—looking for animals to kill; *scanned*—looked out over an area.)

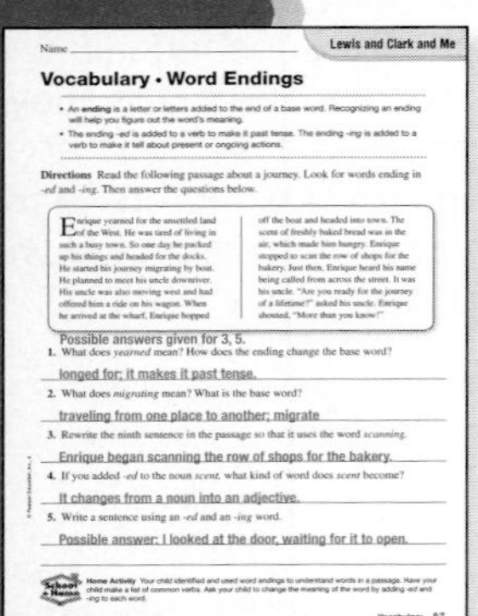
Name ______ Lewis and Clark and Me

Vocabulary • Word Endings

- An **ending** is a letter or letters added to the end of a base word. Recognizing an ending will help you figure out the word's meaning.
- The ending *-ed* is added to a verb to make it past tense. The ending *-ing* is added to a verb to make it tell about present or ongoing actions.

Directions Read the following passage about a journey. Look for words ending in *-ed* and *-ing*. Then answer the questions below.

Enrique yearned for the unsettled land of the West. He was tired of living in such a busy town. So one day he packed up his things and headed for the docks. He started his journey migrating by boat. He planned to meet his uncle downriver. His uncle was also moving west and had offered him a ride on his wagon. When he arrived at the wharf, Enrique hopped off the boat and headed into town. The scent of freshly baked bread was in the air, which made him hungry. Enrique stopped to scan the row of shops for the bakery. Just then, Enrique heard his name being called from across the street. It was his uncle. "Are you ready for the journey of a lifetime?" asked his uncle. Enrique shouted, "More than you know!"

Possible answers given for 3, 5.

1. What does *yearned* mean? How does the ending change the base word?
   longed for; it makes it past tense.
2. What does *migrating* mean? What is the base word?
   traveling from one place to another; migrate
3. Rewrite the ninth sentence in the passage so that it uses the word *scanning*.
   Enrique began scanning the row of shops for the bakery.
4. If you added *-ed* to the noun *scent*, what kind of word does *scent* become?
   It changes from a noun into an adjective.
5. Write a sentence using an *-ed* and an *-ing* word.
   Possible answer: I looked at the door, waiting for it to open.

School + Home **Home Activity** Your child identified and used word endings to understand words in a passage. Have your child make a list of common verbs. Ask your child to change the meaning of the word by adding *-ed* and *-ing* to each word.

Vocabulary 57

Reader's and Writer's Notebook p. 57

Corrective Feedback

If... students have difficulty using word structure to determine meanings,
then... use the model to help them understand how to use word structure.

Model the Skill

Think Aloud Read the second sentence in paragraph 3 on p. 58 aloud. Write *scanned* on the board. When I come to the verb *scanned,* I see that it has an *-ed* ending. What does the ending *-ed* tell you about this verb? (The action happened in the past.)

The river was low, and the men had to pole much of the way. When they weren't poling, they were digging channels for our boat or hiring oxen to pull the boat from the shore.

We were only a couple of weeks down the river when I had my first great day of hunting. The river wasn't quite as shallow and the current not too strong, so the crew rowed along leisurely.

I was lying on the back deck of the boat. I had just scanned the shore—nothing of interest, just a few beaver and a deer. I decided to close my eyes for a nap. I blinked a few times and was ready to lay my head on my paws when something on the water up ahead caught my eye.

58

Student Edition pp. 58–59

OPTION 2 Think Critically, continued

Higher-Order Thinking Skills

Word Endings • Analysis Use context clues to determine the meaning of the word *poling* in paragraph 1 on page 58. I see the ending *-ing* and the base word *pole*. Possible response: The text says that the men had to pole and dig channels for the boat. So, I think poling must be a way of rowing the boat in shallow water by sticking a pole in the water to help push the boat along.

Generalize • Synthesis On page 59 Seaman says: *It is impossible to describe the urge I felt. It was as strong as anything I had ever known. I had to get those squirrels.* What can you generalize or infer about Seaman? Possible response: Seaman is a hunting dog with very strong instincts to hunt.

To help me understand this word, I'll cover up the ending. What is the base word? (scan) I know *scan* has to do with looking. *Scanned* probably means "looked at." To check, I'll try this meaning in the context of the sentence: "I had just looked at the shore." Does that make sense? (yes)

I stuck my nose in the air and sniffed. I recognized the scent immediately. Squirrel.

A squirrel on water? That was unusual. I had seen plenty of squirrels, but I had never seen one swim. There was something else strange. The smell of squirrel was especially strong. I had never known one squirrel to project so powerful a scent.

I stood to take a look. Right away I spotted a squirrel off the starboard side. He was swimming across the river. Another squirrel followed close behind. Without a second thought, I leaned over the side of the boat to get a better look.

I saw another squirrel. And another. I could not believe my eyes; hundreds of squirrels were crossing the river. The water up ahead was almost black with them. Every muscle in my body tightened to full alert.

Lewis was on the other side of the boat, talking to two of the men. I turned to him and barked.

"What is it?" he asked.

It is impossible to describe the urge I felt. It was as strong as anything I had ever known. I had to get those squirrels.

I barked again. Lewis scanned the water ahead.

"Look at that," he said to the men. "Squirrels crossing the river. Now why would they do that?"

"Food?" one man suggested.

Lewis paused for a moment. "There are hickory nuts on both banks."

"Migrating?" suggested the other.

Lewis nodded. "Maybe. Or perhaps they're—"

I barked again. They were wasting time wondering why the squirrels were crossing. It didn't matter. The squirrels were there. Hundreds of them, right in front of us. Sometimes men spend too much time thinking. They miss the fun of life.

59

Literary Elements: Character • Analysis The last paragraph on page 59 describes Seaman's thoughts as the men guess why the squirrels are crossing the river. What inferences can you make about Seaman's character? Possible response: He likes action. He doesn't like thinking about why it's happening. He wants to do something about it.

On Their Own

Have students list two or three words with *-ed* and *-ing* endings on p. 59. Then have them write the base word and give the meaning of the word. For additional practice, use *Reader's and Writer's Notebook* p. 57.

Connect to Social Studies

In the Midwest, summer and winter temperatures can differ greatly and weather changes may happen rapidly. Because land heats up and cools down more quickly than bodies of water, inland regions like the Midwest may have extreme temperature differences between their warmest and coldest months of the year. For example, North Dakota may have a summer high of 111°F and a winter low of -44°F. The Midwest can experience sudden violent weather, such as tornadoes, blizzards, hailstorms, and rapid temperature changes. The climate of the Midwest may affect the lives of the people and the animals who live there.

ELL

English Language Learners

Build vocabulary Direct students to the last sentence in paragraph 1 on p. 59. Read the sentence aloud. Explain that *project* is used as a verb here. Reread the sentence substituting *give off* for *project*. Point out that its pronunciation and meaning is different from the more familiar noun *project*. Ask: Can you find another word in the first paragraph on page 58 that can be either a noun or a verb? (pole) Have students pantomime the action *pole* and describe the noun *pole*. Encourage students to find another example of a word that can be either a noun or a verb in paragraph 2 on p. 59. (look, thought)

Objectives

- Sequence the plot's main events.

Let's Practice It
TR DVD•14

OPTION  Skills and Strategies, continued

Teach Sequence

Review **Sequence** Have students think about the events that happened when Seaman went to fetch a squirrel on p. 60. Ask students to summarize the information in sequence.

Corrective Feedback

If... students are unable to summarize the events in sequence,
then... use the model to help them use sequence to understand the text.

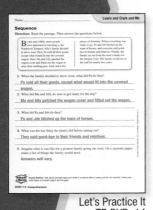

Model the Skill

Think Aloud When I summarize the information on page 60, I know I need to make sense of what I read. I learned that if I summarize the events in order, it will help me remember what happened in the story. What happened first?

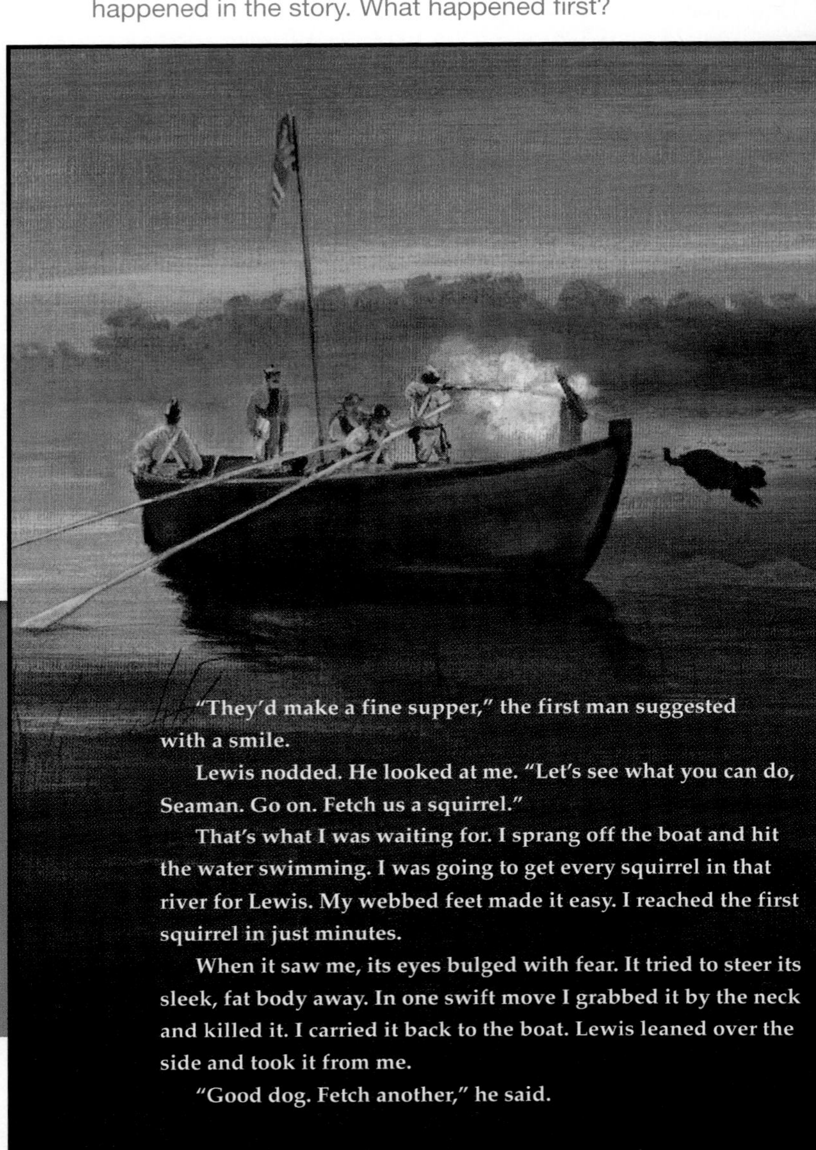

"They'd make a fine supper," the first man suggested with a smile.

Lewis nodded. He looked at me. "Let's see what you can do, Seaman. Go on. Fetch us a squirrel."

That's what I was waiting for. I sprang off the boat and hit the water swimming. I was going to get every squirrel in that river for Lewis. My webbed feet made it easy. I reached the first squirrel in just minutes.

When it saw me, its eyes bulged with fear. It tried to steer its sleek, fat body away. In one swift move I grabbed it by the neck and killed it. I carried it back to the boat. Lewis leaned over the side and took it from me.

"Good dog. Fetch another," he said.

60

Student Edition pp. 60–61

OPTION 2 Think Critically, continued

Higher-Order Thinking Skills

Review **Sequence • Synthesis** Reread Seaman's description of how he hunted for squirrels in paragraph 6 on page 61. Why do you think the author chose to have Seaman describe the sequence of events this way? Possible response: I think that it shows how excited Seaman was and how important this event was to him. He lost track of time because he was so happy getting squirrels for Lewis.

Sensory Words • Analysis Reread paragraphs 3 and 4 on page 60. What words appeal to your senses and help you feel like you are experiencing the hunt with Seaman? Possible response: The author uses words like *sprang* and *swift* to tell how Seaman moved. The author also describes the squirrel with vivid words saying that its *eyes bulged with fear,* and that it had a *sleek, fat body.*

(Lewis told Seaman to go fetch a squirrel.) Next, I read that Seaman jumped into the water and swam toward a squirrel. Then I remember how the squirrel reacted when it saw Seaman. What did it do? (Its eyes bulged with fear and it tried to swim away.) Finally, Seaman caught the squirrel and brought it back to the boat.

The crew had stopped rowing, and the boat drifted slowly toward the mass of squirrels.

"Look at Captain Lewis's dog!" yelled one of the rowers.

I turned and started swimming again. I could hear the men cheering me on. In two strokes I was on another squirrel.

"Good dog!" Lewis yelled. "Go!"

"Go," the crew echoed. "Go, Seaman, go!"

I went. And went. Over and over, I went. I went until I was exhausted. I don't know how long it lasted. Maybe one hour. Maybe four.

All I know is that when I finished, there was a pile of squirrels in the boat. Lewis and the crew were laughing and cheering. All the rest of the day the men were patting me and saying, "Good dog" and "Good boy" and "We'll be eatin' good tonight." The admiration of the crew was great, but the look of pride on Lewis's face was better than all the men's praise added together.

That night the men fried the squirrels, and we ate well.

In the three years that followed, I hunted almost every day. But the squirrels on the Ohio were my favorite.

...observed a number of squirrels swiming the Ohio... they appear to be making to the south;... I made my dog take as many each day as I had occation for, they wer fat and I thought them when fryed a pleesent food... he would take the squirel in the water kill them and swiming bring them in his mouth to the boat....

Meriwether Lewis September 11, 1803

61

On Their Own

Have students use a graphic organizer to list the sequence of events on p. 61. For additional practice, use *Let's Practice It!* p. 14 on the *Teacher Resources DVD-ROM.*

Background Knowledge • Evaluation • Text to Self Seaman likes to do things that please his owner. Do you or someone you know own a pet? How do pets show their love for their owners? How do owners show their love for their pets? Possible response: Pets show their love for their owners by obeying them and wanting to be near them. Owners show their love for their pets by taking very good care of them, praising them, and giving them treats.

Check Predictions Have students look back at the predictions they made earlier and discuss whether they were accurate. Then have students preview the rest of the selection and either adjust their predictions accordingly or make new predictions.

Differentiated Instruction

Strategic Intervention

Sequence Arrange students in small groups. Have one student say a sentence that tells what happened first. Then, the next student shares a sentence, telling something that happened next. The students continue taking turns until they have told the main events of the plot in sequence.

Advanced

Have students come up with a list of questions they would ask Lewis about the expedition or about his relationship with Seaman.

English Language Learners

Vocabulary: Idioms Focus students' attention on the idiom *cheering me on* in paragraph 3 on p. 61. Explain the ideas of *cheering me on* and *cheering me up*. *Cheering me on* means "to encourage me to continue on." *Cheering me up* is another common expression in English. It means "to make someone happy." Have students tell about a time when they either cheered someone on or cheered someone up.

Sequence Help students use the illustration to retell the sequence of events on pp. 60–61. Encourage students to use the words *first*, *next*, and *then* as they explain the sequence of events.

If you want to teach this selection in two sessions, stop here.

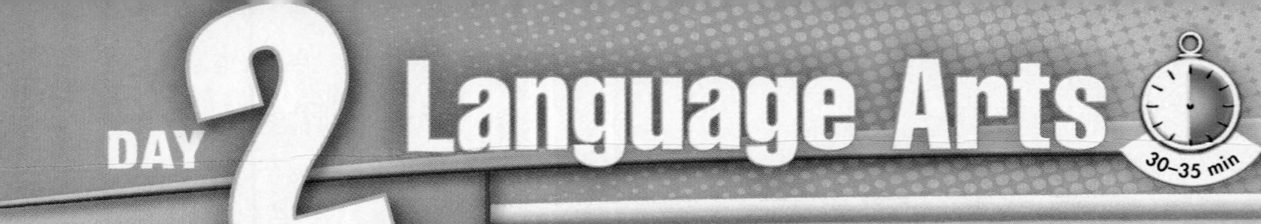

Objectives

- Find pertinent information from online and print sources.
- Recognize and correctly use imperative and exclamatory sentences.
- Practice correctly spelling words with long *a* and *i*.

Research and Inquiry
Navigate/Search

Teach Have students search the Internet using their inquiry questions and keywords from Day 1. If possible, have students also go to the library and look for books or other print sources on the discoveries of Lewis and Clark. Tell them to skim and scan each site or print source to find the main idea of the text and locate specific information about their topic. Point out that looking for bold or italicized words can help them figure out what kind of information the source will provide. Have students look for other features, such as headings, illustrations, captions, and highlighting. Remind students to take notes as they gather information.

Model Think Aloud When looking for information on how Lewis and Clark learned to communicate and trade with Native American tribes they met, I typed in the keywords *Lewis and Clark*, *communicate*, *trade*, and *Native Americans*. I found too many Web sites to read all of the information, so I skimmed the text for main ideas and I scanned for keywords in bold or italic type. The name *Sacagawea* came up several times. I think I will try using *Sacagawea* as a keyword and see if that helps me find more relevant information for my topic.

Guide practice Have students continue their search of appropriate Web sites or other print sources. Guide students in identifying the author, title, publisher, and publication year of a Web site, book, or other print source. Point out that students may have to search a Web site to find the author or organization that publishes the site and to find the date that the site was last updated. Explain that sometimes this information is written in small print at the bottom of the site.

On their own Have students write short summaries of useful information from the sources they find so that they will be able to create a report later. Remind students to also record the appropriate information from each source to begin a Works Cited page.

Conventions

Imperative and Exclamatory Sentences

Teach Write these sentences: *Put on the light now. What a bright light!* Show that the first sentence is imperative because it is a command and ends in a period. The second is exclamatory because it shows excitement and ends with an exclamation point.

Guide practice Students can make their writing strong and exciting using imperative and exclamatory sentences. In the sentences below, have students change the weak voice to a strong voice, and the boring style to an exciting style.

> **Weak Voice: I want you to bring me a pizza now.**
> **Boring Style: The sunset is beautiful.**

Daily Fix-It Use Daily Fix-It numbers 3 and 4 in the right margin.

Connect to oral language Have students look for, read, and identify imperative and exclamatory sentences in *Lewis and Clark and Me. (Fetch us a squirrel,* p. 60; *"Good dog!"* p. 60)

On their own For additional practice, use *Reader's and Writer's Notebook* p. 54.

Spelling

Long *a* and *i*

Teach Remind students that the long *a* and long *i* sounds can be spelled in different ways. Write *highway.* Underline *igh* and *ay.* Explain that *igh* spells the long *i* sound and *ay* spells the long *a* sound.

Guide practice Have students work in pairs.They should write each spelling word and underline the letters that spell the long *a* and long *i* sounds.

On their own For additional practice, use the *Reader's and Writer's Notebook,* p. 55.

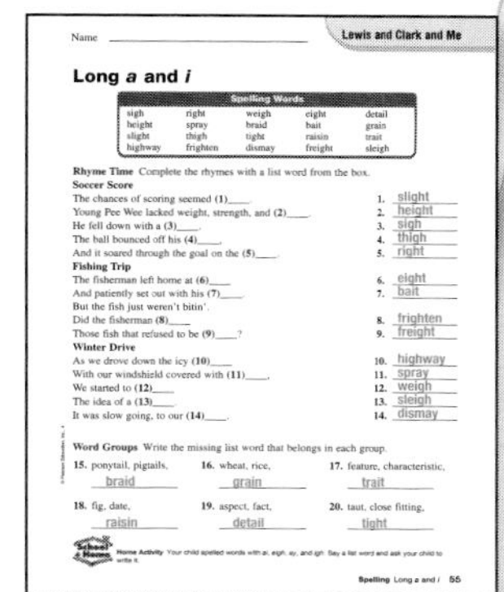
Name ______ Lewis and Clark and Me

Long *a* and *i*

Spelling Words				
sigh	right	weigh	eight	detail
height	spray	braid	bait	grain
slight	thigh	tight	raisin	trait
highway	frighten	dismay	freight	sleigh

Rhyme Time Complete the rhymes with a list word from the box.

Soccer Score
The chances of scoring seemed (1)____. 1. slight
Young Pee Wee lacked weight, strength, and (2)____. 2. height
He fell down with a (3)____. 3. sigh
The ball bounced off his (4)____, 4. thigh
And it soared through the goal on the (5)____. 5. right

Fishing Trip
The fisherman left home at (6)____ 6. eight
And patiently set out with his (7)____. 7. bait
But the fish just weren't bitin'.
Did the fisherman (8)____ 8. frighten
Those fish that refused to be (9)____? 9. freight

Winter Drive
As we drove down the icy (10)____ 10. highway
With our windshield covered with (11)____, 11. spray
We started to (12)____ 12. weigh
The idea of a (13)____ 13. sleigh
It was slow going, to our (14)____. 14. dismay

Word Groups Write the missing list word that belongs in each group.

15. ponytail, pigtails, braid
16. wheat, rice, grain
17. feature, characteristic, trait
18. fig, date, raisin
19. aspect, fact, detail
20. taut, close fitting, tight

School + Home **Home Activity** Your child spelled words with ai, eigh, ay, and igh. Say a list word and ask your child to write it.

Spelling Long *a* and *i* 55

Reader's and Writer's Notebook p. 55

Daily Fix-It

3. What a enormous country this is. *(an; is!)*
4. The state of California. Is one of the biggest state in the country. *(California is; states)*

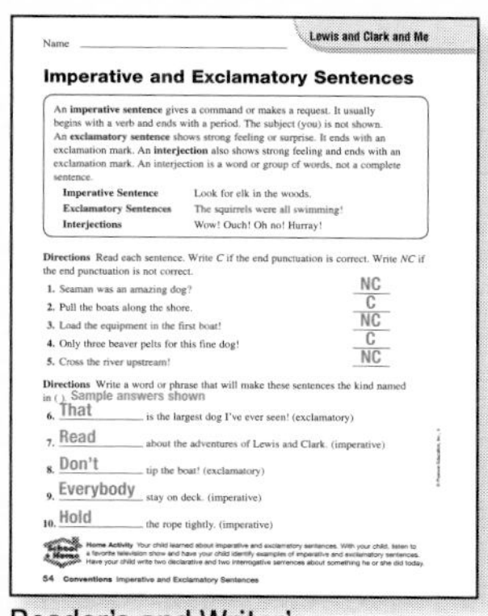
Name ______ Lewis and Clark and Me

Imperative and Exclamatory Sentences

An **imperative sentence** gives a command or makes a request. It usually begins with a verb and ends with a period. The subject (you) is not shown. An **exclamatory sentence** shows strong feeling or surprise. It ends with an exclamation mark. An **interjection** also shows strong feeling and ends with an exclamation mark. An interjection is a word or group of words, not a complete sentence.

Imperative Sentence	Look for elk in the woods.
Exclamatory Sentences	The squirrels were all swimming!
Interjections	Wow! Ouch! Oh no! Hurray!

Directions Read each sentence. Write *C* if the end punctuation is correct. Write *NC* if the end punctuation is not correct.

1. Seaman was an amazing dog? NC
2. Pull the boats along the shore. C
3. Load the equipment in the first boat! NC
4. Only three beaver pelts for this fine dog! C
5. Cross the river upstream! NC

Directions Write a word or phrase that will make these sentences the kind named in ( ). Sample answers shown

6. That is the largest dog I've ever seen! (exclamatory)
7. Read about the adventures of Lewis and Clark. (imperative)
8. Don't tip the boat! (exclamatory)
9. Everybody stay on deck. (imperative)
10. Hold the rope tightly. (imperative)

School + Home **Home Activity** Your child learned about imperative and exclamatory sentences. With your child, listen to a favorite television show and have your child identify examples of imperative and exclamatory sentences. Have your child write two declarative and two interrogative sentences about something he or she did today.

54 **Conventions** Imperative and Exclamatory Sentences

Reader's and Writer's Notebook p. 54

English Language Learners

Conventions To provide students with practice on imperative and exclamatory sentences, use the modified grammar lessons in the *ELL Handbook* and the Grammar Jammer online at www.ReadingStreet.com

Language transfer: Exclamatory sentences
Students with literacy skills in Spanish may be accustomed to writing an introductory (upside-down) exclamation point at the beginning of an exclamation. Point out that in English, the exclamation point appears only at the end of the sentence.

Objectives

- Organize ideas to prepare for writing.

Writing—Expository Composition

Writing Trait: Organization

Introduce the prompt Remind students that although the selection they'll be reading this week, *Lewis and Clark and Me,* is an example of historical fiction, it is based on true events, so it has features of expository composition. Review the key features of an expository composition. Remind students to think about these features as they plan their own writing. Then explain that they will begin the writing process for an expository composition today. Read aloud the writing prompt.

Writing Prompt

Think about another time in history when people found opportunity in a new place. Now write an expository composition about it.

Select a topic

To help choose a topic, let's make a chart with a list of times and places, opportunities, and people to write about. Display a three-column chart. In *Lewis and Clark and Me,* you read about explorers seeing new lands. I'll put that information in my chart. Have students brainstorm other historical events they know about. Fill in the chart as they give their suggestions.

Gather information Remind students that they can do research to help them find more events to include in their chart. Remember to keep this chart as students will refer back to it tomorrow as they draft.

Time and Place	Opportunity	People
western U.S., 1800s	new land	explorers
western U.S., 1800s	railroad jobs	workers from China
California, 1800s	discover gold	settlers

Corrective feedback Circulate around the room as students use their charts to help them plan what they will write about. Talk individually with students who seem to be having difficulty completing their charts or choosing a topic. Ask struggling students to think about historical events they have read about in class.

MINI-LESSON

Main Idea and Details

- I'll write about Chinese workers who worked on the transcontinental railroad. I'll use the Internet, books, and print resources to gather facts and a main idea chart to organize my theme.
- Display chart. Write, *The first Chinese workers hired by the railroad were already living in California.* in the *Main Idea* box.
- In the *Supporting Details* boxes, write facts that support this main idea. One detail that supports this main idea is that many people from China came to California as early as 1850 to escape poverty. Then I'll write that many first worked in gold mines.
- Have students begin their own chart using the *Reader's and Writer's Notebook,* p. 56. Explain that they will fill in their chart with information about the historical events they have chosen.

Teacher Tip

Check students' quick writes to be sure they are communicating clearly about the historical events they have chosen.

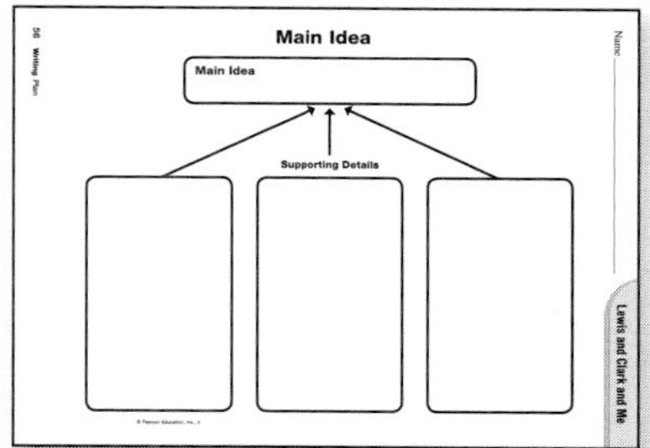

Reader's and Writer's Notebook p. 56

ROUTINE

Quick Write for Fluency

Team Talk

1. **Talk** Have pairs discuss the historical events they have researched.
2. **Write** Each student writes a sentence about one event.
3. **Share** Each partner reads each other's sentence. Then each partner asks the other one question about the event.

Routines Flip Chart

Wrap Up Your Day

- ✔ **Build Concepts** What characteristics did you learn about Lewis's dog?
- ✔ **Author's Purpose** After determining the author's purpose, how did it help you read the story?
- ✔ **Questioning** How did stopping to ask questions about the text help you understand what you read?

Tell students that tomorrow they will read more about the adventures of Lewis's dog on the expedition.

Objectives

- Expand the weekly concept.
- Develop oral vocabulary.

Today at a Glance

Oral Vocabulary
experiences, prepared

Comprehension Check/Retelling
Discuss questions

Reading
Lewis and Clark and Me

Thinking Critically
Retelling

Fluency
Appropriate phrasing

Research and Study Skills
Skim and scan

Research and Inquiry
Analyze

Spelling
Long *a* and *i*

Conventions
Imperative and exclamatory sentences

Writing
Expository composition

Concept Talk

Question of the Week

What opportunities can be found in new places?

Expand the concept Remind students of the weekly concept question. Discuss how the question relates to the expedition of Lewis and Clark and the dog Seaman. Remind students to make pertinent comments in discussion. Tell students that today they will read about an interesting encounter that Lewis and Seaman had with a group of Native Americans.

Anchored Talk

Develop oral vocabulary Use text features—illustrations, extracts, heads—to review pp. 52–61 of *Lewis and Clark and Me: A Dog's Tale.* Discuss the Amazing Words *seek* and *fortune.* Add these and other concept-related words to the concept map. Use the following questions to develop students' understanding of the concept. Remind students to ask and answer questions with appropriate detail and to give suggestions based on the ideas of others.

- What opportunities do people going to new lands *seek?*
- When people go to a new place to *seek* their *fortune,* what are some ways they could accomplish this goal?

Oral Vocabulary
Amazing Words

Amazing Words Oral Vocabulary Routine

Teach Amazing Words

1. **Introduce** Write the word *experiences* on the board. Have students say it with you. Yesterday, we read about one of Seaman's favorite *experiences* when he was able to hunt squirrels for the first time on the expedition. Have students use the context of the sentence to determine a definition of *experiences.* (Experiences are what happens to someone; what is seen, done, or lived through.)
2. **Demonstrate** Have students answer questions to demonstrate understanding. What kinds of new *experiences* did Seaman have when Lewis became his master? (Seaman got to travel on a boat, he got to hunt squirrels, and he got to see new animals and places he never saw before.) Why are new *experiences* good? (We can learn new things or go somewhere we have never been.)
3. **Apply** Have students apply their understanding. What was one of your favorite *experiences* during summer vacation?

See p. OV•2 to teach *prepared*.

Routines Flip Chart

Amazing Words

pioneer	fortune
traveled	experiences
settlers	prepared
territories	foreign
seek	improve

Apply Amazing Words

As students read pp. 62–67 of *Lewis and Clark and Me,* have them consider how the Amazing Words *experiences* and *prepared* apply to Seaman and the expedition of Lewis and Clark.

Connect to reading

Explain that today students will read about an interesting encounter that Lewis and Seaman had with a group of Native Americans. As they read, students should think about how the Question of the Week and the Amazing Words *experiences* and *prepared* apply to this encounter.

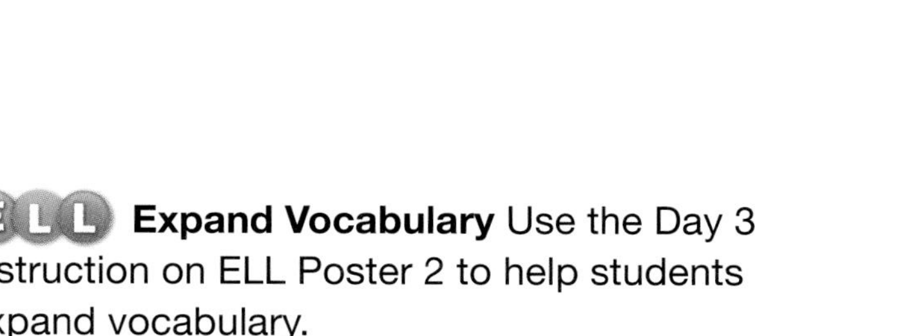

ELL Expand Vocabulary Use the Day 3 instruction on ELL Poster 2 to help students expand vocabulary.

ELL Poster 2

Objectives

- ◎ Determine the author's purpose to aid comprehension.
- ◎ Use the questioning strategy to aid comprehension.
- ◎ Use word structure and word endings to determine meanings of words.

Comprehension Check

Have students discuss each question with a partner. Ask several pairs to share their responses.

☑ **Genre • Analysis**
Why do you think the author chose to include excerpts from Meriwether Lewis's journal in the story? Possible response: The journal entries help to show that some of the events actually happened.

☑ **Author's Purpose • Analysis**
What do you think the author's purpose is for writing this story from Seaman's point of view? Possible response: I think the author is trying to entertain as well as inform. I think the writer chose to write from Lewis's dog's point of view because it is a very entertaining way to inform about part of Lewis's journey.

☑ **Questioning • Synthesis**
Ask yourself literal, interpretive, and evaluative questions about the characters in the story so far to monitor and adjust your comprehension. Possible response: Will Seaman continue to be as excited as the expedition goes on? Will Seaman find other animals that he likes to hunt as much as squirrels?

☑ **Word Endings • Analysis**
What is the base word and meaning of the word *migrating*? Tell how you could use word structure to figure out the meaning of the word. Possible response: I could cover up the ending and figure out the base word. The base word is *migrate* which means "to move from one place to another." So, *migrating* means "moving from one place to another."

☑ **Connect text to self**
If you were going on an expedition like Captain Lewis, would you have chosen to take a dog with you? Explain why or why not. Possible response: Yes, I would have taken a dog because a dog makes the journey more fun. Dogs also help hunt for food.

Strategy Response Log

INTERACT with TEXT

Have students write questions about the characters or events of *Lewis and Clark and Me* on p. 8 in the *Reader's and Writer's Notebook.*

Check Retelling

Have students retell *Lewis and Clark and Me,* summarizing information in the text in a logical order. Encourage students to describe the setting in their retellings.

Corrective feedback

If... students leave out important details,
then... have students look back through the illustrations in the selection.

Small Group Time

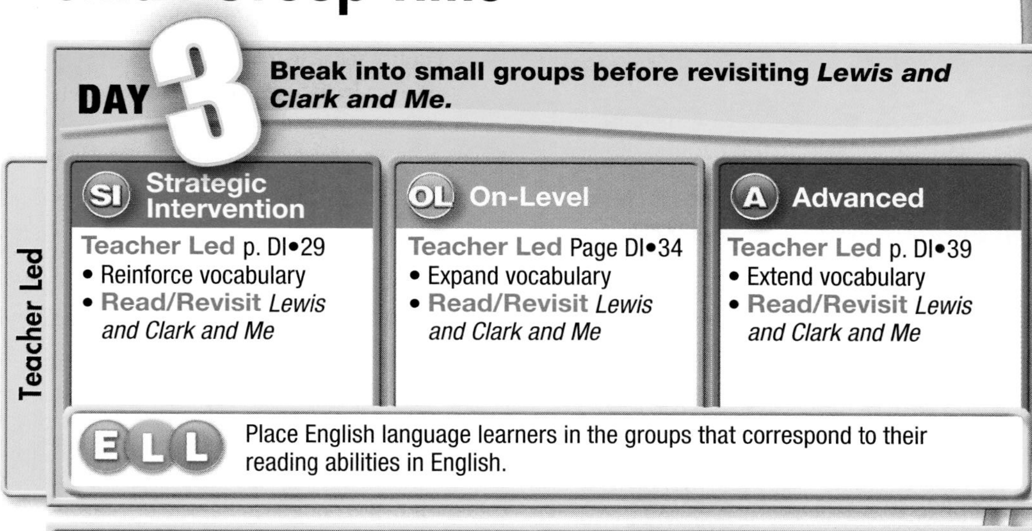

DAY 3 **Break into small groups before revisiting *Lewis and Clark and Me.***

Teacher Led

SI Strategic Intervention	OL On-Level	A Advanced
Teacher Led p. DI•29 • Reinforce vocabulary • **Read/Revisit** *Lewis and Clark and Me*	**Teacher Led** Page DI•34 • Expand vocabulary • **Read/Revisit** *Lewis and Clark and Me*	**Teacher Led** p. DI•39 • Extend vocabulary • **Read/Revisit** *Lewis and Clark and Me*

ELL Place English language learners in the groups that correspond to their reading abilities in English.

Practice Stations
- Let's Write
- Get Fluent
- Word Work

Independent Activities
- AudioText: *Lewis and Clark and Me*
- *Reader's and Writer's Notebook*
- Research and Inquiry

English Language Learners

Check retelling To support retelling, review the multilingual summary for *Lewis and Clark and Me* with the appropriate Retelling Cards to scaffold understanding.

Read and Comprehend

45–50 min

Objectives

◎ Use word endings to determine meanings of unknown words.

OPTION 1 Skills and Strategies, continued

Teach Word Endings

◎ **Word Endings** Have students use word structure to identify the base words and meanings for *concerned* and *staring* on p. 62. (Base words: *concern; stare.* Meanings: *concerned*—worried; *staring*—looking)

Corrective Feedback

If… students have difficulty using word structure to determine base words and meaning,
then… use the model to guide students in using word structure.

Model the Skill

Think Aloud Read paragraph 5 on p. 62 aloud. Write *staring* on the board. When I come to the verb *staring,* I'm not sure what this word means. To help me understand this word, I'll divide it into its base word and ending. What are the two word parts? (*star* and *-ing*)

Bear-Dog

"Indians."

We had not been on the shore very long before I heard Lewis say the word.

Lewis and Clark and I had crossed the river to make some observations. That's when these Indians appeared. They were different from other people I had known—the boatmen and city folk.

I didn't sense that Lewis or Clark were concerned, so I wasn't. The Indians seemed friendly enough. Lewis talked to them. It wasn't until later that I realized Lewis gave the same talk to every group of Indians we met. He talked about the "great white father" in Washington.

The Indians listened patiently as one of the English-speaking Indians translated. Lewis used hand motions to help. As he talked on, it became obvious to me that the Indians were not interested in Lewis or what he was saying. They were staring at me. Finally, Lewis realized what was going on, and he invited the Indians to take a closer look.

They gathered around. They touched me. They whispered about me. They acted like they had never seen a dog before. Then I noticed an Indian dog standing to the side. I took one look at that animal and realized why they were so interested in me.

That dog could not have been more than twenty pounds. Newfoundlands can weigh up to 150 pounds, and I'm a large Newfoundland. If that scrawny dog was the only dog they had seen, then I was a strange sight indeed.

62

Multidraft Reading

If you chose…
Option 1 Return to Extend Thinking instruction starting on p. 54–55.
Option 2 Read pp. 62–67.
Use the Guide Comprehension and Extend Thinking instruction.

Student Edition pp. 62–63

OPTION 2 Think Critically, continued

Higher-Order Thinking Skills

◎ **Word Endings • Analysis** What is the meaning of the word *translated* in paragraph 5 on p. 62? Possible response: If I divide the word, the base word is *translate* and the ending is *-ed*. I know the ending means "in the past." From the context, I can tell that Lewis is communicating with the help of an English-speaking Indian. The English-speaking Indian is changing the English language into the Indian language to help them understand. I think the base word *translate* means "to put the meaning of words from one language into the words of another language." *Translated* means the words were "changed after they were spoken."

Inferring • Analysis When Lewis is talking about the *great white father* in Washington, to whom is he referring? What clue does this detail give you about what Lewis might be saying in his speeches to Indians they encounter? Possible response: Lewis is referring to President Thomas Jefferson. I think this detail suggests that Lewis is trying to explain the purpose of their expedition to the Indians since President Jefferson sent them to explore.

I know that *-ing* means "the action of." *Star* makes me think of a star in the sky, but I remember that the spelling of base words changes when endings are added, so I think the base word is *stare* which means "to look." So *staring* must mean "the action of look," or "looking." If I replace *staring* with *looking*, does the sentence make sense? (yes)

"Bear," one of the English-speaking Indians said.

I looked up. He was pointing at me.

"Dog," Lewis replied patiently.

The Indian looked at his own dog. He looked back at me.

"Bear," he said again.

Lewis looked at me and smiled. Clark was smiling, too. I lifted my head.

"I guess he does look like a bear," Lewis said.

Lewis picked up a stick and threw it.

"Fetch," he said.

I fetched.

"Stay," he said.

I stayed.

63

Draw Conclusions • Evaluation Is it reasonable for the Indians to think that Seaman is a bear? Why or why not? Possible response: Yes, because Seaman is large and hairy like a bear, and he doesn't look like the dog the Indians have.

On Their Own

Have students identify and sort words ending in *-ed* and *-ing* on pp. 62–63. Beside each word, have students write its base word. Then ask students to use each word in a context sentence that shows its meaning.

English Language Learners

Monitor comprehension Reread p. 63. Have students use context clues to figure out the meaning of *fetch* in paragraph 9. Ask students to pantomime playing fetch with a dog. Ask: If someone says "stay" to a dog, should the dog stand still and wait or should the dog run off? (stand still and wait) Have students pantomime asking a dog to stay. Then have students summarize what is happening with the Indians and Seaman. Ask: Why do you think Lewis had Seaman fetch and stay for the Indians? (to try and show them that he is a dog who can obey normal commands and is not a bear)

Objectives

◎ Determine the author's purpose.

OPTION 1 Skills and Strategies, continued

Teach Author's Purpose

Author's Purpose Remind students that an author writes to entertain, to persuade, to express an idea, or to provide information. Have students identify why the author uses dialogue as well as Lewis's journal entry on pp. 64–65. What is the author's purpose?

Corrective Feedback

If... students have difficulty evaluating the author's purpose,
then... use the model to guide students in understanding author's purpose.

Model the Skill

Think Aloud When I read the dialogue on page 64, I feel like I am in the story and part of the conversation. What can I learn from this dialogue? (I can learn how the Indians name Seaman and how they use beaver skins as a way to trade for things.)

"Sit," he said.

I sat.

The Indians were impressed.

"Dog," Lewis said politely. Lewis was always nice.

The Indian who had called me "bear" turned to consult with his friends.

Finally, he turned.

"Bear-dog," he said with satisfaction.

Lewis smiled.

"Yes, I guess you could call him bear-dog."

Later, George Drouillard explained to us that the Indians don't have a separate word for *horse*. They call a horse "elk-dog." I guess it made sense for them to call me a bear-dog.

The Indian suddenly turned and walked through the crowd to his horse. He pulled out three beaver skins. He held them out to Lewis.

"For bear-dog," he said.

It wasn't often that I saw Lewis surprised. He was then.

I took a step closer to Lewis.

Lewis looked the Indian square in the eye and said, "No trade. Bear-dog special."

As we rode back to camp in the boat, Lewis said to me, "Three beaver skins! Can you believe that?"

No, I could not. The idea that Lewis and I would ever separate was unthinkable. Not many dogs and men fit together like Lewis and I. If you have ever experienced it, then you know what I'm talking about. And if you haven't, well, it's hard to explain. All I can tell you is that when a dog and a man fit like Lewis and I did, nothing can separate them. Lewis said it best.

"No trade."

64

Student Edition pp. 64–65

OPTION 2 Think Critically, continued

Higher-Order Thinking Skills

Author's Purpose • Evaluation Do the details on page 64 support the idea that one of the author's purposes for writing this story is to express her appreciation for the special relationship that dogs and people can have? Explain why or why not. Possible response: Yes, I think the author uses both the speech and action of both characters to express this purpose. The last paragraph is written with strong words that express Seaman's feelings about the relationship that he and Lewis have.

Draw Conclusions • Analysis Why do the Indians call Seaman a "bear-dog"? Possible response: The Indians don't have a word for a large dog like Seaman. For horse, they combined two words they had to describe something new. Since Seaman is a dog that is big like a bear, they use the word *bear-dog* to describe him.

What do we learn from reading Captain Lewis's journal on page 65? (We learn that this event really happened.) I think the author's purpose is to inform the reader about how the Indians used to name things and how they used to get something they wanted.

. . . one of the Shawnees a respectable looking Indian offered me three beverskins for my dog with which he appeared much pleased. . . of course there was no bargan, I had given 20$ for this dogg myself—
Meriwether Lewis November 16, 1803
65

Inferring • Synthesis What can you infer about the value of three beaver skins? How does Lewis's refusal show the value of Seaman to him? Possible response: I can infer from Lewis's reaction and from his journal entry that three beaver skins was a lot to have offered for a dog. Lewis's refusal shows that Seaman is more valuable than any goods that could be offered to him.

On Their Own

Have students discuss another purpose that the author might have had for writing pp. 64–65 the way she did.

Connect to Social Studies

As Lewis and Clark met with Native Americans during their expedition, they often traded with them for goods they needed. This system of trading one set of goods for another instead of money is called a barter system. The fur trade between the Native Americans and the Europeans was an example of a barter system at work. In exchange for beaver, mink, and other pelts the Native Americans had, French, Dutch, and American traders gave the Native Americans goods that they produced, such as iron axes and glass beads.

ELL

English Language Learners

Cognates Point out the Spanish cognates for these English words on p. 64: *Indian/Indio*, *satisfaction/satisfaccíon*, and *special/especial*.

DAY 3 Read and Comprehend

Objectives

◎ Ask questions to monitor and adjust comprehension.

OPTION 1 Skills and Strategies, continued

Teach Questioning

◎ **Questioning** Have students generate an evaluative question about the map on pp. 66–67 and the author's purpose for including it.

Corrective Feedback

If… students have difficulty generating evaluative questions,
then… use the model to guide students in using the questioning strategy.

Model the Strategy

Think Aloud I look at these pages and wonder why the author chose to end the story this way. What evaluative question could I ask about these last two pages?

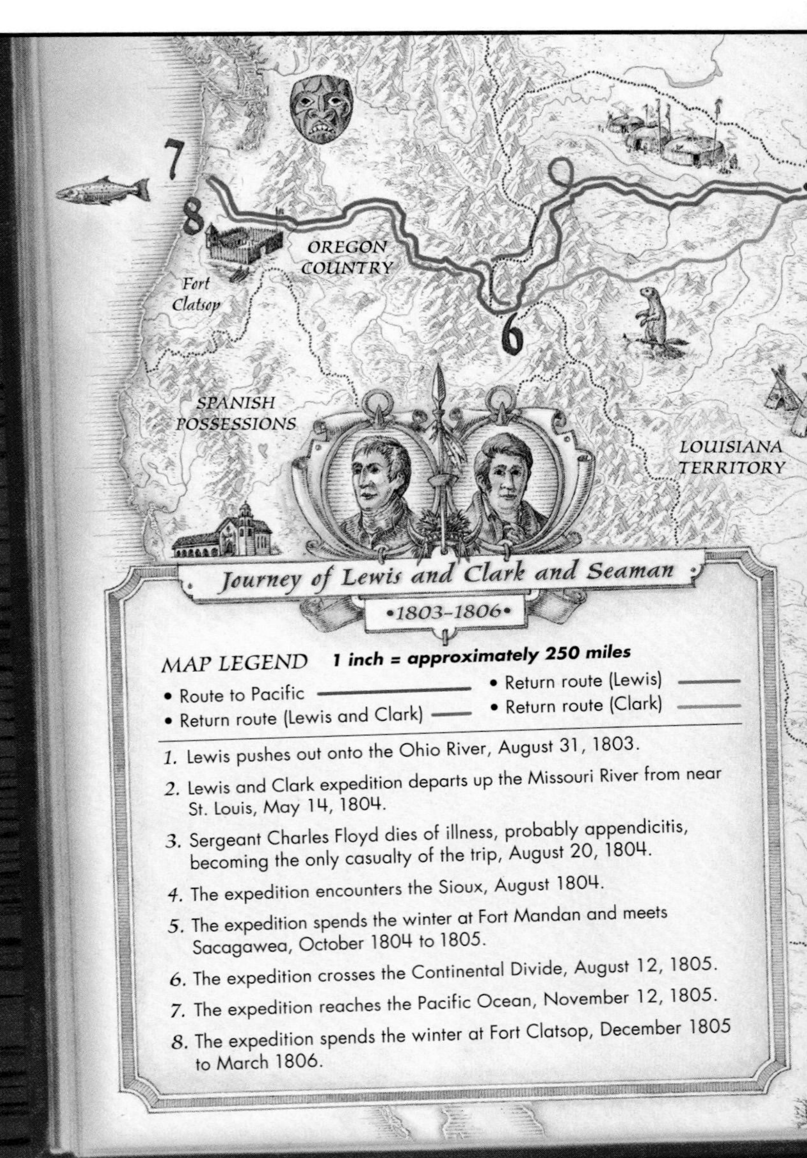

Student Edition pp. 66–67

OPTION 2 Think Critically, continued

Higher-Order Thinking Skills

◎ **Questioning • Synthesis** What questions can you ask after reading the map legend? Possible response: Why did Lewis and Clark split apart on the return route? Why did the author choose to end the story with a map? Was this a good way to end the story?

Graphic Sources • Analysis What does the map on pages 66–67 show? How is it similar and different to a U.S. map today? It shows the routes of Lewis and Clark's 1803–1806 journey west to the Pacific and back east across what is now the United States. Some of the states east of the Mississippi look the same as they do today. The rest of the land on the map shows how it looked before the States were decided.

Comprehension Check

Spiral Review

Literary Elements: Character and Plot • Evaluation Would you recommend this story to someone else? Use details about the characters and plot to explain why you would or would not recommend this story. Possible response: I would recommend this story to someone else. It was very interesting to read a story told by a dog. I thought that Seaman and Lewis were interesting characters. I think that the plot was also interesting. It was exciting to read about the adventures of Seaman, such as the squirrel hunting and the meeting with the Indians. I enjoyed reading about his relationship with Lewis.

(Possible response: Was it a good idea for the author to include the map in this text?) I think the author wanted to inform readers about the route that Lewis, Clark, and Seaman took. I think the author wanted to show how far they explored together, so yes, I think it was a good idea to include the map here.

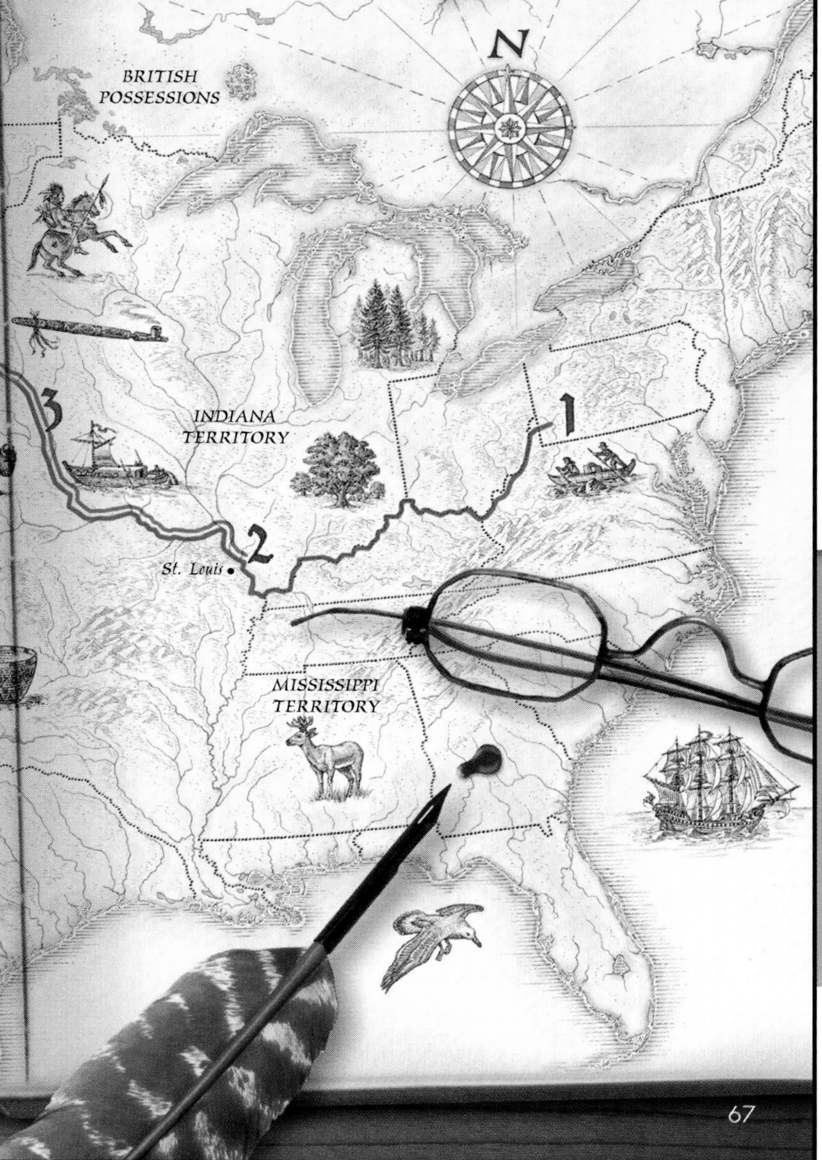

On Their Own

Have students ask other literal, interpretive, and evaluative questions about the map and why it is included in the text. Have them state how it adjusts their comprehension of the text.

Compare and Contrast • Synthesis Compare and contrast this story to another historical fiction text that you have read. How are the texts similar? How are they different? Possible response: In both stories, the setting was very important to the action of the story. In *Lewis and Clark and Me* and in the other story, some of the main events actually happened. The stories are different because the other story was told more realistically. In this story, a dog narrates, which is impossible in real life.

Check Predictions Have students return to the predictions they made earlier and confirm whether they were accurate.

Differentiated Instruction

 Strategic Intervention

Graphic sources Have students work in pairs to read pp. 66–67. Have one student read the numbered steps in the legend while the other student follows the route on the map.

A Advanced

Author's purpose Have students evaluate the way the author ends the story. Have students write an alternative ending to the story.

ELL

English Language Learners

Monitor Comprehension: Graphic sources With students, trace the route of Lewis and Clark using the sequence on the map. Ask students to look at the pictures along the route. Have students stop at each picture and use the picture to explain what happened along the way to the Pacific Ocean.

Read and Comprehend

Objectives

- Identify the author's purpose to aid comprehension.
- Use the questioning strategy to check understanding.

Check Retelling
SUCCESS PREDICTOR

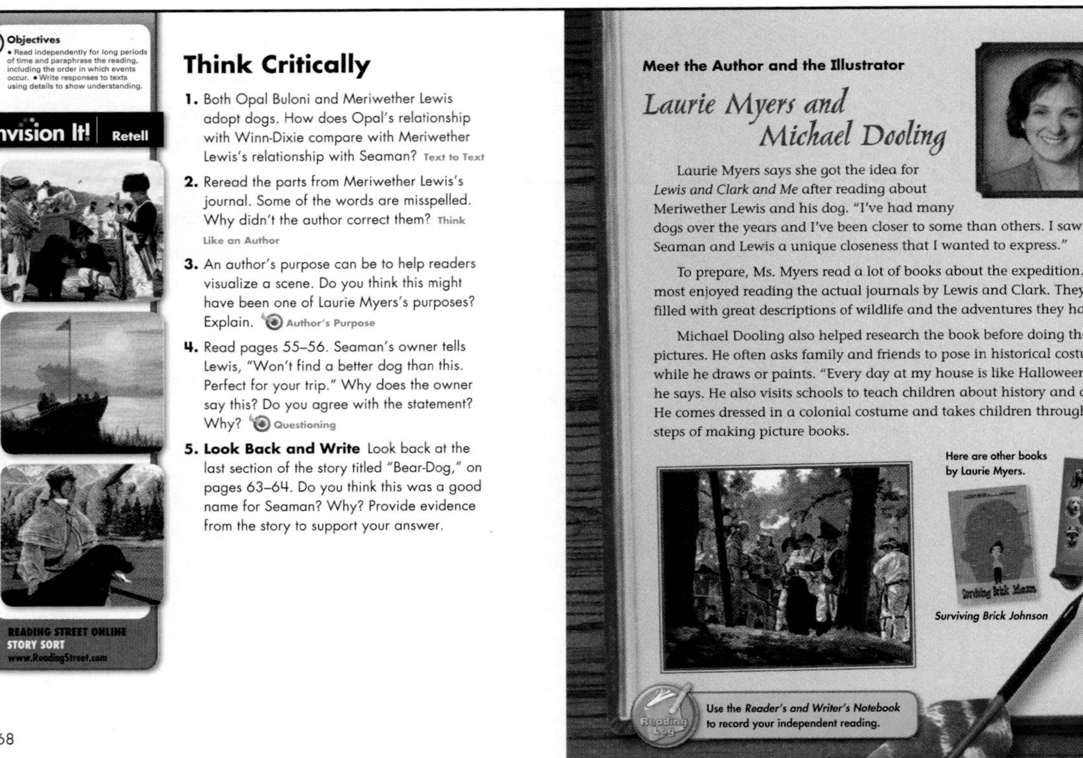

Student Edition pp. 68–69

Retelling

Envision It! Have students work in pairs to retell the selection, using the Envision It! Retelling Cards as prompts. Remind students that they should accurately describe the plot and characters in a logical order and use key vocabulary in their retellings. Monitor students' retellings.

Scoring rubric

Top-Score Response A top-score response makes connections beyond the text and describes the plot and characters, using the author's purpose and the questioning strategy.

Plan to Assess Retelling

- ☑ **Week 1** Assess Strategic Intervention students.
- ☑ **This week assess Advanced students.**
- ☐ **Week 3** Assess Strategic Intervention students.
- ☐ **Week 4** Assess On-Level students.
- ☐ **Week 5** Assess any students you have not yet checked during this unit.

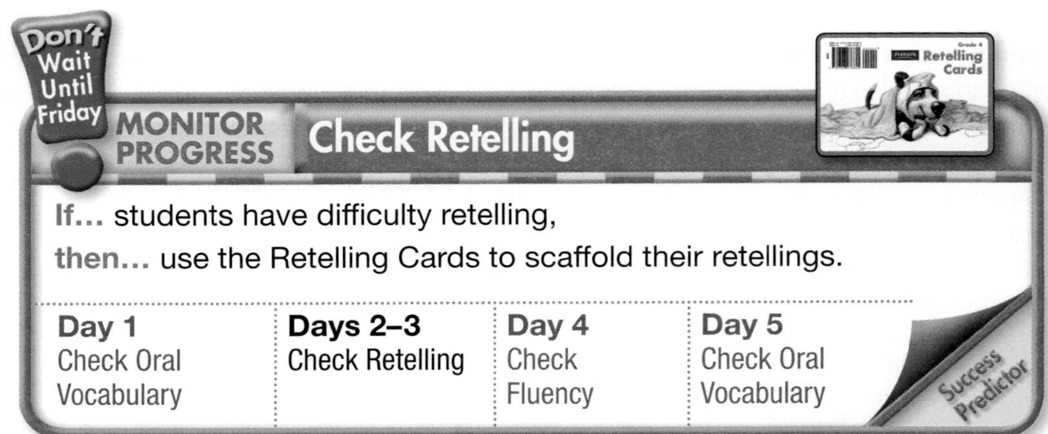

If... students have difficulty retelling,
then... use the Retelling Cards to scaffold their retellings.

Day 1	Days 2–3	Day 4	Day 5
Check Oral Vocabulary	Check Retelling	Check Fluency	Check Oral Vocabulary

Think Critically

Text to text

1. Both Lewis and Opal have a very special relationship with their dogs. The dogs go with them wherever they go and the dogs love their owners. Winn-Dixie helps Opal meet her first friend in town and Seaman also is the cause for Lewis's meeting with a group of Native Americans.

Think like an author

2. The author wanted to show the words exactly as Lewis wrote them in his journal, and spellings were different at that time.

Author's purpose

3. Responses will vary but should include details from the text that support students' thinking. Students might mention the scene when Seaman first hunts for squirrels as an example to support the author's purpose to help readers visualize a scene.

Questioning

4. The owner says this because he is trying to sell Seaman to Lewis. I agree with the statement because Seaman is a type of dog that is very well suited for this journey because he can swim and his feet and coat are perfect for being in the water.

5. **Look Back and Write** To build writing fluency, assign a 10–15 minute time limit.

Suggest that students use a prewriting strategy, such as brainstorming or using a graphic organizer, to organize their ideas. Remind them to establish a topic sentence and support it with facts, details, or explanations. As students finish, encourage them to reread their responses, revise for organization and support, and proofread for errors in grammar and conventions.

Scoring rubric

Top-Score Response A top-score response uses details from the story to explain why "Bear-Dog" was a good name for Seaman.

A top-score response should include:

- The Indians have never seen a large dog like Seaman and so it makes sense that they named him by combining two words they know to describe him.
- Seaman does look similar to a bear because of his color and size. So, using bear in the name makes sense.
- Seaman also showed the Indians that he did things like a normal dog would do such as fetch and stay. So, combining dog and bear in the name makes sense.

Differentiated Instruction

Strategic Intervention

Have students work in pairs to reread pp. 63-64. Have them come up with reasons why "Bear-Dog" is a good name for Seaman.

Meet the Author and Illustrator

Model identifying similarities and differences between the real-life events and experiences Laurie Myers had with dogs and the events and characters' experiences in *Lewis and Clark and Me.* Point out Myers's feelings of closeness with some of her pets and that this inspired her to write the story about Seaman.

Independent Reading

After students enter their independent reading information into their Reading Logs, have them paraphrase a portion of the text they have just read. Remind students that when we paraphrase, we express the meaning of a passage, using other words and maintaining logical order.

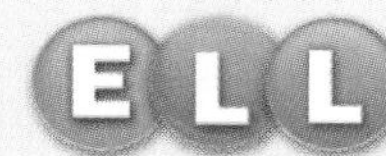

English Language Learners

Retelling Use the Retelling Cards to discuss the selection with students. Divide the students into small groups. Have a different small group explain what is happening in each card.

Retelling
Success Predictor

DAY 3 Read and Comprehend

Objectives

- Read grade-level text with appropriate phrasing.
- Reread for fluency.
- Use skimming and scanning techniques to locate information using text features.

Model Fluency
Appropriate Phrasing

Model fluent reading Have students turn to p. 54 of *Lewis and Clark and Me: A Dog's Tale*. Have students follow along as you read the paragraphs after the introduction on this page. Tell them to notice how you use periods, dashes, and commas to provide clues for pausing as you read about how Lewis found Seaman.

Guide practice Have students follow along as you read the page again. Then have them reread the page as a group until they read with appropriate phrasing and no mistakes. Ask questions to be sure students comprehend the text. Continue in the same way on p. 55.

Reread for Fluency

Corrective feedback

If… students are having difficulty reading with appropriate phrasing,
then… prompt:

- Where can we break up this sentence? Which words are related?
- Read the sentence again. Pause after each group of words.
- Tell me the sentence. Now read it with pauses after each group of words.

ROUTINE Choral Reading

1. **Select a passage** For *Lewis and Clark and Me*, use p. 58.
2. **Model** Have students listen as you read the page aloud with appropriate phrasing.
3. **Guide practice** Have students read along with you.
4. **On their own** Have the class read aloud without you. For optimal fluency, students should reread three or four times with appropriate phrasing.

Routines Flip Chart

Research and Study Skills
Skim and Scan

Teach

Have students imagine they are writing a research report on Lewis and Clark. Point out that if they found many articles that might be helpful, they wouldn't have time to read them all. Explain that good researchers skim and scan a text to decide if it is useful.

You may skim, or read text very quickly, to find main ideas. When you skim, pay attention to these text features to get an overview of the contents of the text:

- **first and last paragraphs** in a selection
- **topic and concluding sentences** of paragraphs
- **headings and subheads**
- **guide words** and any words set off in bold or italic print
- **summaries** at the end of a selection

You may scan, or move your eyes quickly down the page to find answers to specific questions. Use multiple text features, such as specific guide words or phrases, names, numbers, or dates, to locate information in the text.

Have students skim a passage from a social studies or science textbook. After a few minutes, have students tell what main topics the text covers. Then have students scan the passage to find five facts about specific people, places, dates or ideas included in it.

Guide practice

Discuss these questions:

When you first skimmed the passage, what text features helped you identify the main topic of the text? (topic and concluding sentences, headings, subheads)

When you scanned the text for five facts, what did you do to find the information quickly? (I looked for guide words, the names of people and places, and dates.)

On their own

Have students complete pp. 58–59 of the *Reader's and Writer's Notebook*.

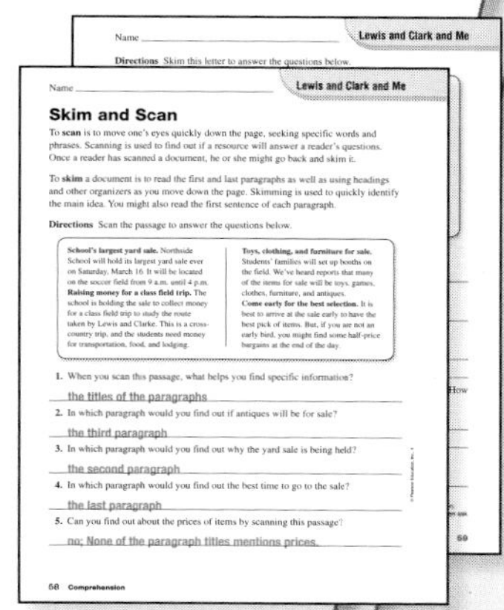

Name ______ Lewis and Clark and Me

Skim and Scan

To **scan** is to move one's eyes quickly down the page, seeking specific words and phrases. Scanning is used to find out if a resource will answer a reader's questions. Once a reader has scanned a document, he or she might go back and skim it.

To **skim** a document is to read the first and last paragraphs as well as using headings and other organizers as you move down the page. Skimming is used to quickly identify the main idea. You might also read the first sentence of each paragraph.

Directions Scan the passage to answer the questions below.

School's largest yard sale. Northside School will hold its largest yard sale ever on Saturday, March 16. It will be located on the soccer field from 9 a.m. until 4 p.m. **Raising money for a class field trip.** The school is holding the sale to collect money for a class field trip to study the route taken by Lewis and Clarke. This is a cross-country trip, and the students need money for transportation, food, and lodging.

Toys, clothing, and furniture for sale. Students' families will set up booths on the field. We've heard reports that many of the items for sale will be toys, games, clothes, furniture, and antiques. **Come early for the best selection.** It is best to arrive at the sale early to have the best pick of items. But, if you are not an early bird, you might find some half-price bargains at the end of the day.

1. When you scan this passage, what helps you find specific information?
the titles of the paragraphs
2. In which paragraph would you find out if antiques will be for sale?
the third paragraph
3. In which paragraph would you find out why the yard sale is being held?
the second paragraph
4. In which paragraph would you find out the best time to go to the sale?
the last paragraph
5. Can you find out about the prices of items by scanning this passage?
no; None of the paragraph titles mentions prices.

58 Comprehension

Reader's and Writer's Notebook pp. 58–59

Academic Vocabulary

skim read text very quickly to find main ideas

scan move your eyes quickly down the page to find answers to specific questions

ELL

English Language Learners

Professional Development: Access content Use graphic organizers such as T-charts to scaffold learning when possible. These visuals are a way to modify content. They make complex academic English vocabulary more understandable.

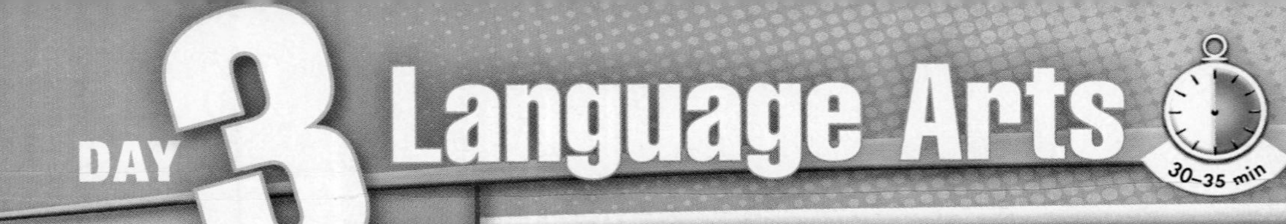

Objectives

- Analyze data for usefulness.
- Identify and correctly use imperative and exclamatory sentences.
- Spell frequently misspelled words correctly.

Research and Inquiry
Analyze

Teach Tell students that today they will analyze their findings and may need to change the focus of their original inquiry question.

Model 

My inquiry question was *How did Lewis and Clark learn to communicate and trade with Native American tribes they met?* My search turned up so much information that it was hard to narrow the focus. Then I came upon some specific information about Sacagawea, a Native American woman who helped Lewis and Clark communicate with other tribes. Further research about Sacagawea led me to even more information about how Lewis and Clark communicated with tribes and learned from them. I realized that I needed to refocus my inquiry question on communication alone. So now my inquiry question is *What strategies did Lewis and Clark discover for communicating with Native Americans?*

Guide practice Have students analyze their findings. They may need to refocus their inquiry question to better fit the information they found. Remind students to use skimming and scanning techniques to identify data by looking at text features as they continue their search for relevant information. Have students create their Works Cited page from the information they identified yesterday. Be sure students include the author, title, publisher, and publication year for each source.

On their own Have students review their notes and compare the information they have gathered from various sources. Students may use a concept web or chart to organize the information they want to include in their report.

Conventions
Imperative and Exclamatory Sentences

Review Remind students that this week they learned about imperative and exclamatory sentences.

- An imperative sentence gives a command or makes a request. It ends with a period. The first word is usually a verb.
- An exclamatory sentence shows strong feeling or surprise. It ends with an exclamation point.

Daily Fix-It Use Daily Fix-It numbers 5 and 6 in the right margin.

Connect to oral language Have students choose a person or character from the story and give a command or make an exclamation to the person or character. (e.g., *What a smart dog you are, Seaman!)*

People or characters: Seaman, Lewis, Clark, George Drouillard, the Indian

On their own For additional support, use *Let's Practice It!* p. 15 on the *Teacher Resources DVD-ROM.*

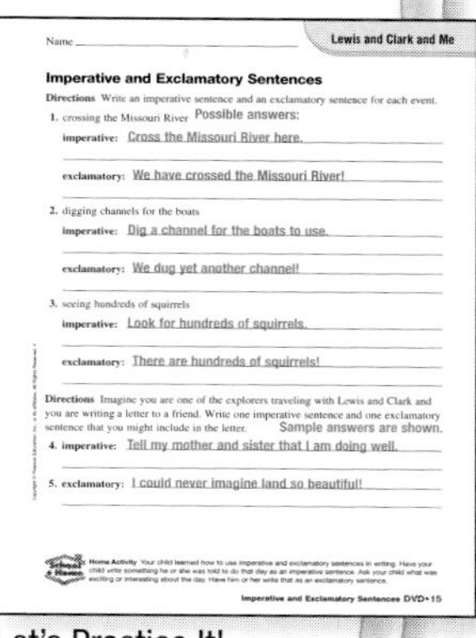

Name ______ Lewis and Clark and Me

Imperative and Exclamatory Sentences

Directions Write an imperative sentence and an exclamatory sentence for each event.

1. crossing the Missouri River Possible answers:
   imperative: Cross the Missouri River here.
   exclamatory: We have crossed the Missouri River!
2. digging channels for the boats
   imperative: Dig a channel for the boats to use.
   exclamatory: We dug yet another channel!
3. seeing hundreds of squirrels
   imperative: Look for hundreds of squirrels.
   exclamatory: There are hundreds of squirrels!

Directions Imagine you are one of the explorers traveling with Lewis and Clark and you are writing a letter to a friend. Write one imperative sentence and one exclamatory sentence that you might include in the letter. Sample answers are shown.

4. **imperative:** Tell my mother and sister that I am doing well.
5. **exclamatory:** I could never imagine land so beautiful!

Home Activity Your child learned how to use imperative and exclamatory sentences in writing. Have your child write something he or she was told to do that day as an imperative sentence. Ask your child what was exciting or interesting about the day. Have him or her write that as an exclamatory sentence.

Imperative and Exclamatory Sentences DVD•15

Let's Practice It!
TR DVD•15

Spelling
Long *a* and *i*

Frequently misspelled words The words *vacation, always,* and *might* are words that students often misspell. *Vacation* ends with *ion. Always* is one word. *Might* follows the *igh* spelling pattern. Choose *vacation, always,* or *might* to complete the sentence and write it correctly.

1. **You should ________ be polite to adults.** (always)
2. **The coach ________ ask the players to stay late.** (might)
3. **We went to the beach for our summer ________.** (vacation)

On their own For additional support, use the *Reader's and Writer's Notebook,* p. 60.

Differentiated Instruction

A Advanced
Have students create imperative and exclamatory sentences using difficult-to-spell spelling words.

Daily Fix-It

5. Many people left there hometowns with hopes of become rich. *(their; becoming)*
6. Tell me more about why they made her expedition? *(their expedition)*

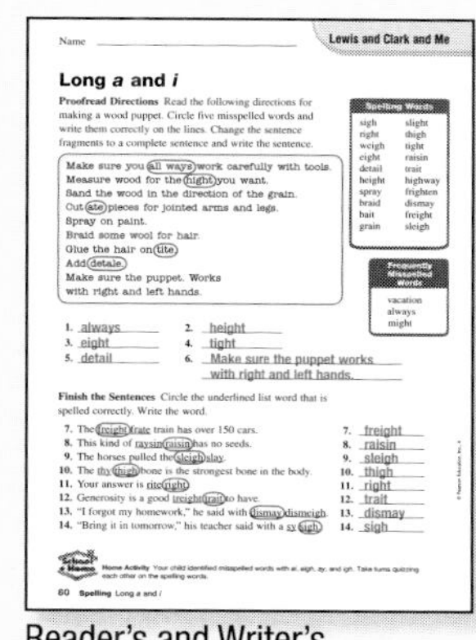

Name ______ Lewis and Clark and Me

Long *a* and *i*

Proofread Directions Read the following directions for making a wood puppet. Circle five misspelled words and write them correctly on the lines. Change the sentence fragments to a complete sentence and write the sentence.

Make sure you all ways work carefully with tools.
Measure wood for the hight you want.
Sand the wood in the direction of the grain.
Cut ate pieces for jointed arms and legs.
Spray on paint.
Braid some wool for hair.
Glue the hair on tite.
Add detale.
Make sure the puppet. Works
with right and left hands.

Spelling Words: sigh, right, weigh, eight, detail, height, spray, braid, bait, grain, slight, thigh, tight, raisin, trait, highway, frighten, dismay, freight, sleigh

Frequently Misspelled Words: vacation, always, might

1. always
2. height
3. eight
4. tight
5. detail
6. Make sure the puppet works with right and left hands.

Finish the Sentences Circle the underlined list word that is spelled correctly. Write the word.

7. The freight/frate train has over 150 cars. — freight
8. This kind of raysin/raisin has no seeds. — raisin
9. The horses pulled the sleigh/slay. — sleigh
10. The thy/thigh bone is the strongest bone in the body. — thigh
11. Your answer is rite/right. — right
12. Generosity is a good treight/trait to have. — trait
13. "I forgot my homework," he said with dismay/dismeigh. — dismay
14. "Bring it in tomorrow," his teacher said with a sy/sigh. — sigh

Home Activity Your child identified misspelled words with ai, eigh, ay, and igh. Take turns quizzing each other on the spelling words.

60 Spelling Long a and i

Reader's and Writer's Notebook p. 60

Objectives

- Understand the criteria for writing an effective expository composition.

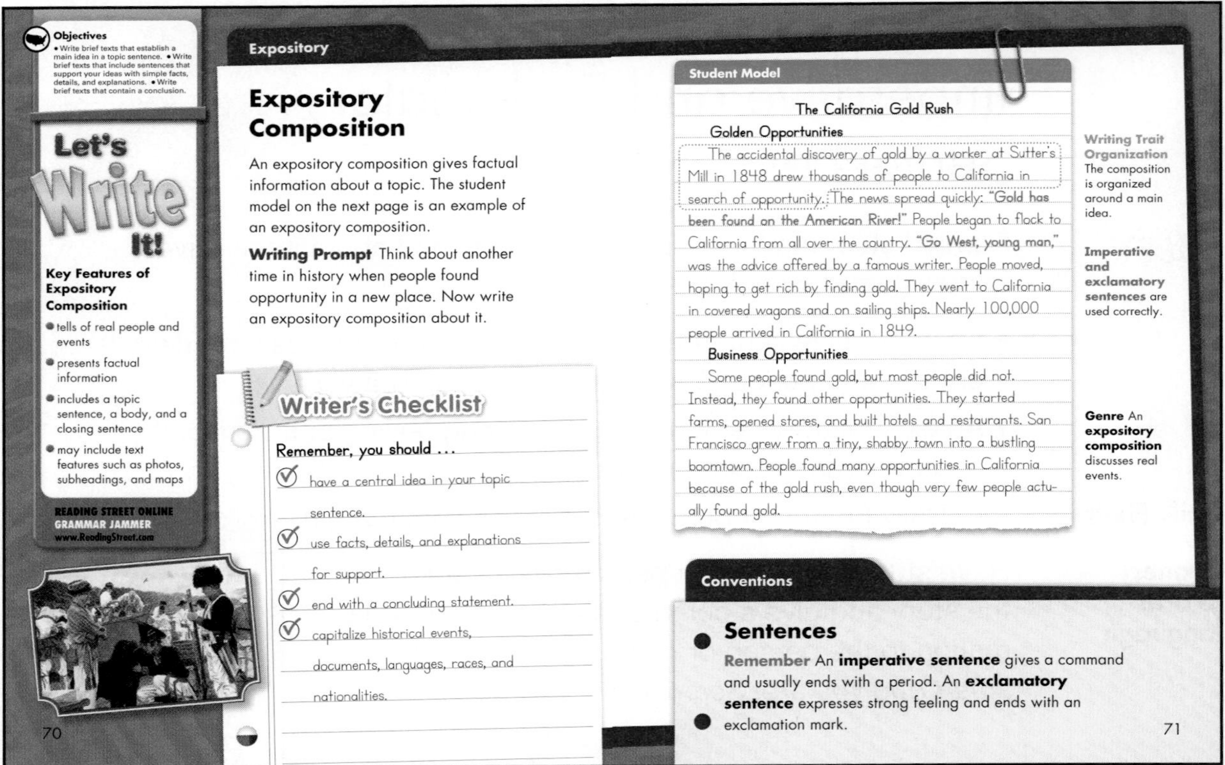

Objectives
• Write brief texts that establish a main idea in a topic sentence. • Write brief texts that include sentences that support your ideas with simple facts, details, and explanations. • Write brief texts that contain a conclusion.

Let's Write It!

Key Features of Expository Composition
- tells of real people and events
- presents factual information
- includes a topic sentence, a body, and a closing sentence
- may include text features such as photos, subheadings, and maps

READING STREET ONLINE
GRAMMAR JAMMER
www.ReadingStreet.com

Expository

Expository Composition

An expository composition gives factual information about a topic. The student model on the next page is an example of an expository composition.

Writing Prompt Think about another time in history when people found opportunity in a new place. Now write an expository composition about it.

Writer's Checklist

Remember, you should ...
- have a central idea in your topic sentence.
- use facts, details, and explanations for support.
- end with a concluding statement.
- capitalize historical events, documents, languages, races, and nationalities.

70

Student Model

The California Gold Rush

Golden Opportunities

The accidental discovery of gold by a worker at Sutter's Mill in 1848 drew thousands of people to California in search of opportunity. The news spread quickly: "Gold has been found on the American River!" People began to flock to California from all over the country. "Go West, young man," was the advice offered by a famous writer. People moved, hoping to get rich by finding gold. They went to California in covered wagons and on sailing ships. Nearly 100,000 people arrived in California in 1849.

Business Opportunities

Some people found gold, but most people did not. Instead, they found other opportunities. They started farms, opened stores, and built hotels and restaurants. San Francisco grew from a tiny, shabby town into a bustling boomtown. People found many opportunities in California because of the gold rush, even though very few people actually found gold.

Writing Trait Organization The composition is organized around a main idea.

Imperative and exclamatory sentences are used correctly.

Genre An **expository composition** discusses real events.

Conventions

Sentences

Remember An **imperative sentence** gives a command and usually ends with a period. An **exclamatory sentence** expresses strong feeling and ends with an exclamation mark.

71

Student Edition pp. 70–71

Let's Write It!
Expository Composition

Teach Use pp. 70–71 in the Student Edition. Direct students to read the key features of an expository composition, which appear on p. 70. Remind students that they can refer to the information in the Writer's Checklist as they write their own expository composition.

Read the student model on p. 71. Point out the topic sentence for each paragraph in the model.

Connect to conventions Remind students that an imperative sentence gives a command or makes a request and an exclamatory sentence shows surprise. Point out the correct use of a period and exclamation point at the end of these sentences in the model.

Writing — Expository Composition
Writer's Craft: Chronological Order

Display rubric

Display Scoring Rubric 2 from the *Teacher Resources DVD* and review the criteria for each trait under each score. Then, using the model in the Student Edition, have volunteers explain why the model should score a 4 for one of the traits. If a student offers that the model should score below 4 for a particular trait, the student should offer support for that response. Remind students that this rubric will be used to evaluate their expository compositions.

Scoring Rubric: Expository Composition

	4	3	2	1
Focus/Ideas	Clear, focused composition; stays on topic and presents essential information	Composition stays mostly on topic	Some repeated or off-topic information; leaves reader with several big questions	Composition lacking clarity, focus, and essential information
Organization	Paragraphs organized around a main idea with strong topic sentences and supporting details	Good paragraphs with clear topic sentences including main ideas with supporting details	Some paragraphs with unclear or missing topic sentences, few supporting details	No paragraphs; no topic sentences, main ideas, or supporting details
Voice	Involved throughout; engages readers	Involved most of the time	Tries to be involved	No involvement
Word Choice	Exact, descriptive; conveys strong impressions	Clear language; conveys strong impressions	Some vague or repetitive words	Incorrect or limited word choice
Sentences	Varied, well-crafted sentences	Clear language; conveys strong impressions	Many short, choppy sentences	Many fragments and run-ons
Conventions	Excellent control and accuracy	Good control; few errors	Errors that hamper understanding	Errors that obstruct meaning

Main idea and detail charts

Have students take out the main idea and detail charts they created on Day 2. If they need more information, have them use the Internet and print resources to complete their charts.

Write

You will use your main idea and supporting details charts to help you write the draft of your expository composition. As you write your draft, focus on getting all of your ideas down on paper. You will have time to revise your draft tomorrow.

Differentiated Instruction

 Advanced

Evaluate organization Have students discuss how the events in the student model are organized. Encourage them to evaluate the organization and support their judgments with reasons.

English Language Learners

Leveled support: Organization Help students organize their paragraphs.

Beginning Read information from resources that students might want to include in their main idea and detail charts. Limit the number of words in each sentence.

Intermediate Have students limit their paragraphs to one main idea and two supporting details. Ask them to number the sentences in the order they will write them before writing.

Advanced/Advanced High Have students use transition words to show the order of the supporting details in each paragraph.

Objectives

- Write a first draft of an expository composition.
- Organize main idea and details in chronological order.

Writing, continued
Writer's Craft: Chronological Order

MINI-LESSON

Chronological Order

■ **Introduce** Explain to students that when writing each paragraph in their composition, they should organize the details of each paragraph around a main idea. Explain that they should write a topic sentence that states the main idea. Then they need to provide details that the reader must know to understand the main idea. Point out that often they will organize their supporting details in chronological order. Remind them to use their main idea and detail charts to work on their drafts. Display the Drafting Tips for students. Then display Writing Transparency 2A.

Chinese Workers In America

Central Pacific Railroad

The Central Pacific Railroad began building the Transcontinental Railroad from the western U.S. in the 1800s. After they started to build it eastward from Sacramento, California they knew they needed more workers.

Chinese Workers in California

The railroad struggled to find enough workers. They looked very hard for people. Soon they realized that there were people from China living in California. People from China had originally come because they had heard of great opportunities. Many people left China to escape poverty. At first, the people from China worked in the gold mines, but their jobs soon ended. Many of them needed work. It was hard to find work, because many people did not want to work with immigrants from China. The railroad decided to give them a chance and were happy that they did. The immigrant from China were hard and dependable workers.

Chinese Workers Come From China

When the Central Pacific Railroad could no longer find workers from China in California, they began advertising in China. The workers were that good. The bosses described immigrants from China as terrific workers. Jealous of the praise given to the people from China, other workers treated them badly. You just think of the truble that caused. The bosses soon threatened that the other workers would lose their jobs if they continued to harass workers from China.

A Commemoration

In May, 1869 the Union Pacific and Central Pacific railroads connected in Utah. This was the completion of the first transcontinental railroad. Finally in 1965, The Golden Spike National Historic Site in Utah commemorated the history of the building of the railroad.

Unit 1 Lewis and Clark and Me   Writing: Model **2A**

Writing Transparency 2A, TR DVD

Drafting Tips

- ✔ To get started, review your main idea and detail chart.
- ✔ Keep your purpose in mind as you write, and be sure you include essential information to support your main ideas.
- ✔ Don't worry too much about grammar and mechanics when drafting. You will concentrate on these things during the editing stage.

I'm going to write a body paragraph of my expository composition about people from China who worked on the transcontinental railroad. When I draft, I develop my ideas. I will look at my chart to include the main idea and details. To organize my paragraph, first I'll write the main idea, then the details in the order in which they happened. I won't worry about revising or proofreading my composition now because I will do those parts of the editing process later.

Direct students to use the drafting tips to guide them in writing their drafts. Remind them to make sure that each paragraph has a topic sentence that states the main idea and relevant details that support the main idea in chronological order.

ROUTINE **Quick Write for Fluency** Team Talk

1. **Talk** Pairs talk about what features they included in their compositions.
2. **Write** Each partner writes an imperative sentence telling his or her partner to include a specific feature and an exclamatory sentence about the feature he or she included.
3. **Share** Have partners read one another's writing and check that they wrote both the imperative and exclamatory sentences correctly.

Routines Flip Chart

Wrap Up Your Day

- ✔ **Build Concepts** What did you learn about how the Indians named their animals?
- ✔ **Author's Purpose** How did the author's decision to tell about the expedition through the dog's eyes help you understand what happened in the story?
- ✔ **Questioning** How is the Indians asking questions about the dog similar to you asking questions about the text?

Preview DAY 4

Tell students that tomorrow they will read about the first Hispanic woman to become an astronaut.

Objectives

- Expand the weekly concept.
- Develop oral vocabulary.

Today at a Glance

Oral Vocabulary
foreign, improve

Genre
Biography

Reading
"Ellen Ochoa: Space Pioneer"

Let's Learn It!
Fluency: Appropriate phrasing
Vocabulary: Word endings
Listening/Speaking: Introduction

Research and Inquiry
Synthesize

Spelling
Long *a* and *i*

Conventions
Imperative and exclamatory sentences

Writing
Expository composition

Concept Talk

Question of the Week

What opportunities can be found in new places?

Expand the concept Remind students that this week they have read about the experiences of pioneers and explorers and the opportunities they found going to new places. Tell students that today they will read a biography about a remarkable woman who followed her dream and became an astronaut.

Anchored Talk

Develop oral vocabulary Use text features–illustrations, maps, heads–to review pp. 62–67 of *Lewis and Clark and Me: A Dog's Tale.* Discuss the Amazing Words *experiences* and *prepared.* Add these and other concept-related words to the concept map. Use the following questions to develop students' understanding of the concept. Remind students to answer questions with appropriate detail and build responses upon the ideas of others.

- What *experiences* would you expect to have traveling with Lewis and Clark on their exploration of the Louisiana Territory?
- Think about how Lewis and Clark *prepared* for their expedition. What do you think pioneers and explorers did in order to be prepared for their journeys?
- When you go to a new place you cannot always be *prepared* for the *experiences* you will have. What kind of attitude do you think it helps to have when you come across something unexpected in a new place?

Strategy Response Log

INTERACT with TEXT

Have students complete p. 8 in the *Reader's and Writer's Notebook.* Then have students work with a partner to answer their questions.

Concept Talk Video

Oral Vocabulary
Amazing Words

Amazing Words Oral Vocabulary Routine

Teach Amazing Words

1. **Introduce** Write the Amazing Word *foreign* on the board. Have students say it aloud with you. We read about how Newfoundlands were *foreign* to the Native Americans that Lewis and Seaman encountered. What context clues show that this type of dog was *foreign* to the Native Americans? (They have no name for this kind of dog and they decide to call Seaman "bear-dog.")
2. **Demonstrate** Have students answer questions to demonstrate understanding. What makes a land *foreign*? (place is unfamiliar, people speak another language and have different customs) How could you prepare for a visit to a *foreign* land? (read about their customs, learn a few words in the language spoken there)
3. **Apply** Have students apply their understanding. Ask students to say words they know in a *foreign* language.

See p. OV•2 to teach *improve*.

Routines Flip Chart

Apply Amazing Words As students read "Ellen Ochoa: Space Pioneer" on pp. 72–75, have them think about how hard work and education *improve* our opportunities and make realizing big dreams seem less *foreign* and more possible.

Connect to reading As students read today's selection about Ellen Ochoa, have them think about how the Question of the Week and the Amazing Words *foreign* and *improve* apply to one woman's journey to becoming a space pioneer.

Amazing Words

pioneer	fortune
traveled	experiences
settlers	prepared
territories	foreign
seek	improve

ELL Produce Oral Language Use the Day 4 instruction on ELL Poster 2 to extend and enrich language.

ELL Poster 2

Objectives

- Introduce biography.

Let's Think About Genre

Literary Nonfiction: Biography

Introduce the genre Explain to students that what we read is structured differently depending on the author's reasons for writing and what kind of information he/she wishes to convey. Different types of texts are called genres. Tell them that a biography is one type of genre.

Discuss the genre Think Aloud Biographies can cover a person's entire life or only part of it. The author creates a narrative, or story, based on true events from the person's life. Biographies are often organized in sequence to show how the events of a person's life happened. They may also include examples of cause-and-effect relationships to show why a person made certain choices in his or her life.

Draw a web on the board, like the one below. Label the center circle *biography*. Ask the following questions, reminding students to answer questions with appropriate detail.

- What does a biography cover? Possible responses: It can cover all or part of a person's life; it can tell true events in a person's life.
- How is a biography structured? Possible responses: It is a narrative; it tells events in sequence; it has examples of cause-and-effect relationships.
- What else do you know about biographies? Possible responses: They are written about famous people today or in the past.

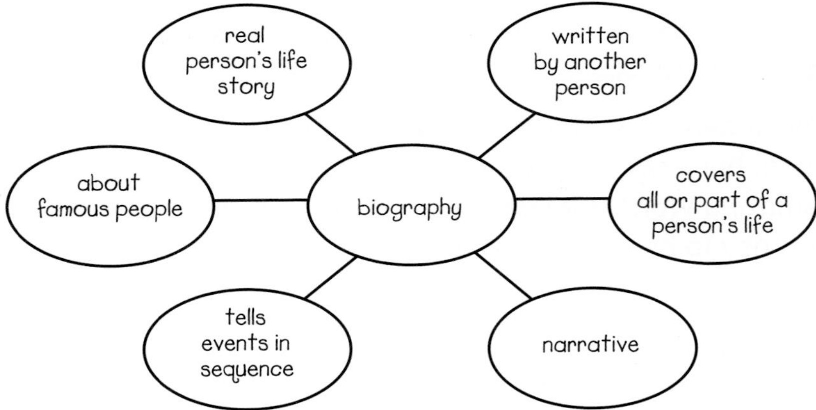

Guide practice Have students discuss the following questions in pairs: *What person would they like to read a biography about? Why do they think a writer might choose to write a biography about that person?* Then have students share their answers with the class.

Connect to reading Tell students that they will now read a biography about a woman who is an astronaut, inventor, and a scientist. Have the class think about times when they have been inspired by someone's life story.

Small Group Time

DAY 4 **Break into small groups before reading or revisiting "Ellen Ochoa: Space Pioneer."**

Teacher Led

SI Strategic Intervention

Teacher Led p. DI•30
- Practice retelling
- Genre focus
- Read/Revisit "Ellen Ochoa: Space Pioneer"

OL On-Level

Teacher Led p. 35
- Practice retelling
- Genre focus
- Read/Revisit "Ellen Ochoa: Space Pioneer"

A Advanced

Teacher Led Page DI•40
- Genre focus
- Read/Revisit "Ellen Ochoa: Space Pioneer"

ELL Place English language learners in the groups that correspond to their reading abilities in English.

Practice Stations
- Read for Meaning
- Get Fluent
- Words to Know

Independent Activities
- AudioText: "Ellen Ochoa: Space Pioneer"
- *Reader's and Writer's Notebook*
- Research and Inquiry

Academic Vocabulary

biography A biography is the story of a real person's life that is written by another person.

ELL

English Language Learners

Cognates The Spanish word *biografía* may be familiar to Spanish speakers as the cognate for *biography.*

Objectives
- Identify features of a biography.

Objectives
- Make connections between literary and informational texts with similar ideas and support your ideas with details from the texts.

Science in Reading

Genre
Biography
- A biography tells the story of a person's life.
- Biographies usually organize a person's life events in the order, or sequence, in which they happened.
- Some biographies may include examples of cause-and-effect relationships. Ask yourself: What events caused that person to make a specific choice?
- Read "Ellen Ochoa: Space Pioneer." As you read, look for elements in the text that make this a biography. What events caused Ellen to become an astronaut?

Ellen Ochoa: Space Pioneer

by David Arroyo

In 1958, a baby girl was born in Los Angeles, California. Little did her parents know that she would grow up to become the world's first female astronaut of Hispanic American heritage. Her name was Ellen Ochoa, and this is her story.

Born and raised in California, Ellen was an excellent student. At school, she loved math and music. She went to college at San Diego State University. There, she earned a degree in physics. After college, she had a decision to make. Would she become a scientist or a musician? She was so good at the flute that she could have become a professional flutist.

72

As much as Ellen loved music, she listened to her mother. Her mother always said that education is the key to a successful career. So Ellen went on to graduate school. At Stanford University, Ellen studied electrical engineering. She did not know what type of job she would pursue—until she heard about Sally Ride. In 1985, Sally Ride became the first female astronaut in the United States. Suddenly, Ellen knew what she wanted to do. She set her sights on becoming an astronaut.

It takes many years of hard work to become an astronaut. First, you have to develop expertise in engineering. Ellen's expertise is in building systems that can see "objects" in space. Her inventions helped NASA to find and understand objects in space better.

Let's Think About...
How does the sequence of life events on this page help you understand Ellen Ochoa's life? **Biography**

1

73

Student Edition pp. 72–73

Guide Comprehension

Teach the genre

Genre: Biography Have students preview "Ellen Ochoa: Space Pioneer" by looking at the title and the photos. What elements show that this is a biography? What do you think the biography will be about?

Corrective feedback

If... students are unable to identify the elements of biography,
then... use the model to guide students in the features of biographies.

Model the genre

I notice that the title is the name of a woman and then it says "Space Pioneer." The title is a clue that this is a biography about a woman who is probably an astronaut. The pictures show a woman doing different things in space. One picture even shows her playing the flute—I bet that will be an interesting detail about her life! I also noticed that the first sentence mentions the date a baby girl was born. Telling events about a person's life in sequence is another feature of a biography. I think this will be a story that tells important events about how this woman became an astronaut.

On their own

Have students work in pairs to write literal questions they have about this person's life story. Have students list their questions in a chart and then record the answers as they read.

Extend Thinking
Think Critically

Higher-order thinking skills

Author's Purpose • Evaluation What do you think the author's purpose was for choosing to write about Ellen Ochoa? Possible response: Ellen Ochoa could be inspiring to young people because she was the first woman of Hispanic descent to become an astronaut. She has an interesting life story that the author wants readers to know about.

Cause and Effect • Analysis What events influenced Ellen and caused her to want to be an astronaut? Possible response: Ellen decided to go to graduate school instead of becoming a professional musician. Then she heard about Sally Ride and this inspired her to become an astronaut.

Let's Think About...

I Possible response: It helps me understand that Ellen Ochoa was a very talented and smart person who worked hard. She cared about education and once she knew that she wanted to be an astronaut, she worked even harder to design things for NASA.

Differentiated Instruction

Strategic Intervention

Summarize Have students work in pairs to summarize the important details they have learned about Ellen Ochoa.

Advanced

Biography Have students use the Internet to explore the life stories of other astronauts or explorers. Have them list five interesting facts they learned about the person's life.

English Language Learners

Vocabulary: Acronyms Read the last sentence on p. 73 and direct students' attention to *NASA.* NASA is the name of our government's space exploration program. Write *NASA* on the board. NASA is a special abbreviation called an acronym. An acronym is a short word formed from the first letters of other words. *NASA* stands for *National Aeronautics and Space Administration.* Ask: Why do you think people use the acronym NASA instead of the longer name? (It's easier and quicker to say.)

DAY 4 Read and Comprehend

Objectives

- Understand how biographies are organized by sequence.
- Make connections across texts to aid comprehension.

NASA was impressed with Ellen's engineering talent. In 1990, NASA accepted Ellen into its astronaut training program. She became an official astronaut in 1991. In 1993, Ellen took her first flight into space. She spent nine days on the space shuttle *Discovery* as a mission specialist. The next year, she traveled on another space shuttle mission.

There is a lot more to being an astronaut than taking a trip on a space shuttle. While on her shuttle missions, Ellen studied the sun's effect on the Earth's climate and atmosphere. She examined the Earth's ozone layer. All of her years of school and her scientific knowledge helped her to do this important research.

74

Today, Ellen Ochoa is still working for NASA. This remarkable woman is a pioneer in spacecraft technology, an inventor, an astronaut, and a scientist. Out of respect for her accomplishments, two schools have been named after her. The students and staff at one of the schools said they wanted her name because Ellen Ochoa was an inspiration to them. Without a doubt, Ellen Ochoa will continue to inspire people for a long time to come.

Let's Think About...

What similarities and differences are there between the events and experiences told in Ellen Ochoa's biography and the events and characters' experiences in *Lewis and Clark and Me*? **Biography**

2

Let's Think About...

Reading Across Texts Look back at *Lewis and Clark and Me* and "Ellen Ochoa: Space Pioneer." What characteristics do Lewis, Clark, and Ellen Ochoa all share? Make a list.

Writing Across Texts Use your list to write a paragraph about what makes a good explorer.

75

Student Edition pp. 74–75

Guide Comprehension

Teach the genre

Genre: Biography Have students reread the first paragraph on p. 74. Ask: How are the ideas in this paragraph organized? Why is this type of organization common to biographies?

Corrective feedback

If... students are unable to identify how the ideas in the paragraph are organized,
then... use the model to guide students in recognizing when ideas in a text are ordered by sequence.

Model the genre

I read the text and notice a lot of dates. I see that each sentence tells an important event that happened, and then the next sentence tells about the next important event. The paragraph is organized by sequence. Biographies are often organized by sequence so readers can understand the important events and experiences in a person's life.

On their own

Have students think about four important events that have happened in their lives. Then have them write a short paragraph that tells these events in sequence.

Extend Thinking
Think Critically

Higher-order thinking skills

Author's Purpose • Analysis What do you think the author's purpose was for including the detail that two schools have been named after Ellen Ochoa? Possible response: I think the author wants to express that it is important to recognize people like Ellen Ochoa who are inspiring to others.

Graphic Sources • Evaluation Did the photographs help you understand the text? Do you think authors should include photographs in a biography? Tell why. Possible response: The photographs helped me understand what Ellen Ochoa does for NASA. I think that photographs should be included because they make the biography more interesting and real for readers.

Let's Think About...

2 Model identifying similarities and differences between the actual events and experiences told in the biography "Ellen Ochoa: Space Pioneer Astronaut" and the events and characters' experiences in the fictional work *Lewis and Clark and Me:* Ochoa and Seaman both traveled to new places (similarity). Ochoa traveled in space, but Seaman traveled in the United States, west of the Mississippi River (difference). Call on students to identify additional similarities and differences between the actual events and experiences described in the biography "Ellen Ochoa: Space Pioneer Astronaut" and the events and characters' experiences in the fictional work *Lewis and Clark and Me.*

Reading Across Texts

Have students create a T-chart and list characteristics of Lewis and Clark and then characteristics of Ellen Ochoa. Have students note the similarities when the chart is finished.

Writing Across Texts

Have students share their paragraphs about what makes a good explorer. Then ask students to write another paragraph explaining whether or not they think they would be a good explorer. Have students support their reasons with details.

Connect to Social Studies

President Dwight D. Eisenhower created NASA in 1958. NASA's mission is to pioneer the future in space exploration, scientific discovery, and aeronautics research. NASA has sent astronauts to the moon and to the International Space Station and continues to send astronauts on various space missions. Scientists at NASA research and develop technology so that space can be further explored. In addition to sending crews into space, NASA also has robotic missions such as sending robots to explore Mars.

ELL

English Language Learners

Graphic organizer Provide support to students as they work on their T-charts. Work together to add characteristics about Lewis and Clark and then about Ellen Ochoa.

DAY 4 Read and Comprehend

Objectives

- Read with fluency and comprehension.
- ◎ Use word endings and structure to determine the meanings of words.
- Present an introduction.

Check Fluency WCPM

SUCCESS PREDICTOR

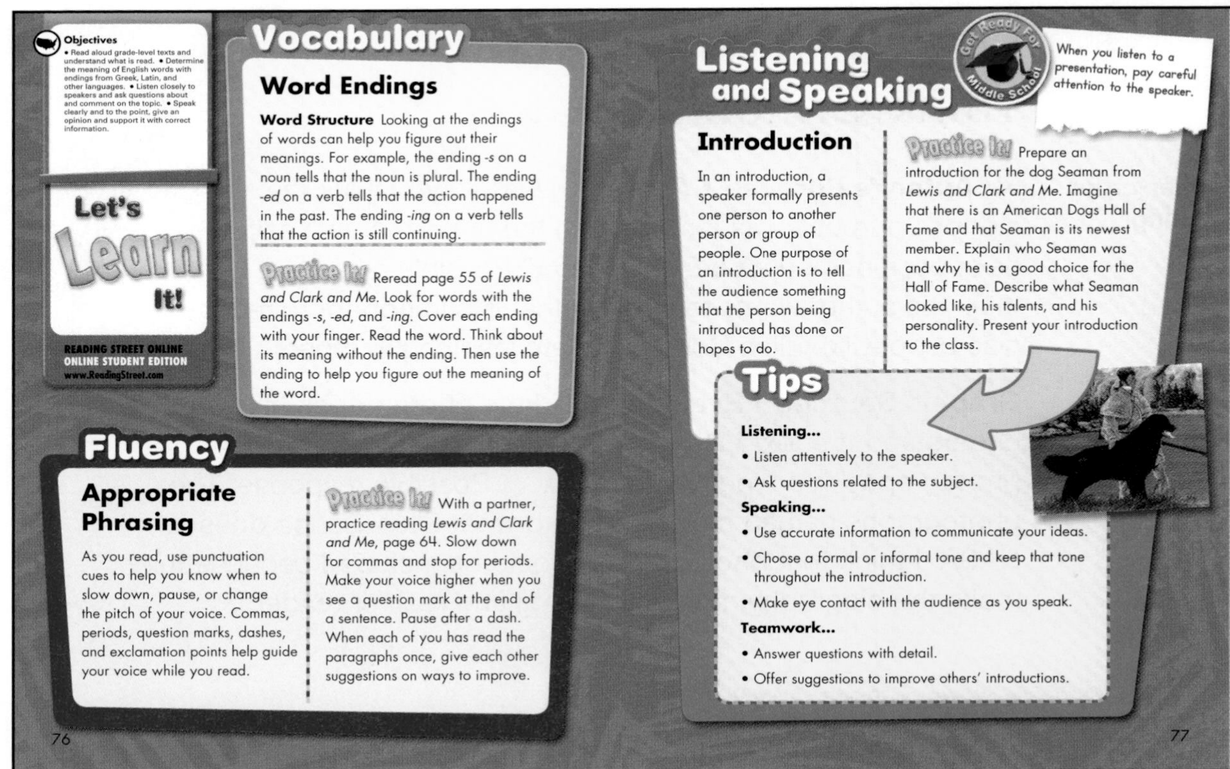

Let's Learn It!

READING STREET ONLINE
ONLINE STUDENT EDITION
www.ReadingStreet.com

Vocabulary

Word Endings

Word Structure Looking at the endings of words can help you figure out their meanings. For example, the ending *-s* on a noun tells that the noun is plural. The ending *-ed* on a verb tells that the action happened in the past. The ending *-ing* on a verb tells that the action is still continuing.

Practice It! Reread page 55 of *Lewis and Clark and Me.* Look for words with the endings *-s*, *-ed*, and *-ing*. Cover each ending with your finger. Read the word. Think about its meaning without the ending. Then use the ending to help you figure out the meaning of the word.

Fluency

Appropriate Phrasing

As you read, use punctuation cues to help you know when to slow down, pause, or change the pitch of your voice. Commas, periods, question marks, dashes, and exclamation points help guide your voice while you read.

Practice It! With a partner, practice reading *Lewis and Clark and Me,* page 64. Slow down for commas and stop for periods. Make your voice higher when you see a question mark at the end of a sentence. Pause after a dash. When each of you has read the paragraphs once, give each other suggestions on ways to improve.

Listening and Speaking

Get Ready for Middle School

When you listen to a presentation, pay careful attention to the speaker.

Introduction

In an introduction, a speaker formally presents one person to another person or group of people. One purpose of an introduction is to tell the audience something that the person being introduced has done or hopes to do.

Practice It! Prepare an introduction for the dog Seaman from *Lewis and Clark and Me.* Imagine that there is an American Dogs Hall of Fame and that Seaman is its newest member. Explain who Seaman was and why he is a good choice for the Hall of Fame. Describe what Seaman looked like, his talents, and his personality. Present your introduction to the class.

Tips

Listening...

- Listen attentively to the speaker.
- Ask questions related to the subject.

Speaking...

- Use accurate information to communicate your ideas.
- Choose a formal or informal tone and keep that tone throughout the introduction.
- Make eye contact with the audience as you speak.

Teamwork...

- Answer questions with detail.
- Offer suggestions to improve others' introductions.

76 77

Student Edition pp. 76–77

Fluency
Appropriate Phrasing

Guide practice Use the Student Edition activity as an assessment tool. Make sure the reading passage is at least 200 words in length. As students read aloud with partners, walk around to make sure they are using punctuation cues to pause at appropriate places to aid comprehension.

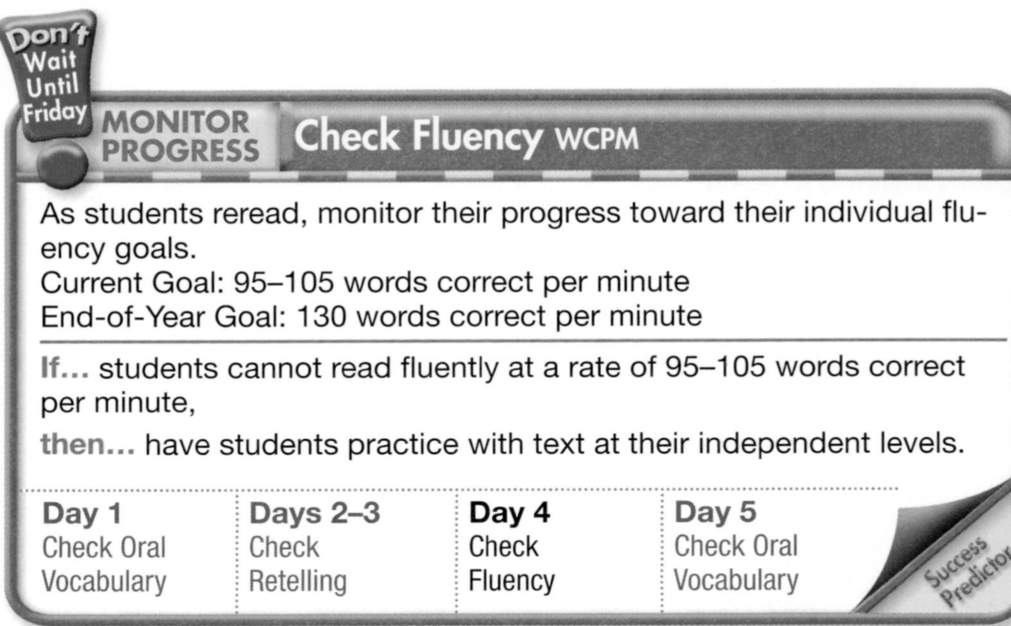

Don't Wait Until Friday

MONITOR PROGRESS **Check Fluency** WCPM

As students reread, monitor their progress toward their individual fluency goals.
Current Goal: 95–105 words correct per minute
End-of-Year Goal: 130 words correct per minute

If... students cannot read fluently at a rate of 95–105 words correct per minute,
then... have students practice with text at their independent levels.

Day 1 Check Oral Vocabulary	**Days 2–3** Check Retelling	**Day 4** Check Fluency	**Day 5** Check Oral Vocabulary

Success Predictor

Vocabulary
 Word Endings

Teach word endings

Word Structure Write the following words on the board:

employers	embarking	intended	attempted

Ask volunteers to identify the endings and base words.

Guide practice

Have students determine the meanings of the base words. Have them use a dictionary or glossary if necessary. Then have them use the ending to figure out the meaning of the word.

On their own

Walk around the room as students work to find words from *Lewis and Clark and Me.* Check to make sure that students are correctly identifying the base words and their meanings.

Listening and Speaking
Introduction

Teach

Tell students that an introduction is effective when the speaker presents accurate, interesting information about the person or thing being introduced. Have students review *Lewis and Clark and Me* to recall what Seaman was like. Remind students that when they plan their introductions, they should include details that will help their listeners visualize how Seaman looks and acts. Suggest that they share a story about Seaman that will entertain their audience and show why he should be included in the Hall of Fame. Remind speakers to use vivid verbs and strong adjectives to add interest to their introductions.

Guide practice

Have students practice their introductions with a partner. Remind students to speak with appropriate volume, maintain a consistent tone, and make eye contact with their listeners. Audience members should listen attentively and be prepared to ask relevant questions and make pertinent comments in response to the speaker's message.

On their own

Have students present their introductions to the class.

Introduction

Remind students that it is important to be aware of the audience. Tell students that they should vary the rate and tone of their voice as they speak with feeling to convince the audience to share their opinion.

Academic Vocabulary

eye contact the act of looking at another person directly in the eye to establish a connection when speaking and listening

ELL

English Language Learners

Practice pronunciation Assist pairs of students by modeling the correct pronunciations of the words from the lesson vocabulary and then having students repeat after you.

Objectives

- Write a report to present information.
- Review imperative and exclamatory sentences.
- Spell words with long *a* and long *i* correctly.

Research and Inquiry
Synthesize

Teach Have students synthesize their research findings and draw conclusions through a brief written explanation. Review with students how to organize their information and conclusions into a brief report. Remind students that their explanation should have a clear main idea and supporting details. Suggest that students find or draw pictures to include in their report if it is appropriate to their topic. Remind them to include captions, subheads, and other graphic sources, as appropriate.

Guide practice Have students use a word processing program to write their reports and create their Works Cited page. If students do not have access to a word processing program, remind them to write a final copy of the report that is appropriate for presentation. Check to see that students are including the necessary information in their Works Cited page: title, author, publisher, date of publication (or date when Web site was last updated).

On their own Have students organize and combine information to write their report. When students have finished writing, have them plan how they will present their report to the class.

Conventions
Imperative and Exclamatory Sentences

Test practice Tell students that grammar skills, such as the use of imperative and exclamatory sentences, are often assessed on important tests. Remind students of the definitions.

- Imperative sentences give a command or make a request and end in a period.
- Exclamatory sentences show surprise and end in an exclamation point.

Daily Fix-It Use Daily Fix-It numbers 7 and 8 in the right margin.

On their own For additional practice, use the *Reader's and Writer's Notebook* p. 61.

Reader's and Writer's Notebook p. 61

Spelling
Long *a* and *i*

Practice spelling strategy Have partners write the spelling words on cards. Each student should write half of the words and then cut apart the words he or she has written, making the cuts in such a way that the letters spelling the long vowel sound are isolated. Have students exchange their cards and reassemble them.

On their own For additional practice, use *Let's Practice It!* p. 16 on the *Teacher Resources DVD-ROM.*

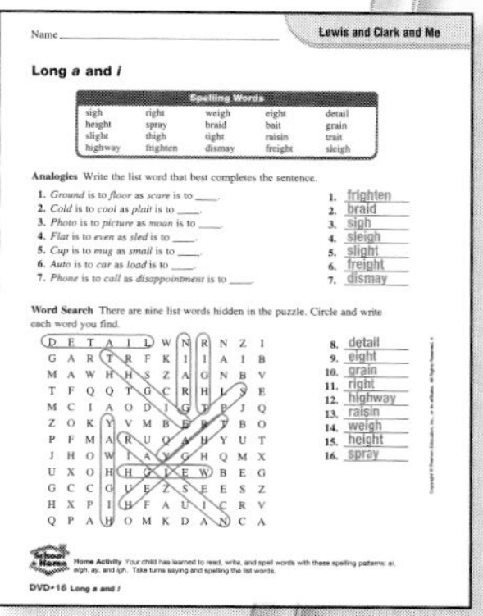
Name ____________ Lewis and Clark and Me

Long *a* and *i*

Spelling Words				
sigh	right	weigh	eight	detail
height	spray	braid	bait	grain
slight	thigh	tight	raisin	trait
highway	frighten	dismay	freight	sleigh

Analogies Write the list word that best completes the sentence.

1. *Ground* is to *floor* as *scare* is to ____. 1. frighten
2. *Cold* is to *cool* as *plait* is to ____. 2. braid
3. *Photo* is to *picture* as *moan* is to ____. 3. sigh
4. *Flat* is to *even* as *sled* is to ____. 4. sleigh
5. *Cup* is to *mug* as *small* is to ____. 5. slight
6. *Auto* is to *car* as *load* is to ____. 6. freight
7. *Phone* is to *call* as *disappointment* is to ____. 7. dismay

Word Search There are nine list words hidden in the puzzle. Circle and write each word you find.

D E T A I L W N R N Z I
G A R T R F K I I A I B
M A W H H S Z A G N B V
T F Q Q T G C R H L S E
M C I A O D I G T P J Q
Z O K Y V M B E R T B O
P F M A R U Q A H Y U T
J H O W I A Y G H Q M X
U X O H H G I E W B E G
G C C G U E Z S E E S Z
H X P I H F A U I C R V
Q P A H O M K D A N C A

8. detail
9. eight
10. grain
11. right
12. highway
13. raisin
14. weigh
15. height
16. spray

Home Activity Your child has learned to read, write, and spell words with these spelling patterns: ai, eigh, ay, and igh. Take turns saying and spelling the list words.

DVD•16 Long *a* and *i*

Let's Practice It!
TR DVD•16

Daily Fix-It

7. Can you polished this man's shoes *(polish; shoes?)*
8. she was only 16 years old, her brother moved far away. *(She; old; Her)*

Objectives

- Revise draft of expository composition.
- Apply revising strategy of adding.
- Include supporting sentences with facts, details, and explanations.

Writing—Expository Composition

Revising Strategy

MINI-LESSON

Revising Strategy: Adding

- Yesterday we drafted an expository composition. Today we will revise our drafts.
- Display Writing Transparency 2B. Remind students that revising does not include corrections of grammar and mechanics. Then introduce the revising strategy Adding.
- When we revise, we ask ourselves what information is missing that would help the reader better understand the topic. Adding is the revising strategy by which additional important information is included. In this example, readers might want to know the name of the railroad. I'll add that information.
- Point out to students that if they do include photos, maps, or illustrations, they should label each item.

Revising Marks			
Take Out		Uppercase letter	═
Add	^	Lowercase letter	/
Period	⊙	New paragraph	¶
Move	⌒		

The ^Central Pacific railroad struggled to find enough workers. They looked very hard for people. Soon they realized that there were people from China living in California. ^People from China started to come to the United States in 1850. Many came ~~People from China had originally come~~ because they had heard of great opportunities. Many people left China to escape poverty. At first, the people from China worked in the gold mines, but their jobs soon ended. Many of them needed work. It was hard to find work, because many people did not want to work with immigrants from China. ^They were afraid they would lose their jobs. The railroad decided to give ^Immigrants from China ~~them~~ a chance and were happy that they did. The immigrants from China were hard and dependable workers.

Unit 1 Lewis and Clark and Me Writing: Revise 2B

Writing Transparency 2B, TR DVD

Tell students that as they revise, not only should they look for places where they can add information to make their writing clearer and more interesting, they should also check that their paragraphs include main ideas and details in chronological order as well as a concluding statement.

Revising Tips

✔ Stay focused on the purpose of your composition, which is to provide factual information.

✔ Add facts as needed to provide additional important information about the people, places, and events you mention.

✔ Think about how you can add details to answer readers' possible questions about the topic.

Peer conferencing

Peer Revision Have pairs of students exchange papers for peer revision. Partners can then spend a few minutes telling each other what the composition is about and what their partner could add to make it more interesting or understandable.

Have students revise their compositions. They should use the information their partner gave during the Peer Revision as well as the key features of an expository composition to guide their revision. Be sure that students are using the revising strategy Adding and that they have a concluding statement.

Corrective feedback Circulate around the room to monitor students and confer with them as they revise. Remind students correcting errors that they will have time to edit tomorrow. They should be working on adding important information, content, and organization today.

ROUTINE Quick Write for Fluency **Team Talk**

1. **Talk** Have students discuss how Seaman became Meriwether Lewis's dog.
2. **Write** Each student should write a paragraph telling the details of the event the group discussed.
3. **Share** Have partners read one another's writing to check that the details are in time-order.

Routines Flip Chart

Write Guy *Jeff Anderson*

Trait-by-Trait: Organization

Organization is a trait of good writing, but let's not be so concerned with form that we forget about meaning. A student may develop a good way to communicate ideas that does not precisely follow the format we expect. There isn't only one way to reach the goal. And there isn't just one way to organize your writing. Reward creativity and help students see what other writers do in mentor texts.

ELL

English Language Learners

Support revising Help students see that they can provide more information by adding factual details such as names of people, places, and dates. Have students look at the notes for any specific information that they can use to add to their drafts.

Wrap Up Your Day

- ✔ **Build Concepts** What did you learn about Ellen Ochoa?
- ✔ **Oral Vocabulary** Monitor students' use of oral vocabulary as they respond to this question: What route did Ellen take to become an astronaut?
- ✔ **Text Features** Discuss how the photographs help students understand the text.

Preview DAY 5

Remind students to think about what opportunities can be found in new places.

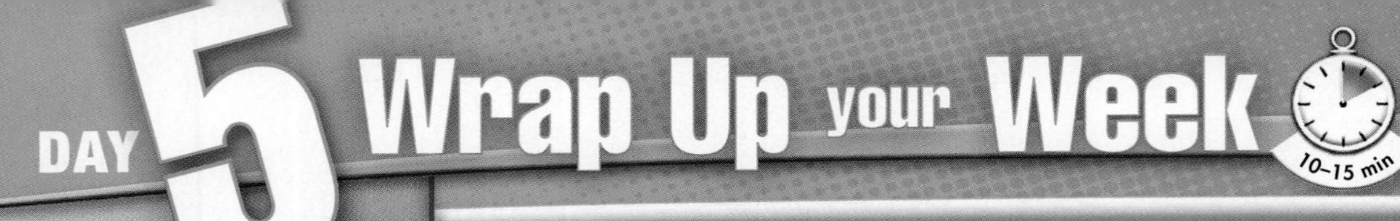

Objectives

- Review the weekly concept.
- Review oral vocabulary.

Today at a Glance

Oral Vocabulary

Comprehension
◉ Author's purpose

Lesson Vocabulary
◉ Word endings

Word Analysis
Suffixes *-or, -er*

Literary Terms
Sensory words

Assessment
Fluency
Comprehension

Research and Inquiry
Communicate

Spelling
Long *a* and *i*

Conventions
Imperative and exclamatory sentences

Writing
Expository composition

Check Oral Vocabulary
SUCCESS PREDICTOR

Concept Wrap Up

Question of the Week

What opportunities can be found in new places?

Review the concept Have students look back at the reading selections to find examples that demonstrate the kinds of opportunities that can be found in new places.

Review Amazing Words Display and review this week's concept map. Remind students that this week they have learned ten Amazing Words related to opportunities. Have students use the Amazing Words and the concept map to answer the question *What opportunities can be found in new places?*

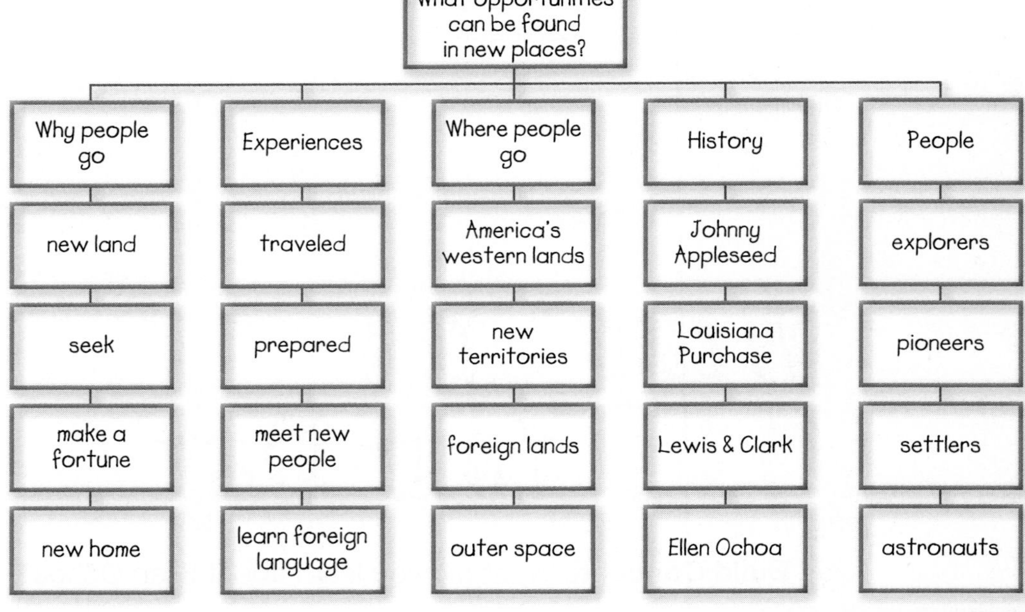

ELL Check Concepts and Language
Use the Day 5 instructions on ELL Poster 2 to monitor students' understanding of the lesson concept.

ELL Poster 2

Amazing Ideas

Connect to the Big Question

Have pairs of students discuss how the Question of the Week connects to the Big Question: *What can we discover from new places and people?* Tell students to use the concept map and what they have learned from this week's Anchored Talks and reading selections to form an Amazing Idea—a realization or "big idea" about Turning Points. Remind partners to pose and answer questions with appropriate detail and to give suggestions that build on each other's ideas. Then ask pairs to share their Amazing Ideas with the class.

Amazing Ideas might include these key concepts:

- New places bring new opportunities such as discovering a different way to make a fortune or make new friends.
- Throughout history people have gone to new places to make a better life.
- Pioneers in the past created a new life that gave people hope. Today people are still looking for opportunities to create something new and are exploring ways to make life better.

Write about it

Have students write a few sentences about their Amazing Idea, beginning with "This week I learned . . ."

It's Friday

MONITOR PROGRESS Check Oral Vocabulary

Have individuals use this week's Amazing Words to describe opportunities found in new places. Monitor students' abilities to use the Amazing Words and note which words you need to reteach.

If... students have difficulty using the Amazing Words,

then... reteach using the Oral Vocabulary Routine, pp. 47a, 50b, 62b, 72b, OV•2.

Day 1	Days 2–3	Day 4	Day 5
Check Oral Vocabulary	Check Retelling	Check Fluency	Check Oral Vocabulary

Success Predictor

Amazing Words

pioneer	fortune
traveled	experiences
settlers	prepared
territories	foreign
seek	improve

ELL

English Language Learners

Concept map Work with students to add new words to the concept map.

DAY 5 Wrap Up your Week

20–25 min

Objectives

- Review author's purpose.
- Review word endings.
  - Review suffixes *-or* and *-er.*
  - Review sensory words.

Comprehension Review

Author's Purpose

Teach author's purpose Review the definition of author's purpose on p. 48. Remind students that authors write to persuade, to inform, to express ideas or feelings, and to entertain. Authors can have more than one purpose for writing a text. For additional support have students review p. EI•2 on author's purpose.

Envision It!

Envision It! Visual Skills Handbook

Author's Purpose

An author writes for many purposes, some of which are to inform, entertain, persuade, or express a mood or feeling. An author may have more than one purpose for writing. Sometimes the author's purpose is directly stated, but other times you have to figure it out on your own.

EI•2

Student Edition p. EI•2

Guide practice Have partners identify the author's purposes for writing *Lewis and Clark and Me.* Have student pairs find details that support the author's purpose in the story. Then have pairs tell how they know the author's reasons for writing the historical fiction text.

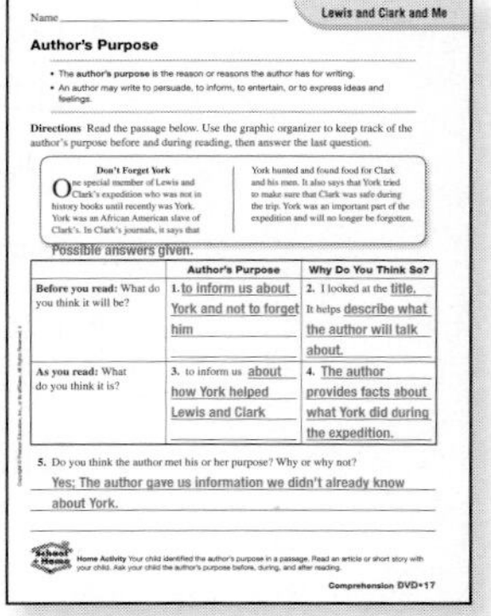
Name ________ Lewis and Clark and Me

Author's Purpose

- The **author's purpose** is the reason or reasons the author has for writing.
- An author may write to persuade, to inform, to entertain, or to express ideas and feelings.

Directions Read the passage below. Use the graphic organizer to keep track of the author's purpose before and during reading, then answer the last question.

Don't Forget York

One special member of Lewis and Clark's expedition who was not in history books until recently was York. York was an African American slave of Clark's. In Clark's journals, it says that York hunted and found food for Clark and his men. It also says that York tried to make sure that Clark was safe during the trip. York was an important part of the expedition and will no longer be forgotten.

Possible answers given.

	Author's Purpose	Why Do You Think So?
Before you read: What do you think it will be?	1. to inform us about York and not to forget him	2. I looked at the title. It helps describe what the author will talk about.
As you read: What do you think it is?	3. to inform us about how York helped Lewis and Clark	4. The author provides facts about what York did during the expedition.

5. Do you think the author met his or her purpose? Why or why not?

Yes; The author gave us information we didn't already know about York.

Home Activity Your child identified the author's purpose in a passage. Read an article or short story with your child. Ask your child the author's purpose before, during, and after reading.

Comprehension DVD•17

Let's Practice It!
TR DVD•17

On their own For additional practice with author's purpose, use *Let's Practice It!* p. 17 on the *Teacher Resources DVD-ROM.*

Vocabulary Review

Word Endings

Teach word endings Remind students that the ending *-ed* is added to a verb to show action that happened in the past. The ending *-ing* is used for verbs telling about ongoing actions.

Guide practice Review with students how to find the base word and ending in the vocabulary word *yearned.* Have students use the base word and the word ending to explain the meaning of *yearned.*

On their own Have students work in pairs to find five verbs in *Lewis and Clark and Me* that end in *-ed* or *-ing.* Have them write the verb and the base word and then create a new verb by adding *-ed* or *-ing.* Then have partners take turns using the original and new forms of the verbs in example sentences.

Word Analysis Review
Suffixes *-or, -er*

Teach suffixes *-or, -er*

Review that the suffixes *-or* and *-er* came from Old High German and Middle English and are added to the end of verbs to create nouns. These suffixes can mean "someone who." Discuss the meanings of the words *contractor* and *seeker.*

Guide practice

Display the following words: *manager, designer, advisor,* and *supervisor.* Use the Strategy for Meaningful Word Parts to teach the word *advisor.*

ROUTINE Strategy for Meaningful Word Parts

1. **Identify word parts** Display the word *advisor.* I will circle the suffix *-or* and underline *advis*.
2. **Connect to meaning** I know that sometimes the spelling of a base word changes when endings are added, so I think the base word is *advise.* This verb means "to offer advice." The suffix *-or* means "one who." By combining these definitions, I know that *advisor* means "someone who offers advice."
3. **Read the word** Blend the meaningful word parts together to read the word *advisor.*

Routines Flip Chart

On their own

Have students identify the base word and use the suffix to generate a definition for each of the remaining words.

Literary Terms Review
Sensory Words

Teach sensory words

Remind students that sensory words, or imagery, are words or phrases that help the reader experience the way things look, smell, taste, sound, or feel.

Guide practice

Help students identify sensory words used to describe Lewis on p. 54, paragraphs 4 and 5, and describe how the words appeal to their senses.

On their own

Have students find examples of sensory words on p. 59. Have them explain how the imagery helps them better understand what they are reading.

Lesson Vocabulary

docks platforms built on the shore or out from the shore; wharves; piers
migrating going from one region to another with the change in seasons
scan to glance at; look over hastily
scent smell
wharf platform built on the shore or out from the shore beside which ships can load or unload
yearned felt a longing or desire

English Language Learners

Author's purpose If students have trouble understanding the different reasons why authors write, compare and contrast the purposes of *Lewis and Clark and Me* with "Ellen Ochoa: Space Pioneer." Ask: Why did the author write *Lewis and Clark and Me*? (to entertain, to inform) Why did the author write "Ellen Ochoa: Space Pioneer"? (to inform) Are any of these reasons the same? (yes) How are they different? (*Lewis and Clark and Me* is a story told by a dog that is written to also entertain readers.)

Sensory words Help students understand the purpose of sensory words by working with them to describe a vivid object you have in the classroom in a way that would appeal to the senses. Then have students add sensory words to the following sentence: *The dog went to his owner.* (The big, wet dog ran happily to his owner.)

Objectives

- Read aloud grade-level text with fluency.

Assessment

Check words correct per minute

Fluency Make two copies of the fluency passage on p. 77k. As the student reads the text aloud, mark mistakes on your copy. Also mark where the student is at the end of one minute. To check the student's comprehension of the passage, have him or her retell what was read. To figure words correct per minute (WCPM), subtract the number of mistakes from the total number of words read in one minute.

WCPM

Corrective feedback

If... students cannot read fluently at a rate of 95–105 WCPM,
then... make sure they practice with text at their independent reading level. Provide additional fluency practice by pairing nonfluent readers with fluent readers.

If... students already read at 130 WCPM,
then... have them read a book of their choice independently.

Plan to Assess Fluency

- ☑ **Week 1** Assess Advanced students.
- ☑ **This week assess Strategic Intervention students.**
- ☐ **Week 3** Assess On-Level students.
- ☐ **Week 4** Assess Strategic Intervention students.
- ☐ **Week 5** Assess any students you have not yet checked during this unit.

Set individual goals for students to enable them to reach the year-end goal.

- Current Goal: 95–105 WCPM
- Year-End Goal: 130 WCPM

Small Group Time

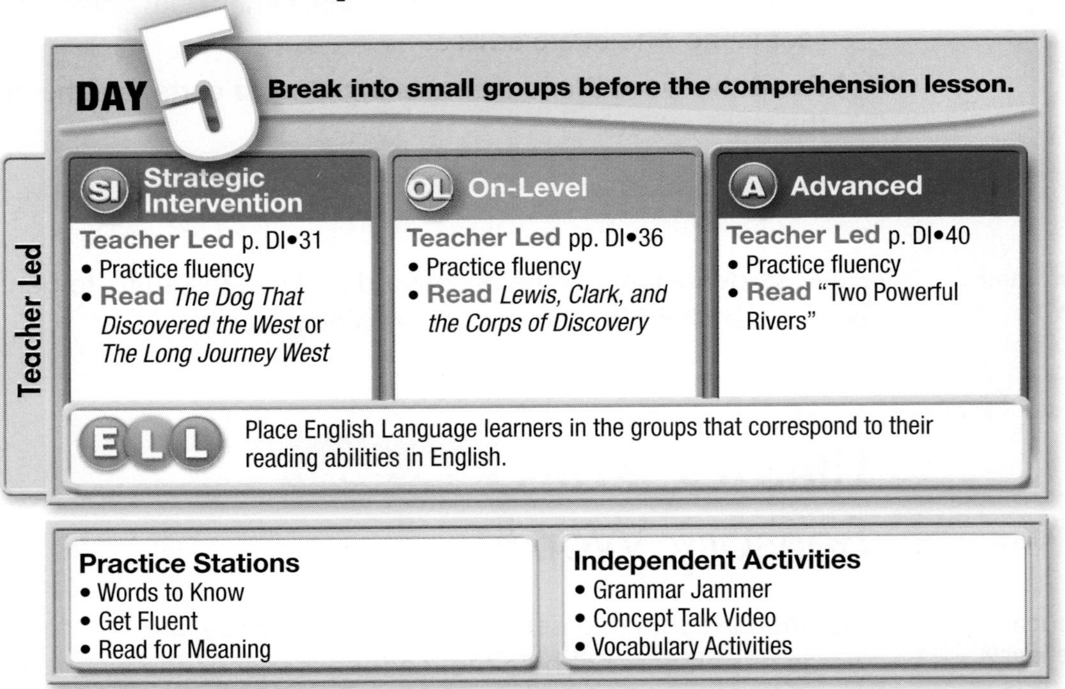
DAY 5
Break into small groups before the comprehension lesson.
Teacher Led
SI Strategic Intervention
Teacher Led p. DI•31
• Practice fluency
• Read The Dog That Discovered the West or The Long Journey West
OL On-Level
Teacher Led pp. DI•36
• Practice fluency
• Read Lewis, Clark, and the Corps of Discovery
A Advanced
Teacher Led p. DI•40
• Practice fluency
• Read "Two Powerful Rivers"
ELL
Place English Language learners in the groups that correspond to their reading abilities in English.
Practice Stations
• Words to Know
• Get Fluent
• Read for Meaning
Independent Activities
• Grammar Jammer
• Concept Talk Video
• Vocabulary Activities

Name ______________________________

Always a Doctor

It can be hard to change who you are. Juan Romagoza of El 13
Salvador had a love for helping people. He was studying to be a 26
surgeon. Then, during a civil war in his country, the military kidnapped 38
him. They did not like that Juan had been giving care to farm workers. 52
The military treated him badly. They hurt him so that he would not be 66
able to do surgery any more. 72

Juan lived through the civil war. In the 1980s he fled from his 85
country and came to the United States. Here, he met a doctor in 98
Washington, D.C. The doctor found Juan to be a kind and caring man. 111
He hired Juan to run a free clinic one night a week. Juan would give 126
care to those who could not pay for it. Juan showed kindness toward the 140
people he cared for. He found that he loved his work. 151

Now, twenty years later, Juan's clinic gives care to people full time. 163
They even have a new building. Juan's clinic helps Latino people who 175
might not be able to pay for a doctor's care. They are grateful for his 190
help and see him as a hero. And Juan Romagoza is grateful to be a 205
doctor. 206

MONITOR PROGRESS

- **Check Fluency**

Objectives

- Read grade-level text with comprehension.

Assessment

Check author's purpose

Author's Purpose Use "Eve Bunting: Hope in Hard Times" on p. 77m to check students' understanding of author's purpose.

1. Why does Eve Bunting write books about children who are going through hard times? Possible response: She knows that life can be hard sometimes and she wants to offer children hope when they are going through hard times.
2. Is the author's purpose stated or implied in the passage? Explain. Possible response: The author's purpose is implied. The author does not directly state the purpose for writing this passage, so readers have to infer the author's purpose using clues from the text.
3. What do you think is the author's implied purpose for writing this passage? Possible response: The author wrote to inform readers about Eve Bunting and her work.

Corrective feedback

If... students are unable to answer the comprehension questions,
then... use the Reteach lesson in the *First Stop* book.

Name ______________________________

Eve Bunting: Hope in Hard Times

Eve Bunting's father often told her that life was hard. Life was hard for Eve at times. But this Irish immigrant used her experience to become a well-loved author. She wrote over two hundred books for children.

Eve was born in Northern Ireland in 1928. Her childhood was a happy one. Many nights were spent by the fireplace as her father read poems. Later, when Eve was at boarding school, World War II broke out. German planes bombed the city. Eve and her classmates hid in bomb shelters under the ground.

When she grew up, Eve got married and had three children. Life in Northern Ireland was not easy, though. There was much hatred. Groups with different religions and beliefs did not get along. Eve and her husband, Ed, made a hard choice. They would leave the troubles of Ireland and come to America.

They moved in 1958 with no money and no job. Eve missed Ireland, though, and felt lonely in her new home. Eve decided to take a class in writing. She rewrote an Irish tale about two giants that she had loved as a child and it became her first book for children.

After that, Eve found many ideas for books. She thought of her hard times growing up. Life was hard for other children too, she knew. When Eve read news about hard times, she wrote about them. She wrote one book about a homeless father and son. Another was about riots in Los Angeles. Eve hopes that her books will help give children hope when life is hard.

MONITOR PROGRESS

• Author's Purpose

DAY 5 Wrap Up your Week

10–15 min

Objectives

- Communicate inquiry results.
- Administer spelling test.
- Review imperative and exclamatory sentences.

Research and Inquiry
Communicate

Present ideas Have students share their inquiry results by presenting their information and giving a brief talk on their research. Have students display their reports or point out any special features they included in their report.

Listening and speaking Remind students how to be good speakers and how to communicate effectively with their audience.

- Respond to relevant questions with appropriate details.
- Speak with fluent rate, volume, and enunciation.
- Keep eye contact with audience members.

Remind students of these tips on how to be a good listener.

- Listen attentively by staying focused on the speaker.
- Wait until the speaker is finished before raising your hand to ask a relevant question or make a pertinent comment.
- Be polite, even if you disagree.

Spelling Test
Long *a* and *i*

Spelling test To administer the spelling test, refer to the directions, words, and sentences on p. 49c.

Conventions
Extra Practice

Teach Remind students that an imperative sentence gives an order or makes a request and ends in a period and that an exclamatory sentence shows strong feeling or surprise and ends in an exclamation point.

Guide practice Have partners write an imperative sentence and an exclamatory sentence in no particular order, with no punctuation. Then have them exchange sentences and fill in the correct punctuation.

Give me the book to read

This was such a great story

Daily Fix-It Use Daily Fix-It numbers 9 and 10 in the right margin.

On their own Write these sentences relating to the story *Lewis and Clark and Me.* Have students fill an initial word and the end punctuation in each. Remind students that an imperative sentence ends in a period and an exclamatory sentence ends in an exclamation point. Students should complete *Let's Practice It!* p.18 on the *Teacher Resources DVD-ROM.*

1. ________ **a wonderful dog that Seaman was** (What) (!)
2. ________ **after the squirrel** (Go) (.)
3. ________ **at that beautiful water** (Look) (!)
4. ________ **the boat here** (Stop) (.)

Daily Fix-It

9. Its interesting to read a story about people who maked history. *(It's; made)*
10. Ask the librarian for more books about the california Gold Rush? *(California; Rush.)*

Let's Practice It!
TR DVD•18

Objectives

- Proofread revised drafts of an expository composition, including use of imperative and exclamatory sentences.
- Create and present final draft.

Writing—Expository Composition
Imperative and Exclamatory Sentences

Review revising Remind students that yesterday they revised their expository compositions, focusing on adding words and information to make the writing interesting and more informative. Today they will proofread their compositions.

MINI-LESSON

Proofread Imperative and Exclamatory Sentences

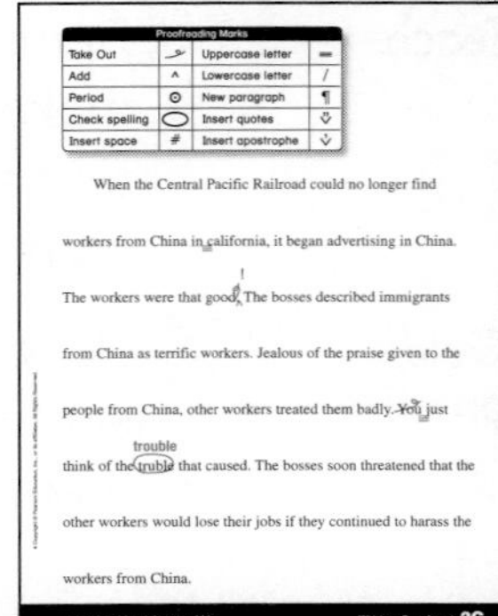
Writing Transparency 2C, TR DVD

- **Teach** When we proofread, we look closely at our work, searching for errors in spelling, capitalization, punctuation, and grammar. Today we will focus on making sure our imperative and exclamatory sentences are used correctly.

- **Model** Let's look at another paragraph from the story we revised yesterday. Display Writing Transparency 2C. Explain that you will look for errors in the use of imperative and exclamatory sentences. I see a problem in the sentence *The workers were that good.* The sentence is an exclamatory sentence. It needs an exclamation point at the end. Point out that the sentence *You just think of the trouble that caused* would work well as an imperative sentence. Delete the word *You.* Explain to students that they should reread their composition several times, looking for errors in spelling, punctuation, capitalization, and grammar. Remind them to capitalize any proper nouns, such as names of historical events, languages, and nationalities.

Proofread Display the Proofreading Tips. Ask students to proofread their compositions, using the Proofreading Tips and paying attention to imperative and exclamatory sentences. Circulate around the room to answer questions. Have pairs proofread each other's compositions.

Proofreading Tips

- ✓ Be sure all imperative and exclamatory sentences are punctuated and used correctly.
- ✓ Double-check spelling with a dictionary.
- ✓ Begin postwriting only after drafting, revising, and editing have been completed.

Present Have students incorporate revisions and proofreading edits into their compositions to create a final draft.

Give students two options for presenting: reading their compositions aloud to each other in small groups, or writing their compositions and displaying printouts of them around the room. For oral presentations, have students create a picture to show the main topic of the compositions. For printed compositions, have students post them on self-designed backing such as poster board or construction paper. When students have finished, have each complete a Writing Self-Evaluation Guide.

ROUTINE Quick Write for Fluency — Team Talk

1. **Talk** Have students discuss what opportunities in history they learned about this week.
2. **Write** Each student writes a paragraph summarizing what he or she learned.
3. **Share** Partners read one another's writing.

Routines Flip Chart

Teacher Note

Writing self-evaluation Make copies of the Writing Self-Evaluation Guide on p. 39 of the *Reader's and Writer's Notebook* and hand out to students.

ELL

English Language Learners

Support editing Provide editing practice for students. Write the following and have them identify the sentences that need an exclamation point:

1. I can't wait to go to the circus
2. What a terrific game she played
3. Cats have sharp claws

Poster preview Prepare students for next week by using Week 3, ELL Poster 3. Read the Poster Talk-Through to introduce the concepts and vocabulary. Ask students to identify and describe objects and actions in the art.

Selection summary Send home the summary of *On the Banks of Plum Creek,* in English and the students' home languages, if available. Students can read the summary with family members.

Preview NEXT WEEK

Why do we want to explore new places? Tell students that they will read about sisters who explore and discover the banks along Plum Creek.

DAY 5 Assessment Checkpoints for the Week

Weekly Assessment

Weekly Tests

Use pp. 7–14 of *Weekly Tests* to check:

- ✔ **Word Analysis** Suffixes *-or, -er*
- ✔ **Comprehension Skill** Author's Purpose
- ✔ Review **Comprehension Skill** Sequence
- ✔ **Lesson Vocabulary**

docks	scent
migrating	wharf
scan	yearned

Differentiated Assessment

Advanced

On-Level

Strategic Intervention

Fresh Reads for Fluency and Comprehension

Use pp. 7–12 of *Fresh Reads for Fluency and Comprehension* to check:

- ✔ **Comprehension Skill** Author's Purpose
- ✔ Review **Comprehension Skill** Sequence
- ✔ **Fluency** Words Correct Per Minute

Managing Assessment

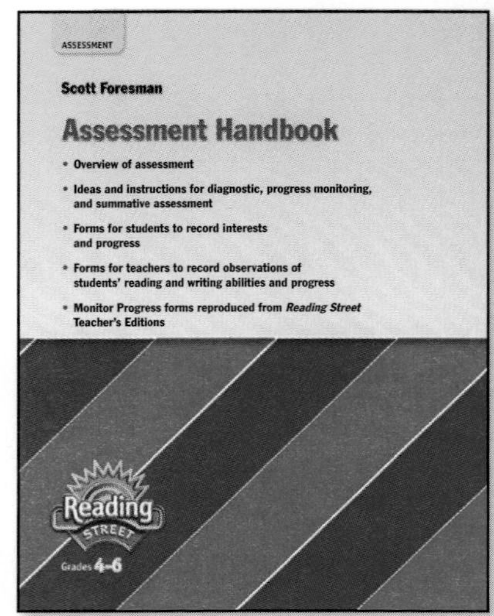

Assessment Handbook

Use *Assessment Handbook* for:

- ✔ **Weekly Assessment Blackline Masters for Monitoring Progress**
- ✔ **Observation Checklists**
- ✔ **Record-Keeping Forms**
- ✔ **Portfolio Assessment**

Johnny Appleseed

Continued from p. 47b

interested in looks. He was interested in apples. He was a happy man who shared his love of apples with others. It's been many years since John Chapman roamed the Midwest planting trees. We may never be able to separate the fact from the fiction of his life. But, he will always be remembered as a spirited American pioneer who planted apple trees. He will always be an American legend. He will always be Johnny Appleseed.

Pacing Small Group Instruction

5-Day Plan

DAY 1	• Reinforce the concept • Read Leveled Readers Concept Literacy Below Level
DAY 2	• Author's Purpose • Questioning • Revisit Student Edition pp. 52–61
DAY 3	• Word Endings • Revisit Student Edition pp. 62–67
DAY 4	• Practice Retelling • Read/Revisit Student Edition pp. 72–75
DAY 5	• Reread for fluency • Reread Leveled Readers

3- or 4-Day Plan

DAY 1	• Reinforce the concept • Read Leveled Readers Concept Literacy Below Level
DAY 2	• Author's Purpose • Questioning • Revisit Student Edition pp. 52–61
DAY 3	• Word Endings • Revisit Student Edition pp. 62–67
DAY 4	• Practice Retelling • Read/Revisit Student Edition pp. 72–75 • Reread for fluency • Reread Leveled Readers

3-Day Plan: Eliminate the shaded box.

DAY 1

Build Background

- **Reinforce the Concept** Discuss the weekly question *What opportunities can be found in new places?* One opportunity you can find in new places is the chance to explore the unknown. For example, by exploring mountains or caves you can discover animals or sights you've never seen before. In new places, you may also have the opportunity to have entirely new experiences. For example, the first time you see snow, you might touch it and form it into a snowball. What else could you do if you had never seen snow before? Discuss the words in the concept map.

- **Connect to Reading** This week you will read about how some people explored the new land that the United States had just bought in 1803. Because they had never seen it before, they had to be prepared to travel on water as well as on land.
  - How did Johnny Appleseed travel in the late 1700s? (*The Read Aloud suggests that he walked.*)
  - What other means of transportation were available to people in the early 1800s? (*horseback, wagon, boat*)

Objectives

- Participate in teacher-led discussions by answering questions with appropriate detail.

DAY 1

For a complete literacy instructional plan and additional practice with this week's target skills and strategies, see the **Leveled Reader Teaching Guide.**

Concept Literacy Reader

- **Read** *The Dog That Discovered the West*
- **Before Reading** Preview the story with students, focusing on key concepts and vocabulary. Then have them set a purpose for reading.
- **During Reading** Read the first two pages of the story aloud while students track the print. Then have students finish reading the story with a partner.
- **After Reading** After students finish reading the story, connect it to the weekly question. What did Seaman have a chance to do in the West? (*get food, keep travelers safe, make friends*)

Below-Level Reader

- **Read** *The Long Journey West*
- **Before Reading** Have students preview the story, using the illustrations. Then have students set a purpose for reading.
- **During Reading** Do a choral reading of pp. 5–8. If students are able, have them read and discuss the remainder of the book with a partner. Have partners discuss the following questions:
  - Why do you think the author wrote this? (*to explain why Lewis and Clark made their journey*)
  - Why did the Corps need horses? (*They needed horses to cross the mountains.*)
- **After Reading** Have students look at and discuss the concept map. Connect the Below-Level Reader to the weekly question *What opportunities can be found in new places?* In *The Long Journey West*, what opportunities did Lewis and Clark find in new places? (*exploring new territory, meeting Native Americans, and discovering new plants and animals*)

MONITOR PROGRESS

If... students have difficulty reading the selection with a partner,
then... have them follow along as they listen to the Leveled Readers DVD-ROM.

If... students have trouble understanding the goals of the Corps of Discovery,
then... review pp. 4–7 and discuss the need to learn about the Louisiana Purchase.

Objectives

- Participate in teacher-led discussions by answering questions with appropiate detail.

Student Edition, p. EI•2

More Reading

Use additional Leveled Readers or other texts at students' instructional levels to reinforce this week's skills and strategies. For text suggestions, see the Leveled Reader Database or the Leveled Readers Skills Chart on pp. CL 24–CL 29.

Reinforce Comprehension

Skill Author's Purpose Review with students *Envision It!* p. EI•2 on Author's Purpose. Then use p. 48 to review the definition of author's purpose. Authors usually have more than one purpose for writing. For example, they may express an idea in an entertaining way or inform readers about an issue as part of persuading them.

Strategy Questioning Review the information about questioning on p. 48. For additional support, refer students to *Envision It!* p. EI•21.

Revisit *Lewis and Clark and Me* on pp. 52–61. As students read, have them apply the comprehension skill and strategy to the story.

- From whose point of view does the author tell the story? (*the dog Seaman*)
- Why do you think the author wrote the story? (*to entertain the reader and inform the reader about Lewis and Clark's journey*)
- At the bottom of p. 56, the author shows a piece from Captain Lewis's journals. Why do you think the author includes this? (*It shows that the story is based on an actual event.*)
- On p. 59, what is the author's purpose in writing, "It is impossible to describe the urge I felt. It was as strong as anything I had ever known. I had to get those squirrels"? (*It was to remind us that Seaman is a dog. Seaman goes on to say that humans think too much and miss the fun of life.*)

Use the During Reading Differentiated Instruction for additional support for struggling readers.

MONITOR PROGRESS

If... students have difficulty reading along with the group,
then... have them follow along as they listen to the AudioText.

Objectives
- Identify an author's purpose(s) for writing.
- Ask literal questions of text.

DAY 3

Reinforce Vocabulary

Word Endings/Word Structure Refer to p. 57, paragraph 2. Model using word endings to understand meaning. Write *boarded* on the board. When I come to the verb *boarded,* I see it has an *-ed* ending, so this action happened in the past. To understand this word, I'll cover the ending. I know the base word *board* has something to do with climbing aboard something. *Boarded* probably means "climbed onto." I'll try this meaning in the sentence, ". . . the day we climbed onto the boat . . .." That makes sense.

Revisit *Lewis and Clark and Me* on pp. 62–67. Then review *Words!* on p. W•6. Have students practice using word endings to figure out word meanings.

Point out the word *nodded* on p. 60.

- What is the base word? (*nod*) How does the word ending *-ed* change the meaning of the base word? (*It shows that it happened in the past.*)
- Look at the word *bulged* on this page. Cover up the word ending. What does the base word mean? (Bulge *means "stick out."*) When did this action happen? (*in the past*) How do you know? (-ed *word ending signals an action that already happened*)
- Why wouldn't Lewis trade Seaman to the Indian? (*Seaman was Lewis's special dog.*)

Use the During Reading Differentiated Instruction for additional support for struggling readers.

MONITOR PROGRESS

If... students need more practice with the lesson vocabulary,
then... use *Envision It! Pictured Vocabulary Cards*.

Objectives
- Recognize an ending on a base word.
- Use word structure to analyze and decode new words.

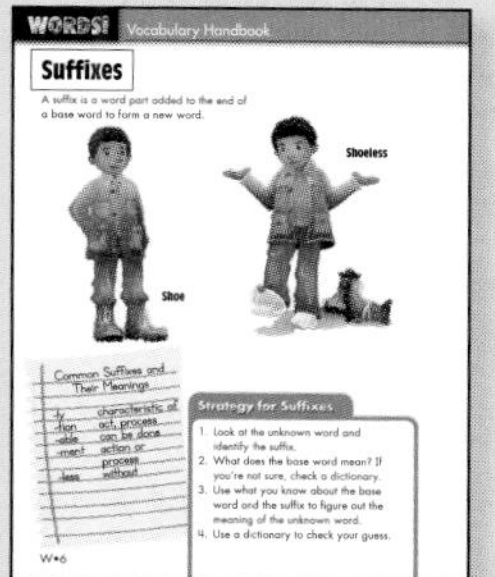

Student Edition, p. W•6

More Reading

Use additional Leveled Readers or other texts at students' instructional levels to reinforce this week's skills and strategies. For text suggestions, see the Leveled Reader Database or the Leveled Readers Skills Chart on pp. CL 24–CL 29.

Practice Retelling

- **Retell** Have students work in pairs and use the Retelling Cards to retell *Lewis and Clark and Me.* Monitor retelling and prompt students as needed.
  - Who are the main characters in the story?

  If students struggle, model a fluent retelling.

Genre Focus

- **Before Reading or Revisiting** "Ellen Ochoa: Space Pioneer" on pp. 72–75, read aloud the information about biography on p. 72. Explain that a biography is the story of a person's life as told by another person. Biographies are usually told in chronological order, describing events in the order they happened. A biography includes only the facts about a person's life that shaped his or her personality.

  Then have students preview "Ellen Ochoa: Space Pioneer." Ask: What pictures do you see? (*Ellen Ochoa at different ages and pictures of space equipment*) Ask students to set a purpose for reading based on their preview.

- **During Reading or Revisiting** Have students read along with you while tracking the print. Stop to discuss any unfamiliar words, such as *heritage* and *expertise.*

- **After Reading or Revisiting** Have students share their reactions to the biography. Then guide them through the Reading Across the Texts and Writing Across Texts activities.
  - What are some words that show the order of the events in Ellen Ochoa's life? (*after college, until, suddenly, first, in 1990, in 1991, in 1993, the next year*)
  - What characteristics do Lewis, Clark, and Ellen Ochoa all share? (*adventurous, determined, courageous*)

MONITOR PROGRESS

If... students have difficulty retelling the main selection,
then... have them review the story using the illustrations.

Objectives

- Describe explicit relationships among ideas in texts organized by sequence.

DAY 5

For a complete literacy instructional plan and additional practice with this week's target skills and strategies, see the **Leveled Reader Teaching Guide.**

Concept Literacy Reader

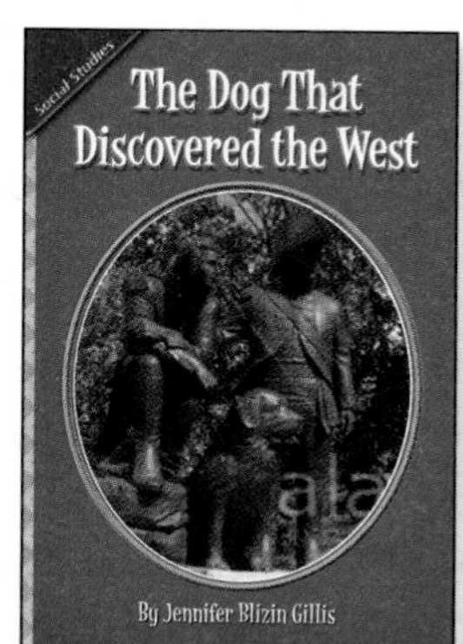
The Dog That Discovered the West

- **Model** Model the fluency skill of appropriate phrasing for students. Ask students to listen carefully as you read aloud the first two pages of *The Dog That Discovered the West.* Have students note the grouping of your words and the rise and fall of your voice.
- **Fluency Routine**

1. Have students reread passages from *The Dog That Discovered the West* with a partner.
2. For optimal fluency, students should reread three to four times.
3. As students read, monitor fluency and provide corrective feedback. Remind students to pause at commas, dashes, and the ends of sentences.

See *Routines Flip Chart* for more help with fluency.

- **Retell** Have students retell *The Dog That Discovered the West.* Prompt as necessary.

Below-Level Reader

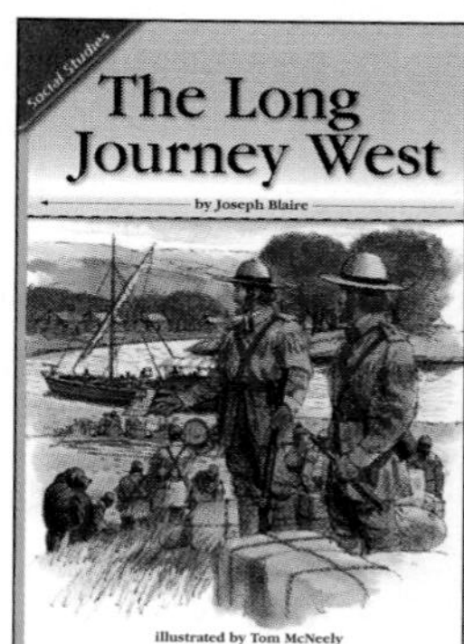
The Long Journey West

- **Model** Ask students to listen carefully as you read aloud the first two pages of *The Long Journey West,* emphasizing appropriate phrasing.
- **Fluency Routine**

1. Have students reread passages from *The Long Journey West* with a partner or individually.
2. For optimal fluency, students should reread three to four times.
3. As students read, monitor fluency and provide corrective feedback. Point out that commas require a shorter pause than periods. Discuss how punctuation gives pacing clues to the reader.

See *Routines Flip Chart* for more help with fluency.

- **Retell** For additional practice, have students retell *The Long Journey West* page by page, using the illustrations. Prompt as necessary.
  - What happens in this part?
  - What is the problem in the story?

MONITOR PROGRESS

If... students have difficulty reading fluently,
then... provide additional fluency practice by pairing nonfluent readers with fluent ones.

Objectives
- Read aloud grade-level stories with fluency.

Small Group Time

Pacing Small Group Instruction

15–20 min

5-Day Plan

DAY 1	• Expand the concept • Read On-Level Reader
DAY 2	• Author's Purpose • Questioning • Revisit Student Edition pp. 52–61
DAY 3	• Word Endings • Revisit Student Edition pp. 62–67
DAY 4	• Practice Retelling • Read/Revisit Student Edition pp. 72–75
DAY 5	• Reread for fluency • Reread On-Level Reader

3- or 4-Day Plan

DAY 1	• Expand the concept • Read On-Level Reader
DAY 2	• Author's Purpose • Questioning • Revisit Student Edition pp. 52–61
DAY 3	• Word Endings • Revisit Student Edition pp. 62–67
DAY 4	• Practice Retelling • Read/Revisit Student Edition pp. 72–75 • Reread for fluency • Reread On-Level Reader

3-Day Plan: Eliminate the shaded box.

OL On-Level

DAY

Build Background

■ **Expand the Concept** Connect the weekly question *What opportunities can be found in new places?* and expand the concept. When we go to new places, we have opportunities for new experiences. New places invite us to explore and learn new things. What new experiences can you have when you visit a new country? Discuss the meanings of the words on the concept map.

On-Level Reader

For a complete literacy instructional plan and additional practice with this week's target skills and strategies, see the **Leveled Reader Teaching Guide.**

■ **Before Reading** *Lewis, Clark, and the Corps of Discovery*, have students preview the reader by looking at the title, cover, and pictures in the book. Ask:

- What is the topic of this book?
- Do you think it was easy or difficult for Lewis and Clark to explore the Louisiana Territory? Why?

Have students create K-W-L charts based on the Lewis and Clark expedition.

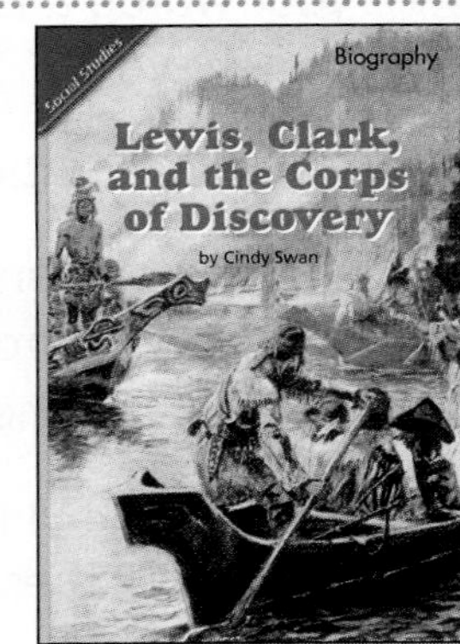

Lewis, Clark, and the Corps of Discovery

In the first column, What I Know, write what you already know about the Lewis and Clark expedition. In the second column, What I Want to Know, write what you hope to learn from this book. Leave the third column, What I Learned, blank for now.

■ **During Reading** Read aloud the first three pages of the book as students follow along. Then have them finish reading the book on their own. Remind students to look for answers to their questions as they read.

■ **After Reading** Have students complete their K-W-L charts.

- Did the story contain information you wanted to know? In the third column of your chart, write what you learned.
- How does the topic relate to the weekly question *What opportunities can be found in new places?*

Objectives

- Participate in teacher-led discussions by answering questions with appropriate detail.

DAY 2

Expand Comprehension

Skill Author's Purpose Use p. 48 to review the definition of author's purpose. For additional review, see Author's Purpose in *Envision It!* p. EI•2. An author usually has more than one purpose for writing. For example, an entertaining story can also express ideas and feelings. A persuasive article may also inform the reader.

Strategy Questioning Review the strategy of questioning. Encourage students to look in the text and think about what they already know to find answers to their questions. During reading, use Extend Thinking and the *Envision It!* p. EI•21 for additional support.

Revisit *Lewis and Clark and Me* on pp. 52–61. Have students discuss and ask questions about the author's purpose.

- Why do you think the author tells this story from Seaman's point of view? (*to make the story entertaining*)
- On p. 56, what could the author's purpose be for using dialogue as well as Lewis's journal entry? (*The dialogue tells readers how the American Indians created new words. The journal entry shows that this event really happened and shares Lewis's thoughts.*)

Student Edition, p. EI•2

More Reading

Use additional Leveled Readers or other texts at students' instructional levels to reinforce this week's skills and strategies. For text suggestions, see the Leveled Reader Database or the Leveled Readers Skills Chart on pp. CL 24–CL 29.

Objectives

- Identify an author's purpose(s) for writing.
- Ask literal questions of text.

Expand Vocabulary

Word Endings/Word Structure Write the word *blinked* as you say it aloud. Ask students to identify the word ending (*-ed*). What word is the base word? (*blink*) What does the word ending *-ed* do to the meaning of the base word? (*changes it to past tense*)

- **Revisit** *Lewis and Clark and Me* on pp. 62–67. Have students pause on p. 64, locate all the words with the ending *–ed,* and tell you what they are. Write the words on the board: *impressed, called, turned, smiled, explained, walked, pulled, surprised, looked,* and *experienced.* Then review each word in its context. Point out that not every word with the *-ed* ending is used as the past tense of a verb. For example, in "The Indians were impressed," the word *impressed* is an adjective. In "It wasn't often that I saw Lewis surprised," *surprised* is an adjective as well. Ask students to finish reading *Lewis and Clark and Me,* using word endings to help them understand unfamiliar words as they read.

- Regarding the squirrel incident, the author writes that ". . . the look of pride on Lewis's face was better than all the men's praise added together." Why does the author tell you this? (*She wants readers to connect to Seaman's feelings.*)

- Why does the author tell the story about "bear-dog"? (*to show how special Seaman is to Lewis*)

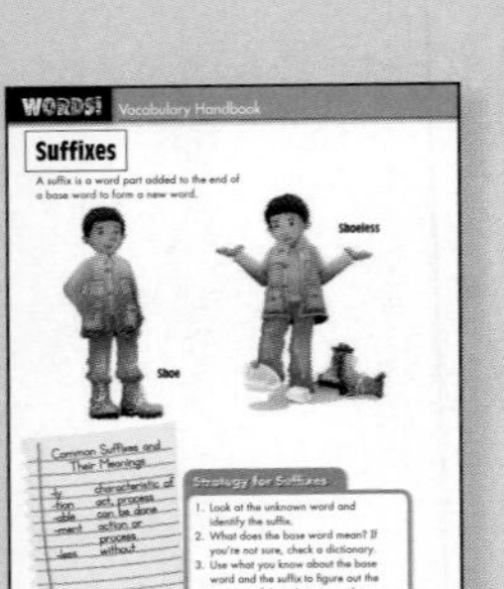
Student Edition, p. W•6

More Reading

Use additional Leveled Readers or other texts at students' instructional levels to reinforce this week's skills and strategies. For text suggestions, see the Leveled Reader Database or the Leveled Readers Skills Chart on pp. CL 24–CL 29.

Objectives

- Recognize an ending on a base word.
- Use word structure to analyze and decode new words.

On-Level

DAY 4

Practice Retelling

- **Retell** To assess students' comprehension, use the Retelling Cards. Monitor retelling and prompt students as needed.

Genre Focus

- **Before Reading or Revisiting** "Ellen Ochoa: Space Pioneer" on pp. 72–75, read aloud the genre information on p. 72. Have students preview "Ellen Ochoa: Space Pioneer" and set a purpose for reading.
  - What features do you see that suggest this is a biography? (*pictures of Ellen Ochoa*)
  - Why do you think the story includes so many photographs?
- **During Reading or Revisiting** Have students read along with you while tracking the print.
  - What cause-and-effect relationships appear in this biography? (*Ellen decides to go to graduate school because her mother "said that education is the key to a successful career."*)
  - How does this biography compare to *Lewis and Clark and Me*? (*Both are about adventurers and explorers; one is historical fiction and the other is a biography.*)
- **After Reading or Revisiting** Have students share their reactions to the biography. Then have them write a paragraph that might appear in a biography of one of their friends.

Objectives

- Describe explicit relationships among ideas in texts organized by sequence.

On-Level Reader

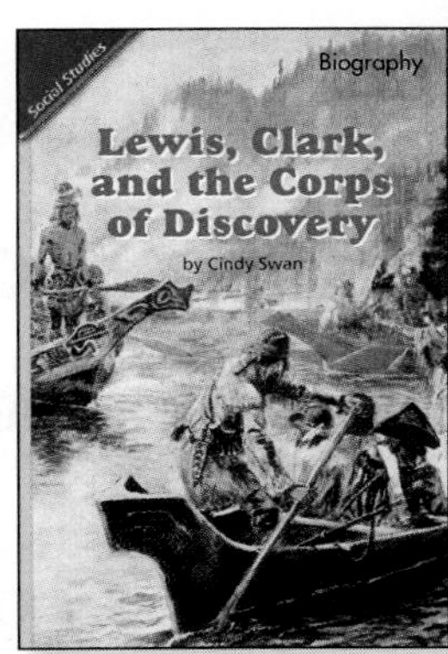

Lewis, Clark, and the Corps of Discovery

- **Model** Read aloud the first three pages of *Lewis, Clark, and the Corps of Discovery,* emphasizing appropriate phrasing. Encourage students to note how you use punctuation and paragraph breaks to guide your phrasing.
- **Fluency Routine**

1. Have students reread passages from *Lewis, Clark, and the Corps of Discovery* with a partner.
2. For optimal fluency, students should reread passages three to four times.
3. As students read, monitor fluency and provide corrective feedback. Have students note the grouping of their words into phrases and the rise and fall of their voices. Discuss how reading with a natural rhythm is much more pleasing than reading word by word.

See *Routines Flip Chart* for more help with fluency.

- **Retell** For additional practice, have students use headings and visual features to retell *Lewis, Clark, and the Corps of Discovery.* Prompt as necessary.
  - What is this section mostly about?
  - What did you learn from reading this section?
  - What part did this expedition play in United States history?

Objectives

- Read aloud grade-level stories with fluency.

DAY 1

Build Background

- **Extend the Concept** Discuss the weekly question *What opportunities can be found in new places?* In history, how have people developed newly discovered places to meet their needs? For example, why have people built dams on some rivers? (*to control the flow of water for crop irrigation and other purposes*)

Advanced Reader

For a complete literacy instructional plan and additional practice with this week's target skills and strategies, see the **Leveled Reader Teaching Guide.**

- **Before Reading** *Two Powerful Rivers*, have students preview the reader by skimming the book, reading the headings and looking at the illustrations. Have them use these elements to predict what will happen in the text. Then have students set a purpose for reading.

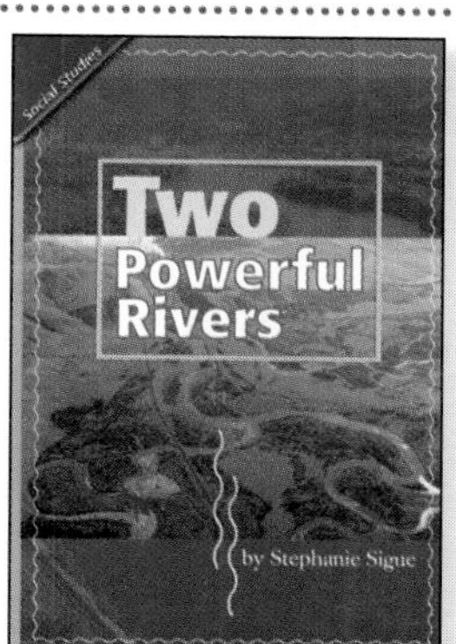

Two Powerful Rivers

- **During Reading** As students read the book independently, encourage them to think critically. For example, ask:
  - What arguments could someone have made in favor of building levees along the Mississippi?
  - Why do you think some people might oppose using areas near rivers for agriculture and industry?
  - What arguments might someone offer in favor of removing dams from the Missouri River?
- **After Reading** Have students review the concept map and explain how *Two Powerful Rivers* helps answer the weekly question *What opportunities can be found in new places?* Prompt as necessary.
  - What opportunities might early settlers have seen for land development near rivers?
  - What changes came after people started using the Missouri and the Mississippi?
- **Now Try This** Assign "Now Try This" at the end of the Advanced Reader.

Objectives

- Participate in teacher-led discussions by answering questions with appropriate detail.

Pacing Small Group Instruction

15–20 min

5-Day Plan

DAY 1	• Extend the concept • Read Advanced Reader
DAY 2	• Author's Purpose • Questioning • Revisit Student Edition pp. 52–61
DAY 3	• Word Endings • Revisit Student Edition pp. 62–67
DAY 4	• Genre Focus • Read/Revisit Student Edition pp. 72–75
DAY 5	• Reread for fluency • Reread Advanced Reader

3- or 4-Day Plan

DAY 1	• Extend the concept • Read Advanced Reader
DAY 2	• Author's Purpose • Questioning • Revisit Student Edition pp. 52–61
DAY 3	• Word Endings • Revisit Student Edition pp. 62–67
DAY 4	• Genre Focus • Read/Revisit Student Edition pp. 72–75 • Reread for fluency • Reread Advanced Reader

3-Day Plan: Eliminate the shaded box.

More Reading

Use additional Leveled Readers or other texts at students' instructional levels to reinforce this week's skills and strategies. For text suggestions, see the Leveled Reader Database or the Leveled Readers Skills Chart on pp. CL 24–CL 29.

A Advanced

DAY 2

Extend Comprehension

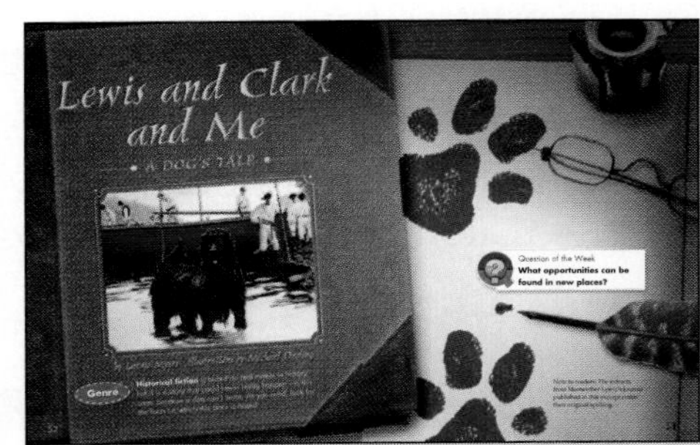

Skill Author's Purpose Review the definition of author's purpose. Invite students to think about how reading affects them. Explain that their reactions to a piece of writing offer clues to what the author intended. Think of *Two Powerful Rivers,* which you just read. What did it teach you? Did it persuade you that any action needs to be taken? Do you think the author had more than one purpose?

Strategy Questioning Review the definition of the strategy. Remind students to ask and answer questions as they continue reading *Lewis and Clark and Me.* During reading, use the Extend Thinking questions and the During Reading Differentiated Instruction for additional support.

- **Revisit** *Lewis and Clark and Me* on pp. 52–61. Have students analyze the author's purpose as they read. Encourage them to speculate on the author's motivations. Why did the author include excerpts from Lewis's journal? (*The contrast between Seaman's and Lewis's viewpoints makes the story interesting to read.*)

- **Critical Thinking**
  - Why do you suppose the author uses a dog, rather than a human crew member, as the narrator of this story?
  - In your opinion, does this narrator's point of view limit the story or make it more interesting? Explain.

Objectives

- Identify an author's purpose(s) for writing.
- Ask literal questions of text.

DAY 3

Extend Vocabulary

Word Endings/Word Structure Read a sentence containing a word with an *-ed* or *-ing* ending, such as this one: "Then I noticed an Indian dog standing to the side."

- How does knowing the meaning of the ending *-ed* help you understand the meaning of a whole word? (*It tells me the action occurred in the past.*)
- How does it help to know the meaning of the ending *-ing*? (*It tells me the action that is happening.*)

Remind students to use word endings to understand actions as they read *Lewis and Clark and Me.*

- **Revisit** *Lewis and Clark and Me* on pp. 62–67. Have students recall what has happened in the selection so far and then finish reading.
- **Critical Thinking** Encourage students to think critically. How would the story change if Meriwether Lewis were the narrator?
- **Creative Thinking** Prompt students to think creatively. We learn that these American Indians have no word in their language for *horse,* so they call a horse an *elk-dog.* Why would that be an appropriate term for them to use? As you read, think about things the Europeans might bring with them on their expedition that the American Indians would probably be unfamiliar with, and think of other new and imaginative terms the American Indians might use to describe them.

Objectives

- Recognize an ending on a base word.
- Use word structure to analyze and decode new words.

More Reading

Use additional Leveled Readers or other texts at students' instructional levels to reinforce this week's skills and strategies. For text suggestions, see the Leveled Reader Database or the Leveled Readers Skills Chart on pp. CL 24–CL 29.

Genre Focus

"Ellen Ochoa: Space Pioneer"

- **Before Reading or Revisiting** "Ellen Ochoa: Space Pioneer" on pp. 72–75, read the panel on biography. Then have students use text features to set a purpose for reading.
- **During Reading or Revisiting** Have students write down important dates that they would add to a time line. Ellen Ochoa's accomplishments are impressive. What are some of them? (*She learned to play the flute, earned a degree in physics, developed expertise in engineering, became an astronaut, and invented systems that can see "objects" in space.*)
- **After Reading or Revisiting** Have students discuss Reading Across Texts. Then have them do Writing Across Texts independently.

Objectives

- Describe explicit relationships among ideas in texts organized by sequence.

DAY 5

Two Powerful Rivers

- **Reread for Fluency** Have students silently reread passages from *Two Powerful Rivers.* Then have them reread aloud with a partner or individually. As students read, monitor fluency and provide corrective feedback. If students read fluently on the first reading, they do not need to reread three to four times. Assess the fluency of students in this group using p.77j.
- **Retell** Have students summarize the main idea and key details from the Advanced Reader *Two Powerful Rivers.*
- **Now Try This** Have students complete their projects. You may wish to review their projects to see if they need additional ideas. Have them share their projects with classmates.

Objectives

- Read aloud grade-level stories with fluency.

The ELL lessons are organized by strands. Use them to scaffold the weekly curriculum of lessons or during small group time instruction.

Academic Language

Students will read the following academic language in this week's core instruction. As students encounter the vocabulary, provide a simple definition or concrete example. Have students speak giving an example or synonym of the word and identify available cognates. This allows students to internalize new English words.

Skill Words	biography *(biografía)* contact *(contacto)* historical *(historico)* imperative	exclamatory *(eclamativo)* organization purpose
Concept Words	communicate journey	opportunity *(oportunidad)*

* *Spanish cognates in parentheses*

Concept Development

What opportunities can be found in new places?

- **Preteach Concept**
  - **Prior Knowledge** Have students turn to pp. 46–47 in the Student Edition. Call attention to the picture of the ships and tap into students' prior knowledge of the Mayflower. What do you notice about these ships? Do they look like ships of today or long ago? How can you tell?
  - **Discuss Concept** Elicit students' prior knowledge and experience of opportunities that can be found in new places. What do you think made people take those ships to America all those years ago? What were they hoping to find in a new place? Why do people move to new places today? Supply background information as needed.
  - **Poster Talk-Through** Read aloud the Poster Talk-Through on ELL Poster 2 and work through the Day 1 activities.
- **Daily Concept and Vocabulary Development** Use the daily activities on ELL Poster 2 to build concept and vocabulary knowledge.

Objectives
- Use prior knowledge and experiences to understand meanings in English.
- Listen to and derive meaning from a variety of media such as audio tape, video, DVD, and CD ROM to build and reinforce concept and language attainment.

Content Objectives
- Use concept vocabulary related to finding opportunities in new places.

Language Objectives
- Use prior knowledge to understand meanings.

Daily Planner

DAY 1	• **Frontload Concept** • **Preteach** Comprehension Skill, Vocabulary, Phonics/Spelling, Conventions • **Writing**
DAY 2	• **Review** Concept, Vocabulary, Comprehension Skill • **Frontload Main Selection** • **Practice** Phonics/Spelling, Conventions/Writing
DAY 3	• **Review** Concept, Comprehension Skill, Vocabulary, Conventions/Writing • **Reread Main Selection** • **Practice** Phonics/Spelling
DAY 4	• **Review Concept** • **Read ELL/ELD Readers** • **Practice** Phonics/Spelling, Conventions/Writing
DAY 5	• **Review** Concept, Vocabulary, Comprehension Skill, Phonics/Spelling, Conventions • **Read ELL/ELD Readers** • **Writing**

**See the ELL Handbook for ELL Workshops with targeted instruction.*

Concept Talk Video

Use the Concept Talk Video Routine (*ELL Handbook*, p. 477) to build background knowledge about bringing diverse people together.

Support for English Language Learners

Language Objectives

- Understand and use basic vocabulary.
- Learn meanings of grade-level vocabulary.

Cognates

For Spanish learners, point out that the word for *opportunity* is spelled *oportunidad* in Spanish. Reinforce the concept that these languages share many words that are the same or similar.

ELL Workshop

Allow students further practice with expanding and internalizing high-frequency English vocabulary and developing basic sight vocabulary with *Learn New Words* (*ELL Handbook*, pp. 402–403).

ELL English Language Learners

Basic Vocabulary

- **High-Frequency Words** Use the ELL Vocabulary Words Routine on p. 471 of the *ELL Handbook* to systematically teach newcomers the first 300 sight words in English. Students who began learning ten words per week at the beginning of the year are now learning words 11–20 (*ELL Handbook*, pp. 447). Page 446 of the handbook contains a bank of strategies that you can use to ensure students' mastery of High-Frequency Words and learn basic vocabulary.

Lesson Vocabulary

- **Preteach** Introduce the Lesson Vocabulary using this routine:

1. Distribute copies of this week's Word Cards (*ELL Handbook*, p. 35).
2. Display ELL Poster 2 and reread the Poster Talk-Through.
3. Using the poster illustrations, model how a word's meaning can be expressed with other similar words: The *docks*, or places where boats park, were very crowded today.
4. Use these sentences to reveal the meanings of the other words.
   - Many people *yearned* for a better life when they went west from Missouri. (wanted or hoped)
   - Everyone watched as the ship pulled up to the *wharf*. (landing place for boats)
   - I watched him *scan* the wharf looking for his friend. (look around)
   - It was fall and the geese were *migrating*. (moving from one place to another when the season changes)
   - The dog enjoyed the *scent* of the animals. (smell)
5. Have students draw a picture illustrating two of the lesson words listed above to ensure that they have acquired the meaning of the vocabulary

Objectives

- Expand and internalize initial English vocabulary by learning and using high-frequency English words necessary for identifying and describing people, places, and objects, by retelling simple stories and basic information represented or supported by pictures, and by learning and using routine language needed for classroom communication.
- Use accessible language and learn new and essential language in the process.

ELL English Language Learners

■ **Reteach** Use a matching game to check and reinforce students' understanding of the vocabulary.

- Distribute a copy of the Word Cards and 6 blank cards to each pair of students. Have partners write a clue or simple picture on a blank card for each word. Have students mix the Word Cards and clue cards together and lay them face up, spread out on a table. Students can take turns matching the Word Card with its clue. Have students explain their choices.

■ **Writing** Place students into mixed proficiency groups. Provide them with a Web graphic organizer. Give each group a different vocabulary word for a jigsaw activity. Have students write their word in the center. Then have them write words they associate with the vocabulary word in all the outer circles. Remind them to keep the weekly concept in mind when thinking of synonyms. Have groups share their Webs. Encourage students to suggest other words that could be added to the outer circle.

Beginning Have students draw pictures in the outer circles. Then help them label their pictures with the appropriate Lesson Vocabulary word.

Intermediate Have students write words in the outer circles.

Advanced/Advanced High Have students write descriptive phrases instead of individual words in the outer circles. Then have them write a sentence using the vocabulary word and one of their phrases to show the meaning of the word.

MINI-LESSON

Subject-Verb Agreement

In each sentence the subject and verb must agree. If a noun has an *s,* it often is a plural. In most cases, to agree with the verb, the verb must not have an *s.* Sometimes we must edit our writing to make the subject and verb agree. Write these sentences on the board: *The boys runs. The girls jumps.* Have students identify the subject and the verb in each sentence. Then have students edit the sentences to have correct subject-verb agreement. Have them write the newly edited sentences.

Objectives

- Edit writing for standard grammar and usage, including subject-verb agreement, pronoun agreement, and appropriate verb tenses commensurate with grade-level expectations as more English is acquired.

Language Objectives

- Produce drawings, phrases, or short sentences to show an understanding of Lesson Vocabulary.

ELL Teacher Tip

Creating daily opportunities for students to listen to and use the language they are learning in the classroom helps their learning. One way to do this is through role-playing. Have pairs of students take on the roles of characters in a story they are reading, or have them act out a vocabulary word. Role-playing motivates students to use oral language creatively. You can also have students draw pictures and then describe them.

Graphic Organizer

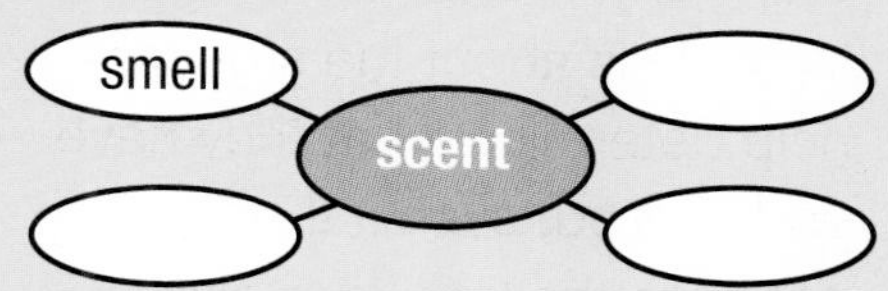

ELL Workshop

As students speak using new vocabulary, they may need assistance knowing how to adapt spoken English for informal purposes. *Use Informal English* (*ELL Handbook*, pp. 390–391) provides extra support.

Support for English Language Learners

Content Objectives

- Monitor and adjust oral comprehension.

Language Objectives

- Discuss oral passages to confirm understanding.
- Use a graphic organizer to take notes and summarize spoken messages.

Graphic Organizer

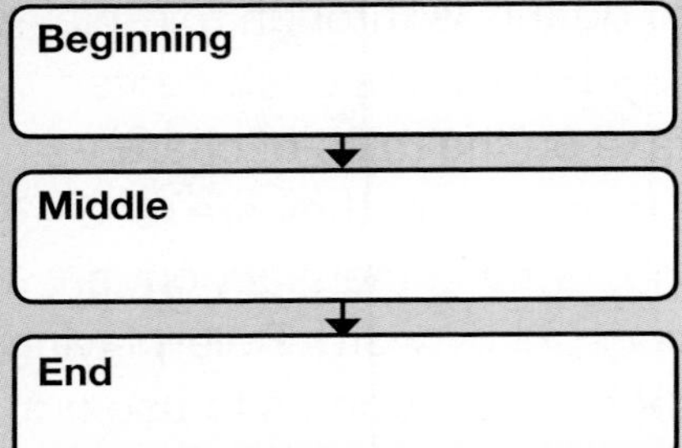

ELL Teacher Tip

Have students supplement their verbal responses by drawing details about the story to help determine what they have understood, even if they do not have the language skills to share answers to the questions verbally.

ELL Workshop

Encourage students to demonstrate listening comprehension of the Read Aloud and other spoken messages. Provide *Retell or Summarize* (*ELL Handbook*, pp. 408–409) for practice.

ELL English Language Learners

Listening Comprehension

Read Aloud

Planting Apple Trees

John Chapman was a boy during the American Revolution. He lived in Massachusetts. When he was a young man, he left home. He traveled west by himself. He planted apple trees everywhere. He became known as Johnny Appleseed.

Johnny Appleseed collected apple seeds. He traveled through Ohio and Indiana. He looked for good land that could support trees. He claimed the land. He took care of the soil and planted apple seeds. Soon Johnny owned over 1,000 acres of orchards. Johnny worked hard caring for his orchards. He traveled hundreds of miles to take care for them.

Johnny made friends with people everywhere. He became friends with Native Americans and with settlers. He sold apple seeds and small apple trees to the people he met. Sometimes he even gave them away.

Prepare for the Read Aloud The modified Read Aloud above prepares students for listening to the oral reading "Johnny Appleseed" on p. 47b.

- **First Listening: Listen to Understand** Write the title of the Read Aloud on the board. This is about a man named John Chapman who became known as Johnny Appleseed. Listen to find out why John Chapman was given a nickname. Where did he travel? What did he do? Afterward, ask the questions again and have students share their answers.
- **Second Listening: Listen to Check Understanding** Using Story Map A *(ELL Handbook,* p. 483), help students fill in what happened by using linguistic support using the phrases *beginning of the story, middle of the story,* and *end of the story* to enhance understanding. This summary will demonstrate listening comprehension. Now listen again to see if you listed events in the right order. Have students read aloud their Story Maps to confirm understanding of "Johnny Appleseed."

Objectives

- Use visual, contextual, and linguistic support to enhance and confirm understanding of increasingly complex and elaborated spoken language.
- Demonstrate listening comprehension of increasingly complex spoken English by following directions, retelling or summarizing spoken messages, responding to questions and requests, collaborating with peers, and taking notes commensurate with content and grade-level needs.

Phonics and Spelling

- **Long *a* and long *i*** Use Sound-Spelling Cards 74 and 80 to teach the sounds, pronunciations, and spelling relationships of long *a* and long *i*.
  - Display card 74 to teach long a. This is a *rake*. The sound of the letter *a* is /ā/. Say it with me: /ā/. We call this sound the long *a*. Repeat these /ā/ words after me: *grape*, *rain*, and *tray*.
  - Point out that there are different ways of spelling long *a* words. Write a 3-column chart on the board with the headings *a, e, ai,* and *ay.* List the words *rake, grapes, rain,* and *tray* in the columns where they belong. Here are some other long a words. Repeat them after me: *train, whale, clay.* Have students add these to the chart and write other long a words they know.
  - Have students write their own 3-colunm chart and repeat this process with Sound-Spelling Card 80 to teach the long i sound by using the following words: *bike, night, sky, mice,* and *high.*

Word Analysis: Suffixes *-or, -er*

- **Teach and Model** Use Sound-Spelling Cards 176 and 165 to teach the suffixes *-or* and *-er*. Display card 176 to teach *-or*. This is a *sailor*. The word *sailor* is made up of a base word and a suffix. A suffix is a word part that is added to the end of the word to change its meaning. Write *sailor* on the board with a line between *sail* and *or*. Point to *sail*. This is the base word. Point to the suffix *-or*. This is the suffix. Repeat using card 165 to teach *-er*. The suffixes *-or* and *-er* give a word the meaning "a person or thing that does something." A *sailor* is someone who sails. A *painter* is someone who paints.
- **Practice** Write the words *buyer, rower, editor,* and *actor* on the board with a line between the base word and the suffix. Have students read each word and say its meaning. Then have them write the base word and the suffix.

Leveled Support

Beginning/Intermediate Provide pairs of cards with the base word on one card and the suffix on another. Have Beginning students put the cards together and say the word. Have Intermediate students define the words.

Advanced/Advanced High Challenge students to work in pairs to write sentences using both the base word and the word with the suffix.

Objectives

- Learn relationships between sounds and letters of the English language to represent sounds when writing in English.
- Learn relationships between sounds and letters of the English language and decode (sound out) words using a combination of skills such as recognizing sound-letter relationships and identifying cognates, affixes, roots, and base words.

Content Objectives

- Identify and define words with the suffixes *-or* and *-er*.
- Identify various spelling relationships with the long a and long *i* sounds.

Language Objectives

- Apply phonics and decoding skills to vocabulary.
- Learn meanings of words with the *-or* and *-er* suffixes.

Transfer Skills

Long Vowel Sounds Some long vowel sounds in English are similar to the sounds made by different vowels or vowel combinations in Spanish. Spanish speakers may spell words with long *a* with *e* or words with long *i* with *ai*. For more practice pronouncing these sounds, use the Modeled Pronunciation Audio CD Routine *(ELL Handbook,* p.477).

ELL Teaching Routine

To provide students additional instruction and practice in suffixes *-or* and *-er,* use the lesson in the *ELL Handbook* p. 296.

Content Objectives

- Identify the author's purpose to aid understanding.
- Determine how to identify the author's purpose.

Language Objectives

- Identify the author's purpose to aid understanding.
- Determine how to identify the author's purpose.

ELL Workshop

Encourage students to ask questions to monitor their understanding of instruction of comprehension skills. Use *Ask Clarifying Questions* (*ELL Handbook*, pp. 404–405) for practice.

ELL Workshop

Discuss that authors often express feelings in writing. Give students the opportunity to express feelings about the selection. *Express Feelings* (*ELL Handbook*, pp. 416–417) provides extra support.

ELL English Language Learners

Comprehension
Author's Purpose

- **Preteach** An author's purpose is the reason an author writes something. Have students turn to p. 48 in the Student Edition. Read aloud first point on the page for students to learn and become familiar with the academic language. An author may write to persuade, to inform, to entertain, or to express ideas and feelings.
- **Reteach** Distribute copies of the Picture It! (*ELL Handbook,* p. 36). Have students read the paragraph and look at the picture. Guide students to use inductive and deductive learning strategies by reading the questions aloud and then by having students complete the practice exercises at their language proficiency level. (1. b 2. c)

Beginning/ Intermediate Reread the paragraph as students read along. Help them identify facts. Then have them write down place names.

Advanced/Advanced High Have students reread the paragraph aloud, looking at the picture as they do so. Have them underline facts. Then have them write down and read aloud the facts that are place names.

MINI-LESSON

Social Language

Tell students that there is a common way to talk about or explain an author's purpose. We usually say that an author's purpose is either to inform, to entertain, to persuade, or to express. Have students look at the four pictures on Envision It! p. EI•2 in the Student Edition to understand spoken language. Define the terms if necessary. For each picture, have students describe what the readers are doing using increasingly specific details and by using deductive learning. Use the reader's response to the book to predict the author's purpose. Model an example using simple words to clarify meaning and details and to explain the author's purpose. The boys are laughing and smiling. They are having fun reading the book. This book must be funny, so I think the author's purpose is to entertain. Check to see that students understand the terms. Have students ask for assistance if they do not understand.

Objectives

- Monitor understanding of spoken language during classroom instruction and interactions and seek clarification as needed.
- Narrate, describe, and explain ideas with increasing specificity and detail as more English is acquired.

ELL English Language Learners

Reading Comprehension
Lewis and Clark and Me

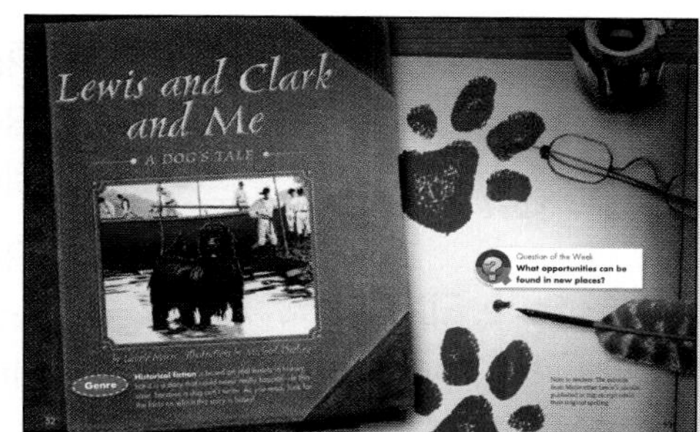

Student Edition pp. 52–53

■ **Frontloading** Have students look through the *Lewis and Clark and Me,* a historical fiction, pp. 52–67 in the Student Edition. Explain the selection is a story set in the past that portrays people and events that could have happened. Distribute copies of the English summary of *Lewis and Clark and Me (ELL Handbook,* p. 37). Read aloud the summary, making sure that students understand the general meaning. Encourage them to ask questions about any unfamiliar language. Preview the selection by having students look at the pictures for contextual support. Use the Graphic Organizer (side column) to ensure comprehension.

Sheltered Reading Ask the following questions to guide understanding.

- p. 55: Where is Lewis headed? (out west, up the Missouri River)
- p. 56: How much does Lewis pay for the dog? (twenty dollars)
- p. 59: Where were the squirrels that Seaman hunted? (They were swimming across the river.)
- p. 64: Why did the Indian hold out three beaver skins to Lewis? (He wanted to buy Seaman.)
- p. 64: Why was it unthinkable that Lewis and Seaman would ever separate? (Because the man and the dog have a special relationship.)

■ **Fluency: Appropriate Phrasing/Punctuation Cues** Remind students that punctuation marks give clues about how to read. Punctuation marks tell you when to pause for a short time or a long time. They tell you when to raise or lower your voice. Read the last three paragraphs on p. 64, modeling reading with appropriate phrasing. Have pairs take turns reading p. 60. Have them read with appropriate phrasing using punctuation cues. Then have students reread using shared reading. For more practice, use the Fluency: Choral Reading Routine (*ELL Handbook,* p. 474).

■ **After Reading** Help students summarize the text with the Retelling Cards. Give each student a card. Have students retell in the correct sequence.

Objectives

- Understand the general meaning, main points, and important details of spoken language ranging from situations in which topics, language, and contexts are familiar to unfamiliar.

Content Objectives

- Monitor and adjust comprehension.
- Make and adjust predictions.

Language Objectives

- Read with appropriate phrasing with punctuation cues.
- Summarize text using visual and contextual support for general understanding.

Graphic Organizer

Beginning
↓
Middle
↓
End

Audio Support

Students can prepare for reading *Lewis and Clark and Me* by using the eSelection or the AudioText CD. See the AudioText CD Routine (*ELL Handbook*, p. 477).

ELL Teaching Routine

For more practice summarizing, use the Retelling/Summarizing Nonfiction Routine (*ELL Handbook*, p. 476).

For additional leveled instruction, see the **ELL/ELD Reader Teaching Guide.**

Comprehension
Talking to Lewis and Clark

- **Before Reading** Distribute copies of the ELL and ELD Readers, *Talking to Lewis and Clark*, to students at their reading level.
  - **Preview** Read the title aloud with students: This is a nonfiction text about Lewis and Clark and how they talked to the Native Americans. Have students to look through the pictures and name what they see. Have them identify where Louis and Clark traveled and how they talked to the Native Americans based on the picture clues and their prior knowledge.
  - **Set a Purpose for Reading** Let's read to learn more about Lewis and Clark.
- **During Reading** Follow this Reading Routine for both reading groups.

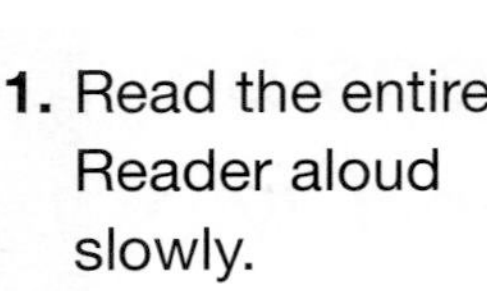

ELD Reader ELL Reader

1. Read the entire Reader aloud slowly.
2. Reread pp. 1–4, pausing to build background or model comprehension. Have Beginning students finger-point as you read. Use the questions in the chart below to check students' comprehension.
3. Have students reread pp. 1–4, taking turns reading alternate pages.
4. Repeat steps 2–3 above for pp. 5–8 of the Reader.

- **After Reading** Use the exercises on the inside back cover of each Reader and invite students to share their writing. In a whole-group discussion, ask students, How did Lewis and Clark talk to the Native Americans? Record their answers on the board and invite them to point to pictures in the book to support their answers.

ELD Reader Beginning/Intermediate

- **pp. 2–3** Who asked Lewis to take the trip? (President Thomas Jefferson)
- **p. 5** How did some Native Americans talk with each other? (They used sign language.)
- **p. 8** Who helped Lewis and Clark talk to some of the Native Americans? (Sacajawea)

Writing Find a sentence in the Reader that helps show the author's purpose. Copy the sentence. Then read it aloud to your partner.

ELL Reader Advanced/Advanced High

- **pp. 2–3** Why did Lewis and Clark take their trip? (President Jefferson asked them to find out what was in the new territory.)
- **p. 5** Why did the Native Americans invent Plains Sign Language? (The groups spoke different languages.)
- **p. 8** What was the language chain? (translations that made it possible for Lewis to speak to Sacajawea)

Study Guide Distribute copies of the ELL Reader Study Guide (*ELL Handbook*, p. 40). Scaffold comprehension of author's purpose by helping students look back through the Reader and fill in the graphic organizer. (**Answers** See *ELL Handbook*, pp. 209–212.)

Objectives

- Demonstrate comprehension of increasingly complex English by participating in shared reading, retelling or summarizing material, responding to questions, and taking notes commensurate with content area and grade level needs.

ELL English Language Learners

Conventions
Imperative and Exclamatory Sentences

- **Preteach** Display the following sentences on the board: *Give me your book, Maria. I loved that movie.* An imperative sentence tells someone to do something. Which of these sentences tells someone to do something? An exclamatory sentence ends in an exclamation point. Is the second sentence an exclamatory sentence? Why is it not an exclamatory sentence? What is missing?
- **Practice** Have partners say simple commands that they can give to each other. Provide the following examples: Pick up your coat. Eat your lunch. Run faster. Then, have students give directions for a simple action using imperative sentences.

Beginning Read the sentence and have students identify it as imperative or exclamatory.

Intermediate Have students read the sentences and identify them as imperative or exclamatory.

Advanced/Advanced High Have students read the sentences, identify them as imperative or exclamatory, and write a sentence of each type on their own.

- **Reteach** Display sentences on the board: *Talk to your sister. She talks so much!* Have students identify the imperative and exclamatory sentences.
- **Practice** Display the following chart, and help students revise each example to make an imperative sentence and to make an exclamatory sentence.

Imperative	Exclamatory
It is snowing	It is snowing
What a day	What a day
Juan, come here	Juan, come here

Beginning Read the heading and a sentence. Have a student come up and insert the correct punctuation. Help guide students toward changing the verb if necessary.

Intermediate Have students read the sentences aloud and insert the correct punctuation and verb.

Advanced/Advanced High Have students read the sentences aloud, insert the correct punctuation and verb, and write two more sentences of their own.

Objectives

- Speak using a variety of grammatical structures, sentence lengths, sentence types, and connecting words with increasing accuracy and ease as more English is acquired.

Content Objectives

- Decode and identify imperative and exclamatory sentences.

Language Objectives

- Read imperative and exclamatory sentences.
- Write imperative and exclamatory sentences.

Transfer Skills

Imperative and Exclamatory Sentences If students continue to use home-language patterns such as beginning a sentence with punctuation, model correct English usage and have students practice with similar examples.

Grammar Jammer

For more practice with sentences, use the Grammar Jammer for this target skill. See the Grammar Jammer Routine (*ELL Handbook*, p. 478) for suggestions on using this learning tool.

Content Objectives

- Identify the ideas organized around a main idea.

Language Objectives

- Write by organizing ideas around a main idea.
- Share feedback for editing and revising.

ELL Teaching Routine

For practice spelling words related to finding opportunities, use the Spelling Routine (*ELL Handbook*, p. 476).

ELL Workshop

Students may use classroom resources to respond to questions they have about their writing. *Use Classroom Resources* (*ELL Handbook*, pp. 406–407) provides extra support.

ELL Workshop

Provide students with the opportunity to orally express their opinions and ideas. *Express Opinions* (*ELL Handbook*, pp. 414–415) supports student practice.

ELL English Language Learners

Organize Ideas Around a Main Idea

- **Introduce** Display the title and paragraph model and read them aloud. Review how ideas are organized around an important idea or detail. What is the main idea of the passage? (Lewis had a dog.) What ideas are organized around it? (Lewis took his dog on his trip west. The dog's name was Seaman. Seaman swam well. He loved to hunt. Seaman was important to Lewis.) Underline the main idea. This is a main idea. Main ideas include information and facts that provide clues to the author's purpose. The other ideas are organized around it. They elaborate on, or add to, the main idea.

Writing Model

Lewis took his dog on his trip west. The dog's name was Seaman. Seaman swam well. He loved to hunt. Seaman was important to Lewis.

- **Practice** Write these words on the board. Work together to organize ideas around a main idea. (Possible answer: Main Idea: Seaman and the Squirrels; Ideas: Seaman liked to hunt. He hunted squirrels. He caught them in the water.)

Seaman	liked	hunt	squirrels	caught	water

- **Write** Have students write a paragraph explaining something they found interesting about Lewis and Clark. Have them tell why they thought it was interesting by using specific details. For ideas, they can use *Lewis and Clark and Me* and *Talking to Lewis and Clark.*

Beginning Have students write a main idea title at the top of their paper. Then have them draw pictures to show ideas related to it. Have them dictate a sentence for each picture. Write out their sentences and have students copy them.

Intermediate Have partners work together to write a main idea title. Then have them organize related ideas in the form of a paragraph. For prewriting, students can use a Concept Web for organizing their ideas.

Advanced/Advanced High Have students develop their titles and paragraphs independently. Then have pairs exchange papers and provide feedback for revising and editing.

Objectives

- Narrate, describe, and explain with increasing specificity and detail to fulfill content area writing needs as more English is acquired.

This Week's ELL Overview

Grade 4 • Unit 1 • Week 3
On the Banks of Plum Creek
78a–109r and DI•66–DI•75

ELL Handbook

- Maximize Literacy and Cognitive Engagement
- Research Into Practice
- Full Weekly Support for Every Selection

On the Banks of Plum Creek
- Multi-Lingual Summaries in Five Languages
- Selection-Specific Vocabulary Word Cards
- Frontloading/Reteaching for Comprehension Skill Lessons
- ELD and ELL Reader Study Guides

- Transfer Activities
- Professional Development

Daily Leveled ELL Notes

ELL notes appear throughout this week's instruction and ELL Support is on the DI pages of your Teacher's Edition. The following is a sample of an ELL note from this week.

English Language Learners

Beginning Say two word sentences such as: *Eagles fly; Cars move.* Have students identify the subject and predicate in each.

Intermediate Say a subject and have students complete the sentence with a predicate. Then say a predicate and have them fill in the subject. For example: *The boys* _______; _______ *came to visit.*

Advanced Have students complete the intermediate activity in writing.

Advanced High Have students write four sentences that each have one subject and one predicate. Then have them underline the subject once and the predicate twice.

ELL by Strand

The ELL lessons on this week's Support for English Language Learners pages are organized by strand. They offer additional scaffolding for the core curriculum. Leveled support notes on these pages address the different proficiency levels in your class. See pages DI•66–DI•75.

ELL Guy
Dr. Jim Cummins

The Three Pillars of ELL Instruction

ELL Strands	Activate Prior Knowledge	Access Content	Extend Language
Vocabulary pp. DI•67–DI•68	Preteach	Reteach	Leveled Writing Activities
Reading Comprehension p. DI•72	Frontloading	Sheltered Reading	After Reading
Phonics, Spelling, and Word Analysis p. DI•70	Preteach	Teach/Model	Leveled Practice Activities
Listening Comprehension p. DI•69	Prepare for the Read Aloud	First Listening	Second Listening
Conventions and Writing pp. DI•74–DI•75	Teach/Model	Teach/Model	Leveled Practice Activities/ Leveled Writing Activities
Concept Development p. DI•66	Activate Prior Knowledge	Discuss Concept	Daily Concept and Vocabulary Development

This Week's Practice Stations Overview

Six Weekly Practice Stations with Leveled Activities can be found at the beginning of each week of instruction. For this week's Practice Stations, see pp. 78h–78i.

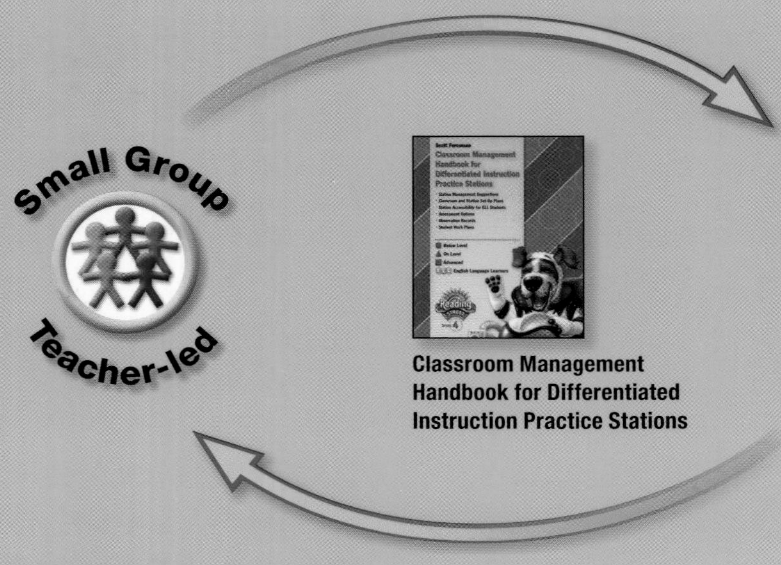

Classroom Management Handbook for Differentiated Instruction Practice Stations

Practice Stations

Daily Leveled Center Activities

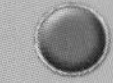 Below
 On-Level
Advanced

Practice Stations Flip Charts

Word Wise	**Word Work**	**Words to Know**	**Let's Write**	**Read for Meaning**	**Get Fluent**

	Word Wise	Word Work	Words to Know	Let's Write	Read for Meaning	Get Fluent
Objectives	• Spell words with long *a* and long *i* vowels.	• Identify and write words with long *a* and long *i* vowel sounds.	• Use word endings to help determine the meaning of words.	• Write an expository composition.	• Determine an author's purpose for writing.	• Read aloud with expression.
Materials	• *Word Wise* Flip Chart Activity 3 • Teacher-made word cards • paper • pencil	• *Word Work* Flip Chart Activity 3 • Teacher-made word cards • paper • pencil	• *Words to Know* Flip Chart Activity 3 • Teacher-made word cards • paper • pencil	• *Let's Write* Flip Chart Activity 3 • paper • pencil	• *Read for Meaning* Flip Chart Activity 3 • Leveled Readers • paper • pencil	• *Get Fluent* Flip Chart Activity 3 • Leveled Readers for each level

This Week on Reading Street!

Question of the Week

Why do we want to explore new places?

Daily Plan

Whole Group

- Literary Elements: Character & Setting & Plot
- Multiple-Meaning Words
- Fluency/Rate and Accuracy
- Research and Inquiry

MONITOR PROGRESS Success Predictor

Day 1	Days 2–3	Day 4	Day 5
Check Oral Vocabulary	Check Retelling	Check Fluency	Check Oral Vocabulary

Small Group

- Reading Support
- Skill Support
- Fluency Practice

Practice Stations

Independent Activities

Customize Literacy More support for a Balanced Literacy approach, see pp. CL•1–CL•47

Customize Writing More support for a customized writing approach, see pp. CW•1–CW•10

Whole Group

- Writing: Parody
- Conventions: Complete Subjects and Predicates
- Spelling: Long *e* and *o*

Assessment

- Weekly Tests
- Day 5 Assessment
- Fresh Reads

This Week's Reading Selections

Main Selection
Genre: **Historical Fiction**

Paired Selection
Online Reference Sources

Leveled Readers

ELL and ELD Readers

Resources on Reading Street!

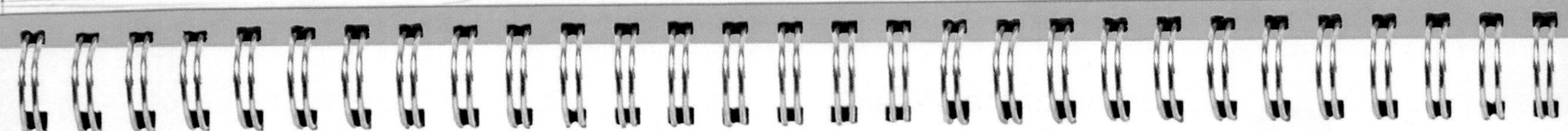

	Build Concepts	 Comprehension
Whole Group	 Let's Talk About pp. 78–79	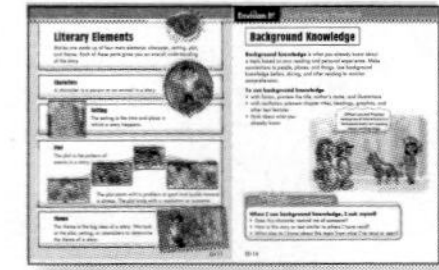 Envision It! Skills/ Strategies 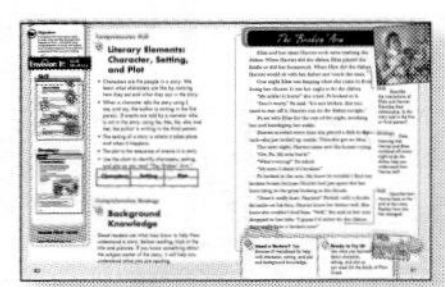 Comprehension Skills Lesson pp. 80–81
 Go Digital	• Concept Talk Video	• Envision It! Animations • eSelections
Small Group and Independent Practice	 On the Banks of Plum Creek pp. 84–85  ELL and ELD Readers  Leveled Readers	 On the Banks of Plum Creek pp. 84–85  ELL and ELD Readers  Leveled Readers 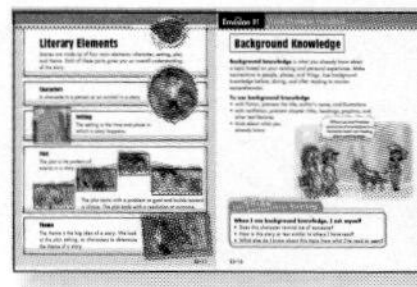 Envision It! Skills/ Strategies  Reader's and Writer's Notebook  Practice Station Flip Chart
 Go Digital	• eReaders • eSelections	• Envision It! Animations • eSelections • eReaders
Customize Literacy	• Leveled Readers	• Envision It! Skills and Strategies Handbook • Leveled Readers
 Go Digital	• Concept Talk Video • Big Question Video • eReaders	• Envision It! Animations • eReaders

Question of the Week

Why do we want to explore new places?

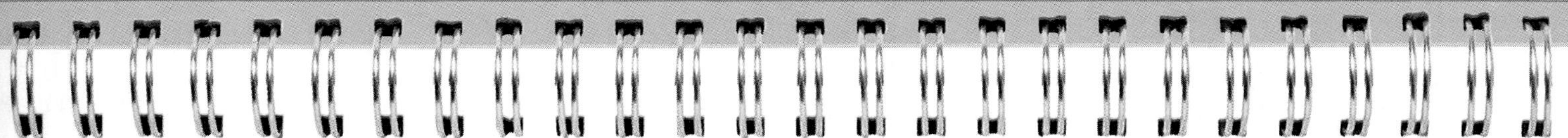

Vocabulary

Envision It! Vocabulary Cards

Vocabulary Skill Lesson pp. 82–83

- Envision It! Vocabulary Cards
- Vocabulary Activities

Envision It! Vocabulary Cards

On the Banks of Plum Creek pp. 84–85

Practice Station Flip Chart

Words! W•10

Reader's and Writer's Notebook

- Envision It! Vocabulary Cards
- Vocabulary Activities
- eSelections

- Envision It! Vocabulary Cards

- Vocabulary Activities

Fluency

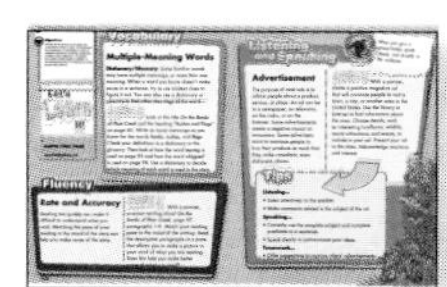

Let's Learn It! pp. 108–109

- eSelections
- eReaders

On the Banks of Plum Creek pp. 84–85

Practice Station Flip Chart

Leveled Readers

ELL and ELD Readers

- eSelections
- eReaders

- Leveled Readers

- eReaders

Conventions and Writing

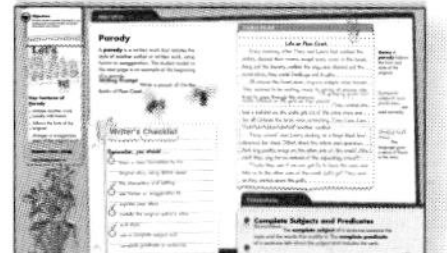

Let's Write It! pp. 102–103

- Grammar Jammer

Reader's and Writer's Notebook

On the Banks of Plum Creek pp. 84–85

Practice Station Flip Chart

- Grammar Jammer

- Reader's and Writer's Notebook

- Grammar Jammer

Week 3

My 5-Day Planner for Reading Street!

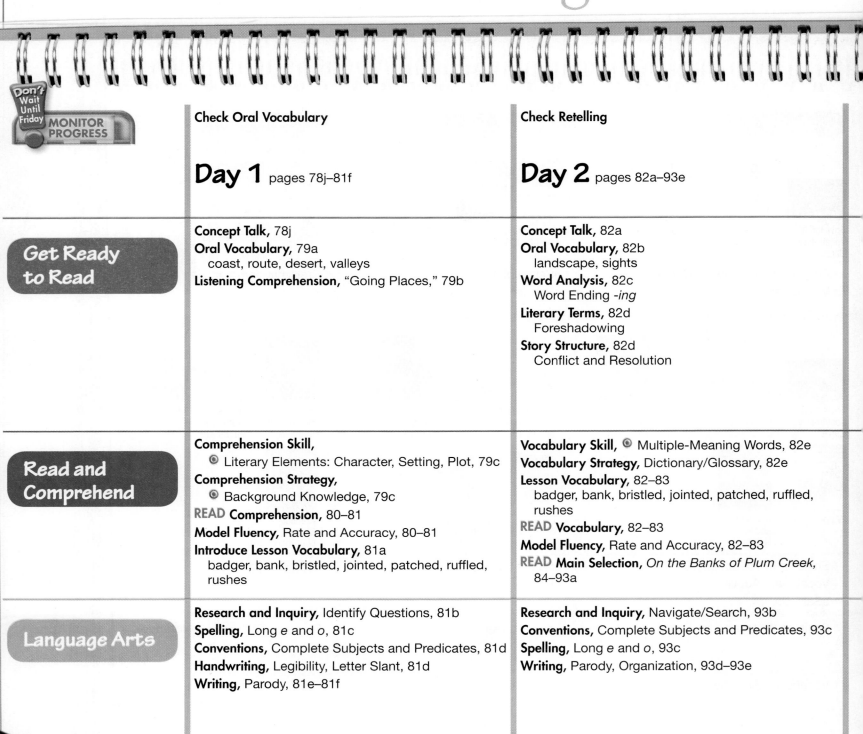

Don't Wait Until Friday MONITOR PROGRESS

	Check Oral Vocabulary **Day 1** pages 78j–81f	Check Retelling **Day 2** pages 82a–93e
Get Ready to Read	**Concept Talk,** 78j **Oral Vocabulary,** 79a coast, route, desert, valleys **Listening Comprehension,** "Going Places," 79b	**Concept Talk,** 82a **Oral Vocabulary,** 82b landscape, sights **Word Analysis,** 82c Word Ending *-ing* **Literary Terms,** 82d Foreshadowing **Story Structure,** 82d Conflict and Resolution
Read and Comprehend	**Comprehension Skill,** ◎ Literary Elements: Character, Setting, Plot, 79c **Comprehension Strategy,** ◎ Background Knowledge, 79c READ **Comprehension,** 80–81 **Model Fluency,** Rate and Accuracy, 80–81 **Introduce Lesson Vocabulary,** 81a badger, bank, bristled, jointed, patched, ruffled, rushes	**Vocabulary Skill,** ◎ Multiple-Meaning Words, 82e **Vocabulary Strategy,** Dictionary/Glossary, 82e **Lesson Vocabulary,** 82–83 badger, bank, bristled, jointed, patched, ruffled, rushes READ **Vocabulary,** 82–83 **Model Fluency,** Rate and Accuracy, 82–83 READ **Main Selection,** *On the Banks of Plum Creek,* 84–93a
Language Arts	**Research and Inquiry,** Identify Questions, 81b **Spelling,** Long *e* and *o*, 81c **Conventions,** Complete Subjects and Predicates, 81d **Handwriting,** Legibility, Letter Slant, 81d **Writing,** Parody, 81e–81f	**Research and Inquiry,** Navigate/Search, 93b **Conventions,** Complete Subjects and Predicates, 93c **Spelling,** Long *e* and *o*, 93c **Writing,** Parody, Organization, 93d–93e

Question of the Week

Why do we want to explore new places?

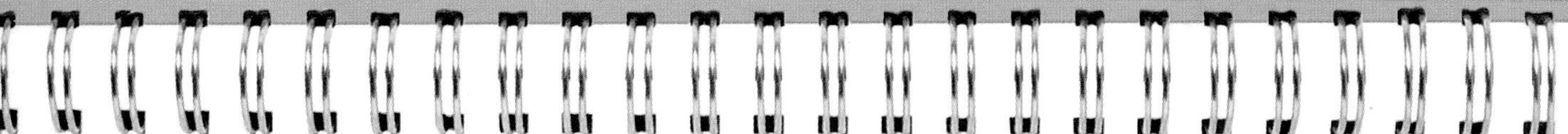

Check Retelling **Day 3** pages 94a–103c	Check Fluency **Day 4** pages 104a–109e	Check Oral Vocabulary **Day 5** pages 109f–109q
Concept Talk, 94a **Oral Vocabulary,** 94b landmarks, enormous **Comprehension Check,** 94c **Check Retelling,** 94d	**Concept Talk,** 104a **Oral Vocabulary,** 104b magnificent, navigate **21st Century Skills,** Online Reference Sources, 104c	**Concept Wrap Up,** 109f **Check Oral Vocabulary,** 109g coast, route, desert, valleys, landscape, sights, landmarks, enormous, magnificent, navigate **Amazing Ideas,** 109g Review ◎ Literary Elements: Character, Setting, Plot, 109h Review ◎ Multiple-Meaning Words, 109h Review **Word Analysis,** 109i Review **Literary Terms,** 109i
READ **Main Selection,** *On the Banks of Plum Creek,* 94–99a **Retelling,** 100–101 **Think Critically,** 101a **Model Fluency,** Rate and Accuracy, 101b **Research and Study Skills,** Electronic Media, 101c	READ **Paired Selection,** "Laura Ingalls Wilder," 104–107a **Let's Learn It!** 108–109a Fluency: Rate and Accuracy Vocabulary: Multiple-Meaning Words Listening and Speaking: Advertisement	**Fluency Assessment,** WCPM, 109j–109k **Comprehension Assessment,** ◎ Literary Elements: Character, Setting, Plot, 109l–109m
Research and Inquiry, Analyze, 101d **Conventions,** Complete Subjects and Predicates, 101e **Spelling,** Long *e* and *o*, 101e **Let's Write It!** Parody, 102–103a **Writing,** Parody, Voice, 103a–103c	**Research and Inquiry,** Synthesize, 109b **Conventions,** Complete Subjects and Predicates, 109c **Spelling,** Long *e* and *o*, 109c **Writing,** Parody, Revising, 109d–109e	**Research and Inquiry,** Communicate, 109n **Conventions,** Complete Subjects and Predicates, 109o **Spelling Test,** Long *e* and *o*, 109o **Writing,** Parody, Complete Subjects and Predicates, 109p–109q **Quick Write for Fluency,** 109q

Week 3

Grouping Options for Differentiated Instruction

Turn the page for the small group time lesson plan.

Planning Small Group Time on Reading Street!

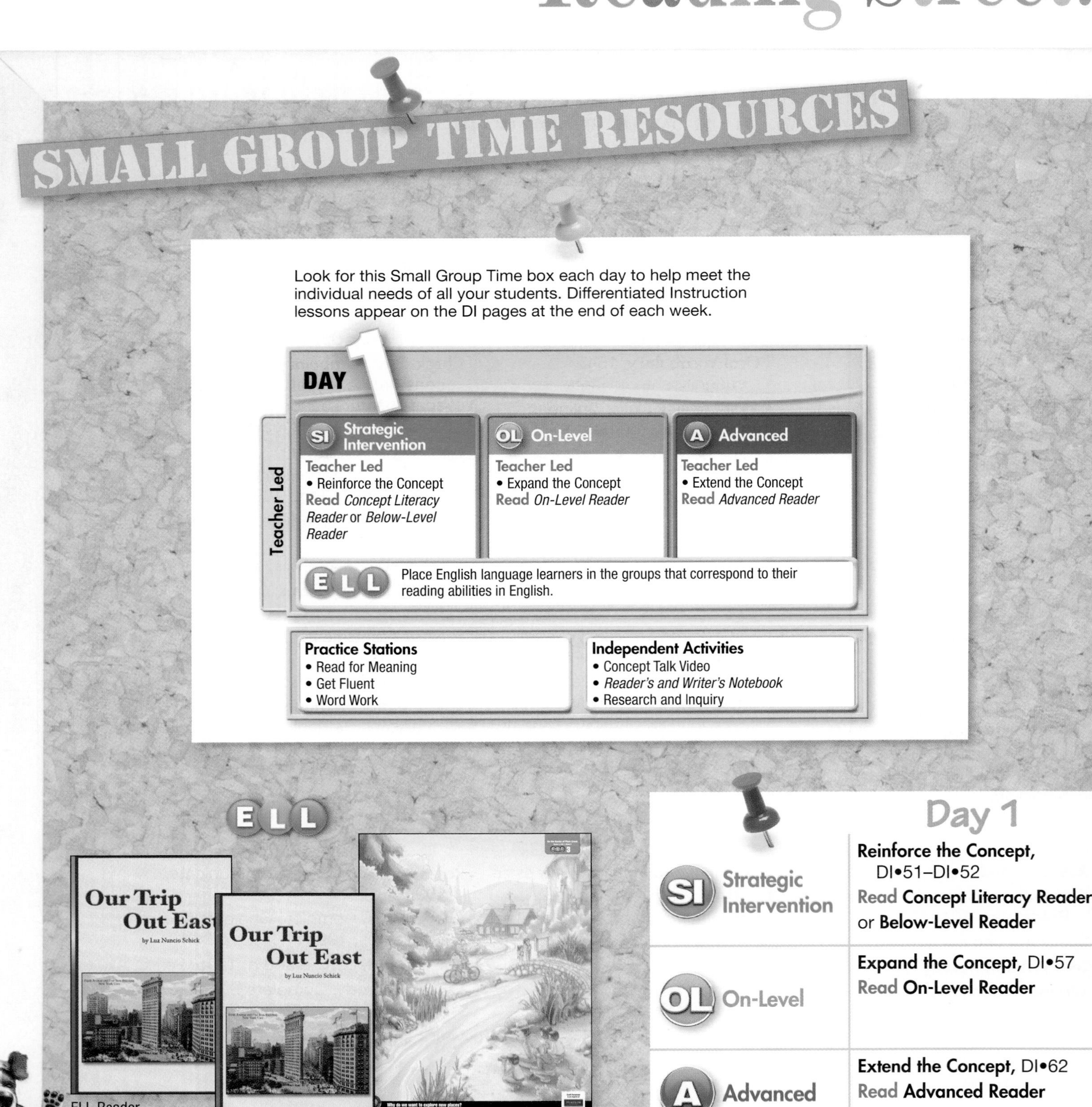
SMALL GROUP TIME RESOURCES
Look for this Small Group Time box each day to help meet the individual needs of all your students. Differentiated Instruction lessons appear on the DI pages at the end of each week.
DAY 1
Teacher Led
SI Strategic Intervention
Teacher Led
• Reinforce the Concept
Read Concept Literacy Reader or Below-Level Reader
OL On-Level
Teacher Led
• Expand the Concept
Read On-Level Reader
A Advanced
Teacher Led
• Extend the Concept
Read Advanced Reader
ELL
Place English language learners in the groups that correspond to their reading abilities in English.
Practice Stations
• Read for Meaning
• Get Fluent
• Word Work
Independent Activities
• Concept Talk Video
• Reader's and Writer's Notebook
• Research and Inquiry
ELL
Our Trip Out East
by Luz Nuncio Schick
Our Trip Out East
by Luz Nuncio Schick
Why do we want to explore new places?

ELL Reader
Advanced
Advanced High

ELD Reader
Beginning
Intermediate

ELL Poster

	Day 1
SI Strategic Intervention	**Reinforce the Concept,** DI•51–DI•52 Read **Concept Literacy Reader** or **Below-Level Reader**
OL On-Level	**Expand the Concept,** DI•57 Read **On-Level Reader**
A Advanced	**Extend the Concept,** DI•62 Read **Advanced Reader**
ELL English Language Learners	DI•66–DI•75 **Frontload Concept** **Preteach Skills** **Writing**

You Are Here!
Unit 1
Week 3

Reading Street Response to Intervention Kit

Reading Street Practice Stations Kit

Question of the Week

Why do we want to explore new places?

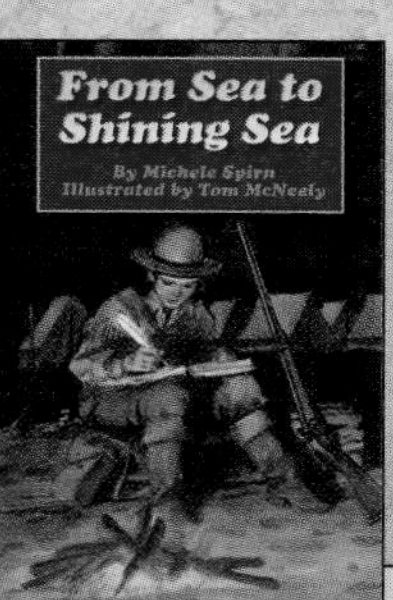

Below-Level Reader

Laura Ingalls Wilder: Pioneer Girl
By Mary Lindeen

Concept Literacy Reader

On the Banks of Plum Creek pp. 84–85

OL On-Level

On-Level Reader

A Advanced

Advanced Reader

Laura Ingalls Wilder pp. 104–105

Small Group Weekly Plan

Day 2	Day 3	Day 4	Day 5
Reinforce Comprehension, DI•53 Revisit **Main Selection**	**Reinforce Vocabulary,** DI•54 Read/Revisit **Main Selection**	**Reinforce Comprehension,** Practice Retelling, DI•55 Genre Focus Read/Revisit **Paired Selection**	**Practice Fluency,** DI•56 Reread **Concept Literacy Reader** or **Below-Level Reader**
Expand Comprehension, DI•58 Revisit **Main Selection**	**Expand Vocabulary,** DI•59 Read/Revisit **Main Selection**	**Expand Comprehension,** Practice Retelling, DI•60 Genre Focus Read/Revisit **Paired Selection**	**Practice Fluency,** DI•61 Reread **On-Level Reader**
Extend Comprehension, DI•63 Revisit **Main Selection**	**Extend Vocabulary,** DI•64 Read/Revisit **Main Selection**	**Extend Comprehension,** Genre Focus, DI•65 Read/Revisit **Paired Selection**	**Practice Fluency,** DI•65 Reread **Advanced Reader**
DI•66–DI•75 **Review Concept/Skills** **Frontload Main Selection** **Practice**	DI•66–DI•75 **Review Concept/Skills** Reread **Main Selection** **Practice**	DI•66–DI•75 **Review Concept** Read **ELL/ELD Readers** **Practice**	DI•66–DI•75 **Review Concept/Skills** Reread **ELL/ELD Readers** **Writing**

Week 3

Practice Stations for Everyone on Reading Street!

Word Wise
Words with long *a* and long *i*

Objectives
- Spell words with long *a* and long *i* vowels.

Materials
- *Word Wise* Flip Chart Activity 3
- Teacher-made word cards
- paper • pencil

Differentiated Activities

● Choose four word cards. Write the words. Circle the letter or letters that spell the long *a* or long *i* in each word. Write a sentence for each word.

▲ Choose six word cards, and write the words. Circle the letter or letters that spell the long *a* or long *i* in each word. Write a sentence for each word.

■ Choose eight word cards, and write the words in a list. Circle the letter or letters that spell the long *a* or long *i* in each word. Write a sentence for each word.

Technology
- Online dictionary

Word Work
Words with long *a* and long *i* vowels

Objectives
- Identify and write words with long *a* and long *i* vowel sounds.

Materials
- *Word Work* Flip Chart Activity 3
- Teacher-made word cards
- paper • pencil

Differentiated Activities

● Choose six word cards. Say each word. Make a two-column chart with headings *Long a* and *Long i.* Write each word in the correct column.

▲ Choose ten word cards, and say each word. Make a two-column chart with headings *Long a* and *Long i.* Write each word in the correct column.

■ Choose twelve word cards. Group your words by long vowel sounds. Write each group in a list. Say each word. Add other words with these long-vowel sounds to the lists.

Technology
- Modeled Pronunciation Audio CD

Words to Know
Word endings

Objectives
- Use word endings to help determine the meanings of words.

Materials
- *Words to Know* Flip Chart Activity 3
- Teacher-made word cards
- paper • pencil

Differentiated Activities

● Choose five word cards. Write the words. Circle the word ending in each word. Use a dictionary to check meanings. Write a sentence for each word.

▲ Choose seven word cards, and write the words. Circle the word ending in each word. Use the dictionary to check definitions. Write a sentence for each word.

■ Choose seven word cards, and write the words. Use the dictionary to check definitions. Write a sentence for each word. Add a different ending to each word, and write new sentences.

Technology
- Online dictionary

Use this week's materials from the Reading Street Leveled Practice Stations Kit to organize this week's stations.

Key

- Below-Level Activities
- On-Level Activities
- Advanced Activities

Practice Station Flip Chart

Let's Write!
Expository composition

Objectives
- Write an expository composition.

Materials
- *Let's Write!* Flip Chart Activity 3
- paper • pencil

Differentiated Activities

● Think about a job you would like to have. Write an expository composition that tells about a job you would like to have. Describe what you would do. Organize your ideas around a main idea.

▲ Write an expository composition about a job that interests you. Explain the responsibilities of the job. Organize your ideas around a main idea.

■ Write an expository composition describing a job you would like to have. Explain the responsibilities of this job and how you would get the job.

Technology
- Online graphic organizers

Read for Meaning
Author's purpose

Objectives
- Determine an author's purpose for writing.

Materials
- *Read for Meaning* Flip Chart Activity 3
- Leveled Readers • paper • pencil

Differentiated Activities

● Choose a book from those your teacher provided. Think about the author's purpose for writing the story. Write one sentence that tells the author's purpose.

▲ Read one of the books your teacher provided, and think about the author's purpose for writing the story. Write one sentence stating the author's purpose. Explain whether you think the purpose was achieved.

■ Choose and read a leveled reader, and think about the author's reason for writing. Write a short paragraph stating the author's purpose and whether you think the purpose was achieved.

Technology
- Leveled Reader Database

Get Fluent
Practice fluent reading

Objectives
- Read aloud with expression.

Materials
- *Get Fluent* Flip Chart Activity 3
- Leveled Readers for each level

Differentiated Activities

● Work with a partner. Choose a Concept Literacy Reader or Below-Level Reader. Take turns reading a page from the book. Use the readers to practice correct expression. Provide feedback as needed.

▲ Work with a partner. Choose an On-Level Reader. Take turns reading a page from the book. Use the reader to practice correct expression. Provide feedback as needed.

■ Work with a partner. Choose an Advanced Reader. Take turns reading a page from the book. Use the reader to practice correct expression. Provide feedback as needed.

Technology
- Reading Street Readers CD-ROM
- Leveled Reader Database

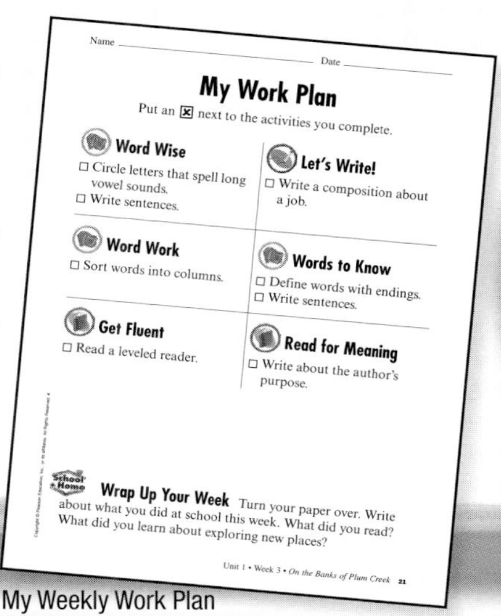

Name ______ Date ______

My Work Plan

Put an ☒ next to the activities you complete.

Word Wise
☐ Circle letters that spell long vowel sounds.
☐ Write sentences.

Let's Write!
☐ Write a composition about a job.

Word Work
☐ Sort words into columns.

Words to Know
☐ Define words with endings.
☐ Write sentences.

Get Fluent
☐ Read a leveled reader.

Read for Meaning
☐ Write about the author's purpose.

School + Home **Wrap Up Your Week** Turn your paper over. Write about what you did at school this week. What did you read? What did you learn about exploring new places?

Unit 1 • Week 3 • *On the Banks of Plum Creek*

My Weekly Work Plan

Week 3

Objectives

- Introduce the weekly concept.
- Develop oral vocabulary.

Today at a Glance

Oral Vocabulary
route, coast, desert, valleys

Comprehension
◎ Literary elements: Character, setting, plot
◎ Background knowledge

Reading
"The 'Broken' Arm"

Fluency
Rate and accuracy

Lesson Vocabulary
Multiple-meaning words

Research and Inquiry
Identify questions

Spelling
Long *e* and *o*

Conventions
Complete subjects and predicates

Handwriting
Legibility: Letter slant

Writing
Parody

Concept Talk

Question of the Week

Why do we want to explore new places?

Introduce the concept

To further explore the unit concept of Turning Points, this week students will read, write, and talk about why people are motivated to explore new locations. Write the Question of the Week on the board.

ROUTINE Activate Prior Knowledge — Team Talk

1. **Think** Have students think about the different reasons why people might explore new places.
2. **Pair** Have pairs of students discuss the Question of the Week.
3. **Share** Call on a few students to share their ideas with the group. Guide the discussion and encourage elaboration with prompts such as:
   - Where are some places in the world that you would enjoy exploring?
   - What things might you discover in those places?

Routines Flip Chart

Anchored Talk

Develop oral vocabulary

Have students turn to pp. 78–79 in their Student Editions. Look at each of the photos. Then, use the prompts to guide discussion and create the *Why do we want to explore new places?* concept map. Remind students to ask and answer questions with appropriate details.

- In addition to trains, what are other methods that people in the past used to travel across the country and around the world? (boat, horse, covered wagons, hot air balloons, airplanes) People have always had the urge to travel. Today they can journey to different locations much faster than in the past. Let's add *Ways People Travel* to our concept map.
- What reasons do you think this family at the Golden Gate Bridge had for traveling to a new place? (They took a vacation to sightsee and visit landmarks.) Let's add *Why People Travel* to the concept map.

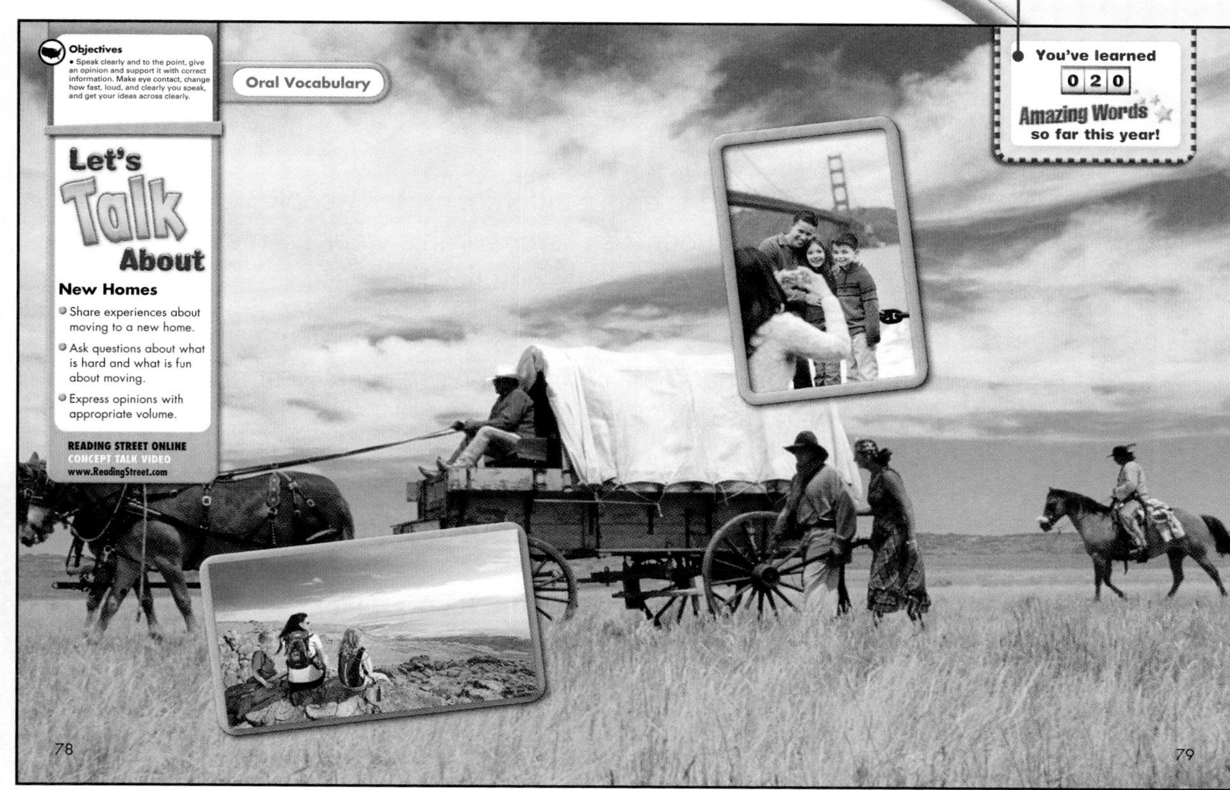

Objectives
• Speak clearly and to the point, give an opinion and support it with correct information. Make eye contact, change how fast, loud, and clearly you speak, and get your ideas across clearly.
Oral Vocabulary
Let's Talk About
New Homes
Share experiences about moving to a new home.
Ask questions about what is hard and what is fun about moving.
Express opinions with appropriate volume.
READING STREET ONLINE
CONCEPT TALK VIDEO
www.ReadingStreet.com
You've learned
0 2 0
Amazing Words
so far this year!
78
79

Student Edition pp. 78–79

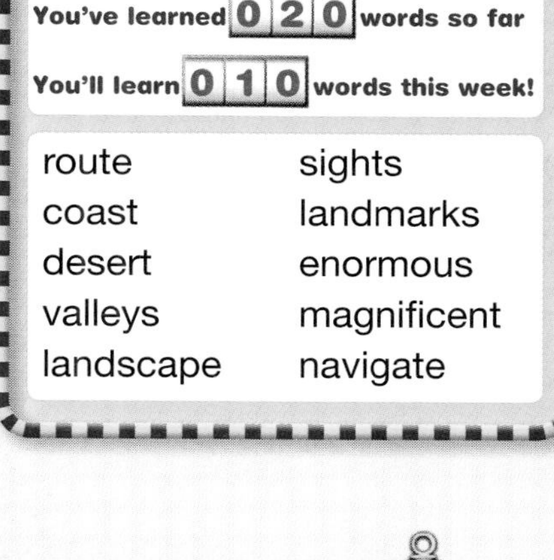

Writing on Demand

Writing Fluency
Ask students to respond to the photos on pp. 78–79 by writing as well as they can and as much as they can about why people want to explore new locations.

- Why do you think the mother and her two children climbed to the top of the mountain? (They wanted to admire the view of the ocean.) Let's add *Where People Travel* to the concept map.
- After discussing the photos, ask: Why do we want to explore new places?

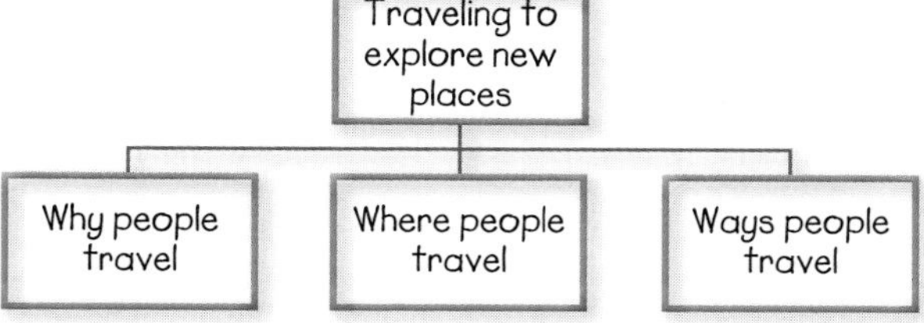

Connect to reading To further explore the unit concept of Turning Points, this week students will read, write, and talk about why people are motivated to explore new locations. Write the Question of the Week on the board.

ELL Visual Learning: Concept Talk Use the Day 1 instructions on ELL Poster 3 to assess and build background knowledge, develop concepts, and build oral vocabulary.

ELL Poster 3

ELL

English Language Learners

ELL support Additional ELL support and modified instruction is provided in the *ELL Handbook* and in the ELL Support lessons on pp. DI•66–DI•75.

Listening comprehension English learners will benefit from additional visual support to understand the key terms in the concept map. Use the pictures on pp. 78–79 to scaffold understanding.

Frontload for Read Aloud Use the modified Read Aloud on p. DI•69 of the ELL Support lessons to prepare students to listen to "Going Places."

Objectives

- Develop listening comprehension.
- Build oral vocabulary.

Check Oral Vocabulary
SUCCESS PREDICTOR

Oral Vocabulary
Amazing Words

Introduce Amazing Words "Going Places" on p. 79b is about different routes people travel across the United States. Tell students to listen for this week's Amazing Words—*route, coast, desert,* and *valleys*—as you read.

Model fluency As you read "Going Places," model appropriate rate by reading at a speed that is appropriate to the text and will improve the listener's comprehension, and model accuracy with smooth, fluent reading.

Teach Amazing Words

Amazing Words Oral Vocabulary Routine

route
coast
desert
valleys

1. **Introduce** Write the word *route* on the board. Have students say the word aloud with you. In "Going Places," we learn that you can travel many *routes* across the United States. Does the author include any context clues that tell me the meaning of this word? Supply a student-friendly definition.
2. **Demonstrate** Have students answer questions to demonstrate understanding. How can a map help you find a *route* to take during vacation? Why would you want to take a scenic *route*?
3. **Apply** Ask students to give a personal example of *route*.

See p. OV•3 to teach *coast, desert,* and *valleys.*

Routines Flip Chart

Apply Amazing Words To develop oral vocabulary, lead the class in a discussion about the Amazing Words' meanings. Remind students to listen attentively to speakers and to build on the ideas of others in a discussion.

MONITOR PROGRESS Check Oral Vocabulary

During discussion, listen for students' use of Amazing Words.

If... students are unable to use the Amazing Words to discuss the concept,
then... use Oral Vocabulary Routine in the Routines Flip Chart to demonstrate words in different contexts.

Day 1	Days 2–3	Day 4	Day 5
Check Oral Vocabulary	Check Retelling	Check Fluency	Check Oral Vocabulary

Going Places

by Harriet Webster

Our country stretches 1,600 miles from north to south and 2,800 miles from east to west. Coast to coast, that's nearly the same distance as from New York to London, passing over the Atlantic Ocean. Or think of it this way: If you traveled by car at a steady speed of sixty miles an hour, never once stopping for a break, it would take nearly forty-seven hours to cross the country. If you were to choose jet travel instead, the nonstop trip would take about five hours. From the edge of the Atlantic Ocean, you'd head inland and soar above the gentle rises of the Appalachian Mountains and the fertile farmlands of the Midwest. Depending upon your route, you might catch a glimpse of the Great Lakes to the north. Farther west, you'd look down on the endless prairies and cattle-grazing land. On the southern route, you might see desert below. Then you'd climb above the snow-capped Rockies before passing over the lush green valleys of California and the shores of the great Pacific Ocean.

That's a lot of territory! Think how challenging a cross-country expedition must have been for our forebears, who made their treks without the benefit of modern transportation. Parts of the Great Plains were so featureless and so flat that settlers drove stakes into the ground to show others where to go. Even today, that area is called Staked Plains. Another way they left directions for those who would follow was to sprinkle mustard seeds through the western valleys in the hope that a trail of bright yellow plants would signal the way.

There is so much to explore in the U.S.A. that you need never run out of discoveries to make or places to explore. A good way to keep track of what you have seen and to build on your knowledge is to keep a naturalist's scrapbook.

DAY 1 Read and Comprehend

30–35 min

Objectives

- ◎ Understand literary elements—character, setting, and plot—to aid comprehension.
- ◎ Use background knowledge to aid comprehension.
- Read grade-level text with rate and accuracy.

Skills Trace

◎ **Literary Elements**

Introduce U1W3D1; U4W5D1; U5W3D1

Practice U1W3D2; U1W3D3; U4W5D2; U4W5D3; U5W3D2; U5W3D3

Reteach/Review U1W3D5; U1W4D2; U1W4D3; U2W1D3; U5W5D2; U5W5D3; U5W3D5

Assess/Test
Weekly Tests U1W3; U4W5; U5W3
Benchmark Tests U5

KEY:
U=Unit W=Week D=Day

Skill ↔ Strategy

◎ Literary Elements: Character, Setting, and Plot

◎ Background Knowledge

Student Edition p. EI•11

Introduce literary elements

Envision It!

Explain to students that characters are the people in a story. Readers learn about the characters by noticing how they interact with each other and the changes they undergo. Setting is where the story takes place and when it happens. The plot is the sequence of events in a story. Have students turn to p. EI•11 in the Student Edition to review literary elements. Then read "The 'Broken' Arm" with students.

Model the skill

Think Aloud I read that the characters in the story are Eliza, Harriet and Pa. I can learn about them by how they interact together. Eliza and Harriet did different things while the other did the dishes and Pa cared for them both. The setting takes place at their home that has a yard and happens during the night. The plot is the sequence of events. The girls take turns doing the dishes. Eliza gets hurt and Harriet has to do the dishes for her. When Harriet tries to pretend being hurt, she is too honest to lie to her Pa.

Guide practice

Have students read "The 'Broken' Arm" on their own. After they read, have them use a graphic organizer like the one on p. 80 to identify literary elements from the passage.

Strategy check

Background Knowledge Remind students that if they have difficulty understanding "The 'Broken' Arm," they can use their background knowledge to monitor and adjust comprehension. Model the strategy.

Model the strategy

Think Aloud As I read the first paragraph, I remember how I had to do the dishes while my brothers got to play. I didn't like it when that happened. But one time I had a friend over and my brothers had to do the dishes while we got to play. Have students review the strategy of background knowledge on p. EI•16 of the Student Edition.

On their own

Use p. 62 in the *Reader's and Writer's Notebook* for additional practice with literary elements: character, setting, and plot.

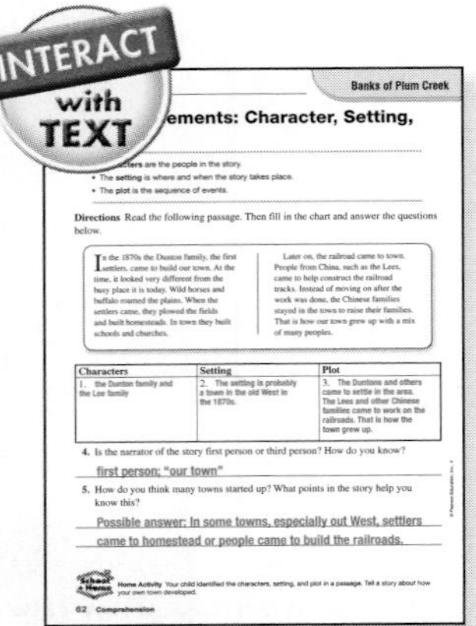

Reader's and Writer's Notebook p. 62

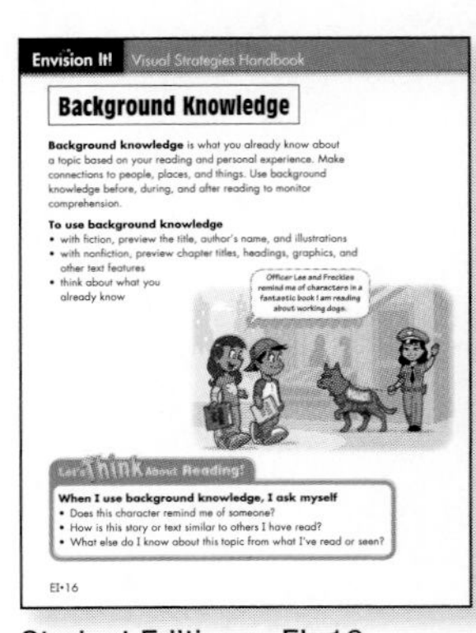

Student Edition p. EI•16

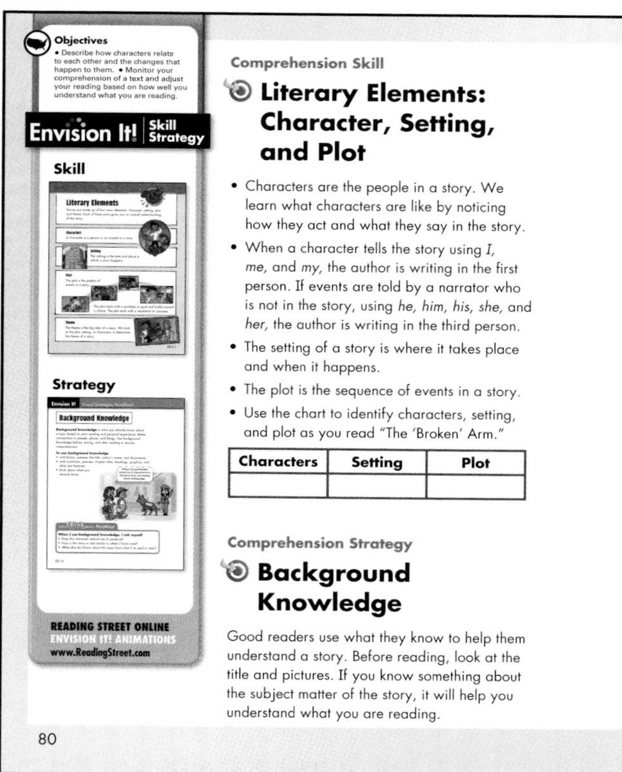

Objectives
• Describe how characters relate to each other and the changes that happen to them. • Monitor your comprehension of a text and adjust your reading based on how well you understand what you are reading.

Envision It! Skill Strategy

Skill

Strategy

READING STREET ONLINE
ENVISION IT! ANIMATIONS
www.ReadingStreet.com

Comprehension Skill

Literary Elements: Character, Setting, and Plot

- Characters are the people in a story. We learn what characters are like by noticing how they act and what they say in the story.
- When a character tells the story using *I*, *me*, and *my*, the author is writing in the first person. If events are told by a narrator who is not in the story, using *he*, *him*, *his*, *she*, and *her*, the author is writing in the third person.
- The setting of a story is where it takes place and when it happens.
- The plot is the sequence of events in a story.
- Use the chart to identify characters, setting, and plot as you read "The 'Broken' Arm."

Characters	Setting	Plot

Comprehension Strategy

Background Knowledge

Good readers use what they know to help them understand a story. Before reading, look at the title and pictures. If you know something about the subject matter of the story, it will help you understand what you are reading.

80

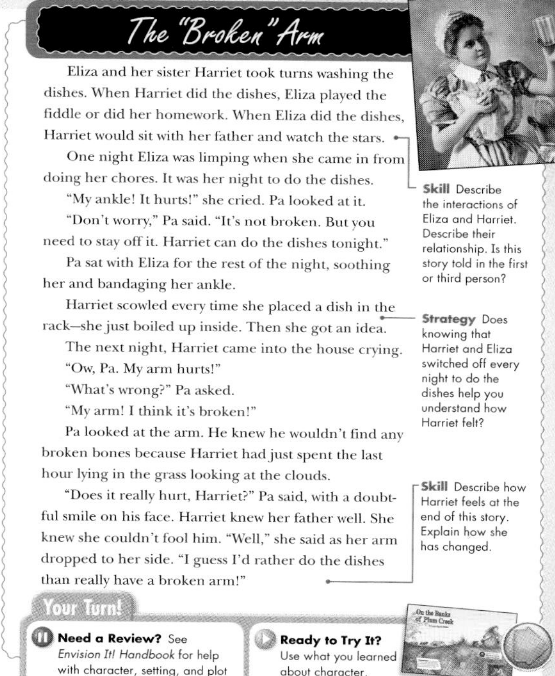

The "Broken" Arm

Eliza and her sister Harriet took turns washing the dishes. When Harriet did the dishes, Eliza played the fiddle or did her homework. When Eliza did the dishes, Harriet would sit with her father and watch the stars.

One night Eliza was limping when she came in from doing her chores. It was her night to do the dishes.

"My ankle! It hurts!" she cried. Pa looked at it.

"Don't worry," Pa said. "It's not broken. But you need to stay off it. Harriet can do the dishes tonight."

Pa sat with Eliza for the rest of the night, soothing her and bandaging her ankle.

Harriet scowled every time she placed a dish in the rack—she just boiled up inside. Then she got an idea.

The next night, Harriet came into the house crying.

"Ow, Pa. My arm hurts!"

"What's wrong?" Pa asked.

"My arm! I think it's broken!"

Pa looked at the arm. He knew he wouldn't find any broken bones because Harriet had just spent the last hour lying in the grass looking at the clouds.

"Does it really hurt, Harriet?" Pa said, with a doubtful smile on his face. Harriet knew her father well. She knew she couldn't fool him. "Well," she said as her arm dropped to her side. "I guess I'd rather do the dishes than really have a broken arm!"

Skill Describe the interactions of Eliza and Harriet. Describe their relationship. Is this story told in the first or third person?

Strategy Does knowing that Harriet and Eliza switched off every night to do the dishes help you understand how Harriet felt?

Skill Describe how Harriet feels at the end of this story. Explain how she has changed.

Your Turn!

Need a Review? See *Envision It! Handbook* for help with character, setting, and plot and background knowledge.

Ready to Try It? Use what you learned about character, setting, and plot as you read *On the Banks of Plum Creek.*

81

Student Edition pp. 80–81

Skill Eliza likes to play the fiddle or do her homework. Harriet likes to sit with her father and watch the stars. They both take turns doing the dishes. This is told in the third person.

Strategy Yes. If I were Harriet, I would feel like it was unfair that I had to do dishes on Eliza's night to do them.

Skill Harriet feels grateful that she really doesn't have a broken arm. She has changed by realizing that doing the dishes isn't much to complain about.

Academic Vocabulary

background knowledge what a reader already knows about a given topic, gathered from personal experience

Model Fluency

Rate and Accuracy

Model fluent reading

Have students listen as you read the last paragraph of "The 'Broken' Arm," focusing on the rate and accuracy. Tell students that you are reading the paragraph at a moderate rate, pausing between phrases and between sentences, and reading precisely by avoiding errors.

ROUTINE Oral Rereading

1. **Read** Have students read "The 'Broken' Arm" orally.
2. **Reread** To achieve optimal fluency, students should reread the text three or four times with appropriate rate and accuracy.
3. **Corrective Feedback** Have students read aloud without you. Provide feedback about their rate and accuracy and encourage them to adjust the speed at which they read and avoid errors. To achieve optimal fluency, students should reread the text three or four times.

Routines Flip Chart

ELL

English Language Learners

Literary elements Provide oral practice by having students give brief synopses of plots of their favorite folk tales. Have students identify the conflict that motivates the action of the plot.

Objectives

- Activate prior knowledge of words.
- Identify questions for research.

Vocabulary
Tested Vocabulary

Lesson vocabulary

Have students create word rating charts using the categories *Know, Have Seen* and *Don't Know.*

Activate prior knowledge

Word Rating Chart

Word	Know	Have Seen	Don't Know
badger			✔
bank	✔		
bristled		✔	
jointed		✔	
patched			
ruffled			
rushes			

Read each word to students and have them rate their knowledge of the word by placing a checkmark in one of the three columns: *Know* (know and can use); *Have Seen* (have seen or heard the word; don't know meaning); *Don't Know* (don't know the word).

Have students provide sentences for the words they checked in the *Know* column. By the end of the week, have them revise their charts and demonstrate their understanding by using each word in a sentence.

Preteach Academic Vocabulary

Academic Vocabulary Write the following words on the board:

multiple-meaning word	**advertisement**
background knowledge	**volume**
foreshadowing	**letter slant**

Have students share what they know about this week's Academic Vocabulary. Use the students' responses to assess their prior knowledge. Preteach the Academic Vocabulary by providing a student-friendly description, explanation, or example that clarifies the meaning of each term. Then ask students to restate the meaning of the Academic Vocabulary term in their own words.

Research and Inquiry
Identify Questions

Teach Discuss the Question of the Week: *Why do we want to explore new places?* Tell students they will research why people want to explore new places. They will present a brochure with their findings to the class on Day 5.

Model Think Aloud: I'll start by generating a topic that interests me, such as exploring lighthouses. Then I'll formulate a list of open-ended questions about why people want to explore new places. I know that one reason I like to explore new places is to discover different landmarks and landscapes. Some possible questions could be *What landmark or landscape would I want to explore on vacation?*, *What would I learn during my exploration?*, and *What new activities could I try while exploring?*

Guide practice After students have generated topics and brainstormed inquiry questions, explain that tomorrow they will conduct an online research of their questions. Help students identify keywords that will guide their search.

On their own Have students work individually, in pairs, or in small groups to narrow their research topics to one topic and write an inquiry question.

Small Group Time

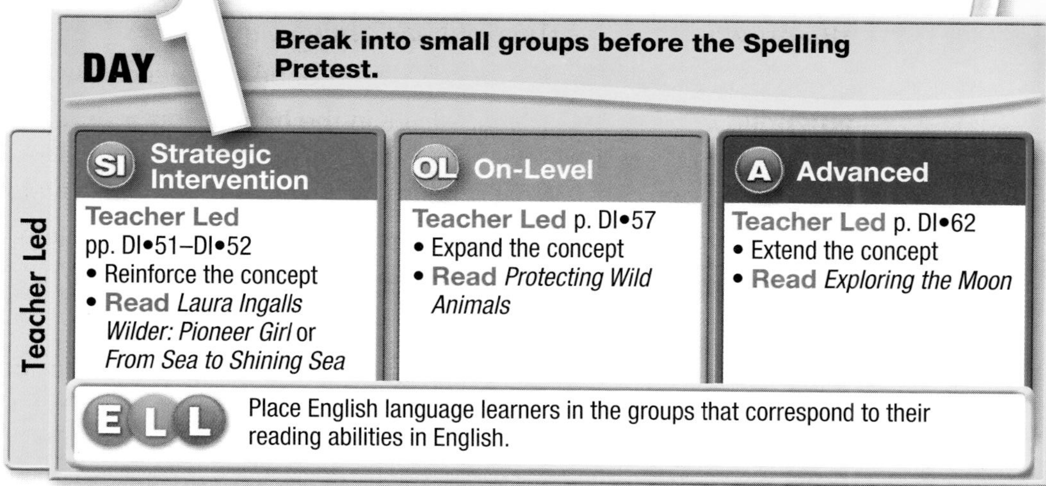

DAY 1 Break into small groups before the Spelling Pretest.

Teacher Led

SI Strategic Intervention	OL On-Level	A Advanced
Teacher Led pp. DI•51–DI•52 • Reinforce the concept • Read *Laura Ingalls Wilder: Pioneer Girl* or *From Sea to Shining Sea*	Teacher Led p. DI•57 • Expand the concept • Read *Protecting Wild Animals*	Teacher Led p. DI•62 • Extend the concept • Read *Exploring the Moon*

ELL Place English language learners in the groups that correspond to their reading abilities in English.

Practice Stations
- Read for Meaning
- Get Fluent
- Word Work

Independent Activities
- Concept Talk Video
- *Reader's and Writer's Notebook*
- Vocabulary Activities

INTERNET GUY
Don Leu

21st Century Skills

Weekly Inquiry Project

Day 1 Identify Questions
Day 2 Navigate/Search
Day 3 Analyze
Day 4 Synthesize
Day 5 Communicate

Differentiated Instruction

 Advanced

Advanced Have students identify keywords for their search by listing elements such as the name of a city, landform, or national park and its location. After meeting with students and reviewing their keywords, have them enter their keywords into a student-friendly search engine.

English Language Learners

Multilingual vocabulary Students can apply knowledge of their home languages to acquire new English vocabulary by using the Multilingual Vocabulary Lists (*ELL Handbook*, pp. 431–432).

Objectives

- Spell words with long *e* and *o*.
- Use and understand complete subjects and predicates.
- Practice writing letters using proper slant.

Spelling Pretest
Long *e* and *o*

Introduce Tell students to think of words with the long *e* sound *(team)* and long *o* sound *(moan)*. This week we will spell words with the long *e* sound and words with the long *o* sound.

Pretest Use these sentences to administer the spelling pretest. Say each word, read the sentence, and repeat the word.

1. sweet	Honey tastes **sweet.**
2. each	I think **each** of us has a sister.
3. three	Jake made **three** baskets.
4. least	At **least** it's not raining.
5. freedom	The army fought for **freedom.**
6. below	A basement is **below** the house.
7. throat	Do you have a sore **throat?**
8. float	Can you **float** on your back?
9. foam	My mom drinks coffee topped with milk **foam.**
10. flown	The baby birds have **flown** away.
11. greet	Did you **greet** your mom with a smile?
12. season	What **season** do you like best?
13. croak	Some frogs **croak** at night.
14. shallow	The water is too **shallow** for swimming.
15. eagle	The **eagle** flew across the sky.
16. indeed	Your story is very good **indeed.**
17. rainbow	We saw a **rainbow** after the storm.
18. grown	The plant has **grown** very tall.
19. seaweed	We saw **seaweed** under the water.
20. hollow	A mouse lives in the **hollow** log.

Challenge words

21. Halloween	What costume will you wear for **Halloween?**
22. speedometer	The **speedometer** on the car was broken.
23. underneath	The slippers are **underneath** the bed.
24. seacoast	We live on the **seacoast** of Maine.
25. cocoa	After building the snowman, we had hot **cocoa.**

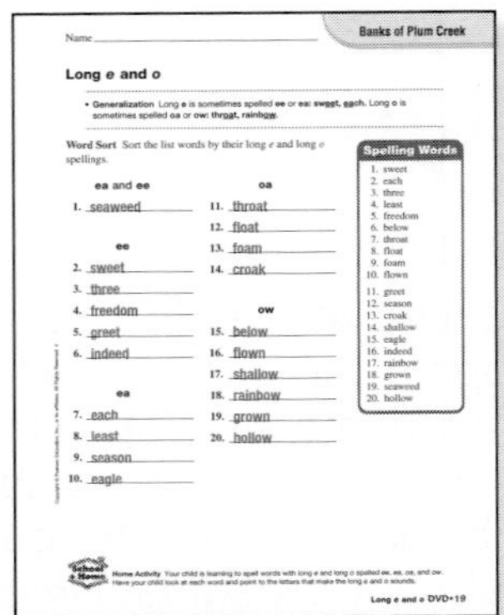
Let's Practice It!
TR DVD•19

Self-correct After the pretest, you can either display the correctly spelled words or spell them orally. Have students self-correct their pretests by rewriting misspelled words correctly.

On their own For additional practice, use *Let's Practice It!* p. 19 on the *Teacher Resources DVD-ROM*.

Conventions

Complete Subjects and Predicates

Teach Display Grammar Transparency 3, and read aloud the explanation and examples in the box. Explain that a subject tells whom or what the sentence is about. Some sentences have more than one subject. These are compound subjects. Point out that all the words in the subject are the complete subject. Next explain that a predicate tells what the subject does. If a sentence has more than one predicate, it has a compound predicate. All the words in the predicate are the complete predicate.

Model Write the correct answers to numbers 1 and 2. Explain how you applied the rules for identifying the complete subjects and predicates in sentences.

Guide practice Guide students to complete items 3 and 4. Remind them to identify the complete subjects and predicates in sentences correctly. Record the correct responses on the transparency.

Daily Fix-It Use Daily Fix-It numbers 1 and 2 in the right margin.

Connect to oral language Have students read sentences 5–8 on the transparency and circle the simple subject and predicate in each sentence.

Handwriting

Legibility: Letter Slant

Explain letter slant Display lowercase *f, h, l.* Explain that letters can slant to the right, left, or straight up and down. Point out that to write legibly, letters should slant in the same direction. If they did not they would bump into each other.

Model letter slant Write *f, h,* and *l* several times. Draw an arrow along the upstroke of each to show the direction of your letter slant.

Guide practice Have students evaluate their letter slant by writing their full name in cursive on a piece of paper. Have them also write *f, h,* and *l* several times, and draw arrows if necessary to find their letter slant. Circulate around the room, guiding students.

Academic Vocabulary

Letter slant is the proper angle at which letters in words are written.

Daily Fix-It

1. The hot springs at Yellowstone National Park is amazing? (*are amazing.*)
2. We saw an eagle. At our campsite. (*eagle at*)

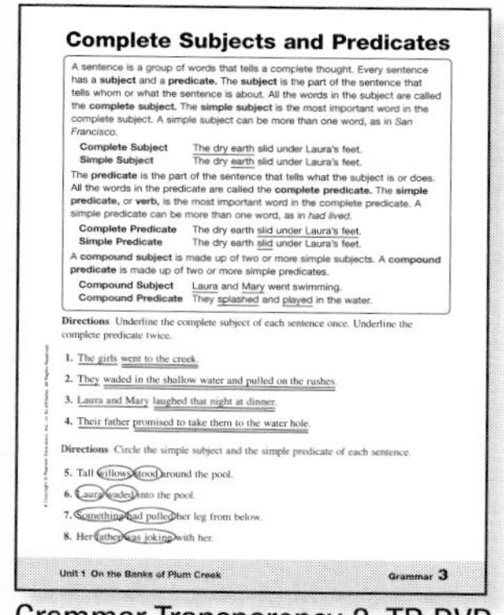

Complete Subjects and Predicates

A sentence is a group of words that tells a complete thought. Every sentence has a **subject** and a **predicate.** The **subject** is the part of the sentence that tells whom or what the sentence is about. All the words in the subject are called the **complete subject.** The **simple subject** is the most important word in the complete subject. A simple subject can be more than one word, as in *San Francisco.*

Complete Subject The dry earth slid under Laura's feet.
Simple Subject The dry earth slid under Laura's feet.

The **predicate** is the part of the sentence that tells what the subject is or does. All the words in the predicate are called the **complete predicate.** The **simple predicate,** or **verb,** is the most important word in the complete predicate. A simple predicate can be more than one word, as in *had lived.*

Complete Predicate The dry earth slid under Laura's feet.
Simple Predicate The dry earth slid under Laura's feet.

A **compound subject** is made up of two or more simple subjects. A **compound predicate** is made up of two or more simple predicates.

Compound Subject Laura and Mary went swimming.
Compound Predicate They splashed and played in the water.

Directions Underline the complete subject of each sentence once. Underline the complete predicate twice.

1. The girls went to the creek.
2. They waded in the shallow water and pulled on the rushes.
3. Laura and Mary laughed that night at dinner.
4. Their father promised to take them to the water hole.

Directions Circle the simple subject and the simple predicate of each sentence.

5. Tall willows stood around the pool.
6. Laura waded into the pool.
7. Something had pulled her leg from below.
8. Her father was joking with her.

Unit 1 On the Banks of Plum Creek Grammar 3

Grammar Transparency 3, TR DVD

English Language Learners

Leveled support: Subjects and predicates Have students identify and complete subject-predicate patterns in sentences.

Beginning Say two word sentences such as: *Eagles fly; Cars move.* Have students identify the subject and predicate in each.

Intermediate Say a subject and have students complete the sentence with a predicate. Then say a predicate and have them fill in the subject. For example:

The boys ________; ________ *came to visit.*

Advanced/Advanced High Have students complete the intermediate activity in writing.

Handwriting If students have difficulty writing their names in cursive, write samples for them to follow.

Objectives

- Understand and identify the features of a parody.

MINI-LESSON

5-Day Planner

Guide to Mini-Lessons

DAY 1	Read Like a Writer
DAY 2	Order of Events
DAY 3	Use Language to Match Purpose
DAY 4	Revising Strategy: Consolidating
DAY 5	Proofread for Complete Sentences

Writing—Parody
Introduce

MINI-LESSON

Read Like a Writer

INTERACT with TEXT

Reader's and Writer's Notebook p. 63

Introduce This week you will write a parody. A parody is a written work that imitates the style of another author or written work, using humor or exaggeration.

Prompt	Write a parody of *On the Banks of Plum Creek.*
Trait	Voice
Mode	Narrative

Examine Model Text Let's read a parody of *Lewis and Clark and Me.* Have students read "Lewis and Clark and NOT ME," on p. 63 of the *Reader's and Writer's Notebook.*

Key Features A parody is a humorous or exaggerated imitation of another written work. Have students draw a box around a humorous or exaggerated part of this parody that reminds them of an event in *Lewis and Clark and Me.*

A parody follows the style and voice of the original written work. Have volunteers read aloud parts of this model that are similar to the style and voice in *Lewis and Clark and Me.*

A parody makes a clear **connection** with the characters, setting, or subject of the original written work. Have students circle characters, setting, and events in this model that remind them of those in *Lewis and Clark and Me.* Explain that a parody is an imaginative story that contains details about the characters and setting and that is related to the original story in a humorous or exaggerated way.

Review
Key features

Review the key features of a parody with students. You may want to post the key features in the classroom for students to refer to as they work on their stories.

Key Features of a Parody

- imitates another work, usually with humor
- follows the form of the original
- changes or exaggerates parts of the original work

ROUTINE **Quick Write for Fluency** Team Talk

1. **Talk** Have partners talk about the important features of a parody.
2. **Write** Each student writes a sentence summarizing what a parody is.
3. **Share** Have partners read their own writing to each other.

Routines Flip Chart

Wrap Up Your Day

- **Build Concepts** What did you learn about why we want to explore new places?
- **Oral Vocabulary** Have students use the Amazing Words they learned in context sentences.
- **Homework** Send home this week's Family Times Newsletter in *Let's Practice It!* pp. 20–21 on the *Teacher Resources DVD-ROM.*

Let's Practice It!
TR DVD•20–21

Writing to Learn

When a student writes a sentence, provide her with at least one reader so that she learns how her language communicates. That reader may be a partner, a family member, the teacher, or a group of classmates. Writing comes alive and has a purpose when it has an audience.

English Language Learners

Leveled support: Activate prior knowledge Prepare students to begin their parodies of *On the Banks of Plum Creek.*
Beginning Ask students yes/no questions about characters and events in the story.
Intermediate Ask students multiple-choice questions about the characters, setting, and events of the story.
Advanced/Advanced High Have partners take turns telling each other the events that took place in the story.

Tell students that tomorrow they will read about a girl who explores her new home on the prairie.

Objectives

- Expand the weekly concept.
- Develop oral vocabulary.

Today at a Glance

Oral Vocabulary
landscape, sights

Word Analysis
Word ending *-ing*

Literary Terms
Foreshadowing

Story Structure
Conflict and resolution

Lesson Vocabulary
◎ Multiple-meaning words

Reading
"Foggy River Schoolhouse"
On the Banks of Plum Creek

Fluency
Rate and accuracy

Research and Inquiry
Navigate/Search

Spelling
Long *e* and *o*

Conventions
Complete subjects and predicates

Writing
Parody

Concept Talk

Question of the Week

Why do we want to explore new places?

Expand the concept

Remind students of the weekly concept question. Tell students that today they will begin reading *On the Banks of Plum Creek.* As they read, encourage students to think about why people have wanted to explore new places throughout history.

Anchored Talk

Develop oral vocabulary

Use the photos on pp. 78–79 and the Read Aloud, "Going Places," to talk about the Amazing Words: *route, coast, desert,* and *valleys*. Add the vocabulary words to the concept map to develop students' knowledge of the topic. Discuss the following questions. Remind students to listen attentively to other students and answer with appropriate detail. Encourage students to build on others' ideas when they answer.

- Why might you want to travel along a *route* that winds beside the *coast*?
- If you visited a *desert* in the United States, what different features would you write about or photograph?
- Why might you find rivers or streams running through *valleys*?

Oral Vocabulary
Amazing Words

Amazing Words

route
coast
desert
valleys
landscape
sights
landmarks
enormous
magnificent
navigate

Teach Amazing Words

Amazing Words Oral Vocabulary Routine

1. **Introduce** Write the Amazing Word *landscape* on the board. Have students say it aloud with you. Relate *landscape* to the photographs on pp. 78-79 and "Going Places." What type of *landscape* would you photograph in your neighborhood? When you visit your favorite vacation spot, what type of *landscape* would be featured on a postcard you mail to your friend? Have students determine the definition of the word. (A *landscape* is the land and natural scenery that can be seen in one glance.)
2. **Demonstrate** Have students answer questions to demonstrate understanding. What might the *landscape* look like if you climbed up to a high point? What type of *landscape* would you see if you took a boat ride along a coast?
3. **Apply** Have students apply their understanding. What type of *landscape* do you find most inspiring?

See p. OV•3 to teach *sights*.

Routine Flip Chart

Apply Amazing Words

As students read "Foggy River Schoolhouse" on p. 83, have them think about the *landscape* outside the narrator's schoolroom and the different *sights* along the creek.

Connect to reading

Explain that today students will read about a curious pioneer girl. Help students establish purpose for reading. As they read, they should think about how the Question of the Week and the Amazing Words *landscape* and *sights* apply to the curious pioneer girl.

ELL Reinforce Vocabulary Use the Day 2 instruction on ELL Poster 3 to teach lesson vocabulary and discuss the lesson concept.

ELL Poster 3

Objectives

- Use word affix *-ing* to determine meanings of grade-level academic English words.
- Understand foreshadowing in fiction to explain the plot's main events' influence on future events.
- Understand conflict and resolution in the plot by summarizing the plot's main events.

Word Analysis
Word Ending *-ing*

Teach word ending *-ing* Tell students that the word ending *-ing* has different functions. This affix can be added to verbs to form nouns or adjectives. Display the word *towering.* Have students underline the base word and circle the word ending *-ing.*

Model Think Aloud This word is *towering.* The word ending *-ing* has been added to the verb *tower. Tower* means "to rise high." When I add the word ending *-ing* to *tower,* it becomes an adjective. I think *towering* describes something that is very high. When I look up *towering* in the dictionary, I find that its meaning is the same as my definition.

Guide practice Use the Routine to guide practice in reading and understanding multisyllabic words with the word ending *-ing.*

On their own Display the words *barking, smiling, grazing,* and *fishing.* Have students work in pairs to circle the word endings and underline the base words. Then have students generate a definition for each word. Have students check their definitions with a dictionary. Follow the Strategy for Meaningful Word Parts to teach the word *sewing.*

ROUTINE Strategy for Meaningful Word Parts

1. **Introduce word parts** Display the word *sewing.* Circle the word ending *-ing* and underline the base word *sew.*
2. **Connect to meaning** I see the word *sew*. I know that the verb *sew* means "to work with a needle and thread." When we add the word ending *-ing*, the new word can be a noun, a verb, or an adjective. As a noun, I think that *sewing* means "the work done with a needle and thread." As an adjective, I think *sewing* describes a place or thing that is for sewing, such as a sewing room or a sewing machine. I check a dictionary to confirm my definitions.
3. **Read the word** Blend the meaningful word parts together to read *sewing.* Continue the Routine with the words *amazing* and *ringing.*

Routines Flip Chart

Literary Terms
Foreshadowing

Teach foreshadowing Tell students that hints and clues about what will happen later in a story are called *foreshadowing.* We can use foreshadowing to explain the plot's main events' influence on future events. Foreshadowing is used mainly in fiction.

Model foreshadowing Think Aloud Let's look at "The 'Broken' Arm" on page 81. What hints or clues does the author give us about Harriet before she pretends to have a broken arm? (Harriet boils up inside about having to do the dishes two nights in a row. Then she gets an idea.) The author uses foreshadowing to help us guess that Harriet will attempt to get out of washing dishes the following evening.

Guide practice Find an example of foreshadowing in *On the Banks of Plum Creek.* Be sure to point out the hints and clues the author provides.

On their own Have students look for examples of foreshadowing in other selections in their Student Edition.

Story Structure
Conflict and Resolution

Teach conflict and resolution In stories, the events of a plot develop as a result of a **conflict,** or a force that sets the story in motion. The outcome or conclusion of the conflict is the **resolution.** Summarizing the plot's main events can help us determine the conflict and resolution.

Model the strategy Think Aloud When I read *On the Banks of Plum Creek,* I'll discover the problem, or conflict, that sets the events of the story in motion. As I read further, I can summarize the main events. That will help me explain how the conflict reached a resolution.

Guide practice Have students identify the conflict and resolution in "The 'Broken' Arm."

On their own Have students discuss with partners a conflict they faced and the events that lead to its resolution. Encourage volunteers to share a story with the class.

Academic Vocabulary

foreshadowing hints or clues given beforehand about what will happen later in a story

Objectives

- ◎ Use a dictionary or glossary to confirm the meanings of multiple-meaning words.
- Read grade-level text with rate and accuracy.

Vocabulary Strategy for ◎ Multiple-Meaning Words

Student Edition p. W•10

Teach multiple-meaning words

Envision It!

Tell students that when they encounter a multiple-meaning word, or a word with more than one meaning, they can look at the context of the sentence to determine its meaning. Then they should use the strategy of looking up the word in a dictionary or glossary to confirm that they have used the word's correct meaning. Refer students to *Words!* on p. W•10 in the Student Edition for additional practice. Then read "Foggy River Schoolhouse" on p. 83 with students.

Model the strategy

Think Aloud Write on the board: *The flat creek bank was warm, soft mud.* I know one meaning of *bank* is "a business that lends, exchanges, and takes care of money." That meaning doesn't make sense here. The clues in the sentence suggest that *bank* has something to do with a creek and mud. To confirm the word's meaning, I will use the dictionary/glossary strategy for help. When I look up *bank* in a dictionary, I see that there is more than one entry for *bank*. I read through the definitions and realize how *bank* is used in the text. It means "the rising ground at the edge of a lake, river, or sea."

Guide practice

Write this sentence on the board: *The rushes in the wind made a wild, lonely sound.* Have students determine the meaning of *rushes* by looking the word up in a dictionary and reading through the entries until they discover the definition that makes sense in the context of the sentence. For additional support, use *Envision It! Pictured Vocabulary Cards* or *Tested Vocabulary Cards.*

On their own

Read "Foggy River Schoolhouse" on p. 83. Have students use context clues, along with a dictionary or glossary, to list the definitions for the lesson vocabulary. For additional practice use *Reader's and Writer's Notebook* p. 64.

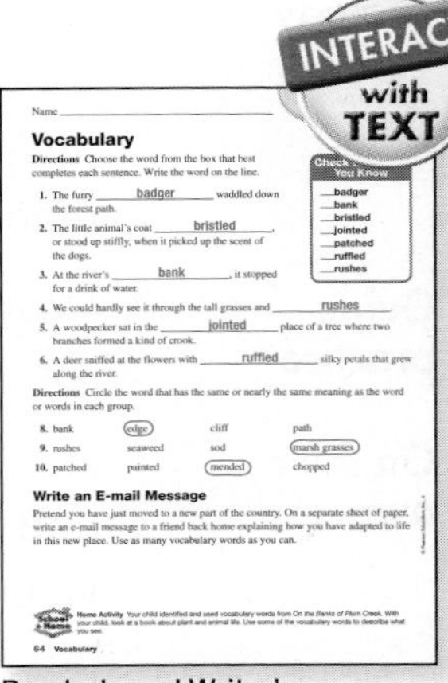
INTERACT with TEXT

Name ______

Vocabulary

Directions Choose the word from the box that best completes each sentence. Write the word on the line.

Check the Words You Know: badger, bank, bristled, jointed, patched, ruffled, rushes

1. The furry __badger__ waddled down the forest path.
2. The little animal's coat __bristled__, or stood up stiffly, when it picked up the scent of the dogs.
3. At the river's __bank__, it stopped for a drink of water.
4. We could hardly see it through the tall grasses and __rushes__.
5. A woodpecker sat in the __jointed__ place of a tree where two branches formed a kind of crook.
6. A deer sniffed at the flowers with __ruffled__ silky petals that grew along the river.

Directions Circle the word that has the same or nearly the same meaning as the word or words in each group.

8.	bank	(edge)	cliff	path
9.	rushes	seaweed	sod	(marsh grasses)
10.	patched	painted	(mended)	chopped

Write an E-mail Message

Pretend you have just moved to a new part of the country. On a separate sheet of paper, write an e-mail message to a friend back home explaining how you have adapted to life in this new place. Use as many vocabulary words as you can.

Home Activity Your child identified and used vocabulary words from *On the Banks of Plum Creek*. With your child, look at a book about plant and animal life. Use some of the vocabulary words to describe what you see.

64 Vocabulary

Reader's and Writer's Notebook p. 64

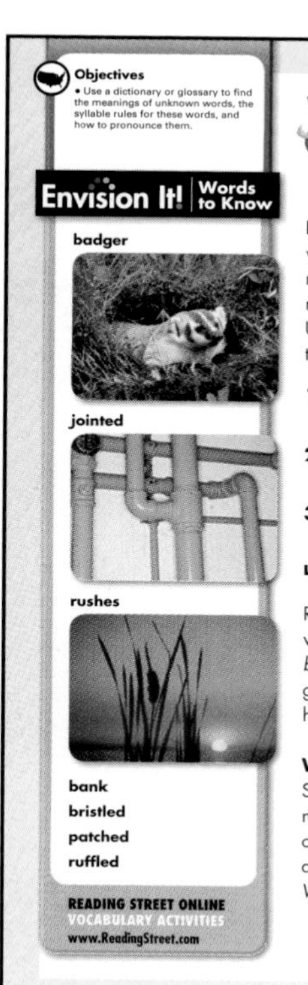

Objectives
- Use a dictionary or glossary to find the meanings of unknown words, the syllable rules for these words, and how to pronounce them.

Envision It! | **Words to Know**

badger

jointed

rushes

bank

bristled

patched

ruffled

READING STREET ONLINE
VOCABULARY ACTIVITIES
www.ReadingStreet.com

Vocabulary Strategy for

Multiple-Meaning Words

Dictionary/Glossary You may read a word whose meaning you know, but the word doesn't make sense in the sentence. The word may have more than one meaning, or multiple meanings. Use a dictionary or glossary to find the meaning that fits.

1. Try the meaning that you know. Does it make sense in the sentence?
2. If it doesn't, look up the word to see what other meanings it has.
3. Read all the meanings given for the word. Try each meaning in the sentence.
4. Choose the one that makes the most sense.

Read "Foggy River Schoolhouse." Stop at any words that have multiple meanings, such as *bank* or *ruffled.* Look them up in a dictionary or glossary to see what other meanings they could have.

Words to Write Reread "Foggy River Schoolhouse." Imagine that you live in the nineteenth century and go to school in a one-room schoolhouse. Write a journal entry describing a typical day. Use words from the *Words to Know* list.

82

Foggy River Schoolhouse

My older brother, Edward, got me in trouble today. He wanted to make me laugh, so he threw sticky burrs at me during Miss Osgood's arithmetic lesson. Some of the burrs landed on my desk and were easy to throw right back at Edward, but a few of those bristled burrs got caught in the folds of my ruffled petticoat. I had such trouble getting them unstuck from the cloth that Edward couldn't hold in his laughter. Miss Osgood was not happy and she sent both of us to the corner to face the wall.

My teacher, Miss Osgood, calls me a "country girl" because I'd rather play outside in the rushes than sit inside and learn arithmetic. Who would blame me! That schoolroom can get pretty cramped. All of the students from Foggy River learn in the same room. I do love to practice drawing the jointed letters of the alphabet, but I'd much rather do it on the soft bank of the open creek where I might catch a glimpse of a badger or a beaver.

Maybe when I get older I'll like being at school more. Then I'll be able to chop wood for the stove and fetch water, which means I'll get to go outside! Edward is older, so he gets to do these chores. My school chore is to clap the erasers.

Even at home, my chores keep me inside. Tonight I have to mend the hole in Edward's patched flannel shirt. Maybe I'll choose a mismatched color for his patch!

Your Turn!

Need a Review? For additional help with using a dictionary or glossary to determine the meaning of multiple-meaning words, see *Words!*

Ready to Try It? Read *On the Banks of Plum Creek* on pp. 84–99.

83

Student Edition pp. 82–83

Lesson Vocabulary

badger a burrowing, flesh-eating mammal

bank the rising ground at the edge of a lake, river, or sea

bristled stand up straight, as hair or fur

jointed having one or more places where two things or parts are joined

patched mended with a scrap of material

ruffled made to look as if trimmed with strips of material gathered together like ruffles

rushes marsh plants with hollow stems

Differentiated Instruction

Strategic Intervention

Multiple-meaning words Have students select a word from this week's lesson vocabulary and write two definitions for it, using a dictionary to check meanings.

Reread for Fluency

Rate and Accuracy

Model fluent reading Read the first paragraph of "Foggy River Schoolhouse" aloud, focusing on rate and accuracy. Tell students that you are reading the paragraph at a moderate rate, pausing between phrases and between sentences, and reading precisely by avoiding errors.

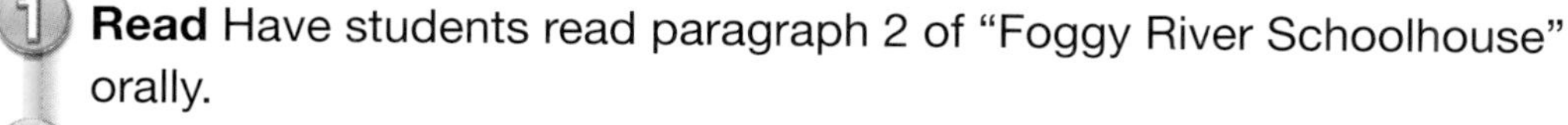

ROUTINE Oral Rereading

1. **Read** Have students read paragraph 2 of "Foggy River Schoolhouse" orally.
2. **Reread** To achieve optimal fluency, students should reread the text three or four times with appropriate rate and accuracy.
3. **Corrective Feedback** Listen as students read. Provide corrective feedback regarding their oral reading, paying attention to rate and accuracy.

Routines Flip Chart

English Language Learners

Build Academic Vocabulary Use the lesson vocabulary pictured on p. 82 to teach the meanings of *badger, jointed,* and *rushes.* Call on pairs to write the words on sticky notes and use them to label images of the words on the ELL Poster.

Objectives

- Understand the elements of historical fiction.
- Use text features to preview and predict.
- Set a purpose for reading.

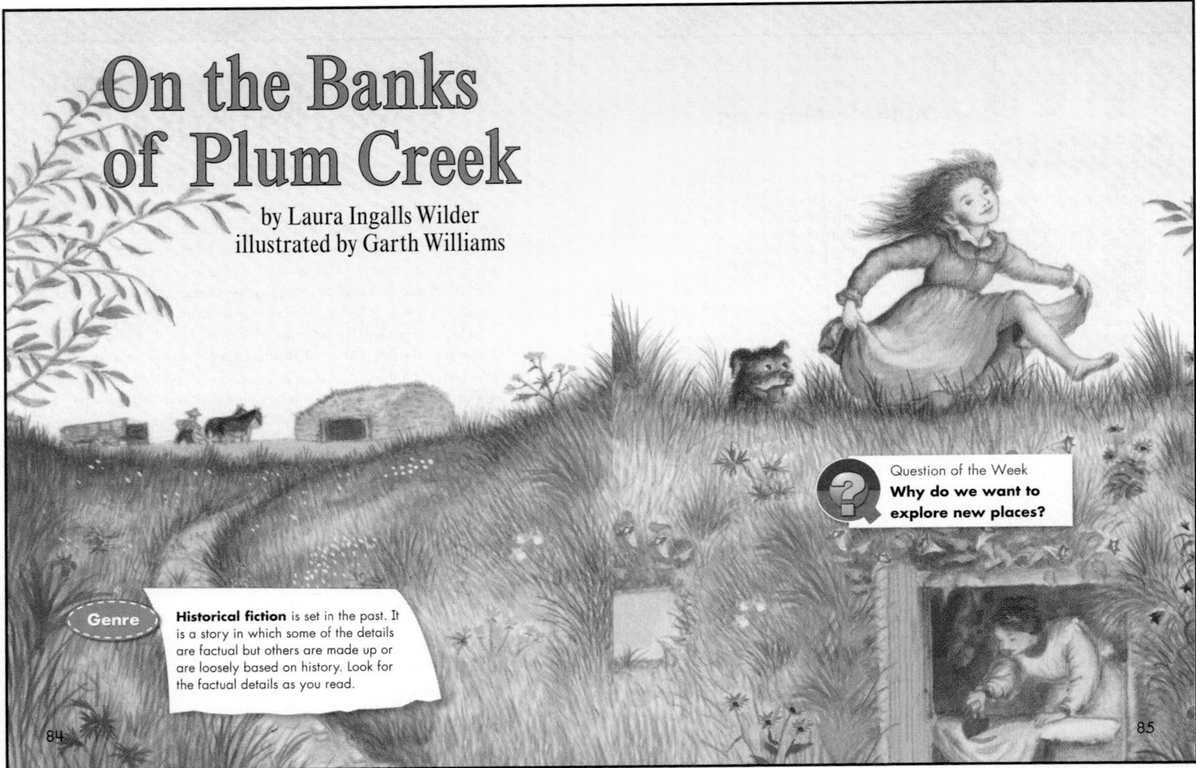

On the Banks of Plum Creek
by Laura Ingalls Wilder
illustrated by Garth Williams
Question of the Week
Why do we want to explore new places?
Genre
Historical fiction is set in the past. It is a story in which some of the details are factual but others are made up or are loosely based on history. Look for the factual details as you read.
84
85

Student Edition pp. 84–85

Build Background

Discuss new places

Team Talk Have students turn to a partner and discuss the Question of the Week and these questions about new places. Guide students in answering the questions with appropriate detail and providing suggestions that build upon the ideas of others.

- What new place would you like to visit on vacation?
- How would you travel there?
- How did people in the past travel to new places?
- What do people explore and visit after arriving at new places?

Connect to selection

Have students discuss their answers with the class. Possible responses: I would like to visit the Grand Canyon on vacation. I would take an airplane to Colorado. People in the past rode to new places on trains and in stage-coaches. When people arrive at new places, they explore the landscape and visit the landmarks. For additional opportunities to build background, use the Background Building Audio.

Prereading Strategies

Genre Explain that **historical fiction** is realistic fiction that takes place in the past. It is a combination of imagination and fact, for fictional characters are placed in a historically factual setting to act out a fictional plot.

Preview and predict Have students preview the title, illustrations, and headings in *On the Banks of Plum Creek*. Have them predict what they think the story is about.

Set purpose Prior to reading, have students set their own purposes for reading this selection, based on their own desired outcome to enhance comprehension. To help students set a purpose, ask them to think about how new places can be exciting to explore.

Strategy Response Log

INTERACT with TEXT

Have students begin filling out the *Know* column on their KWL Charts on p. 9 in the *Reader's and Writer's Notebook*. Then have them think about what they want to find out and list it in the *What* column.

Small Group Time

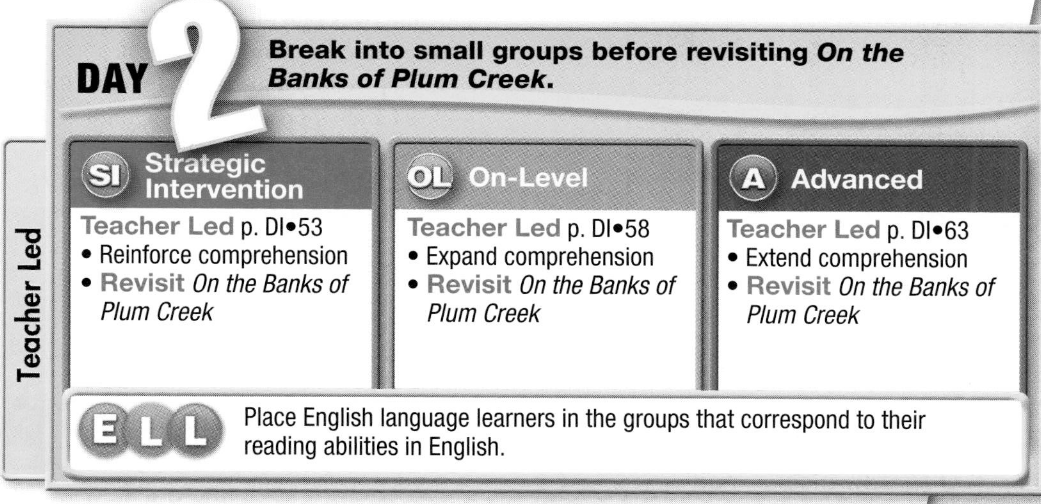

DAY 2 **Break into small groups before revisiting *On the Banks of Plum Creek.***

Teacher Led

SI Strategic Intervention	OL On-Level	A Advanced
Teacher Led p. DI•53 • Reinforce comprehension • **Revisit** *On the Banks of Plum Creek*	**Teacher Led** p. DI•58 • Expand comprehension • **Revisit** *On the Banks of Plum Creek*	**Teacher Led** p. DI•63 • Extend comprehension • **Revisit** *On the Banks of Plum Creek*

ELL Place English language learners in the groups that correspond to their reading abilities in English.

Practice Stations
- Words to Know
- Get Fluent
- Word Wise

Independent Activities
- Background Building Audio
- *Reader's and Writer's Notebook*
- Research and Inquiry

Differentiated Instruction

A Advanced

Have students make a time line showing different methods of transportation. They should write dates for each transportation method in time order from left to right and then add details along the line.

Multidraft Reading

For **Whole Group** instruction, choose one of the reading options below. For each reading, have students set the purpose indicated.

Option 1

Day 2 Read the selection. Use Guide Comprehension to monitor and clarify understanding.

Day 3 Reread the selection. Use Extend Thinking to develop higher-order thinking skills.

Option 2

Day 2 Read the first half of the selection, using both Guide Comprehension and Extend Thinking instruction.

Day 3 Read the second half of the selection, using both Guide Comprehension and Extend Thinking instruction.

English Language Learners

Build background To build background, review the selection summary in English *(ELL Handbook*, p. 43). Use the Retelling Cards to provide visual support for the summary.

DAY 2 # Read and Comprehend

Objectives

- Determine the meaning of multiple-meaning words using the context of the sentence.

OPTION 1 Guide Comprehension Skills and Strategies

Teach Multiple-Meaning Words

Multiple-Meaning Words Have students use a dictionary and the context of the sentence to determine the meaning of the multiple-meaning word *rushes* on p. 86.

Corrective Feedback

If… students are unable to figure out the meaning of *rushes*,
then… model how to determine its meaning.

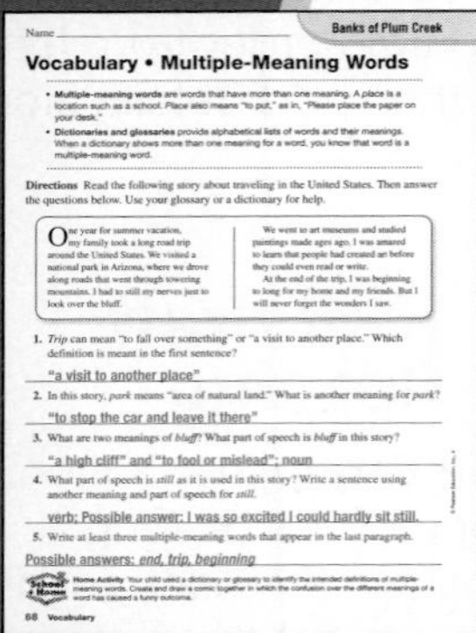
Name

Banks of Plum Creek

Vocabulary • Multiple-Meaning Words

- **Multiple-meaning words** are words that have more than one meaning. A *place* is a location such as a school. *Place* also means "to put," as in, "Please place the paper on your desk."
- **Dictionaries and glossaries** provide alphabetical lists of words and their meanings. When a dictionary shows more than one meaning for a word, you know that word is a multiple-meaning word.

Directions Read the following story about traveling in the United States. Then answer the questions below. Use your glossary or a dictionary for help.

One year for summer vacation, my family took a long road trip around the United States. We visited a national park in Arizona, where we drove along roads that went through towering mountains. I had to still my nerves just to look over the bluff.

We went to art museums and studied paintings made ages ago. I was amazed to learn that people had created art before they could even read or write.

At the end of the trip, I was beginning to long for my home and my friends. But I will never forget the wonders I saw.

1. *Trip* can mean "to fall over something" or "a visit to another place." Which definition is meant in the first sentence?
"a visit to another place"
2. In this story, *park* means "area of natural land." What is another meaning for *park*?
"to stop the car and leave it there"
3. What are two meanings of *bluff*? What part of speech is *bluff* in this story?
"a high cliff" and "to fool or mislead"; noun
4. What part of speech is *still* as it is used in this story? Write a sentence using another meaning and part of speech for *still*.
verb; Possible answer: I was so excited I could hardly sit still.
5. Write at least three multiple-meaning words that appear in the last paragraph.
Possible answers: *end, trip, beginning*

Home Activity Your child used a dictionary or glossary to identify the intended definitions of multiple-meaning words. Create and draw a comic together in which the confusion over the different meanings of a word has caused a funny outcome.

68 Vocabulary

Reader's and Writer's Notebook p. 68

Model the Skill

Think Aloud I am not sure what the word *rushes* means. When I look up the word in a dictionary, it has two possible meanings. It could mean "to move quickly" or "a marsh plant with a hollow stem."

Rushes and Flags

Every morning after Mary and Laura had done the dishes, made their bed and swept the floor, they could go out to play.

All around the door the morning-glory flowers were fresh and new, springing with all their might out of the green leaves. All along Plum Creek the birds were talking. Sometimes a bird sang, but mostly they talked. "Tweet, tweet, oh twitter twee twit!" one said. Then another said, "Chee, Chee, Chee," and another laughed, "Ha ha ha, tiraloo!"

Laura and Mary went over the top of their house and down along the path where Pa led the oxen to water.

There along the creek rushes were growing, and blue flags. Every morning the blue flags were new. They stood up dark blue and proud among the green rushes.

Each blue flag had three velvet petals that curved down like a lady's dress over hoops. From its waist three ruffled silky petals stood up and curved together. When Laura looked down inside them, she saw three narrow pale tongues, and each tongue had a strip of golden fur on it.

Sometimes a fat bumble-bee, all black velvet and gold, was bumbling and butting there.

The flat creek bank was warm, soft mud. Little pale-yellow and pale-blue butterflies hovered there, and alighted and sipped. Bright dragonflies flew on blurry wings. The mud squeezed up between Laura's toes. Where she stepped, and where Mary stepped, and where the oxen had walked, there were tiny pools of water in their footprints.

86

Student Edition pp. 86–87

Literary Elements: Setting • Analysis In what type of place does Laura live? Use details from the selection in your answer. Possible response: Laura lives on the prairie near Plum Creek, where rushes and flowers grow.

OPTION 2 Extend Thinking Think Critically

Higher-Order Thinking Skills

Multiple-Meaning Words • Analysis Using the context of the sentence, determine the meaning of the multiple-meaning word *shallow* on page 87. Possible response: Since Laura and Mary were wading in the water, it must not be very deep. I think that *shallow* means "not very deep."

Which meaning do you think the author means? (a marsh plant with a hollow stem) In the context of the sentence, a marsh plant makes more sense as something that would grow along a creek.

Where they waded in the shallow water a footprint would not stay. First a swirl like smoke came up from it and wavered away in the clear water. Then the footprint slowly melted. The toes smoothed out and the heel was only a small hollow.

There were tiny fishes in the water. They were so small that you could hardly see them. Only when they went swiftly sometimes a silvery belly flashed. When Laura and Mary stood still these little fishes swarmed around their feet and nibbled. It was a tickly feeling.

On top of the water the water-bugs skated. They had tall legs, and each of their feet made a wee dent in the water. It was hard to see a water-bug; he skated so fast that before you saw him he was somewhere else.

The rushes in the wind made a wild, lonely sound. They were not soft and flat like grass; they were hard and round and sleek and jointed. One day when Laura was wading in a deep place by the rushes, she took hold of a big one to pull herself up on the bank. It squeaked.

For a minute Laura could hardly breathe. Then she pulled another. It squeaked, and came in two.

87

Genre • Evaluation Should you expect this selection to be realistic or imaginary? Why? Possible response: It will be realistic. Historical fiction takes place in a factual setting that shows us how the characters lived and contains details that fit the time and the place.

On Their Own

Have students use a dictionary to figure out the meaning of the word *flags* on p. 86. (plants of the iris family with large flowers) For additional practice, use *Reader's and Writer's Notebook*, p. 68.

Differentiated Instruction

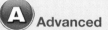

Strategic Intervention

Author's craft Explain that the author, Laura Ingalls Wilder, was an American author who wrote a series of books about her pioneer childhood. Tell students that these stories are fictional, as the author often combined several characters into one and put incidents side by side. Have students discuss reasons why the author might have done this, such as to make her stories more exciting.

Advanced

Critical thinking Have students discuss what chores pioneer children performed and what pastimes they enjoyed. How do these compare to modern-day chores and pastimes?

English Language Learners

Activate prior knowledge Use a T-chart to record students' prior knowledge of houses on the prairie in the mid-1800s and today. We're going to read about how a pioneer family moved to a homestead and lived in a sod house and then in a new cabin with real glass windows. Ask students questions about housing and record their answers in the chart, adding to them as students read the selection.

Objectives

- Sequence the plot's main events to improve comprehension.

OPTION 1 Skills and Strategies, continued

Teach Sequence

Review **Sequence** Explain that sometimes it helps to picture the events in our minds in order to understand the sequence. Have students determine the sequence of events, or order in which things happen, on p. 89. (The family travels past the cattle path, down a steep bank, across a grassy spot, past the tableland, and to the creek bank.)

Corrective Feedback

If... students have a problem determining the sequence of the plot's main events,
then... model how to identify the order of events in the story.

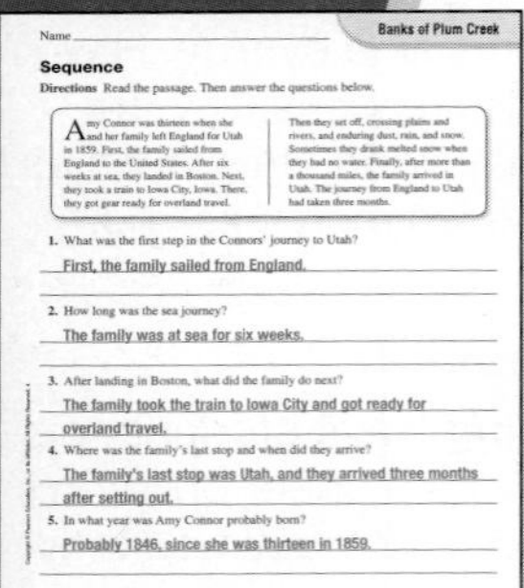
Name ______ Banks of Plum Creek

Sequence

Directions Read the passage. Then answer the questions below.

Amy Connor was thirteen when she and her family left England for Utah in 1859. First, the family sailed from England to the United States. After six weeks at sea, they landed in Boston. Next, they took a train to Iowa City, Iowa. There, they got gear ready for overland travel. Then they set off, crossing plains and rivers, and enduring dust, rain, and snow. Sometimes they drank melted snow when they had no water. Finally, after more than a thousand miles, the family arrived in Utah. The journey from England to Utah had taken three months.

1. What was the first step in the Connors' journey to Utah?
First, the family sailed from England.
2. How long was the sea journey?
The family was at sea for six weeks.
3. After landing in Boston, what did the family do next?
The family took the train to Iowa City and got ready for overland travel.
4. Where was the family's last stop and when did they arrive?
The family's last stop was Utah, and they arrived three months after setting out.
5. In what year was Amy Connor probably born?
Probably 1846, since she was thirteen in 1859.

Home Activity Your child identified sequence in a story about a pioneer girl. Talk with your child about what it would have been like to move far away to a new home in the 1800s.

Comprehension DVD•23

Let's Practice It!
TR DVD•23

Model the Skill

Think Aloud In this passage, the events happen in an order that I can visualize. I can picture in my mind what is happening to figure out the order of events. Then I can reread to see if the order that I have figured out makes sense.

The rushes were little hollow tubes, fitted together at the joints. The tubes squeaked when you pulled them apart. They squeaked when you pushed them together again.

Laura and Mary pulled them apart to hear them squeak. Then they put little ones together to make necklaces. They put big ones together to make long tubes. They blew through the tubes into the creek and made it bubble. They blew at the little fishes and scared them. Whenever they were thirsty, they could draw up long drinks of water through those tubes.

Ma laughed when Laura and Mary came to dinner and supper, all splashed and muddy, with green necklaces around their necks and the long green tubes in their hands. They brought her bouquets of the blue flags and she put them on the table to make it pretty.

"I declare," she said, "you two play in the creek so much, you'll be turning to water-bugs!"

Pa and Ma did not care how much they played in the creek. Only they must never go upstream beyond the little willow valley. The creek came around a curve there. It came out of a hole full of deep, dark water. They must never go near enough to that hole, even to see it.

"Some day I'll take you there," Pa promised them. And one Sunday afternoon he told them that this was the day.

88

Student Edition pp. 88–89

OPTION 2 Think Critically, continued

Higher-Order Thinking Skills

Review **Sequence • Analysis** Describe, in sequential order, how Laura and Mary used the reeds as straws. Possible response: First they pulled apart the reeds and then they fit together big tubes to make longer tubes. Next, they blew through the tubes to make bubbles and scare the fish. When they became thirsty, they drank creek water through the tubes.

Foreshadowing • Evaluation The main character, Laura, often gets in trouble. What clues hint at what trouble she might get into later in the story? Explain how they may influence future events. Possible response: Laura's parents forbid her to go near or even to look at the hole of deep, dark water. I think that Laura might disobey and go near the water because she is curious.

Deep Water

In the dugout Laura and Mary took off all their clothes and over their bare skins they put on old patched dresses. Ma tied on her sunbonnet, Pa took Carrie on his arm, and they all set out.

They went past the cattle path and the rushes, past the willow valley and the plum thickets. They went down a steep, grassy bank, and then across a level place where the grass was tall and coarse. They passed a high, almost straight-up wall of earth where no grass grew.

"What is that, Pa?" Laura asked; and Pa said, "That is a tableland, Laura."

He pushed on through the thick, tall grass, making a path for Ma and Mary and Laura. Suddenly they came out of the high grass and the creek was there.

It ran twinkling over white gravel into a wide pool, curved against a low bank where the grass was short. Tall willows stood up on the other side of the pool. Flat on the water lay a shimmery picture of those willows, with every green leaf fluttering.

89

Draw Conclusions • Evaluation What can you conclude about the region where Laura and her family live? Would you want to be a neighbor? Why or why not? Possible response: I think they must live in a very isolated area because there are no other children for Laura to play with other than her sisters. It sounds like they have fun and enjoy nature, so I'd like to be a neighbor and join in these activities.

On Their Own

Have students continue to visualize to determine the sequence of events as they read. For additional practice, use *Let's Practice It!* p. 23 on the *Teacher Resources DVD-ROM.*

Differentiated Instruction

Strategic Intervention

Foreshadowing Arrange students in small groups to discuss foreshadowing in folk tales and fairy tales. What hints let them guess the fate of the characters, such as the misfortune of the protagonist?

Advanced

Foreshadowing Have students describe how foreshadowing can build suspense by raising questions that encourage them to read onward to discover more about the event being foreshadowed.

English Language Learners

Vocabulary: Unfamiliar words Focus students' attention on the word *tableland* on p. 89. Laura describes this area as high and grassless. A tableland is a flat elevated area, such as a mesa. Ask students what other land features characterize the prairie where the Ingalls family lives.

Background knowledge Read aloud the fifth paragraph on p. 88. Have students think about the setting and how Laura and Mary spend their days. Why would Pa forbid Laura and Mary to go near the water hole? (Pa knows that Laura and Mary enjoy spending hours alone playing in the water, and he is worried that they might drown.)

DAY 2 Read and Comprehend

Objectives

- Understand the interaction between character, setting, and plot.

OPTION 1 Skills and Strategies, continued

Teach Literary Elements

Literary Elements: Character, Setting, Plot Have students determine how the setting and events in the plot affect Laura's character, including the changes she undergoes.

Corrective Feedback

If... students are having difficulty understanding Laura's character,
then... model relating the setting in which she lives and the events in the plot to Laura's character.

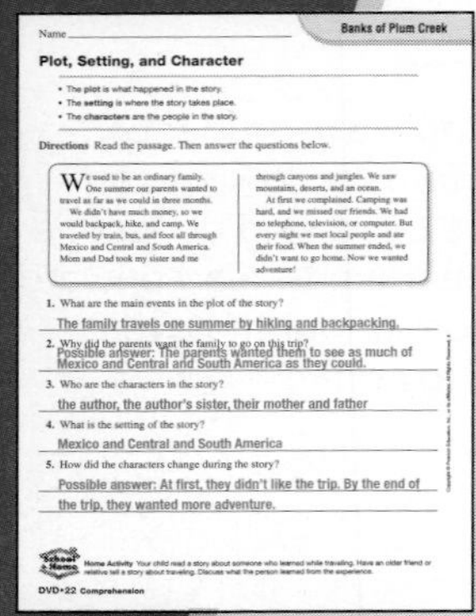

Name ______________ Banks of Plum Creek

Plot, Setting, and Character

- The **plot** is what happened in the story.
- The **setting** is where the story takes place.
- The **characters** are the people in the story.

Directions Read the passage. Then answer the questions below.

We used to be an ordinary family. One summer our parents wanted to travel as far as we could in three months.

We didn't have much money, so we would backpack, hike, and camp. We traveled by train, bus, and foot all through Mexico and Central and South America. Mom and Dad took my sister and me through canyons and jungles. We saw mountains, deserts, and an ocean.

At first we complained. Camping was hard, and we missed our friends. We had no telephone, television, or computer. But every night we met local people and ate their food. When the summer ended, we didn't want to go home. Now we wanted adventure!

1. What are the main events in the plot of the story?
   The family travels one summer by hiking and backpacking.
2. Why did the parents want the family to go on this trip?
   Possible answer: The parents wanted them to see as much of Mexico and Central and South America as they could.
3. Who are the characters in the story?
   the author, the author's sister, their mother and father
4. What is the setting of the story?
   Mexico and Central and South America
5. How did the characters change during the story?
   Possible answer: At first, they didn't like the trip. By the end of the trip, they wanted more adventure.

Home Activity Your child read a story about someone who learned while traveling. Have an older friend or relative tell a story about traveling. Discuss what the person learned from the experience.

DVD•22 Comprehension

Let's Practice It!
TR DVD•22

Model the Skill

Think Aloud Laura and her family have moved to a new place. What kind of environment do they live in? (open prairie, wilderness) Does Laura obey her mother when she says not to go where the creek is deep?

Ma sat on the grassy bank and kept Carrie with her, while Laura and Mary waded into the pool.

"Stay near the edge, girls!" Ma told them. "Don't go in where it's deep."

The water came up under their skirts and made them float. Then the calico got wet and stuck to their legs. Laura went in deeper and deeper. The water came up and up, almost to her waist. She squatted down, and it came to her chin.

Everything was watery, cool, and unsteady. Laura felt very light. Her feet were so light that they almost lifted off the creek bottom. She hopped, and splashed with her arms.

"Oo, Laura, don't!" Mary cried.

"Don't go in any farther, Laura," said Ma.

Laura kept on splashing. One big splash lifted both feet. Her feet came up, her arms did as they pleased, her head went under the water. She was scared. There was nothing to hold on to, nothing solid anywhere. Then she was standing up, streaming water all over. But her feet were solid.

Nobody had seen that. Mary was tucking up her skirts, Ma was playing with Carrie. Pa was out of sight among the willows. Laura walked as fast as she could in the water. She stepped down deeper and deeper. The water came up past her middle, up to her arms.

Suddenly, deep down in the water, something grabbed her foot.

90

Student Edition pp. 90–91

Compare and Contrast • Analysis How does Mary differ from Laura? What would you predict Mary will do next? Possible response: Mary is very obedient and warns Laura not to hop around in the pool. She would probably tell Laura to start obeying her parents.

OPTION 2 Think Critically, continued

Higher-Order Thinking Skills

Literary Elements: Character, Setting, Plot • Evaluation Based on what you know about where Laura lives, or the setting of the story, and what Laura does, or the plot of the story, what do you predict that Laura might do next? Possible response: I think that she will go in even deeper and get into trouble.

(No, she wades in deeper.) What does this tell you about Laura's character? (She is curious and stubborn and likes to challenge the rules.)

On Their Own

Have students continue to use Laura's words and actions to infer character traits and predict what she will do next. For additional practice, see *Let's Practice It!* p. 22 on the *Teacher Resources DVD-ROM*.

The thing jerked, and down she went into the deep water. She couldn't breathe, she couldn't see. She grabbed and could not get hold of anything. Water filled her ears and her eyes and her mouth.

Then her head came out of the water close to Pa's head. Pa was holding her.

"Well, young lady," Pa said, "you went out too far, and how did you like it?"

Laura could not speak; she had to breathe.

"You heard Ma tell you to stay close to the bank," said Pa. "Why didn't you obey her? You deserved a ducking, and I ducked you. Next time you'll do as you're told."

"Y-yes, Pa!" Laura spluttered. "Oh, Pa, p-please do it again!"

Pa said, "Well, I'll—!" Then his great laughter rang among the willows.

"Why didn't you holler when I ducked you?" he asked Laura. "Weren't you scared?"

91

Cause and Effect • Analysis What effect did Pa's ducking have on Laura? Do you think the ducking had its intended purpose? Why or why not? Possible response: She thought it was great fun and asked him to do it again. No, I think Pa ducked Laura in order to scare her and prevent her from going deep into the water again.

Author's Purpose • Synthesis How does the author create a feeling of suspense in the passage where Laura walks deep into the water and is ducked? Possible response: The author places Laura in a dangerous situation and uses many different sensory words to describe Laura's feelings of fear.

Differentiated Instruction

Strategic Intervention

Literary elements: Character, plot, setting Arrange students in small groups, and have them discuss two characters from books and movies who have gotten into predicaments because they were naughty. Students should write a statement relating each character to the events in the plot and the setting of the story. Invite students to share their statements.

Advanced

Literary elements: Character, plot, setting Have students think about whether they'd rather read about an obedient or disobedient young character and then write a paragraph explaining why. Encourage them to discuss how the plot and setting of a story would affect the character differently if he or she were obedient or disobedient.

Connect to Social Studies

Pioneer children played a variety of games still popular today, such as skipping rope and tag. Their toys were homemade dolls and carved wooden toys. In the evening, after chores, children often danced and sang and were entertained by fiddlers.

Objectives

- Use background knowledge to monitor and adjust comprehension.

OPTION 1 Skills and Strategies, continued

Teach Background Knowledge

Background Knowledge Have students read about how Laura spent the remainder of her afternoon on p. 92. Then ask students to use their own knowledge and experience to explain why Laura considered these activities "a wonderful afternoon."

Corrective Feedback

If... students have difficulty connecting to the text,
then... model using background knowledge to monitor and adjust comprehension.

Model the Strategy

Think Aloud I know that Laura is very daring and enjoys taking risks. Based on other kids I know who are similar, I'd imagine that she enjoyed wading close to the deep water and then getting ducked many times.

"I w-was—awful scared!" Laura gasped. "But p-please do it again!" Then she asked him, "How did you get down there, Pa?"

Pa told her he had swum under water from the willows. But they could not stay in the deep water; they must go near the bank and play with Mary.

All that afternoon Pa and Laura and Mary played in the water. They waded and they fought water fights, and whenever Laura or Mary went near the deep water, Pa ducked them. Mary was a good girl after one ducking, but Laura was ducked many times.

Then it was almost chore time and they had to go home. They went dripping along the path through the tall grass, and when they came to the tableland Laura wanted to climb it.

Pa climbed part way up, and Laura and Mary climbed, holding to his hands. The dry dirt slipped and slid. Tangled grass roots hung down from the bulging edge overhead. Then Pa lifted Laura up and set her on the tableland.

It really was like a table. That ground rose up high above the tall grasses, and it was round, and flat on top. The grass there was short and soft.

Pa and Laura and Mary stood up on top of that tableland, and looked over the grass tops and the pool to the prairie beyond. They looked all around at prairies stretching to the rim of the sky.

Then they had to slide down again to the lowland and go on home. That had been a wonderful afternoon.

"It's been lots of fun," Pa said. "But you girls remember what I tell you. Don't you ever go near that swimming-hole unless I am with you."

92

Student Edition pp. 92–93

OPTION 2 Think Critically, continued

Higher-Order Thinking Skills

Background Knowledge • Synthesis Although Laura is "awful scared" when Pa dunks her, she begs him to do it again. When have you been scared yet eager to continue an activity? Possible response: I'm always scared to ride the roller coaster at the amusement park, yet I always ride it at least once each visit.

Draw Conclusions • Evaluation On page 93, the author describes the hot weather, scorching wind, and dusty earth. What can you conclude that Laura is considering after she climbs up the tableland? Possible response: I think that Laura is feeling uncomfortable in the heat and that she is considering how cool the shady swimming hole would feel after her climb.

I also know that Laura enjoys the outdoors, just like I do. The time she spent swimming, hiking, and exploring must have made up a wonderful afternoon.

On Their Own

Have students continue to use background knowledge to connect to what they are reading and adjust their understanding of the story.

Strange Animal

All the next day Laura remembered. She remembered the cool, deep water in the shade of the tall willows. She remembered that she must not go near it.

Pa was away. Mary stayed with Ma in the dugout. Laura played all alone in the hot sunshine. The blue flags were withering among the dull rushes. She went past the willow valley and played in the prairie grasses among the black-eyed Susans and goldenrod. The sunshine was very hot and the wind was scorching.

Then Laura thought of the tableland. She wanted to climb it again. She wondered if she could climb it all by herself. Pa had not said that she could not go to the tableland.

She ran down the steep bank and went across the lowland, through the tall, coarse grasses. The tableland stood up straight and high. It was very hard to climb. The dry earth slid under Laura's feet, her dress was dirty where her knees dug in while she held on to the grasses and pulled herself up. Dust itched on her sweaty skin. But at last she got her stomach on the edge; she heaved and rolled and she was on top of the tableland.

She jumped up, and she could see the deep, shady pool under the willows. It was cool and wet, and her whole skin felt thirsty. But she remembered that she must not go there.

93

Background Knowledge • Synthesis • Text to Text The author vividly describes the setting so that the reader can understand how it affects what happens in the story and influences the main character's behavior. What other story has a setting that is essential to the plot and behavior of the main character? Possible response: The setting of *Anne of Green Gables* is essential to both the plot and the main character, Anne. Green Gables, on Prince Edward Island in Canada, influences both the events and the characters in the story.

Check Predictions Have students look back at the predictions they made earlier and discuss whether they were accurate. Then have students preview the rest of the selection and either adjust their predictions accordingly or make new predictions.

Differentiated Instruction

Strategic Intervention

Draw conclusions Have students talk about Laura's actions in the swimming hole. Then have them draw conclusions about what activities she might enjoy if she lived in modern times. Partners can share their conclusions.

Advanced

Draw conclusions Have students compare Laura's and Mary's behavior in the swimming hole and draw conclusions about their personalities. Students can write a paragraph describing how both characters might behave in the schoolyard during recess or in another situation.

English Language Learners

Multiple-meaning words Focus students' attention on the word *duck* on p. 92. Tell students that this word has a variety of meanings. It can be a noun, meaning "a web-footed swimming bird." It can be a verb, meaning "to dodge or to plunge underwater." Ask students which meaning makes sense in this context.

If you want to teach this selection in two sessions, stop here.

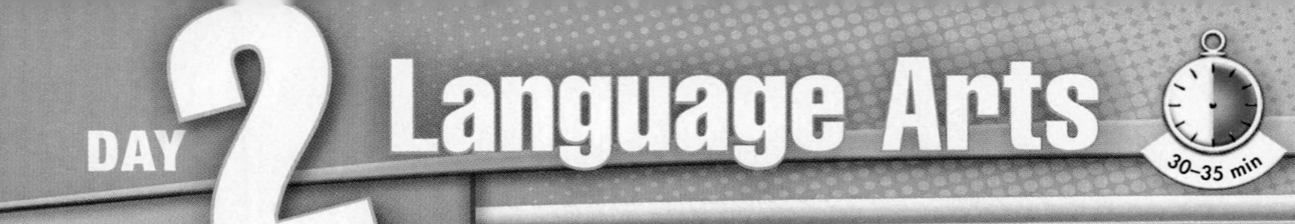

Objectives

- Find pertinent information from online sources.
- Recognize and correctly use complete subjects and predicates.
- Practice correctly spelling words with long *e* and long *o.*

Research and Inquiry

Navigate/Search

Teach

Have students search the Internet using their inquiry questions and keywords from Day 1. Tell them to skim and scan each site, keeping in mind their own reasons for wanting to explore new places. As they skim and scan, they should focus on features such as photographs and illustrations, highlighted, bold, or italic text, maps, and heads and subheads. Remind students to keep track of Web sites they visited and take notes as they gather information.

Model

Think Aloud When searching for information about landscapes and landmarks people might want to explore while on vacation, I found: *People enjoy traveling along the coast and photographing lighthouses.* I will use keywords from this information, such as *coast* and *lighthouse,* to lead me to more specific information. One fact I found using these keywords states: *Although the Gulf of Mexico along the Texas coast has never required many lighthouses, two are still active today.*

Guide practice

Have students continue their review of Web sites they identified. Explain how the Web site's address can specify the nature of the site, which can help you decide if it is a reliable and valid source. Educational sites can include *k12* or *.edu* in the address. Federal government sites end in *.gov,* nonprofit organizations often include *.org,* and commercial businesses usually include *.com.* Have students explain to a partner why it is important to cite valid and reliable sources when completing a research project.

On their own

Have students write down Web addresses, their titles, and the authors of the Web sites to create a Works Cited page.

Grammar Jammer

Conventions
Complete Subjects and Predicates

Teach Write the following sentences on the board: *The dog ran into the house. Max ran into the house.* Demonstrate how to add details to the subjects and predicates and combine the simple sentences into a sentence with a compound subject and predicate: *The frightened dog and his terrified owner ran into the old house in the woods.*

Guide practice Write the sentences below on the board. Have students add details and combine the sentences in cursive. Encourage them to make sure the slant of their letters is uniform.

The dish fell. The dish broke.

Daily Fix-It Use Daily Fix-It numbers 3 and 4 in the right margin.

Connect to oral language Have students identify compound and simple subjects and predicates in *On the Banks of Plum Creek.* (CS: *The rushes in the wind;* SS: *The rushes;* CP: *made a wild, lonely sound;* SP: *made.)*

On their own For additional practice, use *Reader's and Writer's Notebook,* p. 65.

Spelling
Long *e* and *o*

Teach Remind students that the long *e* sound can be spelled *ea* or *ee,* and that the long *o* sound can be spelled *oa* or *ow.*

Guide practice Write *seaweed, float,* and *rainbow*. Guide students in identifying the long *e* spellings in *seaweed,* and the long *o* spellings in *float* and *rainbow.* Point out that since *oa* and *ow* sound the same, and *ea* and *ee* sound the same, they will need to memorize words with these sounds. Have students work in pairs writing each spelling word and underlining the letters that make the long *e* or long *o* sound.

On their own For additional practice, use *Reader's and Writer's Notebook,* p. 66.

Daily Fix-It

3. Mr and mrs. Kim entertained us in San Francisco. (*Mr. and Mrs.*)
4. They, were at the airport to great us. (*They were; greet*)

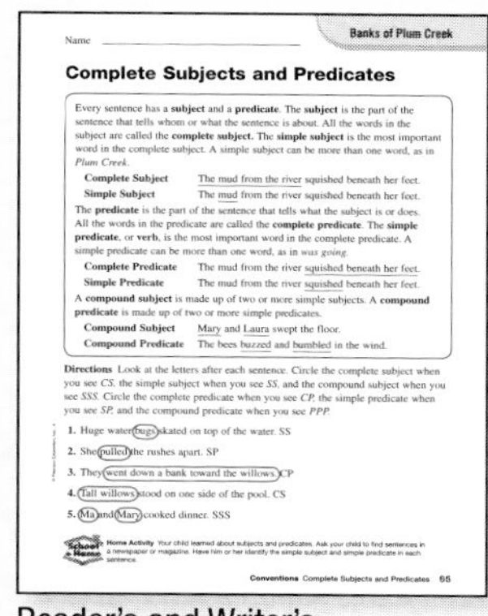

Banks of Plum Creek

Complete Subjects and Predicates

Reader's and Writer's Notebook p. 65

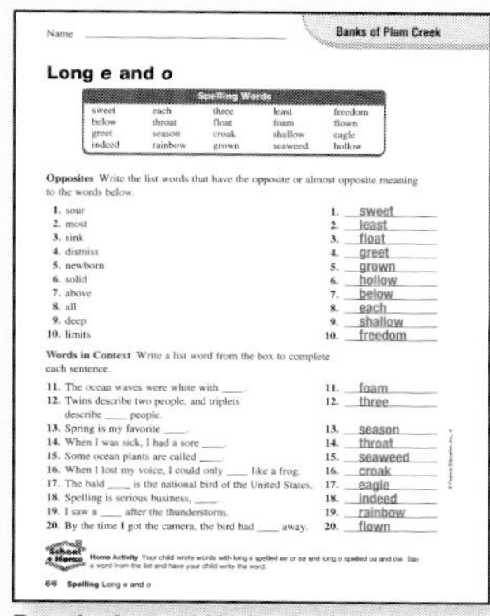

Banks of Plum Creek

Long e and o

Reader's and Writer's Notebook p. 66

English Language Learners

Conventions To provide students with practice on complete subjects and predicates, use the modified grammar lessons in the *ELL Handbook* and the Grammar Jammer online at: www.ReadingStreet.com

Objectives

- Organize ideas to prepare for writing.

Writing—Parody
Writing Trait: Organization

Introduce the prompt

Remind students that the selection they are reading this week, *On the Banks of Plum Creek,* is an example of historical fiction. Explain that their parodies will need to include some of the features of the original selection. Review the key features of a parody. Remind students to think about these features as they plan a first draft. Then explain that they will begin the writing process for a parody today. Read aloud the writing prompt.

Writing Prompt

Write a parody of *On the Banks of Plum Creek.*

Select a topic

Think Aloud One strategy we can use to generate ideas for our first draft is brainstorming different parts of the story we might like to parody. We can use a graphic organizer to list the different parts of the story and the pages where we find those parts. Display a T-chart. In one part of *On the Banks of Plum Creek,* you read a description of the banks as Mary and Laura walked along. I'll put that event and page number in my chart. Add the information to the T-chart. Ask students to brainstorm other events and find the pages they appear on in the story. Fill in the chart as they give their suggestions.

Event	Page
description of what the creek bank was like	86
family trip to the deep water	89
Pa teaches Laura a lesson about going too deep	91

Corrective feedback

Circulate around the room as students use their charts to help them choose the event from the story they will use to write their parody. Talk individually with students who seem to be having difficulty completing their charts or choosing an event. Ask struggling students to start with their favorite parts of the story.

MINI-LESSON

Order of Events

- You can use another T-chart to help you organize your parody. Display a T-chart. I'm going to write a parody about Plum Creek itself. I'll start with a humorous title: *On the Banks of Pomegranate Marsh.* Write the title in the chart.
- In the left column write about the mud described in the original story. The author describes mud as warm and soft. I'll write how I will describe it in my parody. Write *cold, gooey mud* in column 2. Continue to fill in columns 1 and 2 with additional information.
- Have students begin their own T-chart using the form on p. 67 of their *Reader's and Writer's Notebook.* Explain that they will fill in their chart with events from the part of the story they chose to parody. Tell students to write the events in order and use words to make their parody humorous or exaggerated.

ROUTINE

Quick Write for Fluency

Team Talk

1. **Talk** Have pairs discuss how their setting is like the original setting and how it is different.
2. **Write** Each student writes a few sentences comparing and contrasting the settings.
3. **Share** Partners share their writing with each other and other groups.

Routines Flip Chart

Wrap Up Your Day

- ✔ **Build Concepts** What did you learn about why Laura likes to explore new places?
- ✔ **Literary Elements** What have you learned about the characters, setting, and plot in the story?
- ✔ **Background Knowledge** How did background knowledge help you understand the text?

Differentiated Instruction

Advanced

Have students discuss other stories they think would be fun to parody. Have them write the parody for extra credit or to simply to share with the class.

Reader's and Writer's Notebook p. 67

Teacher Tip

Suggest students draw a picture to go with the original story and then a picture to go with their parody to help them see some humorous differences.

Tell students that tomorrow they will read about what happens when Laura goes exploring on her own.

Objectives
- Expand the weekly concept.
- Develop oral vocabulary.

Today at a Glance

Oral Vocabulary
landmarks, enormous

Comprehension Check/Retelling
Discuss questions

Reading
On the Banks of Plum Creek

Think Critically
Retelling

Fluency
Rate and accuracy

Research and Study Skills
Electronic media

Research and Inquiry
Analyze

Spelling
Long *e* and *o*

Conventions
Complete subjects and predicates

Writing
Parody

Concept Talk

Question of the Week
Why do we want to explore new places?

Expand the concept

Remind students of the weekly concept question. Discuss how the question relates to a pioneer girl who lives on the prairie along the banks of a creek. Tell students that today they will read about a girl and the adventures she has exploring her new prairie homestead. Encourage students to think about the landscape she discovers.

Anchored Talk

Develop oral vocabulary

Use story structure to review the conflict and resolution of the story on pp. 84–93 of *On the Banks of Plum Creek.* Discuss the Amazing Words *landscape* and *sights.* Add these words to the concept map. Use the following questions to develop students' understanding of the concept. Remind students to ask and answer questions with appropriate detail and to give suggestions based on the ideas of others.

- The *sights* in and along Plum Creek fascinate Laura and her sister Mary. Discuss what natural *sights* captivate you and why.
- Think about the *landscape* around Laura's homestead. How do you think that the *landscape* in Minnesota has changed since Laura first settled there?

Oral Vocabulary
Amazing Words

Amazing Words

coast
route
desert
valleys
landscape
sights
landmarks
enormous
magnificent
navigate

Teach Amazing Words

Amazing Words Oral Vocabulary Routine

1. **Introduce** Write the Amazing Word *landmarks* on the board. Have students say it with you. Yesterday, we learned that Laura and her family used *landmarks* to navigate their way around their new landscape. Have students determine a definition of *landmarks*. (*Landmarks* are large objects on land that are easy to see and can help a person find the way to a place nearby.)
2. **Demonstrate** Have students answer questions to demonstrate understanding. What were some of the *landmarks* along the creek Laura used to find her way to the swimming hole? (Some of the *landmarks* Laura used were a willow valley, plum thicket, and a tableland.)
3. **Apply** Have students apply their understanding. Would you rather navigate an unfamiliar territory by using natural or human-made *landmarks*? Explain why.

See p. OV•3 to teach *enormous*.

Routines Flip Chart

Apply Amazing Words

As students read pp. 94–99 of *On the Banks of Plum Creek,* have them consider how the Amazing Words *landmarks* and *enormous* apply to the adventures of a girl on the Minnesota frontier.

Connect to reading

Explain that today students will read about how Laura encounters a strange animal as she journeys toward the forbidden swimming hole. Help students establish a purpose for reading.

ELL Expand Vocabulary Use the Day 3 instruction on ELL Poster 3 to help students expand vocabulary.

ELL Poster 3

Objectives

- Use literary elements to aid comprehension.
- Use the background knowledge strategy to aid comprehension.
- Use the strategy for multiple-meaning words to define new vocabulary.

Comprehension Check

Have students discuss each question with a partner. Ask several pairs to share their responses.

☑ **Genre • Analysis**
How can looking at the illustrations in *On the Banks of Plum Creek* help you to imagine life on the prairie in the mid-1800s? Possible response: The illustrations help me to visualize the prairie, her family's dugout house, and the wildlife around Plum Creek.

☑ **Literary elements: Character, setting, plot • Evaluation**
What type of father do you think Pa is? Use details from the story's plot and setting to support your answer. Possible response: Pa is reasonable and fair as a father, with a good sense of humor. He ducks Laura when she disobeys but laughs when she requests another ducking. He allows Laura and her sisters to explore their new home.

☑ **Background knowledge • Synthesis**
How does knowing about the difficulties frontier families faced help you to understand why children were required to help with a variety of daily chores? Possible response: I know that frontier families needed to clear land, build houses, plant crops, and raise livestock. Children had chores both inside and outside the house because every pair of hands was needed.

☑ **Multiple-meaning words • Synthesis**
Use the context of the sentence and what you learned about the prairie to determine the meaning of the word *coarse* on page 89. Then check your definition in a dictionary or glossary. Possible response: I think it must describe the texture of the grasses. When I look up the word *coarse* in a dictionary, I see that it means "thick strands."

☑ **Connect text to self**
Laura spends much of her free time exploring nature. How do you explore nature in your own neighborhood? Possible response: I enjoy bird watching in the park.

Strategy Response Log

INTERACT with TEXT

Have students use p. 9 in the *Reader's and Writer's Notebook* to add information they learned to the *L* column of their KWL Charts. Then have students summarize the selection.

Check Retelling

Have students retell the Deep Water section of *On the Banks of Plum Creek.*

Corrective feedback

If... students leave out important details,
then... have students look back through the illustrations in the selection.

Small Group Time

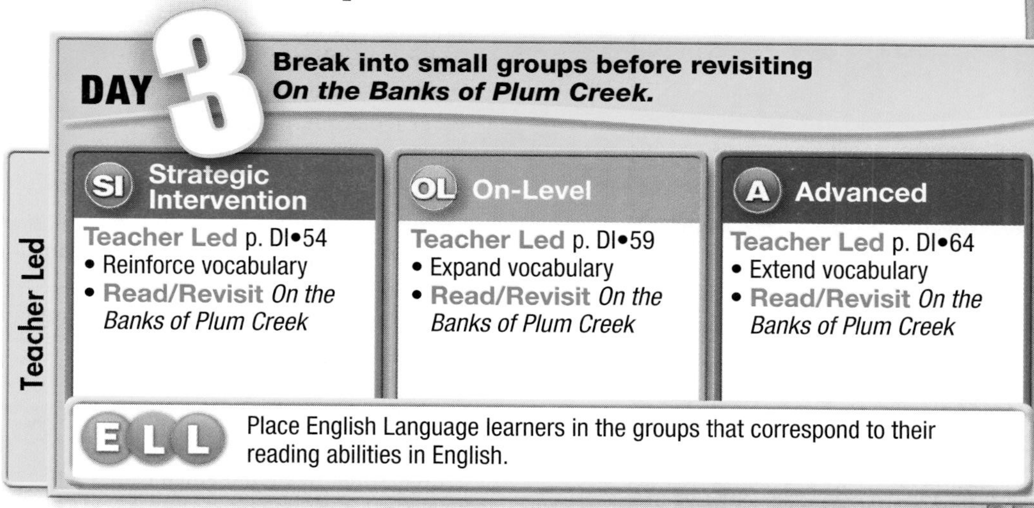

DAY 3 **Break into small groups before revisiting *On the Banks of Plum Creek.***

Teacher Led

SI Strategic Intervention	OL On-Level	A Advanced
Teacher Led p. DI•54 • Reinforce vocabulary • Read/Revisit *On the Banks of Plum Creek*	Teacher Led p. DI•59 • Expand vocabulary • Read/Revisit *On the Banks of Plum Creek*	Teacher Led p. DI•64 • Extend vocabulary • Read/Revisit *On the Banks of Plum Creek*

ELL Place English Language learners in the groups that correspond to their reading abilities in English.

Practice Stations
- Let's Write
- Get Fluent
- Word Work

Independent Activities
- AudioText: *On the Banks of Plum Creek*
- *Reader's and Writer's Notebook*
- Research and Inquiry

ELL

English Language Learners

Check retelling To support retelling, review the multilingual summary for *On the Banks of Plum Creek* with the appropriate Retelling Cards to scaffold understanding.

DAY 3 Read and Comprehend

Objectives

- Sequence the plot's main events and explain how they influence future events in the plot.

OPTION 1 Skills and Strategies, continued

Teach Sequence

Review **Sequence** Have students sequence the plot's main events from when Laura first crosses paths with the strange animal to when she arrives in the dugout.

Corrective Feedback

If... students are unable to determine the correct sequence,
then... model how to identify the order of events in the story.

Model the Skill

I can picture in my mind the order in which things happen. First, Laura meets the strange creature and stares at it. The creature sinks flat onto the ground.

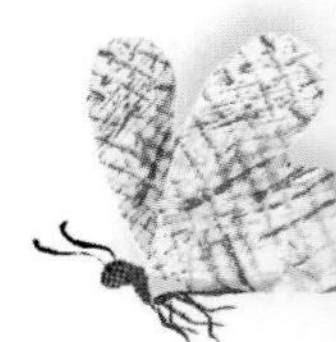

The tableland seemed big and empty and not interesting. It had been exciting when Pa was there, but now it was just flat land, and Laura thought she would go home and get a drink. She was very thirsty.

She slid down the side of the tableland and slowly started back along the way she had come. Down among the tall grasses the air was smothery and very hot. The dugout was far away and Laura was terribly thirsty.

She remembered with all her might that she must not go near that deep, shady swimming-pool, and suddenly she turned around and hurried toward it. She thought she would only look at it. Just looking at it would make her feel better. Then she thought she might wade in the edge of it but she would not go into the deep water.

She came into the path that Pa had made, and she trotted faster.

Right in the middle of the path before her stood an animal.

Laura jumped back, and stood and stared at it. She had never seen such an animal. It was almost as long as Jack, but its legs were very short. Long gray fur bristled all over it. It had a flat head and small ears. Its flat head slowly tilted up and it stared at Laura.

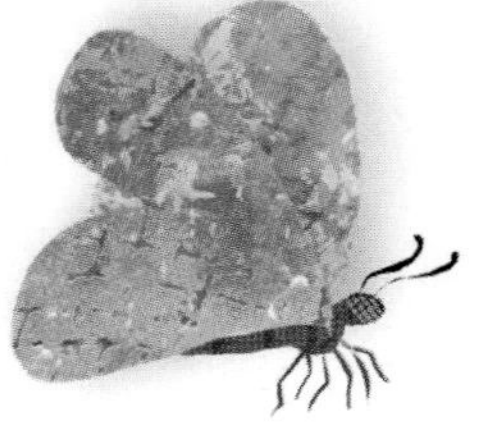

94

Multidraft Reading

If you chose...
Option 1 Return to Extend Thinking instruction starting on p. 86–87.
Option 2 Read pp. 94–99.
Use the Guide Comprehension and Extend Thinking instruction.

Student Edition pp. 94–95

OPTION 2 Think Critically, continued

Higher-Order Thinking Skills

Review **Sequence • Analysis** How did Laura's encounter with the strange animal affect the future events in the plot of the story? Possible response: When Laura got scared by the animal, she ran home, instead of continuing on to the swimming hole.

Draw Conclusions • Evaluation If Laura was "a good little girl" like Mary, where would she have gone and what would she have done after she explored the tableland? Possible response: Laura would have gone home to get a drink of water and do her school lessons.

Next, Laura pokes it with a stick. The creature snarls, scaring Laura. Finally, Laura runs home as fast as she can.

She stared back at its funny face. And while they stood still and staring, that animal widened and shortened and spread flat on the ground. It grew flatter and flatter, till it was a gray fur laid there. It was not like a whole animal at all. Only it had eyes staring up.

Slowly and carefully Laura stooped and reached and picked up a willow stick. She felt better then. She stayed bent over, looking at that flat gray fur.

It did not move and neither did Laura. She wondered what would happen if she poked it. It might change to some other shape. She poked it gently with the short stick.

A frightful snarl came out of it. Its eyes sparkled mad, and fierce white teeth snapped almost on Laura's nose.

Laura ran with all her might. She could run fast. She did not stop running until she was in the dugout.

"Goodness, Laura!" Ma said. "You'll make yourself sick, tearing around so in this heat."

All that time, Mary had been sitting like a little lady, spelling out words in the book that Ma was teaching her to read. Mary was a good little girl.

95

Character • Evaluation How does Laura's opinion of the strange animal change from when she first sees it? Possible response: At first Laura is very curious about the animal. She has never seen such an animal, and she stares at it with curiosity. Then, after poking the animal and seeing its reaction, she is terrified of the animal and its sudden attack.

On Their Own

Have students work with a partner to explain how an event earlier in the plot, such as Laura setting out for the swimming hole, led to the future event of Laura finding the strange animal. (Laura ran into the strange animal on her way to the swimming hole.)

Connect to Social Studies

A variety of animals live in the prairie. The animals have adapted to plains of grass with low rainfall, hot summers, and cold winters. Animals that can be discovered in the North American prairies include the antelope, prairie dog, coyote, shrew, and opossum.

English Language Learners

Monitor understanding Read aloud the third paragraph of p. 95. Why did Laura think that poking the strange animal would change it to another shape? Have students look back at the text to clarify their understanding. (first paragraph: *The animal grew flatter on the ground until it was not like a whole animal, but rather like a strip of gray fur.*)

DAY 3 Read and Comprehend

OPTION 1 Skills and Strategies, continued

Objectives

◎ Understand the interaction between character, setting, and plot to aid comprehension.

Teach Literary Elements

Literary Elements: Character, Setting, and Plot Have students read the text on pp. 96–97. Explain that this section of the plot contains a conflict, or problem. Ask students how the character and setting influence the conflict and resolution of the plot.

Corrective Feedback

If... students have difficulty determining how the interaction of characters and setting influence the main events of the plot,
then... model how to identify the conflict and resolution by summarizing the plot's main events.

Model the Skill

Think Aloud I know that the conflict is a problem that the main character must confront and resolve. Laura, the main character in this story, has disobeyed her parents because the swimming hole is an appealing part of the setting on such a hot day. Laura cannot sleep

Laura had been bad and she knew it. She had broken her promise to Pa. But no one had seen her. No one knew that she had started to go to the swimming-hole. If she did not tell, no one would ever know. Only that strange animal knew, and it could not tell on her. But she felt worse and worse inside.

That night she lay awake beside Mary. Pa and Ma sat in the starlight outside the door and Pa was playing his fiddle.

"Go to sleep, Laura," Ma said, softly, and softly the fiddle sang to her. Pa was a shadow against the sky and his bow danced among the great stars.

Everything was beautiful and good, except Laura. She had broken her promise to Pa. Breaking a promise was as bad as telling a lie. Laura wished she had not done it. But she had done it, and if Pa knew, he would punish her.

Pa went on playing softly in the starlight. His fiddle sang to her sweetly and happily. He thought she was a good little girl. At last Laura could bear it no longer.

96

Student Edition pp. 96–97

Literary Elements: Character • Synthesis What do you think would happen if Laura did not confess the truth to Pa straightaway? Possible response: I think that Laura's guilty conscience would continue to grow. She would feel miserable, especially the next time that her father trusted her. She would probably blurt out the truth eventually.

OPTION 2 Think Critically, continued

Higher-Order Thinking Skills

Literary Elements: Character, Setting, and Plot • Synthesis How do you think Laura would behave if Pa forbade her to explore the shallow creek by herself? Explain why you think this way, using what you know about Laura and the setting of the story. Possible response: I think that Laura would be tempted to splash in the creek alone in spite of Pa's rule. Laura is very headstrong and often gets into trouble because she doesn't listen. She is tempted by the landmarks on the prairie where she and her family live.

because she feels so guilty breaking her father's trust. This conflict is resolved when she finally tells Pa the truth and receives her punishment.

On Their Own

Have students use graphic organizers to show the character, setting, and plot of the story.

She slid out of bed and her bare feet stole across the cool earthen floor. In her nightgown and nightcap she stood beside Pa. He drew the last notes from the strings with his bow and she could feel him smiling down at her.

"What is it, little half-pint?" he asked her. "You look like a little ghost, all white in the dark."

"Pa," Laura said, in a quivery small voice, "I—I—started to go to the swimming-hole."

"You did!" Pa exclaimed. Then he asked, "Well, what stopped you?"

"I don't know," Laura whispered. "It had gray fur and it—it flattened out flat. It snarled."

"How big was it?" Pa asked.

Laura told him all about that strange animal.

Pa said, "It must have been a badger."

Then for a long time he did not say anything and Laura waited. Laura could not see his face in the dark, but she leaned against his knee and she could feel how strong and kind he was.

"Well," he said at last, "I hardly know what to do, Laura. You see, I trusted you. It is hard to know what to do with a person you can't trust. But do you know what people have to do to anyone they can't trust?"

"Wh—at?" Laura quavered.

"They have to watch him," said Pa. "So I guess you must be watched. Your Ma will have to do it because I must work at Nelson's. So tomorrow you stay where Ma can watch you. You are not to go out of her sight all day. If you are good all day, then we will let you try again to be a little girl we can trust."

97

Literary Elements: Theme • Analysis What lesson about life do you think the author wants you to learn from this story? Summarize and explain the lesson or message. Possible response: Not betraying a person's trust can help someone avoid many problems.

Draw Conclusions • Analysis In the last paragraph of page 97, Pa reveals Laura's punishment. Do you think his punishment is fair? Why or why not? Possible response: Yes, I believe his punishment is fair because Laura needs to be taught a lesson so she can be trusted again. The next time she considers disobeying, she will probably remember this punishment and reconsider.

Differentiated Instruction

Strategic Intervention

Literary elements: Plot Tell students they can answer a series of questions to identify the conflict, rising action, climax, and resolution. Helpful questions include: What is the problem? How does Laura try to solve the problem? What happens that helps Laura solve the problem? How does the story end?

Advanced

Explore a topic Have students use the library or Internet to discover more about entertainment during pioneer days, such as fiddling.

ELL

English Language Learners

Vocabulary: Compound words Have students find a compound word on the spread (*starlight, nightgown, nightcap*). Have pairs of students look at a sentence containing a compound word. They can use a dictionary to look up the word and then write a sentence using the compound word. Ask pairs to share their sentences.

Objectives

◎ Use background knowledge to monitor and adjust comprehension.

OPTION 1 Skills and Strategies, continued

Teach Background Knowledge

◎ **Background Knowledge** Ask students to use their background knowledge to explain why they think that Laura believed that "being good could never be as hard as being watched." (Laura was terribly bored being confined indoors under her mother's watchful eyes and felt it would be easier to behave the next time.)

Corrective Feedback

If... students have difficulty understanding the concept,
then... model how to use background knowledge to monitor and adjust comprehension.

Model the Strategy

Think Aloud: Laura is like many people I know; she is happiest exploring the outdoors. When she was confined inside as a punishment, she must have been miserable doing household chores.

"How about it, Caroline?" he asked Ma.

"Very well, Charles," Ma said out of the dark. "I will watch her tomorrow. But I am sure she will be good. Now back to bed, Laura, and go to sleep."

The next day was a dreadful day.

Ma was mending, and Laura had to stay in the dugout. She could not even fetch water from the spring, for that was going out of Ma's sight. Mary fetched the water. Mary took Carrie to walk on the prairie. Laura had to stay in.

Jack laid his nose on his paws and waggled, he jumped out on the path and looked back at her, smiling with his ears, begging her to come out. He could not understand why she did not.

Laura helped Ma. She washed the dishes and made both beds and swept the floor and set the table. At dinner she sat bowed on her bench and ate what Ma set before her. Then she wiped the dishes. After that she ripped a sheet that was worn in the middle. Ma turned the strips of muslin and pinned them together, and Laura whipped the new seam, over and over with tiny stitches.

She thought that seam and that day would never end.

But at last Ma rolled up her mending and it was time to get supper.

"You have been a good girl, Laura," Ma said.

98

Student Edition pp. 98–99

OPTION 2 Think Critically, continued

Higher-Order Thinking Skills

◎ **Background Knowledge • Evaluation** How do you think Laura felt when her dog, Jack, begged her to take him outside to play? Why do you think she felt that way? Possible response: Laura must have felt miserable because she couldn't explain to Jack that she was being punished by staying indoors and doing chores.

◎ **Literary Elements: Character • Evaluation** How does Laura's opinion about misbehaving change after spending the day inside? Possible response: Laura now realizes that once she begins to misbehave, it is difficult to stop and could lead to something terrible happening.

Comprehension Check

Spiral Review

Author's Purpose • Analysis Why do you think the author wrote *On the Banks of Plum Creek*? Did the author have more than one reason for writing this story? Explain why you think that way. Possible response: I think that the author wrote this story for several reasons. The author wanted to entertain readers with her story. She also wanted to express her feelings about people and places in the past. In addition, she wanted to inform readers about life on the prairie in the mid-1800s.

The next time she has an urge to misbehave, she will probably remember the dreary day spent indoors and change her mind.

On Their Own

Have students write a paragraph about what Laura would rather be doing on the day she is punished.

"We will tell Pa so. And tomorrow morning you and I are going to look for that badger. I am sure he saved you from drowning, for if you had gone to that deep water you would have gone into it. Once you begin being naughty, it is easier to go on and on, and sooner or later something dreadful happens."

"Yes, Ma," Laura said. She knew that now.

The whole day was gone. Laura had not seen that sunrise, nor the shadows of clouds on the prairie. The morning-glories were withered and that day's blue flags were dead. All day Laura had not seen the water running in the creek, the little fishes in it, and the water-bugs skating over it. She was sure that being good could never be as hard as being watched.

Next day she went with Ma to look for the badger. In the path she showed Ma the place where he had flattened himself on the grass. Ma found the hole where he lived. It was a round hole under a clump of grass on the prairie bank. Laura called to him and she poked a stick into the hole.

If the badger was at home, he would not come out. Laura never saw that old gray badger again.

99

Summarize • Analysis Summarize what Laura missed while she had to stay inside. What inferences can you make about how she will behave in the future? Possible response: Laura had not seen the sunrise or the shadows of the clouds. She didn't get to see the morning-glories or blue flags. She didn't get to see the creek with little fishes and water-bugs. I can infer that Laura will not disobey again so she doesn't miss being outside.

Check Predictions Have students return to the predictions they made earlier and confirm whether they were accurate.

Differentiated Instruction

SI Strategic Intervention

Draw conclusions Have students work in pairs to draw conclusions about why the badger disappeared from the spot where Laura first discovered it.

A Advanced

Draw conclusions Ask students to explore the badger's habitat, using the library or Internet. Where do they think the badger went after its initial encounter with Laura?

Connect to Social Studies

Pioneer girls had a variety of chores. They quilted and sewed, made soap and candles, cooked, and washed dishes.

ELL

English Language Learners

Figurative language Point out the fifth paragraph on p. 98 and explain to students that "smiling with his ears" is a colorful way to say that the dog, Jack, is using body language to show that he is happy and eager to go outside.

Objectives

- ◎ Use the literary elements of character, setting, and plot to aid comprehension.
- ◎ Use background knowledge to aid comprehension.

Check Retelling
SUCCESS PREDICTOR

Objectives
• Read independently for long periods of time and paraphrase the reading, including the order in which events occur. • Identify whether the narrator or speaker of a story is first person or third person. • Write responses to texts using details to show understanding.

Envision It! Retell

READING STREET ONLINE
STORY SORT
www.ReadingStreet.com

Think Critically

1. Laura Ingalls Wilder's stories have been read and watched worldwide by both adults and children. Why do you think people find her books so appealing? Text to World
2. Is this story told in the first person or the third person? Explain how you know. How would the story have been different if Laura had been the narrator of the events? Think Like an Author
3. Think about Pa's relationship with his family. What are some words you might use to describe his character? Use examples from the story to support your word choices. ◎ Literary Elements: Character, Setting, and Plot
4. Before reading this story, what did you know about families who moved west to settle our country? Did this information help you to understand Laura's life on the prairie? Why? ◎ Background Knowledge
5. **Look Back and Write** Look back at page 97. Describe Pa's feelings when Laura tells him that she has broken her promise to him. Provide evidence to support your answer.

100

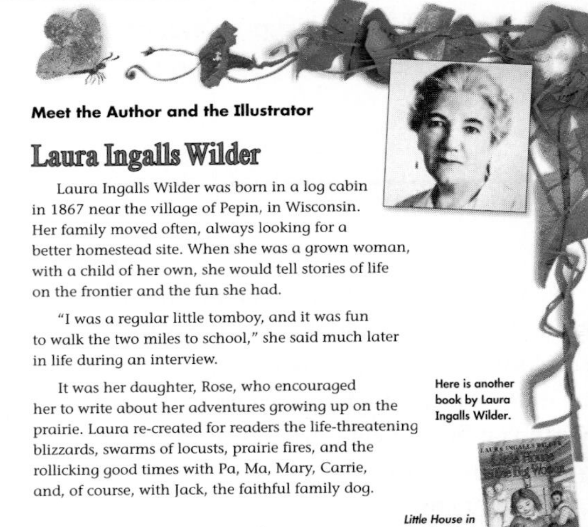

Meet the Author and the Illustrator

Laura Ingalls Wilder

Laura Ingalls Wilder was born in a log cabin in 1867 near the village of Pepin, in Wisconsin. Her family moved often, always looking for a better homestead site. When she was a grown woman, with a child of her own, she would tell stories of life on the frontier and the fun she had.

"I was a regular little tomboy, and it was fun to walk the two miles to school," she said much later in life during an interview.

It was her daughter, Rose, who encouraged her to write about her adventures growing up on the prairie. Laura re-created for readers the life-threatening blizzards, swarms of locusts, prairie fires, and the rollicking good times with Pa, Ma, Mary, Carrie, and, of course, with Jack, the faithful family dog.

Here is another book by Laura Ingalls Wilder.

Little House in the Big Woods

Garth Williams

Garth Williams was born in New York State in 1912. He was a painter, sculptor, and an architect before he became a children's book illustrator. Garth Williams illustrated more than 100 children's books, including *Stuart Little, Charlotte's Web,* and the *Little House* books.

Use the *Reader's and Writer's Notebook* to record your independent reading.

101

Student Edition pp. 100–101

Retelling

Envision It! Have students work in pairs to retell the selection, using the Envision It! Retelling Cards as prompts. Remind students that they should accurately describe the plot and characters and use key vocabulary as they retell. Monitor students' retellings.

Scoring rubric

Top-Score Response A top-score response makes connections beyond the text, describes the plot and characters, using accurate information, and draws conclusions from the text.

Plan to Assess Retelling

- ☑ **Week 1** Assess Strategic Intervention students.
- ☑ **Week 2** Assess Advanced students.
- ☑ **This week assess Strategic Intervention students.**
- ☐ **Week 4** Assess On-Level students.
- ☐ **Week 5** Assess any students you have not yet checked during this unit.

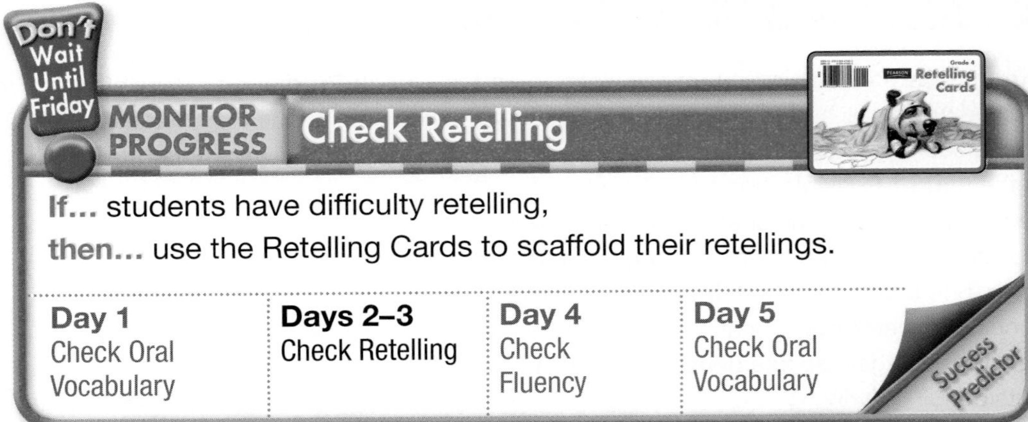

Don't Wait Until Friday **MONITOR PROGRESS** Check Retelling

If... students have difficulty retelling,
then... use the Retelling Cards to scaffold their retellings.

Day 1	Days 2–3	Day 4	Day 5
Check Oral Vocabulary	Check Retelling	Check Fluency	Check Oral Vocabulary

Success Predictor

Think Critically

Text to world

1. I think people find her books appealing because they tell of adventures that took place on the frontier. They give readers a sense of what it must have been like growing up in that time.

Think like an author

2. This story is told in the third person. The author refers to the characters by name and uses words, such as *they, her,* and *his.* If Laura had told the story, she would have referred to herself as I or me, and might have described staying inside differently.

Literary elements: Character, setting, plot

3. Pa is kind, fun-loving, and fair. He enjoys entertaining the family with his fiddle, exploring the prairie with his daughters, and laughing at Laura's antics. When he discovered that Laura betrayed his trust, he dealt out a fair punishment.

Background knowledge

4. I knew that families had to be strong because they often were alone and needed to depend on each other. This helped me to understand why the Ingalls family was so close-knit and why it was important for children like Laura to do various chores.

Writing on Demand

5. **Look Back and Write** To build writing fluency, assign a 10–15 minute time limit.

Suggest that students use a prewriting strategy, such as brainstorming or using a graphic organizer, to organize their ideas. Remind them to establish a topic sentence and support it with facts, details, or explanations. As students finish, encourage them to reread their responses, revise for organization and support, and proofread for errors in grammar and conventions.

Scoring rubric

Top-Score Response A top-score response uses evidence to show Pa's feelings when Laura broke her promise.

A top-score response should include:

- Pa is upset and needs time to think before he responds to Laura's confession.
- Pa is disappointed that Laura broke his trust in her.
- Pa decides that if Laura is good, he will give her another chance to re-establish trust.

Differentiated Instruction

Strategic Intervention

Have students work in pairs to act out the scene on p. 97 between Pa and Laura. Encourage them to use their own words in this scene.

Meet the Author

Have students read about author Laura Ingalls Wilder on p. 101. Ask them to identify similarities and differences between the author's life and her experiences and the character Laura's experiences in *On the Banks of Plum Creek*.

Independent Reading

After students enter their independent reading information into their Reading Logs, have them paraphrase a portion of the text they have just read. Remind students that when we paraphrase, we express the meaning of a passage, using other words and maintaining logical order.

English Language Learners

Retelling Use the Retelling Cards to discuss the selection with students. Place the cards in an incorrect order and have volunteers correct the mistakes. Then have students explain where each card should go as they describe the sequence of the selection.

Read and Comprehend

Objectives

- Read grade-level text with appropriate rate and accuracy.
- Reread for fluency.
- Use electronic media, including online searches, to collect information for a research plan.

Model Fluency
Rate and Accuracy

Model fluent reading

Have students turn to p. 92 of *On the Banks of Plum Creek*. Have students follow along as you read this page. Tell them to listen to the speed, or rate, at which you read and the precise, accurate way that you read the page.

Guide practice

Have the students follow along as you read the page again. Then have them reread the page as a group without you until they read with the correct rate and accuracy with no mistakes. Ask questions to make sure students comprehend the text. Continue in the same way on p. 93.

Reread for Fluency

Corrective feedback

If... students are having difficulty reading at the correct rate and with accuracy,
then... prompt:

- Did you read every word? Where do you see difficult words?
- How can you read with better accuracy?
- Read the sentence again. Make sure you read carefully and do not miss any words.
- Do you think you need to slow down or read more quickly?
- Read the sentence more quickly. Now read it more slowly. Which helps you understand what you are reading?
- Tell me the sentence. Read it at the rate that would help me understand it.

ROUTINE **Oral Rereading**

1. **Read** Have students read p. 96 of *On the Banks of Plum Creek* orally.

2. **Reread** To achieve optimal fluency, students should reread the text three or four times with appropriate rate and accuracy.

3. **Corrective Feedback** Have students read aloud without you. Provide feedback about their rate and accuracy.

Routines Flip Chart

Research and Study Skills
Electronic Media

Teach

Ask students what types of electronic media they have used to obtain news or provide entertainment. Remind them that electronic media include any resources that require electricity to function. Explain that there are two types of electronic media: computer and non-computer sources. Have students brainstorm examples of both types.

- Computer sources include CD-ROMs, DVDs, and the Internet (including online sources, such as Web sites, encyclopedias, newspapers, and so on).
- Non-computer sources include audiotapes, videotapes, DVDs, films, filmstrips, television shows, and radio.

Have groups of students discuss how they might use electronic media to follow a research plan for a class trip to the Laura Ingalls Wilder Historic Home and Museum in Mansfield, Missouri. Encourage them to think about collecting information from multiple sources, including online searches.

Guide practice

Discuss these questions:

How would you use an Internet search engine to research the class trip to the museum? (type in the key words and click on the top results)

What information would you expect to find on a Web site devoted to the museum? (background information, photographs, hours of operation, tour costs, activities, contact information, biography of Laura Ingalls Wilder)

On their own

Have students complete pp. 69–70 of the *Reader's and Writer's Notebook*.

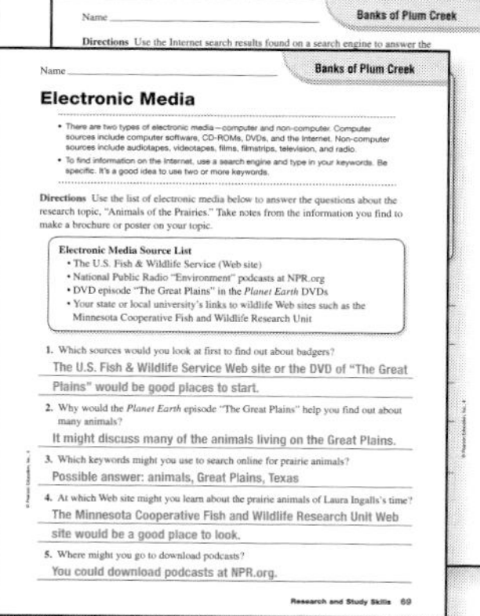

Name ________ Banks of Plum Creek

Directions Use the Internet search results found on a search engine to answer the

Name ________ Banks of Plum Creek

Electronic Media

- There are two types of electronic media—computer and non-computer. Computer sources include computer software, CD-ROMs, DVDs, and the Internet. Non-computer sources include audiotapes, videotapes, films, filmstrips, television, and radio.
- To find information on the Internet, use a search engine and type in your keywords. Be specific. It's a good idea to use two or more keywords.

Directions Use the list of electronic media below to answer the questions about the research topic, "Animals of the Prairies." Take notes from the information you find to make a brochure or poster on your topic.

Electronic Media Source List
- The U.S. Fish & Wildlife Service (Web site)
- National Public Radio "Environment" podcasts at NPR.org
- DVD episode "The Great Plains" in the *Planet Earth* DVDs
- Your state or local university's links to wildlife Web sites such as the Minnesota Cooperative Fish and Wildlife Research Unit

1. Which sources would you look at first to find out about badgers?
The U.S. Fish & Wildlife Service Web site or the DVD of "The Great Plains" would be good places to start.
2. Why would the *Planet Earth* episode "The Great Plains" help you find out about many animals?
It might discuss many of the animals living on the Great Plains.
3. Which keywords might you use to search online for prairie animals?
Possible answer: animals, Great Plains, Texas
4. At which Web site might you learn about the prairie animals of Laura Ingalls's time?
The Minnesota Cooperative Fish and Wildlife Research Unit Web site would be a good place to look.
5. Where might you go to download podcasts?
You could download podcasts at NPR.org.

Research and Study Skills 69

Reader's and Writer's Notebook pp. 69–70

English Language Learners

Professional Development "Think-alouds can be particularly informative when used with second-language students. Through this type of dialogue, the teacher can discover not only the types of challenges that students encounter with the text, but also how they deal with such challenges." —Dr. Georgia Earnest García

Electronic media Have students visit the media center so they may utilize electronic media to search for Web sites about Laura Ingalls Wilder. Help them to discover various electronic media features, such as historic photographs.

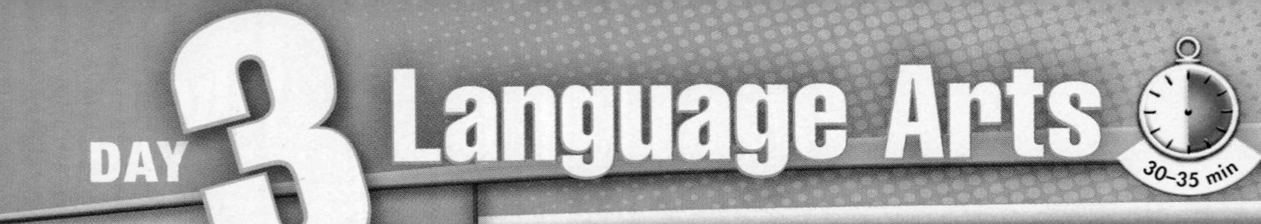

Objectives

- Analyze data for usefulness.
- Identify and correctly use complete subjects and complete predicates.
- Spell frequently misspelled words.

Research and Inquiry
Analyze

Teach Tell students that today they will analyze their findings and may need to change the focus of their original inquiry question.

Model **Think Aloud** Originally I thought that most people explored new places to view various landmarks, such as lighthouses. I collected information from a local travel agent, and she told me that many travelers want to reconnect with nature by observing wild animals on their vacations. I will refocus my inquiry question to include information from the interview with my local expert, from printed brochures and other written information, and my online research. Now my inquiry question is *What animals might people hope to observe when they visit a prairie on vacation?*

Guide practice Have students analyze their findings. They may need to refocus their inquiry question to better fit the information they found. Remind students that if they have difficulty improving their focus, they can ask a reference librarian for reference texts or a local expert for guidance. Encourage students to collect additional information from valid Web sites as necessary.

Remind students that online reference sources can also contain short audio and video clips that can help them to understand information or visualize places they have not seen.

On their own Have students summarize their research by writing a concise paragraph. Ask volunteers to read their paragraphs to the class and then compare their summaries.

Grammar Jammer

Conventions

Complete Subjects and Predicates

Review Remind students that this week they learned how to use a complete subject and a complete predicate in a sentence.

- A subject tells whom or what the sentence is about. The complete subject contains all the words in the subject.
- A predicate tells what the subject is or does. The complete predicate contains all the words in the predicate.

Daily Fix-It Use Daily Fix-It numbers 5 and 6 in the right margin.

Connect to oral language Have students choose a subject from one list and a predicate from the other and combine them into complete simple sentences.

> **Complete subjects: The empty box; A tall, mysterious man; At the end of the day the team**
>
> **Complete predicates: slowly entered the house; decided to meet at the playground; contained a long lost treasure**

On their own For additional support, use *Let's Practice It!* p. 24 on the *Teacher Resources DVD-ROM.*

Spelling

Long *e* and *o*

Frequently misspelled words Students often misspell *whole* and *know,* confusing them with *hole* and *no.* Write the words on the board. In *whole,* the sound /h/ is spelled *wh.* In *know,* the sound /n/ is spelled *kn.* I'm going to read a sentence. Choose the correct word to complete the sentence and then write it correctly.

> 1. **You can see the ________ world from space.** (whole)
> 2. **Astronauts ________ what Earth looks like from space.** (know)
> 3. **The planet Mercury has ________ moons.** (no)
> 4. **Asteroids can strike and leave ________ on planets.** (holes)

On their own For additional support, use the *Reader's and Writer's Notebook,* p. 71.

Differentiated Instruction

Strategic Intervention

Compare and contrast Write these sentences on the board:

Friends play.
All of our friends play together at the park.

Have partners tell how the sentences are alike and how they are different. Encourage them to use the terms *subject, predicate,* and *complete* as they discuss the similarities and differences.

Daily Fix-It

5. What an amazing sity San Francisco is. (*city; is!*)
6. My dad, my mom, my brother, and I. Went to Chinatown. (*I went; Chinatown*)

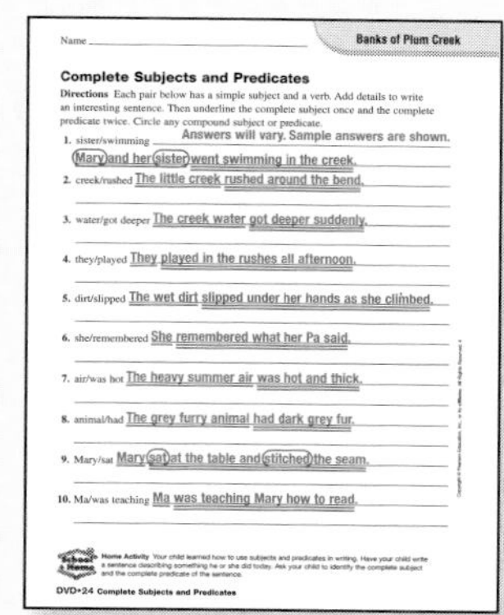

Name ________ Banks of Plum Creek

Complete Subjects and Predicates

Directions Each pair below has a simple subject and a verb. Add details to write an interesting sentence. Then underline the complete subject once and the complete predicate twice. Circle any compound subject or predicate.

Answers will vary. Sample answers are shown.

1. sister/swimming Mary and her sister went swimming in the creek.
2. creek/rushed The little creek rushed around the bend.
3. water/got deeper The creek water got deeper suddenly.
4. they/played They played in the rushes all afternoon.
5. dirt/slipped The wet dirt slipped under her hands as she climbed.
6. she/remembered She remembered what her Pa said.
7. air/was hot The heavy summer air was hot and thick.
8. animal/had The grey furry animal had dark grey fur.
9. Mary/sat Mary sat at the table and stitched the seam.
10. Ma/was teaching Ma was teaching Mary how to read.

DVD•24 Complete Subjects and Predicates

Let's Practice It!
TR DVD•24

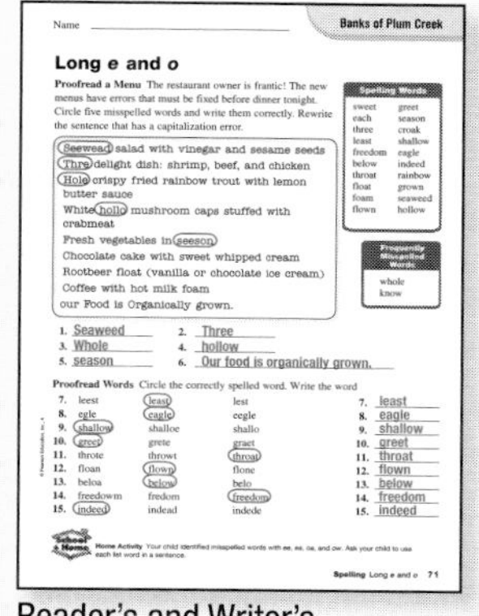

Name ________ Banks of Plum Creek

Long *e* and *o*

Proofread a Menu The restaurant owner is frantic! The new menus have errors that must be fixed before dinner tonight. Circle five misspelled words and write them correctly. Rewrite the sentence that has a capitalization error.

Seewead salad with vinegar and sesame seeds
Thre delight dish: shrimp, beef, and chicken
Hole crispy fried rainbow trout with lemon butter sauce
White hollo mushroom caps stuffed with crabmeat
Fresh vegetables in seeson
Chocolate cake with sweet whipped cream
Rootbeer float (vanilla or chocolate ice cream)
Coffee with hot milk foam
our Food is Organically grown.

Spelling Words: sweet, each, three, least, freedom, below, throat, float, foam, flown, greet, season, croak, shallow, eagle, indeed, rainbow, grown, seaweed, hollow

Frequently Misspelled Words: whole, know

1. Seaweed 2. Three
3. Whole 4. hollow
5. season 6. Our food is organically grown.

Proofread Words Circle the correctly spelled word. Write the word

7.	leest	least	lest	least
8.	egle	eagle	eegle	eagle
9.	shallow	shalloe	shallo	shallow
10.	greet	grete	graet	greet
11.	throte	throwt	throat	throat
12.	floan	flown	flone	flown
13.	beloa	below	belo	below
14.	freedowm	fredom	freedom	freedom
15.	indeed	indead	indede	indeed

Spelling Long *e* and *o* 71

Reader's and Writer's Notebook p. 71

Objectives

- Understand the criteria for writing an effective parody.
- Identify complete subjects and predicates.

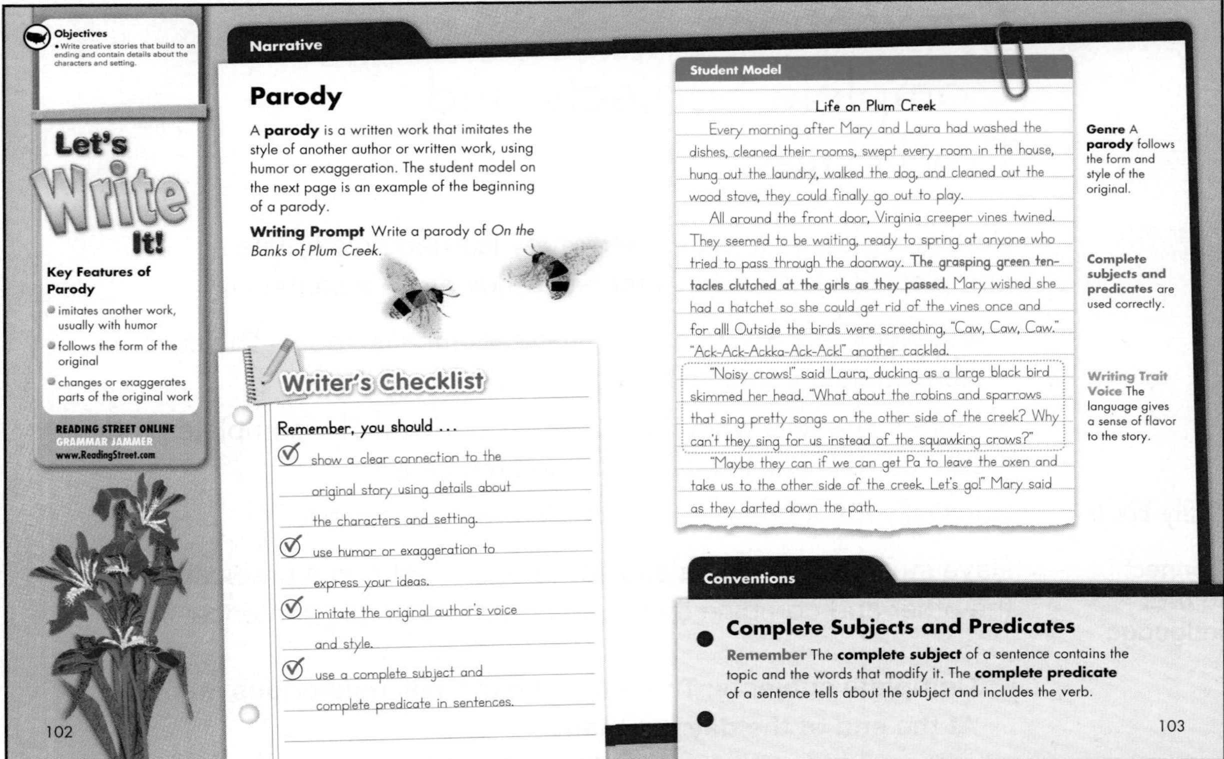

Objectives
- Write creative stories that build to an ending and contain details about the characters and setting.

Let's Write It!

Key Features of Parody
- imitates another work, usually with humor
- follows the form of the original
- changes or exaggerates parts of the original work

READING STREET ONLINE
GRAMMAR JAMMER
www.ReadingStreet.com

Narrative

Parody

A **parody** is a written work that imitates the style of another author or written work, using humor or exaggeration. The student model on the next page is an example of the beginning of a parody.

Writing Prompt Write a parody of *On the Banks of Plum Creek.*

Writer's Checklist

Remember, you should ...
- show a clear connection to the original story using details about the characters and setting.
- use humor or exaggeration to express your ideas.
- imitate the original author's voice and style.
- use a complete subject and complete predicate in sentences.

102

Student Model

Life on Plum Creek

Every morning after Mary and Laura had washed the dishes, cleaned their rooms, swept every room in the house, hung out the laundry, walked the dog, and cleaned out the wood stove, they could finally go out to play.

All around the front door, Virginia creeper vines twined. They seemed to be waiting, ready to spring at anyone who tried to pass through the doorway. **The grasping green tentacles clutched at the girls as they passed.** Mary wished she had a hatchet so she could get rid of the vines once and for all! Outside the birds were screeching, "Caw, Caw, Caw." "Ack-Ack-Ackka-Ack-Ack!" another cackled.

"Noisy crows!" said Laura, ducking as a large black bird skimmed her head. "What about the robins and sparrows that sing pretty songs on the other side of the creek? Why can't they sing for us instead of the squawking crows?"

"Maybe they can if we can get Pa to leave the oxen and take us to the other side of the creek. Let's go!" Mary said as they darted down the path.

Genre A **parody** follows the form and style of the original.

Complete subjects and predicates are used correctly.

Writing Trait Voice The language gives a sense of flavor to the story.

Conventions

Complete Subjects and Predicates

Remember The **complete subject** of a sentence contains the topic and the words that modify it. The **complete predicate** of a sentence tells about the subject and includes the verb.

103

Student Edition pp. 102–103

Let's Write It!
Parody

Teach

Use pp. 102–103 in the Student Edition. Direct students to read the key features of a parody, which appear on p. 102. Remind students that they can refer to the information in the Writer's Checklist as they write their own parody.

Read the student model on p. 103. Point out how the language is used to show humor, and how the parody is related to the ideas in the original story by being organized in the same sequence and having the same form and style of the original story. Emphasize that both the original story and the parody contain related details about the characters and setting.

Connect to conventions

Remind students that a complete subject contains all the words in the subject part of a sentence and the complete predicate contains all the words in the predicate part of the sentence. Point out the correct use of the complete subjects and predicates used in the sentences in the model.

Writing—Parody
Writing Craft: Voice

Display rubric

Display Scoring Rubric 3 from the *Teacher Resources DVD* and review the criteria for each trait under each score. Then, using the model in the Student Edition, have volunteers explain why the model should score a 4 for one of the traits. If a student offers that the model should score below 4 for a particular trait, the student should offer support for that response. Remind students that this is the rubric that will be used to evaluate the parody they write.

Scoring Rubric: Parody

	4	3	2	1
Focus/Ideas	Clear, focused ideas showing connections to original story characters, setting, and events	Focused ideas with some connections to original story setting, characters, and events	Parody has some unclear or unrelated ideas, characters, or events	Parody lacking any relationship to original story
Organization	Well-organized paragraphs that tell events in chronological order similar to order of original story	Good paragraphs with events largely in same order as original story	Some events out of chronological order as original story	No paragraphs, or events in chronological order of original story
Voice	Language and style match the tone and purpose of the original author's voice	Language matches the voice of the original author most of the time	Tries to match the original author's voice	Does not match the original author's style or voice
Word Choice	Vivid adjectives and strong verbs convey the humor and exaggeration	Clear language; mostly using humorous words and exaggeration	Some words that do not match the style or voice of the parody	Incorrect or limited word choice
Sentences	Complete and varied sentences	Smooth sentences, some complex	Too many short, choppy sentences.	Many fragments and run-ons
Conventions	Correct use of complete subjects and predicates, including compound subjects and predicates	Few errors in subjects and predicates	Weak control; some errors in use of complete subjects and predicates, no compound subjects or predicates	Serious errors that obscure meaning; subjects and predicates not used correctly

T-charts

Have students take out the T-charts they created yesterday. If they have more information to add, give them time to add it.

Write

You will use your T-chart to help you write the draft of your parody. As you write your draft, focus on getting of your ideas down and organizing them into paragraphs. You will have time to revise your draft tomorrow.

Differentiated Instruction

Advanced

Rewrite the parody Have students rewrite the parody on the student page, using the same voice the writer uses in the parody on this page. Have students share their new parodies with the class.

English Language Learners

Expression Have partners take turns reading aloud sentences from the parody on the student page that they think is funny. Have them use expression in their voices to show humor.

Objectives

- Use an engaging voice in writing.
- Use voice to show purpose in writing.

Writing, continued
Writing Trait: Voice

MINI-LESSON

Use Language to Match Purpose

Introduce Explain to students that voice is the way the writer sounds to the reader. In a parody the writer uses a voice similar to that of the original author, often exaggerated to add humor. Emphasize that the purpose of a parody is to imitate in a humorous way another piece of writing. Display the Drafting Tips for students. Remind them to use their T-charts to work on their drafts. Then display Writing Transparency 3A.

On the Banks of Pomegranate Marsh

The marsh bank was blanketed in cold, sticky mud. Hungry mosquitoes buzzed the surface of the still, green sludge. The mosquitoes stopped often. They swarmed around the girls legs. As they did they tasted samples of the dark, green slime between the girl's toes. Some of the braver mosquitoes stung the legs of the girls. Laura waded into the shallow water. Mary waded into the shallow water. The sticky smelly bottom sucked at their feet. As the girls walked, their feet released clouds of inky grey-black smoke. Mary stumbled in a sinkhole left by the footprints of the oxen.

"Be careful, Mary," giggled Laura. "You know how clumsy you can be."

Something slithered across the water just ahead of the girls. The silvery tubular thing glided hear and there. Its movement sent cold waves. Slapped against the ankles of the girls. It was hard to see the creature. The water was dark and murky . Moved so very quickly. Startled, Mary turned towards the bank. Her foot caught in sinkhole. She fell. Backwards into the water.

Laura burst out laughing.

"I'm cold, I'm wet, and I want to go home, Laura." Mary cried.

"Okay! Okay! Let me help you up ," replied Laura. Laura dipped her hand into the creek and splashed water at Mary.

Unit 1 On the Banks of Plum Creek Writing: Model 3A

Writing Transparency 3A, TR DVD

Drafting Tips

- ✔ Use details in your parody about characters, setting, and events that are related to the original story, but in a humorous or exaggerated way.
- ✔ As you draft, think about how to use language to reflect the original author's voice.
- ✔ Don't worry about grammar and mechanics when drafting. Focus on getting a complete parody down on paper.

Think Aloud I'm going to start to write a parody called *On the Banks of Pomegranate Marsh.* When I draft, I will refer to my T-chart to help organize my ideas into paragraphs. I'll carefully choose my words to imitate the voice the author used in the original story. I'll add language to match both the author's voice and the humor of a parody.

Ask students to use the drafting tips to guide them in writing their drafts. Remind them to make sure that their characters, setting, and events are all related to the ideas in the original story and to choose words that make the voice match the purpose of the parody.

ROUTINE **Quick Write for Fluency** Team Talk

1. **Talk** Pairs talk about the kinds of words and sentences they used to show a humorous voice in their writing.
2. **Write** Each partner writes a paragraph describing the purpose of the language used in his or her draft.
3. **Share** Have partners read one another's writing and check that they wrote the complete subjects and complete predicates correctly.

Routines Flip Chart

Differentiated Instruction

SI Strategic Intervention

Expand subjects and predicates Have students choose one sentence from their draft and circle the complete subject and the complete predicate. Have them add at least one word to each to help them see how they can expand into compound subjects and predicates.

Wrap Up Your Day

- ✓ **Build Concepts** What did you learn about why Laura goes exploring on her own?
- ✓ **Literary Elements: Character, Setting, Plot** How does the setting of the story and what you know about Laura help you understand the events in the story's plot?
- ✓ **Background Knowledge** How did your own background knowledge of what it's like to explore new places help you understand how Laura felt when she was out by herself?

Preview DAY 4

Tell students that tomorrow they will read more about Laura Ingalls Wilder and her life on the prairie.

Objectives

- Develop the weekly concept
- Develop oral vocabulary

Today at a Glance

Oral Vocabulary
magnificent, navigate

21st Century Skills
Online reference sources

Reading
"Laura Ingalls Wilder"

Let's Learn It!
Fluency: Rate and accuracy
Vocabulary: Multiple-meaning words
Listening/Speaking: Advertisement

Research and Inquiry
Synthesize

Spelling
Long *e* and *o*

Conventions
Complete subjects and predicates

Writing
Parody

Concept Talk

Question of the Week

Why do we want to explore new places?

Expand the concept Remind students that this week they have read about various landmarks and landscapes people encounter as they explore new places. Tell students that today they will read about how to use online reference sources to discover more about the author, Laura Ingalls Wilder.

Anchored Talk

Develop oral language Use the story structure to review the conflict and resolution on pp. 94–99 of *On the Banks of Plum Creek.* Discuss the Amazing Words *landmarks* and *enormous*. Add these words to the concept map. Use the following questions to develop students' understanding of the concept. Remind students to ask and answer questions with appropriate detail and to build on other students' answers.

- Think about how Laura used *landmarks* to navigate her way around a new territory. What are some *landmarks* you would use to help a new student find his or her way around your neighborhood?
- The *enormous* prairie seemed like it stretched on forever, up to the sky. What *enormous* landscape has filled you with a sense of awe?

Strategy Response Log INTERACT with TEXT

Have students use p. 9 in *Reader's and Writer's Notebook* to add information they learned to the L column of their KWL charts. Then have students summarize the selection.

Oral Vocabulary
Amazing Words

Amazing Words

coast	sights
route	landmarks
desert	enormous
valleys	magnificent
landscape	navigate

Amazing Words Oral Vocabulary Routine

Teach Amazing Words

1. **Introduce** Write the Amazing Word *magnificent* on the board. Have students say it aloud with you. We read about how the *magnificent* swimming pool tempted Laura on a hot day. Have students determine a definition of *magnificent*. (To be *magnificent* is to be impressive and splendid in appearance.)
2. **Demonstrate** Have students answer questions to demonstrate understanding. Why did Laura think that the pool was *magnificent*? (It was deep, shady, and cool.)
3. **Apply** Have students apply their understanding. What is a synonym for *magnificent*? (grand)

See p. OV•3 to teach *navigate*.

Routines Flip Chart

Apply Amazing Words As students read "Laura Ingalls Wilder" on pp. 104–107, have them think about what else the author considered *magnificent* and why the Ingalls family decided to *navigate* across the prairie.

Connect to reading Help students establish purpose for reading. As students read today's selection about Laura Ingalls Wilder, have them think about how the Question of the Week and the Amazing Words *magnificent* and *navigate* apply to the author of the "Little House" books.

ELL Produce Oral Language Use the Day 4 instruction on ELL Poster 3 to extend and enrich language.

ELL Poster 3

Objectives

- Introduce online reference sources.

21st Century Skills
Online Reference Sources

Introduce online reference sources

Explain to students that an online reference source is one type of technology we use today. Ask students to share what they already know about online reference sources, such as what they are and how they work.

Discuss the skill

With students, compare the written conventions used for various digital and print media. For example, ask: How could you find out more about animals that live on the prairie? (Possible responses: read a book, use an encyclopedia, use an online reference source, find online or print news articles) Explain: In the past, people weren't able to go to a Web site to obtain information because the technology did not exist. We can compare these types of media to learn how online reference sources have changed the way we gather information about a topic.

On the board, draw a Venn diagram like the one below. Label the sides *Online Reference Sources* and *Print Reference Sources.* Ask the following questions:

- How do you use an online reference source? Possible response: I type the information that I am looking for into a search window and use a mouse to click on the links that will take me to the specific information.
- How do you use print reference sources? Possible response: I look up the information in the index or alphabetically and turn to the pages that contain the specific information.
- How are the sources similar? Possible response: Both are written in a similar fashion and contain features such as maps, pictures, captions, and call-outs. Both also provide links to additional resources.

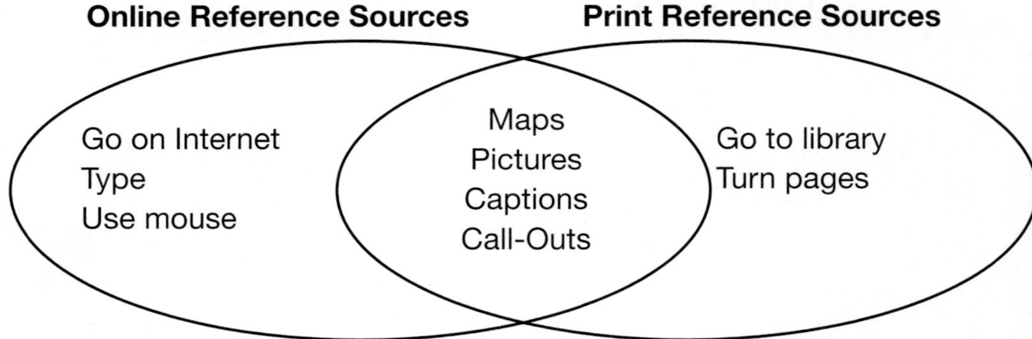

Guide practice

Have students work in pairs to list the benefits of using online reference sources instead of print reference sources to search for information. Ask them to share their lists with the class.

Connect to reading

Tell students that they will now read more about author Laura Ingalls Wilder from a variety of online reference sources. Have the class think about information they hope to discover from these sources.

Small Group Time

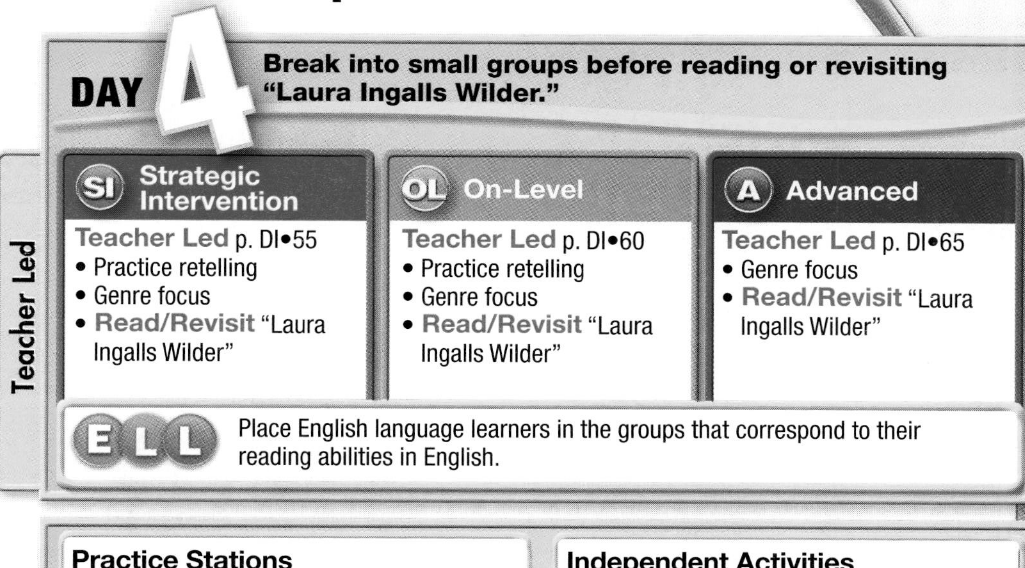

DAY 4 **Break into small groups before reading or revisiting "Laura Ingalls Wilder."**

Teacher Led

SI Strategic Intervention

Teacher Led p. DI•55
- Practice retelling
- Genre focus
- **Read/Revisit** "Laura Ingalls Wilder"

OL On-Level

Teacher Led p. DI•60
- Practice retelling
- Genre focus
- **Read/Revisit** "Laura Ingalls Wilder"

A Advanced

Teacher Led p. DI•65
- Genre focus
- **Read/Revisit** "Laura Ingalls Wilder"

ELL Place English language learners in the groups that correspond to their reading abilities in English.

Practice Stations
- Read for Meaning
- Get Fluent
- Words to Know

Independent Activities
- AudioText: "Laura Ingalls Wilder"
- *Reader's and Writer's Notebook*
- Research and Inquiry

ELL

English Language Learners

Cognates The Spanish word *referencia* may be familiar to Spanish speakers as the cognate for *reference.*

Objectives

- Use online reference sources to find out more information about a topic.

Objectives
• Compare how different writing styles are used to communicate different kinds of information on the Internet.

21st Century Skills INTERNET GUY

Online Reference Sources What is the first thing to do at a new Web site? Find out who wrote the information. Use the "About this site" button. Can you believe them?

- Online reference sources look like print sources, and they are organized the same way. Instead of turning pages by hand, you use a mouse to click from screen to screen.
- Other text features include search windows (you type in the information you are looking for) and links (underlined words, which take you to specific information).
- Use the text features as you read "Laura Ingalls Wilder." Compare the writing seen here with writing in an e-mail.

104

LAURA INGALLS WILDER

After reading the selection from *On the Banks of Plum Creek*, you want to know more about the author, Laura Ingalls Wilder, and about the book. To learn more, you go to an online reference Web site.

105

Student Edition pp. 104–105

Guide Comprehension
Skills and Strategies

Teach online reference sources

21st Century Skills: Online Reference Sources Have students preview "Laura Ingalls Wilder" on pp. 104–107. Have them look at the features of online reference sources and discuss their various parts. Then ask: How do online reference sources help you to better understand what Laura might have been like? Explain how different writing styles are used to communicate different kinds of information on the Internet.

Corrective feedback

If… students are unable to explain how they are better able to understand what Laura might have been like,
then… model exploring online reference sources.

Model the skill

Think Aloud As I read the online reference sources about how Laura Ingalls Wilder based *On the Banks of Plum Creek* on her childhood adventures, I begin to see how she wove actual events into her books. The photographs on the Web site help me to envision the author and her family.

On their own

Have students use online reference sources to find out more information about life in the mid-1880s on the prairie. For example, students could search for chores that children were expected to perform.

Extend Thinking
Think Critically

Higher-order thinking skills

Background Knowledge • Analysis What steps would you follow to learn more about the Little House books from reliable online reference sources? Possible response: Find links to an encyclopedia or other reference source; type "Little House books" into the search window; explore the search results; click on interesting links.

Literary Elements: Character, Setting, Plot • Synthesis As you explore online reference sources, what information would you attempt to discover about the characters, setting, and/or plot of *On the Banks of Plum Creek*? Possible response: I'd like to find out about how the family felt about moving to the prairie—what challenges and difficulties they faced and what role nature played in pioneer life.

Differentiated Instruction

Strategic Intervention

Online reference sources Work with students to find more titles in the Little House book series. Have students read synopses of the books and write about one they might want to read.

Advanced

Online reference sources Have students find information about an invention that was considered modern back in the 1800s, such as a sewing machine or wheat thresher, and describe how the Ingalls family might have used it.

English Language Learners

Online reference sources Remind students that reference sources can help them to quickly discover information, such as finding a new recipe or learning about a new trick for the family pet to perform. Invite volunteers to talk about what information they might want to search for using online reference sources.

Objectives

- Use links and other features found in online reference sources to find out more information about a topic.

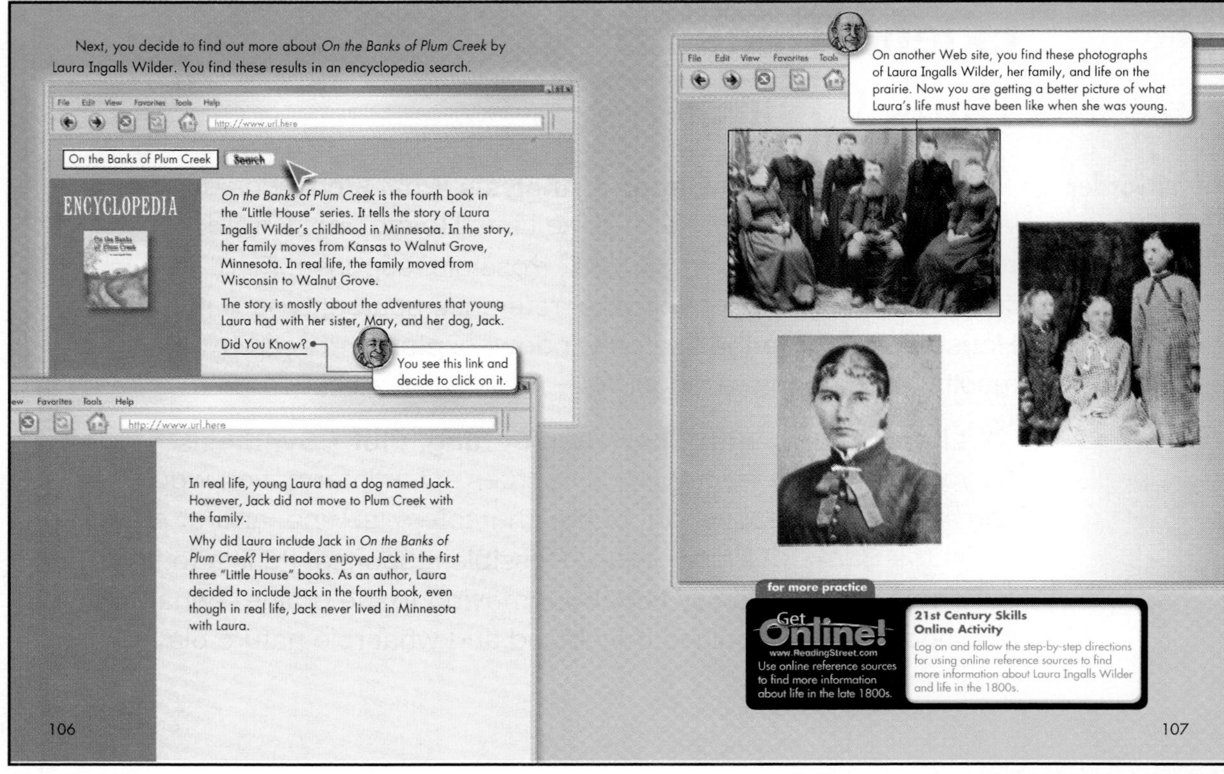

Student Edition pp. 106–107

Guide Comprehension
Skills and Strategies

Teach online reference sources

21st Century Skills: Links Explain that online reference sources may contain links to other Web-based information that is related to the topic being researched. Then ask: If you came across a "Did You Know?" link, how would you open it?

Corrective feedback

If... students are unable to explain how they would open a link found on a Web page,
then... model how to use a link in an online reference source.

Model the skill

I see a "Did You Know?" link beneath a sentence talking about the adventures Laura Ingalls Wilder shared with her sister Mary and her dog Jack. I am curious to discover more about Jack, so I click on this link. When I do this, I open another Web page that explains more about Jack and the role he plays in the Little House books.

On their own

Have students use the media center and practice opening links that they find on Web pages pertaining to Laura Ingalls Wilder. Have students tell why this information is similar or different to other sources on the Internet.

Extend Thinking
Think Critically

Higher-order thinking skills

Cause and Effect • Analysis What caused Laura to include Jack in *On the Banks of Plum Creek*? Possible response: Laura listened to her readers, who enjoyed reading about Jack's antics in the previous Little House books. She took poetic license and included him in her next book, even though he never lived in Minnesota with Laura.

Compare and Contrast • Synthesis Reread page 106. What similarities and differences can you identify between the actual events in Laura Ingalls Wilder's real life and the events that happen in *On the Banks of Plum Creek*? Possible response: In the book, Jack shared all of Mary and Laura's adventures, but I learn from Wilder's biography that Jack didn't live with the Ingalls family in Minnesota.

21st Century Skills
Online Reference Sources

For more practice

Show students how to locate the Web site by clicking on the appropriate links. Be sure that they follow the step-by-step directions for using online reference sources. Discuss with students how to find more information about author Laura Ingalls Wilder and life in the 1800s. Guide students in comparing the resources they find, as well as the written conventions used in each one.

Connect to Social Studies

On the banks of Plum Creek in Minnesota, the Ingalls family faced several natural disasters: a storm of grasshoppers that devoured their wheat crop, followed by a drought with fiery tumbleweeds, and then prairie blizzards in the winter.

ELL

English Language Learners

Online reference sources Help students find other online images of Laura Ingalls Wilder.

DAY 4 Read and Comprehend

Objectives

- Read with fluency and comprehension.
- ◎ Use a dictionary or glossary to find the definitions of multiple-meaning words.
- Create and broadcast an advertisement.

Check Fluency WCPM
SUCCESS PREDICTOR

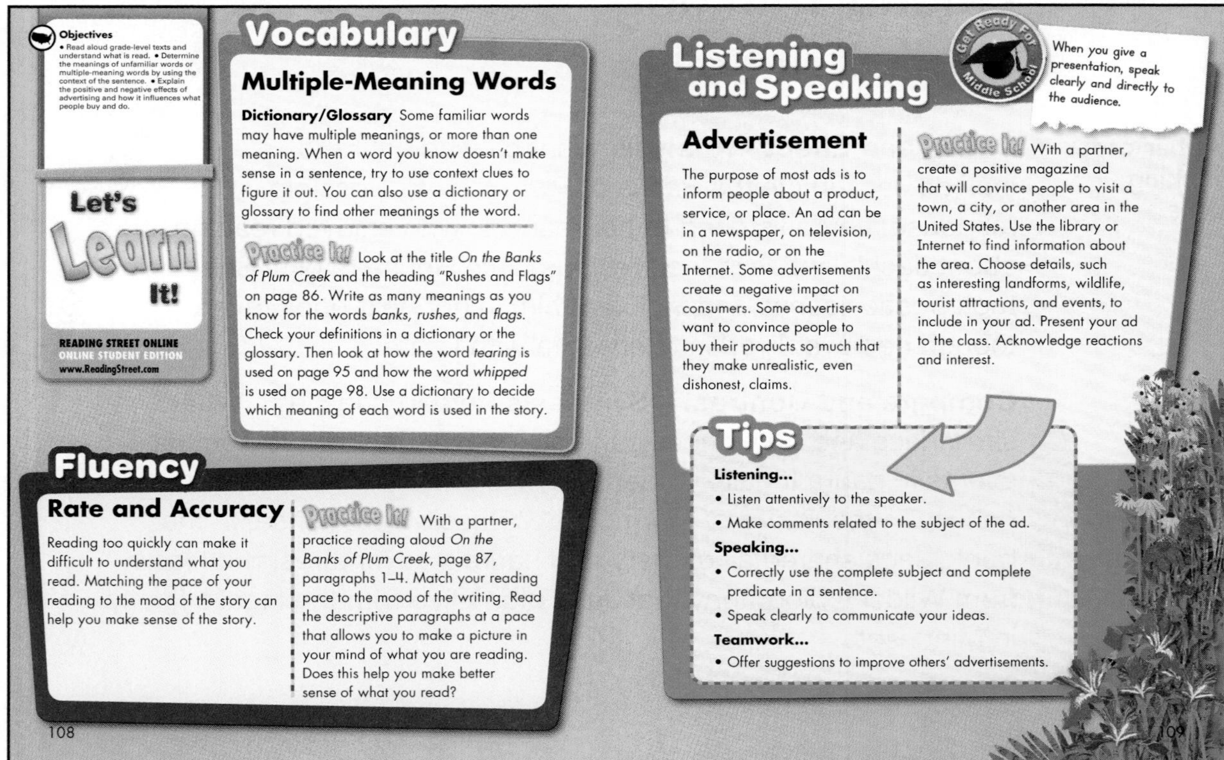

Objectives
• Read aloud grade-level texts and understand what is read. • Determine the meanings of unfamiliar words or multiple-meaning words by using the context of the sentence. • Explain the positive and negative effects of advertising and how it influences what people buy and do.

Let's Learn It!

READING STREET ONLINE
ONLINE STUDENT EDITION
www.ReadingStreet.com

Vocabulary

Multiple-Meaning Words

Dictionary/Glossary Some familiar words may have multiple meanings, or more than one meaning. When a word you know doesn't make sense in a sentence, try to use context clues to figure it out. You can also use a dictionary or glossary to find other meanings of the word.

Practice It! Look at the title *On the Banks of Plum Creek* and the heading "Rushes and Flags" on page 86. Write as many meanings as you know for the words *banks, rushes,* and *flags.* Check your definitions in a dictionary or the glossary. Then look at how the word *tearing* is used on page 95 and how the word *whipped* is used on page 98. Use a dictionary to decide which meaning of each word is used in the story.

Fluency

Rate and Accuracy

Reading too quickly can make it difficult to understand what you read. Matching the pace of your reading to the mood of the story can help you make sense of the story.

Practice It! With a partner, practice reading aloud *On the Banks of Plum Creek,* page 87, paragraphs 1–4. Match your reading pace to the mood of the writing. Read the descriptive paragraphs at a pace that allows you to make a picture in your mind of what you are reading. Does this help you make better sense of what you read?

Listening and Speaking

Get Ready For Middle School

When you give a presentation, speak clearly and directly to the audience.

Advertisement

The purpose of most ads is to inform people about a product, service, or place. An ad can be in a newspaper, on television, on the radio, or on the Internet. Some advertisements create a negative impact on consumers. Some advertisers want to convince people to buy their products so much that they make unrealistic, even dishonest, claims.

Practice It! With a partner, create a positive magazine ad that will convince people to visit a town, a city, or another area in the United States. Use the library or Internet to find information about the area. Choose details, such as interesting landforms, wildlife, tourist attractions, and events, to include in your ad. Present your ad to the class. Acknowledge reactions and interest.

Tips

Listening...
- Listen attentively to the speaker.
- Make comments related to the subject of the ad.

Speaking...
- Correctly use the complete subject and complete predicate in a sentence.
- Speak clearly to communicate your ideas.

Teamwork...
- Offer suggestions to improve others' advertisements.

108 109

Student Edition pp. 108–109

Fluency
Rate and Accuracy

Guide practice Use the Student Edition activity as an assessment tool. Make sure the reading passage is at least 200 words in length. As students read aloud with partners, walk around to make sure that they are reading at a moderate rate by matching the pace of their reading to the mood of the story and reading accurately by avoiding errors.

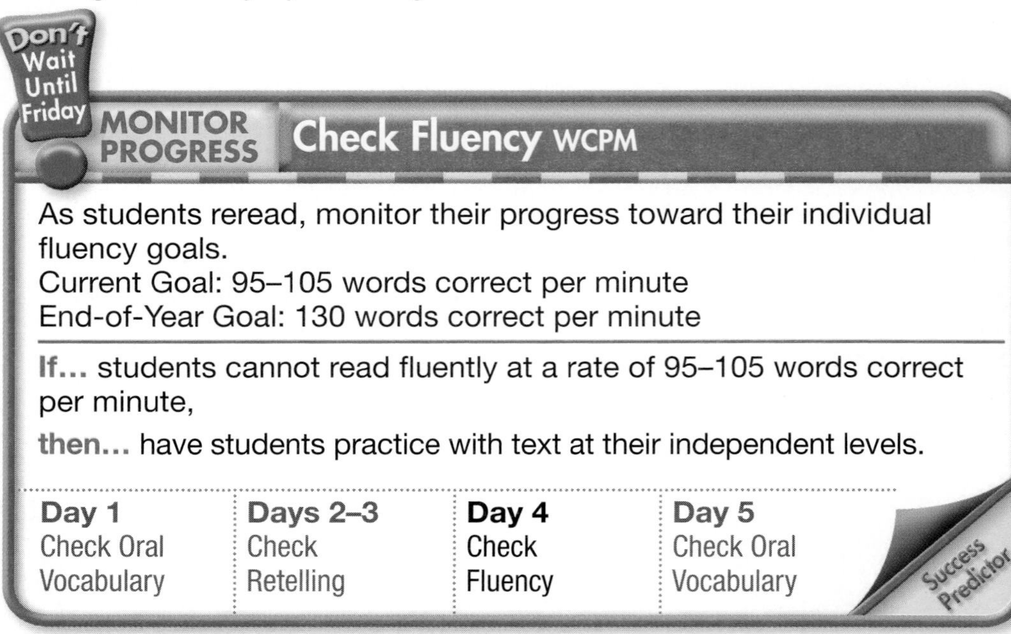

Don't Wait Until Friday

MONITOR PROGRESS **Check Fluency** WCPM

As students reread, monitor their progress toward their individual fluency goals.
Current Goal: 95–105 words correct per minute
End-of-Year Goal: 130 words correct per minute

If... students cannot read fluently at a rate of 95–105 words correct per minute,
then... have students practice with text at their independent levels.

Day 1	Days 2–3	Day 4	Day 5
Check Oral Vocabulary	Check Retelling	Check Fluency	Check Oral Vocabulary

Success Predictor

Vocabulary
Multiple-Meaning Words

Teach multiple-meaning words

Dictionary/Glossary Write these words on the board:

Point out that these words have several, or multiple, meanings, depending upon the context of the sentence.

Guide practice

Have students look up each word in a dictionary or glossary and list the multiple meanings of each word.

On their own

Pairs of students should write two sentences for each word, using a different meaning in each sentence. Check to make sure that each pair uses the words correctly so that they make sense in the sentences.

Listening and Speaking
Advertisement

Teach

Tell students that in order for an advertisement to be convincing, it must persuade people to buy a particular product, use a specific service, or visit a certain place. Remind pairs of students to use details about interesting tourist attractions to create a convincing magazine ad. They should use captivating language and an expressive voice to capture their audience's attention. They should be careful to use positive, not negative, advertisement techniques to impact consumers' behavior.

Guide practice

Be sure students speak clearly and convey an opinion supported by accurate information. Encourage students to employ appropriate eye contact, speaking rate, volume, enunciation, and the conventions of language to communicate their ideas effectively. Remind the audience members to listen attentively, ask relevant questions, and make pertinent comments about whether the ad captured their interest.

On their own

Have students present their ads to the class and explain how a negative or positive technique would affect consumer behavior for their advertisement.

Advertisement

Remind students that their advertisement should spotlight exciting events and fun activities that they believe will encourage people to visit a U.S. town or city. Tell students that they can gauge their audience's interest by verbal and facial reactions to the advertisement.

Academic Vocabulary

Advertisements are public announcements of things that are for sale, such as a product or a service. They appear in publications and on the Internet, radio, and television.

ELL

English Language Learners

Which word? Work with students to use a word such as *badger* as both a noun and a verb. After they look up the multiple meanings in a dictionary, have pairs of students use a T-chart to write the meaning of the word when it is used as a noun and the meaning when it is used as a verb.

Fluency

Success Predictor

Objectives

- Use a brochure to present information.
- Review complete subjects and predicates.
- Spell words with long *e* and long *o* correctly.

Research and Inquiry
Synthesize

Teach

Have students synthesize their research findings and results. Students should use electronic media to find and print illustrations and photographs of prairie animals, along with maps, for brochures they will create. Suggest that students also print out appropriate information they found while researching. Review how to choose relevant information from a number of sources and organize it logically.

Guide practice

Have students create their brochures and prepare their presentations for Day 5. Distribute poster board, scissors, glue, and staplers so students can create brochures. Check that they are including a variety of animals found on the prairie, text about each animal, and a map showing the habitat of the animals.

On their own

Have students include their research findings in their brochures. Then have them organize and combine information and plan their presentations. Have students write a brief explanation of their findings in which they draw conclusions about their research question.

Conventions
Complete Subjects and Predicates

Test practice Remind students that grammar skills, such as using complete subjects and predicates in sentences, are often assessed on important tests. Remind students of the definitions.

- A complete subject contains all the words in the subject.
- A complete predicate contains all the words in the predicate.

Daily Fix-It Use Daily Fix-It numbers 7 and 8 in the right margin.

On their own For additional practice, use *Reader's and Writer's Notebook,* p. 72.

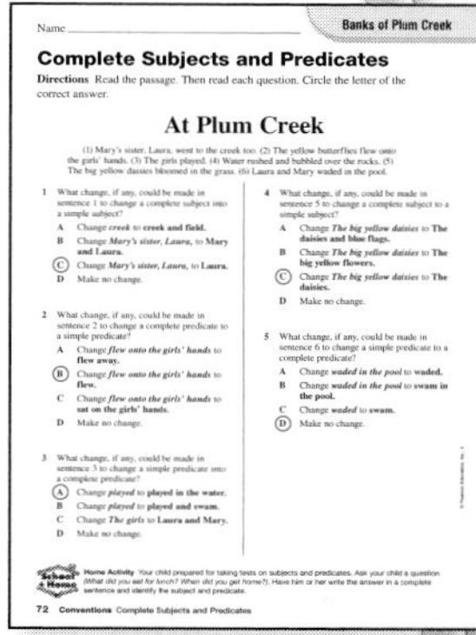

Name ______________________ Banks of Plum Creek

Complete Subjects and Predicates

Directions Read the passage. Then read each question. Circle the letter of the correct answer.

At Plum Creek

(1) Mary's sister, Laura, went to the creek too. (2) The yellow butterflies flew onto the girls' hands. (3) The girls played. (4) Water rushed and bubbled over the rocks. (5) The big yellow daisies bloomed in the grass. (6) Laura and Mary waded in the pool.

1 What change, if any, could be made in sentence 1 to change a complete subject into a simple subject?
- A Change *creek* to **creek and field.**
- B Change *Mary's sister, Laura,* to **Mary and Laura.**
- (C) Change *Mary's sister, Laura,* to **Laura.**
- D Make no change.

2 What change, if any, could be made in sentence 2 to change a complete predicate to a simple predicate?
- A Change *flew onto the girls' hands* to **flew away.**
- (B) Change *flew onto the girls' hands* to **flew.**
- C Change *flew onto the girls' hands* to **sat on the girls' hands.**
- D Make no change.

3 What change, if any, could be made in sentence 3 to change a simple predicate into a complete predicate?
- (A) Change *played* to **played in the water.**
- B Change *played* to **played and swam.**
- C Change *The girls* to **Laura and Mary.**
- D Make no change.

4 What change, if any, could be made in sentence 5 to change a complete subject to a simple subject?
- A Change *The big yellow daisies* to **The daisies and blue flags.**
- B Change *The big yellow daisies* to **The big yellow flowers.**
- (C) Change *The big yellow daisies* to **The daisies.**
- D Make no change.

5 What change, if any, could be made in sentence 6 to change a simple predicate to a complete predicate?
- A Change *waded in the pool* to **waded.**
- B Change *waded in the pool* to **swam in the pool.**
- C Change *waded* to **swam.**
- (D) Make no change.

School + Home **Home Activity** Your child prepared for taking tests on subjects and predicates. Ask your child a question (What did you eat for lunch? When did you get home?). Have him or her write the answer in a complete sentence and identify the subject and predicate.

72 **Conventions** Complete Subjects and Predicates

Reader's and Writer's Notebook p. 72

Spelling
Long *e* and *o*

Practice spelling strategy Have partners write the spelling words and circle each *ea*. Tell them to continue by circling *ee, oa,* and *ow.* Tell partners to use a different color to circle each letter combination.

On their own For additional practice, use *Let's Practice It!* p. 24 on the *Teacher Resources DVD-ROM.*

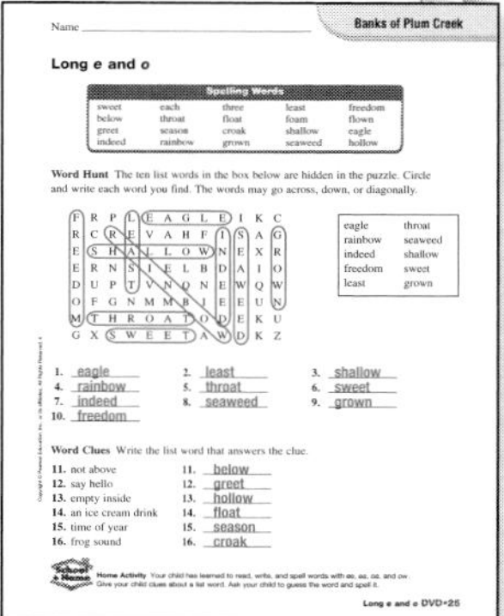

Name ______________________ Banks of Plum Creek

Long *e* and *o*

Spelling Words				
sweet	each	three	least	freedom
below	throat	float	foam	flown
greet	season	croak	shallow	eagle
indeed	rainbow	grown	seaweed	hollow

Word Hunt The ten list words in the box below are hidden in the puzzle. Circle and write each word you find. The words may go across, down, or diagonally.

```
F R P L E A G L E I K C
R C R E V A H F I S A G
E S H A L L O W N E X R
E R N S I E L B D A I O
D U P T V N O N E W Q W
O F G N M M B I E E U N
M T H R O A T O D E K U
G X S W E E T A W D K Z
```

eagle	throat
rainbow	seaweed
indeed	shallow
freedom	sweet
least	grown

1. eagle 2. least 3. shallow
4. rainbow 5. throat 6. sweet
7. indeed 8. seaweed 9. grown
10. freedom

Word Clues Write the list word that answers the clue.

11. not above — 11. below
12. say hello — 12. greet
13. empty inside — 13. hollow
14. an ice cream drink — 14. float
15. time of year — 15. season
16. frog sound — 16. croak

School + Home **Home Activity** Your child has learned to read, write, and spell words with ee, ea, oa, and ow. Give your child clues about a list word. Ask your child to guess the word and spell it.

Long e and o DVD•25

Let's Practice It!
TR DVD•25

Daily Fix-It

7. Mr. Sakata, our neighbor, was borned in Japan? (*born; Japan.*)
8. He speaks English, he speaks and write Japanese. (*English. He; writes*)

Differentiated Instruction

Advanced

Compound subjects and predicates Have one partner write a complete subject that contains a compound subject. Have the other partner write a complete predicate that contains a compound predicate. Have partners combine their complete subjects and predicates into a sentence, regardless of content. Then have them edit the sentence so that it makes sense and still contains a compound subject and predicate.

DAY 4 Language Arts

Objectives

- Revise drafts of a parody.
- Apply the revising strategy.

Writing—Parody
Revising Strategy

MINI-LESSON

Revising Strategy: Consolidating

- Yesterday we drafted a parody of *On the Banks of Plum Creek.* Today we will revise our drafts. The goal is to make our writing clear and well organized.

- Display Writing Transparency 3B. Remind students that revising does not include corrections of grammar and mechanics. Tell them that this will be done tomorrow as they proofread their work. Then introduce the revising strategy of consolidating.

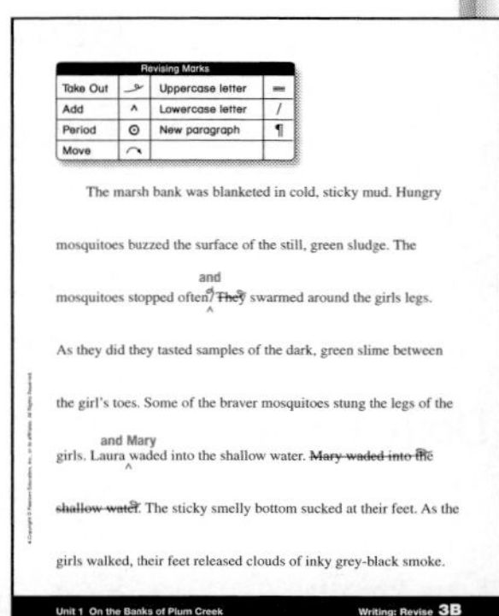

Revising Marks			
Take Out		Uppercase letter	═
Add	^	Lowercase letter	/
Period	⊙	New paragraph	¶
Move			

The marsh bank was blanketed in cold, sticky mud. Hungry mosquitoes buzzed the surface of the still, green sludge. The mosquitoes stopped often. ~~They~~ [and] swarmed around the girls legs. As they did they tasted samples of the dark, green slime between the girl's toes. Some of the braver mosquitoes stung the legs of the girls. Laura [and Mary] waded into the shallow water. ~~Mary waded into the shallow water.~~ The sticky smelly bottom sucked at their feet. As the girls walked, their feet released clouds of inky grey-black smoke.

Unit 1 On the Banks of Plum Creek — Writing: Revise 3B

Writing Transparency 3B

- When you revise, you ask yourself, *How can I make my writing clear and smooth?* Consolidating is the strategy in which text is combined to make writing smoother and less repetitious. Let's look at my first paragraph. I see the third and fourth sentences are related. I can combine them by changing each simple predicate to a compound predicate. I'll cross off *They* in the second sentence and form one sentence. Combine the sentences and read the new sentence aloud. Do the same for the seventh and eighth sentences. Reread your parody and look for places where you can consolidate.

Tell students that as they revise, not only should they look for places where they can consolidate, they should also check that their paragraphs are well organized and clear.

Revising Tips

- ✔ Use a variety of simple and complex sentences.
- ✔ Combine subjects or predicates of related sentences to form one more interesting and smoother sentence.
- ✔ Change language to reflect the humor or exaggeration of the parody.

Peer conferencing

Peer Revision Have groups of students exchange papers for peer revision. Partners can use the Revising Tips as a checklist for listing the areas in which they think their partner needs to improve. Refer to the *Reader's and Writer's Notebook* for more information about peer conferencing.

Have students revise their compositions using the information their classmates gave during the Peer Revision as well as the key features of a parody to guide them. Be sure that students are using the revising strategy consolidating as they revise.

Corrective feedback

Circulate around the room to monitor students and confer with them as they revise. Remind students that they will have time to proofread tomorrow. They should be working on consolidating and on content, coherence, and organization today.

ROUTINE **Quick Write for Fluency** Team Talk

1. **Talk** Have students discuss the part of *On the Banks of Plum Creek* for which they wrote their parody.
2. **Write** Each student writes a paragraph comparing one sentence from the original story and telling how he or she wrote a parody of it.
3. **Share** Partners check each other's comparisons to see if the parody and original sentences have the same form.

Routines Flip Chart

Teacher Tip

If students have difficulty consolidating, have them look for especially short sentences in their parodies to see if they are related.

English Language Learners

Leveled support: Combining sentences

Beginning Limit combining subjects for simple sentences orally, such as saying: *Jen runs. Maria runs.* Have students orally combine to *Jen and Maria run.*

Intermediate Repeat the same activity as beginning learners, but expand to combining predicates from simple sentences.

Advanced/Advanced High Repeat the same activity as intermediate learners, but have students write sentences rather than limiting it to oral practice.

Wrap Up Your Day

- ✔ **Build Concepts** Have students discuss what it must be like to explore the uninhabited land around a new home.
- ✔ **Oral Vocabulary** Monitor students' use of oral vocabulary as they respond to the question: What were important things that Laura noticed around her new home as she explored?
- ✔ **Text Features** Discuss how graphic sources and links help students understand text.

Remind students to think about why people want to explore new places.

Objectives

- Review the weekly concept.
- Review oral vocabulary.

Today at a Glance

Oral Vocabulary

Comprehension
◎ Literary elements: Character, setting, plot

Lesson Vocabulary
◎ Multiple-meaning words

Word Analysis
Word ending *-ing*

Literary Terms
Foreshadowing

Assessment
Fluency
Comprehension

Research and Inquiry
Communication

Spelling
Long *e* and *o*

Conventions
Complete subjects and predicates

Writing
Parody

Check Oral Vocabulary
SUCCESS PREDICTOR

Concept Wrap Up

Question of the Week

Why do we want to explore new places?

Review the concept Have students look back at the reading selections to find examples that best demonstrate how people explore new places.

Review Amazing Words Display and review this week's concept map. Remind students that this week they have learned ten amazing words related to exploring new places. Have students use the Amazing Words and the concept map to answer the question, *Why do we want to explore new places?*

ELL Check Concept and Language
Use the Day 5 instructions on ELL Poster 3 to monitor students' understanding of the lesson concept.

ELL Poster 3

Amazing Ideas

Connect to the Big Question

Have pairs of students discuss how the Question of the Week connects to the Big Question: *What can we discover from new places and people?* Tell students to use the concept map and what they have learned from this week's Anchored Talks and reading selections to form an Amazing Idea—a realization or "big idea" about Turning Points. Remind partners to pose and answer questions with appropriate detail, and to give suggestions that build on each other's ideas. Then ask pairs to share their Amazing Ideas with the class.

Amazing Ideas might include these key concepts:

- People around the world travel to discover different cultures and places.
- The highlight of your trip might be exploring magnificent landmarks and landscapes.
- As you navigate unfamiliar locations, you learn interesting things about people and places.

Write about it

Have students write a few sentences about their Amazing Idea beginning with "This week I learned . . ."

It's Friday

MONITOR PROGRESS — **Check Oral Vocabulary**

Have individuals use this week's Amazing Words to describe exploring new places. Monitor students' abilities to use the Amazing Words and note which words you need to reteach.

If... students have difficulty using the Amazing Words,
then... reteach using the Oral Vocabulary Routine, pp. 79a, 82b, 94b, 104b, OV•3.

Day 1	Days 2–3	Day 4	Day 5
Check Oral Vocabulary	Check Retelling	Check Fluency	Check Oral Vocabulary

Success Predictor

Amazing Words

route	sights
coast	landmarks
desert	enormous
valleys	magnificent
landscape	navigate

ELL

English Language Learners

Concept map Work with students to add new words to the concept map.

Objectives

- ◎ Review literary elements: character, setting, plot.
- ◎ Review multiple-meaning words.
- Review word ending *-ing.*
- Review foreshadowing.

Comprehension Review

Literary Elements: Character, Setting, Plot

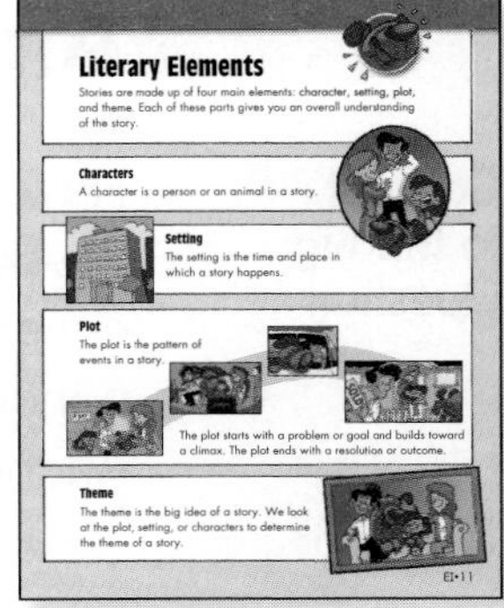

Literary Elements

Stories are made up of four main elements: character, setting, plot, and theme. Each of these parts gives you an overall understanding of the story.

Characters

A character is a person or an animal in a story.

Setting

The setting is the time and place in which a story happens.

Plot

The plot is the pattern of events in a story.

The plot starts with a problem or goal and builds toward a climax. The plot ends with a resolution or outcome.

Theme

The theme is the big idea of a story. We look at the plot, setting, or characters to determine the theme of a story.

EI•11

Student Edition EI•11

Teach literary elements

Envision It!

Review the definitions of the literary elements character, setting, and plot on p. 80. Remind students that characters are who the story is about, the setting is when and where a story takes place, and the plot is the sequence of events that happen in a story. For additional support have students review p. EI•11 on literary elements.

Guide practice

Have partners identify the sequence of events in *On the Banks of Plum Creek.* Have student pairs find an example of how the setting and characters in the story influenced the sequence of main events in the plot.

On their own

For additional practice with literary elements, use *Let's Practice It!* p. 26 on the *Teacher Resources DVD-ROM.*

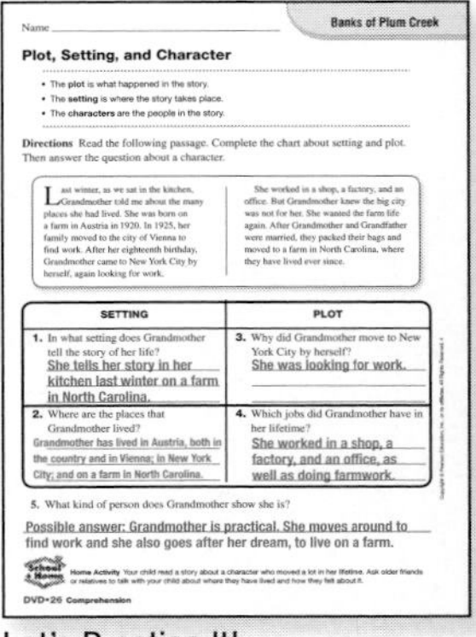

Name ____________ Banks of Plum Creek

Plot, Setting, and Character

- The **plot** is what happened in the story.
- The **setting** is where the story takes place.
- The **characters** are the people in the story.

Directions Read the following passage. Complete the chart about setting and plot. Then answer the question about a character.

Last winter, as we sat in the kitchen, Grandmother told me about the many places she had lived. She was born on a farm in Austria in 1920. In 1925, her family moved to the city of Vienna to find work. After her eighteenth birthday, Grandmother came to New York City by herself, again looking for work.

She worked in a shop, a factory, and an office. But Grandmother knew the big city was not for her. She wanted the farm life again. After Grandmother and Grandfather were married, they packed their bags and moved to a farm in North Carolina, where they have lived ever since.

SETTING	PLOT
1. In what setting does Grandmother tell the story of her life? She tells her story in her kitchen last winter on a farm in North Carolina.	3. Why did Grandmother move to New York City by herself? She was looking for work.
2. Where are the places that Grandmother lived? Grandmother has lived in Austria, both in the country and in Vienna; in New York City; and on a farm in North Carolina.	4. Which jobs did Grandmother have in her lifetime? She worked in a shop, a factory, and an office, as well as doing farmwork.

5. What kind of person does Grandmother show she is?

Possible answer: Grandmother is practical. She moves around to find work and she also goes after her dream, to live on a farm.

Home Activity Your child read a story about a character who moved a lot in her lifetime. Ask older friends or relatives to talk with your child about where they have lived and how they felt about it.

DVD•26 Comprehension

Let's Practice It!
TR DVD•26

Vocabulary Review

Multiple-Meaning Words

Teach multiple-meaning words

Remind students to use a dictionary or glossary to help them understand the meanings of multiple-meaning words.

Guide practice

Review with students how to find the correct meaning of *bank* using a dictionary. Explain that there are several definitions and students should use the context of the sentence to determine which meaning the author intends.

On their own

Have students work with partners to write sentences using this week's lesson vocabulary words. Partners can trade sentences and identify the context clues that help them determine the correct meaning of each word.

Word Analysis Review
Word Ending *-ing*

Teach word ending *-ing* Review the different functions of the word ending *-ing* with students. Display the word *cooking*. Have students underline the base word and circle the word ending.

Guide practice Display the following words: *splashing, laughing, talking,* and *sleeping.* Use the Strategy for Meaningful Word Parts to teach the word *splashing.*

ROUTINE **Strategy for Meaningful Word Parts**

1. **Look for meaningful word parts** Display the word *splashing.* Circle the word ending *-ing* and underline the base word *splash.*
2. **Connect to meaning** Define each smaller part of the word. *Splash* means "to cause something liquid to move and scatter." As an adjective, *splashing* can describe a sound.
3. **Read the word** Blend the meaningful word parts together to read *splashing.*

Routines Flip Chart

On their own Have students work in pairs to circle the base words in *laughing, talking,* and *sleeping.*

Literary Terms Review
Foreshadowing

Teach foreshadowing Have students reread the "Strange Animal" section of *On the Banks of Plum Creek* on pp. 93–95. Remind students that foreshadowing is hints and clues about what will occur later.

Guide practice Find an example of foreshadowing from the "Strange Animal" section. Discuss how the author uses foreshadowing. Have students find other examples of foreshadowing and discuss.

On their own Have students make a T-chart with the headings *Clues* and *What will happen.* Ask them to list clue words or phrases and the events in the story they foreshadow.

Lesson Vocabulary

badger a burrowing, flesh-eating mammal
bank the rising ground at the edge of a lake, river, or sea
bristled stand up straight, as hair or fur
jointed having one or more pieces where two things or parts are joined
patched mended with a scrap of material
ruffled made to look as if trimmed with strips of material gathered together like ruffles
rushes marsh plants with hollow stems

ELL

English Language Learners

Sequence If students have difficulty determining which events happen simultaneously, have them search for clue words such as *meanwhile, while,* and *during.*

Word ending *-ing* Have students practice adding *-ing* to verbs they list from the selection.

DAY 5 Wrap Up your Week

15–20 min

Objectives

- Read grade-level text with fluency.

Assessment

Check words correct per minute

Fluency Make two copies of the fluency passage on p. 109k. As the student reads the text aloud, mark mistakes on your copy. Also mark where the student is at the end of one minute. To check the student's comprehension of the passage, have him or her retell what was read. To figure words correct per minute (WCPM), subtract the number of mistakes from the total number of words read in one minute.

WCPM

Corrective feedback

If... students cannot read fluently at a rate of 95–105 WCPM,
then... make sure they practice with text at their independent reading level. Provide additional fluency practice by pairing nonfluent readers with fluent readers.

If... students already read at 130 WCPM,
then... have them read a book of their choice independently.

Plan to Assess Fluency

- ☑ **Week 1** Assess Advanced students.
- ☑ **Week 2** Assess Strategic Intervention students.
- ☑ **This week assess On-Level students.**
- ☐ **Week 4** Assess Strategic Intervention students.
- ☐ **Week 5** Assess any students you have not yet checked during this unit.

Set individual goals for students to enable them to reach the year-end goal.

- Current Goal: 95–105 WCPM
- Year-End Goal: 130 WCPM

Small Group Time

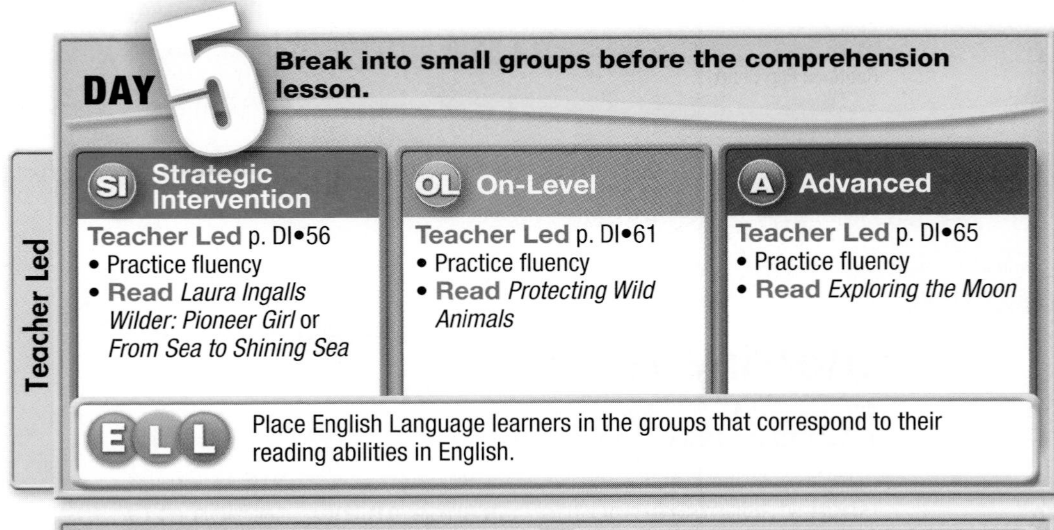

DAY 5
Break into small groups before the comprehension lesson.
Teacher Led
SI Strategic Intervention
Teacher Led p. DI•56
• Practice fluency
• Read Laura Ingalls Wilder: Pioneer Girl or From Sea to Shining Sea
OL On-Level
Teacher Led p. DI•61
• Practice fluency
• Read Protecting Wild Animals
A Advanced
Teacher Led p. DI•65
• Practice fluency
• Read Exploring the Moon
ELL
Place English Language learners in the groups that correspond to their reading abilities in English.

Practice Stations

- Words to Know
- Get Fluent
- Read for Meaning

Independent Activities

- Grammar Jammer
- Concept Talk Video
- Vocabulary Activities

Name ____________________

The Train Man

The steam locomotive whistled and began to move. "I can't wait to 12
visit Salt Lake City," Lilly told her younger brother Ted. 22

An older man in a seat across from them looked up. "Going to 35
Utah?" he asked. "We'll be crossing track I built with my own hands." 48

Ted's eyes widened. 51

"It wasn't easy, building the railroad," the man said. "We worked 62
every day, sometimes sixteen hours a day, laying track. Many lives were 74
lost. Mine was almost one of them." 81

Lilly and Ted waited for more, but the man fell silent and slept. 94

"It was in Omaha, Nebraska, near here, where we started the 105
tracks," the man said when he woke. "Thirty years ago, in 1865. The 118
Union Pacific built tracks west from Omaha. The Central Pacific built 129
them east from Sacramento. Both tried to reach Salt Lake City first." 141

The next day, when Nebraska's plains had turned to Wyoming's 151
hills, the man continued. "We were building a bridge," he said. "I 163
fell 50 feet into a canyon. Broke my back. It could have been worse, 177
though. Other men blasted through mountains. Those explosives were 186
touchy. Many men died." 190

Lilly and Ted learned much from the train man. By the time they 203
reached Salt Lake City, they appreciated the railway that had taken 214
them there. 216

MONITOR PROGRESS

- Check Fluency

DAY 5 Wrap Up your Week

15–20 min

Objectives

- Read grade-level text with comprehension.

Assessment

Check literary elements

Literary Elements: Character, Setting, Plot Use "A Home on the Prairie" on p. 109m to check students' understanding of the literary elements character, setting, and plot.

1. What did Robert think about his new life on the Illinois prairie? Possible response: Although it was hard work to plow the land, helpful neighbors and a field of farm crops started to make Robert feel at home.
2. How does the prairie setting influence the plot? Possible response: The free farm land on the prairie spurred the move from Pennsylvania to Illinois. However, the tough prairie grass roots made living on the prairie difficult.
3. Why do you think members of the Murphy family are such helpful neighbors? Possible response: The Murphy family probably had help with their fields, crops, and family when they first moved to the Illinois prairie. They remember how difficult it was to set up a homestead.

Corrective feedback

If... students are unable to answer the comprehension questions,
then... use the Reteach lesson in the *First Stop* book.

Name ______________________________

A Home On The Prairie

The oxen pulled the wagon to a stop near a grove of trees. Robert climbed out and looked around. Prairie stretched as far as he could see. "So this is Illinois," Robert said, as his little brother Jeff climbed out of the wagon. "I thought we'd never make it."

The three-month journey from Pennsylvania to Illinois had been long and dangerous. First their wagon had gotten stuck in mud. Then they'd gotten lost. Finally, though, on May 18, 1838, they'd arrived. "It'll be worth it," Pop said, unloading the wagon. "There's free land here to farm. And we'll have a home to call our own."

"First things first," Pop told Mom. "We'll plow the land and plant seeds for crops. Then we'll build a proper home."

As they built a temporary shelter in the grove, a neighbor rode up on his horse. The neighbor, Mr. Murphy, helped raise the shelter and told them about his farm not far away. "It's not easy to plow this land," he said. "You'll need a special metal plow."

The next day, Mr. Murphy and his family came by with food and a plow. Robert and Jeff played with Mr. Murphy's sons while Mr. Murphy showed Pop how to plow through the tough roots of the tall prairie grasses.

After a few weeks, Robert and his family had their land plowed and seeds planted. Using wood from the trees nearby, they built a home. Living on the Illinois prairie was hard work, Robert found. However, with neighbors to help and crops growing, it was beginning to feel like a real home.

MONITOR PROGRESS

• Character, Setting, and Plot

Objectives

- Communicate inquiry results.
- Administer spelling test.
- Review complete subjects and predicates.

Research and Inquiry
Communicate

Present ideas Have students share their inquiry results by presenting their information and giving a brief talk on their research. Have students display the brochures they created on Day 4.

Listening and speaking Remind students how to be good speakers and how to communicate effectively with their audience.

- Respond to relevant questions with appropriate details.
- Speak clearly and loudly.
- Keep eye contact with audience members.

Remind students of these tips for being a good listener.

- Listen attentively to speakers.
- Wait until the speaker has finished before raising your hand to ask a relevant question or make a pertinent comment.
- Be polite, even if you disagree.

Spelling Test
Long *e* and *o*

Spelling test To administer the spelling test, refer to the directions, words, and sentences on p. 81c.

Conventions
Extra Practice

Teach Remind students that a complete subject contains all the words in the subject part of a sentence and a complete predicate contains all the words in the predicate part of the sentence.

Guide practice Have students circle the complete subject and underline the complete predicate in each sentence. Have them draw a box around the simple subject and predicate.

The entire class was invited to the party.

Last night my next-door neighbor visited us.

Daily Fix-It Use Daily Fix-It numbers 9 and 10 in the right margin.

On their own Write these sentences. Have students look back in *On the Banks of Plum Creek* to find complete subjects or predicates to fill in the blanks. Remind them to include the correct end punctuation when writing their completed sentences. Students should complete *Let's Practice It!* p. 27 on the *Teacher Resources DVD-ROM.*

1. **The flat reef bank ________ .** (was warm soft mud)
2. **________ flew on blurry wings.** (Bright dragonflies)
3. **The mud ________ .** (squeezed up between Laura's toes)
4. **On top of the water the water-bugs ________ .** (skated)

Daily Fix-It

9. Your going to love the Rocky Mountains in colorado. *(You're; Colorado)*
10. They are higher then the mountains. Where we live. *(than; mountains where)*

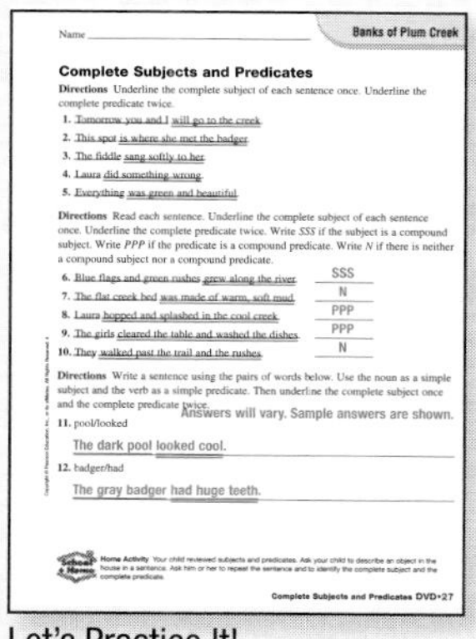

Name ________________ Banks of Plum Creek

Complete Subjects and Predicates

Directions Underline the complete subject of each sentence once. Underline the complete predicate twice.

1. Tomorrow you and I will go to the creek.
2. This spot is where she met the badger.
3. The fiddle sang softly to her.
4. Laura did something wrong.
5. Everything was green and beautiful.

Directions Read each sentence. Underline the complete subject of each sentence once. Underline the complete predicate twice. Write *SSS* if the subject is a compound subject. Write *PPP* if the predicate is a compound predicate. Write *N* if there is neither a compound subject nor a compound predicate.

6. Blue flags and green rushes grew along the river. SSS
7. The flat creek bed was made of warm, soft mud. N
8. Laura hopped and splashed in the cool creek. PPP
9. The girls cleared the table and washed the dishes. PPP
10. They walked past the trail and the rushes. N

Directions Write a sentence using the pairs of words below. Use the noun as a simple subject and the verb as a simple predicate. Then underline the complete subject once and the complete predicate twice.

Answers will vary. Sample answers are shown.

11. pool/looked
The dark pool looked cool.
12. badger/had
The gray badger had huge teeth.

Home Activity Your child reviewed subjects and predicates. Ask your child to describe an object in the house in a sentence. Ask him or her to repeat the sentence and to identify the complete subject and the complete predicate.

Complete Subjects and Predicates DVD•27

Let's Practice It!
TR DVD•27

Objectives

- Proofread revised drafts of parody, including use of complete subjects and predicates.
- Create and present final draft.

Writing—Parody
Complete Subjects and Predicates

Review Revising Remind students that yesterday they revised their parodies, looking especially at where they could consolidate sentences to make their writing clearer and flow more smoothly. Today they will proofread their parodies.

MINI-LESSON

Proofread for Complete Sentences

- **Teach** When we proofread, we search for errors in spelling, capitalization, punctuation, and grammar. Today we will focus on making sure that our sentences all have a complete subject and predicate, and that there are no sentence fragments.

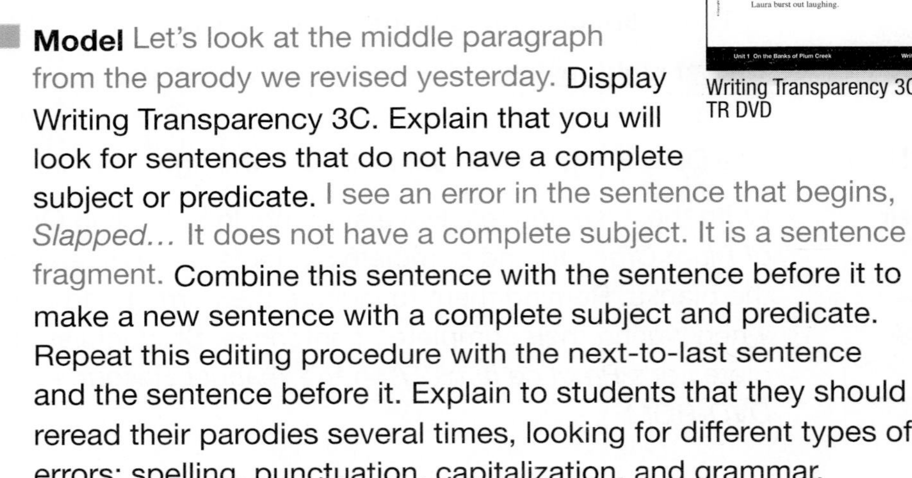

Writing Transparency 3C, TR DVD

- **Model** Let's look at the middle paragraph from the parody we revised yesterday. Display Writing Transparency 3C. Explain that you will look for sentences that do not have a complete subject or predicate. I see an error in the sentence that begins, *Slapped…* It does not have a complete subject. It is a sentence fragment. Combine this sentence with the sentence before it to make a new sentence with a complete subject and predicate. Repeat this editing procedure with the next-to-last sentence and the sentence before it. Explain to students that they should reread their parodies several times, looking for different types of errors: spelling, punctuation, capitalization, and grammar.

Proofread Display the Proofreading Tips. Ask students to proofread their parodies, using the Proofreading Tips and paying particular attention to complete subjects and predicates. Circulate around the room. When students finish editing their own work, have pairs proofread one another's parodies.

Proofreading Tips

- ✓ Be sure all sentences have a complete subject and predicate.
- ✓ Check that all words are spelled correctly. Use a dictionary if you are unsure about any words.
- ✓ Check that all sentences are punctuated correctly.

Present

Have students revise their final drafts in response to the feedback of their classmates.

Give students two options for publishing their written work to a specific audience: An oral presentation to the class or a written final parody. For oral presentations, have a class show. Have an announcer introduce each student, who then "performs" his or her parody as if on stage. Have students rehearse their presentations with a partner before putting on the show. If presenting parodies in written form, have students make printouts of their parodies, using any art tools they are familiar with to decorate their papers before printing. Have printouts available on a table for others to read at their leisure. When students have finished, have each complete a Writing Self-Evaluation Guide.

ROUTINE **Quick Write for Fluency** Team Talk

1. **Talk** Have students discuss what they learned about imitating another writer's work.
2. **Write** Each student writes a sentence telling the most surprising thing he or she learned.
3. **Share** Partners read their own writing to their partner.

Routines Flip Chart

Teacher Note

Writing self-evaluation Make copies of the Writing Self-Evaluation Guide on p. 39 of the *Reader's and Writer's Notebook* and hand out to students.

English Language Learners

Support editing Provide practice with fixing sentence fragments such as *My friend.* or *Stopped talking* by adding the missing subject or predicate. Beginning learners may be more comfortable fixing sentence fragments orally.

Poster preview Prepare students for next week by using Week 4, ELL Poster 4. Read the Poster Talk-Through to introduce the concepts and vocabulary. Ask students to identify and describe objects and actions in the art.

Selection summary Send home the summary of *The Horned Toad Prince* in English and the students' home languages, if available. Students can read the summary with family members.

Preview NEXT WEEK

What can we discover in the landscape of the Southwest? Tell students that next week they will read a story that takes place in the Southwest about a girl who tries to trick a horned toad.

DAY 5 Assessment Checkpoints for the Week

Weekly Assessment

Weekly Tests

Use pp. 15–22 of *Weekly Tests* to check:

✔ **Word Analysis** Word Ending *-ing*

✔ **Comprehension Skill** Literary Elements: Character, Setting, Plot

✔ Review **Comprehension Skill** Sequence

✔ **Lesson Vocabulary**

badger	patched
bank	ruffled
bristled	rushes
jointed	

Differentiated Assessment

Advanced

On-Level

SI
Strategic Intervention

Fresh Reads for Fluency and Comprehension

Use pp. 13–18 of *Fresh Reads for Fluency and Comprehension* to check:

✔ **Comprehension Skill** Literary Elements: Character, Setting, Plot

✔ Review **Comprehension Skill** Sequence

✔ **Fluency** Words Correct Per Minute

Managing Assessment

Assessment Handbook

Use *Assessment Handbook* for:

✔ **Weekly Assessment Blackline Masters for Monitoring Progress**

✔ **Observation Checklists**

✔ **Record-Keeping Forms**

✔ **Portfolio Assessment**

Teacher Notes

Pacing Small Group Instruction

15–20 min

5-Day Plan

DAY 1	• Reinforce the concept • Read Leveled Readers Concept Literacy Below Level
DAY 2	• Character, Setting, and Plot • Background Knowledge • Revisit Student Edition pp. 84–93
DAY 3	• Multiple-Meaning Words • Revisit Student Edition pp. 94–99
DAY 4	• Practice Retelling • Read/Revisit Student Edition pp. 104–107
DAY 5	• Reread for fluency • Reread Leveled Readers

3- or 4-Day Plan

DAY 1	• Reinforce the concept • Read Leveled Readers
DAY 2	• Character, Setting, and Plot • Background Knowledge • Revisit Student Edition pp. 84–93
DAY 3	• Multiple-Meaning Words • Revisit Student Edition pp. 94–99
DAY 4	• Practice Retelling • Read/Revisit Student Edition pp. 104–107 • Reread for fluency • Reread Leveled Readers

3-Day Plan: Eliminate the shaded box.

SI Strategic Intervention — DAY 1

Build Background

- **Reinforce the Concept** Discuss the weekly question *Why do we want to explore new places?* People want to explore new places for all kinds of reasons. We may want to explore a new place simply because we are curious. For example, imagine exploring your new classroom on the first day of school. We also explore places when we think we might benefit from learning about them. For example, one reason people explored the Wild West was because they needed new places to live. The exploration showed that there were good places to live, and settlers moved west to start farms and towns. Discuss the words in the concept map.
- **Connect to Reading** The people you will read about this week helped settle the plains of America. They traveled far and made homes where no towns existed. What does "Going Places" tell us that helps us understand the experiences of early settlers? (*They had to travel great distances without the benefits of modern transportation, maps, or company.*)

Objectives

- Participate in teacher-led discussions by answering questions with appropriate detail.

DAY 1

For a complete literacy instructional plan and additional practice with this week's target skills and strategies, see the **Leveled Reader Teaching Guide.**

Concept Literacy Reader

- **Read** *Laura Ingalls Wilder: Pioneer Girl*
- **Before Reading** Preview the story with students, focusing on key concepts and vocabulary. Then have them set a purpose for reading.
- **During Reading** Read the first two pages of the story aloud while students track the print. If students are able, have them read and discuss the remainder of the book with a partner.
- **After Reading** After students finish reading the story, connect it to the weekly question *Why do we want to explore new places?*

Below-Level Reader

- **Read** *From Sea to Shining Sea*
- **Before Reading** Have students preview the story using the illustrations. Then have students set a purpose for reading.
- **During Reading** Do a choral reading of the first four pages. Then have students finish reading the book with a partner. Have partners discuss these questions:
  - Who approved the Lewis and Clark expedition? (*President Thomas Jefferson*)

  - What is the goal of the expedition? (*to explore the Louisiana Purchase*)
  - Why do Lewis and Clark want to do it? (*to find out more about the country*)
- **After Reading** Have students look at and discuss the concept map. Connect the reader to the weekly question *Why do we want to explore new places?* In *From Sea to Shining Sea,* why do the explorers want to go west? (*to see what is in the country's newest territory*)

MONITOR PROGRESS

If... students have difficulty reading the selection with a partner,
then... have them follow along as they listen to the Leveled Readers DVD-ROM.

If... students have trouble understanding why Lewis and Clark explored the west,
then... reread the pertinent pages and discuss the reasons together.

Objectives

- Participate in teacher-led discussions by answering questions with appropriate detail.

Reinforce Comprehension

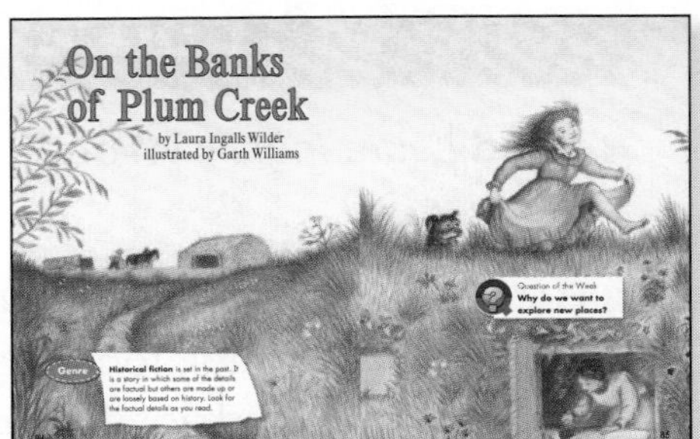

Skill Literary Elements: Character, Setting, and Plot Review the *Envision It!* p. EI•11 on literary elements. Then use p. 80 to review the definitions of character, setting, and plot. Setting includes both place and time. Clues to the time of a story include pictures and descriptions of objects. If an object is familiar to you, the story probably takes place in recent times. If an object is not familiar, the story may take place in the past or in the future.

Strategy Background Knowledge Review the definition of background knowledge. Remind students to think about what they already know about the topic as they read the story. For additional support, refer students to *Envision It!* p. EI•16.

Revisit *On the Banks of Plum Creek* on pp. 84–93. As partners read, have them apply the comprehension skill and strategy to the story.

- Who are the characters in this story? (*Laura, Mary, Pa, and Ma*)
- What is the setting of the story? (*the family's home and surroundings near Plum Creek in the late 1800s*)
- What clues indicate that the setting is in the past? (*The floor of the house is "earthen." Ma does her mending by hand; the sheets are made of muslin. The family fetches water from the spring. For entertainment Pa plays the fiddle—there is no mention of TV, computers, or electricity.*)
- What is the plot about? (*the experiences of Laura and her family as the girls grow up*)

Use the During Reading Differentiated Instruction for additional support for struggling readers.

MONITOR PROGRESS

If... students have difficulty reading along with the group,
then... have them follow along as they listen to the AudioText.

Objectives
- Describe the interaction of characters including their relationships.
- Identify the setting of a story.

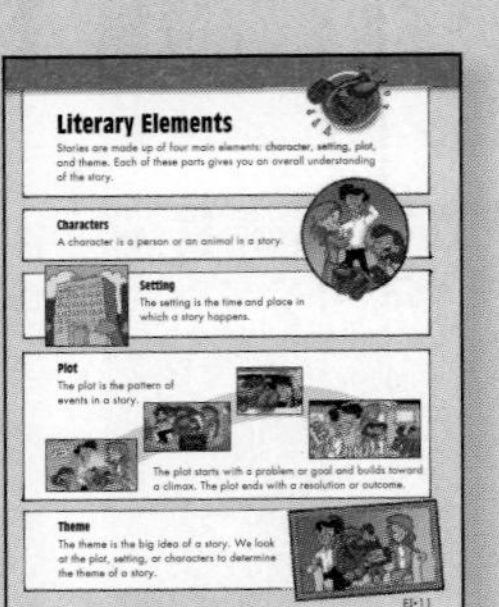

Student Edition, p. EI•11

More Reading

Use additional Leveled Readers or other texts at students' instructional levels to reinforce this week's skills and strategies. For text suggestions, see the Leveled Reader Database or the Leveled Readers Skills Chart on pp. CL 24–CL 29.

Reinforce Vocabulary

Multiple-Meaning Words Say the word *rushes* as you write it on the board. I wonder what this word means. When I look in the dictionary, I see that the word *rush* has many meanings. It can be a noun or a verb. As a noun, it can refer to a type of plant that grows in marshes. As a verb, it can mean "hurry." Review *Words!* on pp. W•10 and W•14.

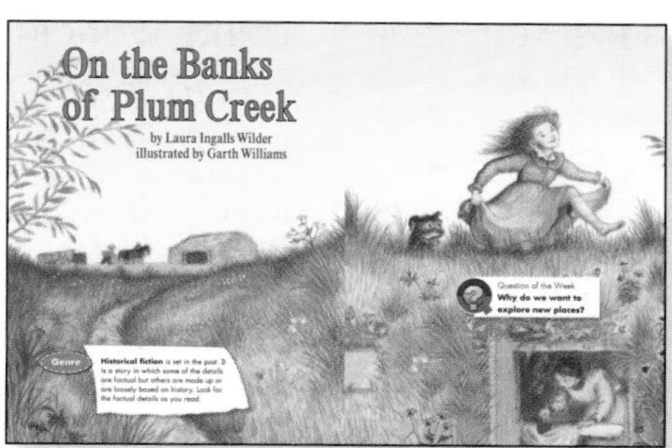

Revisit *On the Banks of Plum Creek* on pp. 94–99. Encourage students to use a dictionary or a glossary.

- Point out the word bank on p. 92. Ask a volunteer to look it up in a dictionary or a glossary. The word *bank* can mean "the land along the edge of a river." What is another meaning of the word? (*a place whose business has to do with exchanging and protecting money*)
- Look at the words *ducked* and *pool* on p. 92. What are two dictionary meanings of the words *duck* and *pool*? (Duck *can mean "to lower one's head" or "a swimming bird."* Pool *can mean "a body of water" or "to share."*)
- What is Laura doing when she meets the strange animal? (*heading toward the pool*)
- Why did Laura feel bad about what she had done? (*She had promised not to go there.*)
- How does Laura like being watched all day? (*She does not like it.*)

Use the During Reading Differentiated Instruction for additional support for struggling readers.

MONITOR PROGRESS

If… students need more practice with the lesson vocabulary,
then… use *Envision It! Pictured Vocabulary Cards.*

Objectives

- Use the context of the sentence to determine meaning of multiple meaning words.
- Use a dictionary or glossary to determine meanings of unknown words.

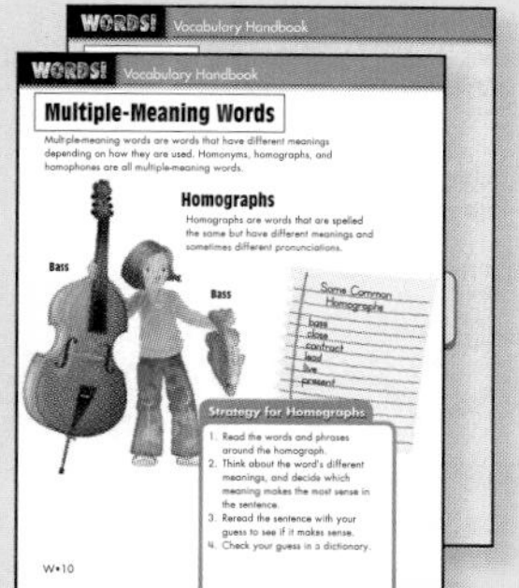

Student Edition, pp. W•10 and W•14

More Reading

Use additional Leveled Readers or other texts at students' instructional levels to reinforce this week's skills and strategies. For text suggestions, see the Leveled Reader Database or the Leveled Readers Skills Chart on pp. CL 24–CL 29.

Practice Retelling

- **Retell** Have students work in pairs and use the Retelling Cards to retell *On the Banks of Plum Creek.* Monitor retelling and prompt students as needed. For example, ask:
  - Tell me what happens in this story.

  If students struggle, model a fluent retelling.

Genre Focus

- **Before Reading or Revisiting** "Laura Ingalls Wilder" on pp. 104–107, read aloud the genre information on p. 104. Reiterate that an online reference source can provide links to dictionaries, encyclopedias, and other sites. For example, a Web site devoted to Laura Ingalls Wilder might include her biography and information about the books she wrote. As you click on links, you find different types of information.

  Then have students preview the reference source on Laura Ingalls Wilder. What pictures, words, and features do you see? (*computer screens, icons, a keyboard, photographs, Search windows, cursors*) Have students set a purpose for reading based on their preview.

- **During Reading or Revisiting** Have students read along with you while tracking the print, or do a choral reading. Stop to discuss any unfamiliar words, such as *click* and *link.*

- **After Reading or Revisiting** Have students share their reactions to the online reference source. Then guide them through the Get Online! activity.
  - What is the subject of the Web site pictured here? (*Laura Ingalls Wilder*)
  - What does this Web site have in common with *On the Banks of Plum Creek*? (*The subject of the Web site is the author of* On the Banks of Plum Creek.)

MONITOR PROGRESS

If... students have difficulty retelling the main selection,
then... have them review the story using the illustrations.

Objectives

- Compare various written conventions used for digital media.

DAY 5

For a complete literacy instructional plan and additional practice with this week's target skills and strategies, see the **Leveled Reader Teaching Guide.**

Concept Literacy Reader

Laura Ingalls Wilder: Pioneer Girl

- **Model** Model the fluency skill of rate and accuracy for students. Ask students to listen carefully as you read aloud the first two pages of *Laura Ingalls Wilder: Pioneer Girl.* Have students note your pace and pronunciation.
- **Fluency Routine**
  1. Have students reread passages from *Laura Ingalls Wilder: Pioneer Girl* with a partner.
  2. For optimal fluency, students should reread three to four times.
  3. As students read, monitor fluency and provide corrective feedback. Advise them to slow down to improve accuracy as necessary.

  See *Routines Flip Chart* for more help with fluency.
- **Retell** Have students retell *Laura Ingalls Wilder: Pioneer Girl* and prompt as necessary.

Below-Level Reader

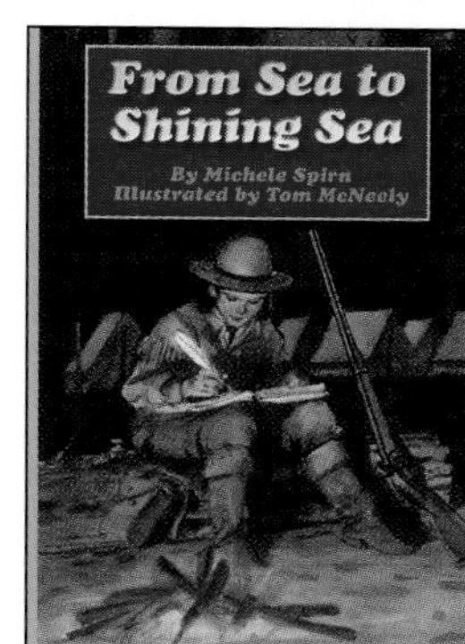

From Sea to Shining Sea

- **Model** Ask students to listen carefully as you read aloud the first two pages of *From Sea to Shining Sea,* emphasizing rate and accuracy.
- **Fluency Routine**
  1. Have students reread passages from *From Sea to Shining Sea* with a partner or individually.
  2. For optimal fluency, students should reread three to four times.
  3. As students read, monitor fluency and provide corrective feedback. Point out that slowing down at the more difficult passages makes it easier for listeners to understand. Discuss how grouping sentences creates a natural rhythm.

  See *Routines Flip Chart* for more help with fluency.
- **Retell** For additional practice, have students retell *From Sea to Shining Sea* page by page, using the illustrations. Prompt as necessary.
  - What happens in this part?
  - What problems do the characters face?

MONITOR PROGRESS

If... students have difficulty reading fluently,
then... provide additional fluency practice by pairing nonfluent readers with fluent ones.

Objectives
- Read aloud grade-level stories with fluency.

Pacing Small Group Instruction

5-Day Plan

DAY 1	• Expand the concept • Read On-Level Reader
DAY 2	• Character, Setting, and Plot • Background Knowledge • Revisit Student Edition pp. 84–93
DAY 3	• Multiple-Meaning Words • Revisit Student Edition pp. 94–99
DAY 4	• Practice Retelling • Read/Revisit Student Edition pp. 104–107
DAY 5	• Reread for fluency • Reread On-Level Reader

3- or 4-Day Plan

DAY 1	• Expand the concept • Read On-Level Reader
DAY 2	• Character, Setting, and Plot • Background Knowledge • Revisit Student Edition pp. 84–93
DAY 3	• Multiple-Meaning Words • Revisit Student Edition pp. 94–99
DAY 4	• Practice Retelling • Read/Revisit Student Edition pp. 104–107 • Reread for fluency • Reread On-Level Reader

3-Day Plan: Eliminate the shaded box.

DAY 1

Build Background

■ **Expand the Concept** Discuss the weekly question (*Why do we want to explore new places?*) and expand the concept. Sometimes when we explore new places, we can help improve them. For example, if we visit a place where the wildlife is in jeopardy, we can find ways to protect the wildlife. Discuss the meanings of the words on the concept map.

On-Level Reader

For a complete literacy instructional plan and additional practice with this week's target skills and strategies, see the **Leveled Reader Teaching Guide.**

■ **Before Reading** *Protecting Wild Animals*, have students preview the reader by looking at the title, cover, and pictures in the book. Ask:

- What is the topic of this book? (*protection of small wild animals*)
- Why do some people want to save threatened or endangered animals? (*The animals contribute to the balance of nature.*)

Have students predict what will happen in the story.

■ **During Reading** Read aloud the first three pages of the book as students follow along. Then have them finish reading the book on their own.

- Why is the family going to Minnesota? (*to help set up a wildlife sanctuary*)
- What problem does Elias have with his parents' plan? (*He doesn't want to leave the comforts of home.*)
- How does Elias change by the time the story ends? (*He catches on to his parents' enthusiasm for helping the animals.*)

■ **After Reading** Have partners discuss the concept map. Then, ask:

- What did the family do to protect wild animals? (*They worked on setting up a sanctuary, a new home for them.*)
- How does the topic relate to the weekly question *Why do we want to explore new places?* (*The family goes to a place that's new to them for the purpose of improving it.*)

Objectives

- Participate in teacher-led discussions by answering questions with appropriate detail.

DAY 2

Expand Comprehension

Skill Literary Elements: Character, Setting, and Plot Use p. 80 to review the definitions of character, setting, and plot. For additional review, see *Envision It!* p. EI•11. The author does not always tell us exactly what a character is like. Instead, the author uses the character's words, thoughts, and actions to reveal the character's personality.

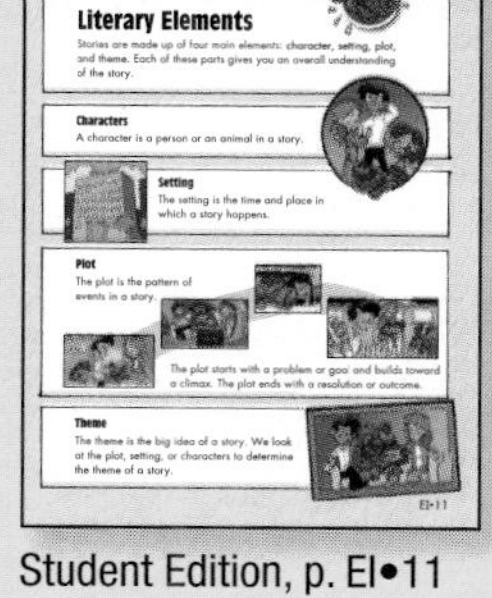
Student Edition, p. EI•11

Strategy Background Knowledge Review the definition of background knowledge. Encourage students to use their background knowledge as they read. For additional support during reading, use the Extend Thinking questions or refer students to *Envision It!* p. EI•16.

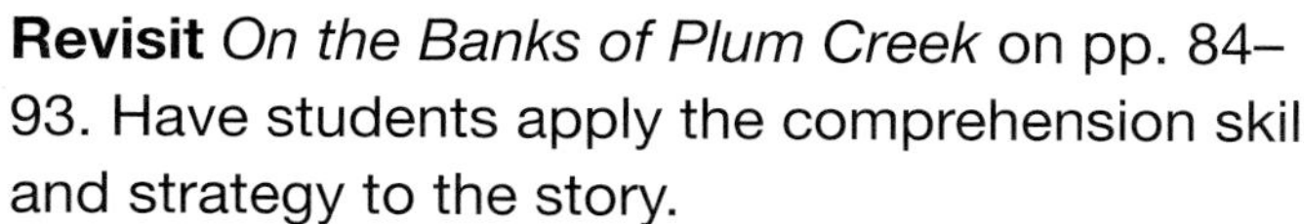

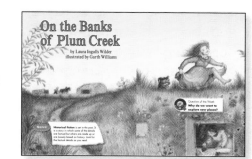

Revisit *On the Banks of Plum Creek* on pp. 84–93. Have students apply the comprehension skill and strategy to the story.

- What was the mud like on the bank of the creek? (*It was warm, soft, and wet.*)
- Based on your own knowledge, why do you think Laura was surprised when a big rush squeaked? (*She did not expect the plant to make a sound.*)
- What can you learn about Laura and Mary from the story of the rushes? (*They were used to being creative.*)

More Reading

Use additional Leveled Readers or other texts at students' instructional levels to reinforce this week's skills and strategies. For text suggestions, see the Leveled Reader Database or the Leveled Readers Skills Chart on pp. CL 24–CL 29.

Objectives

- Describe the interaction of characters including their relationships.
- Sequence the plot's main events.

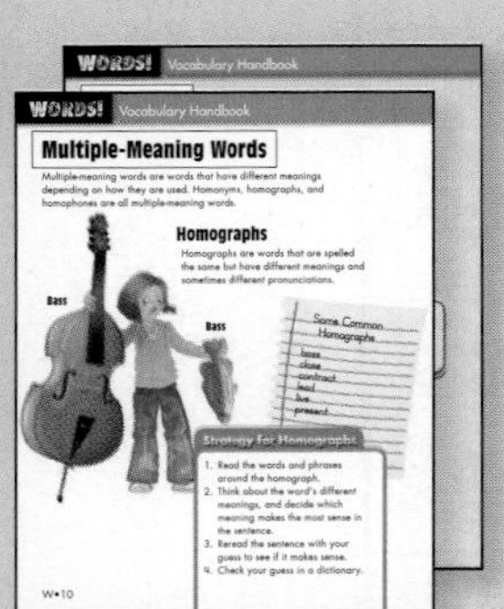

Student Edition, pp. W•10 and W•14

More Reading

Use additional Leveled Readers or other texts at students' instructional levels to reinforce this week's skills and strategies. For text suggestions, see the Leveled Reader Database or the Leveled Readers Skills Chart on pp. CL 24–CL 29.

Expand Vocabulary

Multiple-Meaning Words Write this sentence from the story on the board: "Each blue flag had three velvet petals that curved down like a lady's dress over hoops." Ask students to identify at least three words with multiple meanings (*blue, flag, down, like, dress, over, hoops*). Then model using a dictionary to explore meanings. Two meanings of the word *blue* are "a color" and "sad." The word *down* can mean "the opposite of up" and "soft feathers." To tell which meaning the author intended, I'll see how each word is used in the sentence. The word *blue* is part of *blue flag,* which is the name of a flower. I think that in this sentence, *blue* refers to a color. The petals "curved down," so *down* means "the opposite of up" in this sentence.

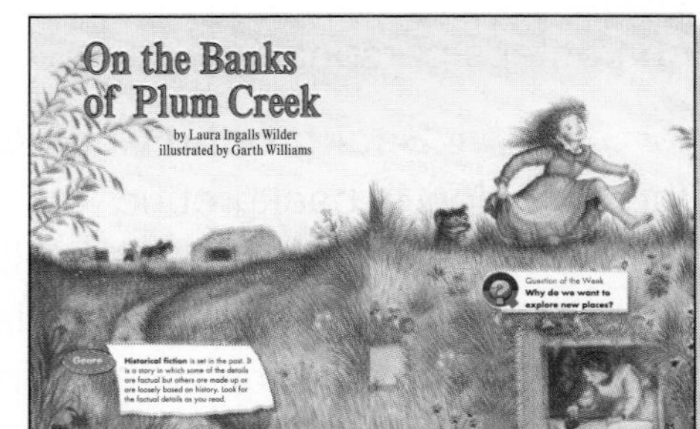

Revisit *On the Banks of Plum Creek* on pp. 94–99. Encourage students to use a glossary or dictionary to determine the appropriate meaning to use for a multiple-meaning word. For example, using the last page of the story, ask them to locate the possible meanings of the words *badger, clouds,* and *clump.* Ask them to explain how studying the words' usage in the sentences helps them understand the words as nouns rather than verbs.

- The girls and Pa stand on top of a tableland and look out at the view. What does this scene tell you about the setting? (*It is a wide-open, sparsely settled prairie environment.*)
- Laura tells her father that she had disobeyed him. What does this tell you about Laura's personality? (*She tells the truth even though she knows she might be punished.*)

Objectives

- Use the context of the sentence to determine meaning of multiple meaning words.
- Use a dictionary or glossary to determine meanings of unknown words.

Practice Retelling

- **Retell** To assess students' comprehension, use the Retelling Cards. Monitor retelling and prompt students as needed.

Genre Focus

- **Before Reading or Revisiting** "Laura Ingalls Wilder" on pp. 104–107, read aloud the genre information on p. 104. Have students preview the selection and set a purpose for reading.
  - What features do you see that are not in printed reference sources? (*computer icons, screens, Search windows, cursors, links*)
  - Why do you think the writer included so many different screens? (*to show that a Web site can offer many kinds of information*)
- **During Reading or Revisiting** Have students read along with you while tracking the print.
  - What are some links on the Web site? (*atlas, almanac, dictionary, encyclopedia*)
  - What would you learn if you clicked on the link "Did You Know"? (*The dog never actually lived at Plum Creek with the family.*)
- **After Reading or Revisiting** Have students share their reactions to the online reference source. Then have them write a short paragraph about an online reference source they have used.

Objectives

- Compare various written conventions used for digital media.

On-Level Reader

Protecting Wild Animals

- **Model** Read aloud the first page of *Protecting Wild Animals,* emphasizing rate and accuracy. Ask students to follow along as you read the second page, noticing how you change your rate to ensure accurate pronunciation. Model reading short passages while students note the rate and clarity of your speech.
- **Fluency Routine**

  1. Have students reread passages from *Protecting Wild Animals* with a partner.
  2. For optimal fluency, students should reread passages three to four times.
  3. As students read, monitor fluency and provide corrective feedback. Discuss parts where students read more quickly and have them explain why.

  See *Routines Flip Chart* for more help with fluency.
- **Retell** For additional practice, have students use graphic features and illustrations as a guide to retell *Protecting Wild Animals.* Prompt as necessary.
  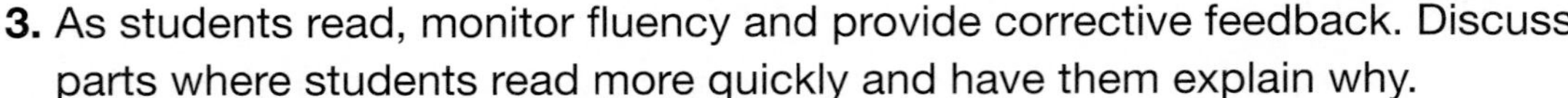
  - What happens in this section?
  - What did you learn from reading this section?
  - How would you describe this book to someone who has not read it yet?

Objectives
- Read aloud grade-level stories with fluency.

Advanced

DAY 1

Build Background

- **Extend the Concept** Discuss the weekly question *Why do we want to explore new places?* What is the most exciting new place you have explored? Why did you go there?

Advanced Reader

For a complete literacy instructional plan and additional practice with this week's target skills and strategies, see the **Leveled Reader Teaching Guide.**

- **Before Reading** *Exploring the Moon*, have students look at the illustrations in the book and use them to predict what will happen in the text. Then have students set a purpose for reading.
- **During Reading** Have students read Exploring the Moon independently. Encourage them to think critically.
  - How do you think the main character felt about going away to summer camp for the first time?
  - Why do you think the camp counselor gathered the campers together to watch the 1969 moon landing on television?
  - Imagine you are the first person on the moon. How do you feel as you set your foot on the surface?

Exploring the Moon

- **After Reading** Have students review the concept map and explain how *Exploring the Moon* helps answer the weekly question *Why do we want to explore new places?* Prompt as necessary.
  - How do you think the moon landing in 1969 changed people's attitudes toward space travel?
  - How did watching the moon landing affect the main character in *Exploring the Moon*?
- **Now Try This** To extend concepts from the reader, invite students to write a journal entry in the voice of the main character.

Objectives

- Participate in teacher-led discussions by answering questions with appropriate detail.

Pacing Small Group Instruction

15–20 min

5-Day Plan

DAY 1	• Extend the concept • Read Advanced Reader
DAY 2	• Character, Setting, and Plot • Background Knowledge • Revisit Student Edition pp. 84–93
DAY 3	• Multiple-Meaning Words • Revisit Student Edition pp. 94–99
DAY 4	• Genre Focus • Read/Revisit Student Edition pp. 104–107
DAY 5	• Reread for fluency • Reread Advanced Reader

3- or 4-Day Plan

DAY 1	• Extend the concept • Read Advanced Reader
DAY 2	• Character, Setting, and Plot • Background Knowledge • Revisit Student Edition pp. 84–93
DAY 3	• Multiple-Meaning Words • Revisit Student Edition pp. 94–99
DAY 4	• Genre Focus • Read/Revisit Student Edition pp. 104–107 • Reread for fluency • Reread Advanced Reader

3-Day Plan: Eliminate the shaded box.

More Reading

Use additional Leveled Readers or other texts at students' instructional levels to reinforce this week's skills and strategies. For text suggestions, see the Leveled Reader Database or the Leveled Readers Skills Chart on pp. CL 24–CL 29.

Extend Comprehension

Skill Literary Elements: Character, Setting, and Plot Review the definitions of character, setting, and plot. Sometimes an author will give you hints about what is going to happen in a story. This technique is called *foreshadowing.* For example, when an author describes characters, he or she may use clue words, such as *naughty* and *sorry,* that give hints about the consequences their actions will have.

Strategy Background Knowledge Review the definition of the strategy. Remind students to use background knowledge as they read. Use the Extend Thinking questions and During Reading Differentiated Instruction for additional support.

- **Revisit** *On the Banks of Plum Creek* on pp. 84–93. Encourage students to use background knowledge to think about the characters, setting, and plot.
  - Why aren't the girls supposed to follow the creek beyond the willow valley? (*There is a deep place there.*)
  - How might the description of the swimming hole foreshadow events later in the story? (*Because the place is forbidden, it might provide a temptation to the girls.*)
  - What main problem does Laura face? (*She wants to be adventurous, but her parents' concern for her safety holds her back.*)
- **Critical Thinking** Prompt students to think critically about how the characters in this story will affect the plot. Pa and Ma are responsible for the girls and for taking care of the house and animals. The girls are free to play and explore after they do chores. How might these ways of spending time come into conflict later in the story? (*The girls may get into trouble while their parents are busy at home.*)

Objectives

- Describe the interaction of characters including their relationships.
- Sequence the plot's main events.

DAY 3

Extend Vocabulary

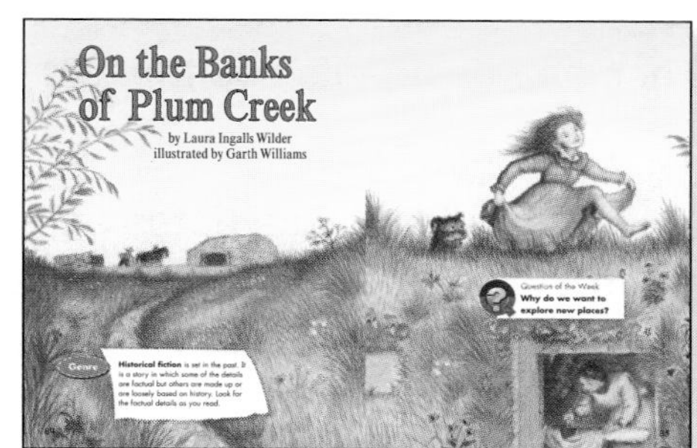

Multiple-Meaning Words Read this sentence from the story: "That ground rose up high above the tall grasses, and it was round, and flat on top." Have students use dictionaries to answer this question: What are two meanings of *rose*? (*past tense of* rise; flower)

Discuss using context to figure out which meaning of the word applies. Remind students to use a dictionary as they read.

- **Revisit** *On the Banks of Plum Creek* on pp. 94–99.
- **Critical Thinking** As students read, encourage them to think critically.
  - How do you know that Laura is a good girl even though she sometimes disobeys? (*She feels so bad that she confesses, even though she knows she'll be punished.*)
  - Listen to this sentence: "Pa was a shadow against the sky and his bow danced among the great stars." How do you know the word *bow* does not refer to a tied ribbon? (*Pa is playing the fiddle, and the bow is what plays the strings.*)
  - How does Pa resolve the problem of Laura's disobedience? (*He makes her stay within Ma's sight for a full day.*)
  - Why is Laura sure that "being good could never be as hard as being watched"? (*When she is watched, her freedom is limited.*)
- **Creative Thinking** Encourage students to speculate about Laura's character.
  - If you were Laura, how would you avoid getting into trouble?
  - What do you think Laura will be like when she becomes an adult? Would she make a good parent? Explain.

Objectives

- Use the context of the sentence to determine meaning of multiple meaning words.
- Use a dictionary or glossary to determine meanings of unknown words.

More Reading

Use additional Leveled Readers or other texts at students' instructional levels to reinforce this week's skills and strategies. For text suggestions, see the Leveled Reader Database or the Leveled Readers Skills Chart on pp. CL 24–CL 29.

DAY 4

Genre Focus

- **Before Reading or Revisiting** "Laura Ingalls Wilder" on pp. 104–107, read aloud the genre information. Then have students use the text features to set a purpose for reading.
- **During Reading or Revisiting** Have students take notes on the different text features used on the Web site. Ask students to share several positive things about the Web site, and jot a list on the board. This Web site has a variety of features. What are some of them? (*links to an atlas, an almanac, a dictionary, and an encyclopedia*) Explain that Web site links lead to other pages with different kinds of information.
- **After Reading or Revisiting** Have students do the Get Online! activity independently.

Objectives

- Compare various written conventions used for digital media.

- **Reread for Fluency** Have students silently reread passages from *Exploring the Moon.* Then have them reread aloud with a partner or individually. As students read, monitor fluency and provide corrective feedback. If students read fluently on the first reading, they do not need to reread three to four times. Assess the fluency of students in this group using p. 109j.
- **Retell** Invite students to retell the main idea and key details from *Exploring the Moon.*
- **Now Try This** Review students' journal entries to provide constructive feedback on their skill at imitating the main character's voice.

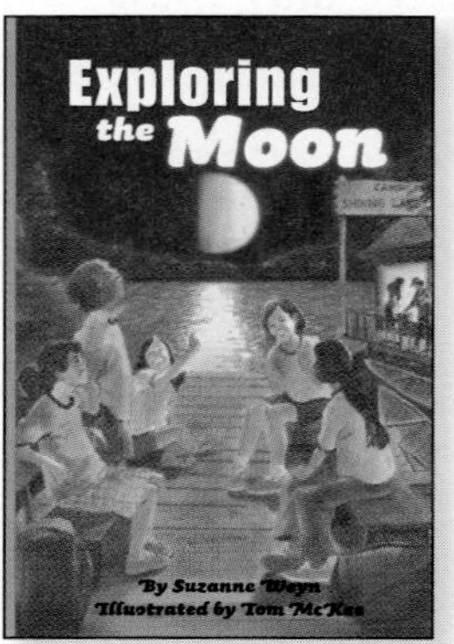

Exploring the Moon

Objectives

- Read aloud grade-level stories with fluency.

English Language Learners

The ELL lessons are organized by strands. Use them to scaffold the weekly curriculum of lessons or during small group time instruction.

Academic Language

Students will internalize new academic language by using and reusing the newly learned words in meaningful ways. To have students begin this process, write the skill and concept words on the board. Have students suggest an example or synonym of each word. Help them identify available cognates.

Skill Words	character setting plot background	knowledge parody *(parodea)* predicate *(predicado)* subject
Concept Words	explore *(explorar)* new *(nuevo)*	places travel

* *Spanish cognates in parentheses*

Concept Development

Why do we want to explore new places?

■ **Preteach Concept**

- **Prior Knowledge** Have students turn to pp. 78–79 in the Student Edition. Call attention to the picture of the covered wagon and tap into students' knowledge of traveling west. Does this wagon look like something people use now or long ago? Why did people travel west in covered wagons like this a long time ago? What were they hoping to find out west?
- **Discuss Concept** Elicit students' knowledge and experience of exploring new places. Would you want to explore a new place, such as a new city or a famous mountain? What would you like to see? What makes people want to explore new places? Supply background information as needed.
- **Poster Talk-Through** Read aloud the Poster Talk-Through on ELL Poster 3 and work through the Day 1 activities.

■ **Daily Concept and Vocabulary Development** Use the daily activities on ELL Poster 3 to build concept and vocabulary knowledge.

Objectives

- Internalize new basic and academic language by using and reusing it in meaningful ways in speaking and writing activities that build concept and language attainment.

Content Objectives

- Use concept vocabulary related to the desire to explore new places.

Language Objectives

- Express ideas in response to art and discussion.

Daily Planner

DAY 1	• **Frontload Concept** • **Preteach** Comprehension Skill, Vocabulary, Phonics/Spelling, Conventions • **Writing**
DAY 2	• **Review** Concept, Vocabulary, Comprehension Skill • **Frontload Main Selection** • **Practice** Phonics/Spelling, Conventions/Writing
DAY 3	• **Review** Concept, Comprehension Skill, Vocabulary, Conventions/Writing • **Reread Main Selection** • **Practice** Phonics/Spelling
DAY 4	• **Review Concept** • **Read ELL/ELD Readers** • **Practice** Phonics/Spelling, Conventions/Writing
DAY 5	• **Review** Concept, Vocabulary, Comprehension Skill, Phonics/Spelling, Conventions • **Reread ELL/ELD Readers** • **Writing**

See the ELL Handbook for ELL Workshops with targeted instruction.

Concept Talk Video

Use the Concept Talk Video Routine (*ELL Handbook,* page 477) to build background knowledge about exploring new places. For more listening practice, see *Use Classroom Resources* (*ELL Handbook*, pp. 406–407).

Support for English Language Learners

Language Objectives

- Internalize new basic language by using it and revising it in meaningful speaking activities.
- Learn meanings of grade-level vocabulary.

Cognates

For Spanish speakers, point out that the word for *explore* is spelled *explorar* in Spanish. Reinforce the concept that these languages share many words that are the same or similar.

ELL Workshop

Provide practice for students to better comprehend English vocabulary used in written classroom materials with *Learn New Words* (pp. 402–403, *ELL Handbook*).

English Opportunity

Help students expand and internalize the high-frequency words. Read each word aloud. Then use each word to identify or describe people, places or objects, such as *The clock hangs by the door.* Then have students repeat the high-frequency word, using it in a sentence if possible.

Basic Vocabulary

■ **High-Frequency Words** Use the ELL Vocabulary Words Routine on p. 471 of the *ELL Handbook* to systematically teach newcomers the first 300 sight words in English. Students who began learning ten words per week at the beginning of the year are now learning words 21–30 (*ELL Handbook*, pp. 447). P. 446 of the handbook contains a bank of strategies that you can use to ensure students' mastery of High-Frequency Words.

Lesson Vocabulary

■ **Preteach** Introduce the Lesson Vocabulary using this routine:

1. Distribute copies of this week's Word Cards (*ELL Handbook*, p. 41).
2. Display ELL Poster 3 and reread the Poster Talk-Through.
3. Using the poster illustrations, model how a word's meaning can be expressed with other similar words: The *badger*, or small furry animal, is eating leaves.
4. Use these sentences to reveal the meaning of the other words.
   - We followed the trail along the *bank* of the river. (land by the side of a river)
   - The angry cat's fur *bristled.* (stood up)
   - The stem of the plant was *jointed* so that it could bend. (made to bend without breaking)
   - She *patched* the hole in her shirt. (sewed a piece of cloth on)
   - The edge of the skirt was *ruffled.* (wrinkled, messed up)
   - The tall *rushes* grew along the side of the creek. (a kind of plant that grows near water)

Objectives

- Use visual, contextual, and linguistic support to enhance and confirm understanding of increasingly complex and elaborated spoken language.
- Understand the general meaning, main points, and important details of spoken language ranging from situations in which topics, language, and contexts are familiar to unfamiliar.
- Understand implicit ideas and information in increasingly complex spoken language commensurate with grade-level learning expectations.

ELL English Language Learners

■ **Reteach** Distribute a copy of the Word Cards (*ELL Handbook*, p. 41) and six blank cards to each pair of students.

- Have partners write a clue or draw a simple picture on a blank card for each word.
- Have students mix the Word Cards and clue cards together and lay them face up on a table. Students can take turns choosing cards, trying to match a word with its clue. Have students explain their choices.

■ **Writing** Place students in mixed proficiency groups. Provide a set of Word Cards for each group and a three-column chart with these headings: *Word*, *Meaning*, *Sentence*. Groups choose a Word Card and place it in the middle of a desk or table where all can see it. Have them pass around the chart in a round robin form. One student writes the word on the chart. The next student writes a short phrase or draws a picture to illustrate the word's meaning. The next student writes a short sentence using the word. Before students begin, model using the graphic organizer: Word: rushes; Meaning: plants; Sentence: The rushes grow by the river. Groups continue until they have used all of the words.

Beginning Have students copy the selected word onto the chart or draw pictures to illustrate the sentences.

Intermediate Have students write a word meaning and orally suggest a sentence using a vocabulary word.

Advanced Encourage students to write a sentence using a vocabulary word.

Advanced High Challenge these students to look up the words in a dictionary. Have them write additional meanings for multiple meaning words such as *badger* (noun and verb), *bank*, *ruffled* (adjective and verb), and *rushes* (noun and verb).

Objectives

- Internalize new basic and academic language by using and reusing it in meaningful ways in speaking and writing activities that build concept and language attainment.
- Learn new language structures, expressions, and basic and academic vocabulary heard during classroom instruction and interactions.
- Speak using grade-level content area vocabulary in context to internalize new English words and build academic language proficiency.

Language Objectives

- Produce drawings, phrases, or short sentences to show understanding of Lesson Vocabulary.

ELL Teacher Tip

Many English words have multiple meanings. Illustrating and creating examples of the ways words are used can build English learners' experiences and understanding of the multiple meanings that words may have. Teachers can help students expand their understanding of multiple meanings by sharing sentences, definitions, and pictures that demonstrate the different meanings.

Graphic Organizer

Word	Meaning	Sentence

ELL Workshop

As students speak using new vocabulary, they may need assistance knowing how to adapt spoken English for formal purposes. *Use Formal English* (*ELL Handbook*, pp. 392–393) provides extra support.

ELL English Language Learners

Content Objectives

- Use contextual support to enhance and confirm understanding of spoken language.

Language Objectives

- Discuss oral passages.
- Use a graphic organizer to take notes.

Graphic Organizer

Sequence	Place
First	Atlantic Ocean

ELL Teacher Tip

Display a map of the United States. Locate the Atlantic Ocean and the East Coast. Demonstrate moving from right to left to show going from east to west. As you read, have volunteers point out the different areas named on the map.

ELL Workshop

Encourage students to demonstrate listening comprehension of the Read Aloud and other spoken messages. Provide *Retell or Summarize* (*ELL Handbook*, pp. 408–409) for practice.

Listening Comprehension

Read Aloud

Travel Across the Country

It is about 2,800 miles from the East Coast to the West Coast of the United States. That is almost the same distance as it is from New York to London, England. Think about traveling in a car across the United States from coast to coast. It would take almost forty-seven hours if you drove sixty miles an hour and never stopped. The same trip would take about five hours in a jet airplane.

If you started at the Atlantic Ocean and flew west, you would go over the Appalachian Mountains first. Then you would fly over the farmlands in the Midwest. You might see the Great Lakes in the north. As you flew farther west, you would see prairies and land where cattle graze. You might see desert to the south. Then you would fly over the snow-covered Rocky Mountains. At last, you would see the green valleys of California and the shores of the Pacific Ocean.

That is a lot of land. Long ago, there were no cars or airplanes. There were no roads. On the Great Plains, people left stakes in the ground to show others where to go. The Great Plains area is still called the Staked Plains. Other people sprinkled mustard seeds through the western valleys. They hoped bright yellow plants would grow to show others a trail.

Prepare for the Read Aloud The modified Read Aloud above prepares students for listening to the oral reading "Going Places" on p. 79b.

- **First Listening: Listen to Understand** Write the title of the Read Aloud on the board. This is about traveling across the United States. What can people see as they travel from the East Coast to the West Coast? Afterward, ask the question again and have students use contextual support to confirm their understanding of what they heard.
- **Second Listening: Listen to Check Understanding** Using a T-chart (*ELL Handbook*, p. 493), work with students to record the sequence of places seen. Have students write numbers or words that show order in the left column and places in the right. Now listen again to check that you identified all the things you can see as you travel across the country from east to west.

Objectives

- Use visual, contextual, and linguistic support to enhance and confirm understanding of increasingly complex and elaborated spoken language.

Phonics and Spelling

- **Long *e* and *o*** Copy and distribute pp. 256 and 258 of the *ELL Handbook.*
  - **Preteach** Have students point to the bee at the top of the page. This is a bee. *Bee* has the sound of /ē/. Say it with me: /ē/, *bee*.
  - **Teach Spellings** Write a four-column chart on the board with the headings *ee*, *e*, *ea*, *y*. List the words *bee*, *beaver*, and *me* in the first three columns. Ask students to help you add the long *e* words from Row 1 to the chart.
  - **Distinguish Sounds** I will say some word pairs. Raise your hand if both words have the /ē/ sound: *team, Tim; meat, met; seen, seat; wheat, wet*.
  - Follow the Preteach and Teach Spellings steps with long *o* words. Then have students use their decoding skills to pronounce these words: *boat, bought; globe, lobe; low, blow; hose, toes; coat, cot; good, gold.* Have students identify which words have the long *o* sound.

Word Analysis: Words Ending in *-ing*

- **Teach/Model** Explain that the suffix *-ing* can be added to a verb to show that an action is happening now. It can also be added to a verb to form a noun. Write these verbs on the board: *paint*, *patch*. Read each word aloud. When I add the suffix *-ing* to the verb *paint*, I make a new word, *painting*. The word *painting* is a noun. When I add *-ing* to the verb *patch*, I make the verb *patching*.
- **Practice** Write these words on the board: *build*, *frost*, *stuff*; *eat*, *sing*, *go*. Have students copy each word and add *-ing*. Discuss whether the new word is a noun (*building*, *frosting*, *stuffing*) or a verb (*eating*, *singing*, *going*).

Beginning/Intermediate Help students read the words, if necessary. Orally discuss sentences using the words, such as: *The building is tall.*

Advanced/Advanced High Ask students to write a sentence using each word.

Objectives

- Distinguish sounds and intonation patterns of English with increasing ease.

Content Objectives

- Identify suffix *-ing*.
- Identify different spellings of /ē/ and /ō/.
- Review spelling patterns and distinguish sounds and intonation patterns of long vowel sounds.

Language Objectives

- Apply phonics and decoding skills to vocabulary.
- Identify the use of words ending in *-ing*.

Long vowels and the vowel digraphs that produce long vowels can be confusing for English language learners. For example, some long vowel sounds in English are similar to the sounds made by different vowels or vowel combinations in Spanish. The long *e* sound is similar to the sound of *i* in Spanish, such as *need/nido* (*nest*); *see/sí* (*yes*). The long *o* sound is similar to the sound of *o* in Spanish, such as *no/no*.

ELL Teaching Routine

For more practice with vowel sounds, use the Sound-by-Sound Blending Routine (*ELL Handbook*, p. 472).

Content Objectives

- Identify the literary elements of a story, including character, setting, and plot.
- Use literary elements to aid comprehension.

Language Objectives

- Identify literary elements.
- Demonstrate knowledge of when to use informal language.

ELL Workshop

Encourage students to ask questions to monitor their understanding of instruction of comprehension skills. Use *Ask Clarifying Questions* (*ELL Handbook*, pp. 404–405) for practice.

ELL English Language Learners

Comprehension

Literary Elements: Character, Setting, Plot

- **Preteach** The characters are the people or animals in a story. The setting is the time and place a story happens. The plot is what happens. Have students turn to *Envision It!* on p. EI•11 in the Student Edition. Read aloud the text together. Have students identify the characters and the setting shown in the illustrations. Discuss the plot using the small illustrations.
- **Reteach** Distribute copies of the Picture It! (*ELL Handbook*, p. 46). Before reading aloud, ask for volunteers to define setting, character, and plot. Tell them to choose one element to think about as you read aloud. After reading, call on volunteers to tell you what they learned about one element. (Setting: on a bus; characters: Raymond and Oliver; problem: Raymond is lonely; solution: He makes friends with Oliver.)

Beginning/Intermediate Have students underline the setting. Have them circle a character name when they see it. Ask students to cross out sentences that tell a problem. Then, have them put a box around sentences that show a solution.

Advanced/Advanced High Pair students together. Have one student name a setting, character, problem, or solution. Have the other partner tell which element they named. For example: Partner 1: “New York City.” Partner 2: “Setting.” The partners can take turns.

MINI-LESSON

Informal Language

Tell students that words that mimic the sounds they make are examples of informal language. Give students examples, such as *buzz, hum,* and *ding.* Tell them that these words are used to make writing more descriptive. Have students turn to p. 86 in the Student Edition. Have students read the first two paragraphs on the page. Have them identify the informal sound words on the page. Then have students demonstrate an ability of when to use informal language by writing a paragraph with sound words properly used in it.

Objectives

- Demonstrate an increasing ability to distinguish between formal and informal English and an increasing knowledge of when to use each one commensurate with grade-level learning expectations.

Reading Comprehension
On the Banks of Plum Creek

Student Edition pp. 84–85

■ **Frontloading**

- Have students look through *On the Banks of Plum Creek*, pp. 84–99 in the Student Edition, and tell what they see that makes the selection historical fiction, a realistic story that takes place in the past. (illustrations, kind of clothes, horses to pull a plow) Distribute copies of the English summary of *On the Banks of Plum Creek* (*ELL Handbook*, p. 43). Help students understand the meaning of spoken language by having students read the summary aloud with you. Preview the selection by having students look at the pictures. Provide students with a Story Map to complete as they read the story.

Sheltered Reading Have students use their Student Editions to answer the questions. Encourage them to seek clarification while referring to the Student Edition as needed.

- pp. 86–88: Who are the characters in the story? (Laura, Mary, Ma, Pa)
- pp. 93–95: What does Pa tell Laura and Mary not to do? (go to the swimming hole without him) What does Laura almost do? (go to the swimming hole alone) What stops her? (a strange animal in the path)
- pp. 96–99: What climax or important moment does the story build up to? (Laura tells Pa what she did.)

■ **Fluency: Read with Appropriate Rate and Accuracy** Remind students that they must read at the right rate (not too slow or fast) to read and comprehend with accuracy or correctness. Model reading the first paragraph on page 87 both too fast and too slow to show how rate affects accuracy. Then have pairs choose a paragraph on p. 94 to read with accuracy and an appropriate rate. Have partners listen and offer feedback.

After Reading Help students summarize the text with the Retelling Cards. Have students express ideas ranging from communicating short phrases to having extended discussions.

Objectives

- Monitor understanding of spoken language during classroom instruction and interactions and seek clarification as needed.

Content Objectives

- Monitor and adjust comprehension.
- Make and adjust predictions.

Language Objectives

- Read grade-level text with an appropriate rate that fosters accuracy.
- Summarize text using visual support.

Graphic Organizer

Title ______________

Characters	Setting

Events

Audio Support

Students can prepare for reading *On the Banks of Plum Creek* by using the eSelection or the AudioText CD (*ELL Handbook*, p. 477).

ELL Teaching Routine

For more practice summarizing, use the Retelling/Summarizing Narrative Routine (*ELL Handbook*, p. 475).

For additional leveled instruction, see the **ELL/ELD Reader Teaching Guide.**

Comprehension
Our Trip Out East

- **Before Reading** Distribute copies of the ELL and ELD Readers, *Our Trip Out East*.
  - **Preview** Read the title aloud with students: This is a nonfiction text about a trip the author takes with her family from Chicago to the East Coast in the summer of 1959. Invite students to look through the pictures and name what they see. Have them employ analytical skills commensurate with content area needs by predicting what the family does and sees.
  - **Set a Purpose for Reading** Let's read to find out where the author goes and what happens.
- **During Reading** Follow the Reading Routine for both reading groups.
  1. Read the entire Reader aloud slowly.
  2. Reread pp. 2–4, to build background and comprehension. Have students identify where to start reading text on a page. Tell students that the directionality of reading English is from left-to-right and top-to-bottom on the page, modeling with your finger. Have students finger-point as you read. Use the questions to check students' comprehension.
  3. Have students reread pp. 1–7 silently.
  4. Repeat steps 2–3 above for pp. 8–12 of the Reader.
- **After Reading** Use the exercises on the inside back cover, leading a whole-group discussion. What were the most interesting things the family saw on their trip? Record students' answers on the board and invite them to point to pictures in the book to support their answers.

ELD Reader

ELL Reader

ELD Reader Beginning/Intermediate

- **p. 3** Who joined the author's family on the trip east? (Abuelita, her grandmother) Read aloud the sentence that tells you. (p. 3)
- **p. 6** Why was the blue station wagon wonderful? (It took them to New Jersey and never broke down.)

Writing What are the different settings in this story? Find and copy the names of places. Read them aloud to your partner.

ELL Reader Advanced/Advanced High

- **p. 5** Why did the author's family leave Chicago? (Her father had a job in New Jersey.)
- **pp. 10–11** How was New York different from Chicago? (The buildings were taller and closer together.)

Study Guide Distribute copies of the ELL Reader Study Guide (*ELL Handbook*, p. 46). Help students recall the events that occurred in each place and write them in order. Review their responses together. (**Answers** See *ELL Handbook*, pp. 209–212.)

Objectives

- Demonstrate comprehension of increasingly complex English by participating in shared reading, retelling or summarizing material, responding to questions, and taking notes commensurate with content area and grade level needs.

Conventions
Complete Subjects and Predicates

■ **Teach/Model** Display this sentence: *The boy rides the bus. The boy* is the subject of the sentence. The sentence is about the boy. A sentence is about its subject. *Rides the bus* is the predicate. What does the boy do? (rides the bus) A predicate tells something about the subject. This follows the pattern of a simple sentence. This follows the pattern of a simple sentence.

■ **Teach/Model** Present the concept and provide examples:

- The subject of a sentence tells whom or what the sentence is about. Two or more subjects connected by *and* or *or* is a compound subject.
- The predicate of a sentence tells what the subject is or does. Two or more verbs joined by a connecting word is called a compound predicate. This follows the pattern of a compound sentence.

Subject	Predicate
Mack	threw the baseball.
The crowd	cheers the team.
Jen and Dena	are in the office.
The cook	washed and cut the carrots.

■ **Oral Language** Write these sentences on strips: *The flowers are beautiful. My cats chase the toy mouse. Dogs or cats are good pets. The football players run and jump.* Cut each strip into subject and predicate. Have students scramble the sentence parts to form new sentences.

Beginning/Intermediate Have pairs take turns writing subjects and predicates. Provide the following sentence frames: The ________. ________ in the class.

Advanced/Advanced High Have students write a variety of sentences with complete subjects and predicates, including compound subjects and predicates. Have them exchange papers with partners who underline their subjects and circle their predicates.

To provide students additional instruction and practice with subjects and predicates, use the lesson in the *ELL Handbook* (p. 348).

Objectives

- Speak using a variety of grammatical structures, sentence lengths, sentence types, and connecting words with increasing accuracy and ease as more English is acquired.

Content Objectives

- Identify complete subjects and predicates.
- Identify compound subjects and predicates.

Language Objectives

- Speak sentences using complete subjects and predicates.
- Write sentences with complete subjects and predicates.
- Write using sentence patterns.

Transfer Skills

Subjects and Predicates The typical English sequence of subject then predicate is not standard in some languages. For example, in Spanish the verb often appears before the subject, while in Korean and Hindi the verb typically appears at the end of a sentence.

Grammar Jammer

For more practice with sentences, use the Grammar Jammer for this target skill. See the Grammar Jammer Routine (*ELL Handbook*, p. 478) for suggestions on using this learning tool.

Content Objectives

- Identify the purpose of a piece of writing.

Language Objectives

- Adapt spoken language appropriately for informal purposes.
- Write with a specific purpose in mind.

ELL English Language Learners

Language Matches Purpose

■ **Introduce** Talk about the purpose of writing. Purpose is the reason for something. What is the purpose of *On the Banks of Plum Creek*? The author tells us this story for two reasons. One reason is to tell a good story that we'll enjoy. Another reason is to teach a lesson. Ask students how the writing would be different if it were for a different purpose. How would this be different if it were written to make you think or believe a certain thing? How would this be different if it were an encyclopedia entry? Then discuss what kind of language they would use in speaking about the selection. Ask students how they might talk to friends about the selection.

Writing Model

Wow! This story was great! It reminded me of a time I got in trouble. My parents told me not to ride my bike to a friend's house. The street was too busy, so they were worried about me. But I rode anyway. I was sorry I did! I wasn't allowed to use my bike for a week.

■ **Practice** Examine the writing model with students. Ask how the language would be different if the writing were an advertisement for the book. How would it be different if the writing was a report about life on the prairie? What if students were telling their parents or a teacher about the book?

■ **Write** Have students choose a paragraph or two in the story to tell a friend about. They can write what they would tell their friends before speaking. Remind them that they are adapting their language for an informal purpose—speaking to a friend.

Beginning Have students tell about the story to a friend as you listen. Record what students say. Have them read aloud from your writing.

Intermediate Have students write about the story as if they were speaking to a friend and then read their work aloud in small groups. Partners can give feedback on the language.

Advanced/Advanced High Have students write as if they were speaking to friends and exchange papers with partners. Partners can give feedback on the language before students read their work aloud. Ask students how they would adapt the language to a formal audience, for formal purposes.

Objectives

- Adapt spoken language appropriately for formal and informal purposes.

Customize Your Writing

Weekly Writing Focus

Writing Forms and Patterns

- Instruction focuses on a different **product** each week.
- Mini-lessons and models help students learn key features and **organizational patterns**.

Grade 4 Products letters, essays, stories, instructions, poems, drama, and so on

Grade 4 Organization Patterns cause and effect, sequence, compare and contrast, main idea and details, narrative story structure, and so on

Daily Writing Focus

Quick Writes for Fluency

- Writing on Demand Use the Quick Write routine for **writing on demand**.
- The Quick Write **prompt and routine** extend skills and strategies from daily writing lessons.

Unit Writing Focus

Writing Process 1 2 3 4 5

- Six **writing process** lessons provide structure to move students through the steps of the writing process.
- One-week and two-week pacing allows lessons to be used in **Writing Workshop**.

Steps of the Writing Process Plan and Prewrite, Draft, Revise, Edit, Publish and Present

Grade 4 Writing Process Products personal narrative, expository composition, compare and contrast essay, story, persuasive essay, research report

Write Guy
Jeff Anderson

Need Writing Advice?

Writing instruction is all about creating effective writers. We don't want to crush the inner writer in a child by over-correcting and over-editing. What makes effective writing instruction? Children need to write, write, write! But is that enough? Probably not. All kinds of instruction and guidance go into making an effective writer.

The Write Guy offers advice on teacher and peer conferencing, focusing on writing traits, revising strategies, editing strategies, and much, much more.

MINI-LESSON

- Daily 10-minute mini-lessons focus instruction on the **traits** and **craft** of good writing.
- Instruction focuses on one writing trait and one writer's craft skill every week.

Traits focus/ideas, organization, voice, word choice, sentences, conventions

Craft drafting strategies, revising strategies, editing strategies

Read Like a Writer

- Use **mentor text** every week as a model to exemplify the traits of good writing.
- **Interact with text** every week to learn the key features of good writing.

Mentor Text Examine literature in the Student Edition.

INTERACT with TEXT Underline, circle, and highlight model text in the *Reader's and Writer's Notebook.*

Customize Your Writing

Alternate Pacing Plan for Unit Writing Projects

Sometimes you want to spend more time on writing—perhaps you do a **Writing Workshop**. This one- or two-week plan for the unit level writing projects can help.

1 Week Plan	Day 1	Day 2	Day 3	Day 4	Day 5
1 Plan and Prewrite					
2 Draft					
3 Revise					
4 Edit					
5 Publish					

2 Week Plan	Day 1	Day 2	Day 3	Day 4	Day 5	Day 6	Day 7	Day 8	Day 9	Day 10
1 Plan and Prewrite										
2 Draft										
3 Revise										
4 Edit										
5 Publish										

Grade 4 Unit Writing Projects

Internet Guy
Don Leu

Unit Writing Project 1–21st Century Project

Unit 1 E-Newsletter

Unit 2 Podcasting

Unit 3 Online Photo Essay

Unit 4 Story Exchange

Unit 5 Electronic Pen Pals

Unit 6 Blogging

Unit Writing Project 2–Writing Process

Unit 1 Personal Narrative

Unit 2 Expository Composition

Unit 3 Compare and Contrast Essay

Unit 4 Story

Unit 5 Persuasive Essay

Unit 6 Research Report

E-Newsletter

Writing Project Create an e-newsletter with articles about a country you would like to visit.

Purpose Enhance skills in Internet research as well as using applications for word processing and design.

Audience students, peers, teacher, family

Introduce genre and key features

In this workshop, we will create an e-newsletter about a country that we would like to visit. We will use the Internet to find information about this country and then design a newsletter that we can share with our friends and family.

Key Features of an E-Newsletter

- includes several factual articles relating to the same topic or theme
- provides interesting details for the reader
- includes illustrations and photographs to make the articles more vivid
- is designed to appeal to a specific audience
- is written, designed, or published electronically

Academic Vocabulary

Newsletter A newsletter is a small newspaper written for a specific audience.

Teacher Tip

Explore Examples Do an online search for "child-friendly" newsletters to show as models in class. Use an LCD projector or equivalent technology to display appropriate results. Show students a variety of styles, and look for opportunities to discuss key features.

ELL

English Language Learners

Introduce the E-Newsletter
Show students examples of child-friendly newsletters. Point out how each article relates to a specific theme or main idea. Show how illustrations and photos make articles more interesting.

21st Century Writing

Objectives

- Understand and identify the features of a newsletter article.
- Organize ideas to prepare for writing.

1 PREWRITE Plan and Prewrite

MINI-LESSON

Reading Like a Writer

- **Examine Model Text** Display several sample newsletters. Different groups and organizations make newsletters that focus on their group and its interests. Discuss the purpose and audience of the newsletters you show students. You are going to write a travel newsletter. It will include fact-based articles about a country you would like to visit.

- **Explore Model Text** Let's look at an example of an article in a travel newsletter. This is the kind of article that you will write. Display and read aloud to students "Visiting Mexico City" on 21st Century Writing Transparency TC1. Ask them to identify key features of a newsletter article in the student model. Make sure that students understand that all sentences in a paragraph should be about the same idea or topic.

Visiting Mexico City

Mexico City is the capital of Mexico. It is one of the world's largest cities. Most of the world's biggest cities are found on rivers. Mexico City, however, is in the Valley of Mexico. In Spanish they call that valley *Mesa Central*. About one-fifth of Mexico's population lives in Mexico City.

It has old neighborhoods that still have ruins from when the Aztec people lived in the area. It also has very new high-rise buildings stretching more than 50 stories into the sky! You can buy packaged groceries at fancy supermarkets. You can also buy live chickens and fresh tortillas at traditional market stands. If you are looking for a taste of the old and the new, Mexico City is the place to go!

Unit 1 E-Newsletter 21st Century Writing TC1

21st Century Transparency TC1, TR DVD

Determine appropriate topics

We will create an e-newsletter about one country we would like to visit. The newsletter will include many articles that focus on different parts of the country. First, we need to choose our country. Encourage students to brainstorm a list of countries they would like to visit and why they would like to go there. Write responses on the board. When the class has generated several ideas, help them to choose the most popular option either through discussion or a vote.

Narrow the topic

Now that we have chosen our country, we need to decide what articles we will put in our newsletter. Organize students into small groups and have each group create a K-W-L chart with at least three things they would like to learn about the chosen country. Suggest topics such as music, school, and important historical events. Have students look at each topic and evaluate why it is or is not a suitable topic for a newsletter article. They might ask: *Will I be able to find enough information on this topic? Will my audience find this topic interesting?* Ask each group to pick the most suitable topic on its list for its contribution to the e-newsletter. Then have each student choose an aspect of that topic as the focus of his or her article.

K	W	L
Mexico has rain forests.	What plants and animals live in Mexico?	
Many professional athletes are from Mexico.	What are the most popular sports in Mexico?	
Tacos, burritos, and tortillas are Mexican foods.	What are other traditional Mexican dishes?	

Corrective feedback

If... students have trouble deciding whether a topic is suitable, **then...** suggest that they answer these questions: *Would I enjoy learning more about this topic? Would my family enjoy reading about it?* Two *yes* answers indicate a possible topic.

Academic Vocabulary

Topic Sentence A topic sentence tells the main idea of a paragraph.

Differentiated Instruction

SI Strategic Intervention

Global Brainstorming If students struggle to choose a country to write about, display a classroom map or globe. Help students locate and name countries. Then have them identify at least one thing they would like to learn about each country.

Teacher Tip

Narrowing Topics If more than one small group chooses the same topic, have each group narrow the topic further. For example, "Sports in Mexico" can become "Baseball in Mexico" and "Soccer in Mexico."

ELL

English Language Learners

Build Vocabulary If students do not know some words in TC1 model, such as *neighborhoods* or *high-rise*, read the words and use them in sentences. Offer definitions for each unfamiliar word.

21st Century Writing

Objectives

- Use electronic research tools effectively and safely.
- Understand basic search engine techniques.
- Organize ideas to prepare to write a first draft.

Plan and Prewrite

Using an E-mail Program

Think Aloud A search engine is a useful tool that allows us to search for information on the World Wide Web. We can find information about the country we've chosen by entering keywords into the search field. The search engine will find Web sites that use those keywords. I want to learn about the history of the Mexican flag.

- Display the home page of a search engine on a projector. Enter *Mexican flag* into the search field and read through the first five results. If the search engine provides image results, display these for students as well. Then help students generate useful key words in order to research material for their articles.

There are too many sites that refer to the Mexican flag for me to look at all of them. I can use special commands to help the search engine narrow my search. Enter *Mexican flag + history* into the search field. Read through the top results with students. Introduce other search engine features to help them effectively narrow their searches.

Common Search Engine Features	
+	Adding "+" before a word makes sure it is included in the search.
~	Adding "~" before a word searches for that word and its synonyms.
OR	Adding "OR" between two search terms looks for sites with either term.
""	Adding quotes around a phrase searches for all of the words together.

Plan and Prewrite

Evaluating Sources

Now that I have narrowed my search, I need to find the Web sites with the most reliable information. Help students discern which sites are credible by asking the following questions:

- Is this site from a respected institution such as a museum or university?
- Is the domain name *.edu, .org*, or *.gov*?
- Is the information on the site up-to-date? When was the site last updated?
- Does the information seem fair, not favoring a particular argument or group?
- Can you find other sources that support the information on the site?

Bookmarking sites

Encourage students to keep a log of keywords and phrases that they use to search for information. Have them use their Internet browser's "bookmarks" or "favorites" function to save useful sites. If they copy and paste relevant information into a document that they can refer to later, remind them to save the URL (Web address) as well. Encourage students to share the best sites with their small group members.

Differentiated Instruction

Strategic Intervention

Newsletter Article Remind students that their newsletter articles must be fact based. Sit with them as they conduct their research and help them differentiate between Web sites with factual and fictitious entries. Guide them to distinguish the differences on their own.

Teacher Tip

Internet Safety Be aware of and follow your school and district guidelines for Internet use. Pay attention to the sites students visit and ensure they are appropriate.

Technology Tip

Domain Names Domain names help Internet users find Web sites and understand their function. The most common domain names are commercial (*.com or .firm*), educational (*.edu*), government (*.gov*), or organizational (*.org* or *.net*).

Objectives

- Organize research and ideas.
- Write a first draft of a newsletter article.
- Revise a draft of a newsletter article.

Draft

Organize ideas Have students make a simple web to organize their ideas and research. Tell them to write their topic in the center and connect it to keywords and supporting information in the outside of the web.

Getting started Have students look at their web organizers and write a topic sentence. Then they can write sentences that provide supporting details. Encourage them to refer to their notes from the sites they bookmarked during their research.

Examine model text Display 21st Century Transparency TC1 and review "Visiting Mexico City."

Think Aloud This student started with a clear topic sentence. The sentences that follow support the topic sentence. The body paragraphs support the topic with details. The conclusion paragraph restates the topic sentence.

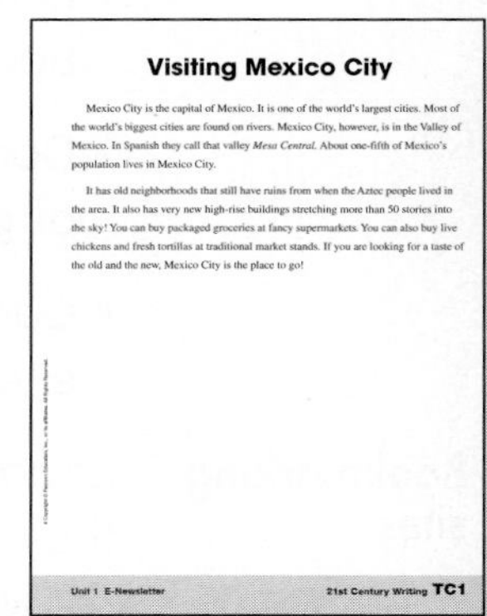

Visiting Mexico City

Mexico City is the capital of Mexico. It is one of the world's largest cities. Most of the world's biggest cities are found on rivers. Mexico City, however, is in the Valley of Mexico. In Spanish they call that valley *Mesa Central.* About one-fifth of Mexico's population lives in Mexico City.

It has old neighborhoods that still have ruins from when the Aztec people lived in the area. It also has very new high-rise buildings stretching more than 50 stories into the sky! You can buy packaged groceries at fancy supermarkets. You can also buy live chickens and fresh tortillas at traditional market stands. If you are looking for a taste of the old and the new, Mexico City is the place to go!

Unit 1 E-Newsletter 21st Century Writing TC1

21st Century Transparency TC1, TR DVD

Develop draft Remind students that the purpose of drafting is to record their ideas. Display or read Use Your Own Words (below) for students. Tell them that as they finish their drafts, they should remember that their conclusion statements can restate their topic sentences. Also encourage them to choose titles that will excite and interest their readers.

Use Your Own Words

- ✔ The author of a Web site is just like the author of a book! Be sure to use your words, not theirs, when writing your article. Using someone else's words without proper citation is called plagiarism.
- ✔ You can paraphrase or summarize the information you find on the Web sites that you use.

Revise

MINI-LESSON

Varying Sentence Length

- One way to revise writing is to vary the length of the sentences. A combination of long and short sentences makes writing more interesting. Read these examples with students:

All the same length	Mexico City is the capital of Mexico. It is one of the world's largest cities. Most of the world's biggest cities are found on a river. Mexico City is in the Valley of Mexico. In Spanish they call that valley *Mesa Central*. About one-fifth of Mexico's population lives in Mexico City.
Different lengths	Mexico City, the capital of Mexico, is one of the world's largest cities. Most of the world's biggest cities are found on a river, but Mexico City is in the Valley of Mexico, or *Mesa Central* in Spanish. About one-fifth of Mexico's population lives in Mexico City.

- Discuss with students how the paragraph was improved by varying the sentence lengths.

Peer Conferencing Have students return to their small groups and exchange their drafts for peer revision. Ask them to write at least three revision suggestions for each group member. Have students consider these suggestions as they revise their articles.

Revise drafts Earlier we wrote drafts of our newsletter articles. Now we will revise our drafts. When we revise, we incorporate comments from peer conferencing and try to make our writing clearer and more interesting. An interesting article has sentences that vary in length and support the topic sentence.

Corrective feedback **If...** students have difficulty varying sentence length, **then...** have them read their article aloud to their small group to determine whether it flows or sounds choppy.

Differentiated Instruction

Advanced

Apply Revising Skills As they revise their work, have students look for ways to improve their writing by using sensory details. Have them think about ways things would look, sound, taste, smell, or feel.

Teacher Tip

Plagiarism and the Internet
Remind students that just as they would not copy text directly from a book, they should paraphrase or restate text they find on a Web page when writing their articles.

ELL

English Language Learners

Supporting Details Have students write their topic sentence as a question. Then have them answer the question using their research to help generate supporting details.

21st Century Writing

Objectives

- Edit a revised draft of a newsletter article to correct errors in grammar, mechanics, and spelling.
- Use the Internet to search for images and illustrations to enhance a newsletter article.

4 Edit

MINI-LESSON

Using the Computer to Edit

- The grammar and spelling checker is a useful tool to identify errors in your writing. Read each suggestion that the checker makes carefully before you accept it to be sure that the correction is appropriate. Have students use the grammar and spelling checker in the word processing program that they used to write their newsletter article.

- Although the grammar and spelling checker is very useful, it does not always identify every mistake. If a word is spelled correctly but is the wrong word to use in that sentence, the spelling checker will not correct it. Type the following sentence in a word processing program and display it on a projector:

  You can see many plants and animals their.

  Use the spelling checker to check the sentence. The spelling checker did not catch the incorrect word because it is spelled correctly, but used incorrectly. What is the word we need? How should it be spelled? Change "their" to "there."

- Have students practice editing the following sentences, first by using the grammar and spelling checker and then by themselves.

  Are tacos you're favorite Mexican food?

  You can here the crowd cheer in the stadium.

  What will the dancers where for the concert?

  You can sea many plants and animals in Mexico.

Edit drafts Ask students to edit their own drafts. After they use the grammar and spelling checker, have them print out their article and read it sentence by sentence to make further edits. Ask them to check their drafts for spelling, grammar, punctuation, and capitalization.

Publish and Present

MINI-LESSON

Finding Images on the Internet

- Display the home page of an Internet search engine on a projector. Photographs and illustrations will make our articles more interesting for our readers. We can look for pictures on the Internet. This search engine will help us find pictures that will make our articles stand out.
- I want to find a picture of the Mexican flag. If available, choose the option for searching images in the search engine. Type the keywords *Mexican flag* into the search field. Display the results on the projector. Click on an option that is appropriate and go to the site that holds the image source.
- Have students search for appropriate images for their articles. Show students how to copy and save images onto their computer desktop. Encourage them to change the file names so that they can easily identify each image. Have them store the images in a special folder to keep them organized and easy to access when it is time to publish the e-newsletter.

Corrective feedback

If… students have difficulty finding appropriate images,
then… have them refer to the list of keywords they made during their initial research for their article and use those words in the search engine's image search option.

Differentiated Instruction

 Advanced

Concepts of Print Have children interested in design work with the final newsletter layout. Encourage them to change fonts and font sizes to draw attention to headings and to use artwork to optimize space.

Technology Tip

Internet Image Search Many images on the Web are protected by copyright. It is good practice for students to be aware of which images are safe to use. Direct them to an image gallery specifically for educational use or help them discern which images are copyrighted while using a search engine's image finder.

English Language Learners

English Conventions Assist students in editing spelling and grammatical errors. Discuss how to correct each error and the reason for the change. Use the appropriate lessons in the *ELL Handbook* to support teaching English conventions.

Objectives

- Use a design program to lay out articles in newsletter format.
- Present an e-newsletter comprising factual articles.

5 Publish and Present

Options for presenting

Offer students two options for presenting their work:

Print out a hard copy of their newsletter to take home to their families and to display in the classroom.	Convert the file to Portable Document Format (PDF) and make it available for download on a class or school Web site or educational file-sharing site.

Laying out the newsletter

Now that we have written and revised our articles about the country we want to visit, it is time to put them together to create our E-Newsletter. We will use a design program to put the articles and pictures we found into a format that our audience will find fun and easy to read.

Help students decide which articles and topics should be on the front page, in the middle, and on the last page. Have students choose which articles should be grouped together. Encourage them to consider the size and color of images and the length of articles as well as the topic.

Give each student an opportunity to use a design application to lay out the articles and images. Assist students in resizing photographs and illustrations and in flowing text into multiple columns, as needed. Help students combine their pages into one complete document. Print a final copy on a color printer to display in the classroom.

Customize Literacy in Your Classroom

Table of Contents
for Customize Literacy

Customize Literacy is organized into different sections, each one designed to help you organize and carry out an effective literacy program. Each section contains strategies and support for teaching comprehension skills and strategies. *Customize Literacy* also shows how to use weekly text sets of readers in your literacy program.

Weekly Text Sets
to Customize Literacy

The following readers can be used to enhance your literacy instruction.

	Concept Literacy Reader	Below-Level Reader	On-Level Reader	Advanced Reader	ELD Reader	ELL Reader
Unit 1 WEEK 1	*Coming Together*	*Florida Everglades: Its Plants and Animals*	*Something to Do*	*The Story of Libraries*	*World Concert*	*World Concert*
Unit 1 WEEK 2	*The Dog That Discovered the West*	*The Long Journey West*	*Lewis, Clark, and the Corps of Discovery*	*Two Powerful Rivers*	*Talking to Lewis and Clark*	*Talking to Lewis and Clark*
Unit 1 WEEK 3	*Laura Ingalls Wilder: Pioneer Girl*	*From Sea to Shining Sea*	*Protecting Wild Animals*	*Exploring the Moon*	*Our Trip Out East*	*Our Trip Out East*

Customize Literacy in Your Classroom

Customize Instruction
to Improve Reading Behaviors

Instruction in comprehension skills and strategies provides readers with avenues to understanding a text. Through teacher modeling and guided, collaborative, and independent practice, students become independent thinkers who employ a variety of skills and strategies to help them make meaning as they read.

Mini-Lessons for Comprehension Skills and Strategies

Unit 1	Sequence, Author's Purpose, Literary Elements, Main Idea and Details, Summarize, Story Structure
Unit 2	Cause and Effect, Draw Conclusions, Fact and Opinion, Main Idea and Details, Background Knowledge, Text Structure, Monitor and Clarify
Unit 3	Graphic Sources, Fact and Opinion, Generalize, Cause and Effect, Important Ideas, Predict and Set Purpose
Unit 4	Compare and Contrast, Sequence, Graphic Sources, Literary Elements, Visualize, Questioning, Inferring
Unit 5	Author's Purpose, Compare and Contrast, Literary Elements, Main Idea and Details, Draw Conclusions, Text Structure, Important Ideas
Unit 6	Cause and Effect, Fact and Opinion, Sequence, Generalize, Graphic Sources, Inferring, Summarize

Envision It! A Comprehension Handbook

Envision It! Visual Skills Handbook
Author's Purpose
Categorize and Classify
Cause and Effect
Compare and Contrast
Draw Conclusions
Fact and Opinion
Generalize
Graphic Sources
Literary Elements
Main Idea and Details
Sequence

Envision It! Visual Strategies Handbook
Background Knowledge
Important Ideas
Inferring
Monitor and Clarify
Predict and Set Purpose
Questioning
Story Structure
Summarize
Text Structure
Visualize

Anchor Chart Anchor charts are provided with each strategy lesson. These charts incorporate the language of strategic thinkers. They help students make their thinking visible and permanent and provide students with a means to clarify their thinking about how and when to use each strategy. As students gain more experience with a strategy, the chart may undergo revision.

See pages 101–126 in the *First Stop on Reading Street* Teacher's Edition for additional support as you customize literacy in your classroom.

Good Readers DRA2 users will find additional resources in the *First Stop on Reading Street* Teacher's Edition on pages 104–105.

Contents

Pacing Guide

This chart shows the instructional sequence from *Scott Foresman Reading Street* for Grade 4. You can use this pacing guide as is to ensure you are following a comprehensive scope and sequence. Or, you can adjust the sequence to match your calendar, curriculum map, or testing schedule.

Grade 4

READING	UNIT 1					REVIEW WEEK	UNIT 2	
	Week 1	Week 2	Week 3	Week 4	Week 5		Week 1	Week 2
Comprehension Skill	Sequence	Author's Purpose	Literary Elements (Character, Setting, Plot)	Author's Purpose	Main Idea/ Details		Cause/Effect	Draw Conclusions
Comprehension Strategy	Summarize	Questioning	Background Knowledge	Story Structure	Text Structure		Background Knowledge	Story Structure
Vocabulary Skill/ Strategy	Suffixes/Word Structure	Word Endings/ Word Structure	Multiple-Meaning Words/ Dictionary	Synonyms, Antonyms/ Context Clues	Suffixes *-ist*, *-ive*, *-ness*/ Word Structure		Prefixes & Suffixes/Word Structure	Unknown Words/ Dictionary-Glossary
Fluency Skill	Expression	Appropriate Phrasing/ Punctuation Cues	Rate/Accuracy	Expression	Appropriate Phrasing		Appropriate Phrasing	Expression
Spelling/ Word Work	Short Vowels VCCV	Long *a* and *i*	Long *e* and *o*	Long *e*	Long *u*		Adding *-s*, *-es*	Irregular Plurals

	UNIT 4					REVIEW WEEK	UNIT 5	
	Week 1	Week 2	Week 3	Week 4	Week 5		Week 1	Week 2
Comprehension Skill	Compare/ Contrast	Compare/ Contrast	Sequence	Graphic Sources	Literary Elements (Character, Plot)		Author's Purpose	Compare/ Contrast
Comprehension Strategy	Visualize	Summarize	Important Ideas	Predict and Set Purpose	Monitor and Clarify		Important Ideas	Visualize
Vocabulary Skill/ Strategy	Synonyms & Antonyms/ Context Clues	Multiple-Meaning Words/ Context Clues	Unknown Words/ Dictionary-Glossary	Greek & Latin Roots/ Word Structure	Synonyms & Antonyms/ Context Clues		Homographs/ Dictionary-Glossary	Greek & Latin Roots/ Word Structure
Fluency Skill	Expression	Appropriate Phrasing/ Punctuation Cues	Expression	Appropriate Phrasing	Expression		Rate and Accuracy	Appropriate Phrasing
Spelling/ Word Work	Contractions	Final Syllable Patterns	Consonant Digraph /sh/	Consonants /j/, /ks/, /kw/	Prefixes *un-*, *dis-*, *in-*		Multisyllabic Words	Words with Double Consonants

Are you the adventurous type? Want to use some of your own ideas and materials in your teaching? But you worry you might be leaving out some critical instruction kids need? Customize Literacy can help."

REVIEW WEEK

Week 3	Week 4	Week 5
Draw Conclusions	Fact and Opinion	Main Idea/ Details
Questioning	Monitor & Clarify	Inferring
Prefixes/ Word Structure	Unknown Words/ Dictionary-Glossary	Unknown Words/ Dictionary-Glossary
Expression	Expression	Expression
Words with *ar, or*	Consonant Patterns *ng, nk, ph, wh*	Words with *ear, ir, our, ur*

UNIT 3

REVIEW WEEK

Week 1	Week 2	Week 3	Week 4	Week 5
Graphic Sources	Fact/ Opinion	Generalize	Cause and Effect	Generalize
Important Ideas	Text Structure	Visualize	Predict and Set Purpose	Inferring
Multiple-Meaning Words/ Context Clues	Multiple-Meaning Words/ Context Clues	Unfamiliar Words/ Context Clues	Root Words/ Word Structure	Suffixes/ Word Structure
Expression	Expression	Appropriate Phrasing	Appropriate Phrasing/ Punctuation Cues	Appropriate Phrasing/ Punctuation Cues
Adding *-ed, -ing*	Homophones	Vowel Sound in *shout*	Compound Words	Possessives

REVIEW WEEK

Week 3	Week 4	Week 5
Literary Elements (Character, Plot, Theme)	Main Idea/ Details	Draw Conclusions
Story Structure	Text Structure	Monitor and Clarify
Unfamiliar Words/ Context Clues	Greek & Latin Prefixes/Word Structure	Synonyms/ Context Clues
Expression	Expression	Rate and Accuracy
Greek Word Parts	Latin Roots	Related Words

UNIT 6

REVIEW WEEK

Week 1	Week 2	Week 3	Week 4	Week 5
Cause/Effect	Fact/Opinion	Sequence	Generalize	Graphic Sources
Questioning	Summarize	Inferring	Predict and Set Purpose	Background Knowledge
Root Words/ Word Structure	Multiple-Meaning Words/ Dictionary-Glossary	Unfamiliar Words/ Context Clues	Unfamiliar Words/ Context Clues	Multiple-Meaning Words/ Context Clues
Appropriate Phrasing	Expression	Expression	Appropriate Phrasing/ Punctuation Cues	Rate and Accuracy
Schwa	Prefixes *mis-, non-, pre-, re-*	Suffixes *-less, -ment, -ness*	Suffixes *-ful, -ly, -ion*	Silent Consonants

Pacing Guide

Grade 4

LANGUAGE ARTS	UNIT 1 Week 1	Week 2	Week 3	Week 4	Week 5	UNIT 2 Week 1	Week 2
Speaking and Listening	Dramatic Retelling	Introduction	Advertisement	Oral Report	Travel Show	Sportscast	Newscast
Grammar	Declarative and Interrogative Sentences	Imperative and Exclamatory Sentences	Complete Subjects and Predicates	Compound Sentences	Clauses and Complex Sentences	Common and Proper Nouns	Regular Plural Nouns
Weekly Writing	Realistic Fiction	Expository Composition	Parody	Friendly Letter	Personal Narrative	Poetry	News Article
Trait of the Week	Organization	Organization	Voice	Conventions	Voice	Figurative Language	Focus/Ideas
Writing	E-Newsletter/Personal Narrative						

REVIEW WEEK

	UNIT 4 Week 1	Week 2	Week 3	Week 4	Week 5	UNIT 5 Week 1	Week 2
Speaking and Listening	Advertisement	TV Commercial	Interview	Retelling	Newscast	Dramatization	Radio Announcement
Grammar	Singular and Plural Pronouns	Pronouns	Pronouns and Antecedents	Possessive Pronouns	Contractions and Negatives	Adjectives and Articles	Adverbs
Weekly Writing	Mystery	Song	Instructions	Problem-Solution Essay	Adventure	Fantasy	Legend
Trait of the Week	Word Choice	Word Choice	Organization	Focus/Ideas	Word Choice	Conventions	Sentences
Writing	Story Exchange/Story						

REVIEW WEEK

REVIEW WEEK

Week 3	Week 4	Week 5
Readers' Theater	Interview	Panel Discussion
Irregular Plural Nouns	Singular Possessive Nouns	Plural Possessive Nouns
Poetry: Free Verse; Cinquain	Expository Composition	Persuasive Essay
Figurative Language	Organization	Organization

Podcast/How-to Report

UNIT 3

REVIEW WEEK

Week 1	Week 2	Week 3	Week 4	Week 5
Persuasive Speech	Interview	Readers' Theater	Weather Broadcast	How-to Demonstration
Action and Linking Verbs	Main and Helping Verbs	Subject-Verb Agreement	Past, Present, and Future Tenses	Irregular Verbs
Narrative Poem	Invitation	Myth	Formal Letter	Summary
Organization	Voice	Sentences	Organization	Sentences

Photo Essay/Compare and Contrast Essay

REVIEW WEEK

Week 3	Week 4	Week 5
How-to Demonstration	Panel Discussion	Talk Show
Comparative & Superlative Adjectives, Adverbs	Time Order Words	Prepositions and Prepositional Phrases
Thank-You Note	Persuasive Ad	Personal Narrative
Word Choice	Focus/Ideas	Sentences

Electronic Pen Pals/Persuasive Essay

UNIT 6

REVIEW WEEK

Week 1	Week 2	Week 3	Week 4	Week 5
Panel Discussion	How-to Demonstration	Debate	Readers' Theater	Informational Speech
Conjunctions	Capitalization and Abbreviations	Commas	Quotations and Quotation Marks	Titles
Cause-and-Effect Essay	Review	Skit	Play	Literary Nonfiction
Focus/Ideas	Sentences	Word Choice	Word Choice	Conventions

Blog/Research Report

Teaching Record Chart

This chart shows the critical comprehension skills and strategies you need to cover. Check off each one as you provide instruction.

Reading/Comprehension	DATES OF INSTRUCTION		
Summarize and explain the lesson or message of a work of fiction is its theme.			
Compare and contrast the adventures or exploits of characters (e.g. the tricksters) in traditional and classical literature.			
Explain how the structural elements of poetry (e.g., rhyme, meter, stanzas, line breaks) relate to form (e.g., lyrical poetry, free verse).			
Describe the structural elements particular to dramatic literature.			
Sequence and summarize the plot's main events and describe their influence on future events.			
Describe the interaction of characters including their relationships and the changes they undergo.			
Identify whether the narrator or speaker of a story is first or third person.			
Identify similarities and differences between the events and characters' experiences in a fictional work and the actual events and experiences described in an author's biography or autobiography.			
Identify the author's use of similes and metaphors to produce imagery.			
Read independently for a sustained period of time and paraphrase what the reading was about, maintaining meaning and logical order (e.g., generate a reading log or journal; participate in book talks).			
Explain the difference between a stated purpose and implied purpose in expository texts.			

"Tired of using slips of paper or stickies to make sure you teach everything you need to? Need an easier way to keep track of what you have taught, and what you still need to cover? **Customize Literacy** can help."

Reading/Comprehension	DATES OF INSTRUCTION		
Summarize the main idea and supporting details in texts in ways that maintain meaning.			
Distinguish fact from opinion in a text and explain how to verify what is a fact.			
Describe explicit and implicit relationships among ideas in texts organized by cause-and-effect, sequence, or comparison.			
Use multiple text features (e.g., guide words, topic and concluding sentences) to gain an overview of the contents of text and to locate information.			
Explain how an author uses language to present information to influence the reader to think or do something.			
Determine the sequence of activities needed to carry out procedure (e.g., following a recipe).			
Explain factual information presented graphically (e.g., charts, diagrams, graphs, illustrations).			
Establish purposes for reading selected texts based on own or others' desired outcome to enhance comprehension.			
Ask literal, interpretive, and evaluative questions of text.			
Monitor and adjust comprehension (e.g., using background knowledge, creating sensory images, rereading a portion aloud, generating questions).			
Make inferences about text and use textual evidence to support understanding.			
Summarize information in text, maintaining meaning and logical order.			
Make connections (e.g., thematic links, author analysis) between literary and informational texts with similar ideas and provide textual evidence.			

Student Edition p. EI•13

Sequence

Objectives:

- Students define sequence.
- Students identify sequence relationships.
- Students understand that some, but not all, sequence relationships are signaled by clue words.

What is it? **Sequence** means the order in which things happen. Sequence can also mean the steps we follow to make or do something. Understanding sequence, or time relationships, is important in understanding certain genres, such as historical fiction and biography. Social studies and science texts use sequence to describe events and processes. At Grade 4, when clue words are not used to explicitly point out sequence, readers need to think about the order in which events occur.

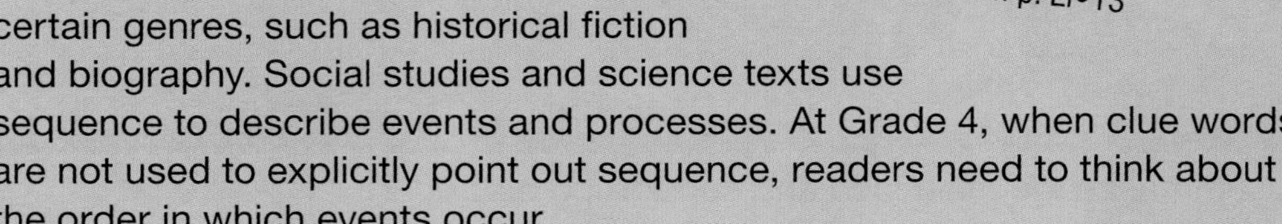

How Good Readers Use the Skill Students experience time relationships every day. Teachers can build on these experiences and help students connect them to reading. At first, students understand sequence as the order of what happens first, next, and last in a selection. Students can then move on to use clue words to decipher more complicated sequence relationships, such as flashbacks and simultaneous events.

Texts for Teaching

Student Edition

- *Because of Winn-Dixie,* 4.1, pages 26–37
- *Navajo Code Talkers,* 4.2, pages 88–103
- *How Tía Lola Came to ~~Visit~~ Stay,* 4.2, pages 388–403

Leveled Readers

- See pages CL 24–CL 29 for a list of Leveled Readers.

Mini-Lesson 1

Teach the Skill

Use the Envision It! lesson on page EI•13 to visually review sequence.

Remind students that:

- **sequence** means the order in which things happen. It can also be the steps we take to do or make something.
- **clue words** such as *first, last,* and *after* can help students figure out order.

Practice

Write the following sentences in random order on the board and have students put them in sequential order using clue words, such as *first, next, then,* and so on. Students might use other words that indicate time as well, such as *last night* or *Monday.*

I made supper for everyone. I got out a jar of sauce and a box of pasta. I boiled the pasta and heated up the sauce. I scooped ice cream for everyone. We all did the dishes.

If... students have difficulty identifying sequence relationships, **then...** use just two sentence and work with them to decide which action would come first.

Apply

As students read the assigned text, have them look for clue words that signal sequence.

Writing

Students can describe their activities yesterday using clue words.

Teach the Skill

Use the Envision It! lesson on page EI•13 to visually review sequence.

Remind students that:

- **sequence** means the order in which things happen. It can also be the steps we take to do or make something.
- **clue words** such as *first*, *last*, and *after* can help students figure out order.
- not all selections that are in time order have clue words.
- clue words such as *while*, *meanwhile*, and *during* signal events that are happening simultaneously.

Practice

Read aloud the following passage and have students listen for three events that happen in sequence and two events that happen simultaneously. Remind students that they may need to use their common sense and prior knowledge to determine sequence, as every event may not include a clue word.

Last night the kids made supper for everyone. I got the ingredients out of the fridge and lined them up. Meanwhile, Jarod set the table. I started the water boiling for pasta. This would take longer than heating the sauce. While the pasta boiled and the sauce bubbled, Jarod and I made a salad. After dinner, Jarod and I washed the dishes. As a treat, Dad took everyone out for dessert.

If... students have difficulty identifying sequence relationships, **then...** chunk the text and have them point out clue words that identify events in each chunk.

Apply

As students read the assigned text, have them complete a sequence graphic organizer to help students order events in the selection.

Writing

Students can make a list of clue words to use in their writing.

Teach the Skill

Use the Envision It! lesson on page EI•13 to visually review sequence.

Remind students that:

- **sequence** means the order in which things happen. It can also be the steps we take to do or make something.
- not all selections that are in time order have clue words.
- clue words such as *while*, *meanwhile*, and *during* signal events that are happening simultaneously.
- sometimes events are told out of order, for example in a flashback, and readers must look at verb tenses for clues to sequence.

Practice

Read aloud the following passage and have students listen for the order of events. Ask students to support their ideas.

The story we read today brought another incident to mind. I was just eight when I got my first guitar, but this was still years after I had been taking piano lessons. I started those lessons shortly after turning five. The guitar sat in my closet until one day when my piano teacher brought her guitar to my lesson. We played a duet! I started playing the guitar that day and haven't stopped.

If... students have difficulty identifying sequence relationships, **then...** provide a graphic organizer for additional practice.

Apply

As students read the assigned text, have them complete a sequence graphic organizer to help students order events in the selection.

Writing

Students can describe an event out of order, using verb tenses as sequence clues.

Objectives:

- Students understand that an author writes for one or more purposes.
- Students identify purposes for writing.
- Students infer an author's purpose from text features and specific language used.
- Students use author's purpose to set a reading rate.

Author's Purpose

Student Edition p. EI•2

What is it? An author may write to persuade, to inform, to entertain, or to express a mood or feeling. Readers can infer an **author's purpose** from text features and from specific language the author uses. At Grade 4, students learn to set/adjust their rate of reading based on their predictions of author's purpose. Evaluating an author's purpose also helps students develop comprehension and appreciation of what they read.

How Good Readers Use the Skill Students know that they read different kinds of selections for different reasons. Teachers can build on these experiences by introducing specific purposes for writing and helping readers classify things they read. At first, students learn that authors write to inform or entertain. More sophisticated readers learn other purposes; they learn that an author may have several purposes. Eventually we want readers to preview a selection for hints to author's purpose, for example, graphics, dialogue, and sample text. They also think critically about whether an author met his or her purpose.

Texts for Teaching

Student Edition

- *Lewis and Clark and Me,* 4.1, pages 52–61
- *The Horned Toad Prince,* 4.1, pages 116–129
- *Smokejumpers,* 4.2, pages 178–191

Leveled Readers

- See pages CL 24–CL 29 for a list of Leveled Readers.

Teach the Skill

Use the Envision It! lesson on page EI•2 to visually review author's purpose.

Remind students that:

- an author may write to **persuade,** to **inform,** to **entertain,** or to **express** a mood or feeling.
- readers can infer an **author's purpose** from text features and language.

Practice

Ask students to name some movies, books, and TV shows they have read or seen lately. Join in, adding your experiences. Together, work to classify the list according to purpose. Have students ask: *Was this created to teach me something? to entertain me? to persuade me to think or act in a certain way? to express a certain mood or feeling?* Talk briefly about what parts of the movie, book, or TV show students used to decide on its purpose. Make a chart for your responses.

If... students have difficulty identifying the purpose,
then... provide two choices for a particular book or show and have students select from the choices.

Apply

As students read the assigned text, have them look at the classification chart you made and think about what purpose the author might have had.

Writing

Students can write their own definitions for *persuade*, *inform*, *express*, and *entertain* to use when classifying selections.

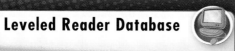

Mini-Lesson 2

Teach the Skill

Use the Envision It! lesson on page EI•2 to visually review author's purpose.

Remind students that:

- an author may write to **persuade,** to **inform,** to **entertain,** or to **express** a mood or feeling.
- readers can infer an **author's purpose** from text features and from specific language the author uses.
- an author may have more than one purpose for writing.

Practice

Provide different reading materials. Include nonfiction informational articles, fictional stories, a poem or two, and at least one advertisement. Have small groups first decide on the purpose behind the piece and then to point out language or text features to support their opinions. Bring the groups together to explain their ideas. Record the language they cite for each kind of writing. Ask: Could an author have more than one purpose for writing? What makes you think as you do?

If... students have difficulty determining purpose from text features and language,

then... have them focus on one kind of writing. List text features and language that help make an inference about author's purpose.

Apply

Have students read the assigned text and complete a graphic organizer to help figure out author's purpose.

Writing

Students can write a few sentences with a purpose in mind and have a classmate say what the purpose is.

Mini-Lesson 3

Teach the Skill

Use the Envision It! lesson on page EI•2 to visually review author's purpose.

Remind students that:

- an author may write to **persuade,** to **inform,** to **entertain,** or to **express** a mood or feeling.
- readers can infer an **author's purpose** from text features and from specific language the author uses.
- an author may have more than one purpose for writing.
- understanding the **author's purpose** can help them determine their reading rate.

Practice

Model reading aloud a portion of a challenging nonfiction article to show students how you use it to determine your reading rate. Show students the article and then think aloud as you preview it to determine your reading rate. Ask: What is this about? What text features does the author include? Why might the author have written this? Will I read slowly or quickly? As you read some of the article, explain to students how you will set your reading rate based on the difficulty of the text and the author's purpose.

If... students have difficulty understanding that previewing can help determine author's purpose and reading rate,

then... go through a nonfiction selection and list text features, discussing their use in the article.

Apply

As students read, have them set their reading rate based on the author's purpose.

Writing

Ask students to review a piece of their writing to determine purpose and strengthen it if necessary.

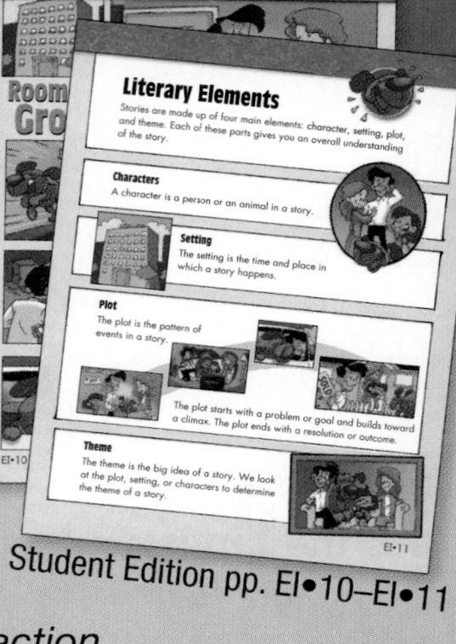

Student Edition pp. EI•10–EI•11

Objectives:

- Students understand that fictional selections include characters, a setting, and a plot.
- Students identify or infer setting and traits and motives of characters.
- Students follow the plot in a story.
- Students identify the theme of a story.

Literary Elements

What is it? **Literary elements** include the characters, setting, plot, and theme of a fictional piece of writing. At Grade 4, students learn that the elements of a story are often related. They make inferences about one element to understand others. Students learn to identify plot elements, such as *conflict* and *rising action.* Students read pieces with no directly stated theme.

How Good Readers Use the Skill Students need experience in understanding the relationships between characters and setting and how they impact plot and theme. Identifying these elements is the first step. Readers ask questions, such as *What is the character's goal? Does he or she achieve it? What message might the author have for me, the reader?* Students learn to use the literary elements and language in a story to preview and make connections as they read. Understanding theme is a way readers connect a story to their own experiences or those of others. Older readers connect themes within stories and make connections between stories that share similar themes.

Texts for Teaching

Student Edition

- *On the Banks of Plum Creek,* 4.1, pages 84–99
- *Encyclopedia Brown and the Case of the Slippery Salamander,* 4.2, pages 146–155
- *Cliff Hanger,* 4.2, pages 234–245

Leveled Readers

- See pages CL 24–CL 29 for a list of Leveled Readers.

Mini-Lesson 1

Teach the Skill

Use the Envision It! lesson on pp. EI•10–EI•11 to visually review literary elements.

Remind students that:

- **characters** are the people or animals in stories. Readers learn about characters through their words and actions and through how other characters act toward them.
- the **setting** is the time and place in which a story takes place.
- the **plot** is the pattern of events in a story that lead to a character fulfilling a goal or solving a problem.
- what happens in a story can often cause a character to change.

Practice

Provide an example of a character from a story you have read. Begin a web about the character, listing details from the story at the beginning of the story and at the end. Ask: What was the character like at the beginning? Did the character change? How? Why? Compare the characters with each other and with real people.

If... students have difficulty identifying character traits, **then...** suggest two traits, such as curious and uninterested, and have students select the one that fits best. Make sure students explain their choices.

Apply

As students read the assigned text, have them record traits of the main character on a graphic organizer. They can use this to talk about how characters change in the story.

Write

Students can write a description of a character. The description should include how the character changes in a story.

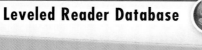

Teach the Skill

Use the Envision It! lesson on pp. EI•10–EI•11 to visually review literary elements.

Remind students that:

- **characters, setting,** and **plot** are the *who*, *where*, and *what* of a story.
- the **plot** is the pattern of events in a story that leads to a character fulfilling a goal or solving a problem.
- the character begins to solve the problem or reach the goal in what is called **rising action.**
- the turning point—usually the most important event in a story—is called the **climax.**
- the **resolution** is the outcome.

Practice

Supply students with a familiar story. Have volunteers retell the story. Jot down the events student recall on a graphic organizer, such as a plot line or story sequence chart. Identify the problem, rising action, climax, and resolution. Ask questions to help students understand kinds of problems characters face: Is there a conflict between two characters? Is there a conflict between a character and something in nature? Is the conflict inside the character, as when a character needs to make a decision about something?

If... students have difficulty identifying parts of the plot,
then... have students work with figuring out these two parts first: the problem or goal and the resolution.

Apply

As students read the assigned text, have them record plot events on a graphic organizer. They can use this to summarize the story.

Writing

Students can write a summary of a favorite book or story. Include the story's problem, rising action, climax, and resolution.

Teach the Skill

Use the Envision It! lesson on pp. EI•10–EI•11 to visually review literary elements.

Remind students that:

- **characters, setting,** and **plot** are the *who*, *where*, and *what* of a story.
- the **theme** is the underlying meaning of a story. Readers use information about characters, setting, and plot from the story to understand this big idea.
- the **theme** is the *why* of a story, or the point the author is trying to make. It may be a generalization, such as, "Honesty is the best policy."
- sometimes themes are not stated.

Practice

Using a familiar story, have students think about what the theme might be. First, have them retell the plot of the story. Then brainstorm with students a general topic for the story. Ask: Is the story about friendship? about growing up? about disappointment? about being steadfast? When students choose one or two topics, have them locate details in the story that would support that topic. Together, think about a theme for the story. Write it as a sentence.

If... students have difficulty choosing a theme,
then... provide one or two choices and have students select one and tell why it is a good choice.

Apply

As students read the assigned text, have them first look to see if the author states a theme; if not, have them think about why the author wrote the story.

Writing

Students can write a paragraph about the theme of a favorite story. Have them include why they think as they do.

Objectives:

- Students identify a summary as the gist of an article or story.
- Students use the strategy of summarizing as they read.
- Students ask questions to help them summarize.

Texts for Teaching

Student Edition

- *Because of Winn-Dixie,* 4.1, pages 26–37
- *Encantado: Pink Dolphin of the Amazon,* 4.2, pages 58–71
- *Jim Thorpe's Bright Path,* 4.2, pages 356–371

Leveled Readers

- See pages CL 24–CL 29 for a list of Leveled Readers.

Summarize

Summarize

We **summarize**, or retell, to check our understanding of what we've read. A summary is a brief statement—no more than a few sentences—and maintains a logical order.

To summarize fiction

- tell what happens in the story
- include the goals of the characters, how they try to reach them, and whether or not they succeed

To summarize nonfiction

- tell the main idea
- think about text structure and how the selection is organized

Let's Think About Reading!

When I summarize, I ask myself

- What is the story or selection mainly about?
- In fiction, what are the characters' goals? Are they successful?
- In nonfiction, how is the information organized?

EI•23

Student Edition p. EI•23

Understand the Strategy

Summarizing means picking out the important ideas in a story or an article and restating them in your own words. Summarizing enables readers to organize information and evaluate the importance of what they read.

Teach

Use the Envision It! lesson on page EI•23 to visually review summarizing.

Remind students that summarizing what they read can help them organize and understand what they read and that this can be a helpful study tool. Using a piece of familiar text, model asking questions to identify important information that should be a part of a summary as well as the unimportant ideas. Then, write a summary in your own words.

Questions for Nonfiction	Questions for Fiction
What is this selection about?	What is this story about?
What are the main ideas?	What do the characters want to do?
Which information is important?	What problems do they face doing it?
Which information is interesting, but not that important? Why?	How do they solve the problem in the end? Or do they?

Practice

Supply students with a text and a good summary of that selection. Have them talk about what parts of the text were important to include and what parts were not important to include and why they thought so. Then provide a new text and have students read the text and write a summary. Using student ideas, work together to write a summary all agree on.

If... students have difficulty summarizing,
then... chunk the text for them and have them determine important points and summarize a small portion of the text. Later they can put their summaries together.

Apply

Ask students to write a summary of a text on their own. Students can use a graphic organizer to help them organize information for a summary.

Anchor Chart

Anchor charts help students make their thinking visible and permanent. With an anchor chart, the group can clarify their thinking about how to use a strategy. Display anchor charts so readers can use them as they read. They may wish or need to review and edit the charts as they gain more experience with strategies. Here is a sample chart for writing a summary.

Writing a Summary

1. Be sure you understand the selection! Reread it if you don't get it.
2. Ask questions to help you understand what you read.
3. Write down the main points.
4. Write down the important details—try to distinguish the important details from the really interesting ones. Sometimes the details you remember aren't the most important ones!
5. If you are summarizing fiction, think about the characters, setting, plot, and theme.
6. If you are summarizing nonfiction, think about the text structure.
7. Try writing a few sentences that tell the main points in your own words.
8. Reread your summary to see how it sounds.

Anchor Chart

Using Multiple Strategies

Good readers use multiple strategies as they read. You can encourage students to read strategically through good classroom questioning. Use questions such as these to help students apply strategies during reading.

Answer Questions

- Who or what is this question about?
- Where can you look to find the answer to this question?

Ask Questions

- What do you want to know about ________?
- What questions to do you have about the ________ in this selection? Use the words *who, what, when, where, why,* and *how* to ask your questions.
- Do you have any questions after reading?

Graphic Organizers

- What kind of graphic organizer could you use to help you keep track of the information in this selection?

Monitor and Clarify

- Does the story or article make sense?
- What don't you understand about what you read?
- Do you need to reread, review, read on, or check a reference source?
- Do you need to read more slowly or more quickly?
- What is a ________? Where could you look to find out?

Predict/Confirm Predictions

- What do you think this story or article will be about? Why do you think as you do?
- What do you think you will learn from this selection?
- Do the text features help you predict what will happen?
- Based on what has happened so far, what do you think will happen next?
- Is this what you thought would happen?
- How does ________ change what you thought would happen?

Preview

- What do the photographs, illustrations, or graphic sources tell about the selection?
- What do you want to find out? What do you want to learn?

Background Knowledge

- What do you already know about ________?
- Have you read stories or articles by this author before?
- How is this selection like others that you have read?
- What does this remind you of?
- How does your background knowledge help you understand ________?
- Did the text match what you already knew? What new information did you learn?

Story Structure

- Who are the characters in this story? the setting?
- What is the problem in this story? How does the problem get solved?
- What is the point of this story?

Summarize

- What two or three important ideas have you read so far?
- How do the text features relate to the important ideas?
- Is there a graphic organizer that can help you organize the information before you summarize?

Text Structure

- How has the author organized the writing?
- What clues tell you that the text is structured ________?

Visualize

- When you read this, what do you picture in your mind?
- What do you hear, see, or smell?
- What do you think ________ looks like? Why do you think as you do?

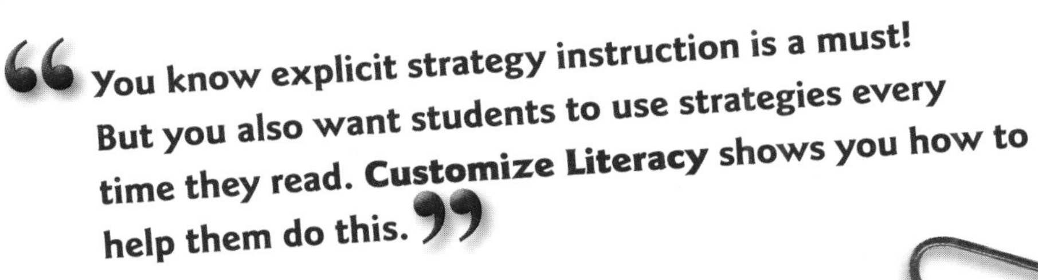

"You know explicit strategy instruction is a must! But you also want students to use strategies every time they read. **Customize Literacy** shows you how to help them do this."

Glossary of Literacy Terms

This glossary lists academic language terms that are related to literacy. They are provided for your information and professional use.

A

alliteration the repetition of a consonant sound in a group of words, especially in poetry

allusion a word or phrase that refers to something else the reader already knows from history, experience, or reading

animal fantasy a story about animals that talk and act like people

answer questions a reading strategy in which readers use the text and prior knowledge to answer questions about what they are reading

antonym a word that means the opposite of another word

ask questions a reading strategy in which readers ask themselves questions about the text to help make sense of what they read

author's point of view the author's opinion on the subject he or she is writing about

author's purpose the reason the author wrote the text

autobiography the story of a real person's life written by that person

B

background knowledge the information and experience that a reader brings to a text

biography the story of a real person's life written by another person

C

cause why something happens

character a person, an animal, or a personified object in a story

chronological order events in a selection, presented in the order in which they occurred

classify and categorize put things, such as pictures or words, into groups

climax the point in a story at which conflict is confronted

compare tell how things are the same

comprehension understanding of text being read—the ultimate goal of reading

comprehension strategy a conscious plan used by a reader to gain understanding of text. Comprehension strategies may be used before, during, or after reading.

conclusion a decision or opinion arrived at after thinking about facts and details and using prior knowledge

conflict the problem or struggle in a story

context clue the words, phrases, or sentences near an unfamiliar word that give the reader clues to the word's meaning

contrast tell how things are different

details small pieces of information

dialect form of a language spoken in a certain region or by a certain group of people that differs from the standard form of that language

dialogue written conversation

diary a day-to-day record of one's activities and thoughts

draw conclusions arrive at decisions or opinions after thinking about facts and details and using prior knowledge

D

effect what happens as the result of a cause

etymology an explanation of the origin and history of a word and its meaning

exaggeration a statement that makes something seem larger or greater than it actually is

expository text text that contains facts and information. Also called *informational text*.

E

fable a story, usually with animal characters, that is written to teach a moral, or lesson

fact piece of information that can be proved to be true

fairy tale a folk story with magical characters and events

fantasy a story that could not really happen

fiction writing that tells about imaginary people, things, and events

figurative language the use of language that gives words a meaning beyond their usual definitions in order to add beauty or force

flashback an interruption in the sequence of events of a narrative to include an event that happened earlier

folk tale a story that has been passed down by word of mouth

foreshadowing the use of hints or clues about what will happen later in a story

F

generalize make a broad statement or rule after examining particular facts

graphic organizer a drawing, chart, or web that illustrates concepts or shows how ideas relate to each other. Readers use graphic organizers to help them keep track of and understand important information and ideas as they read. Story maps, word webs, Venn diagrams, and K-W-L charts are graphic organizers.

graphic source a chart, diagram, or map within a text that adds to readers' understanding of the text

G

H

historical fiction realistic fiction that takes place in the past. It is an imaginary story based on historical events and characters.

humor writing or speech that has a funny or amusing quality

hyperbole an exaggerated statement not meant to be taken literally, such as *I'm so hungry I could eat a horse.*

I

idiom a phrase whose meaning differs from the ordinary meaning of the words. *A stone's throw* is an idiom meaning "a short distance."

imagery the use of language to create beautiful or forceful pictures in the reader's mind

inference conclusion reached on the basis of evidence and reasoning

inform give knowledge, facts, or news to someone

informational text writing that contains facts and information. Also called *expository text*.

interview a face-to-face conversation in which someone responds to questions

irony a way of speaking or writing in which the ordinary meaning of the words is the opposite of what the speaker or writer is thinking; a contrast between what is expected and what actually happens

J

jargon the language of a special group or profession

L

legend a story coming down from the past about the great deeds of a hero. Although a legend may be based on historical people and events, it is not regarded as historically true.

literary elements the characters, setting, plot, and theme of a narrative text

M

main idea the big idea that tells what a paragraph or a selection is mainly about; the most important idea of a text

metacognition an awareness of one's own thinking processes and the ability to monitor and direct them to a desired goal. Good readers use metacognition to monitor their reading and adjust their reading strategies.

metaphor a comparison that does not use *like* or *as*, such as *a heart of stone*

meter the pattern of beats or accents in poetry

monitor and clarify a comprehension strategy by which readers actively think about understanding their reading and know when they understand and when they do not. Readers use appropriate strategies to make sense of difficult words, ideas, or passages.

mood the atmosphere or feeling of a written work

moral the lesson or teaching of a fable or story

motive the reason a character in a narrative does or says something

mystery a story about mysterious events that are not explained until the end, so as to keep the reader in suspense

myth a story that attempts to explain something in nature

N

narrative a story, made up or true, that someone tells or narrates

narrator the character in a selection who tells the story

nonfiction writing that tells about real things, real people, and real events

O

onomatopoeia the use of words that sound like their meanings, such as *buzz* and *hum*

opinion someone's judgment, belief, or way of thinking

oral vocabulary the words needed for speaking and listening

outcome the resolution of the conflict in a story

P

paraphrase retell the meaning of a passage in one's own words

personification a figure of speech in which human traits or actions are given to animals or inanimate objects, as in *The sunbeam danced on the waves.*

persuade convince someone to do or to believe something

photo essay a collection of photographs on one theme, accompanied by text

play a story that is written to be acted out for an audience

P

plot a series of related events at the beginning, middle, and end of a story; the action of a story

poem an expressive, imaginative piece of writing often arranged in lines having rhythm and rhyme. In a poem, the patterns made by the sounds of the words have special importance.

pourquoi tale a type of folk story that explains why things in nature came to be. *Pourquoi* is a French word meaning "why."

predict tell what a selection might be about or what might happen in a text. Readers use text features and information to predict. They confirm or revise their predictions as they read.

preview look over a text before reading it

prior knowledge the information and experience that a reader brings to a text. Readers use prior knowledge to help them understand what they read.

prop an item, such as an object, picture, or chart, used in a performance or presentation

R

reading vocabulary the words we recognize or use in print

realistic fiction a story about imaginary people and events that could happen in real life

repetition the repeated use of some aspect of language

resolution the point in a story where the conflict is resolved

rhyme to end in the same sound(s)

rhythm a pattern of strong beats in speech or writing, especially poetry

rising action the buildup of conflicts and complications in a story

S

science fiction a story based on science that often tells what life in the future might be like

semantic map a graphic organizer, often a web, used to display words or concepts that are meaningfully related

sensory language the use of words that help the reader understand how things look, sound, smell, taste, or feel

sequence the order of events in a selection or the order of the steps in which something is completed

sequence words clue words such as *first*, *next*, *then*, and *finally* that signal the order of events in a selection

S

setting where and when a story takes place

simile a comparison that uses *like* or *as*, as in *as busy as a bee*

speech a public talk to a group of people made for a specific purpose

stanza a group of lines in a poem

steps in a process the order of the steps in which something is completed

story map a graphic organizer used to record the literary elements and the sequence of events in a narrative text

story structure how the characters, setting, and events of a story are organized into a plot

summarize give the most important ideas of what was read. Readers summarize important information in the selection to keep track of what they are reading.

supporting detail piece of information that tells about the main idea

symbolism the use of one thing to suggest something else; often the use of something concrete to stand for an abstract idea

T

tall tale a humorous story that uses exaggeration to describe impossible happenings

text structure the organization of a piece of nonfiction writing. Text structures of informational text include cause/effect, chronological, compare/contrast, description, problem/solution, proposition/support, and ask/answer questions.

theme the big idea or author's message in a story

think aloud an instructional strategy in which a teacher verbalizes his or her thinking to model the process of comprehension or the application of a skill

tone author's attitude toward the subject or toward the reader

topic the subject of a discussion, conversation, or piece of text

V

visualize picture in one's mind what is happening in the text. Visualizing helps readers imagine the things they read about.

Leveled Readers Skills Chart

Scott Foresman Reading Street provides more than six hundred leveled readers. Each one is designed to:

- Practice critical skills and strategies
- Build fluency
- Build vocabulary and concepts
- Develop a lifelong love of reading

Grade 4

Title	Level*	DRA Level	Genre	Comprehension Strategy
Florida Everglades: Its Plants & Animals	K	20	Expository Nonfiction	Summarize
The Long Journey West	K	20	Expository Nonfiction	Questioning
From Sea to Shining Sea	K	20	Realistic Fiction	Background Knowledge
Flash Flood	K	20	Realistic Fiction	Story Structure
America's National Parks	K	20	Expository Nonfiction	Text Structure
Cheers for the Cheetahs	K	20	Realistic Fiction	Background Knowledge
Ranches in the Southwest	L	24	Expository Nonfiction	Background Knowledge
What It Takes to Stage a Play	L	24	Expository Nonfiction	Questioning
Animal Helpers	L	24	Nonfiction	Monitor and Clarify
A Trip to Capitol Hill	L	24	Expository Nonfiction	Inferring
Looking For Changes	L	24	Expository Nonfiction	Important Ideas
The Gray Whale	L	24	Expository Nonfiction	Text Structure
Day For Night	M	28	Narrative Nonfiction	Visualize
Surviving Hurricane Andrew	M	28	Realistic Fiction	Predict
Saving Trees Using Science	M	28	Nonfiction	Inferring
Mini Microbes	M	28	Expository Nonfiction	Visualize
Dolphins: Mammals of the Sea	M	28	Expository Nonfiction	Summarize
Speaking in Code	M	28	Expository Nonfiction	Important Ideas
The Rosetta Stone: The Key to Ancient Writings	M	28	Expository Nonfiction	Predict and Set Purpose
Something to Do	N	30	Realistic Fiction	Summarize
Lewis, Clark, and the Corps of Discovery	N	30	Biography	Questioning
Protecting Wild Animals	N	30	Realistic Fiction	Background Knowledge
From Spain to America	N	30	Expository Nonfiction	Story Structure
Top Hat Tompkins, the Detective	N	30	Mystery Fiction	Monitor and Clarify
Putting a Stop to Wildfires	N	30	Expository Nonfiction	Important Ideas
Let's Get to Know the Incas	N	30	Expository Nonfiction	Visualize
Mountain Rescue	N	30	Fiction	Story Structure
Plants and Animals in Antarctica	N	30	Expository Nonfiction	Text Structure
Stuart's Moon Suit	N	30	Realistic Fiction	Monitor and Clarify
The Wonders of Western Geography	O	34	Expository Nonfiction	Text Structure

* Suggested Guided Reading Level. Use your knowledge of students' abilities to adjust levels as needed.

The chart here and on the next few pages lists titles of leveled readers appropriate for students in Grade 4. Use the chart to find titles that meet your students' interest and instructional needs. The books in this list were leveled using the criteria suggested in *Matching Books to Readers* and *Leveled Books for Readers, Grades 3–6* by Irene C. Fountas and Gay Su Pinnell. For more on leveling, see the *Reading Street Leveled Readers Leveling Guide.*

Target Comprehension Skill	Additional Comprehension Instruction	Vocabulary
Sequence	Draw Conclusions	Word Structure/Suffixes
Author's Purpose	Main Idea and Details	Word Structure/Endings
Setting and Plot	Sequence of Events	Dictionary/Glossary/Multiple Meanings
Author's Purpose	Main Idea and Details	Context Clues/Synonyms/Antonyms
Main Idea and Details	Generalize	Word Structure/Suffixes
Cause and Effect	Plot	Word Structure/Prefixes/Suffixes
Draw Conclusions	Graphic Sources	Unknown Words/Dictionary/Glossary
Draw Conclusions	Generalize	Word Structure/Prefixes/Suffixes
Fact and Opinion	Draw Conclusions	Unknown Words/Dictionary/Glossary
Main Idea and Details	Generalize	Unknown Words/Dictionary/Glossary
Graphic Sources	Compare and Contrast	Context Clues/Multiple Meanings
Fact and Opinion	Main Idea and Details	Context Clues/Multiple Meanings
Generalize	Cause and Effect	Context Clues/Unfamiliar Words
Graphic Sources	Plot and Character	Root Words/Word Structure
Generalize	Main Idea and Details	Word Structure/Suffixes
Compare and Contrast	Fact and Opinion	Context Clues/Synonyms and Antonyms
Compare and Contrast	Generalize	Context Clues/Multiple Meanings
Sequence	Author's Purpose	Unknown Words/Dictionary/Glossary
Graphic Sources	Draw Conclusions	Word Structure/Greek and Latin Roots
Sequence	Draw Conclusions	Word Structure/Suffixes
Author's Purpose	Compare and Contrast	Word Structure/Endings
Setting and Plot	Sequence	Dictionary/Glossary/Multiple Meanings
Author's Purpose	Compare and Contrast	Context Clues/Synonyms/Antonyms
Character and Plot	Fact and Opinion	Context Clues/Synonyms/Antonyms
Author's Purpose	Fact and Opinion	Homographs/Dictionary/Glossary
Compare and Contrast	Main Idea and Details	Word Structure/Greek and Latin Roots
Character, Plot, Theme	Cause and Effect	Context Clues/Unfamiliar Words
Main Idea and Details	Graphic Sources	Word Structure/Greek and Latin Roots
Draw Conclusions	Main Idea and Details	Synonyms/Context Clues
Main Idea and Details	Graphic Sources	Word Structure/Suffixes

Leveled Readers Skills Chart *Continued*

Grade 4

Title	Level*	DRA Level	Genre	Comprehension Strategy
Amazing Female Athletes	O	34	Biography	Background Knowledge
Ranching in the Great American Desert	O	34	Expository Nonfiction	Story Structure
The Black Ensemble Theater	O	34	Nonfiction	Questioning
Dogs on the Job	O	34	Nonfiction	Monitor and Clarify
We Shall Overcome	O	34	Expository Nonfiction	Questioning
The Sauk and Fox Native Americans	O	34	Expository Nonfiction	Summarize
Living with Grandpa Joseph	O	34	Realistic Fiction	Inferring
To Be a Star	O	34	Realistic Fiction	Predict and Set Purpose
Earth's Closest Neighbor	O	34	Expository Nonfiction	Background Knowledge
The United States Government	P	38	Expository Nonfiction	Inferring
Storm Chasers	P	38	Nonfiction	Important Ideas
Migration Relocation	P	38	Expository Nonfiction	Text Structure
Darkness into Light	P	38	Expository Nonfiction	Visualize
Severe Weather: Storms	P	38	Expository Nonfiction	Predict and Set Purpose
Maine Now and Then	P	38	Expository Nonfiction	Inferring
Mysterious Monsters	Q	40	Expository Nonfiction	Visualize
Come Learn About Dolphins	Q	40	Expository Nonfiction	Summarize
The Super Secret Surprise Society	Q	40	Realistic Fiction	Important Ideas
Code Breakers: Uncovering German Messages	Q	40	Expository Nonfiction	Predict and Set Purpose
The Missing Iguana Mystery	Q	40	Mystery	Monitor and Clarify
The Grizzly Bear Hotshots	Q	40	Fiction	Important Ideas
Pompeii, the Lost City	R	40	Expository Nonfiction	Visualize
Bessie Coleman: Queen of the Skies	R	40	Historical Fiction	Story Structure
Let's Explore Antarctica!	R	40	Expository Nonfiction	Text Structure
To the Moon!	R	40	Science Fiction	Monitor and Clarify
The Civil Rights Movement	R	40	Expository Nonfiction	Questioning
The Story of Libraries	S	40	Expository Nonfiction	Summarize
Two Powerful Rivers	S	40	Expository Nonfiction	Questioning
Exploring the Moon	S	40	Realistic Fiction	Background Knowledge
The Diné	S	40	Expository Nonfiction	Story Structure

* Suggested Guided Reading Level. Use your knowledge of students' abilities to adjust levels as needed.

Target Comprehension Skill	Additional Comprehension Instruction	Vocabulary
Cause and Effect	Author's Purpose	Dictionary/Prefixes/Suffixes
Draw Conclusions	Main Idea and Details	Unknown Words/Dictionary/Glossary
Draw Conclusions	Fact and Opinion	Word Structure/Prefixes
Fact and Opinion	Compare and Contrast	Unknown Words/Dictionary/Glossary
Cause and Effect	Sequence	Root Words/Word Structure
Fact and Opinion	Plot and Theme	Multiple Meanings/Dictionary/Glossary
Sequence	Character	Context Clues/Unfamiliar Words
Generalize	Cause and Effect	Context Clues/Unfamiliar Words
Graphic Sources	Main Idea and Details	Multiple Meanings/Context Clues
Main Idea and Details	Generalize	Unknown Words/Dictionary/Glossary
Graphic Sources	Sequence	Context Clues/Multiple Meanings
Fact and Opinion	Draw Conclusions	Context Clues/Multiple Meanings
Generalize	Compare and Contrast	Context Clues/Unfamiliar Words
Cause and Effect	Graphic Sources	Root Words/Word Structure
Generalize	Fact and Opinion	Word Structure/Suffixes
Compare and Contrast	Main Idea and Details	Context Clues/Synonyms and Antonyms
Compare and Contrast	Fact and Opinion	Context Clues/Multiple Meanings
Sequence	Cause and Effect	Unknown Words/Dictionary/Glossary
Graphic Sources	Main Idea and Details	Word Structure/Greek and Latin Roots
Character and Plot	Cause and Effect	Context Clues/Synonyms and Antonyms
Author's Purpose	Sequence	Homographs/Dictionary/Glossary
Compare and Contrast	Generalize	Word Structure/Greek and Latin Roots
Character, Plot, Theme	Generalize	Context Clues/Unfamiliar Words
Main Idea and Details	Generalize	Word Structure/Greek and Latin Affixes
Draw Conclusions	Compare and Contrast	Context Clues/Synonyms
Cause and Effect	Sequence	Root Words/Word Structure
Sequence	Main Idea and Details	Word Structure/Suffixes
Author's Purpose	Compare and Contrast	Word Structure/Endings
Setting and Plot	Sequence	Dictionary/Glossary/Multiple Meanings
Author's Purpose	Compare and Contrast	Context Clues/Synonyms

Leveled Readers Skills Chart *Continued*

Grade 4

Title	Level*	DRA Level	Genre	Comprehension Strategy
Becoming a Melting Pot	S	40	Expository Nonfiction	Summarize
The Seahaven Squids Host a Pet Wash	S	40	Realistic Fiction	Inferring
Birthday Surprise	S	40	Realistic Fiction	Predict and Set Purpose
One Giant Leap	S	40	Narrative Nonfiction	Background Knowledge
John Muir: Protector of the Wilderness	T	50	Biography	Text Structure
Equality in American Schools	T	50	Expository Nonfiction	Background Knowledge
The Legacy of César Chávez	T	50	Biography	Story Structure
Journey to Hong Kong	T	50	Nonfiction	Questioning
Danger! Children at Work	T	50	Expository Nonfiction	Monitor and Clarify
The Power of the People	T	50	Expository Nonfiction	Inferring
Sharing Our Planet	U	50	Expository Nonfiction	Important Ideas
Birds Take Flight	U	50	Expository Nonfiction	Text Structure
Orbiting the Sun	U	50	Expository Nonfiction	Visualize
Wondrously Wild Weather	U	50	Narrative Nonfiction	Predict and Set Purpose
The Alaskan Pipeline	U	50	Expository Nonfiction	Inferring
What in the World Is That?	U	50	Expository Nonfiction	Visualize
How Does Echolocation Work?	U	50	Expository Nonfiction	Summarize
The Incredible Alexander Graham Bell	U	50	Historical Fiction	Important Ideas
The Navajo Code Talkers	V	50	Expository Nonfiction	Predict and Set Purpose
The Salamander Stumper	V	50	Realistic Fiction	Monitor and Clarify
Thor Heyerdahl's Incredible Raft	V	50	Narrative Nonfiction	Important Ideas
Meet the Maya	V	50	Expository Nonfiction	Visualize
A Book of Their Own	V	50	Realistic Fiction	Story Structure
Danger: The World Is Getting Hot!	V	50	Expository Nonfiction	Text Structure
Life on Mars: The Real Story	V	50	Realistic Fiction	Monitor and Clarify
The Women's Movement	V	50	Expository Nonfiction	Questioning
Jim Thorpe: The World's Greatest Athlete	W	60	Biography	Summarize
A New Home	W	60	Realistic Fiction	Inferring
The Show Must Go On!	W	60	Realistic Fiction	Predict and Set Purpose
The Mysteries of Space	W	60	Expository Nonfiction	Background Knowledge

* Suggested Guided Reading Level. Use your knowledge of students' abilities to adjust levels as needed.

Target Comprehension Skill	Additional Comprehension Instruction	Vocabulary
Fact and Opinion	Sequence	Multiple Meanings/Dictionary/Glossary
Sequence	Author's Purpose	Context Clues/Unfamiliar Words
Generalize	Fact and Opinion	Context Clues/Unfamiliar Words
Graphic Sources	Cause and Effect	Context Clues/Homonyms
Main Idea and Details	Generalize	Word Structure/Suffixes
Cause and Effect	Sequence	Word Structure/Prefixes/Suffixes
Draw Conclusions	Sequence	Unknown Words/Dictionary/Glossary
Draw Conclusions	Graphic Sources	Word Structure/Prefixes
Fact and Opinion	Draw Conclusions	Unknown Words/Dictionary/Glossary
Main Idea and Details	Draw Conclusions	Unknown Words/Dictionary/Glossary
Graphic Sources	Theme	Context Clues/Multiple Meanings
Fact and Opinion	Author's Purpose	Context Clues/Multiple Meanings
Generalize	Main Idea and Details	Context Clues/Unfamiliar Words
Cause and Effect	Compare and Contrast	Root Words/Word Structure
Generalize	Sequence	Word Structure/Suffixes
Compare and Contrast	Author's Purpose	Context Clues/Synonyms and Antonyms
Compare and Contrast	Cause and Effect	Context Clues/Multiple Meanings
Sequence	Character and Setting	Unknown Words/Dictionary/Glossary
Graphic Sources	Author's Purpose	Word Structure/Greek and Latin Roots
Character and Plot	Fact and Opinion	Context Clues/Synonyms and Antonyms
Author's Purpose	Fact and Opinion	Homographs/Dictionary/Glossary
Compare and Contrast	Draw Conclusions	Word Structure/Greek and Latin Roots
Character, Plot, Theme	Generalize	Context Clues/Unfamiliar Words
Main Idea and Details	Fact and Opinion	Word Structure/Greek and Latin Roots
Draw Conclusions	Graphic Sources	Synonyms/Context Clues
Cause and Effect	Draw Conclusions	Word Structure/Root Words
Fact and Opinion	Author's Purpose	Multiple Meanings/Dictionary/Glossary
Sequence	Plot	Context Clues/Unfamiliar Words
Generalize	Main Idea and Details	Context Clues/Unfamiliar Words
Graphic Sources	Fact and Opinion	Multiple Meanings/Context Clues

Section 3 Matching Books and Readers

What Good Readers Do

You can use the characteristics and behaviors of good readers to help all your students read better. But what are these characteristics and behaviors? And how can you use them to foster good reading behaviors for all your students? Here are some helpful tips.

Good Readers enjoy reading! They have favorite books, authors, and genres. Good readers often have a preference about where and when they read. They talk about books and recommend their favorites.

Develop this behavior by giving students opportunities to respond in different ways to what they read. Get them talking about what they read, and why they like or dislike it.

This behavior is important because book sharing alerts you to students who are somewhat passive about reading or have limited literacy experiences. Book sharing also helps you when you select books for the class.

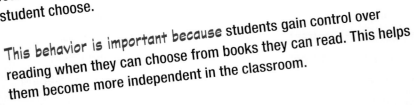

Good Readers select books they can read.

Develop this behavior by providing a range of three or four texts appropriate for the student and then letting the student choose.

This behavior is important because students gain control over reading when they can choose from books they can read. This helps them become more independent in the classroom.

Good Readers read independently for longer periods of time.

Develop this behavior by taking note of the level of support students need during guided reading. Use this information to gauge independent reading time accordingly.

This behavior is important because students become better readers when they spend time reading many texts at their independent level.

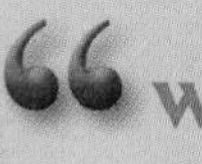

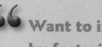

> Want to improve student performance by fostering good reading behaviors? **Customize Literacy** can help.

Good Readers use text features to help them preview and set purposes.

Develop this behavior by having students use the title and illustrations in fiction texts or the title, contents, headings, and other graphic features in nonfiction texts to make predictions about what they will be reading.

This behavior is important because previewing actually makes reading easier! Looking at features and sampling the text enables readers to predict and set expectations for reading.

Good Readers predict and ask questions before and while they read.

Develop this behavior by asking questions. After reading a passage, ask students what they think will happen next in a fiction text. Have them ask a question they think will be answered in a nonfiction text and read on to see if it is.

This behavior is important because when students predict and ask questions as they read, they are engaged. They have a purpose for reading and a basis for monitoring their comprehension.

Good Readers read meaningful phrases aloud with appropriate expression.

Develop this behavior by giving students lots of opportunities to read orally. As they read, note students' phrasing, intonation, and attention to punctuation and give help as needed.

This behavior is important because reading fluently in longer, meaningful phrases supports comprehension and ease in reading longer, more complex texts.

Good Readers read aloud at an appropriate reading rate with a high percent of accuracy.

Develop this behavior by timing students' oral reading to calculate their reading rates. You can also record students' miscues to determine a percent of accuracy. This will help identify problems.

This behavior is important because when students read fluently texts that are "just right," they find reading more enjoyable. A fluent reader is able to focus more on constructing meaning and is more likely to develop a positive attitude toward reading.

Good Readers use effective strategies and sources of information to figure out unknown words.

CH-
QU-
ST-

Develop this behavior by teaching specific strategies for figuring out unknown words, such as sounding out clusters of letters, using context, reading on, and using references.

This behavior is important because when readers have a variety of strategies to use, they are more able to decode and self-correct quickly. Readers who do these things view themselves as good readers.

Good Readers construct meaning as they read and then share or demonstrate their understanding.

Develop this behavior by having students retell what they read or write a summary of what they read in their own words.

This behavior is important because the ability to retell or write a summary is essential for success in reading. It shows how well a student has constructed meaning.

Good Readers locate and use what is explicitly stated in a text.

Develop this behavior by asking questions that require students to go back into the text to find explicitly stated information.

This behavior is important because the ability to recall, locate, and use specific information stated in a text enables readers to respond to literal questions as well as support opinions and justify their responses.

Good Readers make connections.

Develop this behavior by asking questions to help students make connections: *What does this remind you of? Have you ever read or experienced anything like this?*

This behavior is important because making connections helps readers understand and appreciate a text. Making connections to self, the world, and other texts supports higher-level thinking.

Good Readers interpret what they read by making inferences.

Develop this behavior by asking questions to help students tell or write about what they think was implied in the text: *Why do you think that happened? What helped you come to that conclusion?*

This behavior is important because the ability to go beyond the literal meaning of a text enables readers to gain a deeper understanding. When students make inferences, they use background knowledge, their personal knowledge, and the text to grasp the meaning of what is implied by the author.

Good Readers determine importance and evaluate what they read.

Develop this behavior by always having students identify what they think is the most important message, event, or information in a text.

This behavior is important because readers must be able to sort out important from interesting information. The ability to establish and/or use criteria and provide support when making judgments is an important critical-thinking skill.

Good Readers support their responses using information from a text and/or their own background knowledge.

Develop this behavior by always asking students to give the reason(s) they identified an event, message, or idea as most important.

This behavior is important because the ability to justify one's response is important for all learners. It enables others to know the basis for a decision and provides an opening for further discussion.

Conversation Starters

Asking Good Questions When students read interesting and thought-provoking books, they want to share! You can encourage students to think critically about what they read. Use questions such as the following to assess comprehension as well as evoke good class/group discussions.

Author's Purpose

- Why did the author write this piece?
- How does figuring out the author's purpose help you decide how to read the text?

Cause and Effect

- Why did these events happen? How might they have been different if the causes had been different?
- Are there several causes that result in a single effect?
- Is there a single cause that has several effects?

Compare and Contrast

- What clue words show the author is comparing and/or contrasting in this article?
- How are the fictional characters and events in this story like and/or different from real people and events you know of?

Draw Conclusions

- Based on what you have read, seen, or experienced, what can you conclude about this event in the selection?
- This story seems to be a fantasy. Why might you conclude this?
- What words help you draw conclusions about the relationship between the characters?

Fact and Opinion

- What clue word or words signal that this is a statement of opinion?
- How could this statement of fact be proved true or false?

Generalize

- What generalization can you make about the story or the characters in it? What examples lead to that generalization?
- What details, facts, and logic does the author use to support this generalization?
- Is this a valid or a faulty generalization? Explain your ideas.

Graphic Sources

- How does the author use graphic sources (chart, maps, illustrations, time lines, and so on) to support ideas and opinions?
- This selection has many graphic sources. Which one or ones best help you understand the events or ideas in the selection? Why?

Literary Elements: Character, Setting, Plot, Theme

- Describe the main character at the beginning of the story and at the end of the story. How and why does he or she change?
- How is the setting important to the story? How might the story be different if its time or its place were different?
- What does the main character want at the beginning of the story? How does the main character go about trying to achieve this?
- A plot has a conflict, but the conflict isn't always between two characters. What is the conflict in this story? How is it resolved?
- In a few sentences, what is the plot of the story?
- What is the theme of the story? Use details from the story to support your statement.

Main Idea and Details

- What is the main idea of this paragraph or article? What are some supporting details?
- The author makes this particular statement in the article. What details does the author provide to support that statement?

Sequence

- How is the sequence of events important in the text?
- Is the order of events important in this story? Why or why not?
- Based on what has already happened, what will most likely happen next?

Connecting Science and Social Studies

Scott Foresman Reading Street Leveled Readers are perfect for covering, supporting, or enriching science and social studies content. Using these books ensures that all students can access important concepts.

Grade 4 Leveled Readers

Science

Earth and Space Science	Life Science	Life Science
Nonfiction Books • *Danger: The World Is Getting Hot!* • *Darkness Into Light* • *Day for Night* • *Earth's Closest Neighbor* • *Let's Explore Antarctica!* • *Looking For Changes* • *The Mysteries of Space* • *One Giant Leap* • *Orbiting the Sun* • *Putting a Stop to Wildfires* • *Severe Weather: Storms* • *Storm Chasers* • *Wondrously Wild Weather* **Fiction Books** • *Exploring the Moon* • *Flash Flood* • *Life on Mars: The Real Story* • *Stuart's Moon Suit* • *Surviving Hurricane Andrew* • *To the Moon!*	**Nonfiction Books** • *Birds Take Flight* • *Come Learn About Dolphins* • *Dolphins: Mammals of the Sea* • *Florida Everglades: Its Plants and Animals* • *The Gray Whale* • *How Does Echolocation Work?* • *Migration Relocation* • *Mini Microbes* • *Mysterious Monsters* • *Plants and Animals in Antarctica* • *Saving Trees Using Science* • *Sharing Our Planet* • *What in the World Is That?*	**Fiction Books** • *The Missing Iguana Mystery* • *Protecting Wild Animals* • *The Salamander Stumper* • *Top Hat Tompkins, the Detective*

Grade 4 Leveled Readers

Social Studies

Citizenship

Nonfiction Books

- *Equality in American Schools*
- *Danger! Children at Work*
- *Dogs on the Job*

Fiction Books

- *Mountain Rescue*
- *The Super Secret Surprise Society*

Culture

Nonfiction Books

- *The Black Ensemble Theater*
- *The Diné*
- *From Spain to America*
- *What It Takes to Stage a Play*

Fiction Books

- *A Book of Their Own*
- *A New Home*
- *Birthday Surprise*
- *Cheers for the Cheetahs*
- *The Grizzly Bear Hotshots*
- *Living with Grandpa Joseph*
- *The Show Must Go On!*
- *Something to Do*
- *To Be a Star*

Economics

Nonfiction Books

- *The Alaskan Pipeline*
- *Ranches in the Southwest*
- *Ranching in the Great American Desert*
- *Two Powerful Rivers*

Fiction Books

- *The Seahaven Squids Host a Pet Wash*

History

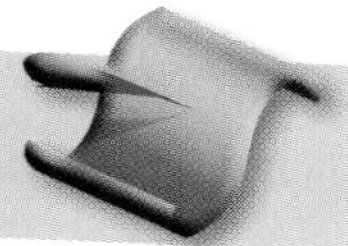

Nonfiction Books

- *Becoming a Melting Pot*
- *The Civil Rights Movement*
- *Code Breakers: Uncovering German Messages*
- *Let's Get to Know the Incas*
- *The Long Journey West*
- *Meet the Maya*
- *The Navajo Code Talkers*
- *Pompeii, the Lost City*
- *The Rosetta Stone: The Key to Ancient Writing*
- *The Sauk and Fox Native Americans*
- *Speaking in Code*
- *The Story of Libraries*
- *Thor Heyerdahl's Incredible Raft*
- *We Shall Overcome*
- *The Women's Movement*

History

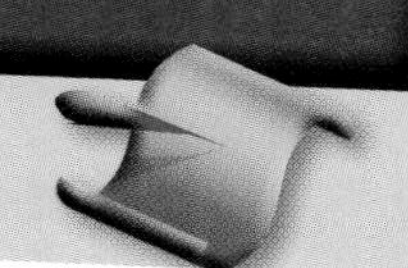

Fiction Books

- *Bessie Coleman*
- *The Incredible Alexander Graham Bell*

Geography

Nonfiction Books

- *America's National Parks*
- *Maine, Now and Then*
- *A Trip to Capital Hill*
- *The Wonders of Western Geography*

Fiction Books

- *From Sea to Shining Sea*

Government

Nonfiction Books

- *The Power of the People*
- *The United States Government*

More Great Titles

Biography

- *Amazing Female Athletes*
- *Jim Thorpe*
- *John Muir*
- *The Legacy of César Chávez*
- *Lewis and Clark and the Corps of Discovery*

Connecting Science and Social Studies

Need more choices? Look back to grade 3.

Grade 3 Leveled Readers

Science

Earth and Space Science

Nonfiction Books

- *The Frozen Continent: Antarctica*
- *Fun with Hobbies and Science!*
- *Gemstones Around the World*
- *Grandpa's Rock Kit*
- *How to Measure the Weather*
- *Measuring the Earth*
- *Meet the Stars*
- *Pictures in the Sky*

Fiction Books

- *What a Day!*
- *Journey Across the Arctic*

Life Science

Nonfiction Books

- *A Pet Bird*
- *All About Birds*
- *All About Penguins*
- *Animal Tracking: Learn More About It*
- *Animals of the Concrete Jungle*
- *Coral Reefs*
- *Desert Life*
- *The Field Trip*
- *Free in the Sea*
- *Growing Vegetables*
- *Ice Fishing in the Arctic*
- *Largest, Fastest, Lightest, Longest*
- *Life in the Arctic*
- *Raisins*
- *Rescuing Whales*
- *These Birds Can't Fly!*
- *Whales and Other Amazing Animals*

Life Science

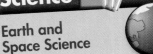

Fiction Books

- *The Best Field Trip Ever!*
- *Bills and Beaks*
- *Buddy Ran Away*
- *Grape Season*
- *The Hunters and the Elk*
- *In the Fields*
- *Swimming in a School*
- *Swimming Like Buck*
- *Toby the Smart Dog*

Grade 3 Leveled Readers

Social Studies

Citizenship

Nonfiction Books

- *Sweet Freedom!*
- *Symbols, Signs, and Songs of America*

Fiction Books

- *Buddy Goes to School*
- *Camping with Aunt Julie*
- *The Opposite Cousins*
- *Our Garden*
- *Puppy Problems*

Culture

Nonfiction Books

- *A Child's Life in Korea*
- *A Walk Around the City*
- *Celebrate Around the World*
- *China's Special Gifts to the World*
- *His Favorite Sweatshirt*
- *Let's Go Have Fun!*
- *Life Overseas*
- *Mixing, Kneading, and Baking*
- *New York's Chinatown*
- *The French Connection*
- *The World of Bread!*

Fiction Books

- *A Tea Party with Obâchan*
- *Bobby's New Apartment*
- *Cowboy Slim's Dude Ranch*
- *E-mail Friends*

Culture

- *Grandmother Spider Steals the Sun*
- *Iguana Takes a Ride*
- *Kapuapua's Magic Shell*
- *The Last Minute*
- *Lily's Adventure Around the World*
- *The Magic of Coyote*
- *One Forest, Different Trees*
- *The Road to New York*
- *The Three Bears and Goldilocks*
- *The Thunder and Lightning Men*

Economics

Nonfiction Books

- *It's a Fair Swap!*
- *It's a World of Time Zones*
- *Let's Make a Trade*
- *What's Money All About?*

Fiction Books

- *A Family of Collectors*
- *Joanie's House Becomes a Home*
- *Let's Surprise Mom*
- *The Market Adventure*
- *The Metal Detective*
- *Mr. Post's Project*
- *The Shopping Trip*

History

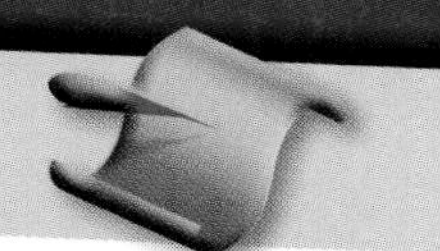

Nonfiction Books

- *Across the English Channel*
- *Celebrate Independence Day/Celebra El Día de la Independencia*
- *Changing Times: Women in the Early Twentieth Century*
- *Greek Myths*
- *The Statue of Liberty: A Gift From France*

Fiction Books

- *A Trip*
- *The Winning Point*
- *With a Twist*

More Great Titles

Biography

- *Extraordinary Athletes*
- *Great Women in U. S. History*
- *Thomas Hart Benton: Painter of Murals*

Connecting Science and Social Studies

Need more choices? Look ahead to grade 5.

Grade 5 Leveled Readers

Science

Earth and Space Science

Nonfiction Books

- *Aim High: Astronaut Training*
- *Astronauts and Cosmonauts*
- *Can Humans Make a Home in Outer Space?*
- *Cheaper, Faster, and Better*
- *Dangerous Storms*
- *Explore with Science*
- *The Inside Story of Earth*
- *Sailing the Stars*
- *The Shaping of the Continents*
- *Space Travel Inventions*
- *Storm Chasing Challenges*
- *Traveling by Plane*
- *Weather Forecasting*

Fiction Books

- *The Journey Through the Earth*
- *The Signs*

Life Science

Nonfiction Books

- *Changing for Survival: Bird Adaptations*
- *Driven to Change*
- *How the Wolves Saved Yellowstone*
- *The Kudzu Invasion*
- *Mixed-Up Vegetables*
- *Our Essential Oceans*
- *Paleontology: Digging for Dinosaurs and More*
- *Sea Life*
- *Searching for Dinosaurs*
- *Surviving the Elements: Animals and Their Environments*
- *What's New with Dinosaur Fossils?*

Fiction Books

- *The Long Trip Home*
- *Toby's California Vacation*

Physical Science

Nonfiction Books

- *George Ferris's Wheel*
- *The Magic of Makeup: Going Behind the Mask*
- *Philo and His Invention*
- *The Search to Build a Perpetual Motion Machine*

Fiction Books

- *A Happy Accident*
- *Jenna and the High Dive*

Grade 5 Leveled Readers

Social Studies

Citizenship

Nonfiction Books

- *Helping Others*
- *The National Guard: Today's Minutemen*
- *The New Kid at School*

Fiction Books

- *Bill Lucks Out*
- *Giant Pumpkin on the Loose*
- *The Sandwich Brigade*

Culture

Nonfiction Books

- *Art's Inspiration*
- *China: Today and Yesterday*
- *Computers in Filmmaking: Very Special Effects*
- *The Root of the Blues*
- *Special Effects in Hollywood*
- *Strange Sports with Weird Gear*
- *The Talker*
- *Unexpected Music*
- *A Visit to the Navajo Nation*

Fiction Books

- *Abuela's Gift*
- *Grandma Betty's Banjo*
- *The Medicine Harvest*
- *Moving*
- *Moving to Mali*

Culture

- *Nathaniel Comes to Town*
- *Operation Inspiration*
- *Our Village*
- *Playing the Game*

Economics

Nonfiction Books

- *Ancient Gold from the Ancient World*
- *The Oceans' Treasures*
- *Precious Goods: From Salt to Silk*

History

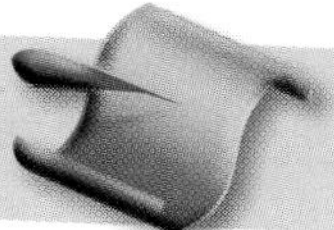

Nonfiction Books

- *The Blues Evolution*
- *The California Gold Rush*
- *The Flight Over the Ocean: Yesterday and Today*
- *From Territory to Statehood*
- *The Golden Spike*
- *The Italian Renaissance and Its Artists*
- *Jazz, Jazz, Jazz*
- *The Land of Opportunity*
- *Let the Games Begin: History of the Olympics*
- *The Most Dangerous Woman in America*

History

- *Paul Revere and the American Revolutionary War*
- *Paul Revere's Ride*
- *A Railroad Over the Sierra*
- *Rube Foster and the Chicago American Giants*
- *Saving an American Symbol*
- *A Spy in Disguise*
- *Stop That Train!*
- *Titanic: The "Unsinkable" Ship*
- *The United States Moves West*
- *What Makes Great Athletes?*

Fiction Books

- *From Slave to Soldier*
- *The Golden Journey*
- *Journey to the New World*
- *The Land of Plenty*

More Great Titles

Biography

- *Blues Legends*
- *The Designs of Da Vinci*
- *Famous Women in Sports*
- *The Journey of African American Athletes*
- *Wilma Rudolph: Running to Win*

Planning Teacher Study Groups

Adventurous teachers often have good ideas for lessons. A teacher study group is a great way to share ideas and get feedback on the best way to connect content and students. Working with other teachers can provide you with the support and motivation you need to implement new teaching strategies. A teacher study group offers many opportunities to collaborate, support each other's work, share insights, and get feedback.

Think About It

A weekly or monthly teacher study group can help support you in developing your expertise in the classroom. You and a group of like-minded teachers can form your own study group. What can this group accomplish?

- Read and discuss professional articles by researchers in the field of education.
- Meet to share teaching tips, collaborate on multi-grade lessons, and share resources.
- Develop lessons to try out new teaching strategies. Meet to share experiences and discuss how to further improve your teaching approach.

Let's Meet!

Forming a study group is easy. Just follow these four steps:

1. **Decide on the size of the group.** A small group has the advantage of making each member feel accountable, but make sure that all people have the ability to make the same commitment!
2. **Choose teachers to invite to join your group.** Think about who you want to invite. Should they all teach the same grade? Can you invite teachers from other schools? Remember that the more diverse the group, the more it benefits from new perspectives.
3. **Set goals for the group.** In order to succeed, know what you want the group to do. Meet to set goals. Rank goals in order of importance and refer often to the goals to keep the group on track.
4. **Make logistical decisions.** This is often the most difficult. Decide where and when you will meet. Consider an online meeting place where group members can post discussion questions and replies if people are not able to meet.

What Will We Study? Use the goals you set to help determine what your group will study. Consider what materials are needed to reach your goals, and how long you think you will need to prepare for each meeting.

How Will It Work? Think about how you structure groups in your classroom. Then use some of the same strategies.

- **Assign a group facilitator.** This person is responsible for guiding the meeting. This person comes prepared with discussion questions and leads the meeting. This could be a rotating responsibility dependent on experience with various topics. This person might be responsible for providing the materials.
- **Assign a recorder.** Have someone take notes during the meeting and record group decisions.
- **Use the jigsaw method.** Not everyone has time to be a facilitator. In this case, divide the text and assign each portion to a different person. Each person is responsible for leading the discussion on that particular part.

Meet Again Make a commitment to meet for a minimum number of times. After that, the group can reevaluate and decide whether or not to continue.

"Have some great teaching tips to share? Want to exchange ideas with your colleagues? Build your own professional community of teachers. **Customize Literacy** gets you started."

Building Community

Trial Lessons

Use your colleagues' experiences to help as you think about new ways to connect content and students. Use the following plan to create a mini-lesson. It should last twenty minutes. Get the support of your colleagues as you try something new and then reflect on what happened.

Be Creative! As you develop a plan for a mini-lesson, use these four words to guide planning: *purpose, text, resources*, and *routine*.

- **Purpose:** Decide on a skill or strategy to teach. Define your purpose for teaching the lesson.
- **Text:** Develop a list of the materials you could use. Ask your colleagues for suggestions.
- **Resources:** Make a list of the available resources, and consider how to use those resources most effectively. Consider using the leveled readers listed on pages CL 24–CL 29 and CL 36–CL 41 of Customize Literacy.
- **Routine:** Choose an instructional routine to structure your mini-lesson. See the mini-lessons in Customize Literacy for suggestions.

Try It! Try out your lesson! Consider audio- or videotaping the lesson for later review. You may wish to invite a colleague to sit in as you teach. Make notes on how the lesson went.

How Did It Go? Use the self-evaluation checklist on page CL45 as you reflect on your trial lesson. This provides a framework for later discussion.

Discuss, Reflect, Repeat Solicit feedback from your teacher study group. Explain the lesson and share your reflections. Ask for suggestions on ways to improve the lesson. Take some time to reflect on the feedback. Modify your lesson to reflect what you have learned. Then try it again.

Checklist for Teacher Self-Evaluation

How Well Did I ...	Very Well	Satisfactory	Not Very Well
Plan the lesson?			
Select the appropriate level of text?			
Introduce the lesson and explain its objectives?			
Review previously taught skills?			
Directly explain the new skills being taught?			
Model the new skills?			
Break the material down into small steps?			
Integrate guided practice into the lesson?			
Monitor guided practice for student understanding?			
Provide feedback on independent practice?			
Maintain an appropriate pace?			
Assess student understanding of the material?			
Stress the importance of applying the skill as they read?			
Maintain students' interest?			
Ask questions?			
Handle student questions and responses?			
Respond to the range of abilities?			

Books for Teachers

Students aren't the only ones who need to read to grow. Here is a brief list of books that you may find useful to fill your reading teacher basket and learn new things.

A Professional Bibliography

Afflerbach, P. "Teaching Reading Self-Assessment Strategies." *Comprehension Instruction: Research-Based Best Practices.* The Guilford Press, 2002.

Bear, D. R., M. Invernizzi, S. Templeton, and F. Johnston. *Words Their Way.* Merrill Prentice Hall, 2004.

Beck, I. L. and M. G. McKeown. *Improving Comprehension with Questioning the Author: A Fresh and Expanded View of a Powerful Approach.* Scholastic, 2006.

Beck, I., M. G. McKeown, and L. Kucan. *Bringing Words to Life: Robust Vocabulary Instruction.* The Guilford Press, 2002.

Blachowicz, C. and P. Fisher. "Vocabulary Instruction." *Handbook of Reading Research,* vol. III. Lawrence Erlbaum Associates, 2000.

Blachowicz, C. and D. Ogle. *Reading Comprehension: Strategies for Independent Learners.* The Guilford Press, 2008.

Block, C. C. and M. Pressley. "Best Practices in Comprehension Instruction." *Best Practices in Literacy Instruction.* The Guilford Press, 2003.

Daniels, H. *Literature Circles.* 2nd ed. Stenhouse Publishers, 2002.

Dickson, S. V., D. C. Simmons, and E. J. Kame'enui. "Text Organization: Instructional and Curricular Basics and Implications." *What Reading Research Tells Us About Children with Diverse Learning Needs: Bases and Basics.* Lawrence Erlbaum Associates, 1998.

Diller, D. *Making the Most of Small Groups: Differentiation for All.* Stenhouse Publishers, 2007.

Duke, N. and P. D. Pearson. "Effective Practices for Developing Reading Comprehension." *What Research Has to Say About Reading Instruction,* 3rd ed. Newark, DE: International Reading Association, 2002.

Fillmore, L. W. and C. E. Snow. *What Teachers Need to Know About Language.* Office of Educational Research and Improvement, U.S. Department of Education, 2000.

Fountas, I. C. and G. S. Pinnell. *Guiding Readers and Writers Grades 3–6: Teaching Comprehension, Genre, and Content Literacy.* Heinemann, 2001.

Guthrie, J. and E. Anderson. "Engagement in Reading: Processes of Motivated Strategic, Knowledgeable, Social Readers." *Engaged Reading: Processes, Practices, and Policy Implications.* Teachers College Press, 1999.

Harvey, S. and A. Goudvis. *Strategies That Work: Teaching Comprehension to Enhance Understanding.* 2nd ed. Stenhouse Publishers, 2007.

Keene, E. O. and S. Zimmerman. *Mosaic of Thought.* 2nd ed. Heinemann, 2007.

Leu Jr., D. J. "The New Literacies: Research on Reading Instruction with the Internet and Other Digital Technologies." *What Research Has to Say About Reading Instruction,* 3rd ed. International Reading Association, 2002.

McKeown, M. G. and I. L. Beck. "Direct and Rich Vocabulary Instruction." *Vocabulary Instruction: Research to Practice.* The Guilford Press, 2004.

McTighe, J. and K. O'Conner. "Seven Practices for Effective Learning." *Educational Leadership,* vol. 63, no. 3 (November 2005).

Nagy, W. E. *Teaching Vocabulary to Improve Reading Comprehension.* International Reading Association, 1998.

National Reading Panel. *Teaching Children to Read.* National Institute of Child Health and Human Development, 1999.

Ogle, D. and C. Blachowicz. "Beyond Literature Circles: Helping Students Comprehend Information Texts." *Comprehension Instruction: Research-Based Practices.* The Guilford Press, 2001.

Pressley, M. *Reading Instruction That Works: The Case for Balanced Teaching,* 3rd ed. The Guilford Press, 2005.

Stahl, S. A. "What Do We Know About Fluency?" *The Voice of Evidence in Reading Research.* Paul H. Brookes, 2004.

Taylor, B. M., P. D. Pearson, D. S. Peterson, and M. C. Rodriguez. "The CIERA School Change Framework: An Evidence-Based Approach to Professional Development and School Reading Improvement." *Reading Research Quarterly,* vol. 40, no. 1 (January/February/March 2005).

Valencia, S. W. and M. Y. Lipson. "Thematic Instruction: A Quest for Challenging Ideas and Meaningful Learning." *Literature-Based Instruction: Reshaping the Curriculum.* Christopher-Gordon Publishers, 1998.

WEEK 1 Oral Vocabulary for

Because of Winn-Dixie

Amazing Words Oral Vocabulary Routine

DAY 1

attention

1. **Introduce** When you focus on something, you are paying *attention* to it.
2. **Demonstrate** If you don't pay *attention*, you won't learn.
3. **Apply** Have students describe times when it's good to pay *attention*.

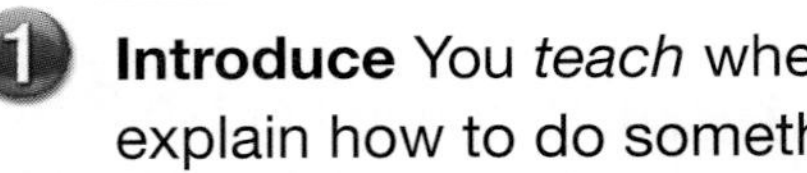

teach

1. **Introduce** You *teach* when you show or explain how to do something.
2. **Demonstrate** My parents *teach* me how to work hard.
3. **Apply** Have students *teach* each other something.

understanding

1. **Introduce** To have an *understanding* of something is to know about it.
2. **Demonstrate** He had a good *understanding* of how to do the work.
3. **Apply** Have students demonstrate their *understanding* of a direction you give.

DAY 2

introduce

1. **Introduce** If you *introduce* someone or something, you make it known to others.
2. **Demonstrate** I *introduce* a new friend to my mom.
3. **Apply** Have students practice *introducing* one person to another.

DAY 3

distinct

1. **Introduce** *Distinct* means "separate, or not the same."
2. **Demonstrate** Roses have a *distinct* smell from other flowers.
3. **Apply** Have students name two *distinct* tastes.

DAY 4

courteous

1. **Introduce** To be *courteous* is to be polite and show good manners.
2. **Demonstrate** Her teacher was impressed with how *courteous* the children were.
3. **Apply** Ask students to describe a time when they were *courteous*.

WEEK 2 # Oral Vocabulary for Let's Learn Amazing Words

Lewis and Clark and Me

Amazing Words Oral Vocabulary Routine

DAY 

traveled

1. **Introduce** *Traveled* means "to move from one place to another."
2. **Demonstrate** The family *traveled* to Florida for their vacation.
3. **Apply** Have students describe a time when they *traveled*.

settlers

1. **Introduce** *Settlers* are people who move to an uninhabited area.
2. **Demonstrate** The *settlers* had to build new homes from trees they chopped down.
3. **Apply** Have students use a U.S. history book to find examples of *settlers*.

---

territories

1. **Introduce** *Territories* are areas of land.
2. **Demonstrate** England has many *territories* under its rule.
3. **Apply** Have students draw a map and talk about the different *territories*.

DAY 

fortune

1. **Introduce** Someone's *fortune* is his or her riches.
2. **Demonstrate** They came to the new country to seek their *fortune*.
3. **Apply** Ask students to describe how someone can have a *fortune*.

DAY 

prepared

1. **Introduce** To be *prepared* means "to make ready or be ready."
2. **Demonstrate** The students *prepared* for their tests.
3. **Apply** Have students discuss different ways to be *prepared* for a test.

DAY 

improve

1. **Introduce** If you *improve* something, you make it better.
2. **Demonstrate** She reads a lot to *improve* her grades.
3. **Apply** Ask students to describe something in their lives that they could *improve*.

Oral Vocabulary for

On the Banks of Plum Creek

Amazing Words Oral Vocabulary Routine

DAY

coast

1 **Introduce** The *coast* is land along the sea.

2 **Demonstrate** The *coast* was very rocky.

3 **Apply** Have students point out the *coast* on a map of the United States.

desert

1 **Introduce** A *desert* is a dry area of land where few plants grow.

2 **Demonstrate** Many snakes and lizards live in the *desert*.

3 **Apply** Have students point to different *deserts* on a world map.

valleys

1 **Introduce** *Valleys* are areas of low land between mountains and hills.

2 **Demonstrate** The water rushed from the mountains into the *valleys*.

3 **Apply** Have students draw two hills with a *valley*.

DAY

sights

1 **Introduce** The *sights* of a location are things that are worth looking at.

2 **Demonstrate** He showed us pictures of all the *sights* he visited on his vacation.

3 **Apply** Have students identify sights in their state to see.

DAY

enormous

1 **Introduce** Something that is *enormous* is very large.

2 **Demonstrate** The Grand Canyon is *enormous*.

3 **Apply** Have students describe *enormous* things they would find in a park.

DAY

navigate

1 **Introduce** To *navigate* means "to steer a ship, airplane, or vehicle toward something."

2 **Demonstrate** Pilots *navigate* airplanes from the cockpit.

3 **Apply** Set up an obstacle course and have students *navigate*.

Acknowledgments

Acknowledgments

Text

Grateful acknowledgment is made to the following for copyrighted material:

26: From *Because of Winn-Dixie* copyright © 2000 by Kate Dicamillo; cover illustration copyright © 2000 by Chris Sheban. Reprinted by permission of Candlewick Press, Inc., Cambridge, MA

52: Text excerpt and selected illustrations from *Lewis and Clark and Me, A Dog's Tale* by Laurie Myers, illustrated by Michael Dooling. Text copyright © 2002 by Laurie Myers, illustrations copyright © 2002 by Michael Dooling. Reprinted by permission of Henry Holt and Company, LLC

84: From On the Banks of Plum Creek by Laura Ingalls Wilder. Reprinted by permission of HarperCollins Publishers

101: Excerpt from an Interview given by Laura Ingalls Wilder to the Missouri Ruralist in 1918. From *Missouri Ruralist 1918*. Reprinted by permission

116: *The Horned Toad Prince* © 2000 by Jackie Mims Hopkins. Illustrations © 2000 by Michael Austin. Reprinted by permission from Peachtree Publishers

144: *Letters Home from Yosemite* by Lisa Halvorsen. Copyright © 2000. Used by permission of Lisa Halvorsen

166: "We're All in the Telephone Book," from *The Collected Poems of Langston Hughes* by Langston Hughes, edited by Arnold Rampersad with David Roessel, Associate Editor, copyright © 1994 by The Estate of Langston Hughes. Used by permission of Alfred A. Knopf, a division of Random House

167: "Speak Up" by Janet S. Wong. Reprinted with the permission of Margaret K. McElderry Books, an imprint of Simon & Schuster Children's Publishing Division from *Good Luck Gold and Other Poems* by Janet S. Wong. Copyright © 1994 Janet S. Wong

168: "City I Love" by Lee Bennett Hopkins. Copyright © 2002 by Lee Bennett Hopkins. First appeared in *Home to Me: Poems Across America*, published by Orchard Books. Reprinted by permission of Curtis Brown, Ltd.

169: "Midwest Town" by Ruth De Long Peterson from *The Saturday Evening Post*, © 1954 Saturday Evening Post Society. Used by permission of Saturday Evening Post Society

178: "What Jo Did," from *Tall Tales: Six Amazing Basketball Dreams* by Charles R. Smith Jr., copyright © 2000 by Charles R. Smith Jr. Used by permission of Dutton Children's Books, A Division of Penguin Young Readers Group, A Member of Penguin Group (USA) Inc., 345 Hudson Street, New York, NY 10014. All rights reserved

202: *Coyote School News* by Joan Sandin. Text and illustrations copyright © 2003 by Joan Sandin. Reprinted by permission of Henry Holt and Company, LLC

262: From *Horse Heroes: True Stories of Amazing Horses* by Kate Petty. Copyright © 1999 Dorling Kindersley Limited. Reprinted by permission

290: From *So You Want to Be President?* by Judith St. George, illustrated by David Small, copyright © 2000 by Judith St. George, text. Copyright © 2000 by David Small, illustrations. Used by permission of Philomel Books, A Division of Penguin Young Readers Group, A Member of Penguin Group (USA) Inc., 345 Hudson Street, New York, NY 10014. All rights reserved

310: "His Hands," from *My Man Blue* by Nikki Grimes, copyright © 1999 by Nikki Grimes. Used by permission of Dial Books for Young Readers, A Division of Penguin Young Readers Group, A Member of Penguin Group (USA) Inc., 345 Hudson Street, New York, NY 10014. All rights reserved

311: "Homework" from *Egg Thoughts and Other Frances Songs* by Russell Hoban. Used by permission of David Higham Associates

312: "Lem Lonnigan's Leaf Machine" from *Here's What You Do When You Can't Find Your Shoe* by Andrea Perry. Reprinted with the permission of Atheneum Books for Young Readers, an imprint of Simon & Schuster Children's Publishing Division. Text copyright © 2003 by Andrea Perry

322: From *The Man Who Named The Clouds* by Joan Holub and Julie Hannah. Text copyright © 2006 by Julie Hannah and Joan Holub. Illustrations copyright © 2006 by Paige Billin-Frye. Used by permission of Albert Whitman & Company

350: From *Adelina's Whales* by Richard Sobol, copyright © 2003 by Richard Sobol. Used by permission of Dutton Children's Books, A Division of Penguin Young Readers Group, A Member of Penguin Group (USA) Inc., 345 Hudson Street, New York, NY 10014. All rights reserved

378: *How Night Came from the Sea* retold by Mary-Joan Gerson, illustrations by Carla Golembe. Text copyright © 1994 by Mary-Joan Gerson. Illustrations copyright © 1994 by Carla Golembe.

Reprinted by permission of Goodman Associates Literary Agents as authorized agent for Mary-Joan Gerson and Carla Golembe

396: "The Ant and the Bear" from *Spirit of the Cedar People: More Stories and Paintings of Chief Lelooska* edited by Christine Normandin. A DK Inc Book, 1998. Reprinted by permission of the Estate of Don Lelooska Smith, Lelooska Foundation

408: From *Eye of the Storm* by Stephen Kramer, copyright © 1997 by Stephen Kramer, text. Used by permission of G.P. Putnam's Sons, A Division of Penguin Young Readers Group, A Member of Penguin Group (USA) Inc., 345 Hudson Street, New York, NY 10014. All rights reserved

436: "Paul Bunyan" from *American Tall Tales* by Mary Pope Osborne, copyright © 1991 by Mary Pope Osborne. Illustrations copyright © 1991 by Michael McCurdy. Used by permission of Alfred A. Knopf, an imprint of Random House Children's Books, a division of Random House, Inc.

460: "Autumn" from *River Winding*. Copyright © 1970 by Charlotte Zolotow. Used by permission of Scott Treimel NY.

462: "spring meadow" by Yu Chang. Used by permission of the author.

463: "Weather" from *Catch a Little Rhyme* by Eve Merriam. Copyright © 1966 by Eve Merriam. Used by permission of Marian Reiner.

Every effort has been made to locate the copyright owner of material reproduced on this component. Omissions brought to our attention will be corrected in subsequent editions.

Illustrations

Cover: Tim Jessel; **EI1–EI13** Bill McGuire; **EI16–EI25** Kenny Kiernan; **86–98** Susan Swan; **134** Amanda Hall; **165–168** Patrick Corrigan; **224** Sachiko Yoshikawa; **234–246** Jimmy Holder; **252** Shelly Hehenberger; **307, 352** Peter Bollinger; **310–312** Lee White; **436–448** Harvey Chan; **W2–W15** Leslie Harrington.

Photographs

Every effort has been made to secure permission and provide appropriate credit for photographic material. The publisher deeply regrets any omission and pledges to correct errors called to its attention in subsequent editions.

Unless otherwise acknowledged, all photographs are the property of Pearson Education, Inc.

Photo locators denoted as follows: Top (T), Center (C), Bottom (B), Left (L), Right (R), Background (Bkgd)

10 ©Dianna Sarto/Corbis; **20** **(CC)** ©Fancy/Veer/Corbis, (B) ©FoodPix/Jupiter Images, (BL) Brand X Pictures; **24** (B) ©Flint/Corbis/Jupiter Images, (C) ©GoGo Images/Alamy, (T) ©Purestock/PhotoLibrary; **26** (C) Everett Collection, Inc.; **27** (R) ©20th Century Fox/Suzanne Tenner/The Kobal Collection, (CL) Getty Images; **28** (C) Everett Collection, Inc.; **29** (BR) Everett Collection, Inc.; **30** (BR) Everett Collection, Inc.; **31** (TR) Getty Images; **32** (CR) Getty Images; **34** (B) ©20th Century Fox Film Corp./Photofest; **35** (T) Dave King/©DK Images; **36** (TL) ©20th Century Fox/Suzanne Tenner/The Kobal Collection; **37** (B) Everett Collection, Inc.; **42** (B) Everett Collection, Inc.; **43** (TR, TL) Everett Collection, Inc.; **46** (BC) ©Nick Hanna/Alamy Images, (B) Corbis; **47** (BR) ©Old Visuals Everett Collection/Jupiter Images; **50** (T) ©Aerial Archives/Alamy Images, (C) ©Jim Zuckerman/Corbis/Jupiter Images, (B) ©Nick Clements/Getty Images; **54** (T) Getty Images; **56** (B) Getty Images; **72** (C) ©Mark M. Lawrence/Corbis; **73** (TL) NASA; **74** (T) ©Mark M. Lawrence/Corbis, (C) JSC/NASA; **75** (B) NASA; **78** (B) ©Jan Butchofsky-Houser/Corbis, (BL) ©Michael DeYoung/Corbis; **79** (TR) ©Randy Faris/Corbis; **81** (TR) ©Bettmann/Corbis; **82** (B) ©Bilderbuch/Alamy, (C) ©Eyecandy Images/Index Open/PhotoLibrary, (T) ©Joe McDonald/Corbis; **93** (C) J. L. Burns/Marine Corps/U.S. Department of Defense; **101** (B) ©AP Photo, (T) ©The Granger Collection, NY; **105** (C) ©Bettmann/Corbis; **107** (CR, CC) ©The Granger Collection, NY; **109** (TR) ©age fotostock/SuperStock, (B) ©ImageState/Alamy Images, (CC) ©Russ Bishop/Stock Connection/Jupiter Images; **114** (T) ©Horizon International Images Limited/Alamy Images, (B) ©INTERFOTO Pressebildagentur/Alamy Images, (C) ©Robert Destefano/Alamy Images; **136** (B) ©Douglas Peebles/Corbis; **137** (BC) ©Douglas Peebles/

Acknowledgments

Corbis, (CR) ©Harvey Lloyd/Getty Images; **142** (T) ©Images&Stories/Alamy Images, (C) ©Peter Barritt/Alamy Images, (B) ©Randy Faris/Jupiter Images; **144** (C) ©David Muench/Corbis, (TR, TL, CR) Getty Images; **145** (CR) Getty Images; **146** (BR) ©Royalty-Free/Corbis, (Bkgd) Getty Images; **147** (TR) ©Royalty-Free/Corbis, (BC) Corel, (CR) Getty Images; **148** (TC, BL) Corel; **149** (TR) ©Royalty-Free/Corbis, (BR) Corel, (TL) Digital Vision; **150** (C) ©Harvey Lloyd/Getty Images; **151** (CR) ©Royalty-Free/Corbis, (TC, BR) Corel; **152** (TL) ©Boyle & Boyle/Animals Animals/Earth Scenes, (CR) ©Don Mason/Corbis; **153** (C, BL) Getty Images; **154** (C) ©Royalty-Free/Corbis; **155** (CR) ©Phil Schermeister/Corbis, (TC) Corel, (TR) Getty Images; **160** (B) Courtesy of Dr. Edward Allen/Texas Tech University; **161** (TL) Sascha Burkard/Shutterstock, (CL) Western History Collections/University of Oklahoma Library; **162** (CL) ©Sascha Burkard/Shutterstock; **163** (B) Rob McCorkle/Texas Parks & Wildlife; **165** (T) ©James Hager/Robert Harding World Imagery/Getty Images; **170** (BC) ©Image Source Limited, (BL) Getty Images; **171** (B) ©Jeremy Horner/Corbis; **176** (B) ©David Madison/Getty Images, (C) Jupiter Images, (T) ©Lawrence Manning/Jupiter Images; **192** (CR) ©Blend Images/SuperStock; **193** (BR) ©Blend Images/SuperStock, (TR) Jupiter Images; **194** (B) Getty Images, (BL) Jupiter Images; **195** (T) ©Jeff Greenberg/Alamy Images, (BR) ©Corbis/Jupiter Images; **200** (B) ©Bill Miles/Corbis, (C) ©Grady Harrison/Alamy Images, (T) ©Paul Edmondson/Getty Images; **226** (B) ©Blend Images/Jupiter Images, (BC) Brand X Pictures; **227** (BR) ©Kevin Dodge/Corbis, (T) ©Nicholas Prior/Getty Images; **232** (C) ©Richard Melloul/Sygma/Corbis, (T) ©John Lund/Getty Images, (B) Jupiter Images; **254** (B) ©Isabelle Vayron/Sygma/Corbis; **255** (CC) ©Royalty-Free/Corbis, (B) ©Corbis/Jupiter Images; **260** (B) ©David Stoecklein/Corbis, (C) ©Paul A. Souders/Corbis, (T) ©Reuters/Corbis; **262** ©Bob Langrish/Animals Animals/Earth Scenes; **264** (BR, BC) Private Collection, Peter Newark American Pictures/Bridgeman Art Library; **265** (CL) Private Collection, Peter Newark American Pictures/Bridgeman Art Library, (BR) Private Collection, Peter Newark Western Americana/Bridgeman Art Library; **266** (B) ©Mary Evans Picture Library/Alamy Images, (TL) ©North Wind Picture Archives/Alamy Images; **267** (BR) Private Collection, The Stapleton Collection/Bridgeman Art Library; **270** (T) ©Bob Langrish; **271** (B) ©Arco Images/Alamy Images, (T) ©Gary Braasch/Getty Images; **272** (T) ©Robert Landau/Corbis, (B) The Kobal Collection; **273** (R, BC) Ronald Grant Archive; **278** ©Phil Schermeister/Corbis; **279** ©Bettmann/Corbis; **280** (BR) ©Bill Manns/The Art Archive, (BL) ©Greg Ryan/Alamy; **282** (BL) ©Brooks Kraft/Corbis, (B) ©Leighton Mark/Corbis; **283** (TR) Getty Images; **288** (T) ©Danilo Calilung/Corbis, (C) ©AlaskaStock/PhotoLibrary Group, Ltd., (B) ©Image Source/Jupiter Images; **306** (TR) Getty Images, (CR, CC) Library of Congress; **307** (TR) ©David Muench/Corbis, (CR) ©Jeffrey Greenberg/Photo Researchers, Inc., (TL, CL) ©Royalty-Free/Corbis, (BL, BC) Getty Images; **314** (B) ©age fotostock/SuperStock, (CC) ©Jon Arnold Images/Alamy Images, (BL) ©Naturbild/Jupiter Images; **318** (CR, CL) Brand X Pictures; **319** (TR) ©Philippe Giraud/Corbis; **320** (B) ©imagebroker/Alamy, (C) ©Holger Winkler/zefa/Corbis, (T) ©Pete Turner/Getty Images; **342** (B) ©blickwinkel/Alamy Images, (TL) ©IFA-Bilderteam/Jupiter Images; **343** (TR) ©Radius Images/Jupiter Images; **347** (C) ©Tom Brakefield/Corbis; **348** (B) ©Bruno Cossa/Grand Tour/Corbis, (C) ©Image Source/Jupiter Images, (T) ©Scott Tucker/Alamy Images; **354** (T) ©Richard Sobol; **366** (TR) ©Natalie Fobes/Corbis; **367** (CR) ©Flip Nicklin/Minden Pictures, (BL) ©Gunter Marx Photography/Corbis, (BC) Alaska Stock; **368** (CR) ©Natalie Fobes/Corbis, (TR) ©Royalty-Free/Corbis; **369** (BL) ©Jeffrey L. Rotman/Corbis, (TR) ©Joel W. Rogers/Corbis; **370** (B) ©R. Ian Lloyd/Masterfile Corporation, (BL) ©Blend Images/Jupiter Images; **371** (TC) ©Claude Steelman/PhotoLibrary Group, Ltd.; **376** (C) ©Daniel Thierry/Photononstop/PhotoLibrary Group, Ltd., (T) ©Tetra Images/Getty Images, (B) ©Tony Howell/PhotoLibrary Group, Ltd.; **400** (BC) ©AFP/Getty Images, (B) ©Eric Nguyen/Corbis; **401** (BC) Jupiter Images; **406** (C) ©SGM SGM/PhotoLibrary Group, Ltd., (T) ©Shaun van Steyn/PhotoLibrary Group, Ltd., (B) ©Surfpix/Alamy Images; **408** (C) ©Warren Faidley/Weatherstock®; **409** (C) ©Warren Faidley/Weatherstock®, (TR, BR, BL) Getty Images; 410 (TR, BR, BL) ©Warren Faidley/Weatherstock®, (B) Getty Images, (BC) ©Warren Faidley/Weatherstock®; **411** (BR, B) ©Warren Faidley/Weatherstock®, (BR) Getty Images; **412** (BL) ©Warren Faidley/Weatherstock®, (BR, BC) ©Warren Faidley/

Weatherstock®; **413** (T) ©Warren Faidley/Weatherstock®; **414** (BR) ©Warren Faidley/Weatherstock®; **415** (TL) Getty Images, (T) ©Warren Faidley/Weatherstock®; **416** (TC) ©Warren Faidley/Weatherstock®, (TL, TCL, CL) ©Warren Faidley/Weatherstock®; **417** (B) ©Warren Faidley/Weatherstock®, (CR) Getty Images; **418** (T) ©Warren Faidley/Weatherstock®; **419** (BR, BL) ©Warren Faidley/Weatherstock®; **428** (B) ©Theo Allofs/Corbis, (BL) ©Tony Waltham/Corbis; **429** (BR) ©Brad Mitchell/Alamy Images, (T) ©George Doyle/Getty Images; **434** (B) ©Jenny Matthews/Alamy Images, (T) ©Richard Baker/Corbis, (C) ©Ron Niebrugge/Alamy Images; **448** (B) ©Momatiuk-Eastcott/Corbis; **449** (BC) ©Panoramic Images/Getty Images; **450** (B) ©Stephen Wilkes/Getty Images; 451 (BC) ©Tom Bean/Corbis.

Teacher's Edition

Text

KWL Strategy: The KWL Interactive Reading Strategy was developed and is used by permission of Donna Ogle, National-Louis University, Skokie, Illinois, co-author of *Reading Today and Tomorrow*, Holt, Rinehart & Winston Publishers, 1988. (See also the *Reading Teacher*, February 1986, pp. 564–570.)

Understanding by Design quotes: Wiggins, G. & J. McTighe. (2005). *Understanding by Design*. Alexandria, VA: Association for Supervision and Curriculum Development.

Illustrations

Cover Tim Jessell

Running Head Linda Bronson

Photographs

Every effort has been made to secure permission and provide appropriate credit for photographic material. The publisher deeply regrets any omission and pledges to correct errors called to its attention in subsequent editions.

Unless otherwise acknowledged, all photographs are the property of Pearson Education, Inc.

UNIT 1

Teacher Notes

Teacher Notes

UNIT 1

Teacher Notes

Teacher Notes

UNIT 1

Teacher Notes

Teacher Notes

UNIT 1

Teacher Notes

Teacher Notes

UNIT 1

Teacher Notes

Teacher Notes

UNIT 1 Teacher Notes

Teacher Resources

Looking for Teacher Resources and other important information?

In the First Stop on Reading Street

- Dear Fourth Grade Teacher
- Research into Practice on Reading Street
- Guide to Reading Street
- Assessment on Reading Street
- Customize Writing on Reading Street
- Differentiate Instruction on Reading Street
- ELL on Reading Street
- Customize Literacy on Reading Street
- Digital Products on Reading Street
- Teacher Resources for Grade 4
- Index

Teacher Resources

Looking for Teacher Resources and other important information?

In the First Stop on Reading Street

- Dear Fourth Grade Teacher
- Research into Practice on Reading Street
- Guide to Reading Street
- Assessment on Reading Street
- Customize Writing on Reading Street
- Differentiate Instruction on Reading Street
- ELL on Reading Street
- Customize Literacy on Reading Street
- Digital Products on Reading Street
- Teacher Resources for Grade 4
- Index